STUDY GUIDE FOR OREGON REAL ESTATE LAW

JOHN JEDDELOH

FOURTH EDITION

Published in the United States of America by
Real Estate Publishers, Inc.
8316 N. Lombard 329
Portland, Oregon 97203-3727

WWW.REALESTATEPUBLISHERS.COM
E-mail: INFO@REALESTATEPUBLISHERS.COM

Library of Congress Catalog Card Number 99-66090
ISBN 1-878572-15-6

First printing, September 2002
Second printing, January, 2003

Cover Design: Architectural elevation of house © 2002 Bruinier & Associates, Inc., Portland, Oregon, 800-379-3828, reproduced with permission. Bruinier & Associates sells stock building plans and plan books for residential, commercial, duplexes, rowhouses and multifamily. Plans are available in traditional format or on CD-ROM. They also do custom architectural design. You can see their work at HTTP://WWW.BRUINIER.COM, or e-mail PLANS@BRUINIER.COM.

Contents

Introduction

The *Study Guide For Oregon Real Estate Law* offers a thorough introduction to the study of Oregon real estate law and is especially structured to prepare students to take the Oregon real estate license examinations. The text is part of the Study Guide series – other texts in the series include *Study Guide For Oregon Real Estate Finance*, *Study Guide For Oregon Real Estate Practices*, *Study Guide For Oregon Real Estate Contracts*, *Study Guide For Oregon Real Estate Agency* and *Study Guide For Oregon Property Management.* Used in conjunction with the other texts in the series, this text will give the reader an excellent foundation in real estate. It is an invaluable tool for anyone interested in real estate investments, property management, mortgage lending, title work, escrow and real estate development.

This book is divided into fourteen sections covering all aspects of the practical side of real estate law, with special consideration to those topics which are covered on Oregon real estate licensing examinations. Because many people using this book will be preparing for the examinations, we have taken great care to ensure that all examination subjects are covered thoroughly, and in proportion to their importance on the real estate examinations. In addition, we have included sample examination questions, many of which have been used on past state exams.

The author, John Jeddeloh, began his real estate career in 1971 and since then has worked in brokerage, property management, appraisal and investing. There is nothing in the field of real estate that he has not done.

The sample questions and text material are from the author's personal knowledge of the real estate licensing examinations in Oregon, from his many years of teaching prelicense courses in both public and private schools in Oregon. The author has 20 years of classroom experience teaching prelicense real estate full-time. There is no one as familiar with the Oregon real estate licensing examinations as he is. Before entering the real estate field, Mr. Jeddeloh worked for a large commercial bank in Oregon and also taught public secondary schools in Oregon. Mr. Jeddeloh has an undergraduate degree in Education and did his graduate work in Business Administration, Law and Finance. Students who have taken his live instruction classes are always impressed by his ability to explain complex subjects clearly and understandably.

The author's combination of knowledge and experience have resulted in this book being the most comprehensive text available for the study of real estate law in Oregon.

Getting a Real Estate License

Real estate brokerage is a relatively young profession compared to other professional fields such as medicine and law. Real estate agents were almost totally unregulated until 1908 when the National Association of Real Estate Boards was formed (currently the National Association of Realtors®. In fact, the chief purpose for which the National Association of Real Estate Boards was formed was to create a Code of Ethics and to encourage government licensing of real estate agents.

Even then, membership and adherence to the Code of Ethics was voluntary. Oregon led the nation by creating the first effective real estate licensing law in 1919. Today, this law is known as the Oregon Real Estate License Law, and is augmented by numerous Administrative rules promulgated by the Oregon Real Estate Agency. The Real Estate License Law requires that you hold one of several different kinds of real estate licenses in order to engage in what the law refers to as "professional real estate activity." Which kind of license you obtain depends on what kind of real estate activity you plan to do, and whether you plan to work for another agent or be independent. Most of these real estate licenses require completion of a separate license examination.

Most persons new to the real estate profession must get a ***brokers license*** as their first license. A brokers license entitles you to engage in all kinds of professional real estate activity except appraisal. (Appraisal is considered a separate field and appraisers are licensed by the Oregon Appraiser Certification and Licensure Board.) A real estate broker can work independently or cooperatively with other brokers. If you wish to run a real estate company and have other brokers working for the company, then you need a ***principal brokers license***. With some exceptions, you cannot get a principal brokers license in Oregon without meeting additional educational requirements and having three years of experience as a broker. The most notable exceptions to these rules are for out of state licensees or for persons who have held a license in another state and now reside in Oregon. Partial or full waiver of the time requirement is also possible if you can demonstrate substantial experience related to real estate, although a full waiver is granted only in exceptional circumstances. Since each individual's situation will be unique, if you feel you might qualify for a waiver, and wish to apply directly for a principal brokers license, you should contact the Oregon Real Estate Agency to determine the exact requirements. Their address is: Oregon Real Estate Agency, 1177 Center Street N.E., Salem, Oregon 97301, Telephone (503) 378-4170.

Assuming, however, that you are new to the profession and do not have significant previous real estate experience, you will need to start with the regular brokers license if you wish to engage in real estate sales. If you wish to conduct property management activity, and your professional real estate activity will be limited to property management, then you may wish to consider the special property managers license (see *Property managers license* below).

There are four requirements to obtain a brokers license. You must

- Be 18 years of age,
- Be of good character,
- Demonstrate competence in Oregon Real Estate Law, Real Estate Finance, Real Estate Practices, Property Management, Real Estate Agency, Real Estate Contracts, and Real Estate Brokerage, and you must
- Take and pass the national and state (Oregon) real estate brokers exams.

Since most persons have no problem with the first two requirements, let us confine our discussion to the last two.

You must demonstrate competence in the seven subject areas by taking and passing a course in each subject area in a school where the course(s) have been approved by the Oregon Real Estate Agency.

The real estate examinations consist of the Oregon exam (also called the state exam) and the national exam. These exams are always given at the same time, which is every month on the third or fourth Saturday (except La Grande test center, which is only three times a year). You must pass both exams with a score of 75% or better. If you pass one exam, but fail the other, you need to retake only the exam you failed, provided that you finally pass it within 12 months of passing the first exam.

Both exams are made up of totally objective multiple choice questions. The Oregon exam consists of 50 questions and the national exam has 150 questions. Most states now split their examinations into a state portion and a national portion (also sometimes called "multi-state" or "uniform" exam). As a result, if you ever move to another state you will usually only have to take the state portion in the new state, since most states now recognize Oregon's national exam as meeting the same requirements as their national, multi-state or uniform exam.

In order for a course to be approved by the Oregon Real Estate Agency it must meet certain requirements. In particular, a course in Oregon Real Estate Law must cover the material presented in this text. Another requirement is that you must actually spend the time taking the course, either in a tape presentation with an instructor present, in a live classroom setting, or by approved distance education (e.g., by the internet or through correspondence).

Property managers license: In early 1988 it became possible to obtain a special license as a property manager. The requirements for the property managers license are the same as for the brokers license, except that the examinations and courses are different. To obtain a property managers license you need to demonstrate competence only in Oregon Property Management. In addition you must take a general examination on property management consisting of 150 questions. You should bear in mind that a property manager licensee is limited strictly to property management; you cannot be involved in any real estate activity that involves a sale. For example, you could lease a property to a tenant, but you could not do a lease-option because if the option is exercised it would result in a sale. Note also that brokers and principal brokers can also do property management, so if you want to be involved in both sales and property management, then the brokers license is the one to get.

Applying for the Examinations: The deadline for applying for any real estate exam is generally the fifth day of the month in which you wish to take the exam. In other words, if you want to take an exam scheduled for the third Saturday in December, you must apply no later than December 5. Note that your application must be postmarked by December 5, not received in Salem by December 5.

However, you should mail your application as soon as possible. Many test centers have limited space (especially the Portland center). If the test center you have chosen is filled when your application is received, then you will be assigned the next closest center where space is available.

The fee for the examination is $75 for the brokers national and state (or either exam separately), and the property managers exam is also $75. In addition, you must submit a fingerprint card the first time you apply to take an examination. The fingerprint card must be completed by an official qualified to take fingerprints. The Real Estate Agency charges $40 for processing the fingerprint card. The fingerprint card will be submitted to the FBI for criminal activity check. You can take the examination(s) at any time, but no license will be issued until the check is completed. This can take several months, so the fingerprint card should be submitted immediately once you have made the decision to obtain the license. You can submit the fingerprint card with the fee for processing it alone and send in the exam application later. The fingerprint card must be obtained from the Real Estate Agency; generic fingerprint cards from other agencies are not acceptable.

You may obtain an exam application, fingerprint card and *Examination Information* booklet from the Oregon Real Estate Agency (see address and phone above). These materials are also available free of charge at the most real estate schools.

Study Hints

Successful students know that if you master the terminology of a given subject area, you will have mastered that subject. This is particularly true of real estate because you will encounter an overwhelming number of new terms to learn. Don't let a new word get by you without learning its meaning and how it is used. About half the exam items are really just vocabulary questions – testing your knowledge of real estate terminology. So if you know the language of real estate thoroughly, you will have the subject well in hand at exam time. To assist you in mastering real estate vocabulary, you will find a *Key terms* section at the end of the reading in each section. Each of the key terms listed is italicized where it first appears in the preceding text, so you can easily check on its meaning and usage.

Always be sure you understand a topic thoroughly before going on to the next topic. Since you will forget material as you progress through the course, you should start a program of systematic review of the material previously studied. A wise man once said "if you want to increase your vocabulary, use a new word three times a day for three days and it will be yours forever." This works because people learn best by a sequence of learning, forgetting, relearning, forgetting, relearning, and so on. Each time you learn-forget-relearn you double the time before you will forget the material.

Another good study trick is to look for common elements and ways to tie information together. If you try to memorize facts in isolation, it is very difficult to remember them for long enough to pass an exam. But if you get an overall picture, the individual facts are easier to remember. After all, individual facts make more sense when you have a framework to place them in.

Do not be alarmed if you find your retention is poor at first. It is not uncommon for students to retain only 20-30% of the information after just one reading. But if you do not give up, you will find that successive readings (plus attendance at the lectures for which this text was designed) will increase your memory remarkably.

Exam Techniques

At the end of each section in this text you will find various sample exam questions which are similar to the type of questions you will find on the real estate exams given by the Real Estate Agency. You should be sure you practice with these questions, as they are the most important part of the text if you are planning on taking licensing exams.

There are three basic question types. Probably the most prevalent type is the *completion* or *fill-in* type of question (see examples below). Almost as common is the *double true-false* format, and occasionally you will encounter a *Roman numeral* type of question. But regardless of the type of question, all test questions are comprised of two parts. The first part is called the ***stem***, and it is the part that actually "asks the question." The stem is followed by three ***distracters*** or ***foils***, which are the three wrong answer choices, and, of course, the correct answer.

For example, in the following question, the stem is in regular print, and the distracters or foils are underlined. The correct answer is in italics:

In real estate, a preliminary sales contract is called

(A) <u>a listing agreement</u>.
(B) <u>a lease-option</u>.
(C) *an earnest money agreement.*
(D) <u>an offering</u>.

Many students make silly mistakes answering questions because they were never taught the simple ground rules for answering questions. The rules are really very easy:

1. Read the stem and the first answer (answer A) as an entire sentence. Then decide whether the statement is true or false. Using your pencil, make a notation of your decision next to the answer.

2. Read the stem again, this time followed by the second answer (answer B). Again, decide whether the statement is true or false and mark your decision next to the answer. Repeat the process for the last two answers (C and D). It is important to remember to read the stem over again each time.

3. When you have finished, the correct answer will be obvious – whichever answer is the "odd man out" is the correct answer. In other words, if you marked three answers false and one answer true, then the one marked true must be the correct answer. Similarly, with some types of negative questions, you may mark three answers true and one answer false. Then the one marked false is the correct answer.

When you finish the above question, it should look like this:

In real estate, a preliminary sales contract is called

f (A) a listing agreement.
f (B) a lease-option.
t (C) an earnest money agreement.
f (D) an offering.

Be sure to mark your decision for each answer. Do not attempt to trust your memory. By the time you finish reading the fourth answer, you could easily have forgotten what you decided about the first answer. This technique is not only useful for avoiding silly mistakes, but also when you are not sure of the answer and must make a partial guess.

Fill-in and completion questions

These questions are really the same type of question. The only difference is that in the fill-in question an actual blank appears in the question, while the completion question contains an assumed blank at the end of the stem. For example –

The _______ is the interest held by the vendor during the term of a land sales contract.

(A) equitable title (C) naked title
(B) marketable title (D) insurable title

or

The interest held by the vendor during the term of a land sales contract is the

(A) equitable title. (C) naked title.
(B) marketable title. (D) insurable title.

After you answered the above questions, your answer section should have looked like this

f (A) equitable title. *t* (C) naked title.
f (B) marketable title. *f* (D) insurable title.

The fill-in or completion format is especially useful for testing knowledge of vocabulary items. Since testing your familiarity with real estate terminology is a fundamental part of the real estate exams, you will find many fill-in and completion questions.

Double true-false questions

The second most commonly encountered exam question type is the double true-false question. These questions come in one of two formats, e.g.

According to the Real Estate License Law, the
- I. Real Estate Commissioner is the seventh member of the Real Estate Board.
- II. decisions of the Real Estate Commissioner cannot be appealed.

(A) I only (C) Both I and II
(B) II only (D) Neither I nor II

or sometimes the format is like this –

According to the Real Estate License Law,
- (A) the Real Estate Commissioner is the seventh member of the Real Estate Board.
- (B) the decisions of the Real Estate Commissioner cannot be appealed.
- (C) both A and B are true.
- (D) neither A nor B is true.

In answering the double true-false question, follow exactly the same rules as for the fill-in or completion question. That is, first read the stem and the first answer (Roman numeral I in the first example, and (A) in the second format). Decide whether the statement is true or false, and mark your decision next to the answer. Then read the stem again, followed by the second answer, and decide whether this statement is true or false. Again mark your decision next to the answer. When you have marked both answers, the correct choice is obvious.

Double true-false questions are popular with test makers because they are easy to write. They are hard on students, however, because if you have to guess at one of the answers, you have only a 50-50 chance.

After you have answered the above question, it should look like this:

According to the Real Estate License Law, the
- *t* I. Real Estate Commissioner is the seventh member of the Real Estate Board.
- *f* II. decisions of the Real Estate Commissioner cannot be appealed.

(A) I only (C) Both I and II above
(B) II only (D) Neither I nor II above

or

According to the Real Estate License Law,
- *t* (A) the Real Estate Commissioner is the seventh member of the Real Estate Board.
- *f* (B) the decisions of the Real Estate Commissioner cannot be appealed.
- (C) Both A and B above are true.
- (D) Neither A nor B above is true.

Roman numeral questions

A third type of question which occasionally occurs on the real estate exams is the Roman numeral question. This question is similar to the double true-false question above, but instead of having two answers (I and II), it has three or more answers. As a result, the choices (A, B, C and D) may have a variety of choice combinations. For example –

Which of the following would be an encumbrance on a real estate title?
- I. A land sales contract
- II. An easement
- III. A trust deed
- IV. A mortgage

(A) I, III and IV only (C) IV only
(B) III and IV only (D) All of the above

Answer the Roman numeral question the same way as you answered the preceding question formats. That is, read the stem followed by each answer in turn and decide whether it is true or false, mark your decision, and continue until you have marked each answer. Always re-read the stem for each answer. When you have marked all the answers, you can easily select the correct answer. After you have completed the above question, the Roman numeral section should look like this –

- *t* I. A land sales contract
- *t* II. An easement
- *t* III. A trust deed
- *t* IV. A mortgage

Notice that regardless of the question format, you always mark your true-false decisions next to each answer and always re-read the stem with each answer. The importance of this technique cannot be overstressed. It is very common for students to let the first answer color their thinking about the second answer. *You cannot do this.* Each answer is distinct and separate from each other and must be considered in isolation. Making your true-false markings as you decide about each answer is the only way to ensure that you will do this properly.

Question sets

On rare occasions, you may encounter on the real estate exams a set of two or more questions which are related to each other. In other words, data from a question is referred to and used in one or more following questions. However, you will never find a set of questions where you must get the answer correct to the first one before you can get the answer correct for the following question(s). In other words, the questions may use common data, but they must be kept separate to the extent that missing a previous question will not cause you to miss a subsequent question.

Frequently, when this technique is employed, there will be a chart or graph to which a number of questions will be directed. These questions are unpopular with test makers because it becomes hard to store the questions individually and they become inflexible when trying to make up a new exam.

One situation on the real estate exams, however, does consistently make use of the question set technique. When testing your knowledge of listing agreements and earnest money receipts, the Real Estate Agency usually includes a "narrative" – that is, a story about how a transaction is to take place. The narrative is followed by a sample listing agreement or earnest money receipt. The listing agreement or earnest money receipt will contain blanks, several of which are numbered. One or more questions then follow, and each question asks what should be placed in one of the numbered blanks. Note that all the questions use the same common data (the narrative), but each question is separate and distinct from the others. That is, you can miss any one question but still have an equal opportunity to get all the others correct.

Ranking the answers

Many times, when answering a test item, you might find that you are unsure of the right answer. Since there is no penalty on the real estate exams for guessing, by all means you should answer the question. But some students have problems deciding which answer to choose. If this happens to you, it may be helpful to use a *ranking technique*, a modification of the true-false marking system discussed above. For example, suppose we had the same completion question we used previously,

> The interest held by the vendor during the term of a land sales contract is the
>
> (A) equitable title. (C) naked title.
> (B) marketable title. (D) insurable title.

Except that this time, suppose you are not sure of the answer. Suppose that you read the stem and answer (A) and decide that it is definitely false, so you mark it false. Then you read the stem again with answer (B), and you decide that the answer is probably true. So you mark (B) as true. When you read the stem again followed by answer (C), you decide that this is a true statement also, so you mark (C) as true. Finally, you read the stem the fourth time followed by answer (D), and this time you also decide the statement is true. When you mark answer (D) as true, you are faced with a dilemma – which is the correct answer among (B), (C) and (D)? Only one answer can be true, but you answered three with true –

> The interest held by the vendor during the term of a land sales contract is the
>
> *f* (A) equitable title. *t* (C) naked title.
> *t* (B) marketable title. *t* (D) insurable title.

The answer is to rank the ones of which you are unsure. It is usually easiest to do this in pairs. For example, ask yourself the question, "Do I like (B) better than (C)?" If you answer yourself that you like (C) better than (B), then eliminate (B) by marking it false. Next, decide between the two remaining choices, (C) and (D). Ask yourself which of these two you think is more likely to be true. If you decide (C) is more likely to be true than (D), then eliminate (D) by marking it false. By this process of elimination you have arrived at the decision that (C) is the correct answer. This method works because it is human nature to get confused when we have too many choices to make, but it is always easy to decide between just two items at a time.

Elimination technique

Sometimes you might encounter a problem where you have no idea whether any of the answers is right or not. In this situation, you might still be able to save the day. Many times you can get at the correct answer to a question by eliminating the answers you know are not correct. If you can eliminate three answers as definitely wrong, then you know the fourth answer has to be the correct one.

Use your subconscious mind

Another trick used by successful test takers is to exert a reluctance to change their answers. Good students know that the subconscious mind is a powerful force. They know that they may not be able consciously to remember the answer, but if they ever read the information in the past it is still stored somewhere in their unconscious mind. Therefore, a good rule of thumb when guessing is to stick by your first answer. Of course, when checking over your test at the end you may discover that you completely misunderstood the question, in which case you are certainly justified in changing your answer.

Work the answers backwards

There is another clever technique which is very useful for certain difficult math questions. While the math questions on the real estate exams are a lot easier than many people fear, still there may occasionally be a math problem that is especially difficult. For example, look at the following problem –

> A seller told an agent that she wanted to net $160,000 from the sale of her lot, which she felt had a market value of about $180,000. She told the agent that the agent could have everything over the $160,000 as commission. However, the agent did not wish to take a listing on this basis, and decided to list it at a set price which would include the amount the seller wished to net plus a commission of 6%. At what price should the agent list?
>
> (A) $160,000 (C) $170,213
> (B) $169,600 (D) $180,000

Now, the way to calculate this correctly is to divide the $160,000 the seller wishes to net by 94%. This is because $160,000 is 94% of what the agent needs to list the property for. However, if you cannot remember how to do the problem, you can still get the right answer another way.

Obviously, one of the four answers above is correct. So you can figure out which is the correct answer just by calculating which one works. Take your calculator, subtract 6% of each answer from that answer in turn, until you find the answer that will leave you with $160,000. As you can see, this technique can make stubborn math problems a breeze.

Learn to smell the answers

Good test takers are usually people who have taken a lot of standardized tests and therefore have come to understand these principles. They have also developed a second sense – they almost seem to be able to "smell" wrong answers put in deliberately to mislead them. The best way for you to develop this second sense is to practice, practice, practice. Go over each and every sample test question without fail.

One thing you can do which will help you develop this second sense is to watch out for key words in a question. Pay particular attention to negative words such as **not, least, except**, and so forth. Also pay close attention to words such as **never**, and **always**. In the real world, things are seldom absolute, so answers containing the words "never" and "always" tend to be untrue.

Pay attention also to the grammatical flow of the question. If there seems to be an abrupt change when you leave the stem and start reading the answer, this can be a clue that the answer is not true. On the other hand, answers which are long, wordy or full of qualifications tend to be true statements. Of course, all of this advice can really only be useful in those cases where you are reduced to guessing anyway. If you know the material, you won't need to worry about second-guessing the test makers.

Choosing the best answer

Many students complain that the test questions seem to have more than one correct answer. They report that one answer may be better than another, but it confuses them when two or more answers are both technically correct. In reality, students who find more than one correct answer are students who really do not understand the material thoroughly. In fact, very few questions have two correct answers and force you to choose the better of the two. The fact is that students who have learned some of the material, but not all of it, find they are able to discriminate down to the last two choices, both of which sound correct to them. But if they knew the material better, they would realize that only one of these last two is really correct.

Incomplete answers

Don't let an incomplete statement fool you. For example, suppose you read the stem of a question and the first answer and it reads "For a valid escrow to exist, there must be: (A) an escrow agent and escrow instructions." You immediately conclude that this is a false statement, because there are several other requirements to create a valid escrow in addition to "an escrow agent and escrow instructions." Wrong! If you read the statement all by itself, it is a true statement, because an escrow agent and escrow instructions are required for a valid escrow. The fact that there are other requirements is irrelevant to the truth of this statement.

Don't "what if" the question

One of the most common mistakes students make is to add material or facts to a question that is not stated. People tend to jump to conclusions and make unwarranted assumptions. This can lead to errors. Consider the following question –

> An office manager has assigned all the leads during one afternoon to Hans Schmidt, a broker licensed with the company. Consuelo Moreno, another of the broker's brokers is also in the office at the same time. In the middle of the afternoon, Mr. and Mrs. Gomez come in to inquire about buying a property. If the office manager assigns the buyers to Moreno,
>
> (A) this is steering.
>
> (B) the broker has violated the Fair Housing Act.
>
> (C) both A and B above are correct.
>
> (D) neither A nor B above is correct.

The correct answer is (C), because assigning clients to brokers on the basis of race, religion, national origin, sex, mental or physical handicap or familial status (having children), is a called *steering* and is a violation of the Fair Housing Act. But many students read this question and add the assumption that the buyers do not speak English. Then they add the assumption that the buyers do speak Spanish, that Schmidt does not speak Spanish, and that Moreno does speak Spanish! Notice that the stem and the answers do not address the language issue at all, so you must assume that everyone speaks English.

Do the easy questions first

You can maximize your probability of success if you do not let the difficult questions slow you down. If you are taking the national and Oregon exams, you will have almost two whole minutes per question. Since most questions won't take more than about 30 seconds, this will be plenty of time. But if you spend 15 minutes on one tough question, and as a result lack time to finish all of the easy questions, you will be the loser.

To avoid this, the best technique is to answer all the easy questions first. Leave the more difficult questions for a second pass later. After you have finished the easy ones, you will find that you have lots of time left to go back and do the harder ones. Furthermore, you will be more relaxed, more mentally conditioned to the test, and you may have found some material which jogged your memory about one of the harder questions you skipped earlier. Some students still skip some of the especially difficult questions on their second pass and save them for a third pass later. If you follow this approach, you can be sure that, if you run out of time, the questions you didn't have time to finish were the questions you had the least chance of getting right anyway.

Double-check your work

When you finally finish the exam, make a final double-check of your work. Don't forget to check your answer sheet – remember that you get no credit for the right answer unless it is clearly marked with pencil in the proper place on the answer sheet. If you skip a question, be especially careful to place your answers in the right space on the answer sheet. Also be sure that your name and other information is correct. When students talk over the exam afterwards with other students, they usually realize that they made at least one, stupid, silly mistake. In fact, the average error rate is about one silly mistake per 50 exam questions, even when you are trying your best to be careful. If you have time remaining, check your work over carefully; this is no time to get sloppy.

Get ahead of the game

As the day for the exam draws near, you will quite naturally feel nervous and apprehensive. This is really a senseless time for you to feel this way! If you studied well, then you are as prepared to take the exams as any of the other people you will meet at the test center. If you haven't done your work by now, well, it's probably too late anyway. So whether you are prepared or not, it makes no sense to worry. The best course of action for the last couple of days before the exams is to continue to review and study, but *relax*! Of course, it also helps to get plenty of rest, watch your diet, and don't let the rest of the world get in your way, but the most important factor is to stay relaxed.

Make your final preparations for the exam several days in advance. Since you may have to drive some distance, be sure to set the alarm clock early enough. Also tend to other mundane matters such as getting together your pencils, admission ticket, identification, calculator (don't forget fresh batteries), and even fill up the car with gas. Get your family to help you for the last couple of days by taking the rest of your usual chores off your back to allow you time to review in peace and quiet. If you can do all this, you can sit down to take the exam feeling confident that you are as prepared as it is possible to be and that ***nothing is going to stand in the way of your success!***

SOURCES OF REAL ESTATE LAW

Since the very beginning of history man has found the need to create rules to live by. In our modern society, the rules have become codified into a complex legal system. A basic understanding of how that system works is essential for persons engaging in business endeavors, especially if the business is real estate.

Most laws relating to real estate are the result of court decisions. This is sometimes referred to as ***common law***, or ***case law***. Whenever two individuals have a dispute and that dispute is brought to court, the judge will render a decision. Now, the interesting thing is that whenever a decision is made which involves a new problem which the court has never addressed before, the case usually creates a ***precedent***. When a precedent has been established, all subsequent cases involving essentially the same problem must be decided the same way. The decision which creates this precedent is called a ***landmark decision***, or ***landmark case***. Today landmark cases are normally decided by a court of appeals (appellate court) or by the Oregon or U.S. Supreme Court, depending on jurisdiction. Since the early colonists brought English common law with them, judges in this country frequently rely on decisions made centuries ago in England. However, most decisions today are based on the great body of American case law, which by now has become substantial.

The common law of the land is, unfortunately, not uniform throughout the United States. Since each state has its own court system, the precedents established in one state tend to vary slightly from those established in another state. In spite of this, a decision rendered in one state usually commands attention in other states, even though a judge in another state is not bound to follow it. Oregon has a small population, and therefore has a shortage of case law of its own. As a result, Oregon courts tend sometimes to look strongly at decisions from other states.

NOTES

A second source of law is that law which is created by elected officials. In the United States, the basis of this law is the Constitution, upon which all legal authority in this country ultimately rests. The Constitution authorizes Congress to create law by the democratic vote of duly elected Senators and Representatives. Each state also has a constitution and a legislature, patterned after the federal model. Even at the local level (city or county), there are elected officials who are given the power to create laws. Law created by these elected officials is called ***statutory law***. Individual state laws are called ***statutes***, while local laws are generally referred to as ***ordinances***.

What happens when there is a conflict between the common law and a statute? The major purpose of a statute is to modify the common law, so statutes take precedence over the common law. But there is always an interesting interplay between the common law and statutory law. While the statutes modify the existing law, the courts have the power to declare a statute or ordinance unconstitutional, and the courts also have the power to interpret statutes. However, if the courts interpret a statute in a manner which the elected officials did not intend, the elected body can simply rewrite the statute or ordinance, and if necessary can even ask the people to amend the constitution. Ultimately the people, through their elected officials, can force the courts to change the law.

Sometimes a statute is created which gives some appointed or elected officials the authority to create additional rules or regulations in order to implement the purposes of the statute. For example, many times the purpose for which the statute was created requires the creation of detailed rules which are too involved for the legislature itself to take the time to consider. Or sometimes it is desirable to allow other appointed or elected officials to make rules or regulations so the law can easily be kept up to date. Statutes which create this authority are called ***enabling statutes***. The rules created under the authority of an enabling statute are called ***administrative law***, or ***administrative rules and regulations***. In your real estate studies you will come across many enabling statutes. The most important enabling statute you will encounter is the Real Estate License Law, which empowers the Oregon Real Estate Agency to create administrative rules which real estate licensees must adhere to, just as if the rules were part of the statute itself.

Statutes tend to be written down in volumes which are relatively easy for lay persons to use. Common law, on the other hand, generally requires a law library and knowledge of how to use it. Therefore, attorneys are the proper specialists to consult when most questions of law come up. In the real estate profession we frequently find ourselves giving advice which borders on the unauthorized practice of law. Always remember that it is illegal for a real estate agent to give legal advice, even if the legal question involves real estate. Real estate agents are permitted to fill in blanks on some standard contracts such as listings and earnest money agreements, but cannot select which standard form to use and the work must be essentially that of following the instructions of the parties.

As we have seen, our system of jurisprudence in the United States today is based largely on English common law traditions. Some states, however, have borrowed heavily from French or Spanish common law. As you can imagine, such states would be those which at one time were French or Spanish colonies. Always bear in mind that your knowledge of Oregon real estate law will help you when you deal in Oregon real estate, but it could create great problems if you try to apply it in another jurisdiction.

Exercise 1a

Law created by court decisions is called ______________ ________ or sometimes ________ ________. When a law is created by local officials it is generally called an ______________. The Oregon Legislature sometimes creates an ______________ ______________ in order to allow other offiicials to create ______________ ________. When a case is decided by the Oregon Supreme Court, a ______________ decision is rendered, which establishes a ______________.

KEY TERMS

The key to understanding any new field is the vocabulary used in that field. To maximize your comprehension of the material presented in this chapter, be sure you know the meaning and significance of the following terms. Remember that the majority of test questions primarily test knowledge of vocabulary.

Administrative law
Case law
Common law
Enabling statute
Landmark case
Landmark decision
Ordinance
Precedent
Statute
Statutory law

ANSWERS

To chapter exercises. If you couldn't figure out what to put in the blanks, find the answer here!

Exercise 1a

Law created by court decisions is called COMMON LAW *or sometimes* CASE LAW. *When a law is created by local officials it is generally called an* ORDINANCE. *The Oregon Legislature sometimes creates an* ENABLING STATUTE *in order to allow other offiicials to create* ADMINISTRATIVE RULES. *When a case is decided by the Oregon Supreme Court, a* LANDMARK *decision is rendered, which establishes a* PRECEDENT

PRACTICE QUESTIONS

The following practice questions are representative of the questions you will find on the final examination and on the licensing examinations given by the Oregon Real Estate Agency.

1. Laws governing real estate come principally from
   (A) state legislatures.
   (B) the courts.
   (C) the Oregon Real Estate Agency.
   (D) referendum of the people.

2. A type of statute which creates a commission, board or other entity which has the authority to make additional rules or regulations to implement the purposes of the statute is called
   (A) an enabling statute.
   (B) an equitable statute.
   (C) a common law statute.
   (D) bureaucratic law.

3. The Oregon Real Estate Agency has created rules which have the force and effect of law. These rules are an example of
   (A) bureaucratic law.
   (B) a body of ordinances.
   (C) administrative law.
   (D) state statutes.

ANSWERS

To practice questions. If you chose the wrong letter, here's the right one! The explanations are designed to clarify your understanding.

1. **B** Most of the law we must live with, and the ultimate basis for all law, is the sum total of all decisions rendered by our courts. The definition of this kind of law is common law or case law. The Oregon Legislature enacts statutes, but there are not as many statutes as there are court decisions. The Oregon Real Estate Agency creates administrative law in the form of administrative rules, but they are only a few pages long. In Oregon, the people have the power to create statutes by referendum, but statutes created by this process are relatively few in number.

2. **A** The special kind of statute that permits the creation of administrative rules is called an enabling statute or ordinance. The other kinds of statutes listed as answers do not exist.

3. **C** When a duly authorized entity makes rules to implement the purposes of an enabling statute, the rules are referred to as administrative law. While the rules may have been created by bureaucrats, "bureaucratic law" is not the proper term to describe such rules. Ordinances are part of statutory law and are commonly created by cities and counties. While administrative law is created by a special type of statute (enabling statute), it cannot be called a statute itself, since it was not created by vote of elected legislators.

REAL AND PERSONAL PROPERTY

BASIC TO AN UNDERSTANDING OF REAL ESTATE LAW IS A CLEAR DEFINITION OF what ***real estate*** is. Many times you will hear people refer to real estate as ***real property*** or as ***realty***, or even as ***land***. While there are technical distinctions in the meanings of these terms, for our purposes we will use them interchangeably. Likewise, ***personal property*** (things which are not real property) are often referred to as ***personalty*** or as ***chattels***.

The entire universe is divided legally into real property and personal property. The definition of personal property is "that which is not real property." Now, if you think about it for a minute, you will realize that this is a very neat definition because it leaves out nothing – everything must fit into one category or the other. But at the same time, it places a great burden on the definition of real property. In other words, if we define personal property as "that which is not real" then we have to know exactly what is real in order to know what is personal.

Most people would agree that a parcel of bare land is real property. But what about the improvements on the land? And how deep does your ownership extend? How high? These are some of the questions we will explore in this section.

Real property consists of the land and everything that is ***appurtenant*** to the land. When we say that something is appurtenant to the land we mean that the item is part of the land and is conveyed automatically to the buyer when the land is sold, even if it is not mentioned in the deed or sales agreement. In other words, if you own a lot which has a house on it, the house is considered an ***appurtenance*** to the land. If you sell the lot to your neighbor, the neighbor is automatically presumed to be entitled to the house as well as the lot. Of course, if you specifically exclude the structure, it is possible to sell the

NOTES

house and the lot separately. Remember though, that the legal presumption is that the house is part of the real estate, so if you wish to keep it you must say so in the sales (earnest money) agreement. Things which are appurtenant to the land are said to "run with the land."

Most appurtenances are obvious and present no problems. A house, or other major physical improvement is clearly part of the real estate. However, some appurtenances are more subtle. Many times an appurtenance will not be a physical improvement, but rather a right which runs with the land, such as an easement over adjacent land. Appurtenances which have no physical existence are said to be ***incorporeal*** – that is, they are intangible, cannot be touched. Physical improvements, on the other hand, are said to be ***corporeal*** – they are tangible and have physical existence. Typical incorporeal appurtenances include not only easements, but water and mineral rights, the right to lateral support from adjacent land, and many others.

Appurtenances are usually corporeal. In this country setting the house and other buildings are part of the real estate. So are the fences and permanent plantings. Perennial crops are also real property, although annual crops are personal. Things which are appurtenant do not need to be stated in the deed, as they run with the land and are conveyed automatically.

Fixtures

Many times you will be faced with a questionable item. For example, suppose you are selling a house and there is a swag lamp in the living room. It is hanging from a hook which is securely fastened to the ceiling. Is the lamp part of the real estate? Or is just the hook part of the real estate? Or are both the lamp and the hook personal property? Consider also a television antenna on a roof, a drop-in range, unattached carpeting cut to fit a room, or any of numerous other items which leave you wondering. You can imagine countless such problems which a real estate agent would be likely to encounter in the daily practice of selling real estate. Knowing when these items are real and when they are personal is crucial to anyone involved with real estate.

These items are referred to as ***fixtures*** and a complex set of legal rules exist to determine if they should be part of the real estate or not. If it is determined that an item is a fixture, then it is real. If it is not a fixture, then it is personal.

Usually a fixture started out as personal property and became a fixture because someone decided to make it part of the real estate. For example, consider a deposit of clay lying beneath the ground. While it is in the ground, it is clearly real. If the owner of the land removes the clay and turns it into bricks, then the bricks are personal property, so the owner has converted real property into personalty. Now suppose a builder comes along, buys the bricks and uses them to construct a brick barbecue. The bricks have now become real estate again. As you can see, a fixture usually started out as personal property and became real property later because of someone's actions.

Note, however, that we are usually only concerned about the item at the point of a sale or lease. If you own a house with a brick barbecue, you probably don't really care if the barbecue is real or personal – either way you may use and enjoy the barbecue. But if you sell or lease the property to someone, it suddenly becomes important to know if you must leave the barbecue, or if you may dismantle and remove it when you leave.

There are various rules involved in determining if an item is a fixture. These rules are commonly referred to as the ***tests of a fixture***. The tests of a fixture are to be applied by a judge in making a decision.

The most basic test is the test of ***annexation***. Annexation refers to how firmly the item is physically attached to the real estate. We refer to the party who installed or involved the item with the real estate as the ***annexor***.

Make careful note that Oregon courts normally recognize the modern concept that the item need not always be physically attached to the real estate to be a fixture. For example, equipment which is designed to be used with the land and is not readily usable elsewhere would probably be held to be a fixture, even though the equipment was not in the least attached. An everyday example might include the separate remote control unit for an automatic garage door opener. The idea is that if the garage door and the opener motor are part of the real estate, and if the control unit is essential to their operation, then the control unit must be considered part of the real estate as well.

On the other hand, it is possible that an item which is firmly attached may be construed to be personal property. This could occur because the intent of the annexor was that the item remain personal or because there was an agreement relative to the item (see below). The point you must grasp here is that if it is not attached it still may be a fixture, and if even if it is attached, it may sometimes remain personal. You cannot assume that if it is attached it is always real estate, and if it is not attached it is always personal property.

The second test is the adaptability of the item (***adaptation***). Stated simply, if an item has been customized or is vital to the use of the real estate, then it will likely be considered a fixture. For example, think of a gas range in a house. While it may be connected to the real estate via the gas pipe, it is not considered a fixture because it has not been customized, it is not vital to the use of the property, and it is easily replaced with a substitute range which would serve as well. But now consider draperies which were custom made to fit a window of an unusual shape. Since the draperies cannot readily be used elsewhere, they would normally be considered part of the real estate. Note that they are also an example of fixtures which are not physically attached.

The third, and most powerful, test of a fixture is ***intention***. Intention refers to the intent of the annexor in installing or involving the item with the real estate. Intention is so powerful an argument that in some cases annexation and adaptation are really just evidence of the intention of the annexor. For example, if the annexor installs an item so firmly that it cannot be removed without irreparable harm to the premises, is this not evidence that the annexor intended for the item to remain permanent? And if the annexor has an item custom made for the property, should this not be considered as evidence that the annexor intended to leave the item with the real estate?

The relationship between the parties is another important factor in determining the intent of the annexor. If an owner installs an item on his or her real estate, there is normally a presumption that the owner did so in order to improve the value of the property, and therefore intended for the item to become a fixture.

But if the item is installed by a tenant, then we must conclude that the tenant probably intended to remove the item at the end of the tenancy. Of course, if the tenant has a long term lease, and installs an item which would normally be worn out by the end of the lease, we might draw a different conclusion. When such items are installed on com-

NOTES

mercial premises they are referred to as ***trade fixtures***. You may also occasionally hear the terms ***domestic fixture*** and ***agricultural fixture*** to refer to items installed by a tenant on residential or agricultural premises respectively. Of course, as would seem logical, if the tenant is to be allowed to remove the items, then it is only fair that the tenant restore the premises and repair any damage caused by the removal.

Another important consideration in determining the intent of the annexor is the existence of an agreement. In other words, if a buyer and a seller (or lessor and lessee) enter into an agreement that an item will or will not be considered a fixture, the courts will generally hold them to their bargain. In fact, the courts will not only enforce the agreement, but will usually even ignore other evidence such as provided by the tests of annexation and adaptation. In other words, if you have an agreement, you can normally assume that it will render other factors irrelevant.

The fact that an agreement relative to an item is generally enforceable is crucial to real estate agents. Questions about fixtures are constantly arising in real estate practice. As a result, standard form contracts for the sale and leasing of real estate contain places for the parties to list which items are included with the real estate (called ***inclusions*** by real estate agents), and which items are not included (commonly referred to as ***exclusions***).

While the law of fixtures is vital for real estate agents to know, there are practical considerations as well. For example, what should you do if the seller, when listing a property for sale, wants to exclude the chandelier in the dining room? It is common for sellers to want to remove certain prized possessions, including even shrubs and trees. A good practice is to have the seller remove the items before the first potential buyers ever see the premises. In the case of shrubs and trees, it is common practice for the seller to mark them with tags so buyers can see which shrubs and trees will be removed.

Exercise a

Real estate could also be called real __________ *or* __________.

Personal property is also called __________ *and it could also be referred to as* __________.

Personal property is defined as __________.

When you buy or sell real estate, the __________ *automatically go with it. Most of the time these are* __________, *but if they have no physical existence, they are called* __________.

Sometimes an item has become involved with the real estate in such a manner that we consider it to be a __________. *The tests to determine this are:* __________ __________, *and* __________.

NOTES

Attributes of real property

Ownership of real estate is really the ownership of a volume of space. This space extends from the surface boundaries down to the center of the earth. Originally, the common law concept of ownership extended to "the heavens above forever and ever." However, if we still followed this concept, air travel would be impossible because anyone flying over your land would be guilty of trespass. Therefore, your ownership interest today extends above the surface only to a height necessary for the ordinary and reasonable use and enjoyment of the property.

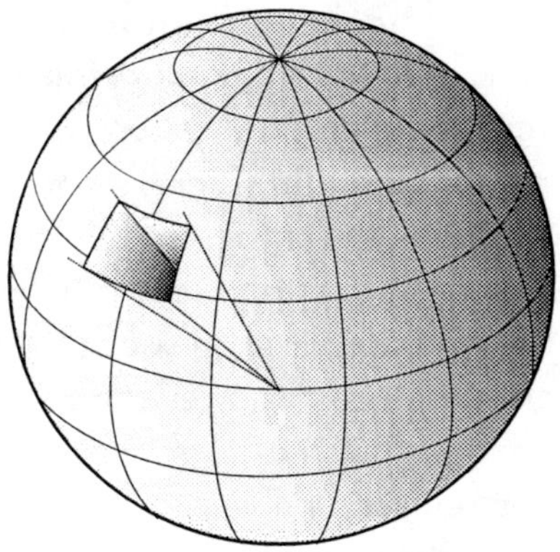

One of the attributes of real estate is that it is a volume of space. Your ownership of real estate extends to the center of the earth and to a height above the land necessary for the ordinary and reasonable use and enjoyment of the property.

Because the owner of land really owns a volume of space, we say that real estate is ***indestructible*** and ***immobile***. After all, no one can destroy space, nor can you move a piece of real estate to another location. In contrast, personal property is easily destroyed or moved.

What about the material which happens to be located within the volume of space? The soil, improvements and other features of an owner's real estate clearly affect the nature, character and value of the property, but they do not change how much property is owned. The concept that real estate is a volume of space and therefore immovable and indestructible is sometimes referred to as ***the legal definition of real estate***

An interesting concept is that an owner can sell any part of the property separately from the rest. Thus, an owner could sell the ***mineral rights*** or the ***air rights*** while retaining ownership of the rest of the land. Air rights are commonly sold in urban areas. For example, a railroad might need the surface only to a height necessary for their trains to clear. The space above could be sold for development as offices, commercial retail space, or even residential purposes. Or rail lines could be elevated above the surface as in urban areas where elevated mass transit lines run above the surface streets.

Real property also has another feature in that it is always unique. No two pieces of real property are ever exactly the same. Even if the value, size and appearance are identical, at least the location is always different. This is not necessarily true of personal property. It is possible for two chattels to be identical in every significant respect. Personal property that is of a sort which consists of identical units is said to be ***fungible***.

Sometimes we have personal property which is closely related to real property. For example, a lease is really nothing more than a piece of paper. But since it involves an interest in real property, we refer to it as a ***chattel real***. Other examples of chattels real include deeds, mortgages, easements, and the like.

Mineral rights

Rules regarding mineral rights depend on whether the minerals are solid or not. In the case of solid minerals, an owner can sell them easily simply by designating the space below the surface where they lie. Oil and gas rights, on the other hand, are considerably more difficult.

NOTES

Oil and gas are usually under great pressure, so when a well is drilled into the land, the oil or gas tends to migrate toward the point at the bottom of the well. This makes it difficult for the owner to take just the oil and gas which lies beneath his or her own land. As a result, oil and gas are usually governed by the ***rule of capture***. The rule of capture means that you own all the oil and gas that you can produce from wells on the surface of your own land, even including oil and gas which comes from under your neighbor's land. Once you have removed the oil or gas it becomes your personal property. Naturally, this rule forces your neighbors to drill their own wells quickly, in order to get their fair share.

Crop rights

Growing plants are legally categorized as those which are naturally occurring (called ***fructus naturales***), and those which are planted or cultivated (called ***fructus industriales***). Both naturally occurring plants and perennial cultivated crops are considered real property until ***severance***. Severance means the physical severing of the crop from the land, and in this case normally refers to the harvest. Once you have severed the plants from the land they are still yours, but now they are personal property. Annual crops, however, are considered personal property, even while still in the ground.

On the other hand, what if you planted a crop on land you were renting or leasing? In this case, we must address what happens if the lease or rental arrangement should be terminated prior to the time when the crops are ready to harvest. It would not be fair for the landlord to deprive a tenant of the fruits of the tenant's labors by terminating a rental agreement just before the crops were ready to harvest. Therefore, the law grants the tenant the ***right of emblement***, that is, the right to return to cultivate and harvest the crops even after the tenancy is terminated. Of course, the tenant only has this right if the tenancy did not have a fixed term or if the tenancy was terminated through an act of God or other problem not caused by the tenant. A lease, for example, is a tenancy for a fixed term. If the tenant plants a crop that would take longer to harvest than the remaining term on the lease, then the tenant presumably knew this before planting the crop, and therefore has no right of emblement.

Crop liens are a potential real estate problem. It is common for farmers to borrow money in the spring to purchase seed and fertilizer and hire labor to cultivate the crops. The loans are then paid off from the proceeds of the sale of the crop. Most such loans are secured by the future crop, giving the lender a lien on the crop. The problem occurs when the property is sold before the loan is paid off. If the seller defaults on the loan, the buyer may find that the lender has the right to enter the premises and harvest the crop even after the sale has closed.

Agricultural property is frequently rented on a year-to-year basis or leased for several years at a time. This can create a problem when the owner goes to sell the land. As will be discussed in more detail later, when you sell a leased or rented property, the buyer takes title subject to the rights of the tenant. To avoid problems, real estate agents who sell agricultural property should inquire when taking a listing if the property is subject to any leases, rental agreements, potential rights of emblement or crop liens.

Water rights

If you own real estate you may also have a water right which is an appurtenance to your property. Water rights are normally granted by the Oregon Water Resources Department. Obtaining and keeping a water right granted by the Water Resources Department is an extensive subject which will be covered in detail in the next section.

NOTES

In a few cases a water right consists of a share of stock in a mutual water company. For example, a developer may wish to build some houses in an area which is not served by public water. Rather than develop the land so that each house has its own well, the developer may create a community well which will be owned by a corporation (mutual water company). Each home owner will own a share of stock in the mutual water company. The arrangement is structured so that the share of stock is an appurtenance to the title, and therefore passes automatically with a sale of the property.

Lateral and subjacent support

When you own real estate one of the rights you enjoy is the right to ***lateral support***, that is, the right to insist that adjacent owners do nothing to cause your land to collapse. For example, if your neighbor excavates a hole and, as a result, your land collapses into the hole, it is your neighbor's responsibility to shore up the side to prevent the collapse of your land.

However, the absolute right to lateral support only exists when your land remains in its natural condition. If you place improvements on your land and the weight of the improvements causes your land to subside into your neighbor's excavation, then your neighbor is liable to you only if the neighbor failed to give you reasonable advance notice before excavating. Similarly, even if you place no structures on your land, but you alter the grade or contour of the land, as with landscaping, the result is the same – your neighbor only need give you proper advance notice of the excavation. The responsibility to shore up the land to prevent a loss is then yours.

A parallel problem is the matter of ***subjacent support***. Subjacent support refers to the support of the land from underneath, as where a mine has been excavated beneath the surface. Oregon is not a state in which a great deal of underground mining activity occurs, so there is little case law on the subject of subjacent support. However, most authorities agree that the principles are generally the same as for lateral support. An owner has the right to expect support from beneath the land, but the right is only absolute if the land remains in its natural conditions. If there are improvements whose weight increases the possibility of collapse, then the person creating the mine is only obligated to give reasonable advance notice.

Exercise b

When you own a parcel of land, you own a ______________ of ___________ which extends to the ___________ of the ___________ and to a height above the land necessary for the ________________ and reasonable use and enjoyment of the land. Because you own a _______________ of ___________, we say that your real estate is ____________________ and immovable.

Rights above the land are called _______ rights. Subsurface rights include the ________________ rights. In contrast, personal property is ________________ and destructible and is also sometimes ______________.

A ____________ __________ is an interest in real property which is nevertheless classed as personal property.

Oil and gas are subject to the _________ of ________________ and when they are removed from below the surface they become ________________ ________________. When a tenant harvests crops this is called ________________. If a tenant plants a crop the tenant has a right of ____________________, that is, the right to return to harvest the crop even after termination of the tenancy.

A share of stock could be real estate if it is a share in a ____________ ____________ ________________.

KEY TERMS

The key to understanding any new field is the vocabulary used in that field. To maximize your comprehension of the material presented in this chapter, be sure you know the meaning and significance of the following terms. Remember that the majority of test questions primarily test knowledge of vocabulary.

Adaptation
Agricultural fixture
Air rights
Annexation
Appurtenance
Appurtenant
Chattel real
Chattels
Corporeal
Domestic fixture
Exclusion
Fixture
Fructus industriales
Fructus naturales
Fungible
Immobile
Inclusion
Incorporeal
Indestructible
Intention
Land
Lateral support
Mineral rights
Personal property
Personalty
Real property
Real estate
Realty
Right of emblement
Rule of capture
Severance
Subjacent support
Tests of a fixture
Trade fixture

ANSWERS

To chapter exercises. If you couldn't figure out what to put in the blanks, find the answer here!

Exercise a

Real estate could also be called real PROPERTY *or* REALTY.
Personal property is also called PERSONALTY *and it could also be referred to as* CHATTELS.
Personal property is defined as THAT WHICH IS NOT REAL PROPERTY.
When you buy or sell real estate, the APPURTENANCES *automatically go with it. Most of the time these are* COPOREAL, *but if they have no physical existence, they are called* INCORPOREAL.
Sometimes an item has become involved with the real estate in such a manner that we consider it to be a FIXTURE. *The tests to determine this are:* ANNEXATION ADAPTATION, *and* INTENTION.

Exercise b

When you own a parcel of land, you own a VOLUME *of* SPACE *which extends to the* CENTER *of the* EARTH *and to a height above the land necessary for the* ORDINARY *and reasonable use and enjoyment of the land. Because you own a* VOLUME *of* SPACE, *we say that your real estate is* INDESTRUCTIBLE *and immovable.*
Rights above the land are called AIR *rights. Subsurface rights include the* MINERAL *rights. In contrast, personal property is* MOVABLE *and destructible and is also sometimes* FUNGIBLE.
A CHATTEL REAL *is an interest in real property which is nevertheless classed as personal property.*
Oil and gas are subject to the RULE *of* CAPTURE *and when they are removed from below the surface they become* PERSONAL PROPERTY. *When a tenant harvests crops this is called* SEVERANCE. *If a tenant plants a crop the tenant has a right of* EMBLEMENT, *that is, the right to return to harvest the crop even after termination of the tenancy.*
A share of stock could be real estate if it is a share in a MUTUAL WATER COMPANY.

PRACTICE QUESTIONS

The following practice questions are representative of the questions you will find on the final examination and on the licensing examinations given by the Oregon Real Estate Agency.

1. The land and all the improvements on it can be called
   (A) realty.
   (B) real property.
   (C) real estate.
   (D) any of the above.

2. Items of personal property are called
   (A) hereditaments.
   (B) freeholds.
   (C) chattels.
   (D) incorporeal appurtenances.

3. The term "chattels" refers to
   (A) the right of a wife in the estate of her deceased husband.
   (B) the right of a husband in the estate of his deceased wife.
   (C) either A or B.
   (D) personal property.

4. Personal property can be
   (A) transferred to another person or entity.
   (B) become real property even if it is not physically attached.
   (C) be pledged as collateral for a loan.
   (D) All of the above are true.

5. Which of the following statements concerning personal property is true?
   I. Chattels are excluded from personal property.
   II. Personal property should be adequately described in the purchase agreement to avoid legal problems.
   (A) I only
   (B) II only
   (C) Both I and II
   (D) Neither I nor II

6. An owner purchased some stones, sand and cement and built a concrete walk on his parcel of real estate. This walk was
   (A) personal property.
   (B) real property.
   (C) both personal and real property.
   (D) neither personal or real property.

7. What does the term "improvements" mean in a real estate transaction?
   (A) Everything except the land
   (B) Additions to property since the last sale
   (C) Fixtures and personal property
   (D) Streets, curbs, sidewalks, and utilities

8. In real estate, the term "improvements" most nearly means
   (A) fences, wells, drains, and roadways.
   (B) additions to the original structure.
   (C) everything artificial or constructed except the land.
   (D) outbuildings.

9. An important characteristic of land is that it may be modified or improved. Such improvements tend to increase the value of real estate. Which of the following is not an improvement?
   (A) New access roads
   (B) Utilities
   (C) New houses
   (D) Planted crops

10. Real property includes
    I. appurtenances.
    II. rights that belong to the land.
    (A) I only
    (B) II only
    (C) Both I and II
    (D) Neither I nor II

11. Appurtenances refer to
    (A) those rights that go with the land.
    (B) encumbrances on the use of the property.
    (C) contractual limitations.
    (D) proposed easements.

12. The term "real property" could include
    (A) claims and judgments.
    (B) covenants and restrictions.
    (C) attachments and liens.
    (D) land and buildings.

13. When referring to real estate, the term "appurtenant" means
(A) adjoining.
(B) incidental.
(C) correlated.
(D) connected.

14. Deeds and other documents dealing with real estate describe only the land because
(A) the buildings and other improvements are transferred separately by a bill of sale.
(B) the buildings and other improvements are not considered to be part of the land.
(C) all appurtenances are automatically included.
(D) All of the above are correct.

15. An appurtenance is part of the real estate. Which of the following would be classified as an appurtenance?
(A) Anything which is used for the benefit of the land by a legal right to do so
(B) Rights of way over adjoining land
(C) A share in a limited partnership which owns development land
(D) Both A and B

16. Which of the following would be considered real property?
(A) An orange tree planted in a tub
(B) Large house plants which are left outside during the summer
(C) Annual crops such as corn and tomatoes planted by a tenant
(D) None of the above

17. When you attach personal property to a building so that in a legal sense it becomes real property it is called
(A) an attachment.
(B) a fixture.
(C) an appurtenance.
(D) an encumbrance.

18. An article of personal property that has become part of the real estate by virtue of its attachment to the real estate is called
(A) a fixture.
(B) an attachment.
(C) an encroachment.
(D) an emblement.

19. Personal property can be
I. converted into real property.
II. hypothecated.
(A) I only
(B) II only
(C) Both I and II
(D) Neither I nor II

20. Items of personal property used in connection with the real estate such as appliances or furniture are called
(A) chattels.
(B) fixtures.
(C) realties.
(D) appurtenances.

21. Which of the following is usually included with the sale of a residence?
I. Fixtures
II. Personal property
(A) I only
(B) II only
(C) Both I and II
(D) Neither I nor II

22. A house has Venetian blinds and removable window screens. After a sale, the seller can remove
(A) the window screens.
(B) the Venetian blinds.
(C) both the window screens and the Venetian blinds.
(D) neither the window screens nor the Venetian blinds.

23. If aluminum storm windows are custom made and installed on a particular building, they become what may properly be described as a
I. fixture.
II. part of the real property.
(A) I only
(B) II only
(C) Both I and II
(D) Neither I nor II

24. Which of the following would be considered a fixture?
(A) A fence around a pasture
(B) A pasture without a fence around it
(C) A tractor on a farm
(D) A pond on a farm

25. Which of the following is least likely to be considered a fixture?
(A) A fireplace grate and andirons
(B) A set of fireplace tools for a built-in fireplace
(C) Custom made storm doors
(D) A built-in kitchen range

26. All of the following would normally be considered personal in nature except
(A) a portable electric space heater.
(B) an installed gas water heater.
(C) a television set connected to a cable outlet.
(D) an electric clothes dryer.

27. All of the following may properly be considered items of personal property except
    (A) a portable electric space heater.
    (B) a gas water heater.
    (C) a television set connected to a cable outlet.
    (D) an electric dryer.

28. Which of the following may properly be considered to be real property?
    (A) Draperies suspended from ornamental rods above windows in a living room
    (B) Apple trees in the back yard
    (C) House plants growing in tubs on the porch
    (D) A plug-in microwave oven sitting on a kitchen counter

29. All of the following are tests to determine whether personal property becomes a fixture except the
    (A) initial cost of the item.
    (B) intent of the person placing the item.
    (C) manner of annexation.
    (D) nature of use or adaptation.

30. All of the following are factors generally applied when determining whether an item of personal property has become real property, except
    (A) cost of the article.
    (B) permanence of annexation.
    (C) agreement between the parties.
    (D) relationship between the parties.

31. Which of the following would be a test of whether or not an item is a fixture?
    (A) The nature or type and the value of the item
    (B) The manner in which the owner(s) hold title to the land
    (C) The length of time the item has been involved with the land
    (D) The intention of the party who involved the item with the land

32. The test for whether or not an article is a fixture depends upon the
    I. intent of the person who placed it.
    II. method of annexation.
    III. damage caused by removal.
    (A) I and II only
    (B) I and III only
    (C) II and III only
    (D) I, II and III

33. All of the following would be considered valid tests to determine if an item is a fixture except the
    (A) marital status of the annexor.
    (B) intention of the annexor when the item was installed.
    (C) manner in which the item was annexed to the real estate.
    (D) nature of the use or adaptation to the real estate.

34. The three tests of annexation, adaptation, and intention enable one to determine if an item is
    (A) littoral property.
    (B) an emblement.
    (C) a fixture.
    (D) an encumbrance.

35. In law, a trade fixture is
    (A) real property.
    (B) personal property.
    (C) an easement.
    (D) both real and personal property.

36. Trade fixtures are
    I. a permanent part of the building.
    II. owned by the owner of the real estate.
    (A) I only
    (B) II only
    (C) Both I and II
    (D) Neither I nor II

37. Items that may properly be termed trade fixtures
    I. are intended to remain the property of the tenant.
    II. must be removed when the lease expires.
    (A) I only
    (B) II only
    (C) Both I and II
    (D) Neither I nor II

38. Which of the following is a legal test applied by the courts to determine whether an article is a fixture or a trade fixture?
    I. Method of annexation to the property
    II. Intention of the parties
    III. Character of the article and its adaptation to the real estate
    (A) II only
    (B) III only
    (C) I and II only
    (D) I, II and III

39. Donovan leased store space to Hollis for a restaurant. Hollis installed his ovens, booths, counters and other equipment to operate the restaurant. When would these items become the property of the store owner?
   (A) When they were installed
   (B) Within a reasonable amount of time if Hollis does not remove them when the lease expires
   (C) Never, because these items are not permanently affixed to the property
   (D) None of the above

40. Joseph Adams decided to move his business to a new location when the term of his lease expired. He wanted to move his display cases, which he purchased as equipment for the store, before the lease expired and install them in his new store. Adams may
   (A) not remove the display cases if they are attached to the premises.
   (B) not remove the cases unless he reimburses the landlord for their value.
   (C) remove the cases prior to the expiration of the lease.
   (D) remove the cases only with written consent of the landlord.

41. Which of the following would be classed as a trade fixture?
   (A) A toilet for sale in a hardware store
   (B) An installed garment rack
   (C) A garden hose in a nursery
   (D) A commercial floor polisher

42. Which of the following is not an appurtenance?
   (A) A barn (C) An orchard
   (B) A fence (D) A trade fixture

43. DeeDee Love installs plush shag carpeting for her own pleasure and comfort in a house she is renting. She has
   I. converted the carpeting from personal property into real estate.
   II. lost the right to remove the carpeting when her tenancy is over.
   (A) I only (C) Both I and II
   (B) II only (D) Neither I nor II

44. Max Gauche is a tenant in a leased house. He installs green and pink wall-to-wall carpeting for his own pleasure. He may remove the carpet
   I. on the termination of the lease, only if the lease provides a clause allowing him to do so.
   II. if he does so prior to the end of the lease and repairs any damage caused by the removal.
   (A) I only (C) Both I and II
   (B) II only (D) Neither I nor II

45. A tenant who installs a window air conditioner for his own pleasure and comfort has
   I. converted the air conditioner from an item of personal property to an item of real estate.
   II. lost the right to remove the air conditioner on vacating the building.
   (A) I only (C) Both I and II
   (B) II only (D) Neither I nor II

46. Which of the following statements best describes the concept of land ownership?
   (A) You own property to the sky above and downward to the center of the earth, as well as the surface.
   (B) You only own the surface of the property and no portion of the airspace.
   (C) You have lateral support but no rights to underground minerals unless specifically granted to you.
   (D) Your rights are limited to the surface.

47. When you own real property, your rights
   (A) extend to the center of the earth.
   (B) extend above the property to a height necessary for the ordinary and reasonable use and enjoyment of the property.
   (C) include all of the appurtenances.
   (D) include all of the above.

48. In terms of basic physical characteristics, land may properly be described as
   (A) immobile.
   (B) indestructible.
   (C) non-homogeneous.
   (D) having all of the above characteristics.

49. Real property is said to be indestructible. This means that
   (A) when you own real estate, you really own a volume of space.
   (B) the law cannot change the land or the appurtenances.
   (C) anything which can be destroyed, such as a house, is not part of the real estate.
   (D) it cannot be moved elsewhere.

50. Ownership of a parcel of land includes the right to use its surface, however, another person may own the
   I. subsurface rights.   II. air rights.
   (A) I only   (C) Both I and II
   (B) II only   (D) Neither I nor II

51. Which of the following statements regarding air rights is true?
   (A) Air rights can be reserved to the grantor in the deed.
   (B) Air rights can be sold separately from the surface rights.
   (C) Air rights can be restricted by zoning ordinances.
   (D) All of the above are true.

52. The Blue Skies Company has all the air rights over land owned by Bill Doaks. The Blue Skies Company has
   (A) an easement right.
   (B) an encumbrance.
   (C) an ownership interest in land.
   (D) both A and B.

53. Which of the following would be the least likely to be classed as real property?
   (A) Mineral rights
   (B) A recently planted ornamental tree
   (C) A share in a real estate investment trust
   (D) The air space over an airport

54. Real property is considered to be
   I. fixtures.   III. appurtenances.
   II. land.   IV. buildings.
   (A) I and III   (C) I II and III
   (B) I and IV   (D) I II, III, and IV

55. Which of the following best defines real property?
   (A) Land and the air above it
   (B) Land and the area below and above the surface and all the improvements thereon
   (C) The land, buildings thereon, and anything permanently affixed to the land and/or buildings
   (D) Land and mineral rights in the land

56. Real estate is a term that refers to
   (A) land in the physical sense and improvements thereto.
   (B) rights to own land and the improvements on it.
   (C) air space above the earth's surface and minerals below the surface.
   (D) all of the above.

57. Which of the following is classed as real property?
   I. Unextracted crude oil
   II. Easements appurtenant
   III. Leasehold estates in residential property
   IV. Uncultivated groves of trees
   (A) I and II only   (C) I, II and IV only
   (B) III and IV only   (D) I, III and IV only

58. Which of the following is not real estate?
   (A) Growing trees
   (B) Air rights
   (C) Coal in the ground
   (D) Lessee's interest under a year-to-year lease

59. Crops that are grown on land and require annual planting and cultivation are called
   I. emblements.   II. personal property.
   (A) I only   (C) Both I and II
   (B) II only   (D) Neither I nor II

60. Trees and crops
   (A) are real estate.
   (B) are personal property.
   (C) may be real estate or personal property, depending on the circumstances.
   (D) are neither personal property nor real estate; they are a form of fructus naturales.

61. Smith owned 40 acres of land on which he grew onions. He sold the crop of onions to Williams who agreed to harvest the onions. Before the onions were harvested, Smith sold his land to Jones and the deed was recorded. The crop of onions belongs to
(A) Smith.
(B) Jones.
(C) Williams.
(D) Williams and Jones in joint tenancy.

62. The word "emblements" means
(A) improvements to buildings.
(B) farm machinery.
(C) an additional provision in a contract.
(D) annual crops.

63. The word "emblements" in some types of real estate leases means
(A) inlaid work.
(B) the tenant's right to remove permanently attached fixtures.
(C) farm or ranch equipment and machinery.
(D) right of a tenant farmer to go on the land to harvest a crop.

64. A right of emblement is
(A) the right of a tenant farmer to harvest crops after the termination of a rental agreement which was of indefinite duration.
(B) decorations used in and about a structure to enhance its appearance and value.
(C) fixtures and part of the real property.
(D) the right to use and appropriate water from a surface source.

65. If a lease of uncertain duration is terminated by the landlord after a crop has been planted, who has the right to harvest the crop?

I. Lessor	II. Lessee
(A) I only	(C) Both I and II
(B) II only	(D) Neither I nor II

66. When a farm is operated by a tenant under a lease, crops requiring annual plantings and cultivation would be the property of the

I. landlord.	II. tenant.
(A) I only	(C) Both I and II
(B) II only	(D) Neither I nor II

67. Farmer Jones leased a farm from his neighbor for one year starting on January 1. In March he planted a crop which would be harvested the following September. However, in April the farmhouse was destroyed by a fire, forcing Jones to leave the premises. In this case, who has the right to harvest the crop?
(A) The lessor
(B) The lessee
(C) Both the lessor and the lessee who must share the profits
(D) Neither the lessor nor the lessee

68. Lynden Baum sold the rights to timber on his land to the Stumpwhacker Lumber Company, Inc. Later, but before the company cut any of the timber, he sold the land. The timber
(A) is now owned by the buyer.
(B) is still owned by the Stumpwhacker Lumber Company, Inc.
(C) remained real property after the sale.
(D) is now owned by the buyer and is now personal property.

69. Which of these items is not normally considered real property?

(A) Perennial plantings	(C) Fixtures
(B) Annual plantings	(D) Easements

70. Which of the following is real property?
(A) Standing timber on improved land
(B) Grape crops sold on contract to a winery
(C) Wheat crop on leased land
(D) Trade fixtures

71. Which of the following would be considered personal property?

(A) Bathtubs	(C) Tree
(B) Harvested crops	(D) Stream

72. Which of the following may properly be considered to be real estate?
(A) A crop of apples harvested and ready for market
(B) A hedge of lilac that bloom annually
(C) House plants growing in tubs on the porch
(D) Tools used in the cultivation of creeping red fescue

73. The only item of personalty among the following is
(A) a stack of lumber on a lot.
(B) a wooden prefabricated home built on a lot.
(C) a fence on a lot.
(D) standing timber.

74. Which of the following is always considered to be personal property?
I. Appurtenances
II. Trade fixtures
III. Standing timber
(A) I only
(B) II only
(C) III only
(D) I, II, and III

75. All of the following are real property, except
(A) a mortgage.
(B) an easement.
(C) land.
(D) fixtures.

76. All of the following would normally be considered real property except
(A) a mortgage.
(B) an easement.
(C) submerged land.
(D) fixtures.

77. All of the following are usually considered to be personal property except
(A) trade fixtures.
(B) easement appurtenant.
(C) trust deeds.
(D) mortgages.

78. Which of the following is considered to be personal property?
(A) An easement
(B) Mineral rights
(C) An existing mortgage
(D) A fixture

79. Which of the following would be a chattel real?
(A) A mortgage
(B) A lease
(C) An automobile
(D) Both A and B

80. A lessee's interest in a rented store is best described as a
(A) chattel real.
(B) reversion.
(C) remainder.
(D) freehold.

81. Which of the following would not be real property?
(A) A share of stock in a mutual water company
(B) A share of stock in a land investment company
(C) Both A and B
(D) Neither A nor B

82. Betty Grypes mistakenly built a fence on her neighbor's property. The fence
(A) was real property.
(B) belonged to the neighbor.
(C) could be removed by the neighbor with or without Betty's permission.
(D) All of the above are correct.

83. The protection of not having your property disturbed by losing support from below your property is your
(A) right to subjacent support.
(B) right to lateral support.
(C) right of contribution.
(D) riparian right.

84. The law guarantees a property owner a right to
I. subjacent support.
II. lateral support.
(A) I only
(B) II only
(C) Both I and II
(D) Neither I nor II

85. Which of the following statements regarding personal property is true?
I. Personal property may not be sold in the same transaction with real property.
II. Timber that is standing is considered personal property.
(A) I only
(B) II only
(C) Both I and II
(D) Neither I nor II

86. Which of the following is correct?
(A) Property is either real or personal.
(B) A fixture is personal property.
(C) A trade fixture is real property.
(D) Only the surface element of land is considered real property; air and mineral rights are personal property.

87. All of the following statements are true, except
(A) fixtures bought, paid for, and installed by a property owner after the execution of a mortgage usually become subject to the lien of the mortgage.
(B) if a landowner tears down a fence with the intention that it be permanently removed, and then piles the material on the land, such material remains real property.
(C) trade fixtures installed by a tenant are removable by the tenant.
(D) installed gas stoves become a fixture.

ANSWERS

To practice questions. If you chose the wrong letter, here's the right one! The explanations are designed to clarify your understanding.

1. **D** Although the terms real estate, real property, realty, tenement(s), and the like have certain technical distinctions, they are usually used synonymously by real estate agents.

2. **C** A synonym for personal property is "chattels." If it is appurtenant, regardless of whether corporeal or incorporeal, then it runs with the land and is considered part of the real estate. Hereditaments refer to the rights of an owner of real estate to leave it to heirs. A freehold is the normal ownership estate in real property.

3. **D** When a spouse dies, the surviving spouse has rights in the estate of the deceased spouse, however, these rights are not called chattels. The term "chattels" is a synonym for personal property.

4. **D** A fundamental right which is incidental to ownership of any property is the right to transfer the property to another. Another fundamental right inherent in the ownership of property is to pledge it as collateral for a loan. Personal property can easily become real property when it is physically attached to the real estate, but it can also become a fixture, even when not physically attached, when the intention of the annexor or adaptation of the item to the real estate leaves little doubt that it must be used in conjunction with the particular parcel.

5. **B** A synonym for personal property is "chattels." A sale agreement normally contains a description of the land. Therefore, the real estate is all that is being sold, unless specific mention is made of personal property that is to be included. Failing to describe personal property in a contract is just as likely to cause problems as failing to describe the real property adequately.

6. **B** The real estate is deemed to include the land itself, plus everything that is appurtenant to the land. Appurtenances include items that were personal property (e.g., building materials purchased at a store) but which were annexed to the real property.

7. **A** The real estate is deemed to include the land itself, plus all rights that are appurtenant to the land. Appurtenances can be corporeal (tangible, i.e., a structure), or incorporeal (intangible, i.e., an easement). Streets, curbs, sidewalks and utilities, as well as fixtures, are improvements, but they are not the only improvements, so the best answer is "everything except the land."

8. **C** The real estate is deemed to include the land itself, plus all rights that are appurtenant to the land. Appurtenances can be corporeal (tangible, i.e., a structure), or incorporeal (intangible, i.e., an easement). Streets, curbs, sidewalks and utilities, as well as fixtures, are improvements, but they are not the only improvements, so the best answer is "everything artificial or constructed except the land.

9. **D** The real estate includes the land and its appurtenances. Appurtenances are items that are said to "run with the land." Growing plants are considered real property, unless they are planted as annual crops, in which case they are called emblements and remain personal property. Annual crops remain legally separate from the land, and can be sold, mortgaged, or otherwise disposed of separately.

10. **C** The real estate is deemed to include the land itself, plus all rights that are appurtenant to the land. An appurtenance is something which "runs with the land," i.e., if you sell the land, the buyer automatically gets all of the appurtenances. It is not necessary to describe the appurtenances in the deed; they pass to the buyer automatically.

11. **A** The real estate is deemed to include the land itself, plus everything that is appurtenant to the land. Appurtenances can be corporeal (tangible, i.e., a structure), or incorporeal (intangible, i.e., an easement). Encumbrances are personal property interests which burden the title and are conceptually the opposite of appurtenances. Contractual limitations are probably encumbrances, i.e., a deed restriction.

12. **D** Improvements, such as buildings, become part of the real estate. Claims, judgments, covenants, restrictions, attachments and liens are all examples of encumbrances. While encumbrances affect the title to the real estate, and are frequently referred to as "chattels real," they are not themselves real property.

13. **B** An appurtenance need not necessarily be "adjoining." For example, your property could have

an easement appurtenant to it which gives you the right to cross over several other parcels, yet your land may not be adjoining or adjacent to all the affected parcels. Similarly, the appurtenance would not necessarily be connected or correlated. An appurtenance, however, is considered an incident of ownership, so it is frequently referred to as "incidental."

14. **C** Buildings and improvements which alter the land from its natural state, whether they increase or decrease the market value, become part of and are considered appurtenant to the real estate. Therefore, a deed conveys them automatically and it is not necessary to describe them in the deed. All the rest of the rights of ownership, including the rights to the center of the earth and the air rights above the land, are also automatically conveyed. Therefore, a deed only need describe the surface boundaries. A bill of sale is used to transfer ownership of personal property.

15. **D** The definition of "appurtenance" is something which runs with the land, i.e., it is considered part of the real estate. Appurtenances can be corporeal (tangible), such as physical improvements, or incorporeal (intangible), such as rights that run with the land. Ownership interests in partnerships and corporations are personal property, even if the partnership or corporation owns real estate.

16. **D** Assuming that the orange tree and house plants are not planted in the ground, are movable, and there is no special intent or agreement to make them part of the real estate, they remain personal property. Annual crops are generally considered personal property, regardless of whether they were planted by a tenant or the owner.

17. **B** A fixture is an item of real estate that at one time was personal property but, because of the nature of its involvement with the real estate, we now consider it to be appurtenant to the real estate. An attachment is a claim against the real estate of a defendant in a lawsuit. An encumbrance is any interest which burdens the title. An appurtenance is any object or interest which runs with the land.

18. **A** Fixtures are items that were personal property at one time, but have become involved with the real estate to the point where they are considered appurtenances. An attachment is a claim filed by a party to a lawsuit. An encroachment occurs when improvements are placed on another's land. A tenant whose tenancy was of indefinite duration is said to have a right of emblement, which is the right to return after the termination of the tenancy to harvest crops.

19. **C** A fixture is an item of real estate that at one time was personal property, but because of the nature of its involvement with the real estate, is now considered to have become part of the real estate. Hypothecation means to pledge as collateral, as when a borrower gives a lender a mortgage on the real estate. Both real and personal property can be hypothecated.

20. **A** A fixture is an item that at one time was personal property, but has become involved with the real estate to the point where we now construe it to be part of the real estate. If an item is a fixture, it is appurtenant. Furniture and appliances are not generally considered fixtures and therefore are not appurtenances.

21. **A** Fixtures are items that were personal property at one time, but have become involved with the real estate to the point where they are considered appurtenances. Appurtenances are considered real property and run with the land automatically. Certain items of personal property may occasionally be included (i.e., range and refrigerator), but if they are to be included, they must be specifically stated on the agreement because they are not real property.

22. **D** Mostly due to the issues of adaptation and annexation, the storm windows and Venetian blinds would be considered fixtures, unless there were some agreement to the contrary.

23. **C** A fixture, by definition, is an item that was personal property, but has become involved with the real estate to the point where we now consider it to be part of the real estate.

24. **A** A fixture is an item that once was personal property, but has become involved with the real estate in some manner that makes it part of the real estate. Clearly the pasture itself and the pond are part of the real estate, but they are not fixtures because they were never personal property that was later involved with the real estate. The fence around the pasture qualifies under the definition of a fixture. The tractor is personal property.

25. **B** A fireplace grate and andirons could well have been custom made or at least purchased of the proper size to fit the fireplace, so they could easily be fixtures. Custom made storm doors would almost always be fixtures due to the tests of annexation and adaptation. Since it is normal custom to leave a built-in range as part of the real estate, this, too would be likely to be considered a fixture. The fireplace tools, however, are probably usable with any fireplace, and

therefore, of the choices, the most likely to be considered personal property.

26. **B** Items used with the real estate are normally considered personal property unless they have been involved in some manner that we consider them to be fixtures. Items become fixtures according to the law of fixtures. A great portion of the law of fixtures has to do with what is ordinary and customary. Although not the case in all states, in Oregon it is good custom for the seller to leave the water heater.

27. **B** A fixture is an item of real estate that at one time was personal property. There are three tests to determine if an item is a fixture: Annexation (manner of attachment, or if it is attached at all), adaptation (can it be used on another property), and intent of the annexor. In this case, none of the items is attached, except the water heater, all are adaptable to be used elsewhere, and the intent of the annexor is clearly that none be considered real except the water heater.

28. **B** A fixture is an item of real estate that at one time was personal property. There are three tests to determine if an item is a fixture: Annexation (manner of attachment, or if it is attached at all), adaptation (can it be used on another property), and intent of the annexor. The draperies would be personal property unless they were custom made in some manner so they could not be used elsewhere.

29. **A** A fixture is an item of real estate that at one time was personal property. There are three tests to determine if an item is a fixture: Annexation (manner of attachment, or if it is attached at all), adaptation (can it be used on another property), and intention of the annexor.

30. **A** The three tests for a fixture are annexation, adaptation and intention. If there is a specific agreement between the parties, courts hold this to be the clearest expression of the intent of the parties. Intent generally takes precedence over the other tests. If there is no agreement, the relationship between the parties can be significant. If an item was installed by a seller, the presumption is that the seller's intention was to make it part of the real estate. If it was installed by a tenant, the presumption is that the tenant intended to remove the item at the termination of the tenancy.

31. **D** There are three legal tests to determine if an item is a fixture – annexation, adaptation, and intention. Intention refers to the intent of the party who installed or involved the item with the real estate (the annexor). The nature, type or value of the item, the manner in which the parties hold title, and the length of time involved, could all be evidence of intent, but by themselves are not tests of a fixture.

32. **A** Of the three tests to determine if an item is a fixture (annexation, adaptation and intention), the most powerful is intention. Intention refers to the intent of the party who installed or involved the item with the real estate (the annexor). Damage caused by removal is not considered a test, although it can be used as an argument that there was no intent if the annexor installed the item in a manner that would cause great damage to remove it.

33. **A** There are three legal tests to determine if an item is a fixture – annexation, that is, how the item has been attached or involved with the real estate; adaptation, or how the item has been adapted to be used with the real estate; and intention. Intention refers to the intent of the party who installed or involved the item with the real estate (the annexor). The relationship between the parties, the method of annexation, and the possible existence of an agreement between the parties are all used to determine the intention of the annexor. The marital status of the annexor is irrelevant, except that it might be used as evidence of intention.

34. **C** Fixtures are items that were personal property at one time, but have become involved with the real estate to the point where they are considered appurtenances. The three tests to determine if an item is a fixture are annexation, adaptation and intention. Littoral property is property along the shore of a lake or the ocean. A tenant whose tenancy was of indefinite duration is said to have a right of emblement, which is the right to return after the termination of the tenancy to harvest crops. An encumbrance is any right of another which burdens the title and which survives a sale.

35. **B** Items installed by a tenant on rented or leased property remain personal property, unless there is an agreement to the contrary. If the tenancy is for business purposes, the items are called trade fixtures.

36. **D** Fixtures are items that were personal property at one time, but have become involved with the real estate to the point where they are considered appurtenances. Items installed by a tenant on rented or leased property remain personal property, unless there is an agreement to the contrary. If the tenancy is for business purposes, the items are called trade fixtures. It does not matter how the tenant attached the items, the tenant may remove them.

37. **C** Fixtures are items that were personal property at one time, but have become involved with the real estate to the point where they are considered appurtenances. Items installed by a tenant on rented or leased property remain personal property, unless there is an agreement to the contrary. It does not matter how the tenant attached the items, the tenant may remove them. The tenant merely has the obligation to restore the premises and to remove the items before the termination of the tenancy.

38. **D** Fixtures are items that were personal property at one time, but have become involved with the real estate to the point where they are considered appurtenances. The three tests for a fixture are annexation (whether or not it is attached, and the manner in which it is attached), adaptation (can it be used on another property), and intention (the intention of the annexor). A trade fixture is an item installed by a tenant and remains personal property on the theory that a tenant would not have the intention to improve someone else's real estate.

39. **B** Fixtures are items that were personal property at one time, but have become involved with the real estate to the point where they are considered appurtenances. Items installed by a tenant on rented or leased property remain personal property, unless there is an agreement to the contrary. It does not matter how the tenant attached the items, the tenant may remove them. The tenant merely has the obligation to restore the premises and to remove the items by the termination of the tenancy.

40. **C** Fixtures are items that were personal property at one time, but have become involved with the real estate to the point where they are considered appurtenances. Items installed by a tenant on rented or leased property remain personal property, unless there is an agreement to the contrary. It does not matter how the tenant attached the items, the tenant may remove them. The tenant merely has the obligation to restore the premises and to remove the items before the termination of the tenancy.

41. **B** The idea of a trade fixture is that the item was attached or adapted so we would normally consider it an appurtenance, but since it was installed by a tenant, we allow it to remain personal and give the tenant the right to remove it. If the item was never attached or adapted in the first place, then it simply remains an ordinary chattel, not a fixture.

42. **D** The real estate includes the land and its appurtenances. Appurtenances are items that are said to "run with the land." Items installed by a tenant on rented or leased property remain personal property, unless there is an agreement to the contrary. If the tenancy is for business purposes, the items are called trade fixtures.

43. **D** Domestic fixtures are items installed by a tenant in leased or rented premises. Such items normally remain personal property. The tenant has the right to remove a domestic fixture, but must do so within a reasonable period of time after the termination of the tenancy, lest it be construed as abandoned. In addition, the tenant must restore the premises to the same condition they were in before the start of the tenancy. A domestic fixture follows the same rules as a trade fixture, except that it is installed by a tenant in residential premises rather than commercial property.

44. **B** Domestic fixtures are items installed by a tenant in leased or rented premises. Such items normally remain personal property. The tenant has the right to remove a domestic fixture, but must do so within a reasonable period of time after the termination of the tenancy, lest it be construed as abandoned. In addition, the tenant must restore the premises to the same condition they were in before the start of the tenancy. A domestic fixture follows the same rules as a trade fixture, except that it is installed by a tenant in residential premises rather than commercial property.

45. **D** A fixture is an item of real estate that at one time was personal property but which has become involved with the real estate and is now considered real property. If the party installing the item is a tenant, the presumption is that the intent of the tenant was to remove the item at the end of the tenancy, so the item remains personal property. The tenant must merely repair any damage caused by the removal, and must remove the item before the termination of the tenancy.

46. **A** Real estate includes all the space between the surface down to the center of the earth, and to a height above the surface necessary for the ordinary use and enjoyment of the property. An owner can sell, rent, lease, give away, mortgage, will, or keep all or any portion of the property.

47. **D** The most important concept of real estate is that your ownership of real estate extends from the surface down to the center of the earth, and even above the surface to a height necessary for the ordinary and reasonable use and enjoyment of the prop-

erty. The definition of an appurtenance is something which runs with the land, i.e., is part of the real estate and conveyed with it automatically.

48. **D** Real estate is said to have "fixity," that is, it cannot be moved. It is also indestructible. Even if you removed all the soil from your land, clear to the center of the earth, you would still own the space. We cannot destroy space, therefore the real estate is indestructible. Real estate is also always unique (non-homogenous). No two parcels are ever completely alike; they must be different because their location, at least, is different.

49. **A** The legal concept of real estate encompasses several ideas. First, real property cannot be destroyed because you own a volume of space and space cannot be destroyed. Second, the land is immovable, in contrast with personal property which is always movable. The most important concept is that your ownership of real estate extends from the surface down to the center of the earth, and even above the surface to a height necessary for the ordinary and reasonable use and enjoyment of the property.

50. **C** Real estate includes all the space between the surface down to the center of the earth, and to a height above the surface necessary for the ordinary use and enjoyment of the property. An owner can sell, rent, lease, give away, mortgage, will, or keep all or any portion of the property.

51. **D** Real estate includes all the space between the surface down to the center of the earth, and to a height above the surface necessary for the ordinary use and enjoyment of the property. An owner can sell, rent, lease, give away, mortgage, will, or keep all or any portion of the property. The government may restrict the owners use of all or any portion of the property. The grantor in a deed is the seller. The seller is free to sell all the land or any portion of it, including selling the surface rights but keeping the air rights.

52. **C** The fact that the air rights are part of the real estate does not preclude the sale of the air rights separately from the rest of the real estate. All corporeal and incorporeal components of the real estate are real property and can be sold or otherwise bargained for separately from the rest. Air rights, therefore, are simply real estate, not an easement or an encumbrance. Of course it is also possible to create an easement for the air rights, but in this case the question stated that the Blue Skies Company owns the air rights, not that they have a right to use the air space. Ownership is not the same as a right to use, which is what an easement is.

53. **C** Mineral rights, trees (whether deliberately planted and cultivated or natural), and air space are all part of the real property. However, any other ordinary ownership of a share as a partner or stockholder in a company is personal property, even if the partnership or corporation owns real estate.

54. **D** The real estate is deemed to include the land itself, plus all rights that are appurtenant to the land. An appurtenance is something which "runs with the land," i.e., if you sell the land, the buyer automatically gets all of the appurtenances. It is not necessary to describe the appurtenances in the deed; they pass to the buyer automatically. Appurtenances can be corporeal (tangible, i.e., a structure), or incorporeal (intangible, i.e., an easement right). Fixtures are corporeal appurtenances that were personal property but which have become involved with the real estate to the point where they are now appurtenant.

55. **B** Real estate includes all the space, and everything contained therein, between the surface down to the center of the earth, and to a height above the surface necessary for the ordinary use and enjoyment of the property. Real estate also includes all the appurtenances that run with the land, which includes both corporeal (tangible) and incorporeal (intangible) matters.

56. **D** Real estate includes all the space, and everything contained therein, between the surface down to the center of the earth, and to a height above the surface necessary for the ordinary use and enjoyment of the property. It also includes all the appurtenances to the land such as improvements or rights that run with the land.

57. **C** Oil and gas, as well as subsurface minerals, are real property until removed from the land. An appurtenance is something which "runs with the land," and is therefore real estate. Trees are considered real property. A leasehold interest is a right of possession, but without ownership. It is not classed as real property.

58. **D** Real estate includes all the space, and everything contained therein, between the surface down to the center of the earth, and to a height above the surface necessary for the ordinary use and enjoyment of the property. Growing plants are considered part of the real estate if growing naturally (fructus naturales). If planted (fructus industriales), they are still considered real property, unless they are annual crops. All plants and crops become personal property

upon severance (harvest). A leasehold interest is an encumbrance and is considered personal property.

59. **C** Growing plants are considered real property, unless they are planted as annual crops, in which case they are called emblements and remain personal property. When a tenant has a tenancy of indefinite duration, the tenant has the right of emblement, that is, the right to return to harvest the crop, even after the termination of the tenancy.

60. **C** Growing plants are considered part of the real estate if growing naturally (fructus naturales). If planted (fructus industriales), they are personal property. All plants and crops become personal property upon severance (harvest).

61. **C** Growing plants are considered real property, unless they are planted as annual crops, in which case they are called emblements and remain personal property. Annual crops remain legally separate from the land (personal property), and can be sold, mortgaged, or otherwise disposed of separately.

62. **D** Growing plants are considered real property, unless they are planted as annual crops, in which case they are called emblements and remain personal property.

63. **D** Growing plants are considered real property, unless they are planted as annual crops, in which case they are called emblements and remain personal property. If a crop is planted by a tenant, the crops remain the personal property of the tenant. A tenant under a tenancy of indefinite duration has a right of emblement, that is, the right to return after the termination of the tenancy to harvest the crop.

64. **A** If a tenancy is of indefinite duration (as opposed to a lease which has a definite expiration date), and the tenancy is terminated before a crop planted by the tenant is ready to harvest, the tenant will have a "right of emblement," that is, the right to return to cultivate and harvest the crop even after the termination of the tenancy. This right also exists even if the tenancy was for a fixed term but, due to act of God or other matter beyond the tenant's control, the tenancy was terminated prior to the harvest. The right of emblement does not exist where the tenancy had a fixed duration because the tenant should have realized that there would not be ample time to harvest the crop and should not have planted it in the first place.

65. **B** Growing plants are considered real property, unless they are planted as annual crops, in which case they are called emblements and remain personal property. When a tenant has a tenancy of indefinite duration, the tenant has the right of emblement, that is, the right to return to harvest the crop, even after the termination of the tenancy.

66. **B** Growing plants are considered real property, unless they are planted as annual crops, in which case they are called emblements and remain personal property. If a crop is planted by a tenant, the crops remain the personal property of the tenant.

67. **B** If a tenancy is of indefinite duration (as opposed to a lease which has a definite expiration date), and the tenancy is terminated before a crop planted by the tenant is ready to harvest, the tenant will have a "right of emblement," that is, the right to return to cultivate and harvest the crop even after the termination of the tenancy. This right also exists even if the tenancy was for a fixed term but, due to act of God or other matter beyond the tenant's control, the tenancy was terminated prior to the harvest. The right of emblement does not exist where the tenancy had a fixed duration because the tenant should have realized that there would not be ample time to harvest the crop and should not have planted it in the first place.

68. **B** Growing timber is normally part of the real estate. However, it is possible to sell any part or interest in the real estate separately. It is not possible to sell something which you do not own. Since the timber had already been sold to the lumber company, the company continued to own it. A contract of sale for a crop, even one that is ordinarily real property, such as timber, converts the crop to personal property, even if it remains standing.

69. **B** The real estate includes the land and its appurtenances. Appurtenances are items that are said to "run with the land," and include physical improvements (corporeal appurtenances) as well as intangible rights (incorporeal appurtenances). An easement right would be an appurtenance. Fixtures are items that were personal property but which have become involved with the real estate so they are now considered appurtenances. Growing plants are considered real property, unless they are planted as annual crops, in which case they are called emblements and remain personal property.

70. **A** Growing plants are considered real property, unless they are planted as annual crops, in which case they are called emblements and remain personal property. Upon severance (harvest) crops always become personal property. Crops may be con-

sidered personal property even before severance if sold under contract. Items installed by a tenant (fixtures) on rented or leased property remain personal property, unless there is an agreement to the contrary. If the tenancy was for business purposes, then the fixtures are called trade fixtures.

71. **B** Permanent improvements are appurtenant, unless installed by a tenant. Similarly, natural features of the land are part of the real estate. Growing plants are always considered part of the real estate, unless planted as an annual crop. Once plants have been severed (i.e., harvested), they become personal property.

72. **B** Growing plants are considered part of the real estate if growing naturally (fructus naturales). If planted as annual crops (fructus industriales), they are considered personal property. Perennial plants are real property, however. Once severed plants and trees are always personal property.

73. **A** A synonym for personal property is "personalty." Growing plants are always considered part of the real estate if growing naturally. Permanent improvements are also appurtenant, unless installed by a tenant. A home is permanent, even though it was prefabricated. If it was still on wheels, it would be considered personal, however.

74. **B** Fixtures are items that were personal property at one time, but have become involved with the real estate to the point where they are considered appurtenances. Items installed by a tenant on rented or leased property remain personal property, unless there is an agreement to the contrary. If the tenancy was for business purposes, then the fixtures are called trade fixtures. Growing plants are always real property, unless they are annual crops or if they have been severed (harvested).

75. **A** The real estate is deemed to include the land itself, plus all rights that are appurtenant to the land. An appurtenance is something which "runs with the land," i.e., if you sell the land, the buyer automatically gets all of the appurtenances. It is not necessary to describe appurtenances in the deed; they pass to the buyer automatically. Appurtenances can be corporeal (tangible, i.e., a structure), or incorporeal (intangible, i.e., an easement right). Fixtures are corporeal appurtenances. A mortgage, however, while an interest in real property is considered personal property.

76. **A** Easements and fixtures are normally appurtenant to the real estate. Submerged land is real estate; the fact that it is submerged is merely a characteristic of the particular parcel. A mortgage, however, although it is an interest in real property, is nevertheless classed as personal property.

77. **B** If it is appurtenant, then it runs with the land and is considered part of the real estate. Fixtures are items that were personal property at one time, but have become involved with the real estate to the point where they are considered appurtenances. Trade fixtures, however, are items installed by a tenant. Since they were installed by a renter or lessee, they are an exception and remain personal property. Liens are interests in property, but are considered personal. Mortgages and trust deeds are examples of liens.

78. **C** If it is appurtenant, i.e., an easement appurtenant, then it runs with the land and is considered part of the real estate. Ownership of real estate extends to the center of the earth and includes everything contained in that space. Fixtures are items that were personal property at one time, but have become involved with the real estate to the point where they are considered appurtenances. Liens are interests in property, but are considered personal property.

79. **D** A chattel real is defined as personal property which involves an interest in real property. A leasehold and a mortgage are both examples of this. However, an automobile has nothing to do with real estate.

80. **A** A mortgage, leasehold estate, and various other encumbrances are considered personal property. Nevertheless, they are interests in real property, so they are sometimes referred to as "chattels real." Estates in reversion and remainders are rights to retake possession of a property at some point in the future. Any ownership interest is said to be a freehold but the interest of a lessee is a less than freehold.

81. **B** Mutual water companies are normally corporations which are created to appropriate and distribute water to various properties from a common well. The share of stock is considered an appurtenance to the real estate. However, any other ordinary ownership of a share as a partner or stockholder in a company is personal property, even if the partnership or corporation owns real estate.

82. **D** Since the fence was permanently attached to the real estate with the intent that it become part of the real estate, it is a fixture and therefore real property. Under the law, if you innocently make improvements which are an encroachment on another person's land, you have the right to enter and remove the im-

provements (at your expense) within a reasonable period of time after learning of your error, even though the fence technically becomes the property of the person who owns the land it was installed on. Because the owner of the land on which the encroachment was placed is the owner of the item, he or she has the right to remove the encroachment and may not even be required to give notice before doing so.

83. **A** The right to support of the sides of one's land is the right of lateral support. The right to support from beneath (as where an adjacent owner has a mine under your land), is called the right of subjacent support. Both rights exist only so long as the land is in its natural state. Riparian rights are the rights of an owner to a stream which passes by.

84. **C** The right to support of the sides of one's land is the right of lateral support. The right to support from beneath (as where an adjacent owner has a mine under your land), is called the right of subjacent support. Both rights exist only so long as the land is in its natural state.

85. **D** Earnest money agreements, land sales contracts, and even other financing instruments very frequently include personal property. Planted annual crops are considered personal property but perennial plants are real property. Standing timber is real property until severance.

86. **A** The definition of personal property is "that which is not real," so everything is either real or personal. Fixtures are items that were personal property at one time, but have become involved with the real estate to the point where they are considered appurtenances. Trade fixtures, however, are items installed by a tenant in rented or leased property. Since they were installed by a tenant, they are an exception and remain personal property. Real estate includes all the space, and everything contained therein, between the surface down to the center of the earth, and to a height above the surface necessary for the ordinary use and enjoyment of the property.

87. **B** Fixtures are items that were personal property at one time, but have become involved with the real estate to the point where they are considered appurtenances. The opposite can also happen; portions of the real property can be removed and thereby become personal property. Items installed by a tenant on rented or leased property remain personal property, unless there is an agreement to the contrary. When a lien is created, it reaches all the property in existence at that time, plus any future additions to the property, unless the document creating the lien specifically excludes future improvements. Appliances, even gas appliances that are connected via a gas pipe, are considered personal property.

WATER RIGHTS

THE USE OF WATER IS AN IMPORTANT PUBLIC CONCERN WHICH THE LAW HAS addressed since the earliest recorded history. Until recently water laws have involved merely the quantity of water and how it should be distributed. Modern legislation, however, is now beginning to address the issue of water quality as well. In this chapter we will focus on water rights as they constitute appurtenances to real property in Oregon.

Since the beginning of our legal heritage the law has recognized the distinction between ***surface water*** and ***ground water***. The meanings are fairly obvious – surface water is that water which naturally occurs on the surface of the land, including lakes and streams. Ground water is generally all water located beneath the surface. Ground water is also occasionally referred to as ***percolating water*** or ***subterranean water***. The distinction between ground water and surface water is important because in Oregon a landowner's rights to ground water and surface water are very different.

In most states east of the Mississippi rights to surface water, as in a stream, are based on a law known as the ***Doctrine of Riparian Right***. Under the Doctrine of Riparian Right a property owner has the right to use and appropriate water from a stream only if the owner's property abuts the stream. Properties which lie adjacent to a stream are said to be ***riparian*** properties and their owners are described as riparian owners. The word "riparian" is derived from the Latin word *ripa*, meaning "the bank of a stream." In similar fashion, properties which lie along a lake are called ***littoral*** properties and the rights to the lake water enjoyed by their owners are called ***littoral rights***.

How the water rights of a riparian owner are reconciled with the rights of upstream and downstream owners is the subject of laws which differ substantially from state to state.

NOTES

The most significant problem with the Doctrine of Riparian Right is the plight of a non-riparian owner. In most riparian right states, only riparian owners are allowed to appropriate and use water from the stream. Non-riparian owners can use stream water in some states, although not in all cases. However, ground water is generally available for appropriation, so a non-riparian owner can simply dig a well to obtain water.

The Doctrine of Riparian right predominates in eastern states where there is moderate to heavy precipitation that is relatively evenly spread throughout the year. In these states, if an owner does not have riparian rights, the water table is usually high enough that it is easy to obtain ground water from a well. In the western states, however, the climate tends to be arid, so ground water is not necessarily always available. In many instances, the land would simply be unusable unless the owner could divert water from a stream and transport it across the riparian land to use on a non-riparian property.

Doctrine of Prior Appropriation

The ***Doctrine of Prior Appropriation*** was created to resolve the problems of non-riparian owners. Under the Doctrine of Prior Appropriation water is not apportioned to an owner merely because the owner's land happens to be riparian. Instead, water rights are granted according to the date of the first use. In other words, water rights are on a first-come, first-served basis. The first property owner to use water from a stream establishes the oldest priority date for that stream. In times of inadequate supply the holder of the oldest water right will be the last to be shut off.

In Oregon there is no preference in priority as to one type of use over another, the priority is merely by date of first use. However, in times of inadequate supply, and where there is a conflict between users with the same priority date, use of water for domestic and stock watering purposes will receive first preference.

Of course, if an owner has a right to appropriate water from a stream, but his or her property is not riparian, then a ditch or pipeline must be created across the land in between. The owner of the riparian property cannot refuse an easement for the ditch or pipeline. However, it is legal for the riparian owner to demand just compensation for the loss of market value as a result of having the easement across his or her land.

A major advantage of this system is not only that it allows use of stream water on non-riparian land, but that it also encourages development. Property owners realize that the older the water right, the more valuable it is. A water right, once established, is appurtenant to the property, which makes the property more desirable.

In most prior appropriation states (including Oregon) another benefit of the Doctrine of Prior Appropriation is that, by statute, all water is owned by the state. This allows the state to create a system of permits and certificates in order to keep clear records of water rights. The state also has the duty to maintain minimum stream and ground water levels.

Water Rights Acts

The first significant legislation affecting water rights in Oregon came with the passage of the ***Water Rights Act of 1909***. The Water Rights Act of 1909 established Oregon as a prior appropriation state and further established the ***Water Resources Department***. In the preamble it also specified that all water lying within the boundaries of the state of Oregon is owned by the state in the name of the people, thus clarifying the right of the state to regulate the appropriation of water. Property owners must now obtain a water right by making application to the Water Resources Department.

NOTES

However, the Water Rights Act of 1909 addressed only surface water rights. Nevertheless, appropriating ground water now requires the same basic procedures as for surface water. This requirement was added with the passage of the ***Ground Water Act of 1955***.

Obtaining a water right

All waters within the state may be appropriated except those which have been closed to appropriation. In order to preserve minimum stream flows and ground water levels it has become necessary to stop accepting applications for water rights in certain geographic areas, so a property owner should check with the Water Resources Department before submitting an application.

Certain uses of water, however, are exempt. The most common exemption for surface water is for water from a natural spring which, under natural conditions (not artificially enlarged or altered) does not form a natural channel and flow off the property where it originates. Note that spring water, is normally considered surface water, but if the owner artificially alters the opening, then it is considered ground water and the rules for ground water apply (see below).

Stock watering from surface water sources is also exempt if it is directly from the source and there is no diversion or other modification of the source. There is also a statutory exemption for certain egg incubation projects.

Ground water uses are exempt if they are for:

- Stock watering,
- A lawn or non-commercial garden up to one-half acre,
- A single or group domestic use for not more than 15,000 gallons per day,
- A single commercial or industrial use for not more than 5,000 gallons per day,
- Down-hole heat exchangers (heat pumps which use ground water as the heat source), and
- Watering up to ten acres of the grounds of schools located in an area identified as a critical ground water area.

Uses of ground water for the above purposes are exempt and a certificate will not be issued, even if applied for.

The sprinklers in this farmer's field are probably using water from a stream or a well. Commercial crop watering is not exempt, regardless of the source of the water. The water right was no doubt obtained from the Water Resources Department, either by the present owner or some previous owner years ago. Water rights are an appurtenance to the title so, unless the water right is lost by abandonment, future owners will automatically enjoy the same water right.

Normally, the first step in obtaining a water right is to apply to the Water Resources Department for a ***water right permit***. A water right permit is not a title right and does not run with the land. No water rights can be granted unless the landowner actually makes a beneficial use of the water, so the purpose of a water right permit is to allow an owner to make a legal use of water to the extent necessary to prove that there is water to be taken, and the owner did, indeed, make a beneficial use of the water.

NOTES

Even if an owner makes application for a water right permit it is not issued automatically. Assuming that the property is not in an area which has been closed, the Water Resources Department will then give other water right holders and the public an opportunity to object to the issuance of a permit. In some cases, a hearing will be held. And applications for large uses will trigger a public interest review to determine if issuing the permit would cause damage to public resources such as fish and wildlife habitat.

Once the permit has been issued it will have time limits (generally three years) and sometimes other conditions. Substantial completion of the improvements necessary to begin appropriating water must usually be accomplished within one year.

When the property owner has actually made a beneficial use of the water, the owner must hire a ***certified water right examiner*** to complete a ***final proof survey***. The survey will indicate the quantity of water that was actually used and the use(s) to which it was put. The final water right will stipulate these as the quantity which can be used without waste and the use(s) for which the water can be used. When the process is completed, the Water Resources Department will issue a ***water right certificate***, which is the evidence of the existence of the water right as an appurtenance to the title.

The water right certificate will stipulate the amount of water allowed both as an instantaneous rate (rate of flow), and if used for irrigation, as an annual maximum amount. The instantaneous rate is usually expressed as a number of cubic feet per second of flow. The annual maximum is expressed in acre-feet. One ***acre-foot*** is the amount of water necessary to cover one acre to a depth of one foot.

Surface water rights established before the Water Rights Act of 1909 was passed are still valid. In order to determine the quantity and priority date, an ***adjudication*** process was required, i.e., the matter had to be submitted to a court hearing. This process resulted in nearly 100 decrees, most of which resulted in the establishment of a water right. However, any claim to a pre-1909 water right had to be filed by the end of 1992, so all future water rights must be established by application to the Water Resources Department.

Prior to the enactment of the Ground Water Act of 1955 ground water uses could be registered if the owner desired, but registration was not required in order to establish the water right. Such registered uses were automatically grandfathered and remain recognized today as long as the use has not been abandoned.

Nature of water rights

All water rights in Oregon are based on certain principles. Some of these principles find their source in common law traditions, yet others are from legislation. Regardless of the source, these four principles summarize Oregon water rights law:

- Water may be appropriated only for a beneficial use; a water right for an amount in excess of what can be used will not be granted and no water right can be granted until a beneficial use has been made.
- The older the priority date of a water right, the longer water will remain available in a time of shortage.
- A water right is appurtenant to the land for which it was established, so that as long as the water is used, the water right goes with the land to the new owner.
- A water right is valid as long as it is used, but if it is not used, is subject to cancellation.

Once a water right certificate is issued it is a water right which is an appurtenance to the title and runs with the land forever. However, it is possible for a water right to be voluntarily canceled. It is also possible for a water right to be canceled if the owner does not make beneficial use of the water at least once every five years. Unless the cancellation is voluntary, a legal proceeding will be required. These proceedings will be commenced by the Water Resources Department upon receiving a sworn complaint. In other words, if you have

NOTES

not used your water right at least once in the past five years, another owner with a later priority date is likely to file a complaint in attempt to have your water right canceled.

Water rights are only appurtenant to the property for which established. For example, if you own a section of land (640 acres), but have a water right for only 40 acres, then the water right can only be used on the 40 acres, not the other 600. The legal description of the property to which the water right is appurtenant must be included in the application for the permit and will appear on the final water right certificate.

While a water right is established for a specific property, a water right can be transferred. To transfer a water right to another property, or even to change a point of diversion or the nature of the use, requires the property owner to file an application with the Water Resources Department. Assuming that the transfer will not injure other water right holders and that the water right has been used continuously for at least the past five years, the Water Resources Department will issue a new water right certificate.

You can check on whether a water right exists for a property by contacting the Water Resources Department in Salem where all water rights are kept on record. Copies of water rights are also kept on file in the office of county water masters.

Real estate agents should take note that when an owner sells a property which has a water right for irrigation, the seller is obligated to tell the buyer upon accepting an offer to buy that the property has a water right. The seller is also obligated to deliver a copy of the water right certificate to the buyer at closing. Therefore, a real estate agent should be sure to inquire of the seller about water rights at the time of taking the listing and assist the seller in verifying the existence of a water right, if necessary.

Exercise a

Rights of an owner to water in an adjacent stream are called ______________ rights.

Oregon is a __________ ______________ state, so priority is based on the __________ ______ of the water. This also means that all water in Oregon is owned by ______________.

In order to use and appropriate water in Oregon, an owner must apply for a __________ __________ permit. After making ______________ use of the water, the owner can apply for a __________ __________ certificate which will be issued by the __________ ______________ Department in Salem. When issued, the water right ______________ becomes an ______________ to the real estate. A water right can only be used for the ______________ for which it was granted and on the land identified in the ______________.

After passage of the __________ __________ Act of 1955, a water right must be obtained in order to use __________ __________. Name the four most common exemptions to this legislation:

1. ______________________________
2. ______________________________
3. ______________________________
4 ______________________________

A water right can be ______________ to another property, but only by receiving the approval of the __________ ______________ Department. You can check locally on whether or not a property has a water right at the office of the county ______________.

KEY TERMS

The key to understanding any new field is the vocabulary used in that field. To maximize your comprehension of the material presented in this chapter, be sure you know the meaning and significance of the following terms. Remember that the majority of test questions primarily test knowledge of vocabulary.

Acre-foot
Adjudication
Certified water right examiner
Doctrine of Riparian Right
Doctrine of Prior Appropriation
Final proof survey
Ground water
Ground Water Act of 1955
Littoral
Littoral rights
Percolating water
Riparian
Riparian owner
Riparian right
Subterranean water
Surface water
Water Rights Act of 1909
Water Resources Department
Water right
Water right certificate
Water right permit

ANSWERS

To chapter exercises. If you couldn't figure out what to put in the blanks, find the answer here!

Exercise a

Rights of an owner to water in an adjacent stream are called __RIPARIAN__ *rights.*
Oregon is a __PRIOR__ __APPROPRIATION__ *state, so priority is based on the* __FIRST__ __USE__ *of the water. This also means that all water in Oregon is owned by* __THE STATE OF OREGON__.
In order to use and appropriate water in Oregon, an owner must apply for a __WATER__ __RIGHT__ *permit. After making* __BENEFICIAL__ *use of the water, the owner can apply for a* __WATER__ __RIGHT__ *certificate which will be issued by the* __WATER__ __RESOURCES__ *Department in Salem. When issued, the water right* __CERTIFICATE__ *becomes an* __APPURTENANCE__ *to the real estate. A water right can only be used for the* __PROPERTY__ *for which it was granted and on the land identified in the* __CERTIFICATE__.
After passage of the __GROUND__ __WATER__ *Act of 1955, a water right must be obtained in order to use* __GROUND__ __WATER__. *Name the four most common exemptions to this legislation:*

1. STOCK WATERING
2. A LAWN OR NON-COMMERCIAL GARDEN UP TO ONE-HALF ACRE
3. A SINGLE OR GROUP DOMESTIC USE FOR NOT MORE THAN 15,000 GALLONS PER DAY
4 A SINGLE COMMERCIAL OR INDUSTRIAL USE UP TO 5,000 GALLONS PER DAY

A water right can be __APPURTENANT__ *to another property, but only by receiving the approval of the* __WATER__ __RESOURCES__ *Department. You can check locally on whether or not a property has a water right at the office of the county* __WATERMASTER__.

PRACTICE QUESTIONS

The following practice questions are representative of the questions you will find on the final examination and on the licensing examinations given by the Oregon Real Estate Agency.

1. The right of a landowner whose land borders on a river to use that water is called
   (A) a surface right.
   (B) a littoral right.
   (C) an emblement right.
   (D) a riparian right.

2. A riparian owner is one who owns lands bounding on
   (A) municipal property.
   (B) a national forest.
   (C) the seashore.
   (D) a waterway.

3. Which of the following statements concerning riparian rights is true?
   (A) They are listed in the warranty deed.
   (B) They are found in the public records.
   (C) They are the absolute and exclusive right to use water which touches one's land.
   (D) They are the right to reasonable use of water which touches one's land.

4. Under current legal thinking riparian rights include
   I. the right to use an unlimited amount of water.
   II. the absolute ownership of water abutting to property.
   (A) I only
   (B) II only
   (C) Both I and II
   (D) Neither I nor II

5. The right of an owner of real property to use water from an adjacent stream is known as
   (A) a surface right.
   (B) a riparian right.
   (C) an emblement right.
   (D) a mineral right.

6. A riparian owner
   I. must be granted a reasonable use of the water in a stream if the stream borders the land.
   II. cannot use ground water until the riparian rights have been exhausted.
   (A) I only
   (B) II only
   (C) Both I and II
   (D) Neither I nor II

7. "Littoral" property is located
   (A) on a hillside.
   (B) on a seashore.
   (C) on a boundary line.
   (D) on a stream.

8. When discussing water rights, the term "water table" refers to the
   (A) level of water stored in an agricultural reservoir.
   (B) quantity of water passing through a ditch or pipe.
   (C) distance below the surface where water is found.
   (D) average annual rainfall in a drainage basin.

9. Water in Oregon is considered to be owned by the
   (A) person who uses it.
   (B) general public.
   (C) water master.
   (D) Bureau of Reclamation.

10. Which of the following statements is correct?
    I. All surface water in Oregon is owned by the people.
    II. All ground water in Oregon is owned by the owner of the land under which it lies.
    (A) I only
    (B) II only
    (C) Both I and II
    (D) Neither I nor II

11. Regarding water rights in Oregon, which of the following statements is true?
    (A) Oregon follows the Doctrine of Riparian Right with modifying statutes.
    (B) Oregon follows the Doctrine of Prior Appropriation with modifying statutes.
    (C) Both the Doctrine of Riparian Right and the Doctrine of Prior Appropriation have been abolished in Oregon and they have been replaced with special statutes covering water rights.
    (D) The Doctrine of Prior Appropriation applies in those counties which lie east of the Cascade Range and the Doctrine of Riparian Right applies in those counties west of the Cascade Range.

12. In the United States it is true that
(A) all states subscribe to the common-law doctrine of riparian rights.
(B) the ownership and use of water in states where water is scarce is often determined by the doctrine of prior appropriation.
(C) Congress has declared all water to be privately owned, except spring water which flows in a well-defined channel.
(D) water on the surface of the earth (e.g. lakes, rivers and streams) is known as ground water.

13. Concerning water rights in Oregon, it is true that
I. Oregon is an appropriation doctrine state.
II. the water right is appurtenant.
(A) I only (C) Both I and II
(B) II only (D) Neither I nor II

14. Which of the following statements concerning water rights in Oregon is true?
I. If there is a conflict between two water right holders with the same priority, the domestic user would be favored.
II. Water right priorities are on a «first come, first served» basis.
(A) I only (C) Both I and II
(B) II only (D) Neither I nor II

15. The State gives permission to a non-riparian owner of a farm to use water from a nearby lake. The owner has received this right under which of the following legal concepts?
(A) Eminent domain (C) Percolation
(B) Estoppel (D) Appropriation

16. In Oregon, which of the following statements is true when a dry year does not produce enough water in a drainage basin to fill the needs of all the water right holders?
I. Domestic users are favored over industrial users if the right holders were issued permits with identical dates of claims.
II. Junior right holders may have to do without water during the deficit condition.
(A) I only (C) Both I and II
(B) II only (D) Neither I nor II

17. Three property owners all own properties along a stream. Due to the fact that their ownership dates back to before 1909, they all obtained water rights on the same day following the passage of the Water Rights Act of 1909. If there should be inadequate stream flow to meet all their needs, then
(A) domestic use and livestock watering will take priority over other uses.
(B) they must share the available water equally.
(C) they must share the available water pro-rata according to the quantity of their water rights.
(D) the priority will be determined by the locations of their properties along the stream.

18. Spring water in Oregon is considered to be
I. surface water if it flows in a normal channel over a property, or off the property on which it surfaces.
II. ground water if the natural opening is altered artificially.
(A) I only (C) Both I and II
(B) II only (D) Neither I nor II

19. The Ground Water Act of 1955
(A) regulates the use of water in flowing streams.
(B) requires that an owner obtain a water right permit to use stream water.
(C) requires an owner to obtain a water right certificate for wells dug prior to 1955.
(D) requires a water right certificate for new uses of ground water commenced after 1955.

20. Water right permits in Oregon are
I. appurtenant to the place of use for which the right was established.
II. necessary for all uses of ground water.
(A) I only (C) Both I and II
(B) II only (D) Neither I nor II

21. The Ground Water Act of 1955
(A) controls water uses in streams, creeks and lakes.
(B) requires a permit to use ground water for livestock watering.
(C) requires a permit for all uses of water.
(D) requires a permit on wells.

22. Water right permits are granted by the
    (A) watermaster for the county where the property is located.
    (B) Oregon Water Resources Department.
    (C) Oregon Real Estate Agency.
    (D) Oregon State Land Board.

23. A use permit would be required on a proposed well used
    (A) for livestock, regardless of the number of gallons to be pumped.
    (B) to pump 2,000 gallons a day for a hundred foot square non-commercial garden.
    (C) to pump 6,000 gallons a day for a commercial use.
    (D) to pump 6,000 gallons a day for six families as a community well.

24. A water right permit for ground water is required in Oregon for
    I. industrial or commercial use of water regardless of amount.
    II. livestock watering.

    (A) I only (C) Both I and II
    (B) II only (D) Neither I nor II

25. A water right is not needed for a use of ground water for
    (A) livestock watering.
    (B) a single or group domestic use not to exceed 15,000 gallons per day.
    (C) 100,000 gallons per day to water a non-commercial garden up to one-half acre in size.
    (D) any of the above.

26. Patti LaPata decided to make a duck pond on her land. In order to do so she bulldozed an excavation which then filled up with water. She may use the water without a water right permit for
    (A) domestic purposes not to exceed 15,000 gallons per day.
    (B) any agricultural purposes.
    (C) any single commercial purpose not to exceed 5,000 gallons per day.
    (D) none of the above.

27. Mrs. Flowers has land adjacent to a stream on which she grew one-half acre of daffodils. One year the well went dry, so she temporarily pumped water from the stream. Mrs. Flowers
    (A) needs a water right permit to take water from the stream.
    (B) is exempt from needing a water right permit to take water from the stream.
    (C) needs either a water right permit or the permission of downstream users to take water from the stream.
    (D) cannot take water from the stream under any circumstances.

28. Abel owned land adjacent to a stream and holds a water right for the use of 10,000 gallons of water a day for domestic purposes. Baker owned land behind and adjacent to Abel's land, but did not have a water right. Which of the following is correct in this case?
    (A) Abel could sell water up to the amount of Abel's water right to Baker for use on Baker's land for domestic purposes.
    (B) Baker could not use any water from the stream, even though Abel gave permission, without first obtaining a water right permit.
    (C) Baker could drill a well and use ground water for domestic use up to 15,000 gallons a day without a water right.
    (D) Both B and C are correct.

29. Mr. Farmer owned two parcels of property, one 10 acres and one 50 acres. Both properties lay along a stream. He had a water right certificate to use 50,000 gallons of water a day from the stream on the 50-acre parcel, but no specific water right for the 10-acre parcel. The 10-acre parcel, however, was used exclusively as Mr. Farmer's personal residence, including a one-half acre lawn and garden. In this case, Mr. Farmer could
    (A) use all the stream water he wanted on the 10-acre parcel, so long as his total use on both parcels did not exceed 50,000 gallons per day.
    (B) use ground water on the 10-acre parcel for the lawn and garden and for the domestic use in the house.
    (C) use up to 20,000 gallons of ground water a day from the 10-acre parcel for watering crops on the 50-acre parcel.
    (D) do any of the above.

30. Which of the following statements concerning water rights is correct?
    I. All spring water located in Oregon is owned by the general public.
    II. A water permit is not required to use ground water to water a lawn or non-commercial garden less than one-half acre in size.
    (A) I only (C) Both I and II
    (B) II only (D) Neither I nor II

31. Which of the following statements is true about a person who holds a certificate of water right issued by the Water Resources Department of the state of Oregon?
    I. The owner may use the right on any new property the owner acquires.
    II. The owner may lose the right after a specified period of non-use.
    (A) I only (C) Both I and II
    (B) II only (D) Neither I nor II

32. Which of the following statements is correct about water rights in Oregon?
    I. The property receives the right and it passes with title.
    II. The water right remains valid as long as the beneficial use is continued.
    (A) I only (C) Both I and II
    (B) II only (D) Neither I nor II

33. A water right may be invalidated
    I. if beneficial use of the water is discontinued for five or more consecutive years.
    II. by a change in ownership of the property for which the water right was established.
    (A) I only (C) Both I and II
    (B) II only (D) Neither I nor II

34. Which of the following statements about Oregon water rights is true?
    I. Domestic use of water always takes precedence over commercial use of water if there is insufficient water for both.
    II. A water right is subject to cancellation after five consecutive years of non-use.
    (A) I only (C) Both I and II
    (B) II only (D) Neither I nor II

35. A water right is subject to cancellation
    I. after five consecutive years of non-use.
    II. through a statement of abandonment.
    (A) I only (C) Both I and II
    (B) II only (D) Neither I nor II

36. An Oregon water right, once established, may be lost by non-use over a continuous period of
    (A) three years. (C) five years.
    (B) four years. (D) six years.

37. Harlan Jones sold his land to Adrienne Smith. The property had a water right for the use of 100,000 gallons a day of ground water for commercial farming purposes. In this case,
    (A) Jones is required to deliver a copy of the water right certificate to Smith at or before closing of the sale.
    (B) Smith must make a sworn statement to the Water Resources Department that the use of the water will continue for at least five years before a new certificate can be issued.
    (C) The use of 100,000 gallons per day of ground water for commercial irrigation is now illegal and must be discontinued upon the sale.
    (D) Jones must endorse the water right certificate to Smith at closing.

38. Which of the following statements concerning water rights in Oregon is false?
    (A) The right to surface water can only be established through issuance of a water rights permit from the Water Resources Director.
    (B) The beneficial use of water shall be the basis, measure and limit for the use of water.
    (C) A water right is appurtenant to the place of use for which the right was established.
    (D) A water right may be rendered invalid by two years of non-use.

39. A water right is granted according to several underlying legal concepts. Which of the following is not one of these concepts?
    (A) The beneficial use of the water is the basis, measure and limit of the water right.
    (B) An owner must use the water at least once every five years in order to maintain a water right.
    (C) A water right permit is appurtenant.
    (D) The priority of the original use will determine the quantity of water allowed.

ANSWERS

To practice questions. If you chose the wrong letter, here's the right one! The explanations are designed to clarify your understanding.

1. **D** The term "riparian" comes from the Latin word "ripa," which means "bank of a stream." Therefore, a property which touches a stream is a riparian property. Surface rights refer to the owner's right to use the surface of the land, as opposed to the air or subsurface rights. Littoral rights are similar to riparian rights, but for property which touches a lake or the seashore. A right of emblement is the right of a tenant to come back after the termination of the tenancy in order to harvest a crop.
2. **D** The term "riparian" comes from the Latin word "ripa," which means "bank of a stream." Therefore, a property which touches a stream is a riparian property.
3. **D** The term "riparian" comes from the Latin word "ripa," which means "bank of a stream." Therefore, a property which touches a stream is a riparian property, and the owner may enjoy certain riparian rights to the stream, including sometimes the right to take water. Water rights today are created by the Water Resources Department, and become an appurtenance to the title when properly filed. Water rights are conveyed automatically by any deed, and therefore need not be recited in the deed.
4. **D** The term "riparian" comes from the Latin word "ripa," which means "bank of a stream." Therefore, a property which touches a stream is a riparian property. At common law, riparian rights included the right to unlimited use of water, unlimited navigation, etc. Today the right to take water is limited by the Doctrine of Prior Appropriation.
5. **B** The term "riparian" comes from the Latin word "ripa," which means "bank of a stream." Therefore, a property which touches a stream is a riparian property. Surface rights refer to the owner's right to use the surface of the land, as opposed to the air or subsurface rights. Mineral rights would be part of the subsurface rights. A right of emblement is the right of a tenant to come back after the termination of the tenancy in order to harvest a crop.
6. **D** Since Oregon no longer follows the Doctrine of Riparian Right, an owner of land which lies adjacent to the stream has no special right to the water in the stream. When surface water is not available, ground water may always be appropriated, although many uses will require the owner to obtain a water right from the state.
7. **B** Where "riparian" refers to property along the bank of a stream. "Littoral" is used to describe property which touches a lake or the seashore.
8. **C** The water table is the point beneath the surface where the ground becomes saturated with water.
9. **B** All water lying within the boundaries of the state of Oregon is owned by the state, therefore, except for exempted uses, in order to use water a permit is needed. The permit will be obtained from the Water Resources Department.
10. **A** The Water Rights Act of 1909 declared that all water lying within the boundaries of the State of Oregon is owned by the State of Oregon in the name of the people of the State of Oregon. As to ownership of water, there is no distinction between ground water and surface water.
11. **B** The original water rights law which applied in Oregon was the Doctrine of Riparian Right, a law which had its roots in early English law. This was replaced in Oregon, as in most western states, with the Doctrine of Prior Appropriation. The replacement occurred as one of the provisions of the Water Rights Act of 1909. The law applies equally to all parts of Oregon, including both east and west of the Cascade Range.
12. **B** The Doctrine of Riparian Right is English common law. Most western states have adopted the Doctrine of Prior Appropriation to replace at least some of the original common law concepts. In Oregon, state law declares that all water lying within the boundaries of the State of Oregon is owned by the state in the name of the people of the state. Ground water (sometimes called percolating water) is water which must be obtained by a well. Lakes and streams constitute surface water.
13. **C** The original water rights law was the Doctrine of Riparian Right. "Riparian" means that the property is along a stream. Riparian rights meant that any owner of land along a stream was entitled to all the water he or she could make a beneficial use of. Downstream users were always at the mercy of upstream users. In order to encourage develop-

ment, western states adopted the Doctrine of Prior Appropriation. According to this concept, the first owner in the chain of title to make a use of water establishes a water right. The water right has a priority date as of the date of the first use. Once established, a water right becomes an appurtenance to the land.

14. **C** In order to encourage development, western states adopted the Doctrine of Prior Appropriation. According to this concept, the first owner in the chain of title to make a use of water establishes a water right. The water right has a priority date as of the date of the first use. This is a "first come, first served" approach to rationing the available water resources.

15. **D** Oregon follows the Doctrine of Prior Appropriation. According to this concept, the first owner in the chain of title to make a use of water establishes a water right. The water right has a priority date as of the date of the first use. Once established, a water right becomes an appurtenance to the land.

16. **C** The Water Rights Act of 1909 was the first legislation to establish the need for water right permits and certificates. Many people obtained water rights immediately, so it is not unusual to find more than one water right on a stream with the same priority date. In case of drought with inadequate water to meet the needs of all the users who have the same priority date, domestic use and stock watering take priority. If there is still water available after domestic and stock watering needs of all have been met, the balance is prorated according to the size of their water rights.

17. **A** The location of the property along a stream may be important in some riparian right states, but has no bearing on water rights in prior appropriation states such as Oregon. In prior appropriation states the priority is determined solely by the date of first use. When several persons have the same priority date and there is inadequate supply to meet all their needs, then Oregon law provides that domestic purposes and livestock watering take precedence.

18. **C** Once the water is on the surface, it is clearly surface water. It is difficult to determine how much alteration constitutes material alteration. For example, if an owner drills a well and water comes to the surface, should the water now be considered surface water? Obviously not. Therefore, to eliminate arguments, any alteration of the opening at all is considered as having the same effect as drilling a well, that is, the water is now considered ground water.

19. **D** The Ground Water Act of 1955 essentially did nothing more than add ground water to the types of water for which a water right certificate must be obtained. Pre-existing wells that the property owner had registered were grandfathered.

20. **A** Once a water right certificate has been issued by the Water Resources Department, it is an appurtenance to the land and is good indefinitely. There are several exemptions for ground (well) water. These include 1) stockwatering, 2) a lawn or non-commercial garden up to one-half acre, 3) domestic use up to 15,000 gallons per day, 4) any single commercial or industrial use up to 5,000 gallons per day, 5) a ground hole heat exchanger and, 6) certain irrigation and other uses for rural schools.

21. **D** An owner must obtain a water permit or water right certificate from the Water Resources Department before any use of water can be made. Prior to the Ground Water Act of 1955, all uses of ground water were exempt. There are still several exemptions for ground (well) water. These include 1) stockwatering, 2) a lawn or non-commercial garden up to one-half acre, 3) domestic use up to 15,000 gallons per day, 4) any single commercial or industrial use up to 5,000 gallons per day, 5) a ground hole heat exchanger and, 6) certain irrigation and other uses for rural schools. The Act also requires a permit for the construction of a well.

22. **B** All water right permits and final certificates are issued by the Water Resources Department of the State of Oregon. Copies of certificates are available for inspection in the office of the Water Resources Department in Salem with copies in the office of the county watermaster.

23. **C** A water permit or water certificate must be obtained from the Water Resources Department before any use of water can be made. However, there are several exemptions for ground (well) water. These include 1) stockwatering, 2) a lawn or non-commercial garden up to one-half acre, 3) domestic use up to 15,000 gallons per day, 4) any single commercial or industrial use up to 5,000 gallons per day, 5) a ground hole heat exchanger and, 6) certain irrigation and other uses for rural schools. An acre is 43,560 square feet, so a garden one hundred feet square would be well under the one-half acre limit (100 × 100 = 10,000 square feet).

24. **D** There are several exemptions for ground (well) water. These include 1) stockwatering, 2) a lawn or non-commercial garden up to one-half acre, 3) do-

mestic use up to 15,000 gallons per day, 4) any single commercial or industrial use up to 5,000 gallons per day, 5) a ground hole heat exchanger and, 6) certain irrigation and other uses for rural schools.

25. **D** Water right permits are not issued if the use being made is exempt. Oregon law exempts ground water uses for domestic purposes not to exceed 15,000 gallons, per day, for commercial purposes not to exceed 5,000 gallons per day, and unlimited quantities as necessary for watering a lawn or non-commercial garden not over one-half acre in size or for stockwatering.

26. **D** If the pond is spring-fed, does not leave the boundaries of her property, and is completely natural, any use of the water would be exempt. But since she created an excavation, the pond is not natural so the exemption does not apply.

27. **A** Watering a non-commercial garden up to one-half acre in size from a well is exempt. However, her garden is commercial, so she presumably has a water right for her normal use of the ground water. However a water right for ground water is just that – for ground water only. She would need a separate water right for the surface water, even if the garden were non-commercial.

28. **D** A water right in Oregon is appurtenant to one particular property, and therefore cannot be used on another property without a formal transfer approved by the Water Resources Department. Most uses of surface water require the owner to obtain a water right permit before any use of the water can be made. Appropriating ground water up to 15,000 gallons per day for domestic purposes is exempt and no water right permit or certificate is required.

29. **B** Water rights are appurtenant to the specific property for which they were granted. Part of the application for a water right permit includes a map of the property showing where the water will be applied. Any use of the water other than on the property to which the water right is appurtenant is illegal. The appropriation of ground water for domestic purposes not to exceed 15,000 gallons per day and in an unlimited amount for a lawn or non-commercial garden up to one-half acre in size is exempt.

30. **C** All water lying within the boundaries of the state of Oregon is owned by the state. Therefore a water permit/certificate must be obtained from the Water Resources Department before any use of water can be made. There are several exemptions for ground (well) water. These include 1) stockwatering, 2) a lawn or non-commercial garden up to one-half acre, 3) domestic use up to 15,000 gallons per day, 4) any single commercial or industrial use up to 5,000 gallons per day, 5) a ground hole heat exchanger and, 6) certain irrigation and other uses for rural schools.

31. **B** Once a water right certificate has been issued by the Water Resources Department, it is an appurtenance to the land and is good indefinitely. It is nevertheless subject to cancellation after five years of non-use. Since it is an appurtenance, it can be used only on the property to which it is appurtenant.

32. **C** Once a water right certificate has been issued by the Water Resources Department, it is an appurtenance to the land and is good indefinitely. It is nevertheless subject to cancellation after five years of non-use.

33. **A** Once established, a water right becomes an appurtenance to the title and runs with the land. It can be lost by five years of non-use.

34. **C** The Water Rights Act of 1909 was the first legislation to establish the need for water right permits and certificates. Many people obtained water rights immediately, so it is not unusual to find more than one water right on a stream with the same priority date. In case of drought with inadequate water to meet the needs of all the users who have the same priority date, domestic use and stock watering take priority. Once a water right certificate has been issued by the Water Resources Department, it is an appurtenance to the land and is good indefinitely. It is nevertheless subject to cancellation after five years of non-use.

35. **C** Once a water right certificate has been issued by the Water Resources Department, it is an appurtenance to the land and is good indefinitely. It is nevertheless subject to cancellation after five years of non-use, or the owner could voluntarily relinquish it.

36. **C** Once a water right certificate has been issued by the Water Resources Department, it is an appurtenance to the land and is good indefinitely. It is nevertheless subject to cancellation after five years of non-use.

37. **A** Oregon statutes require the owner of property which has a water right for irrigation to notify the buyer of the existence of the water right upon accepting an offer to purchase, and to deliver a copy of the water right certificate to the buyer at the closing of the transaction. Any use of water is legal as long as the landowner has a water right or is within statutory exemptions. Water rights are appurtenant to the title and pass to a buyer automatically.

38. **D** All water lying within the boundaries of the state of Oregon is owned by the state, therefore, except for exempted uses, in order to use water a permit or water right certificate is needed. In order to obtain a water right the process is first to acquire the permit, then make the use of the water and, having made the use of the water, apply for a water right certificate. The permit is temporary; the certificate is a permanent appurtenance to the title. Note that beneficial use had to precede the issuance of a permanent water right. A water right can be lost after five years of non-use.

39. **C** Water rights in Oregon are based on four underlying legal concepts: 1) water may be appropriated only for a beneficial use and only in the quantity for which a beneficial use can be made, 2) priority of a water right is based on the date of first use, 3) water rights are appurtenant to the real estate, and 4) water rights are valid indefinitely, but subject to forfeiture if not used at least once every five years. The process to obtain a water right is to start with a permit. Once the permit is issued the landowner can then make a beneficial use of the water and apply for a water right certificate. The certificate is appurtenant to the land, but the permit is not.

INTERESTS IN REAL PROPERTY

MANY DIFFERENT KINDS OF INTERESTS CAN EXIST IN REAL ESTATE AT THE same time. For example, an owner may have leased the property to a tenant, so both the owner and the tenant have interests in the same property simultaneously. Or perhaps the owner has mortgaged the property to a bank. Then the bank clearly has an interest in the property also. The word ***interest*** is a broad term that encompasses any kind of right in the real property.

There are many kinds of interests that can exist in the same property simultaneously. In addition to leasing or mortgaging your property, you can give your neighbor an easement across it, you can give a buyer an option to buy it, and you can even list it for sale with a real estate broker, among many other possibilities.

Most of these interests will be discussed in more detail later, but one particular kind of interest that we will explore in detail in this section is an ***estate***. An estate is a possessory interest in real estate. In other words, if you have a right of possession, your interest is properly referred to as an estate. A possessory interest could arise through ownership of the property, or by being a renter or lessee.

Estates are further classified as ***present estates*** and ***future estates***, that is, the right to current possession, or the right to possession at some time in the future. For example, if you own a property, but lease it to a tenant, the tenant has the present estate, and you have the future estate – the right to possession after the lease is over. There are many ways to create a future estate, as we shall see later.

Modern Oregon real estate law is based on English common and statutory legal principles. Early England was a class society with serfs at the bottom of the social scale and various levels of lords rising up to the king or queen at the top. In the beginning,

NOTES

serfs were not permitted to own real estate – only the lords were allowed that privilege. Later, a third class arose, called "freemen." A freeman was not a lord, but did have the right to own real property. With the signing of the Magna Charta in 1215, all Englishmen who were not lords became freemen – the serf class was abolished. From that point on, any Englishman could own real property. For the most part, women were accorded the same rights in real property as men.

What does all this have to do with modern real estate? Today we still use the terms and concepts developed during this early period of history. One important concept is ***ownership***. In early England ownership was a right which could only be held by a freeman or better, so ownership interests today are still called ***freeholds*** or ***freehold estates***. Possessory interests which are not ownerships are called ***less than freehold estates***, or sometimes ***leaseholds***.

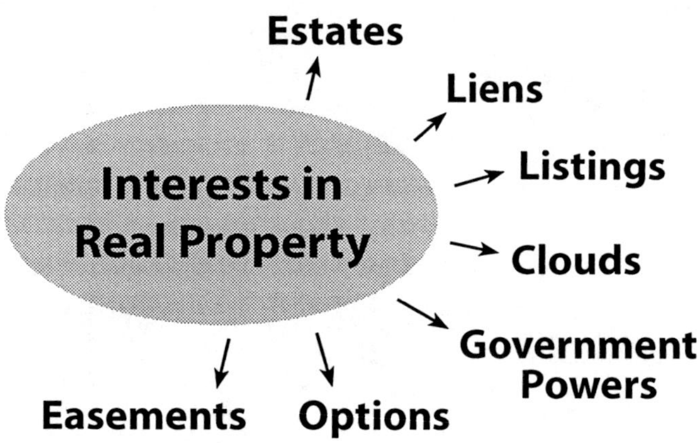

There can be an unlimited number of interests in a given piece of real estate, most of which can exist at the same time. For example, you can own the property (an estate), but have a mortgage to the bank (a lien), lease it to a tenant, grant your neighbor an easement across it, give your brother an option to buy it, and list it with a real estate broker.

There are so many possible interests that we categorize them. There are many different kinds of estates, for example, so many that we will devote this entire section of the book to them. The diagram shows only some of the major groups of interests.

Feudal vs. allodial system of land tenure

In feudal English society, an owner held the land only at the pleasure of the sovereign. This is referred to as the ***feudal system of land tenure***. The word ***tenure*** means "holding," so this really implies that the king or the queen was the ultimate owner of all the land. Freeholders did not even have the right to sell or will their property without the permission of the lord from whom they held the land until the year 1290. Of course, this means that, since the land already belonged to the sovereign, if the king or queen wished to place a road across your land, there was no legal need to pay you any compensation.

By the time of the American revolution, totally new social and legal concepts had become popular. In fact, these concepts were, in large part, the cause of the American revolution. The thrust of these new ideas was a lessening of the powers of the sovereign and the democratization of society – placing more power in the hands of the people. As this developed, a new concept of land tenure came into being, called the ***allodial system of land tenure***. The allodial system of land tenure is just the opposite of the feudal system. That is, the owner is a true owner and not just a holder of the land at the pleasure of the government. While the government does retain certain incidents of sovereignty, true ownership is vested in the citizen who holds title to the land.

Some of the rights the government has retained include the right to take property for the public good (***eminent domain*** or ***condemnation***). But eminent domain can be exercised today only by paying the owner just compensation. The government also has

Notes

the right to regulate an owner's use of the land in order to maintain public order (an example of a regulation would be ***zoning ordinances***). One of the government's major rights is the right to tax privately owned land. And the government has the right to acquire all property for which no owner can be found (***escheat***). While these powers are not technically encumbrances, they nevertheless restrict an owner's use of the property, so we will discuss them in more detail in a later section on encumbrances.

Exercise a

An ____________ is an interest in real property in which the holder has a right of ____________________.

Ownership estates in real property are called ________________ and non-ownership estates are called ____________ ____________ ________________ estates, or ________________.

The early English system of land tenure was called the ______________ system of land tenure. In America, we have always followed the ________________ system of land tenure.

Today, the government has the right of ________________ ________________ (taking property for the public good), the right to __________ property (regulate its use), and the right of ______________ (take property for which there is no owner or heir of an owner).

Estates of inheritance

As we have seen, estates in real property are divided into freeholds and less than freeholds (leaseholds). Let us begin our discussion of these interests with the freehold estates. Freeholds are further classed as ***estates of inheritance*** (usually called ***fees***) and ***estates not of inheritance*** (more commonly referred to as ***life estates***).

A fee estate (or estate in fee) is said to be an estate of inheritance because the owner can leave it to his or her heirs. A life estate, on the other hand, is said to be an estate not of inheritance because the estate terminates upon the death of the owner. That is, if you have a life estate, you own the property, but only for your lifetime. Your ownership ends upon your death. And if your ownership ends upon your death, then there is nothing for you to leave to your heirs. Of course, ownership must continue to be vested in someone even after your death. Who the property would go to after your death (the future possessory estate) is determined by rules which we will discuss later.

Fees are further divided into ***fees tail*** and ***fees simple***. A fee tail (also sometimes called an ***estate in fee tail*** or an ***entailed estate***) is an estate which is granted to the holder and to a certain class of the holder's heirs, normally the children or other family members. The idea is to keep the property in the family. Therefore, if a holder of a fee tail were to attempt to deed the property outside of the class of heirs, the deed would be void. Fees tail are not recognized in Oregon. If you wish to keep property within the family, then the modern approach is to set up a family trust. The advantage of a trust is that the trust is a separate legal entity which can also own stocks, bonds and other personal property as well.

The word "simple" in the expression "fee simple" really just means "not tail." In other words, if you have a fee simple, you can leave the estate to whomever you wish and you can also sell or give away the property during your lifetime. Because the fee tail

NOTES

is not recognized in Oregon, the only kind of fee that still exists is the fee simple. As a result, many knowledgeable persons leave the word "simple" out. In Oregon today, a "fee title" is a "fee simple title."

Fees simple are further divided into those fees which are ***absolute*** and those which are ***defeasible*** (also called ***qualified fees*** or fees which are ***subject to divestiture***). The words "absolute" and "defeasible" refer to how the owner's title is vested. The vesting of title means delivery of the ownership rights and is normally accomplished by a deed. The opposite of vesting is ***divestiture*** (or ***divestment***). In other words, when you buy a property you are vested in title, and when you no longer own it, we say that you are divested.

If your title is vested absolutely, this means that the only way you can be divested is your voluntary act (you deed or will it to someone else), or involuntarily through an operation of law (condemnation, foreclosure, etc.). But if your title is defeasible, then the person you acquired title from has created a ***condition*** and if you violate the condition, you can be divested. Therefore, a defeasible title can be divested voluntarily or involuntarily the same as a title which is vested absolutely, and in addition can be divested if the owner violates the condition. Fortunately, defeasible fees are very rare, so real estate agents are unlikely to run into them in a normal real estate practice.

Of course, if a title is defeasible, then there is a question as to who will gain ownership if the present owner violates the condition and is divested. Normally, the title will revert to the person who set up the condition in the first place. For example, suppose someone deeds property to you and adds to the deed a clause which says that the conveyance is "only so long as the premises shall be used for residential purposes, and if they should cease to be used for residential purposes, then the estate herein granted shall automatically revert to the grantor or the grantor's heirs." Now, if you violate the condition, the title will automatically go back (revert) to the person you got it from. The right to take the title back is called a ***right of reverter, estate in reversion, reversionary interest (estate)*** or just simply a ***reverter.***

In some cases, the grantor does not wish to get the property back, but rather wishes it to go to a third party. But if the property goes to a third party we can't call the future estate a right of reverter, since the word "revert" implies that it returns to the grantor. Instead, if the property is to go to a third party we say that the third party has an ***executory interest***.

As a practical matter, Oregon law recognizes three types of defeasible fees. A ***fee simple determinable*** or ***determinable fee simple***, which is also sometimes called a ***fee simple upon special limitation***, is created by using words such as "for so long as," "while," "during" and the like, together with a statement of the grantor's automatic right of reverter. For example, the language "only so long as the premises shall be used for residential purposes, and if they should cease to be used for residential purposes, then the estate herein granted shall *automatically* revert to the grantor or the grantor's heirs" is an example of a determinable fee. Note that the fee reverts to the grantor automatically upon the violation of the condition.

A ***fee simple on a condition subsequent*** is similar, except that the right of reverter is actually is a ***right of entry***, sometimes also called a ***power of termination*** or ***possibility of reverter.*** The grantor has the right to get the property back, but the right is not automatic. Upon violation of the condition, the grantor must re-enter the premises and take action to recover the estate. Language used to create this interest typically includes phrases such as "on condition that," "provided" and the like. The same residential-only restriction as in the fee simple determinable above could be recast as a fee simple on a condition subsequent by changing it to read "on condition that the premises are used for residential purposes, and if they should not be used for residential purposes, then the grantor or the grantor's heirs may re-enter and terminate the estate herein created."

Notes

When it is desired to have the property go to a third party in the event the condition is breached, then the grantor can create a ***fee simple subject to an executory interest***. This estate is frequently used when the grantor wishes to make the conveyance force someone to act in a certain way, e.g., "I hereby convey this property to Suzie, provided that she marry within the next ten years, and if she should fail to do so, then the fee shall vest absolutely in her brother, Joe." In this case Joe has an executory interest and Suzie has a fee simple subject to her brother's executory interest.

By special statute in Oregon, a determinable fee or a fee simple subject to a condition subsequent become absolutely vested if the condition is not violated within 30 years, even if the grantor places a longer time limit on it. This statute does not apply to estates which are subject to an executory interest, however.

From the preceding discussion, you can see that a fee simple title which is vested absolutely is the highest ownership interest in real property that is possible. You will commonly hear people refer to this interest as a "fee simple absolute" as a short way of describing it. In fact, since the word "simple" is unnecessary in Oregon, you could really shorten this to just "fee absolute." And since defeasible fees are rare, if you say just "fee" or "fee title," everyone normally assumes that you mean a fee simple title absolutely vested.

Exercise b

Freehold estates are categorized as ________ estates (estates of inheritance) and as ____________ ______________

(estates not of inheritance).

The fee ____________ is not recognized in Oregon, leaving us with nothing but a fee ______________ .

In Oregon an estate can be vested ____________________ or the vesting can be ________________ to ________________________ . There are three kinds of these fees, which are:

1. ____

2. ____

3. ____

These must be followed by a right of ________________ or by an ________________ ______________ .

The highest interest in real estate is the ________ ______________ ________________ .

Estates not of inheritance

A fee title is called an estate of inheritance because the owner can leave it to his or her heirs. A life estate, on the other hand, is said to be an estate not of inheritance because the estate terminates upon the death of the owner. Nevertheless, always remember that life estates are ownership interests in real property (freeholds). The difference is that the duration of a fee title is potentially perpetual, where life estates have a duration measured by someone's life. The life which measures the ownership period is called the ***governing life***. This can be the life of the donor, of the recipient, or it can be the life of an unrelated third party. It can even be for the life of the survivor of a stipulated group of persons.

NOTES

The governing life is normally simply the life of the holder of the life estate – called the ***life tenant***. In fact, unless there is some language stating otherwise, the legal presumption is that the governing life is that of the life tenant. If the life estate is for another person's life, then it is called a life estate ***pur autre vie***. The term pur autre vie is Old French which, literally translated, means "for another life." A life estate pur autre vie can be created directly by the grantor – e.g., "I hereby convey this property to you for the life of your brother." But the life tenant can sell the life estate, and if the life tenant were to do so, a life estate pur autre vie would also be created.

For example, suppose you convey a life estate to your sister. Since you specify no other governing life, we presume the governing life is the life of the life tenant, in this case, your sister. Now suppose your sister deeds the property to your brother. An ordinary Oregon deed, without any special language, is presumed to convey all of the grantor's right, title and interest in the property. Therefore, your brother has now received exactly the interest your sister had, no more and no less. Since your sister held an ownership interest for her life, that is exactly what your brother now holds – an ownership interest for your sister's life. In other words, your brother now has a life estate pur autre vie.

Your brother in the preceding example may also be motivated to see that your sister lives a long and healthy life since, upon her death, fee title reverts to you. Life estates always terminate upon the death of the governing life and thereafter fee title must vest in someone. The presumption is (unless there is language to the contrary), that the life estate reverts to the grantor. Note then, that the life estate is normally followed by a right of reverter (also called an estate in reversion or reversionary interest). Of course, these are the same familiar terms we used previously to describe the right of the grantor to get the property back when the estate was a defeasible fee.

When the life estate is to go to a third party rather than back to the grantor, then the future interest is called a ***remainder***. Notice here that the concept of the remainder and the concept of the executory interest we discussed above are the same. Nevertheless, when the future estate follows a life estate it is called a remainder and when it follows a fee estate it is called an executory interest.

Life estates are sometimes created when an owner in fee title conveys a remainder to someone but retains a life estate in the property. Parents frequently convey a remainder in their property to their children, reserving a life estate. This reduces the dollar value of their estate and thereby lowers future estate taxes. At the same time that they are lowering future estate taxes, the parents can take advantage of the gift exclusions which allow them to give substantial sums to any individual without any tax liability. A tax benefit also accrues when you donate property to a qualified charitable or religious organization. Older people frequently donate property to such organizations, but reserve a life estate in the property. The donation gives them a tax break while they are alive and can still enjoy the tax savings.

You can also create a life estate that is defeasible. For example, suppose you want to grant a life estate to someone, but you also want to receive monthly income from the life tenant, and you want the life estate to terminate if the rent is not paid. Then you might grant a life estate "for so long as the sum of X dollars is paid monthly, and if not so paid, then the estate herein created shall automatically terminate and revert and revest in the grantor." This would create a determinable life estate. Note that you now have two rights of reverter – you have the right to get the property back when the life tenant dies, and you also have the right to get the property back if the life tenant violates the condition by not paying the monthly rent.

Since a life estate is an ownership interest, the life tenant is free to use the property in any way, including selling it. The only restriction is that the life tenant cannot do anything which would be injurious to the interests of the holder of the future estate.

NOTES

And, of course, the life tenant has no power or authority to bind the holder of the future estate to any agreements with others.

Even though the rights of the life tenant are subsidiary to the rights of the holder of the future estate, the life tenant can mortgage or lease the life estate or create other interests within it. But what would happen if a life tenant mortgaged the property on a 30-year mortgage, and then died before the mortgage was paid off? In this case, the lender's mortgage would be extinguished. The holder of the future interest would become vested in fee simple absolute and unencumbered by the mortgage. The logic is that the lender took a mortgage on a life estate, so the lender should have known that the life estate could terminate at any time. If the mortgage is an interest which depends on the life estate, then it is extinguished if the life estate is extinguished. The same results would occur if the life tenant were to lease the life estate. If the life tenant dies, the lessee may be forced to move even if the lease is not yet over. Lenders and lessees in these situations commonly protect themselves by obtaining the signature of the holder of the future interest on the mortgage or lease. Then the future interest is also mortgaged or leased so, if the property reverts, the mortgage or lease remains intact.

Anyone who holds a future interest in real estate has a right to expect that the holder of the present interest will maintain the premises in reasonable condition and not allow ***waste***. Waste occurs when a holder of a present possessory estate acts (or fails to act) in such a fashion as to cause a lowering of the value of the interest of those who have a future estate in the property. So while a life tenant can do anything with the property, this right does not extend to waste.

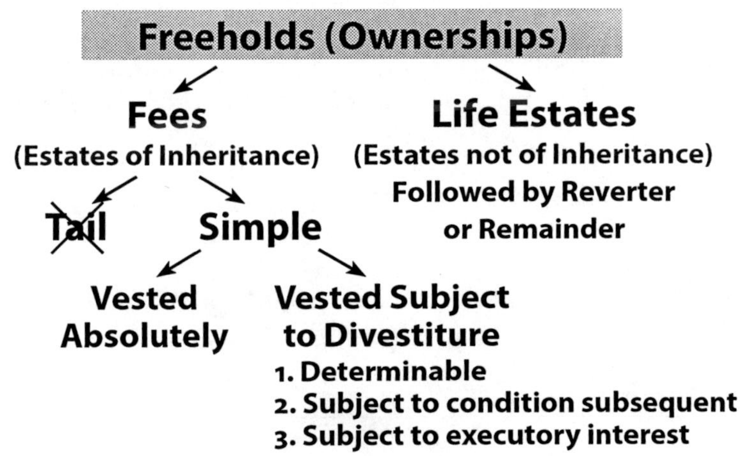

Estates are categorized as freeholds and less than freeholds. Here we see a diagram showing how the freeholds are further categorized as fees and life estates. Fees were originally either tail or simple, but the fee tail is not recognized in Oregon, leaving us with only the fee simple. Ordinarily a fee simple is vested absolutely, but if the grantor wishes it can be vested with a condition. Violating the condition makes the grantee lose the title, so if there is a condition we say the vesting is subject to divestiture, or defeasible. There are three ways to vest the title subject to divestiture.

The bundle of rights

All freeholders (owners) are said to be vested with ***seizin*** (also frequently spelled "seisin") to the property they own. A legal expression commonly used is to say that the owner is "seized of the estate."

Seizin makes the person vested with it responsible for the property. Chief among these responsibilities is the duty to pay the taxes. The owner's responsibilities also include liability for certain damages that might be caused by the land. For example, if the handrail is loose and, as a result, the local letter carrier falls and is injured, the owner is liable. Even if the letter carrier was delivering mail to a renter in the property, the owner is still liable. The owner also has the responsibility to obey the law and to abate any nuisances caused by the land.

On a more pleasant note, the party vested with seizin also has rights. These rights are referred to as the ***bundle of rights***. The bundle of rights is like a bundle of sticks,

NOTES

each of which represents one of the rights of ownership. These sticks include the right to do anything the owner wishes with the property. The owner may use and enjoy it, rent or lease it, mortgage it, sell it, or give it away. Every conceivable thing that could be done with the property is another stick in the bundle of rights. The bundle of rights even includes the right of the owner to do nothing at all.

The owner may exercise any of these rights with the entire property or just part of it. And the owner may simultaneously exercise one or more rights on part of the land while exercising other rights on another part of the land. The owner may exercise some or all the rights for a period of time and then change the use in the future. All or part of the rights may be granted to another for a period of time, for life, or forever. Or the owner may divide the rights and grant them to different individuals, again, for a period of time, for life or forever. The possibilities are endless.

When we refer to an owner granting one of these rights we say that the owner has given one of the "sticks from the bundle of rights." The concept that an owner can give or keep any stick is a concept that is used throughout the study of real estate. For example, when an owner gives a real estate broker a listing, the owner has given the broker one of the sticks from the bundle of rights – the right to sell the property. Always remember that any single stick or combination of sticks can be granted to anyone for any period of time the owner desires.

Exercise c

The length of a life estate is measured by the ____________ *life. If this life is other than the life of the* ______ ____________, *then we say the life estate is a life estate* ______ ____________ ______.

Life estates are always followed by a future interest which will be either a right of ____________ *or a* ____________.

All freeholders, including life tenants, are said to be vested with ____________ *to the property, which gives them responsibilities and a* ____________ *of* ____________, *except that a life tenant is not allowed to commit* ____________ *on the property.*

Leasehold estates

Leaseholds are created by a ***lease*** or ***rental agreement***. The act of leasing or renting the property is legally referred to as a ***demise***. When the leasehold terminates, the owner retakes possession of the property. The right of the owner to retake possession is called a right of reverter (or estate in reversion, reversionary interest or estate, etc.) – the same term we encountered for the future interest after a defeasible fee or a life estate.

A leasehold estate is frequently referred to as a ***tenancy***. This term describes the act of possessing the property by the ***tenant***. A tenant is the party in possession. Legally, we use the word tenant to describe even an owner when the owner is in possession. Note that an "estate" is the possessory interest or right, and the "tenancy" is the act of possessing. While these concepts are slightly different, from a practical standpoint, when describing different interests in property, most people use the terms interchangeably.

NOTES

In the rest of this section we will discuss the various leasehold tenancies and the rights and duties of landlords and tenants generally. However, there is a special statute in Oregon called the "Oregon Residential Landlord and Tenant Law" governing residential tenancies, which is too detailed for the scope of this text.

Creating a less than freehold

To create a less than freehold estate generally requires only the signature of the owner. The tenant signifies acceptance of the terms by taking possession and paying rent. The common practice today, however, is to have the tenant sign the lease or rental agreement as well. If the tenant did not sign the lease, the tenant always has the potential claim that certain provisions of the lease were unknown, and therefore should not be binding.

If the agreement provides that any part of the tenancy is to last longer than a year in the future the agreement must be in writing in Oregon. This is required by a law called the Statute of Frauds. Of course, even though the law does not require a short lease to be in writing, it is always a good idea to take any important contract in writing.

Responsibilities of the parties

A common question is the issue of maintenance. The original English common-law rule provided that the landlord had no responsibility for maintenance of the premises. Today, modern courts give the landlord the responsibility to provide at least some maintenance, particularly of items which involve health or safety hazards. The Oregon Residential Landlord and Tenant Law places extensive maintenance requirements on the landlord. However, in a non-residential setting, the landlord is usually only obligated to maintain the premises if there is an agreement to that effect, although the landlord may be liable for defects unknown to the tenant and for maintenance of common areas under the control of the landlord.

By the same token, the tenant is only obligated to maintain the premises as necessary to prevent waste. The tenant is not obligated to make extensive additions or improvements. Again, the Oregon Residential Landlord and Tenant Law, which only applies to residential rentals, relieves the tenant of most of the burden to maintain the premises and places it on the shoulders of the landlord.

What would happen if someone were injured on the premises during the tenancy? The general rule is that the landlord is liable unless the injury was caused by something under the tenant's control or by some improvement made by the tenant. For example, if you rent a property to a tenant and there is a loose step which causes a visitor to be injured, you are normally liable. If the rental agreement contains language which requires the tenant to perform all maintenance, then the tenant and you would most likely both be liable. On the other hand, if the stair was in good condition at the start of the tenancy, but the tenant damages it beyond ordinary wear and tear, then any resulting injury could conceivably be just the responsibility of the tenant. The issue of responsibility for injuries to each other and to third parties is an area of law where it is difficult to escape liability. The best course for both landlord and tenant is to assume that they will always be liable and plan accordingly.

The law recognizes an implied ***covenant of quiet enjoyment*** on which the tenant may rely. The covenant of quiet enjoyment means that the landlord is obligated to defend the landlord's title against any claims which would interfere with the tenant's right to uninterrupted possession of the premises. If the landlord cannot meet this requirement, then the tenant is relieved of the responsibility to pay rent. For example, suppose you

NOTES

have leased space from the owner of a shopping center in which you operate a business. An owner whose property is adjacent to the shopping center claims an easement through the shopping center and, in fact, right through your space. If the owner of the shopping center is not successful in warding off the claim, and as a result you are forced to leave your space, then your lease is terminated and you have no further obligations to the lessor.

Types of less than freehold estates

Conceptually, there are two categories of less than freeholds. There is a ***tenancy at sufferance*** (without the owner's permission), and there is a ***tenancy at will*** (with permission). There are also two special types of tenancies at will, called a ***tenancy for years*** (for a fixed term, i.e., a lease) and a ***tenancy from period to period*** (periodic tenancy, which has a period that continuously renews until one party gives notice to the other, i.e., a month-to-month rental). It is also possible to be in possession with permission, but without either a fixed term or a period – as though the owner gave the tenant permission, but neglected to stipulate the specific terms.

Although the tenancy for years and tenancy from period to period are actually types of tenancies at will, we don't generally say "tenancy at will for years," or "tenancy at will from period to period." We just say "tenancy for years" or "tenancy from period to period." At the same time, we reserve the phrase "tenancy at will" to mean permission, but with neither a fixed term nor a period. Most people just operate as though there were four separate types and define them individually.

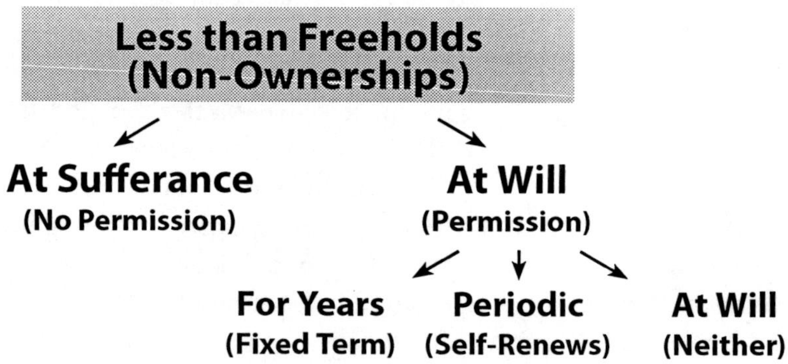

There are two kinds of less than freeholds. If the tenant is in possession without the permission of the owner it is at sufferance. If the tenant has permission it is at will. Tenancy at will can be for a fixed term, i.e., a lease, in which case it is a tenancy for years. Or a tenancy at will can have a period which continuously renews until one party gives notice. This would be called a periodic tenancy. If there is no fixed term and no period, then we call it a tenancy at will. Technically, a tenancy for years and a periodic tenancy are also "at will," but when the phrase is used alone it implies that there is no fixed term or period.

Tenancy for years

The tenancy which gives the most rights to the tenant is the ***tenancy for years***. Do not be confused by the word "years" – a tenancy for years is a tenancy for any fixed term, whether the term is a day, a month, a year, or longer. The tenancy for years is what most people think of when they think of a ***lease***. As everyone knows, a lease has a definite term with a beginning and an ending date. How often the rent is paid, or even whether there is rent, is irrelevant; it is the fixed term which makes the agreement a lease.

Leases also occasionally call for a fixed dollar amount during the term (a ***straight lease***). As a result, lay people commonly presume that there is some legal requirement that this be so. The truth is that leases usually contain cost-of-living clauses or tie the rent to some index or provide that the rent will be a percentage of the tenant's gross sales, among other possibilities. It is unusual to find a lease with a fixed amount of rent.

NOTES

Although most less than freeholds require the parties to give proper notice to each other in order to terminate the agreement, this is not the case with a tenancy for years. No notice is required to terminate a tenancy for years because it has a definite expiration date and the parties obviously knew when it would be over at the time they entered into the lease. Of course, if either party wishes to terminate the lease sooner, then notice may be required. Note that a party wishing to terminate a lease before its expiration has to have a valid reason, such as a breach by the other party.

When the tenant holds a tenancy for years, the owner's title is encumbered by the leasehold. Therefore, if the owner subsequently sells the property, the buyer will take title subject to the lease. Of course, it is possible to place a special termination clause in a lease which allows the lessor to cancel the lease upon a sale. It is also common to find leases where the tenant also has a right to cancel the lease upon the happening of some event such as the death or incapacity of the lessee, for example.

Unless a lease contains language prohibiting it, a lessee may ***assign*** his or her interest to another. An ***assignment*** occurs when you transfer rights under a contract to another. In the case of a lease, this means that you would transfer all of your rights for the entire premises and for the entire remaining term to a new tenant. Many times a lease will contain a clause requiring the lessor's approval for an assignment. The lessor, in this case, cannot unreasonably withhold consent without the risk of becoming liable to the tenant for damages the tenant might suffer as a result.

What if you transfer your rights to just a portion of the premises, or for only a part of the remaining term of the lease? Then this is called a ***sublease*** and, as with the assignment, the lessee may sublease unless the lease specifically prohibits it. Make note that a prohibition on assignment does not create a prohibition on subleasing, and vice-versa. And as with the assignment, if the lease requires the lessor's approval for a sublease, the approval cannot be unreasonably withheld. When a sublease has been created there will be two leases in existence. The lessee of the original lease will have become the lessor to the new tenant. In this situation we say the original lessee holds a ***sandwich lease***.

When the tenant assigns or subleases to another, this does not normally relieve the tenant from the obligation to pay the rent. If the new tenant fails to pay, the landlord has the right to look to the original tenant for payment. However, it is possible for the lessor to accept the new tenant and release the original tenant from liability, This is called a ***novation***. A novation occurs when an original contract is extinguished and replaced with a new contract.

When a lessee abandons the premises the lessor is nevertheless entitled to demand that the rent continue uninterrupted. The common-law rule is that the lessor can hold the tenant to the tenant's promise to pay the rent, regardless of whether the tenant has possession, because moving out was the tenant's own choice. However, in Oregon a landlord has a duty to ***mitigate***. To mitigate means to lessen a loss. Therefore, if the tenant moves out, the lessor must make a good faith attempt to locate a new tenant. When an acceptable tenant is found, the lessor must offset the obligations of the old tenant with whatever the new tenant pays. Of course, the old tenant remains liable for the period when the premises were vacant, and for the expenses the lessor incurred in obtaining the new tenant.

Another factor which may hinder the landlord's right to collect rent from the tenant is the possibility of a ***surrender***. A surrender occurs any time a holder of a present possessory interest relinquishes the premises and allows the holder of the future estate to take over immediately. A surrender of a lease would occur when the lessee moves out and gives possession of the premises back to the lessor prior to the termination of the lease. Of course the lessor need not accept the surrender. However, if the lessor does accept the surrender, the lessee is relieved of any further obligation under the lease.

NOTES

Tenancy from period to period

A more common tenancy (particularly in residential property) is the ***tenancy from period to period***, or ***periodic tenancy***. This type of tenancy is characterized by a rental period, rather than a fixed term as in the tenancy for years. The period may be any period desired by the parties, such as month-to-month, week-to-week and the like. Agricultural properties are frequently rented on a year-to-year basis. Sometimes we refer to this type of tenancy by the period involved. For example, a ***month-to-month tenancy*** is a type of periodic tenancy where the period is monthly, and so on. Usually the parties in a periodic tenancy are referred to as ***landlord*** and ***tenant*** rather than as lessor and lessee, although the distinction is not carefully observed today.

A tenancy from period to period continues for an indefinite period, but can be terminated by either party upon giving proper notice to the other. At common law, the amount of the notice required is the amount of the period, so for a month-to-month tenancy, the notice required would be one month. However, there are several special statutes in Oregon which modify the common law rule. Nonresidential tenancies require a 60-day notice if from year to year and a 30-day notice if month-to-month. The Oregon Residential Landlord and Tenant Law provides for 31 days notice if the tenancy is month-to-month and ten days notice for week-to-week tenancies. Note that the ten day requirement for week-to-week tenancies applies only in residential rentals. Residential tenancies are also subject to shorter notice periods for certain breaches such as nonpayment of rent, damaging the premises, unpermitted pets, and the like.

Since proper notice is required to terminate a periodic tenancy, it is also required if there is to be a substantial modification of the tenancy. This would include matters such as rent increases.

Tenancies from period to period are encumbrances on the owner's title, the same as tenancies for years, so if the owner sells the property, the buyer must respect the rights of the tenant. Of course, the new owner can terminate a periodic tenancy with a relatively short notice, so the matter is not as significant as where a long term lease is involved.

Also as with leases, a periodic tenancy can be assigned or subleased, assuming there is no provision in the rental agreement which prohibits assignment or subleasing. Again, if the landlord declines to allow an assignment or sublease, the matter is not significant because the tenant can just give notice and terminate the tenancy.

Tenancy at will

A ***tenancy at will*** is created when an owner gives someone permission to occupy the premises. Note that a tenancy for years and a periodic tenancy are both tenancies at will, since the owner has given permission. However, it is still a tenancy at will even if there is no fixed term or period. Notice that permission to occupy the premises can be given without stipulating how long the permission is good for, and without even charging rent.

Tenancies at will can be terminated by the owner only by giving proper notice, which is generally held to be 30 days. After all, the owner did give permission for the tenant's occupancy, so it is only fair that the owner give reasonable notice to vacate the premises.

A tenancy at will (unless for years or periodic) cannot be assigned or subleased. Tenancies at will which are not for years or periodic are not considered encumbrances on the owner's title, so a sale of the property extinguishes the tenant's rights and converts the tenancy into a tenancy at sufferance (see below).

NOTES

Tenancy at sufferance and trespass

When a right of possession is terminated, but the tenant does not leave, this is called a ***tenancy at sufferance***. Actually, this does not constitute a true interest in the property since the tenant has no legal grounds upon which to base a right of possession. Therefore, the owner can terminate a tenancy at sufferance without notice.

In order to create a tenancy at sufferance, the tenant must have originally entered into possession lawfully through some prior right which is now ended. For example, if you own the house you live in, sell the house to another, but then not leave after your sales contract requires you to deliver possession to the buyer, you are a tenant at sufferance. The term ***holdover tenant*** is sometimes applied to a tenant at sufferance.

When a tenant never had a legal right, but instead just takes possession of the property, it is called a ***trespass***. A trespasser, the same as a tenant at sufferance, has no legal right to possession, so the owner can terminate the tenancy without notice. A tenancy at sufferance and a trespass are both civil wrongs, so the owner can sue the tenant at sufferance or trespasser for possession or damages. But, unlike a tenancy at sufferance, a trespass is also a criminal act.

An owner faced with a tenant at sufferance or trespasser should be careful. What if the tenant at sufferance or trespasser offers money to the owner? Accepting money from a tenant at sufferance or trespasser may be held to constitute granting permission. Permission means the tenancy is at will (or better), so the owner must now give the tenant proper notice to terminate the tenancy.

Eviction

An ***eviction*** occurs when an owner forces a tenant to leave the premises. This can be an ***actual eviction*** (filing a suit) or a ***constructive eviction*** (forcing the tenant out). Actual evictions occur when the owner files a suit called a ***forcible entry and detainer***, (frequently abbreviated "F.E.D."). Sometimes you encounter the term with a extra word, such as ***forcible entry and wrongful detainer*** or ***forcible entry and unlawful detainer***. In this expression, the term "forcible" does not necessarily mean that the tenant is using force to enter or hold (detain) the premises, but only that the possession is without permission.

Assuming that the owner files a suit for forcible entry and detainer and wins the suit, the judge will grant the owner an ***order of restitution***. This means that the tenant is required to restore possession to the owner. If the tenant still refuses to comply, then the owner can ask the court to order the sheriff to remove the tenant and the tenant's possessions, by force if necessary.

When the owner takes matters into his or her own hands and forces the tenant out, this is called a ***constructive eviction***. For example, if the owner cuts off essential services or locks the tenant out, these actions would constitute constructive eviction. Constructive eviction of a residential tenant causes the landlord to be liable to the tenant for actual and punitive damages, plus the tenant's attorney's fees, so the use of constructive eviction is generally limited to non-residential tenancies.

Where the rental agreement or lease requires the owner to maintain the premises, and the owner fails to do so to the point where the premises become unusable or uninhabitable, this also constitutes constructive eviction. A claim that the owner has constructively evicted the tenant by failure to maintain the premises is a common complaint by a residential tenant.

Another remedy is a ***landlord's lien*** on certain chattels owned by the tenant and brought upon the premises. By statute, the lien attaches to the chattels 20 days after the

NOTES

rent becomes due and remains unpaid. Thereafter the landlord may retain the chattels to enforce collection of rent. If necessary, the landlord may have the chattels sold to satisfy the tenant's obligations. Whenever a party holds the personal property of another in order to force the payment of money, it is called ***distraint***. In this case, enforcement of the landlord's lien is really ***distraint for rent***. Distraint for rent is permitted only if the tenancy is non-residential, and would subject the owner to action by the tenant for actual and punitive damages if it is a residential tenancy.

Lease-options

In an ***option to buy*** the owner grants a buyer the right to buy the property at a certain price and terms for a period of time. For an option to be enforceable, the buyer must give something of value to the seller as consideration. Note that an option does not have to be an option to buy; it can be an option to sell, option to lease, or option to do anything else the parties desire. For example, suppose a buyer gives you a written document stating that the buyer will buy your property for $500,000 any time you are ready to sell it provided that you agree to sell it within the next 90 days and provided that you give the buyer $10. Upon receipt of the offer, you tender the $10 to the buyer. You now hold an option to sell.

Options to buy are frequently coupled with a lease. This is commonly called a ***lease-option***. In a lease-option, the optionee (holder of the option right) also has possession of the property through a lease. Always remember that a lease-option is really two separate documents – a lease and an option to buy. Either the lease or the option can stand on its own. This can create a problem if the tenant breaches the lease. Since the option is a separate agreement, the tenant could still exercise the option. To avoid this, most lease-option agreements provide that a breach of the lease extinguishes the option.

Exercise d

Less than freehold estates are created by a ______________ or, if for an indefinite time or on a periodic basis, by a ______________ ______________________. The creation of a less than freehold estate is called a ______________. The party in possession of the is called a ________________ and the act of possessing is referred to as the __________________. If a tenancy is for more than a year, its creation must be in __________________. This is required by the Oregon __________________ of ______________.

Normally, the ______________ is the party who must maintain the premises, although under the Oregon _______________________ __________________ and ________________ Act, the responsibility to maintain lies with the __________________. The landlord also owes the tenant an implied __________________ of ____________ ______________________.

When a tenancy is for a fixed term, it is called a tenancy ________ ____________ and it constitutes an _______________________ on the owner's title. Normally, the lessee can ______________ his or her interest or can ________________ the premises, in which case a __________________ lease is created. If the lessor accepts a new tenant, this is called a __________________. In Oregon, if a tenant moves out of the premises, the lessor must attempt to ____________________. If the lessor accepts a ____________________ of the premises, the tenant's obligations under the lease are canceled.

When the tenancy continuously self-renews, it is called a ____________________ tenancy. This type of tenancy can be terminated upon proper ____________________ from one party to the other. If the tenancy is month-to-month, the required ____________________ is _____ days. For year-to-year tenancies, a _____ -day ____________________ is required.

When there is permission, but neither a fixed term nor a period, a tenancy _____ ______________ is created. This is not an ____________________ on the owner's title and cannot be ____________________ or ____________________. A _____ - day notice is required to terminate it.

A tenancy _____ ____________________ is created when a tenant lawfully in possession fails to leave at the termination of the tenancy. Such a tenant is also called a ____________________ tenant. If the party in possession did not enter the premises legally, this constitutes a ____________________ which is also a ____________________ act, in addition to a civil wrong.

To force a tenant to move out, the owner can ______________ the tenant. This can be ________________, as where the owner files a suit, called a ____________________ ______________ and ____________________. By filing the suit, the owner is asking the court for an ______________ of ____________________. If the owner attempts to force the tenant out, it is called ____________________ eviction. In a non-residential tenancy, the owner is entitled to a ____________________ lien against certain chattels belonging to the tenant. If the owner retains the chattels, it is called ________________ ________ ______________.

A ______________ - ______________ gives the tenant possession of the property and an option to buy it.

KEY TERMS

The key to understanding any new field is the vocabulary used in that field. To maximize your comprehension of the material presented in this chapter, be sure you know the meaning and significance of the following terms. Remember that the majority of test questions primarily test knowledge of vocabulary.

Absolute
Actual eviction
Allodial system of land tenure
Assign
Assignment
Bundle of rights
Condemnation
Condition
Constructive eviction
Covenant of quiet enjoyment
Defeasible
Demise
Determinable fee
Distraint for rent
Divestiture (Divestment)
Eminent domain
Entailed estate
Escheat
Estate
Estate in fee tail
Estate in reversion
Estate not of inheritance
Estate of inheritance
Eviction
Executory interest
Fee
Fee simple
Fee simple determinable
Fee simple on a condition subsequent
Fee simple subject to an executory interest

Fee simple upon special limitation
Fee tail
Feudal system of land tenure
Forcible entry and (unlawful) detainer
Freehold
Freehold estate
Future estate
Governing life
Holdover tenant
Interest
Landlord
Landlord's lien
Lease
Leasehold
Lease option
Less than freehold estate
Life estate
Life tenant
Mitigate
Month-to-month tenancy
Novation
Option to buy
Order of restitution
Ownership
Periodic tenancy
Possibility of reverter
Power of termination
Present estate
Pur autre vie
Qualified fee
Remainder
Rental agreement
Reversionary interest
Reverter
Right of entry
Right of reverter
Sandwich lease
Seizin
Statute of Frauds
Straight lease
Subject to divestiture
Sublease
Surrender
Tenancy
Tenancy from period to period
Tenancy for years
Tenancy at will
Tenancy at sufferance
Tenure
Trespass
Vesting
Waste
Zoning ordinance

ANSWERS

To chapter exercises. If you couldn't figure out what to put in the blanks, find the answer here!

Exercise a

An ESTATE *is an interest in real property in which the holder has a right of* POSSESSION *.*
Ownership estates in real property are called FREEHOLDS *and non-ownership estates are called* LESS THAN FREEHOLD *estates, or* LEASEHOLDS *.*
The early English system of land tenure was called the FEUDAL *system of land tenure. In America, we have always followed the* ALLODIAL *system of land tenure.*
Today, the government has the right of EMINENT DOMAIN *(taking property for the public good), the right to* ZONE *property (regulate its use), and the right of* ESCHEAT *(take property for which there is no owner or heir of an owner).*

Exercise b

Freehold estates are categorized as FEE *estates (estates of inheritance) and as* LIFE ESTATES *(estates not of inheritance).*
The fee TAIL *is not recognized in Oregon, leaving us with nothing but a fee* SIMPLE *.*

In Oregon an estate can be vested ABSOLUTELY or the vesting can be SUBJECT to DIVESTITURE. There are three kinds of these fees, which are:

1. FEE SIMPLE DETERMINABLE (FEE SIMPLE ON SPECIAL LIMITATION)
2. FEE SIMPLE ON CONDITION SUBSEQUENT
3. FEE SIMPLE SUBJECT TO AN EXECUTORY INTEREST

These must be followed by a right of REVERTER or by an EXECUTORY INTEREST.
The highest interest in real estate is the FEE SIMPLE ABSOLUTE.

Exercise c

The length of a life estate is measured by the GOVERNING life. If this life is other than the life of the LIFE TENANT, then we say the life estate is a life estate PUR AUTRE VIE.
Life estates are always followed by a future interest which will be either a right of REVERTER or a REMAINDER.
All freeholders, including life tenants, are said to be vested with SEIZEN to the property, which gives them responsibilities and a BUNDLE of RIGHTS, except that a life tenant is not allowed to commit WASTE on the property.

Exercise d

Less than freehold estates are created by a LEASE or, if for an indefinite time or on a periodic basis, by a RENTAL AGREEMENT. The creation of a less than freehold estate is called a DEMISE. The party in possession of the is called a TENANT and the act of possessing is referred to as the TENANCY. If a tenancy is for more than a year, its creation must be in WRITING. This is required by the Oregon STATUTE of FRAUDS.
Normally, the TENANT is the party who must maintain the premises, although under the Oregon RESIDENTIAL LANDLORD and TENANT Act, the responsibility to maintain lies with the LANDLORD. The landlord also owes the tenant an implied COVENANT of QUIET ENJOYMENT.
When a tenancy is for a fixed term, it is called a tenancy FOR YEARS and it constitutes an ENCUMBRANCE on the owner's title. Normally, the lessee can ASSIGN his or her interest or can SUBLEASE the premises, in which case a SANDWICH lease is created. If the lessor accepts a new tenant, this is called a NOVATION. In Oregon, if a tenant moves out of the premises, the lessor must attempt to MITIGATE. If the lessor accepts a SURRENDER of the premises, the tenant's obligations under the lease are canceled.
When the tenancy continuously self-renews, it is called a PERIODIC tenancy. This type of tenancy can be terminated upon proper NOTICE from one party to the other. If the tenancy is month-to-month, the required NOTICE is 31 days. For year-to-year tenancies, a 60 -day NOTICE is required.
When there is permission, but neither a fixed term nor a period, a tenancy AT WILL is created. This is not an ENCUMBRANCE on the owner's title and cannot be ASSIGNED or SUBLEASED. A 30 - day notice is required to terminate it.
A tenancy AT SUFFERANCE is created when a tenant lawfully in possession fails to leave at the termination of the tenancy. Such a tenant is also called a HOLDOVER tenant. If the party in possession did not enter the premises legally, this constitutes a TRESPASS which is also a CRIMINAL act, in addition to a civil wrong.
To force a tenant to move out, the owner can EVICT the tenant. This can be ACTUAL, as where the owner files a suit, called a FORCIBLE ENTRY and DETAINER. By filing the suit, the owner is asking the court for an ORDER of RESTITUTION. If the owner attempts to force the tenant out, it is called CONSTRUCTIVE eviction. In a non-residential tenancy, the owner is entitled to a LANDLORD'S lien against certain chattels belonging to the tenant. If the owner retains the chattels, it is called DISTRAINT FOR RENT.
A LEASE - OPTION gives the tenant possession of the property and an option to buy it.

PRACTICE QUESTIONS

The following practice questions are representative of the questions you will find on the final examination and on the licensing examinations given by the Oregon Real Estate Agency.

1. A possessory right or ownership interest in real estate is called an
   (A) abstract of title. (C) ad valorem.
   (B) estate. (D) affidavit.

2. Which of the following would be classified as an estate?
   (A) Mortgage (C) Lease
   (B) Real estate taxes (D) All of the above

3. Which of these words describes an interest but not an estate in real property?
   (A) Reversion (C) Mortgage
   (B) Remainder (D) Lease

4. An estate in real property
   (A) may exist simultaneously with another person who holds another estate in the same property.
   (B) involves a present or future right of possession.
   (C) may be of definite, indefinite, or unlimited duration.
   (D) All of the above are correct.

5. The system of land ownership whereby the land is owned and controlled by individuals is known as the
   (A) feudal system. (C) allodium system.
   (B) commercial system. (D) torrens system.

6. Which of the following is a freehold estate?
   (A) Estate at will (C) Estate for years
   (B) Life estate (D) Leasehold

7. A freehold may be which of the following?
   I. A life estate
   II. A fee simple estate
   (A) I only (C) Both I and II
   (B) II only (D) Neither I nor II

8. Which of the following is considered to have a freehold estate?
   I. The owner of a life estate
   II. Lessee of an apartment
   III. Beneficiary of a trust deed
   (A) I only (C) I and II only
   (B) II only (D) II and III only

9. Which of the following would be an absolutely vested ownership interest which lasts for the duration of someone's life?
   (A) A leasehold estate
   (B) A remainder
   (C) A life estate
   (D) An executory interest

10. A fee simple estate
    I. may be freely transferred.
    II. is of definite duration.
    (A) I only (C) Both I and II
    (B) II only (D) Neither I nor II

11. Which of the following is not a characteristic of a fee simple estate?
    (A) It must be free of all encumbrances.
    (B) It must be inheritable.
    (C) It must be transferable.
    (D) It is of indefinite duration.

12. The kind of estate that is the most freely inheritable and transferable is
    (A) an estate in remainder.
    (B) a life estate.
    (C) a fee simple estate.
    (D) an estate in reversion.

13. When we say that an owner has a qualified fee, we mean that the owner has
    (A) a property subject to one or more easements.
    (B) the right of possession for a fixed term only.
    (C) an ownership interest which is subject to a restriction on the use of the property.
    (D) tenure by authority of the recorder of deeds.

14. An estate which could be divested if the owner failed to comply with a requirement in the deed might be
(A) a fee simple defeasible subject to a condition subsequent.
(B) a fee simple determinable.
(C) a fee simple defeasible subject to an executory interest.
(D) any of the above.

15. A conveyance of a fee simple determinable
I. creates the possibility of an automatic reversion of title.
II. terminates upon the death of the grantee.
(A) I only (C) Both I and II
(B) II only (D) Neither I nor II

16. A private use restriction which contains a reverter clause as an enforcement device is called a
(A) condition.
(B) covenant for benefit of land.
(C) general plan restriction.
(D) personal restriction.

17. Jones conveyed property to Smith as long as Smith maintains a church on the land. Jones has a
(A) remainder.
(B) possibility of reverter.
(C) fee simple.
(D) leasehold.

18. James Patrick devised a piece of property through his will to City Hospital for so long as the property was used for medical purposes. Several years later the City Hospital conveyed this property to a real estate development company. The development company built a shopping center on the property. As a result, the development company has
(A) a fee simple interest in the property.
(B) no interest at all in the property.
(C) a tenancy in common in the property.
(D) a remainder interest in the property.

19. The interest of a lessee could be described as
(A) a chattel real. (C) an estate in reversion.
(B) a freehold estate. (D) a remainder.

20. The interest that a landlord has during a valid tenancy is known as
I. profitable interest. II. reversionary interest.
(A) I only (C) Both I and II
(B) II only (D) Neither I nor II

21. Under a long term lease, the lessor has
(A) remainder rights. (C) an estate for years.
(B) reversionary rights. (D) a ground interest.

22. An instrument which transfers possession of real property but does not transfer ownership is a
(A) deed. (C) mortgage.
(B) lease. (D) satisfaction piece.

23. A lease is an instrument used to transfer
I. possession and use of real property for a specific consideration.
II. ownership of trade fixtures for a specific period.
(A) I only (C) Both I and II
(B) II only (D) Neither I nor II

24. Which of the following is a less than freehold estate?
(A) Fee simple absolute (C) Estate for years
(B) Estate of inheritance (D) Estate in remainder

25. Which of the following is a less than freehold estate?
(A) Property that has an easement on it
(B) Property held under a lease
(C) Real estate minus the mineral, oil and gas rights
(D) All of the above

26. All of the following are non-freehold estates except
(A) estate at sufferance.
(B) estate from period to period.
(C) estate at will.
(D) estate at appurtenance.

27. In real estate law the term "tenancy" refers to
(A) the holding of a possessory interest in real estate.
(B) a position where an owner refuses to grant possession.
(C) the right of the owner to regain possession after a lease.
(D) an estate of inheritance.

28. The lessor of a leasehold estate may be
(A) a fee simple owner. (C) a lessee.
(B) a life tenant. (D) any of the above.

29. A tenant's lease provided that the lessor guaranteed the right to use the property without interference. This is called a covenant
(A) of quiet enjoyment. (C) of title.
(B) of seizin. (D) against nuisances.

30. When a residential property has been rented to a tenant in Oregon, the tenant automatically has the landlord's assurance
(A) of quiet enjoyment.
(B) that the property will meet minimum standards of habitability.
(C) of both A and B.
(D) of neither A nor B.

31. A leasehold would be
I. a chattel real. III. personalty.
II. an estate in remainder.
(A) I only (C) I and III only
(B) I, II and III (D) II and III only

32. If the tenant should allow harm to come to the premises, either willfully or by negligence, this is
(A) waste.
(B) functional obsolescence.
(C) unlawful trespass.
(D) violating a covenant.

33. A lease that has a definite termination date is known as a
(A) tenancy for years. (C) tenancy at will.
(B) periodic tenancy. (D) tenancy at sufferance.

34. An estate for years
(A) automatically terminates at the stated expiration date.
(B) must be for at least two years.
(C) must be in increments of one year.
(D) terminates at the death of either principal.

35. A tenant has an agreement for possession of an owner's property for a period of 30 days. This is
(A) an estate for years.
(B) a month-to-month tenancy.
(C) a periodic tenancy.
(D) an estate at sufferance.

36. If a tenant rents a building from April 1st to July 1st, his or her tenancy is
(A) month to month. (C) an estate for years.
(B) a fee simple estate. (D) a periodic tenancy.

37. Finessa LaVauntelle owned a vacant lot adjacent to a school in fee title. She deeded the lot to the school "so long as the school uses the property for educational purposes, but if the educational use should cease, then the title shall automatically revest in the grantor." The school now has
(A) a fee simple estate absolutely vested.
(B) an easement to use the lot for educational purposes.
(C) a license to use the lot for educational purposes.
(D) a fee simple determinable.

38. Which of the following would be used to enforce a condition that was created at the time the real property was conveyed?
(A) Cease and desist order
(B) Zoning board of appeals
(C) Reverter clause
(D) Violation citation

39. A life tenant is one who has
(A) a lease.
(B) a freehold estate.
(C) an easement.
(D) no interest in the property.

40. The owner of a fee simple estate who conveys his real estate and reserves to himself a life estate in the entire property, grants to the grantee an estate called
(A) homestead.
(B) dower.
(C) an incorporeal interest.
(D) a remainder interest.

41. The right to future possession by the person creating a life estate is known as
(A) alienation. (C) reversion.
(B) hypothecation. (D) contingent.

42. Reversion means
(A) land passes to grantee's heirs and assigns.
(B) land returns to the grantor.
(C) property is alienated.
(D) escheat.

43. Unless there exists a deed restriction to the contrary, the holder of a life estate may do all of the following to his or her holding except
(A) sell it. (C) mortgage it.
(B) rent it. (D) devise it.

44. A life tenant may
I. sell his or her life interest.
II. not commit waste on the property
(A) I only (C) Both I and II
(B) II only (D) Neither I nor II

45. During the term of a life estate, the life tenant
(A) is responsible for paying the taxes on the property.
(B) must accept legal liability for the property as an owner.
(C) must not allow the property to deteriorate.
(D) must do all of the above.

46. Nevah Saydie was deeded some real estate for the rest of her life. Which of the following statements is not true in this case?
(A) She has a freehold estate.
(B) She has a fee simple estate.
(C) Her estate endures only for the length of her life.
(D) She may encumber the estate, but only for a period of time not exceeding her lifetime.

47. A woman granted a life estate in her property to her son but reserved a life estate for herself. Later the woman moved out. The son then claimed a right of possession, asserting that his mother abandoned the property. In this case, the
(A) son is entitled to possession, since moving out subjected the property to waste.
(B) mother retains her life estate even if she moves out of the property.
(C) life estate escheats to the State of Oregon until the mother's death.
(D) son's interest escheats to the State of Oregon.

48. Campbell willed the benefits of his real property to Baker for Baker's lifetime after which the property will pass to Evans. Evans has
(A) a life estate.
(B) an estate at sufferance.
(C) an estate in remainder.
(D) an estate in reversion.

49. If Tom dies and wills his real estate to his wife for her life and upon her death it passes to their son, the type of estate Tom's wife owns is called
(A) life estate.
(B) curtesy.
(C) homestead.
(D) determinable fee estate.

50. If Jones conveys a house to Brown for life, then to Smith, Brown's heirs have
(A) no estate or interest.
(B) an interest equivalent to Brown's.
(C) a reversion.
(D) a remainder.

51. A widow is willed the use of the family home for the rest of her natural life with provision that title shall go to the children upon her death. She holds
(A) a fee simple estate. (C) an easement.
(B) a leasehold. (D) a life estate.

52. A man devised his residence to his widow, and upon her death, it was to go to his three children. The children received a
(A) life estate. (C) partial estate.
(B) reversion. (D) remainder estate.

53. Bill DePrez is the sole stockholder of Lawn Order, Inc., which specializes in landscaping services. Lawn Order, Inc. owned a property in fee simple absolutely vested. Upon his duly authorized signature, Lawn Order, Inc. sold the property to Bill DePrez for his life with remainder to his brother. Thereafter, Bill DePrez sold his interest in the property. When his brother learned of the sale he demanded possession of the property. In this situation, who is entitled to possession?
(A) Bill DePrez, since the life estate was based on his life.
(B) the brother, since the sale canceled the life estate.
(C) the buyer, who is entitled to possession until Bill DePrez dies.
(D) the State of Oregon, since the property now escheats to the state.

54. Rod Stamm left property to his daughter in his will and provided that she was to own it for life and at her death to her children. After his death the daughter deeded a fee simple absolute to her husband. Her husband has
(A) a life estate.
(B) a fee simple absolute.
(C) a fee tail.
(D) no interest in the property.

55. Bill Clinton deeded some property he owned in Wasco, Oregon to Hillary Clinton for her life, with the understanding that the property would go to Chelsea Clinton after Hillary's death. In this situation,
I. as long as Hillary is alive, Chelsea has a remainder interest.
II. when Hillary dies, Chelsea will gain a fee simple absolute.
III. as long as Hillary is alive, Bill Clinton retains a right of reverter.
(A) I only
(B) I and II only
(C) I, II and III
(D) II and III only

56. Jones, a life tenant, sells his estate to Smith. Jones dies. Title is in
(A) Smith.
(B) the remainderman.
(C) Jones' heirs.
(D) Smith's heirs.

57. An estate was granted "to A, for the life of X." A dies while X is still living. The estate
(A) ceases to exist.
(B) escheats to the state.
(C) vests in X for X's life.
(D) vests in the heirs or devisees of A.

58. Mr. Snook who had a fee simple estate sold it to Mr. Dunn but kept a life estate in the property based upon his own life and remained in possession. Mr. Snook then sold his interest to Mr. Britt and gave possession to Mr. Britt. When Mr. Dunn heard of the sale he demanded possession of the property. Who is entitled to possession?
(A) Mr. Snook, since the life estate was based on his life.
(B) Mr. Dunn, since the sale to Mr. Britt canceled the life estate.
(C) Mr. Britt, who may possess the property until Mr. Snook dies.
(D) The property escheats to the state.

59. Joseph Marino leased his life estate in a parcel of real property for five years. He died prior to the expiration of the five-year lease. Upon Marino's death it became apparent that the lease is
(A) still valid until the expiration date, and the lessee will continue to pay the previously agreed rental installments into Marino's estate.
(B) invalid because Marino only had a life estate in the property.
(C) invalid unless ratified by the Marino estate administrator.
(D) still valid until the expiration date, but the lessee must begin paying the previously agreed upon rental installments to the remainderman.

60. Mr. Turner, who had a life estate, leased the property for five years. One year later he died. Mr. Barrett, who had the remainder interest, wants the lessee out. Which of the following is true?
(A) The lease is valid for four more years.
(B) The lease is invalid at its inception (holder of life estate can't lease).
(C) The lease was valid only so long as Mr. Turner was alive.
(D) None of the above.

61. Max DeFraude leased some property to Candide L'Innocence on a five-year lease. Two years thereafter, DeFraude died, at which time his heirs discovered that he held a life estate in the property. DeFraude's heirs ask L'Innocence to vacate the property. If she contests their right to ask her to leave, a court would most likely find that the lease
(A) was valid for the remainder of its term.
(B) was invalid from the start, since a life estate cannot be leased.
(C) expired upon DeFraude's death.
(D) would be valid until L'Innocence's death.

62. In a deed in which the grantor, Paul Jenkins, stated "to Angelo for his life, and then to Paul Jenkins" the grantor has what type of interest?
(A) A life estate
(B) A remainder
(C) A reversion
(D) A right of re-entry

63. Which of the following statements concerning a life estate is false?
(A) All conveyances for a life estate have to be in writing to be enforceable.
(B) A life estate can never extend beyond the life of the life tenant.
(C) A life estate can be a freehold estate.
(D) A person holding a life estate does not have fee title.

64. Which of the following statements concerning life estates is false?
(A) All life estates are for the life of the tenant.
(B) All contracts for a life estate have to be in writing to be enforceable.
(C) A life estate can be a freehold estate.
(D) The life tenant is responsible to pay taxes on the property.

65. Which of the following statements concerning life estates is true?
I. A life estate is considered to be a freehold estate.
II. A life estate can be measured by the life of someone other than the holder of the life estate.
(A) I only (C) Both I and II
(B) II only (D) Neither I nor II

66. A life estate
(A) cannot be encumbered by the holder.
(B) must be measured by the life of only one person.
(C) can be created by will or deed.
(D) is created by the holder of the life estate.

67. A life estate
I. cannot be encumbered by the holder of the life estate.
II. may be measured by the life of more than one person.
III. is an estate of inheritance.
(A) I only (C) I and III only
(B) II only (D) I, II and III

68. The owner's "bundle of rights" to real property includes
I. the air rights above his property.
II. a tenant farmer's right to harvest emblements.
(A) I only (C) Both I and II
(B) II only (D) Neither I nor II

69. Which of the following are included in the bundle of rights concept of real property ownership?
I. The right to tax and escheat to the state
II. The right to lease
III. The right to devise
(A) I only (C) III only
(B) II only (D) II and III only

70. The rights of ownership, including the right to use, possess, enjoy and dispose of a thing in any legal way and to exclude everyone else without rights from interfering is called
(A) corporeal ownership.
(B) incorporeal ownership.
(C) bundle of rights.
(D) survivorship.

71. A private owner of land may
(A) refuse to sell the land to the government.
(B) reject a claim for taxes due on the land.
(C) disinherit his or her heirs.
(D) refuse to follow certain zoning ordinances.

72. A homeowners' association in a subdivision adopted a restriction in which "for sale" signs were prohibited. The restriction is unenforceable because it interferes with the
I. right of the government to create such ordinances.
II. owner's right to sell the property.
(A) I only (C) Both I and II
(B) II only (D) Neither I nor II

73. An item that "belongs to" and passes with the title of the real property is
(A) an emblement. (C) a chattel.
(B) personal property. (D) an appurtenance.

74. Rights in personal property are known as
(A) estates. (C) fee simple estates.
(B) common estates. (D) chattel interests.

75. The interest that a tenant has by virtue of a lease is called a
I. leasehold estate.
II. less than freehold estate.
(A) I only (C) Both I and II
(B) II only (D) Neither I nor II

76. Villa agrees to lease a mountain cabin to Hopkins for the summer months of June, July, and August. Hopkins has an estate
(A) at will.
(B) at sufferance.
(C) from period to period.
(D) for years.

77. A lease on real property is generally considered to be
(A) a property lien.
(B) an estate for years.
(C) an estate at sufferance.
(D) a life estate.

78. An estate for years in real estate can also be called a
(A) leasehold.
(B) fee simple conditional.
(C) fee.
(D) joint tenancy.

79. The sale of a property that is under a long term lease has which of the following effects?
(A) It terminates the lease upon 45 days' notice by the new owner.
(B) It has no effect upon the term of the lease as far as the tenant is concerned.
(C) The sale cannot be made unless the present tenant is notified of the intention to sell and given an opportunity to terminate the lease.
(D) It terminates the lease and the tenant must negotiate a new lease with the new owner.

80. Sue Reilly is a lessee in an apartment building owned by Pacific Management, Inc. If Pacific Management sells the building
(A) Reilly would have first option to lease from the new owner.
(B) Reilly's current lease would be unaffected by the sale.
(C) Reilly would have to move out or negotiate a new lease with the new owner.
(D) Reilly would be required to move out.

81. Bill and Elizabeth Morgan owned a 12-unit apartment complex as tenants by the entirety. They signed a two-year lease for one unit with David Crawford. Three months later Bill Morgan died. Elizabeth sold the building to Kathleen Bishop two months later. This transaction
(A) would terminate Crawford's current lease.
(B) would require Crawford to renegotiate his current lease with Bishop.
(C) would have no effect on Crawford's current lease.
(D) could not be completed until all of the tenants' current leases with Elizabeth Morgan were renegotiated with Bishop.

82. A lease of real property is generally considered to be
(A) an encumbrance on the title to the property.
(B) an estate for years.
(C) both A and B.
(D) neither A nor B.

83. If a tenant holds over after the expiration of a lease without the consent of the landlord, the tenant holds a
(A) month-to-month estate.
(B) periodic tenancy.
(C) tenancy in common.
(D) tenancy at sufferance.

84. A man had a one-year lease on an apartment which expired. He stayed on after the expiration with the consent of the landlord and began to pay rent on a monthly basis. He now holds
(A) an estate in remainder.
(B) a tenancy at sufferance.
(C) a month-to-month tenancy.
(D) an easement.

85. Smith leased a residence for a six month term and upon expiration of the lease retained possession of the property without the consent of the landlord. Smith now holds an
(A) estate for years.
(B) estate at will.
(C) estate from period to period.
(D) estate at sufferance.

86. A man had a one-year lease on a residence which expired July 31. He stayed on after that date without the consent of the landlord and did not pay any rent. He now holds
(A) an estate in remainder.
(B) a tenancy at sufferance.
(C) a month-to-month tenancy.
(D) an easement.

87. A lessee had five years remaining on a lease. The lessee wished to enter into an agreement where another person would take over all the remaining rights the lessee had in the property. This would be known as
(A) an assignment of lease.
(B) a gross lease.
(C) a sublease.
(D) a net lease.

88. Typically, a sublease constitutes
(A) the same as an assignment of the lessee's interest.
(B) a transfer of the entire leasehold interest of the lessee.
(C) a transfer of a portion of the leasehold interest of the lessee.
(D) both A and B.

89. A lessee decided to sublet the entire estate to a third party. The new lessee will become a
(A) landlord.
(B) grantor.
(C) trustee.
(D) tenant.

90. When all or part of a tenant's rights in a property are subleased to another,
(A) primary responsibility for the rent payments shifts to the new tenant.
(B) the original tenant remains fully liable to the lessor for the rent payments.
(C) both A and B are correct.
(D) neither A nor B is correct.

91. A tenant assigned the lease to another. The tenant
(A) transferred the right of possession for the entire remaining term of the lease.
(B) retained secondary liability for payment of the rent of the new tenant does not pay.
(C) accomplished the same thing as a sublease.
(D) did both A and B.

92. A landlord and tenant reached a verbal agreement on a five-year lease. The lease was signed by the landlord and delivered to the tenant. On receipt of the lease, the tenant moved in, but did not ever sign the lease. If the tenant does not pay the rent stipulated in the lease, the landlord can
(A) successfully sue to collect the rent.
(B) collect nothing, as the tenant did not sign the lease.
(C) collect nothing, as the tenant had a tenancy at will which does not require consideration.
(D) collect nothing, provided the tenant moves out immediately after being made aware of the landlord's demand for payment.

93. The terms and conditions of a written lease can be changed only by
(A) the surrender and acceptance of the old lease and the creation of a new one.
(B) a written codicil to the original lease.
(C) a modification agreement signed by the lessor only.
(D) a modification agreement signed by the lessee only.

94. A tenant in a commercial building informed the landlord that a crack had developed in the ceiling. The lease provided that any repairs were the responsibility of the tenant. However, to maintain good tenant relations, the landlord agreed to fix the crack. After the landlord repaired the crack plaster fell, injuring the tenant, as a result of the landlord's faulty repair. If the tenant wishes to recover damages, the tenant will be able to recover
(A) nothing, as the landlord was not obligated to repair the ceiling in the first place.
(B) the cost of re-repairing the ceiling, but nothing for the damages.
(C) for damages, but not the cost of re-repairing the ceiling.
(D) for damages as well as the cost of re-repairing the ceiling.

95. Unless prohibited by the terms of the agreement, a lessee may
I. mortgage the leasehold interest.
II. install trade fixtures and remove them upon vacating the premises.
(A) I only
(B) II only
(C) Both I and II
(D) Neither I nor II

96. A tenancy which automatically renews itself on the last day of the term for a further term of the same duration until terminated by either party with proper notice is called a
(A) tenancy at will.
(B) periodic tenancy.
(C) tenancy at sufferance.
(D) term certain tenancy.

97. An estate in land which runs from year to year is called
(A) a freehold estate.
(B) an estate at will.
(C) an estate for years.
(D) a periodic tenancy.

98. A farmer rented a property on a yearly basis where the law provided that either party could terminate the arrangement with 60 days notice. This was most likely
(A) a tenancy for years.
(B) a tenancy from period to period.
(C) a tenancy at will.
(D) a life estate.

99. An estate at will is
(A) an inheritance of property through an estate.
(B) a tenancy of uncertain duration.
(C) both A and B.
(D) neither A nor B.

100. Under an estate at will,
I. 30 days notice is required to terminate the tenancy.
II. the tenancy is created with the permission of the owner.
(A) I only
(B) II only
(C) Both I and II
(D) Neither I nor II

101. An estate which can be terminated by either party at any time would be
(A) an estate for years.
(B) a tenancy at sufferance.
(C) a tenancy at will.
(D) a tenancy from period to period.

102. A tenant possessed a property for five years without the permission of the owner. This means that the tenant's interest was a
(A) tenancy at sufferance.
(B) tenancy for years.
(C) periodic tenancy.
(D) tenancy at will.

103. A person who originally had a lease but stayed on the premises after the termination of the lease is
(A) a tenant at sufferance.
(B) a holdover tenant.
(C) both a tenant at sufferance and a holdover tenant.
(D) neither a tenant at sufferance nor a holdover tenant.

104. Under Oregon law, how much notice is required to terminate a tenancy at sufferance?
(A) No notice is required.
(B) A 24-hour notice is required.
(C) A 30-day notice is required.
(D) The amount of notice required depends on the length of time the tenant has been in possession.

105. The type of tenancy which gives the lessee the fewest rights is the
(A) tenancy at sufferance.
(B) tenancy at will.
(C) tenancy from period to period.
(D) tenancy for years.

106. Hendrickson leased office space from Vulture Enterprises, Inc. on a five-year lease. After three years of the lease, Hendrickson abandoned the premises and ceased making rent payments. Vulture Enterprises, Inc.
I. could sue for the entire unpaid balance of the lease.
II. must make a reasonable effort to re-rent the premises and, if successful, must lower the damages they claim by the amount received from the new tenant.
(A) I only
(B) II only
(C) Both I and II
(D) Neither I nor II

107. When leased premises reach such a physical condition due to lack of attention by the landlord whereby the tenant is unable to occupy them for the purpose intended, the situation is legally recognized as
(A) a dispossess eviction.
(B) an actual eviction.
(C) a constructive eviction.
(D) a passive eviction.

108. An owner of a retail building did not receive the rent when it was due, so the landlord had the water turned off in order to force the tenant out. You would say that
 I. this constituted constructive eviction.
 II. the landlord had a legal right to do this.
 (A) I only (C) Both I and II
 (B) II only (D) Neither I nor II

109. When the tenant under a lease holds over after the termination of the lease, the
 I. landlord may physically remove the tenant and the tenant's personal property.
 II. tenant is considered at law to be merely a trespasser.
 (A) I only (C) Both I and II
 (B) II only (D) Neither I nor II

110. A forcible entry and wrongful detainer action would normally be used by a
 I. lessor. II. lessee.
 (A) I only (C) Both I and II
 (B) II only (D) Neither I nor II

111. A lessee had possession of real property under a five-year lease. During the lease, the lessor died. As a result of the death of the lessor,
 (A) the heirs could evict the tenant as soon as they gain title.
 (B) the lease continued for the remainder of its term.
 (C) as soon as the heirs gain title they must reaffirm the lease or they will lose their right to collect rent from the tenant.
 (D) as soon as the heirs gain title they can evict the tenant after at least 30 days notice.

112. A lessee may terminate an ordinary lease
 (A) if the lessor interferes with the lessee's quiet enjoyment of the property.
 (B) if the lessor sells the property.
 (C) upon the death of the lessor.
 (D) if the lessor becomes delinquent in paying an underlying mortgage.

113. No notice is necessary in Oregon to terminate a
 (A) tenancy at will.
 (B) tenancy from year to year.
 (C) tenancy from month to month.
 (D) tenancy at sufferance.

114. A lessor and lessee got together and agreed to terminate a lease. This would be called a
 (A) rescission.
 (B) surrender and acceptance.
 (C) revocation.
 (D) cancellation.

115. If Fred Shepard owns a freehold estate, which of the following actions would cause his interest to be converted to a less than freehold estate?
 (A) Conveyance of the mineral and oil rights therein to a third party
 (B) Conveyance of easement for right of way over the land
 (C) Leasing of the land for agricultural purposes to a third party for a period of five years
 (D) None of the above

116. If a person holds a fee simple estate in property, which of the following will result in his or her being left with a less than freehold estate?
 (A) Selling the mineral and oil rights
 (B) Leasing the land on a long term lease
 (C) Assigning a right of way to a railroad company
 (D) None of the above

117. Mabel Barres owns a parcel of real property. She can change her fee simple title to less than a freehold estate by
 I. selling the mineral rights.
 II. a sale-leaseback arrangement.
 (A) I only (C) Both I and II
 (B) II only (D) Neither I nor II

118. The maximum estate that a person may hold in land is called
 (A) estate in severalty. (C) an estate for years.
 (B) a fee simple estate. (D) a life estate.

119. The greatest interest one may have in land is called
 (A) an estate for years. (C) a leasehold estate.
 (B) a fee simple estate. (D) a life estate.

120. The most complete form of ownership our law recognizes today is the
 (A) life estate.
 (B) fee simple absolute.
 (C) fee simple determinable.
 (D) adverse possession.

121. Of the following, the largest estate or ownership in real property is
(A) an estate at sufferance.
(B) an estate at will.
(C) a fee simple estate.
(D) a life estate.

122. Which of the following does the law recognize as the greatest interest in real estate?
(A) Conventional life estate
(B) Fee simple estate
(C) Leasehold estate
(D) Estate of survivorship

123. Which of the following are synonymous in real estate?
I. Estate for years — Periodic estate
II. Estate at will — Tenancy at sufferance
(A) I only (C) Both I and II
(B) II only (D) Neither I nor II

124. Which of the following mean the same thing?
(A) Fee simple upon special limitation — Determinable fee
(B) Defeasible fee — Fee subject to divestiture
(C) Leasehold estate — Less than freehold estate
(D) All of the above pairs mean the same thing.

125. Which of the following would be an estate for an indefinite period?
(A) Tenancy for years
(B) Encumbrance
(C) Freehold estate
(D) Easement appurtenant to the land

126. Which of the following would not be an estate in real property?
(A) A remainder
(B) A leasehold
(C) A greater than freehold estate
(D) All of the above are estates in real property.

127. From the point of view of the lessee, the weakest possible tenancy is a
(A) periodic tenancy. (C) tenancy at sufferance.
(B) tenancy for years. (D) tenancy in common.

128. Polly Esther Suitte has some rights in her neighbor's property. Her rights do not constitute an estate. The rights could be
(A) a remainder.
(B) an easement.
(C) a right of reverter.
(D) a lease for less than a year.

129. The owner of a condominium and the lessee of an apartment have many things in common but their legal relationship with the property is different. With respect to their similarities both parties would hold
(A) an estate in real property.
(B) a less than freehold interest.
(C) a fee interest.
(D) an estate of inheritance.

130. A single woman bought a condominium unit in Willamette, Oregon. The land under the units was owned. She probably had
(A) an estate in fee simple absolute in real property.
(B) an estate for years in real property.
(C) a life estate in real property.
(D) a tenancy for years in real property.

131. A tenant under a lease also held an option to buy. If the tenant assigned the lease to a new tenant, the option to buy
(A) could be voided by the owner.
(B) would become illegal under the provisions of the Statute of Frauds.
(C) would render the option unenforceable.
(D) would constitute a transfer of the option to the new lessee.

ANSWERS

To practice questions. If you chose the wrong letter, here's the right one! The explanations are designed to clarify your understanding.

1. **B** An estate is any interest in property which gives the holder a right of possession. An abstract of title is a summary of all events affecting the title to a parcel from the original homestead to date. The term "ad valorem" is used in reference to property taxes, and means "according to value." An affidavit is a statement signed under penalty of perjury.
2. **C** An estate is any interest in property which gives the holder a right of possession. A lease would be such an interest, as would an ownership, but a mortgage and real estate taxes are liens, not rights of possession.
3. **C** An interest is any right that could exist in property, from the slightest stick in the bundle of rights, up to and including full ownership. An estate is any interest which includes a right of possession. Reversions and remainders are future estates which follow life estates, leases, and other possible present estates. A lease is a right of possession, so it is also an estate. A mortgage, however, does not grant the lender the right of possession.
4. **D** An owner can lease or rent the property to a tenant, so the owner holds a right of reverter (future estate), while the tenant has the present possessory interest, thereby creating two estates in the property at the same time. An estate can be for a definite time period (for years), for life (life estate), or forever (fee title).
5. **C** The original English system of land holding was called the feudal system. Under the feudal system, the sovereign owned all property and the subjects had the right to possession, use, enjoyment, profit, etc. but only at the pleasure of the sovereign. One of the reasons for the revolution in the American colonies was to change this to the more modern allodial idea: When you own real estate, it is your real estate. You do not hold real estate today at the pleasure of the government. It is your property, although the government retains rights in it, such as the right of eminent domain, taxation, etc. Allodial is stated as allodium in some textbooks. The Torrens system is a method of registering land titles, as an alternative to title insurance.
6. **B** An estate is any interest in property which gives the holder a right of possession. There are two kinds of estates, freehold (ownership) and less than freehold (non-ownership). A freehold estate could be a fee (ordinary ownership), or a life estate (ownership for a lifetime). Less than freehold estates are divided into estates for years (for a fixed term, i.e., a lease), periodic estates (of indefinite duration), estates at will (with permission, but neither a period nor a fixed term), and estates at sufferance (no permission).
7. **C** An estate is any interest in property which gives the holder a right of possession. There are two kinds of estates, freehold (ownership) and less than freehold (non-ownership). A freehold estate could be a fee (ordinary ownership), or a life estate (ownership for a lifetime).
8. **A** An estate is any interest in property which gives the holder a right of possession. There are two kinds of estates, freeholds and less than freeholds (leaseholds). A freehold is an ownership, where a less than freehold is a rental or lease interest. Freeholds can be estates of inheritance (fees) or estates not of inheritance (life estates). A trust deed is a financing document, used in place of a mortgage today. The beneficiary of a trust deed is the lender.
9. **C** Ownerships are called freeholds, which can be either fee titles (perpetual) or life estates (for a lifetime). Either can be vested absolutely, or vested subject to divestiture (defeasible). If defeasible, it may be followed by a future estate, which is a reverter, remainder or executory interest. A leasehold estate is a right of possession, but without ownership.
10. **A** An estate is any interest in property which gives the holder a right of possession. Any owner of an estate may transfer it to another, regardless of what kind of estate it is. There are two kinds of estates, freehold (ownership) and less than freehold (non-ownership). An ownership is potentially of unlimited duration.
11. **A** An estate is any interest in property which gives the holder a right of possession. Any owner of an estate may transfer it to another, regardless of what kind of estate it is. There are two kinds of

estates, freehold (ownership) and less than freehold (non-ownership). Freeholds are further divided into fees and life estates. A fee is said to be of perpetual duration, as opposed to the life estate, which last for the lifetime of the governing life. A fee title does not have to be free and clear. Do not confuse the quantity of estate (fee) with the quality of the estate (existence of encumbrances).

12. **C** An estate is any interest in property which gives the holder a right of possession. There are two kinds of estates, freehold (ownership) and less than freehold (non-ownership). Freeholds are further divided into fees and life estates. A fee is said to be of perpetual duration, as opposed to the life estate, which last for the lifetime of the governing life. Because the life estate terminates upon the death of the owner, it is said to be non-inheritable, or an "estate not of inheritance." Following the death of the life tenant, the title will usually revert to the original owner, who is said to have a right of reverter, or estate in reversion. If the original owner stipulated in the deed conveying the life estate that it was to go to someone else, that person is said to have a remainder, or estate in remainder. A life estate is always followed by either a right of reverter or a remainder.

13. **C** A defeasible title is one which can revert or vest an executory interest in another because it was created with a condition. "Qualified" is a synonym for "defeasible."

14. **D** A defeasible title is one which can revert or vest an executory interest in another because it was created with a condition. As a practical matter, there are only three defeasible fees which still exist in Oregon. A fee simple determinable (also referred to as a fee simple upon special limitation) causes the title to revert to the grantor automatically if the condition is violated. A fee simple subject to a condition subsequent creates a possibility of reverter if the condition is violated. The reversioner must reenter affirmatively assert the right to take the property back; the reversion is not automatic. A fee simple subject to an executory interest vests title in a third party if the condition is broken.

15. **A** An estate is any interest in property which gives the holder a right of possession. There are two kinds of estates, freehold (ownership) and less than freehold (non-ownership). A freehold estate could be a fee (ordinary ownership), or a life estate (ownership for a lifetime). Freeholds can be vested absolutely (ordinary ownership), or the vesting can be subject to divestiture (a restriction). There are various ways to create restrictions, one of which is to make the estate "determinable," that is, if the buyer violates the condition, the seller can regain title.

16. **A** Fee titles can be vested absolutely (fee simple absolute), or vested subject to divestiture. If vested subject to divestiture, the seller has created a condition, violation of which gives the seller the right to take ownership back. The right to take ownership back is called the "right of reverter," or "estate in reversion," or simply "reverter." However, it is also possible (and far more common), for the seller to deed the property to the buyer absolutely, but create the same restriction via a covenant. A covenant is an encumbrance on the title. Conditions are very rare; covenants are very common.

17. **B** A freehold estate could be a fee (ordinary ownership), or a life estate (ownership for a lifetime). Freeholds can be vested absolutely (ordinary ownership), or the vesting can be subject to divestiture (a restriction). There are various ways to create restrictions, one of which is to make the estate "determinable," that is, if the buyer violates the condition, the seller can regain title. The seller's right is sometimes called a possibility of reverter.

18. **B** A freehold estate could be a fee (ordinary ownership), or a life estate (ownership for a lifetime). Freeholds can be vested absolutely (ordinary ownership), or the vesting can be subject to divestiture (a restriction). There are various ways to create restrictions, one of which is to make the estate "determinable," that is, if the buyer violates the condition, the seller can regain title.

19. **A** An estate in reversion and a remainder (estate in remainder) are what we call the right to recover the real estate if a condition is breached or following the termination of some other present possessory interest such as a life estate or less than freehold. "Chattel real" is a term used to describe a chattel which exists within real estate. Leases, mortgages and other such matters are really personal property, but since they are involved with real estate, we call them chattels real.

20. **B** Any time someone has the right to retake possession of a property in the future, it is called a right of reverter (estate in reversion, or reversionary interest). There is no legal term "profitable interest."

21. **B** Regardless of the length of the lease, a lease creates a less than freehold estate. A less than freehold estate is a right of possession, but without

ownership. Less than freehold estates are divided into estates for years (for a fixed term, i.e., a lease), periodic estates (of indefinite duration), estates at will (with permission, but neither a period nor a fixed term), and estates at sufferance (no permission). While the lessee has an estate for years, the lessor retains a right of reverter (estate in reversion, or reversionary rights).

22. **B** There are two kinds of estates (rights of possession), freehold (ownership) and less than freehold (non-ownership). Less than freeholds are generally created by leases or rental agreements. "Satisfaction piece" is an old term for the document from a lender stating that a lien has been paid in full.

23. **A** A lease grants a right of possession (less than freehold estate) to a tenant. Less than freehold estates are divided into estates for years (for a fixed term, i.e., a lease), periodic estates (of indefinite duration), estates at will (with permission, but neither a period nor a fixed term), and estates at sufferance (no permission). A trade fixture is an item installed by a tenant on rented or leased property. It remains the personal property of the tenant, even if attached.

24. **C** An estate is any interest in property which gives the holder a right of possession. There are two main categories of estates, freehold (ownership) and less than freehold (non-ownership). A freehold estate could be an estate of inheritance, called a fee (ordinary ownership), or an estate not of inheritance, called a life estate (ownership for a lifetime). Less than freehold estates are divided into estates for years (for a fixed term, i.e., a lease), periodic estates (of indefinite duration), estates at will (with permission, but neither a period nor a fixed term), and estates at sufferance (no permission).

25. **B** An estate is any interest in property which gives the holder a right of possession. There are two kinds of estates, freeholds and less than freeholds (leaseholds). A freehold is an ownership, where a less than freehold is a rental or lease interest.

26. **D** There are two kinds of estates, freeholds and less than freeholds (leaseholds). A freehold is an ownership, where a less than freehold is a rental or lease interest. Less than freeholds are further classed as "at will," (with the permission of the owner), and "at sufferance" (without permission). Tenancies at will may have a fixed term (i.e., a lease), in which case we call them tenancies for years. If there is a period, then we call it a periodic tenancy or tenancy from period to period (or sometimes by the period, e.g., "month-to-month tenancy). If there is neither a period nor a fixed term, we call it just "tenancy at will." When discussing less than freehold estates, the words "estate" and "tenancy" are interchangeable.

27. **A** The right of the owner to recover possession after the termination of a less than freehold estate is called a right of reverter (estate in reversion). An estate of inheritance is a fee. "Tenancy" means the act of possessing, or being in possession of, real property. It is applied equally to the owner as to a renter. In other words, whoever is in possession is the tenant, and the tenant's act of possessing is called the tenancy.

28. **D** Clearly, the owner can lease the property to another. A life tenant holds a life estate, which is an ownership interest. The holder of the life estate (life tenant) can lease the premises to another for a term not exceeding the end of the life estate. Also, a lessee can sublease to another, and so would become a lessor as well as a lessee.

29. **A** Even if the lease says nothing, there is an implied covenant of quiet enjoyment in a lease. The covenant of quiet enjoyment means that the lessor will defend his or her title to the property to the extent necessary to protect and guarantee the tenant's right to uninterrupted possession.

30. **C** The covenant of quiet enjoyment means that the lessor will defend his or her title to the property to the extent necessary to protect and guarantee the tenant's right to uninterrupted possession, and is implied in all leases. Habitability standards are required by the Oregon Residential Landlord and Tenant Law, but this law applies only to residential properties. Rentals and leases of non-residential property need contain no promise of habitability.

31. **C** A "chattel real" is an interest in real property which is classified as personal property. A right of possession under a less than freehold is so considered. "Personalty" is a term which is a synonym for "chattels," so a leasehold interest is also personalty. An estate in remainder is the right to the fee title upon the death of a life tenant, and is therefore real property.

32. **A** Any act or failure to act which causes a loss of value or utility is called waste. A fundamental principle of real property law is that whenever there is a future possessory interest, such as the landlord's right of reverter, the holder of the present possessory estate may not allow waste. This is not violating a covenant contained in the lease because the fact that the tenant may not permit waste need not be stated as a covenant; it is common law.

33. **A** Less than freehold estates are divided into estates for years (for a fixed term, i.e., a lease), periodic estates (of indefinite duration), estates at will (with permission, but neither a period nor a fixed term), and estates at sufferance (no permission). Be careful to note that if there is a fixed ending date, even if the rent is paid monthly, it is a lease (estate for years).

34. **A** An estate (tenancy) for years is characterized by a fixed ending date. When the rent is paid (or even if there is rent at all) is irrelevant. There is no requirement that it be for any particular term. It could be for a few days or hundreds of years. It is commonly used in business arrangements because it survives the death of either the lessor or the lessee. A business tenant would not want, for example, his or her lease terminated merely because the landlord died.

35. **A** Do not let the word "period" confuse you. The fact that the possession was for exactly 30 days means it is a tenancy for years, not periodic. Periodic tenancies have no fixed ending date; they renew over and over for each successive period until one of the parties gives notice to the other.

36. **C** There are two main categories of estates, freehold (ownership) and less than freehold (non-ownership). A freehold estate could be an estate of inheritance, called a fee (ordinary ownership), or an estate not of inheritance, called a life estate (ownership for a lifetime). Less than freehold estates are divided into estates for years (for a fixed term, i.e., a lease), periodic estates (of indefinite duration), estates at will (with permission, but neither a period nor a fixed term), and estates at sufferance (no permission). Be careful to note that if there is a fixed ending date, even if the rent is paid monthly, it is a lease (estate for years).

37. **D** A defeasible title is one which can revert or vest an executory interest in another because it was created with a condition. A fee simple determinable (also referred to as a fee simple upon special limitation) is a type of defeasible fee.

38. **C** A freehold estate could be a fee (ordinary ownership), or a life estate (ownership for a lifetime). Freeholds can be vested absolutely or the vesting can be subject to divestiture (a restriction). There are various ways to create restrictions, one of which is to make the estate "determinable," that is, if the buyer violates the condition, the seller can regain title. The deed will state the restriction, and then a clause expressing the seller's right to regain title if the condition is violated. The right to regain title is called the right of reverter, and the clause is the reverter clause.

39. **B** An estate can be either a freehold (ownership) or a less than freehold, also called leaseholds (non-ownership). Freeholds are further divided into fees (ordinary ownership) and life estates (ownership for a lifetime). An easement is a right of use, rather than a right of possession, and is not an estate at all.

40. **D** A life estate can be created merely by an ordinary deed to which the words "for life," or other similar words have been added. As an alternative, an owner can deed property to another, but reserve a life estate. In this case, the future estate (remainder) is what is conveyed, since the seller has kept the present estate (the life estate). "Homestead" means a person's residence. A dower or curtesy interest is the right of a spouse to a life estate in the real property of a deceased spouse, and is no longer legal in Oregon. "Incorporeal" simply means "intangible," and is a term applied to certain appurtenances, such as, for example, an easement.

41. **C** A life estate lasts only for the lifetime of the governing life, so when that life ends, it must vest in someone else. The life estate is the present estate, and the right to the title after the death of the governing life is called the future estate. If it goes back to the original owner, we call the future estate a right of reverter or estate in reversion. If it goes to a third party, we call it a remainder. Alienation is a conveyance of title. Hypothecation means pledging an asset as collateral for a debt.

42. **B** Whenever a seller retains the right to regain title in the future, this is called a right of reverter, or estate in reversion. Typically, this happens when a life estate is granted, but could also happen when a grantor creates a determinable fee. Probably the most common example of a right of reverter is when a property is leased or rented, in which case we say the lessor has retained a right of reverter. Alienation is a term which is just a synonym for conveyance (granting title to another). Escheat occurs when a person dies without a will and no heirs capable of inheriting, in which case title passes to the State of Oregon.

43. **D** A life estate is an ownership interest (freehold), therefore the owner can sell it. Similarly, a life estate can be liened, rented, or otherwise encumbered. Note that the owner of the life estate cannot convey or encumber more than what he or she owns. A devise is a gift of real property in a will.

44. **C** A life estate is an ownership interest, and can therefore be sold or encumbered the same as any

ownership interest. The life tenant (owner of the life estate) has all the rights and privileges of ownership, as well as the responsibilities. A fundamental principle of real property law, however, is that whenever there is a future interest, the holder of the present interest may not commit "waste," i.e., must maintain and preserve the property for the benefit of the future holder.

45. **D** Since the life estate is a freehold, the life tenant is vested with seizin. This means that the life tenant not only has the bundle of rights, but also has the responsibilities of ownership, including accepting legal liability for the property and the responsibility to pay the taxes. Whenever there is a future interest, the holder of the present estate is not allowed to permit waste of the property.

46. **B** Ownerships are called freeholds, which can be either fee titles (perpetual) or life estates (for a lifetime). Life estates and fee estates are both freeholds, but a life estate lasts only for someone's lifetime, where a fee estate is potentially of unlimited duration. The owner of a life estate has the same rights as the owner of a fee title, including the right to encumber it. However, the life estate is extinguished upon the death of the governing life, therefore all interests (including encumbrances) which depend on its existence would be extinguished also.

47. **B** A life estate is a freehold (ownership) interest. Therefore, the mother would no more lose a life estate by moving out of the property than she would lose the title if she held it in fee simple absolute. Merely failing to occupy the premises does not constitute waste.

48. **C** When a life estate is created, unless there is language to the contrary, there is a presumption that the grantor has retained a right of reverter (estate in reversion). If desired, however, the grantor can specify a third party to receive the title upon the death of the governing life. The interest of a third party is called a remainder instead of a right of reverter. An estate at sufferance is a less than freehold estate.

49. **A** A life estate can be created merely by an ordinary deed or will to which the words "for life," or other similar words have been added. If the grantor specifies nothing further, then the estate reverts to the grantor upon the death of the life tenant. If the grantor wishes, the estate could be conveyed to a person for life and then to a third party. In this case, the grantee has the life estate, the third party has the remainder, and the grantor no longer has any estate at all.

50. **A** A freehold estate is an ownership and can be either a fee title or a life estate. A fee title is an estate of inheritance, since it can be left to heirs. A life estate terminates upon the death of the governing life, therefore there is nothing to will to heirs, which is why it is called an "estate not of inheritance."

51. **D** An estate can be either a freehold (ownership) or a less than freehold, also called leaseholds (non-ownership). Freeholds are further divided into fees (ordinary ownership) and life estates (ownership for a lifetime). A life estate is created the same way as any ownership interest, that is, by a deed, or as a gift in a will. Unless there is language specifying otherwise, the presumption is that the life of the grantee is the governing life, and that the grantor has retained a right of reverter. Any person's life can be stipulated to be the governing life, however. And the grantor can stipulate a third party to take the property after the death of the governing life, if desired. If the title is to pass to a third party, he or she is said to hold a remainder, instead of a right of reverter.

52. **D** A life estate lasts only for the lifetime of the governing life, so when that life ends, it must vest in another. The life estate is the present estate, and the right to the title after the death of the governing life is called the future estate. If it goes back to the original owner, we call the future estate a right of reverter or estate in reversion. If it goes to a third party, we call it a remainder. A devise is a gift of real property in a will.

53. **C** The buyer has a life estate pur autre vie (for another life). When Bill DePrez conveyed to the buyer, the buyer received what Bill DePrez held, which was a life estate for the life of Bill DePrez. Therefore, the buyer is entitled to ownership of the property for the remainder of Bill DePrez' life.

54. **A** While the life tenant may do anything with the life estate which the life tenant desires to do, the life tenant cannot create an estate greater than the life estate. Since an ordinary deed conveys all of the grantor's right, title and interest, a deed purporting to convey a fee simple absolute will convey whatever the grantor had. In this case, the grantor had only a life estate, so the life estate is what was conveyed by the deed. Note that the grantee (the husband) has cause of action against his wife for fraud, since she stated that she was conveying a fee simple absolute, when, in fact, all she held was a life estate.

55. **B** When a remainder is created, the grantor deeds the present interest to the life tenant and the fu-

ture interest to the holder of the remainder. Thereafter, the grantor has no further interest in the property.

56. **B** A life tenant is what we call the owner of a life estate. The life tenant can sell his or her estate, but the buyer will receive exactly what the life tenant had. Here, the life tenant had an ownership for his lifetime, so the buyer gets ownership for the same lifetime. When the governing life terminates, the title vests in the holder of the future estate, either a reversionee or remainderman.

57. **D** A life estate terminates upon the death of the governing life, but the governing life does not have to be the life of the owner of the life estate. If the governing life happens to last longer than the life of the life tenant (owner of the life estate), then there is time left on the life estate, which can be left to the heirs of the life tenant.

58. **C** A life estate can be created "by reservation," i.e., by selling the property but keeping (reserving) a life estate in it. In this case the seller becomes a life tenant, and the buyer really gains a remainder. In a life estate, there must be a governing life, that is, the lifetime of the person which measures the duration of the life estate. Normally, this is the life tenant (owner of the life estate), but need not be. When a life estate is created, unless there is language in the deed stating otherwise, the presumption is that the governing life is the life of the grantee, and the grantor retains a right of reverter. If the life tenant later sells the life estate, the buyer gains what the life tenant had, i.e., ownership for the life of the original life tenant. Therefore the new owner can retain possession, but only for the lifetime of the original life tenant.

59. **B** A life estate is an ownership interest (freehold), therefore the owner can sell it. Similarly, a life estate can be liened, rented, or otherwise encumbered. Note that the owner of the life estate cannot convey or encumber more than what he or she owns. The ownership is for the lifetime of the governing life, so if the owner of the life estate sells or encumbers the life estate, the buyer or lienholder will gain ownership or an encumbrance on just the life estate, not the future interest (right of reverter or remainder). Therefore, upon the death of the governing life, any encumbrances on the life estate, such as a mortgage or less than freehold estate, would be extinguished.

60. **C** A life estate is an ownership interest, and can therefore be sold or encumbered the same as any ownership interest. The life tenant (owner of the life estate) has all the rights and privileges of ownership, as well as the responsibilities. A lease is an encumbrance, and there is nothing to stop a life tenant from leasing the life estate. However, no one can lease more property than what he or she owns. The life tenant owns the property for a lifetime. Once that lifetime is over, the ownership ends, and therefore, the lease is extinguished at the same time.

61. **C** Although the life tenant is free to do with the life estate whatever the life tenant desires, the life tenant can nevertheless not create a greater estate than the life estate. In other words, if the life tenant wishes to lease the life estate, then the lessee takes a leasehold on the life estate, since the life tenant had no authority to lease the future interest as well. Therefore, upon the termination of the life estate, the leasehold is also extinguished.

62. **C** A life estate can be created merely by an ordinary deed or will to which the words "for life," or other similar words have been added. If the grantor specifies nothing further, then the estate reverts to the grantor upon the death of the life tenant. In this case, the grantor has specified that the estate is to return to him upon the death of the life tenant. The fact that the words specifying that it return to the grantor were unnecessary is irrelevant.

63. **B** An estate is any interest in property which gives the holder a right of possession. There are two kinds of estates, freehold (ownership) and less than freehold (non-ownership). A freehold estate could be a fee (ordinary ownership), or a life estate (ownership for a lifetime). In a life estate, there must be a governing life, that is, the lifetime of the person which measures the duration of the life estate. It is possible to create a life estate which runs beyond the life of the governing life, simply by stating it as such, e.g., "to X for the life of Y." In this case Y's life is the governing life, although X is the life tenant, and Y might live longer than X. A life estate is created by a deed, which must be in writing to be enforceable.

64. **A** An estate can be either a freehold (ownership) or a less than freehold, also called leaseholds (non-ownership). Freeholds are further divided into fees (ordinary ownership) and life estates (ownership for a lifetime). Unless there is language specifying otherwise, the presumption is that the life of the grantee is the governing life, and that the grantor has retained a right of reverter. Any person's life can be stipulated to be the governing life, however. Any contract involving real property must be in writing to be enforceable in Oregon. A deed is a contract.

Oregon law also requires a will to be in writing. A fundamental principle of real property law is that whenever there is a future interest, the holder of the present interest may not commit "waste," i.e., must maintain and preserve the property for the benefit of the future holder. This includes all legal liabilities of the owner, including the obligation to pay the taxes.

65. **C** A freehold estate is an ownership and can be either a fee title or a life estate. A fee title is an estate of inheritance, since it can be left to heirs. A life estate terminates upon the death of the governing life, therefore there is nothing to will to heirs, which is why it is called an "estate not of inheritance." Since a life estate is an ownership interest, it can be sold or encumbered in the same way as any ownership. In a life estate, there must be a governing life, that is, the lifetime of the person which measures the duration of the life estate. The life of the life tenant (owner of the life estate) is normally the governing life, but it is possible to create a life estate which runs for the longest (or shortest) of several lives. It is even possible to use the life of an animal as the governing life.

66. **C** A life estate is created the same way as any ownership interest, that is, by a deed, or as a gift in a will. It is possible for the life tenant (owner of the life estate) to be the one who created it (i.e., a life estate created by reservation), but the normal way is for the grantor to convey a life estate to someone and retain a right of reverter. A life estate is an ownership interest which can be sold or encumbered in the same way as any ownership. In a life estate, there must be a governing life, that is, the lifetime of the person which measures the duration of the life estate. The life of the life tenant (owner of the life estate) is normally the governing life, but it is possible to create a life estate which runs for the longest (or shortest) of several lives. It is even possible to use the life of an animal as the governing life.

67. **B** A life estate is an ownership interest (freehold), therefore the owner can sell it. Similarly, a life estate can be liened, rented, or otherwise encumbered. Note that the owner of the life estate cannot convey or encumber more than what he or she owns. The ownership is for the lifetime of the governing life, which can be any lifetime, or even the longest (or shortest) lived of several lives. Since a life estate terminates upon the death of the governing life, there is nothing to leave to heirs. Therefore, the life estate is called an estate not of inheritance.

68. **A** Ownership of land extends from the center of the earth to a height above the land for the ordinary use and enjoyment of the property. Growing plants are generally part of the real estate, unless they are annual crops. If crops are planted by a tenant, the tenant is said to have a right of emblement, that is, the right to come back and harvest the crops after the termination of the tenancy.

69. **D** Real estate includes all the space, and everything contained therein, between the surface down to the center of the earth, and to a height above the surface necessary for the ordinary use and enjoyment of the property. An owner can sell, rent, lease, give away, mortgage, will, or keep all or any portion of the property. All rights in the property are referred to as the "bundle of rights." A devise is a gift of real estate in a will. The right to tax and escheat to the state are governmental powers, not rights of the owner.

70. **C** The bundle of rights includes the right to do anything at all with the property, including the right to sell, rent, lease, mortgage, give it away, and anything else. The bundle of rights even includes the right to do nothing at all. Survivorship means that in a concurrent tenancy the surviving co-tenants take the interest of a deceased co-tenant.

71. **C** The bundle of rights does not include certain rights which have been reserved to the government such as the right of eminent domain, the right of escheat, the right to tax the land, and the right to regulate its use. However, the right to leave the property to whomever the owner desires is part of the bundle of rights.

72. **D** In this case neither the association, nor government agencies, nor private parties can restrict the right of the owner to place a "for sale" sign on the property. The right to sell the property can be vested in another, as where there is a deed covenant. To refuse to allow a "for sale" sign would, however, violate constitutional guarantees by infringing on the right to freedom of speech. Even then, it would only be a constitutional issue if a government agency attempted to make the rule. The government cannot restrict freedom of speech, but private parties generally can.

73. **D** Personal property and chattels mean the same thing, i.e., goods, as opposed to real estate. A right of emblement is a tenant's right to crops. Appurtenances are items which are considered to be part of the land, classed as either corporeal (tangible, i.e., a house), or incorporeal (intangible, i.e., an easement, a water right, etc.).

74. **D** A synonym for personal property is "chattels." An estate is a possessory interest in real property.

75. **C** An estate is any interest in property which gives the holder a right of possession. There are two kinds of estates, freeholds and less than freeholds (leaseholds). A freehold is an ownership, where a less than freehold is a rental or lease interest.

76. **D** Be careful to note that if there is a fixed ending date, even if the rent is paid monthly, it is a lease (estate for years), not a periodic tenancy.

77. **B** Less than freehold estates are divided into estates for years (for a fixed term, i.e., a lease), periodic estates (of indefinite duration), estates at will (with permission, but neither a period nor a fixed term), and estates at sufferance (no permission). Estates for years and periodic estates are considered encumbrances on the fee title, but not liens. A lien is a financial encumbrance, such as a mortgage.

78. **A** Less than freehold estates are divided into estates for years (for a fixed term, i.e., a lease), periodic estates (of indefinite duration), estates at will (with permission, but neither a period nor a fixed term), and estates at sufferance (no permission). A fee title is the normal type of ownership. A fee simple conditional is a rare type of fee title where the grantor reserves the right to retake the title if the grantee violates some condition. Joint tenancy refers to the manner in which two or more persons own the property at the same time.

79. **B** A less than freehold estate which is either for years or periodic is considered an encumbrance on the fee title. If the estate is at will or at sufferance, it is extinguished by a sale.

80. **B** A less than freehold estate which is either for years or periodic is considered an encumbrance on the fee title. If the estate is at will or at sufferance, it is extinguished by a sale.

81. **C** A less than freehold estate which is either for years or periodic is considered an encumbrance on the fee title, and therefore survives a sale; that is, a buyer takes title subject to it. If the estate is at will or at sufferance, it is extinguished by a sale.

82. **C** Although some people use the word "lease" as a synonym for "leasehold" and "less than freehold," in common usage it is considered another term for a tenancy for years.

83. **D** Less than freehold estates are divided into estates for years (for a fixed term, i.e., a lease), periodic estates (of indefinite duration), estates at will (with permission, but neither a period nor a fixed term), and estates at sufferance (no permission). They can be called estates or tenancies; the terms are interchangeable. Normally, if a tenant holds over after a lease the tenant becomes a tenant at sufferance. If the landlord agrees to the tenant's continued occupancy, it is a tenancy at will or better.

84. **C** Less than freehold estates are divided into estates for years (for a fixed term, i.e., a lease), periodic estates (of indefinite duration), estates at will (with permission, but neither a period nor a fixed term), and estates at sufferance (no permission). They can be called estates or tenancies; the terms are interchangeable. Normally, if a tenant holds over after a lease the tenant becomes a tenant at sufferance. But if the landlord agrees to the tenant's continued occupancy, it is a tenancy at will or better. In this example, since the tenant paid rent monthly, and the landlord accepted it, the tenancy is considered periodic.

85. **D** Less than freehold estates are divided into estates for years (for a fixed term, i.e., a lease), periodic estates (of indefinite duration), estates at will (with permission, but neither a period nor a fixed term), and estates at sufferance (no permission). They can be called estates or tenancies; the terms are interchangeable. Normally, if a tenant holds over after a lease the tenant becomes a tenant at sufferance. If the landlord agrees to the tenant's continued occupancy, it is a tenancy at will or better.

86. **B** Less than freehold estates are divided into estates for years (for a fixed term, i.e., a lease), periodic estates (of indefinite duration), estates at will (with permission, but neither a period nor a fixed term), and estates at sufferance (no permission). They can be called estates or tenancies; the terms are interchangeable. Normally, if a tenant holds over after a lease the tenant becomes a tenant at sufferance. If the landlord agrees to the tenant's continued occupancy, it is a tenancy at will or better.

87. **A** When all the possessory rights are transferred to the new party, it is an assignment. If the lessee gives a portion of the rights, such as a portion of the space or a portion of the remaining term, then it is a sublease.

88. **C** An assignment places a new party (the assignee) in the shoes of one of the original parties to a contract (the assignor). In the case of a lease, this means that the new tenant takes the place of the original tenant. The new tenant has the same contractual rights, because the lease is still the original lease. A sublease, however is a new lease, where the

original lessee remains a lessee of the owner, and becomes the lessor to the new tenant. In a sublease there will be two leases on the same premises. An assignment transfers all the rights to the new tenant, so if the new tenant is to have only a portion of the premises, or only a portion of the remaining term, or is to pay more or less rent, then the sublease is the appropriate instrument.

89. **D** The term "tenant" refers to the party in possession of the real estate. The original lessee was a tenant, so by granting a right of possession to a third party, the third party gains right of possession, and thereby becomes a tenant.

90. **C** Normally, when a tenant subleases or assigns to a third party, the original tenant is not relieved of the responsibility to pay. Nevertheless, assuming the lessor agreed to the assignment or sublease, the lessor will expect payment to come first from the third party and will only look to the original tenant for payment in the event the new tenant fails to pay.

91. **D** An assignment is a transfer of all rights in a contract to a new party. A sublease is a new lease instrument that grants only a portion of the leasehold interest to the new tenant. The original tenant is not relieved of liability to the landlord in either case.

92. **A** Leases (as well as deeds) need not be signed by the grantee, only by the grantor (lessor or landlord). In other words, the lessee's acceptance of the terms of the lease is evidenced by the fact that the lessor gave the lessee a copy of the lease, whereupon the lessee moved in. The act of taking possession constitutes agreement to the terms.

93. **A** A surrender of a lease occurs when the lessor agrees to release the tenant from further liability under the lease. While the lessor is under no legal obligation to accept the surrender, if the lessor does accept the surrender, the original lease is deemed to be extinguished. If a lessor and a lessee agree mutually to a modification of an existing lease, this is deeded to be the same as surrender and acceptance, followed by the creation of a new lease. Another term for this is "novation."

94. **C** Since this is a commercial lease, the lessor had no obligation to repair. However, you must always accept legal liability for your wrongful acts, even if done gratuitously. Therefore, since the lessor did repair the ceiling, the lessor is now liable for damages caused by the fact that it was not repaired properly.

95. **C** A mortgage is a device which makes property collateral for a debt. Anything you own can be mortgaged, including a leasehold interest in real property. Of course, if the lender holds a mortgage on a leasehold, a foreclosure cannot gain the lender any greater title than the leasehold. Trade fixtures are defined as items installed by a tenant in rented or leased premises, and the tenant is generally permitted to remove them, provided the tenant repairs any damage caused by their removal and restores the premises. Therefore, trade fixtures, unlike ordinary fixtures, are considered personal property.

96. **B** Less than freehold estates are divided into estates for years (for a fixed term, i.e., a lease), periodic estates (of indefinite duration), estates at will (with permission, but neither a period nor a fixed term), and estates at sufferance (no permission). They can be called estates or tenancies; the terms are interchangeable. There is no such thing as a "term certain tenancy."

97. **D** Do not confuse a "tenancy for years" (lease) with a "tenancy from year to year." A tenancy from year to year is a special type of periodic tenancy where the period happens to be a year.

98. **B** By statute in Oregon, a tenancy from year to year can be terminated by either party upon giving 60 days notice to the other. It is the only periodic tenancy which calls for a 60-day notice.

99. **B** An estate at will is a less than freehold estate which has nothing to do with inheritance.

100. **C** Since the owner has given the tenant permission to occupy the premises, the law requires the owner to give the tenant reasonable notice to quit. But since there is no period involved, the notice has been fixed at a flat 30 days.

101. **B** Since a tenant at sufferance has no permission, the owner need give no legal notice to terminate the tenancy. An estate for years (lease) also requires no notice, as the parties knew when it would be over when they entered into the agreement. However, a lease cannot be terminated at any time; it requires a cause.

102. **A** There are four types of less than freehold estates: Estate for years (a fixed term), periodic estate (of indefinite duration, until one party gives notice to the other), estate at will (permission of the owner but without a period or a fixed term, and estate at sufferance. Of these, the estate at sufferance is the only one without the owner's permission.

103. **C** One who holds over wrongfully has no permission, so "holdover tenant" is a synonym for a tenant at sufferance.

104. **A** Since a tenant at sufferance has no permission, the owner need give no legal notice to terminate the tenancy.
105. **A** There are four types of less than freehold estates: tenancy for years (a fixed term), periodic tenancy (of indefinite duration, until one party gives notice to the other), tenancy at will (permission of the owner but without a period or a fixed term, and tenancy at sufferance. Of these, the tenancy at sufferance is the only one without the owner's permission.
106. **C** The lessor is entitled to be made whole, but no more. In Oregon, a lessor must make a good faith attempt to mitigate the loss in the event a tenant abandons the premises. Anything the lessor can get from a new tenant must be used to offset the liability of the old tenant.
107. **C** Actual eviction is when a suit to evict is filed. Constructive eviction is when the landlord forces the tenant out by shutting off the utilities, locking the tenant out, etc. The landlord is not always the one who is required to maintain, although that is usually the case. If the landlord is the one required to maintain, and the landlord fails to maintain to the point where the premises finally become uninhabitable, forcing the tenant out, this is legally considered constructive eviction.
108. **C** To file a suit for eviction (F.E.D. or forcible entry and detainer) is called an actual eviction. When a landlord forces a tenant out some other way, it is called constructive eviction. Even a mere failure to maintain the premises to the point where they become uninhabitable, constitutes constructive eviction, if the landlord was the party responsible for maintenance. Constructive eviction makes a landlord legally liable to a tenant for damages if the tenancy is residential. However, there are no restrictions on constructive eviction for commercial property.
109. **D** The distinction between a tenant at sufferance and a trespasser is twofold. First, a tenant at sufferance is a party who entered the premises originally under some legal right of possession, but has remained in possession after the legal right ended. Second, a tenancy at sufferance and a trespass are both civil wrongs – that is, a landlord can summarily evict either one. A trespass, however, is also a criminal act. As for physically removing the tenant, the law might allow this if it were other than a residential lease and there were extenuating circumstances. Normally, however, the landlord must bring an eviction proceeding and, if the tenant still refuses to leave, ask the court to order the sheriff to move the tenant out.
110. **A** Since a forcible entry and (wrongful) detainer action (F.E.D.) is an eviction proceeding, it would be the lessor would be the plaintiff and the tenant would be the defendant.
111. **B** The death of either party has no effect on a normal lease. The heirs of the lessee may retain possession, provided they continue to perform the lease. Similarly, the heirs of the lessor will automatically take title to the property subject to the lease.
112. **A** When there is an underlying mortgage, then the mortgage normally already existed as an encumbrance on the title at the time the lessee accepted the lease. Therefore, the tenant took the lease subject to the rights of the lender. If the lender should foreclose, the foreclosure will extinguish the lease. However, until the lease is actually extinguished by a foreclosure, the tenant's lease is intact and the obligation to pay continues. A covenant of quiet enjoyment is the lessor's promise that nothing will interfere with the title so as to abridge the tenant's right of possession. Allowing the lender to foreclose would be a breach of the covenant of quiet enjoyment. A tenancy for years and a periodic tenancy are not terminated by the death of either party.
113. **D** Less than freehold estates are divided into estates for years (for a fixed term, i.e., a lease), periodic estates (of indefinite duration), estates at will (with permission, but neither a period nor a fixed term), and estates at sufferance (no permission). A tenancy at will requires 30 days' notice, a periodic tenancy requires generally a notice equal to the length of the period (with some exceptions). A tenancy for years is a lease, and requires no special notice to terminate. A tenant at sufferance does not have a legal right to possession, therefore the landlord is not required to give notice.
114. **B** The result is the same as cancellation or rescission, but it is normally called a surrender and acceptance. The lessee surrenders possession to the lessor, who accepts it. Acceptance of a surrender is deemed to extinguish not only the lease, but also the tenant's obligation to pay.
115. **D** An estate is any interest in property which gives the holder a right of possession. There are two kinds of estates, freehold (ownership) and less than freehold (non-ownership). Conveying mineral or oil rights does not cause a loss of the right of possession, nor does conveyance of an easement,

which is a right of use, not a right of possession. If an owner leases his or her land to someone else, the owner still has a freehold (ownership). The only thing that would cause the ownership to become a leasehold would be to sell the property and lease it back from the buyer.

116. **D** An estate is any interest in property which gives the holder a right of possession. There are two kinds of estates, freehold (ownership) and less than freehold (non-ownership). Conveying mineral or oil rights does not cause a loss of the right of possession, nor does conveyance of an easement, which is a right of use, not a right of possession. If an owner leases his or her land to someone else, the owner still has a freehold (ownership). The only thing that would cause the ownership to become a leasehold would be to sell the property and lease it back from the buyer.

117. **B** An estate is any interest in property which gives the holder a right of possession. There are two kinds of estates, freehold (ownership) and less than freehold (non-ownership). Conveying mineral or oil rights does not cause a loss of the right of possession. If an owner leases his or her land to someone else, the owner still has a freehold (ownership). The only thing that would cause the ownership to become a leasehold would be to sell the property and lease it back from the buyer.

118. **B** An estate is any interest in property which gives the holder a right of possession. There are two kinds of estates, freehold (ownership) and less than freehold (non-ownership). A freehold estate could be a fee (ordinary ownership), or a life estate (ownership for a lifetime). Less than freehold estates are divided into estates for years (for a fixed term, i.e., a lease), periodic estates (of indefinite duration), estates at will (with permission, but neither a period nor a fixed term), and estates at sufferance (no permission). An estate in severalty merely means that whatever the estate is, it is owned by only one individual. Of all the choices, the highest ownership interest is the fee simple estate.

119. **B** An estate is any interest in property which gives the holder a right of possession. There are two kinds of estates, freehold (ownership) and less than freehold, also called leasehold estates (non-ownership). A freehold estate could be a fee (ordinary ownership), or a life estate (ownership for a lifetime). Less than freehold estates are divided into estates for years (for a fixed term, i.e., a lease), periodic estates (of indefinite duration), estates at will (with permission, but neither a period nor a fixed term), and estates at sufferance (no permission). An estate in severalty merely means that whatever the estate is, it is owned by only one individual. Of all the choices, the highest ownership interest is the fee simple estate.

120. **B** An estate is any interest in property which gives the holder a right of possession. There are two kinds of estates, freehold (ownership) and less than freehold, also called leasehold estates (non-ownership). A freehold estate could be a fee (ordinary ownership), or a life estate (ownership for a lifetime). Freeholds can be vested absolutely (ordinary ownership), or the vesting can be subject to divestiture (a restriction). There are various ways to create restrictions, one of which is to make the estate "determinable," that is, if the buyer violates the condition, the seller can regain title. "Adverse possession" refers to a process where a person can gain ownership of another's real property by possessing it for a period of time. Of all the choices, the highest ownership interest is the fee simple estate vested absolutely.

121. **C** An estate is any interest in property which gives the holder a right of possession. There are two kinds of estates, freehold (ownership) and less than freehold, also called leasehold estates (non-ownership). A freehold estate could be a fee (ordinary ownership), or a life estate (ownership for a lifetime). Less than freehold estates are divided into estates for years (for a fixed term, i.e., a lease), periodic estates (of indefinite duration), estates at will (with permission, but neither a period nor a fixed term), and estates at sufferance (no permission). An estate in severalty merely means that whatever the estate is, it is owned by only one individual. Of all the choices, the highest ownership interest is the fee simple estate.

122. **B** An estate is any interest in property which gives the holder a right of possession. There are two kinds of estates, freehold (ownership) and less than freehold (non-ownership). A freehold estate could be a fee (ordinary ownership), or a life estate (ownership for a lifetime). Less than freehold estates are divided into estates for years (for a fixed term, i.e., a lease), periodic estates (of indefinite duration), estates at will (with permission, but neither a period nor a fixed term), and estates at sufferance (no permission). An estate in severalty merely means that whatever the estate is, it is owned by only one individual. A survivorship estate simply means that, regardless of what kind of estate it is, there are more than one owner, and the survivor

will gain full ownership upon the death of the co-tenant. Of all the choices, the highest ownership interest is the fee simple estate.

123. **D** An estate for years is a right of possession for a fixed term, i.e., a lease. A periodic estate is a right of possession that self-renews from period to period until one party gives notice to the other. An estate at will is permission to occupy the property, but without a fixed term or a specified period. An estate (tenancy) at sufferance is possession without permission, as a holdover tenant.

124. **D** "Determinable fee" is a synonym for fee simple upon special limitation. When a title is subject to divestiture, we say that a condition has been created and the title is then said to be defeasible. "Leasehold" is another term for "less than freehold," although sometimes it is also used to mean specifically a lease, as opposed to a periodic rental.

125. **C** An encumbrance is not normally an estate, since an estate must be a possessory interest. An easement is a right of use, not a right of possession, so it is not an estate. A tenancy for years is an estate for a fixed term, not an indefinite period. Freeholds are always estates for an indefinite (although not necessarily perpetual) time.

126. **C** The definition of an estate is any possessory interest, whether through ownership or otherwise. Therefore, remainders (right to possession in the future) and leaseholds (right to present possession without ownership) are estates. However, there is no such thing as a "greater than freehold estate."

127. **C** Less than freehold estates are divided into estates for years (for a fixed term, i.e., a lease), periodic estates (of indefinite duration), estates at will (with permission, but neither a period nor a fixed term), and estates at sufferance (no permission). "Tenancy in common" refers to a method where more than one party owns a property together at the same time.

128. **B** An easement, while an encumbrance on the real property, is a right of use, not a right of possession, so it is not an estate. Remainders and reverters are future estates. A lease, regardless of the term, is a right of possession, so it is an estate.

129. **A** An estate is an interest in property which gives the holder a right of possession. Both a lessee of an apartment and an owner of a condominium have a right of possession, so both have estates. Estates are divided into freeholds (ownerships) and less than freeholds, or leaseholds (non-ownerships). Fee interests are ownerships which can be left to heirs, so "a fee interest" and "an estate of inheritance" are essentially synonymous. Both are ownerships, which is not an interest that the lessee of an apartment enjoys.

130. **A** Tenancy for years and estate for years mean the same thing — a lease with a fixed ending date. To be an owner, you must have either a fee title or a life estate. A life estate is far less common than a fee title.

131. **D** Normally, a lease and option (lease option) is written as one contract where the option is dependent upon the tenant not being in default of the lease. Assuming this to be the case, then an assignment of the lease contract is also an assignment of the option, since the option is part of the same contract.

CO-OWNERSHIP OF REAL PROPERTY

In the previous section we defined the word "tenancy" as the "holding" of the real estate. We discussed it in terms of the extent and duration of a tenant's right of possession (estate). Now we will use the word "tenancy" in terms of how many persons own the property at any given time, and their relationships with each other.

Real estate can be owned by one person at a time, or by more than one. When title is vested in more than one person (or legal entity), this is called a ***concurrent tenancy*** or sometimes ***co-tenancy*** or ***co-ownership***. The parties are referred to as ***co-tenants*** or ***concurrent tenants***.

When one person owns the property alone we call it a ***tenancy*** (or ***estate***) ***in severalty***. Do not let the term "severalty" here confuse you – it sounds as though it should mean "more than one" because of its similarity to the word "several." In reality, it is closely related to the word "sever." In other words, the legal concept of a severalty estate is that the owner's property is severed from all other adjacent property, so the ownership is individual.

In contrast, concurrent tenants enjoy an ***undivided right of possession***, also called a ***unity of possession***. The unity of possession means that all co-tenants have an undivided right to possession of the entire property simultaneously and no individual owner can be restricted from possession of any portion of the property. Therefore, no co-tenant can be charged rent for his or her possession of the property. If any co-tenant is excluded from any portion of the property, then that portion of the property has been severed and the common ownership ends with respect to it. The unity of possession is fundamental to the creation of all concurrent tenancies. Without it, the tenancy reverts to separate severalty estates.

NOTES

In some concurrent tenancies there must also exist certain other unities. A ***unity of time*** means that the co-tenants acquired their interest at the same time. A ***unity of title*** means that they acquired their interests through the same deed. And a ***unity of interest*** means that their interests are equal.

Right of survivorship

Of course, ownership of property by one person or entity (severalty) does not produce many legal problems to resolve. Concurrent tenancies, on the other hand, involve complex rules of law. Of these, none is more important than the ***right of survivorship***, or lack of it. Whether or not there is a right of survivorship determines the disposition of the interest of a co-tenant in the event of the co-tenant's death.

For example, suppose you and your brother own property together as co-tenants. If your brother dies and you survive him, do you receive his half interest in the property automatically, or does it go to the persons named in his will or to his natural heirs if he dies without a will? In some concurrent tenancies his interest would automatically vest in you upon his death. If this is the case we would say that you and he owned it with right of survivorship. But if his interest goes to his heirs (even if you happen to be one of his heirs), then the co-tenancy was without a right of survivorship. The existence of a right of survivorship means that the surviving co-tenant(s) automatically take the interest of the deceased co-tenant, share and share alike.

The type of co-tenancy is established by the words in the deed. In other words, when you buy property in a concurrent tenancy you must instruct the seller how to deed it to you. Naturally, the seller does not normally care how you take title, since the seller gets the same price for the property regardless. The decision is usually made at the time the buyers sign the earnest money agreement, although it is also common to leave the issue until it is time for the transaction to close.

As noted above, some concurrent tenancies have a right of survivorship, while others do not. For example, if you specify that you and your spouse wish to hold title as "tenants by the entirety without right of survivorship," you will likely end up with a right of survivorship anyway. A right of survivorship is a feature of the tenancy by the entirety (defined in detail later), and you and your spouse cannot enter into a contract to change that fact. If you did not wish a right of survivorship, you should have chosen a type of concurrent tenancy which did not have a right of survivorship. Notice that kinship and other relationships are generally irrelevant. The fact that you and your brother in the above example are related did not, in and of itself, create a right of survivorship, nor would it bar you from having as right of survivorship if you should so choose.

Of course, in the example above, if your brother's interest in the property is without right of survivorship, you could still wind up owning it if he makes out a will and leaves it to you. However, owning the property with a right of survivorship is better than mutually leaving your interests to each other in your wills. For one thing, a will can be changed unilaterally, whereas the type of concurrent tenancy can be changed only by mutual agreement in writing. In addition, by making wills leaving your respective interests in the property to each other, you would eventually gain title to his interest if you should survive him, but you would gain title to his half interest only after his will had been probated, Probate proceedings can take considerable time and expense. If you had owned the property with right of survivorship, you would be legally vested in title to his half interest automatically and immediately upon his death.

Exercise a

When one person or entity owns a property, the tenancy is in ____________________.

It is a ______________________ ____________________ or co-tenancy if more than one person or entity owns the property together. There is always a ______________ _____ ________________________ in all co-tenancies. Therefore, if a co-tenant is excluded from a portion of the premises, that portion becomes a ____________________ estate.

If the surviving co-tenants have the right to take the interest of a deceased co-tenant, then the ownership is with a _____________ _____ __________________________.

Tenancy in common

Of the different types of concurrent tenancies, one of the most popular is the ***tenancy in common***. Practically everywhere the English brought their legal system, you will find the tenancy in common. Although the rules for a tenancy in common vary slightly from one jurisdiction to the next, in most states it is virtually the same.

There is no right of survivorship in a tenancy in common. This makes it a favorite vehicle for ownership of small investment properties. Two or more people can get together and create a simple investment just by taking title as tenants in common. Upon the death of a co-tenant, the interest of the deceased co-tenant will simply vest in his or her heirs.

A tenancy in common can have any number of co-tenants and they can be natural persons or other entities such as corporations, government agencies, and the like. They can be husband and wife, or unmarried. There is no restriction on what kind of kinship can exist between or among the co-tenants, nor need there be any kinship at all. A natural person can hold property as tenant in common with any other entity, including corporations. In other words, any kind of legal entity, natural or otherwise, can be a tenant in common with any other. In addition, the percentage of interest held by each co-tenant can be equal or unequal in whatever percentages the parties desire.

In a tenancy in common each co-tenant's interest is freely transferable without the permission of any other co-tenant, another feature which makes the tenancy in common ideal for an investment. Normally, however, no co-tenant has the right to act with respect to the interests of another co-tenant. In other words, co-tenants cannot sign for each other. Nevertheless, it is possible that, if the parties have been acting as though they were a partnership, a court might construe the ownership as tenants in common as really an ownership in partnership. In a partnership, partners generally have the authority to bind each other to contracts with third parties.

Not only is each co-tenant's interest freely transferable without the permission of the other co-tenants, but each interest can also be independently liened as well. In other words, if you own an interest as a tenant in common, you may mortgage it to the bank without affecting the interests of your co-tenants. Similarly, a judgment, income tax levy, or other personal obligation of a co-tenant can only affect the interest of the debtor co-tenant, not the interests of the other co-tenants.

NOTES

In a tenancy in common, each co-tenant is entitled to share (pro-rata according to percentage of ownership) in all the rents and profits from the property. If one co-tenant is managing the property for the others, then the others are entitled to an accounting of all income and benefits received from the property. In the event one of the co-tenants is in possession, and while in possession permits waste or removes produce, shrubs or trees, or improvements on the property, he or she may be liable to the other co-tenants for damages.

By the same token, while each co-tenant is entitled to share in the profits from the property, each co-tenant is also responsible for his or her share of the expenses and liabilities of the property. If one co-tenant pays insurance premiums, property taxes, mortgage payments, and similar expenses which benefit all co-tenants, then he or she is entitled to reimbursement from the other co-tenants for their share of the expense.

An important note should be made of the issue of personal liability. While each co-tenant is only responsible for his or her share of the expenses of the property, there is nevertheless potentially unlimited personal liability for the property. If a visitor, for example, is injured on the premises and it is adjudged to be the fault of the owners, then the visitor can probably obtain judgment against each owner "jointly and severally." This means that the visitor can reach any assets of any co-tenant for an amount up to the total of the judgment. The visitor has no obligation to make any attempt to collect the judgment equally from the co-tenants.

An interesting feature of the tenancy in common is the right of each co-tenant to a ***suit for partition*** (partition action). A suit for partition can be brought by any co-tenant who wishes to terminate the co-tenancy. When a suit for partition has been brought by a co-tenant, the judge must either order the property physically surveyed and parceled out pro-rata to the co-tenants, or the judge must order the property sold and divide the resulting cash sales proceeds. Since dividing the property is not usually practical, and in fact, would probably be a violation of land use and subdivision laws, the normal procedure is to order the property sold and divide the proceeds.

Exercise b

In a tenancy in common the maximum number of co-tenants is ____________________. The co-tenants can be ________________ persons or other legal entities. Their interests in the property can be ____________ or ________________. Each co-tenant's interest can be ____________________ as well as liened freely and separately without the permission of the other co-tenants. Each co-tenant is entitled to share ________________ in the profits from the property, but is also responsible for the expenses and liabilities of the property. Each co-tenant bears full legal ________________ for the property. Any tenant in common may file a ____________ ______ ____________________, which the judge must grant.

NOTES

Joint tenancy

At common law, a survivorship estate in real property known as a ***joint tenancy*** was possible. For the most part, joint tenancy has been abolished in Oregon as to real property, although it is still possible to own personal property jointly. An exception exists for personal representatives of an estate and for trustees, who are still permitted to own real property as joint tenants. Since most owners are not trustees or personal representatives, the use of joint tenancy for real property in Oregon is unusual. Joint tenancy is commonly used in other states, however.

If a joint tenancy to real property is created in Oregon each co-tenant will have a right of survivorship. When there is a right of survivorship the interests must be equal, else it would not be fair. After all, the right of survivorship is a gamble – the survivor will take all. It only makes sense that each tenant invest an equal amount. Also, the law requires that the interests be the same kind of title and that they be acquired through the same document at the same time. And, as with all concurrent tenancies, there must be an equal and undivided right of possession. It is common to refer to these as the four unities of the joint tenancy – interest, time, title and possession.

Tenancy by the entirety

While a joint tenancy as to real property is highly unusual in Oregon, a ***tenancy by the entirety*** (also sometimes called ***tenancy by the entireties***) is perhaps the most frequently used concurrent tenancy in Oregon. The tenancy by the entirety is also a common-law tenancy, and it is used in some other states, but not all. To be tenants by the entirety, the co-tenants must have been legally married to each other at the time they took title.

In a tenancy by the entirety each co-tenant is considered the owner of the entire property, not the owner of just a half-interest. However, each person's ownership of the entire property is subject to the spouse's right of survivorship, which cannot be broken as long as the tenancy remains by the entirety. Therefore, when one spouse dies, the survivor does not "inherit" anything; rather, the interest of the deceased spouse is simply extinguished, leaving the surviving spouse vested in severalty. Although each co-tenant owns the entire property, Oregon law does provide that they must share equally the rents and profits from the property.

While death of either spouse turns a tenancy by the entirety into a severalty estate vested in the survivor, a tenancy by the entirety could also be converted into a tenancy in common. This could occur through the voluntary act of the parties, but occurs more commonly as the result of a divorce. When parties who held property as tenants by the entirety become divorced, but continue to own the property after the divorce, the presumption is that their tenancy by the entirety is converted to a tenancy in common. Once it is a tenancy in common, the right of survivorship is, of course, extinguished.

Either co-tenant may unilaterally encumber or convey the entire property, but only subject to the other's right of survivorship. This can create an interesting situation. Suppose you and your spouse own a property free and clear together as tenants by the entirety. You deed all your right, title and interest in the property to your brother. Your brother now owns a 100% interest in the property, but subject to your spouse's right of survivorship. The right of survivorship is governed by the lives of the married parties, (you and your spouse), not your brother. In other words, if your brother dies, his heirs simply inherit his position. If, on the other hand, you die first, your spouse takes the

Notes

entire property back from your brother because your spouse still has a right of survivorship. On the other hand, if your spouse is the first one to die, then your spouse's interest is extinguished and your brother's ownership is no longer subject to your spouse's right of survivorship.

In today's world, it is not uncommon for people to live together, and even purchase property together, without being married. If they are not married, they usually take title as tenants in common, although there are other possibilities. In any event, they cannot be tenants by the entirety if they were not legally married at the time they took title. It is also not unusual for such couples to marry each other later. In this case, they would remain vested in the same way they originally took title. Getting married in Oregon does not change the vesting of title or automatically create a right of survivorship.

Of course, once a couple are married it is possible for them to become tenants by the entirety. To do so used to require that they both deed to a third party who would then immediately deed back to them as tenants by the entirety. By statute, this is no longer necessary. Today they can just both deed to each other "as tenants by the entirety" and record both deeds to change the vesting of title.

Erickson vs Erickson

It has been many decades since the Oregon Legislature enacted the statute which abolished joint tenancy as to real property. Of course, married persons wanting a right of survivorship could always choose a tenancy by the entirety. Or if married persons did not wish a right of survivorship, they could be tenants in common. Unmarried persons probably did not want a right of survivorship, so they would normally choose tenancy in common. But for those cases where unmarried co-tenants wanted a right of survivorship, there was no easy solution.

In the *Erickson* case [*Erickson vs Erickson* 167 Or 1, 115 P2d 172 (1941)] a deed to two brothers stated "the grantees herein do not take title in common but with the right of survivorship; that is, that the fee shall rest in the survivor of the grantees." At the time of the deed, the Legislature had already abolished joint tenancy, so the tenancy clearly could not be joint. The language also clearly stated that the two brothers would not be in common. The Oregon Supreme Court ruled finally that this language created a tenancy in common in the two brothers to a life estate, with cross-contingent remainders to the fee. Therefore, upon the death of one of the brothers, the surviving brother took the property by remainder. In its finding, the Court ruled that the statute abolishing joint tenancy did not abolish the possibility of creating other survivorship interests such as this.

Following the *Erickson* case above, blank deed forms were printed which echoed the words of the Erickson deed. Subsequently, in 1983 the Legislature amended the statute abolishing joint tenancy (ORS 93.180) to provide that "*... every conveyance to two or more persons [except to a husband and wife, to trustees, or to personal representatives] creates a tenancy in common unless it is in some manner clearly and expressly declared... that the grantees... take the lands with right of survivorship. Such a declaration of a right to survivorship shall create a tenancy in common in the life estate with cross-contingent remainders in the fee simple.*"

Therefore, it would appear that no special language is required to create a survivorship estate as in the *Erickson* case as long as the intention of the grantor is clear. Standard deed forms are available, however, and are commonly used by closing agents when the parties are not married but wish a right of survivorship.

Exercise c

For married persons, a survivorship estate is usually a ______________ *by the* ______________ .
Joint tenancy, as a practical matter has been ______________ *in Oregon. However, unmarried persons can have a right of survivorship by creating a tenancy in common to a* __________ ______________ *with cross-contingent* ______________ *to the fee as in the* ______________ *case.*
When the tenancy is by the entirety, the __________ *of* ______________ *cannot be destroyed, even if one of the parties sells or* ______________ *the property. When married persons hold as tenants by the entirety the entirety owns the entire property, so it only requires* ________ *signature to sell or encumber it.*

Creating tenancies

Fortunately, real estate agents do not normally have to draft a deed. Nevertheless, real estate agents should be familiar with the language used on deeds so they can tell who the owners are when it comes time to take a listing.

In Oregon, if a deed conveys property to two or more persons who are not married at the time they take title, the presumption is that they take title as tenants in common, unless special language is used to created the *Erickson* tenancy. Similarly, if the grantees of a deed are husband and wife at the time of the conveyance, the presumption is that they take title as tenants by the entirety. If a husband and wife wish to be tenants in common, the deed must state this fact clearly. Furthermore, any conveyance is presumed to create equal interests unless the deed specifically states otherwise.

Dower and curtesy

Although the rule has been abolished in Oregon, many states still follow the English rule of ***dower and curtesy***. Dower and curtesy refer to the right of a surviving spouse to a life estate in real property owned by the deceased spouse. The wife's right is called her ***dower right*** and the husband's interest is called his ***curtesy right***. The idea was to ensure that you could not completely disinherit your spouse, while at the same time permitting you to leave the remainder interest to others. You might, for example, have a family inheritance which you wished to leave to your family, rather than have it descend in the future down your spouse's lineage.

The significance of dower and curtesy is that if you own property in a dower and curtesy state, and you are married, your spouse automatically has the right to the life estate if your spouse survives you, even if you alone are in title to the property (own it in severalty). If you sell the property, your signature on the deed will convey all rights in the property, except your spouse's dower or curtesy right. Therefore, your buyer may own the property, but is always at risk that your spouse may survive you and return to claim the life estate. As a result, in dower and curtesy states, as a practical matter, no one will accept a married person's deed to a property, even if held in severalty, without the spouse's signature also to convey the potential dower or curtesy right.

Notes

Community property

In a minority of states (but including all states surrounding Oregon), community property laws are followed. ***Community property*** is a concept from Spanish common law. Under community property laws, each spouse brings certain assets to the marriage, called ***separate property***. Separate property also includes property acquired by either spouse after marriage if it was acquired by gift or inheritance. All other property (i.e., property acquired during the marriage) is community property. Upon the death of either spouse, the surviving spouse has an automatic right to one-half the community property, although the deceased spouse may will his or her separate property to others.

The difficulty with community property laws is that, as a general rule, separate property can become community property by a simple declaration to that effect by the spouse who owns it. Even if no formal declaration is made, separate property can become community property if the rents and profits from it are commingled with community funds, or if the joint efforts of both spouses are used to make the property produce a profit. Of course, a buyer of the property has no way of knowing if the property is still separate property or community property. The result is that, in community property states, no one is likely to accept a deed signed by a married person without the signature of the spouse to convey the spouse's possible community property interest, even if only one spouse is in title.

Vesting title to married persons in Oregon

Since Oregon is not a community property state, nor is dower and curtesy law followed here, there is never a need to have a spouse sign a deed unless the spouse is actually in title as a co-tenant. In other words, the only person(s) who must sign to sell the property are the person(s) named as grantees in the deed.

While this creates a simple situation, it means a spouse could potentially be disinherited. The Oregon Legislature addressed this problem by amending the laws of descent and distribution. A spouse in Oregon can leave all of his or her property to whomever he or she wishes. However, if the will does not leave at least one-half the total estate (real and personal) to the surviving spouse, the surviving spouse can challenge the will and demand at least one-half. Or, if the surviving spouse wishes, he or she may let the will stand and abide by the wishes of the deceased spouse.

Many married couples use this as a technique to save inheritance taxes. The couple arrange their affairs so each has adequate resources in his or her own name. Then each spouse makes out a will leaving all his or her property to their children. When one spouse dies, the surviving spouse does not challenge the will. If they did not make out wills leaving their estate directly to the children, then the surviving spouse would automatically inherit it all. And when the surviving spouse eventually dies, the children would finally inherit. But in the process the assets would have had to go through two estates, thus estate taxes would be levied on the estate twice.

Exercise d

If no special language is used and the co-tenants are not married, they will be ______________ ______ ______________. The presumption for married co-tenants is that they will generally take title as ______________ ______ ________ ______________ unless the deed specifically expresses something to the contrary. The interests created will be __________ unless otherwise stated in the deed. When unmarried persons own property together, getting married (choose one) ❑ DOES ❑ DOES NOT change the vesting of title.

Oregon follows laws of

- ❑ *Community property.*
- ❑ *Dower and Curtesy.*
- ❑ *Both dower and curtesy and community property.*
- ❑ *Neither dower and curtesy nor community property.*

KEY TERMS

The key to understanding any new field is the vocabulary used in that field. To maximize your comprehension of the material presented in this chapter, be sure you know the meaning and significance of the following terms. Remember that the majority of test questions primarily test knowledge of vocabulary.

Co-ownership
Co-tenancy
Co-tenant
Community property
Concurrent tenancy
Concurrent tenant
Curtesy right
Dower right
Dower and curtesy
Estate in severalty
Joint tenancy
Right of survivorship
Separate property
Suit for partition
Tenancy in common
Tenancy in severalty
Tenancy by the entirety (entireties)
Undivided right of possession
Unity of interest
Unity of possession
Unity of time
Unity of title

ANSWERS

To chapter exercises. If you couldn't figure out what to put in the blanks, find the answer here!

Exercise a

When one person or entity owns a property, the tenancy is in SEVERALTY. *It is a* CONCURRENT TENANCY *or co-tenancy if more than one person or entity owns the property together. There is always a* UNITY OF POSSESSION *in all co-tenancies. Therefore, if a co-tenant is excluded from a portion of the premises, that portion becomes a* SEVERALTY *estate.*

If the surviving co-tenants have the right to take the interest of a deceased co-tenant, then the ownership is with a RIGHT OF SURVIVORSHIP.

Exercise b

In a tenancy in common the maximum number of co-tenants is UNLIMITED. *The co-tenants can be* NATURAL *persons or other legal entities. Their interests in the property can be* EQUAL *or* UNEQUAL. *Each co-tenant's interest can be* TRANSFERRED *as well as liened freely and separately without the permission of the other co-tenants. Each co-tenant is entitled to share* EQUALLTY *in the profits from the property, but is also responsible for the expenses and liabilities of the property. Each co-tenant bears full legal* LIABILITY *for the property. Any tenant in common may file a* SUIT FOR PARTITION, *which the judge must grant.*

Exercise c

For married persons, a survivorship estate is usually a TENANCY *by the* ENTIRETY. *Joint tenancy, as a practical matter has been* ABOLISHED *in Oregon. However, unmarried persons can have a right of survivorship by creating a tenancy in common to a* LIFE ESTATE *with cross-contingent* REMAINDERS *to the fee as in the* ERICKSON *case.*

When the tenancy is by the entirety, the RIGHT *of* SURVIVORSHIP *cannot be destroyed, even if one of the parties sells or* ENCUMBERS *the property. When married persons hold as tenants by the entirety the entirety owns the entire property, so it only requires* ONE *signature to sell or encumber it.*

Exercise d

If no special language is used and the co-tenants are not married, they will be TENANTS IN COMMON. *The presumption for married co-tenants is that they will generally take title as* TENANTS BY THE ENTIRETY *unless the deed specifically expresses something to the contrary. The interests created will be* EQUAL *unless otherwise stated in the deed. When unmarried persons own property together, getting married (choose one)* ❑ *DOES* ■ *DOES NOT change the vesting of title.*

Oregon follows laws of

❑ *Community property.*
❑ *Dower and Curtesy.*
❑ *Both dower and curtesy and community property.*
■ *Neither dower and curtesy nor community property.*

PRACTICE QUESTIONS

The following practice questions are representative of the questions you will find on the final examination and on the licensing examinations given by the Oregon Real Estate Agency.

1. An estate in severalty is held by
   I. three or more persons.
   II. two persons.
   (A) I only (B) II only (C) Both I and II (D) Neither I nor II

2. An ownership in severalty of real property exists when
   I. several persons own the same property at the same time.
   II. concurrent owners take title, intending the survivor to become vested in the entire ownership.
   III. only one entity owns a parcel of real estate.
   (A) I only (B) II only (C) III only (D) Both I and II

3. "Severalty ownership" means
   (A) ownership by several parties.
   (B) ownership by one person.
   (C) co-ownership.
   (D) joint tenancy.

4. When someone owns property to the exclusion of all other persons, this person is said to hold the property in
   (A) personalty. (B) common. (C) severalty. (D) secret.

5. In the language of real estate, which of the following terms does not belong with the others?
   (A) Joint tenancy (B) Hypothecation (C) Second trust deed (D) Subordination

6. Ownership in severalty occurs when
   (A) two or more persons have identical interests in the same property concurrently.
   (B) husband and wife share the ownership of real property.
   (C) property is owned by one person or entity.
   (D) two or more persons own the property, regardless of the form of the title.

7. In Oregon, a severalty ownership of land can be held by
   (A) married persons. (B) unmarried persons. (C) corporations. (D) any of the above.

8. Ownership in severalty occurs when
   (A) two or more persons have identical interests in the same property concurrently.
   (B) husband and wife share the ownership of the same property.
   (C) two or more persons own the property in any form of title.
   (D) property is owned by one person.

9. An ownership in severalty means that
   I. there are several owners.
   II. a concurrent tenancy with right of survivorship exists.
   III. it is possible that the owner is a corporation.
   (A) I only (B) I and II only (C) I and III only (D) III only

10. Severalty ownership of real estate means
   (A) ownership by several persons of one piece of property.
   (B) there are several ways to own real estate.
   (C) sole ownership by one person.
   (D) a severance in condemnation proceedings.

11. What is meant by the term severalty?
   (A) Diversified interest
   (B) Group ownership of land
   (C) Land ownership by one person
   (D) A right which a person possesses in the lands of another

12. Which of the following describes a tenancy in severalty?
   I. Property held by several people with right of survivorship
   II. Property held by a husband and wife
   (A) I only (B) II only (C) Both I and II (D) Neither I nor II

13. Which of the following would be an advantage for an individual holding property in severalty?
 (A) Shared liability for taxes and other expenses of the property
 (B) Flexibility in making decisions as to the use or disposition of the property
 (C) The existence of a right of survivorship
 (D) All of the above are all advantages of holding property in severalty.

14. The term "undivided interest" means
 I. each co-owner has a right to possession of the entire property.
 II. when one co-owner dies the remaining owners acquire his interest.
 (A) I only (C) Both I and II
 (B) II only (D) Neither I nor II

15. An undivided interest, without the right of survivorship, is
 (A) tenancy in common.
 (B) tenancy in severalty.
 (C) joint tenancy.
 (D) tenancy by the entirety.

16. The form of property ownership known as tenancy in common implies which of the following?
 I. Automatic ownership of the entire property by the surviving partner in the event one partner dies
 II. All of the owners must have equal interests
 (A) I only (C) Both I and II
 (B) II only (D) Neither I nor II

17. Jones and Smith own property together as tenants in common. The death of Jones during Smith's lifetime would result in which of the following?
 (A) Jones' interest in the property would pass to Smith.
 (B) Jones' interest in the property would pass to Jones' heirs or the person designated in a will.
 (C) Smith would automatically own the property as a tenant in severalty.
 (D) Smith would have to file a lawsuit to claim his interest in the property.

18. If the deed which a married couple has to a parcel of land in Oregon states that each has title as tenants in common, then each party is entitled to
 I. full right of survivorship in the estate of the other.
 II. sell an undivided interest in the land without the consent of the other party.
 (A) I only (C) Both I and II
 (B) II only (D) Neither I nor II

19. Brown and Black, both married men, purchased property as tenants in common. Black then died. As a result
 (A) Black's heirs received his interest and became tenants in common with Brown.
 (B) Brown's wife automatically acquired Black's interest and became a tenant by the entirety with Brown.
 (C) Brown received title alone as a tenant in severalty.
 (D) Black's interest in the property reverted to the state since his wife's name was not on the deed.

20. Two or more persons own land as tenants in common. One co-owner dies. The decedent's share passes to
 (A) the other co-owners.
 (B) the heirs or others as specified in his or her will.
 (C) the county.
 (D) the state.

21. Tom, Dick and Harry are co-owners of a parcel of real estate. Tom dies and his interest passes under his will to become part of his estate. Tom was a
 (A) tenant by the entireties.
 (B) joint tenant.
 (C) tenant in common.
 (D) partner.

22. What happens to real property owned by a married Oregon couple as tenants in common when one of them dies?
(A) The deceased spouse's share automatically passes to the surviving spouse.
(B) The deceased spouse's share will be inherited according to the person's will, or in the absence of a will under the descent and distribution laws of Oregon.
(C) Because the tenants in common were married, the surviving spouse will receive a life estate for the deceased spouse's interest in the property.
(D) The deceased spouse's share of the property will escheat to the State of Oregon which will decide what to do with the property.

23. A brother and sister held title as tenants in common. The sister had a will drafted providing that upon her death her interest in the property is to pass to her son. The two now hold title as
(A) tenants in common. (C) life tenants.
(B) tenants in severalty. (D) tenants by the entirety.

24. Robin DeRiche owned a property as tenant in common with his sister. Each of them
(A) must have an equal interest in the property.
(B) can transfer his or her interest in the property without the other's signature.
(C) need not have an undivided right of possession of the entire property.
(D) must will his or her interest in the property to the survivor.

25. If property is held by two or more owners as tenants in common, upon the death of one owner, ownership of his or her interest would pass to
(A) the remaining owner or owners.
(B) the heirs of the deceased tenant or to whoever is designated under his or her will.
(C) the surviving owner and/or his or her heirs.
(D) none of the above.

26. Six investors wish to buy a property and be able to will their respective interests to their children. They need a
(A) severalty estate.
(B) tenancy in common.
(C) survivorship deed.
(D) tenancy by the entirety.

27. Abel, Baker and Charlie own some development land together. Abel and Baker each have a one-fourth interest, and Charlie has the remaining one-half. You know that they
I. have a tenancy in common.
II. each have a right of survivorship.
III. have equal and undivided right of possession.
IV. each received their interest via different deeds.
(A) I, II, III and IV (C) I, III and IV only
(B) I and III only (D) II and III only

28. Mike Michaels and Bill Williams were both married men. They bought a property together as tenants in common. Mike Michaels then died. Following his death,
(A) Michaels' heirs automatically took his interest and became tenants in common with Williams.
(B) Michaels' wife automatically took his interest and became a joint tenant with Williams.
(C) Michaels' wife automatically took his interest and became a tenant in common with Williams.
(D) Williams owned the property in severalty.

29. In a tenancy in common
(A) the co-tenants do not enjoy a right of survivorship.
(B) there can be different percentages of ownership among the co-tenants.
(C) either natural persons or corporations may hold interests.
(D) all of the above are true.

30. One of the features of taking title to real property as tenants in common is that
(A) ownership interests must be equal.
(B) each co-owner's interest may be conveyed separately.
(C) a co-owner cannot will his or her interest in a property.
(D) the last survivor owns the property in severalty.

31. Tenancy in common
(A) can only be held by husband and wife.
(B) entails a right of survivorship.
(C) is not recognized in many states.
(D) must have at least two co-tenants.

32. Under a tenancy in common relationship
    (A) there is only one unity required for its existence – possession.
    (B) the same rights of survivorship exist as in joint tenancy relationships.
    (C) each party has one-half interest in the rights of the other.
    (D) tenants must equally share ownership costs.

33. A tenancy in common must have the unity of
    (A) time. (C) interest.
    (B) title. (D) possession.

34. Which of the following is correct regarding tenancy in common?
    (A) Each party must have acquired his or her interest at the same time.
    (B) Each party may sell his or her interest without the consent of the other.
    (C) Parties may have unequal rights of possession.
    (D) Each party's interest must be equal.

35. If two persons wish to hold title to real property as tenants in common, it is always essential that
    (A) their interests be acquired at the same time.
    (B) they enjoy equal rights of possession.
    (C) they each have equal, undivided interests.
    (D) the duration of their respective tenancies be for identical periods of time.

36. If four persons hold title to real property as tenants in common, they
    (A) must each own a one-fourth interest.
    (B) would be unable to determine which portion of the land is theirs.
    (C) would have the right of survivorship.
    (D) could not transfer their interest without the consent of the others.

37. If title to real property is held by tenants in common, all tenants have
    (A) equal interest.
    (B) an interest in the land, but no specific interest in any one part of the land.
    (C) possession taken at the same time.
    (D) possession taken by virtue of the same title, but possession not necessarily taken at the same time.

38. In a tenancy in common, the co-owners share only one ownership right, the right of
    (A) possession. (C) equality of interest.
    (B) survivorship. (D) unity of interest.

39. A husband and wife own property as tenants in common. If the husband should die, the wife can sell the entire property if she
    I. signs her name to a deed.
    II. obtains the permission of any others claiming to be her husband's heirs.
    (A) I only (C) Both I and II
    (B) II only (D) Neither I nor II

40. A married couple own property as tenants in common in Oregon. Each of them has
    I. full right of survivorship.
    II. the right to sell an undivided interest in the property without the permission of the other.
    (A) I only (C) Both I and II
    (B) II only (D) Neither I nor II

41. Three friends own property as tenants in common. They
    (A) must each have a one-third interest in the property.
    (B) would be unable to distinguish the portion of the property that belongs to each.
    (C) would enjoy a right of survivorship.
    (D) can transfer their interest to outsiders only with the permission of their co-tenants.

42. A tenancy in common requires
    (A) husband and wife.
    (B) undivided interest.
    (C) equal interest.
    (D) an arrangement for possession.

43. Tenancy in common
    (A) may only be held by husband and wife.
    (B) has a right of survivorship.
    (C) is not recognized in many states.
    (D) may have two or more persons as grantees.

44. To hold real property as tenants in common individuals must
    (A) be husband and wife.
    (B) hold equal interests.
    (C) hold undivided interests.
    (D) arrange for possession.

45. An owner who is a tenant in common
    I. may do nothing regarding his or her interest without the consent of the other co-owners.
    II. may convey all his or her interest without consent of the co-owners.
    III. may devise his or her interest to an heir by will.
    (A) I only
    (B) II only
    (C) III only
    (D) II and III only

46. Which of the following statements regarding tenancy in common is true?
    I. Any co-owner can file suit to partition the property.
    II. The interest of a deceased co-owner is divided among the surviving co-owners.
    III. Each co-owner has the right of undivided possession to the entire property.
    (A) I and II only
    (B) I and III only
    (C) II and III only
    (D) I, II and III

47. If two or more owners have concurrent unequal interests in the same property they can only hold title as
    (A) joint tenants.
    (B) tenants in common.
    (C) tenants by the entirety.
    (D) tenants for years.

48. Where two cousins hold title to property, one having one-third interest and the other having two-thirds interest, title would be held in
    (A) joint tenancy.
    (B) tenancy by the entirety.
    (C) tenancy in common.
    (D) tenancy in severalty.

49. If two corporations and three unrelated individuals take title as tenants in common to a parcel of Oregon land,
    (A) the corporations may sell their interests without regard to the other tenants.
    (B) the individuals may sell their interests without regard to the corporations.
    (C) none of the co-tenants has the right of survivorship.
    (D) their situation is accurately described by all of the above.

50. Ella Jones and Les Carr own a ranch as tenants in common, each has an undivided one-half interest. Carr is in sole possession of the land and is operating the ranch. Carr is not liable to Jones for
    (A) payments of rent to Jones for his own use of the land.
    (B) payments Jones makes on the mortgage executed by both.
    (C) rents received from third parties for the use of a portion of the land.
    (D) money received for the oil and minerals extracted from the land.

51. Mr. and Mrs. Rancher own a section of land in eastern Oregon equally as tenants in common. Mrs. Rancher is in sole possession of the land on which she is growing wheat. She is not responsible to her husband for
    (A) rent for his half-interest in the land.
    (B) mortgage payments which he makes on both half interests.
    (C) profits from the sale of the wheat crop.
    (D) any accounting of receipts and disbursements in connection with the wheat crop.

52. A partition action is
    (A) the creation of two or three parcels out of one original parcel of land.
    (B) the creation of new subdivisions.
    (C) a suit to sever ownership interests in a tenancy in common.
    (D) the dissolution of a partnership.

53. A partition action refers to
    (A) a lawsuit asking the court to dissolve a tenancy in common.
    (B) the erosive action of water on lands adjacent to a stream.
    (C) dividing a structure into multiple units by building common walls
    (D) a court action to terminate a partnership.

54. If a tenant in common wishes to sever his or her interest from all other co-tenants, he or she may
    (A) sue for partition.
    (B) sell to an outsider.
    (C) sell to another co-tenant.
    (D) do any of the above.

55. Three owners hold a property as tenants in common. Any one of them can change or divest his or her interest in the property by
(A) partition.
(B) eminent domain.
(C) deed.
(D) any of the above.

56. A tenant in common may
(A) sell or give away his or her interest in the property.
(B) independently mortgage his or her interest in the property.
(C) successfully bring a suit for partition.
(D) do any of the above.

57. When a seller deeds property to buyers as tenants in common,
(A) all the buyers get separate deeds.
(B) each co-tenant receives an undivided interest which can be set forth in one deed.
(C) each co-tenant has a right of survivorship to the interests of the other co-tenants.
(D) each ownership interest must be equal.

58. Which of the following groups can take title to real property in tenancy by the entirety?
I. Husband and wife
II. Father and son
(A) I only
(B) II only
(C) Both I and II
(D) Neither I nor II

59. In Oregon a tenancy by the entireties can be used by
(A) married couples.
(B) unrelated persons.
(C) persons related by blood.
(D) married couples or persons related by blood.

60. A type of co-ownership where the parties must be husband and wife is
(A) tenancy by the entireties.
(B) tenancy in common.
(C) joint tenancy.
(D) severalty ownership.

61. Mr. Lane and Mr. Harris may not own property together as
I. tenants by the entirety.
II. tenants in common.
III. tenants in partnership.
(A) I only
(B) II only
(C) III only
(D) II and III only

62. Holding property by the entirety is limited to
(A) husband and wife.
(B) corporations.
(C) relatives within the same family unit.
(D) limited partnerships.

63. A husband and wife own property under a right of survivorship which cannot be unilaterally destroyed. They apparently have a
(A) tenancy for years.
(B) tenancy by the entirety.
(C) tenancy in common.
(D) tenancy at will.

64. Tenancy by the entirety can only be
I. created between husband and wife.
II. dissolved by death.
(A) I only
(B) II only
(C) Both I and II
(D) Neither I nor II

65. Tenancy by the entirety provides for which of the following upon the death of one of the tenants?
(A) Inheritance by the heirs
(B) Life estate for the remaining tenants
(C) Surviving tenant acquires property through right of survivorship
(D) Tenancy reverts to the reversionee

66. Sally and Harry own a piece of property as tenants by the entirety. Which of the following is true?
(A) If Sally dies, Harry will automatically become the owner of the whole property.
(B) Sally may transfer her interest by a will.
(C) Harry may transfer his interest by a will.
(D) All of the above statements are true.

67. Under tenancy by the entirety, a husband may
I. transfer his interest by a will.
II. legally convey both his interest and his wife's interest without her permission.
(A) I only
(B) II only
(C) Both I and II
(D) Neither I nor II

68. A husband and wife, who own property as tenants by the entirety, must each sign which of the following documents in order for the documents to be legally binding upon both of them?
I. Deeds
II. Sales agreements
(A) I only
(B) II only
(C) Both I and II
(D) Neither I nor II

69. A tenancy by the entirety is dissolved in Oregon when
    I. one spouse dies.
    II. the couple divorces.
    III. one spouse conveys his or her interest to the other spouse.
    (A) I and II only
    (B) I and III only
    (C) II and III only
    (D) I, II and III

70. When owners of a tenancy by the entireties estate are divorced they
    (A) become tenants at sufferance.
    (B) become tenants in common.
    (C) become joint tenants with right of survivorship.
    (D) remain tenants by the entireties.

71. A couple obtains a divorce and thereby terminates their tenancy by the entirety of a section of Oregon land. If nothing else is said as to their holding, the former husband and wife will find that each has
    (A) a fee simple estate of 320 acres.
    (B) an undivided half interest in 640 acres as tenants in common.
    (C) the right of survivorship in the undivided estate of the other.
    (D) a life estate in 320 acres.

72. Bill and Dovee Coo take title to property as tenants by the entirety. Later they become divorced and the divorce decree orders them to become tenants in common. If Dovee wishes she may
    (A) sue for partition.
    (B) deed her interest separately from Bill's interest.
    (C) will her interest to whomever she wishes.
    (D) do any of the above.

73. Which of the following statements is/are true in Oregon?
    (A) When husband and wife own property as tenants by the entireties, a surviving spouse will acquire the half interest of the deceased spouse.
    (B) A creditor gains no interest in the property held as tenants by the entireties unless the creditor is creditor to both parties.
    (C) Both A and B are true in Oregon.
    (D) Neither A nor B is true in Oregon.

74. Mary and Sam Fields take title to property as tenants by the entirety. If a friend wishes to purchase the property, the
    (A) entire title can be conveyed with just Sam's signature.
    (B) entire title can be conveyed with just Mary's signature.
    (C) entire title can be conveyed with either Sam's or Mary's signature alone, but not the right of survivorship of the one who did not sign.
    (D) signature of the friend is required with at least Sam's or Mary's signature.

75. Tenancy by the entirety is based on
    (A) English common law.
    (B) the concept that husband and wife are one legal unit.
    (C) both A and B.
    (D) neither A nor B.

76. Bill and Polly DeBeck purchased a property together, but they were not married at the time they took title. The deed recited that they took title as husband and wife. They are
    (A) tenants in common.
    (B) tenants by the entirety.
    (C) joint tenants with right of survivorship.
    (D) concurrent tenants to a life estate.

77. John and Marsha Gebrueder are brother and sister. They are co-tenants with right of survivorship to a parcel of land. John died, and following his death, Marsha discovered that he was heavily in debt on several personal notes. In this case, John's creditors
    (A) can sue his estate and possibly even end up owning the property together with Mary.
    (B) can sue his estate and possibly even end up owning the entire property.
    (C) have no claim against Mary's interest provided she files a homestead exemption.
    (D) have no claim against the estate, since the notes were personal loans.

78. In Oregon,
    (A) a survivorship estate for unmarried persons can be created by using special words in the deed.
    (B) a survivorship estate is always a type of joint tenancy.
    (C) a survivorship estate is the same as a tenancy in common.
    (D) it is not possible to create a survivorship estate for unmarried persons.

79. A mother and her son hold title to some property. The deed which conveyed it to them stated that they "do not take title in common, but with right of survivorship." This language created
    (A) a joint tenancy.
    (B) a tenancy in common.
    (C) a concurrent tenancy to a life estate.
    (D) any of the above.

80. In Oregon a deed can create a type of co-tenancy with right of survivorship between unmarried persons if
    I. two or more persons are named as grantees.
    II. the deed clearly states that they take title with right of survivorship.
    (A) I only (C) Both I and II
    (B) II only (D) Neither I nor II

81. A tenant holds an interest in property with other co-tenants. The interest is a survivorship estate for unmarried grantees. This tenant may
    (A) unilaterally deed his or her interest in the property to another.
    (B) will his or her interest in the property to another.
    (C) not convey his or her interest in the property separately from the other co-tenants.
    (D) not separately lease his or her interest in the property.

82. Sam and Abel Smith hold property and the deed through which they acquired title states that they took title "not as tenants in common, but with the right of survivorship." If Sam dies before Abel, his interest will pass to
    (A) his heirs.
    (B) their landlord.
    (C) Abel.
    (D) the State Land Board through escheat.

83. With regard to property held under a survivorship estate for individual grantees, the one thing you cannot do with your interest is
    (A) will it. (C) lease it.
    (B) sell it. (D) any of the above.

84. If two purchasers, who are husband and wife, do not state on the deed how they wish title to be taken, in the state of Oregon title would be conveyed to them as
    (A) tenants in common.
    (B) tenants by the entirety.
    (C) tenants in severalty.
    (D) tenants in common, with right of survivorship.

85. A deed conveying land to "John Doe and Richard Doe" creates a co-ownership known as
    (A) tenancy by the entireties.
    (B) joint tenancy.
    (C) community property.
    (D) tenancy in common.

86. Bill Cash and Billie Cash, his daughter, buy a tract of ground for all cash. Bill and Billie are
    (A) owners of a community property estate.
    (B) joint tenants.
    (C) tenants in common.
    (D) holding in severalty.

87. John and Mary Carlson buy a home in Oregon. Although both of their names are specified in the deed, no mention is made in the deed concerning any preference for holding a title. This married couple will automatically hold the property as
    (A) tenants in common.
    (B) tenants by the entirety.
    (C) tenants in partnership.
    (D) joint tenants.

88. The most common tenancy for married persons in Oregon is
    (A) joint tenancy.
    (B) tenancy in common.
    (C) tenancy by the entirety.
    (D) community tenancy.

89. Mr. and Mrs. John Barr buy a farm in Oregon, and no mention is made in the deed concerning any preference for holding the title. The Barr's will automatically hold a
(A) tenancy in common.
(B) tenancy for years.
(C) joint tenancy.
(D) tenancy by the entirety.

90. A husband and wife bought a parcel of real property in both names. The balance of the purchase price after the initial down payment was secured by a mortgage. Neither the deed nor the mortgage revealed the manner in which the husband and wife were to own the property. The court would deem that the husband and wife took the property as
(A) common property.
(B) joint tenants.
(C) tenants by the entirety.
(D) tenants in common.

91. Two brothers purchased a property together. Their deed recited "to Bill Williams and Albert Williams." No words were used to describe the type of tenancy under which they were to take title. The brothers will
(A) be vested as tenants in common.
(B) be vested as tenants in common unless they create a written agreement to the contrary within ten days.
(C) be vested as concurrent tenants to a life estate with contingent remainders to the survivor.
(D) not be vested, as Oregon law requires that the type of concurrent tenancy be specified.

92. Alfred King and his wife Jane are co-owners of real property. Their deed recites says that they took title as co-tenants, but no other language is used to describe their interests in the property. Their title
(A) is vested as tenants in common.
(B) is vested as tenants by the entirety.
(C) is vested as a survivorship estate for individual grantees.
(D) cannot be vested under Oregon law without stating the type of co-tenancy to be created.

93. Bill and Sue Schwarz are married and they buy themselves a house. The deed names Bill Schwarz and Sue Schwarz as grantees, but does not indicate how they are to take title. If Sue dies, Bill will
(A) automatically take the house as an estate in severalty.
(B) automatically get a life estate in the house.
(C) take his place among Sue's other heirs.
(D) get nothing.

94. John and Joan are brother and sister. If they buy real estate together, they can take title as
(A) tenants in common.
(B) co-tenants with right of survivorship.
(C) tenants by the entirety.
(D) either A or B.

95. A married couple had each been married before and each had children by their previous marriages. They wished to buy a house together, yet be able to leave their interests in the house directly to their children. They need a
(A) tenancy by the entirety.
(B) tenancy in severalty.
(C) tenancy in common.
(D) survivorship estate.

96. Before they were married, Keith and Susan Moyer each owned a house. After their marriage they did not change the deeds, but each kept the houses as rentals and together bought a new house as tenants by the entirety. Two years later Susan died. The property Susan owned prior to marrying Keith will
(A) automatically be inherited by Keith alone.
(B) pass to the state.
(C) be inherited by Susan's heirs excluding Keith.
(D) be inherited by Susan's heirs including Keith.

97. Two individuals accumulate real property in severalty while they are single. After they are married, this property
(A) must be changed to tenancy in common.
(B) becomes joint tenancy property.
(C) remains as their separate property.
(D) cannot be disposed of without the consent of the other.

98. Four unrelated women wish to purchase a parcel of land together and each wants to be able to will her interest to her heirs. They need to take title as which of the following?
(A) Tenants in common
(B) Tenants by the entirety
(C) Tenants in partnership
(D) Either A or C above

99. When owners hold title as tenants in common, all of them have
(A) equal interests in all cases.
(B) an interest in the property, which is not an interest in any specific part of the property.
(C) both A and B.
(D) neither A nor B.

100. Which of the following types of tenancy could a married couple in Oregon hold on real property they purchase together?
I. Tenants by the entirety
II. Tenants in common
(A) I only
(B) II only
(C) Both I and II
(D) Neither I nor II

101. A form of co-ownership with an undivided interest and no right of survivorship is
(A) tenancy by the entirety.
(B) tenancy in common.
(C) joint tenancy.
(D) estate of survivorship.

102. Right of survivorship is a feature of
(A) tenancy in severalty.
(B) tenancy by the entirety.
(C) tenancy in common.
(D) all of the above forms.

103. Ownership of an undivided interest in land with no right of survivorship is found only in
(A) joint tenancy.
(B) severalty.
(C) life estate.
(D) tenancy in common.

104. The form of ownership of real property by two or more persons, each of whom has an undivided interest passable to heirs by will, is called
(A) joint tenancy.
(B) right of survivorship.
(C) an estate for life.
(D) tenancy in common.

105. Mario and Maria Esposi owned a house as tenants by the entirety. They leased the house for two years to Rod Johnson. A few months thereafter, Mario died suddenly. Immediately thereafter, Maria sold the house to her church. The sale to the church
(A) would terminate Johnson's lease.
(B) would require Johnson to renegotiate his lease with the church.
(C) would not affect Johnson's lease.
(D) could not be finalized until Johnson renegotiated his lease with the church.

106. Bill and Mary Williams have been married for ten years. Bill wishes to purchase a small rental house to put in his name only. If he does so, Mary must sign the
I. purchase agreement as well and stipulate that he is to take title alone.
II. deed as well when he later goes to sell the property.
(A) I only
(B) II only
(C) Both I and II
(D) Neither I nor II

107. Which is usually true under commonly accepted principles of tenancy law?
I. Unless otherwise specified, a conveyance of property to a husband and wife is construed as a tenancy by the entirety.
II. Tenancy by the entirety is characterized by a right of survivorship, which may be severed by divorce or by joint conveyance of the husband and wife.
(A) I only
(B) II only
(C) Both I and II
(D) Neither I nor II

108. A form of ownership not recognized in Oregon is
(A) severalty ownership.
(B) tenancy in common.
(C) tenancy by the entirety.
(D) community property.

109. When a city or county owns property such as school buildings and the like, title is usually vested as
(A) tenancy in common.
(B) community property.
(C) tenancy by the entirety.
(D) a severalty estate.

110. Which of the following tenancies do not involve a landlord and tenant relationship?
(A) Tenancy at sufferance
(B) Tenancy for years
(C) Tenancy in common
(D) Tenancy at will

111. Which of the following statements concerning tenancies is true?
I. When a husband and wife own property as tenants by the entirety and one of them dies the survivor becomes the owner of the whole interest.
II. When a husband and wife own property as tenants in common and one of them dies the survivor becomes the owner of the whole interest.
III. A tenancy by the entirety is severed by divorce.
(A) I only
(B) III only
(C) I and II only
(D) I and III only

ANSWERS

To practice questions. If you chose the wrong letter, here's the right one! The explanations are designed to clarify your understanding.

1. **D** When two or more persons own property together, it is called a concurrent tenancy, or co-tenancy. A fundamental principle of all concurrent tenancies is that there must be an equal right of possession, regardless of the percentage of interest held. No co-tenant can ever be excluded from any portion of the premises. To do so, would be the equivalent of severing that portion of the premises from the rest. When one's interest is separate (severed from the rest), it is called a severalty estate, or estate in severalty. Therefore, severalty is ownership by just one person.

2. **C** Severalty ownership means only one person or legal entity owns the property, as opposed to concurrent tenancy (co-tenancy). It is called "severalty" because the interest is severed from all others, i.e., it is a separate property.

3. **B** Severalty ownership means only one person or legal entity owns the property, as opposed to concurrent tenancy (co-tenancy). It is called "severalty" because the interest is severed from all others, i.e., it is a separate property.

4. **C** Severalty ownership means only one person or legal entity owns the property, as opposed to concurrent tenancy (co-tenancy). It is called "severalty" because the interest is severed from all others, i.e., it is a separate property. Personalty is a synonym for personal property.

5. **A** Joint tenancy is a type of concurrent tenancy. Hypothecation is to pledge property as collateral for a debt. A trust deed is a modern instrument used in place of a mortgage. Subordination occurs where one lienholder, although holding a lien which is prior in right, agrees to become junior to another lienholder.

6. **C** The term "severalty" means that the property is severed from all other properties. For a concurrent tenancy to exist, there must be an undivided right of possession. Therefore, any time the property is owned by only one person or entity, the ownership is in severalty.

7. **D** "In severalty" means there is one owner and "concurrent tenancy" means there are two or more owners. Any legal entity, whether a natural person (including a husband or a wife), corporation or government agency may own property in severalty or concurrently.

8. **D** When two or more persons own property together, it is called a concurrent tenancy, or co-tenancy. A fundamental principle of all concurrent tenancies is that there must be an equal right of possession, regardless of the percentage of interest held. No co-tenant can ever be excluded from any portion of the premises. To do so, would be the equivalent of severing that portion of the premises from the rest. When one's interest is separate (severed from the rest), it is called a severalty estate, or estate in severalty. Therefore, severalty is ownership by just one person.

9. **D** The expression "in severalty" is the opposite of "concurrent." That is, when there is only one owner, the ownership is in severalty. When there are more than one owner, the tenancy is concurrent. Any legal entity, whether a natural person, corporation or government agency may own property in severalty or concurrently.

10. **C** Severalty ownership means only one person or legal entity owns the property, as opposed to concurrent tenancy (co-tenancy). It is called "severalty" because the interest is severed from all others, i.e., it is a separate property.

11. **C** Severalty ownership means only one person or legal entity owns the property, as opposed to concurrent tenancy (co-tenancy). It is called "severalty" because the interest is severed from all others, i.e., it is a separate property.

12. **D** Severalty ownership means only one person or legal entity owns the property, as opposed to concurrent tenancy (co-tenancy). It is called "severalty" because the interest is severed from all others, i.e., it is a separate property. If a husband and wife own property together it could not be in severalty because "severalty" means one person owns the property alone.

13. **B** Since the ownership is in severalty (one owner), there can be no sharing of expenses nor can there be a right of survivorship.

14. **A** All concurrent tenancies have an undivided right of possession. This means that no co-tenant can ever be excluded from any portion of the premises. To do so (i.e., by putting up a fence) would effectively sever the property into separate parcels. Since this would be a severalty estate, logic requires that for a tenancy to be concurrent, there must always be an undivided right of possession.

15. **A** All concurrent tenancies have a right of survivorship, except the tenancy in common. A severalty estate is not a concurrent tenancy because it is not an undivided interest.

16. **D** In a tenancy in common the interests may be equal or unequal and any co-tenant can freely transfer or separately lien his or her interest without needing the permission of the other co-tenants. Any co-tenant may also will his or her interest separately, as there is no right of survivorship.

17. **B** A tenancy in common does not give the co-tenants a right of survivorship. Therefore, upon the death of a tenant in common the interest of the tenant passes to his or her heirs, not to surviving co-tenants.

18. **B** In a tenancy in common, any co-tenant may will his or her interest separately, as there is no right of survivorship. The fact that the co-tenants are married to each other is irrelevant. The interests may be equal or unequal and any co-tenant can freely transfer or separately lien his or her interest without needing the permission of the other co-tenants.

19. **A** The fact that the co-tenants are married is irrelevant if they are tenants in common. Even if two tenants in common are husband and wife, it would make no difference. They simply follow the normal rules of a tenancy in common, one of which is that a tenancy in common does not have a right of survivorship. Oregon recognizes neither community property nor dower and curtesy laws. As a result, any partner in a marriage can own property alone or with others, and the spouse never has any interest in property so owned.

20. **B** All concurrent tenancies have a right of survivorship except the tenancy in common. Therefore, the interest of a deceased tenant in common always goes to his or her heirs, not to the surviving co-tenants.

21. **C** All concurrent tenancies have a right of survivorship, except the tenancy in common. A partnership is not a concurrent tenancy because it is not an undivided interest.

22. **B** A married couple may be tenants by the entirety (the presumption, unless otherwise stipulated), or tenants in common (if so stated). A tenancy in common does not have a right of survivorship. The fact that the co-tenants are married to each other is irrelevant; the interest of the deceased co-tenant goes to his or her heirs, according to a will or as provided in Oregon laws of descent and distribution. Escheat means that the property of a deceased person who has no heirs or will passes to the State of Oregon.

23. **A** A tenancy in common does not have a right of survivorship, therefore, any co-tenant is entitled to will his or her interest to anyone. Doing so does not change how the title is vested; the co-tenants remain tenants in common.

24. **B** A tenancy in common is characterized by the undivided right of possession and little else. There can be an unlimited number of co-tenants, each co-tenant's interest can be a different percentage, acquired at the same or at different times. Each tenant may sell or lien his or her interest individually and separately from the others and without their permission. The only characteristic that is essential is that there be an equal and undivided right of possession. A tenancy in common has no right of survivorship, so the interest of a deceased co-tenant goes to his or her heirs. There is no need to create a will, however, as the interest will go to heirs by Oregon laws of descent and distribution if there is no will.

25. **B** All concurrent tenancies have a right of survivorship except the tenancy in common. Therefore, the interest of a deceased tenant in common always goes to his or her heirs, not to the surviving co-tenants.

26. **B** A severalty estate is when there is only one owner. A survivorship deed would give them a right of survivorship, which takes precedence over a will. So does tenancy by the entirety, which they cannot use anyway, since it is restricted to married couples. Tenancy in common has no right of survivorship, so it would allow the co-tenants to will their interests to whomever they wish.

27. **B** In all concurrent tenancies where there is a right of survivorship, the ownership interests must always be equal. Therefore, if the ownership interests are not equal, the co-tenants must own as tenants in common. There is no right of survivorship in a tenancy in common, so if they are tenants in common, their interests can be separately conveyed, encumbered or willed. Tenants in common could receive their interest through separate deeds, but there is no requirement

that this be so and, in fact, it is more common for the co-tenants to receive title under one deed.

28. **A** Since they were tenants in common, there was no right of survivorship. Therefore, the interest of the deceased co-tenant vested in his heirs at the time of his death. The surviving co-tenant now has new co-tenant(s).

29. **D** Any type of legal entity can be a tenant in common, and with any other type of legal entity. For example, corporations, government agencies, single persons and married persons could all be tenants in common at the same time to the same property if they should so desire. The interests may be equal or unequal. Tenancy in common does not have a right of survivorship, so the interest of a deceased co-tenant goes to his or her heirs.

30. **B** In a tenancy in common there may be an unlimited number of owners, who can be any kind of legal entity, including corporations, government agencies, husbands and wives, etc. The interests may be equal or unequal and any co-tenant can freely transfer or separately lien his or her interest without needing the permission of the other co-tenants. Any co-tenant may also will his or her interest separately, as there is no right of survivorship.

31. **D** Any legal entities can be tenants in common; the tenancy by the entirety is the only one where the co-tenants must be husband and wife. Although there are occasionally different rules in other jurisdictions, tenancy in common is found in all states. For there to be a concurrent tenancy there must always be more than one tenant. If there is only one tenant, the ownership is in severalty.

32. **A** In a tenancy in common there may be an unlimited number of owners, which can be any kind of legal entity, including corporations, government agencies, husbands and wives, etc. The interests may be equal or unequal and any co-tenant can freely transfer or separately lien his or her interest without needing the permission of the other co-tenants. Any co-tenant may also will his or her interest separately, as there is no right of survivorship. The co-tenants share the income and expense prorata according to their percentage of interest. They do have an equal and undivided right of possession (unity of possession), regardless of the percentage of interest.

33. **D** The four unities of time, title, interest and possession mean that the property must have been acquired at the same time, through the same legal document, the interests must be equal, and there must be an equal and undivided right of possession. A joint tenancy (rarely used in Oregon for real estate) requires all four. A tenancy in common requires only the unity of possession.

34. **B** The four unities of time, title, interest and possession mean that the property must have been acquired at the same time, through the same legal document, the interests must be equal, and there must be an equal and undivided right of possession. A joint tenancy (rarely used in Oregon for real estate) requires all four. A tenancy in common requires only the unity of possession. Therefore, the interests may be equal or unequal. In a tenancy in common any co-tenant can freely transfer or separately lien his or her interest without needing the permission of the other co-tenants.

35. **B** The four unities of time, title, interest and possession mean that the property must have been acquired at the same time, through the same legal document, the interests must be equal, and there must be an equal and undivided right of possession. A joint tenancy (rarely used in Oregon for real estate) requires all four. A tenancy in common requires only the unity of possession.

36. **B** In a tenancy in common there may be an unlimited number of owners, which can be any kind of legal entity, including corporations, government agencies, husbands and wives, etc. The interests may be equal or unequal and any co-tenant can freely transfer or separately lien his or her interest without needing the permission of the other co-tenants. Any co-tenant may also will his or her interest separately, as there is no right of survivorship. The co-tenants share the income and expense prorata according to their percentage of interest. They do have an equal and undivided right of possession, regardless of the percentage of interest. An undivided right of possession means that no co-tenant can ever be excluded from any portion of the premises.

37. **B** Tenancy in common is the most flexible of all the concurrent tenancies. There may be an unlimited number of owners, which can be any kind of legal entity, including corporations, government agencies, husbands and wives, etc. The interests may be equal or unequal and any co-tenant can freely transfer or separately lien his or her interest without needing the permission of the other co-tenants. Any co-tenant may also will his or her interest separately, as there is no right of survivorship. The co-tenants share the income and expense prorata according to their percentage of interest. They do have an equal

and undivided right of possession, regardless of the percentage of interest. All concurrent tenancies have a right of possession. Possession does not have to be through the same deed (title), nor does it have to be acquired at the same time.

38. **A** Tenancy in common is the most flexible of all the concurrent tenancies. There may be an unlimited number of owners, which can be any kind of legal entity, including corporations, government agencies, husbands and wives, etc. The interests may be equal or unequal and any co-tenant can freely transfer or separately lien his or her interest without needing the permission of the other co-tenants. Any co-tenant may also will his or her interest separately, as there is no right of survivorship. The co-tenants share the income and expense prorata according to their percentage of interest. They do have an equal and undivided right of possession, regardless of the percentage of interest. All concurrent tenancies have the same right of possession.

39. **D** Since the married couple were tenants in common, there was no right of survivorship. Therefore, when the husband died, his wife did not necessarily gain title to his half interest in the property. She would also need more than mere permission if there were others claiming to be her husband's heirs.

40. **B** Whether or not the co-owners are married is irrelevant. If the property is held as tenants in common, there is no right of survivorship and the interests are freely transferable.

41. **B** All co-tenancies have an undivided right of possession, so which portion of the property belongs to which co-tenant is not possible to determine. Tenancy in common does not require equal interests and does not confer a right of survivorship on the tenants.

42. **B** In a tenancy in common there may be an unlimited number of owners, which can be any kind of legal entity, including corporations, government agencies, husbands and wives, etc. The interests may be equal or unequal and any co-tenant can freely transfer or separately lien his or her interest without needing the permission of the other co-tenants. Any co-tenant may also will his or her interest separately, as there is no right of survivorship. The co-tenants share the income and expense prorata according to their percentage of interest. They do have an equal and undivided right of possession, regardless of the percentage of interest. This is usually referred to as an undivided interest.

43. **D** In a tenancy in common there may be an unlimited number of owners, which can be any kind of legal entity, including corporations, government agencies, husbands and wives, etc. The interests may be equal or unequal and any co-tenant can freely transfer or separately lien his or her interest without needing the permission of the other co-tenants. Any co-tenant may also will his or her interest separately, as there is no right of survivorship. The co-tenants share the income and expense prorata according to their percentage of interest. They do have an equal and undivided right of possession, regardless of the percentage of interest. All concurrent tenancies have a right of possession. Of all the possible concurrent tenancies, tenancy in common is the only one that is usually identical, or at least very much the same, in all states.

44. **C** In a tenancy in common there may be an unlimited number of owners, who can be any kind of legal entity, including corporations, government agencies, husbands and wives, etc. The interests may be equal or unequal and any co-tenant can freely transfer or separately lien his or her interest without needing the permission of the other co-tenants. The co-tenants have an equal and undivided right of possession (unity of possession), regardless of the percentage of interest. There is no need to "arrange for possession," as this is an automatic feature.

45. **D** In a tenancy in common the interests may be equal or unequal and any co-tenant can freely transfer or separately lien his or her interest without needing the permission of the other co-tenants. Any co-tenant may also will his or her interest separately, as there is no right of survivorship. To devise is to give a gift of real property in a will.

46. **B** In a tenancy in common any co-tenant may will his or her interest separately, as there is no right of survivorship. This also means that, if an owner fails to make a will, his or her interest still goes to his or her heirs. The co-tenants have an equal and undivided right of possession, regardless of the percentage of interest. One disadvantage of a tenancy in common is that all co-tenants have the right to a suit for partition.

47. **B** The four unities of time, title, interest and possession mean that the property must have been acquired at the same time, through the same legal document, the interests must be equal, and there must be an equal and undivided right of possession. A joint tenancy (rarely used in Oregon for real estate) requires all four. A tenancy in common requires only the unity of possession. Even in a tenancy by the entirety, there cannot be unequal interests. Only the tenancy in common permits equal or unequal shares.

48. **C** The four unities of time, title, interest and possession mean that the property must have been acquired at the same time, through the same legal document, the interests must be equal, and there must be an equal and undivided right of possession. A joint tenancy (rarely used in Oregon for real estate) requires all four. A tenancy in common requires only the unity of possession. Even in a tenancy by the entirety, there cannot be unequal interests. Only the tenancy in common permits equal or unequal shares.
49. **D** Tenancy in common is the most flexible of all the concurrent tenancies. There may be an unlimited number of owners, which can be any kind of legal entity, including corporations, government agencies, husbands and wives, etc. The interests may be equal or unequal and any co-tenant can freely transfer or separately lien his or her interest without needing the permission of the other co-tenants. Any co-tenant may also will his or her interest separately, as there is no right of survivorship.
50. **A** In a tenancy in common the co-tenants share the income and expense pro-rata according to their percentage of interest. The co-tenants do have an equal and undivided right of possession, regardless of the percentage of interest. Since each co-tenant is entitled to possession of the whole, neither can charge the other for rent.
51. **A** Since each co-tenant has an equal and undivided interest in the entire property, no co-tenant can charge rent to another co-tenant. However, all co-tenants, of whatever type, are always responsible to each other for profits received and for expenses paid, and for accounting of them.
52. **C** In a tenancy in common, a suit for partition occurs when one or more co-tenants ask a court to order the property physically divided and parceled out to each co-tenant, or order the property sold with resulting distribution of the cash proceeds. The judge has no choice but to grant the partition; the only option left to the judge is whether to order the property physically divided or order it sold.
53. **A** Any co-tenant in a tenancy in common may file a suit for partition of the property, and the judge must grant it. The judge has the option of physically dividing the land, or of ordering it sold and dividing the proceeds among the co-tenants.
54. **A** Selling to another co-tenant or to an outsider is an option any co-tenant has. However, such a sale would not sever the undivided right of possession. Only a suit for partition or the ultimate sale of all interests to one entity in severalty would sever the undivided right of possession.
55. **D** A suit for partition changes the owner's interest by severing the co-tenancy and converting it to a severalty estate. Eminent domain is the power of the government to take privately owned property for public purposes (condemnation). A co-tenant can also sell his or her interest separately from the others by deeding it to a buyer.
56. **D** Interests in a tenancy in common are always freely transferable and separately lienable. A tenant in common also has the right to petition the court to sever the tenancy by dividing the property physically or by ordering the property sold and dividing the proceeds. This is called a suit for partition.
57. **B** Each time an interest in a property is conveyed there must be a deed. However, more than one co-tenant seller can sign the same deed, and the deed can name multiple parties as buyers. In other words, it does not matter how many deeds there are, as long as all the ownership rights are properly transferred to the buyers. Normally this is done with one deed, signed by all owners and naming all buyers on the same document.
58. **A** Any natural person, married or not, or legal entity can be a tenant in common with any other entity. To be tenants by the entirety requires that the parties be married to each other at the time they take title and remain so.
59. **A** Tenancy by the entirety (entireties) can only be used by persons who are legally married at the time they take title and remain so. If a couple are not married they may hold property as tenants in common or as concurrent tenants with right of survivorship (Erickson case), but not as tenants by the entirety. If such co-tenants later marry, the marriage does not change the vesting of title; they are still in common or concurrent with right of survivorship. Once married, they can deed their respective interests to each other "as tenants by the entirety" and convert their tenancy to a tenancy by the entirety, if they wish.
60. **A** A married couple may be tenants by the entirety (the presumption, unless otherwise stipulated), or tenants in common (if so stated). Any natural person, married or not, or legal entity can be a tenant in common with any other entity. To be tenants by the entirety requires that the parties be married to each other at the time they take title and remain so. Joint tenancy, although rarely used for real estate, requires that the parties be personal representatives

of an estate or trustees. Severalty ownership is individual ownership, not a concurrent tenancy.

61. **A** A married couple may be tenants by the entirety (the presumption, unless otherwise stipulated), or tenants in common (if so stated). Any natural person, married or not, or legal entity can be a tenant in common with any other entity. To be tenants by the entirety requires that the parties be married to each other at the time they take title and remain so. There is no such thing as "tenants in partnership."

62. **A** Any legal entity can be a tenant in common, but tenancy by the entirety is limited to a couple who are husband and wife at the time they take title.

63. **B** Joint tenancy, tenancy by the entirety, and co-tenancy to a life estate with contingent remainders to the fee are the three recognized ways to hold property with right of survivorship in Oregon. If one party sells his or her interest in any of these it terminates the right of survivorship, with the exception of the tenancy by the entirety. In the tenancy by the entirety the right of survivorship cannot be unilaterally destroyed.

64. **A** A married couple may be tenants by the entirety (the presumption, unless otherwise stipulated), or tenants in common (if so stated). To be tenants by the entirety requires that the parties be married to each other at the time they take title. If a married couple own property as tenants by the entirety, but later become divorced, yet continue to own the property together, the tenancy by the entirety becomes a tenancy in common. While death of either party will terminate a tenancy by the entirety, it is not the only way to dissolve it. For example, the parties could voluntarily deed the property to a buyer. Or they could even deed to each other, stipulating that the conveyance is to terminate the tenancy by the entirety and create a tenancy in common instead.

65. **C** A married couple may be tenants by the entirety (the presumption, unless otherwise stipulated), or tenants in common (if so stated). A tenancy in common does not have a right of survivorship, but a tenancy by the entirety does. A right of survivorship means that the surviving co-tenant takes the interest of the deceased co-tenant. If there is no right of survivorship, the interest of the deceased co-tenant goes to his or her heirs.

66. **A** A tenancy in common does not have a right of survivorship, but a tenancy by the entirety does. Right of survivorship means that the surviving co-tenant(s) takes the interest of the deceased co-tenant. If there is no right of survivorship, the interest of the deceased co-tenant goes to his or her heirs. A provision in a will attempting to leave property owned with right of survivorship to others is of no force and effect, as the right of survivorship takes precedence over a will.

67. **D** A tenancy by the entirety has a right of survivorship, which takes precedence over a will. An attempt to will property held as tenants by the entirety is of no force and effect. In a tenancy by the entirety, the "entirety" owns the property. The entirety is an old term for the married unit, harking back to the days when the act of marriage caused the individuals to cease to exist as separate individuals. Although marriage no longer creates the entirety (each party remains a legal entity and can enter into separate contracts), many states (including Oregon) retain the concept of the married unit (the entirety) owning the property. Either partner can bind the entirety with just his or her signature. Thus it only takes one signature to sell property owned as tenants by the entirety. However, the spouse who did not sign will retain his or her right of survivorship. This means that if the spouse who did not sign survives the other, he or she can take the property away from whoever the other spouse sold the property to. For this reason, it is customary to demand both signatures when property is held by the entirety. If both spouses sign, then each has conveyed the right of survivorship. Consider here that "his wife's interest" includes her right of survivorship.

68. **C** In a tenancy by the entirety, the "entirety" owns the property. The entirety is an old term for the married unit, harking back to the days when the act of marriage caused the individuals to cease to exist legally as separate persons. Although the marriage act no longer creates the entirety (each party remains a legal entity and can enter into separate contracts), many states (including Oregon) retain the concept of the married unit (the entirety) owning the property. Either partner can bind the entirety with just his or her signature. Thus it only takes one signature to sell property owned as tenants by the entirety. However, the spouse who did not sign will retain their his or her right of survivorship. This means that if the spouse who did not sign survives the other, he or she can take the property away from whoever the other spouse sold the property to, and extinguish all encumbrances created since the conveyance. For this reason, it is customary to demand both signatures when property is held by the entirety. If both spouses sign, then each has conveyed the right of survivorship.

69. **D** A tenancy by the entirety has a right of survivorship, so death of either party will result in the other owning the property in severalty. One spouse would also own the property in severalty if the other deeded to him or her (a common event upon a dissolution of marriage). To be tenants by the entirety requires that the parties be married to each other at the time they take title and remain so. If a married couple own property as tenants by the entirety, but later become divorced, yet continue to own the property together, the tenancy by the entirety becomes a tenancy in common.

70. **B** A married couple may be tenants by the entirety (the presumption, unless otherwise stipulated), or tenants in common (if so stated). To be tenants by the entirety requires that the parties be married to each other at the time they take title and remain so. If a married couple own property as tenants by the entirety, but later become divorced, yet continue to own the property together, the tenancy by the entirety becomes a tenancy in common. A tenant at sufferance is one who has held over wrongfully and no longer has any legal right to possession, a type of less than freehold estate.

71. **B** A married couple may be tenants by the entirety (the presumption, unless otherwise stipulated), or tenants in common (if so stated). To be tenants by the entirety requires that the parties be married to each other at the time they take title and remain married during their ownership. If a married couple own property as tenants by the entirety, but later become divorced, yet continue to own the property together, the tenancy by the entirety becomes a tenancy in common. A full section of land contains 640 acres.

72. **D** When property is held as tenants by the entirety, a divorce sunders the marriage, and therefore the couple can no longer be tenants by the entirety. Therefore, they automatically become tenants in common. Once they are tenants in common, each owns a half interest to do with as he or she wishes, subject only to the undivided right of possession. Therefore, either one may sell, will, encumber or do anything he or she wishes with his or her interest. Any tenant in common always entitled to a suit for partition.

73. **D** In a tenancy by the entirety the married unit (the entirety) owns the property, so there are no "half-interests." Creditors can always reach all assets of the debtor, regardless of whether there are co-tenants.

74. **C** In a tenancy by the entirety, either party can sell the entire property with his or her signature alone. However, such a sale does not convey the other spouse's right of survivorship. Buyers do not normally need to sign a deed in order for there to be a valid conveyance in Oregon.

75. **C** The basis of most laws in the United States is the common law of various jurisdictions in England, although a few of our laws originated in Spain and France. All laws relating to tenancy in common, joint tenancy, and by the entirety are based on English legal concepts. Community property is derived from Spanish law, but Oregon does not recognize community property laws.

76. **A** If they were not married at the time they took title, then they took title as tenants in common. The fact that the deed erroneously states that they took title as husband and wife is irrelevant.

77. **D** A concurrent tenancy with right of survivorship (as in the Erickson case) is really a concurrent tenancy to a life estate with contingent remainders to the fee. When one of the co-tenants owes money, it could be a personal loan (unsecured), or it could be secured by real or personal property. In this case, the loans were personal, so the real estate was unaffected by their existence. Since the debtor's interest in the property was extinguished by his death, the survivor owns the property free and clear. The creditors could sue the debtor's estate and obtain a judgment, which would be a lien against any real property owned by the debtor. However, even if they did so, the debtor would no longer own any interest in real property to which the judgment lien could attach because ti would pass to the survivor immediately upon his death.

78. **A** Oregon recognizes three types of survivorship estates – joint tenancy (restricted to personal representatives and trustees), tenancy by the entirety (restricted to husband and wife), and concurrent tenancy with right of survivorship (as in the Erickson case). Note that a survivorship estate for unmarried persons would normally have to be the concurrent tenancy with right of survivorship. Oregon law does not require any particular language to create it other than the statement that the parties take title "with right of survivorship" (ORS 93.180). If the buyers are not married, failing to use the special language will result in their taking title as tenants in common.

79. **B** Oregon Revised Statutes 93.180 provides that a concurrent tenancy to a life estate with cross contingent remainders to the fee is created by deeding property to unmarried persons "with right of survivorship."

80. **C** A co-tenancy to a life estate with remainders to the fee can be created by deeding property to two or more persons and stating that the conveyance is "with right of survivorship" (ORS 93.180).

81. **A** A "concurrent tenancy for unmarried grantees" is sometimes used as a synonym for a concurrent tenancy with right of survivorship (Erickson). A concurrent tenancy with right of survivorship is really a concurrent tenancy to a life estate with contingent remainders to the fee. If one co-tenant were to sell or lease all his or her interest in the property the buyer or lessee would obtain a present half-interest, including the remainder interest. The remainder interest will have the same effect as a survivorship interest – upon the death of either co-tenant, the deceased co-tenant's interest in the property is extinguished and fee title is absolutely vested in the survivor. Therefore, an attempt by either co-tenant to will his or her interest will fail.

82. **C** Deeding to two or more unmarried persons "with right of survivorship" conveys to them a concurrent tenancy to a life estate with cross contingent remainders to the fee. Upon the death of either party, the survivor will take fee title in severalty by remainder.

83. **A** A "survivorship state for individual grantees" is another expression for title held as concurrent tenants to a life estate with cross-contingent remainders to the fee, as in the Erickson case. Either party may sell his or her interest. The buyer will receive exactly what the seller held – the life estate and remainder. In this case, however, the governing life remains the life of the original party. A life estate is an ownership interest, so the life tenants may lease the property to another if they wish. However, either party's interest would be extinguished upon their death, so there is nothing that can be willed to heirs.

84. **B** A married couple may be tenants by the entirety (the presumption, unless otherwise stipulated), or tenants in common (if so stated). Since nothing was stated in their deed, they will be tenants by the entirety. Tenancy in severalty means single ownership, and is therefore not a concurrent tenancy.

85. **D** There are four types of concurrent tenancies in Oregon: Tenancy in common, joint tenancy (rarely used for real property), tenancy by the entirety (married persons only), and survivorship estate for unmarried grantees (Erickson case). Community property is a concept that applies to property held in severalty by a married person in some states. Oregon does not recognize community property. When unmarried persons take title and the manner in which they take title is not specified, the presumption is that they become tenants in common.

86. **C** There are four types of concurrent tenancies in Oregon: Tenancy in common, joint tenancy (rarely used for real property), tenancy by the entirety, and survivorship estate for unmarried grantees (Erickson case). Community property is a concept that applies to property held in severalty by a married person in some states. Oregon does not recognize community property. When unmarried persons take title together, and the manner in which they take title is not specified, the presumption is that they become tenants in common. A severalty estate is individual ownership.

87. **B** A married couple may be tenants by the entirety (the presumption, unless otherwise stipulated), or tenants in common (if so stated). They could technically also become automatically joint tenants, but only if they are acting as dual personal representatives of an estate, or trustees. Since this is unlikely, they will undoubtedly be tenants by the entirety. There is no such thing as "tenants in partnership."

88. **C** When the type of estate is not specified, the presumption is that married people will take as tenants by the entirety, and unmarried persons will take as tenants in common. These presumptions are made because they are the most commonly desired results.

89. **D** A married couple may be tenants by the entirety (the presumption, unless otherwise stipulated), or tenants in common (if so stated). Since nothing was stated in their deed, they will be tenants by the entirety.

90. **C** A married couple may be tenants by the entirety (the presumption, unless otherwise stipulated), or tenants in common (if so stated). Since nothing was stated in their deed, they will be tenants by the entirety.

91. **A** The vesting of title is presumed to be as tenants in common if the buyers are not married, or as tenants by the entirety if the buyers are married at the time of the conveyance. Interests are also presumed to by equal unless otherwise specified. If the buyers choose to take title otherwise, then the deed must stipulate their desire by appropriate language. Thus, a deed to "Bill Williams and Albert Williams," without any additional language, vests the title to equal interests as tenants in common.

92. **B** When a deed conveys title to two or more people and the type of tenancy is not specified, the

law presumes that they will be tenants in common, unless married, in which case the presumption is tenancy by the entirety.

93. **A** Since they clearly were vested as tenants by the entirety, then there was a right of survivorship. Therefore, the survivor will own the house in severalty.

94. **D** Oregon recognizes four types of concurrent tenancy. The simplest is a tenancy in common, which can be held by any legal entities and does not involve a right of survivorship. The remaining three contain a right of survivorship – joint tenancy (restricted to trustees and personal representatives of an estate), tenancy by the entirety (restricted to husband and wife) and concurrent tenancy with right of survivorship (as in the Erickson case). Since the co-tenants in the question are not married, they could either take title in common or as concurrent tenants with right of survivorship, but not as tenants by the entirety.

95. **C** If they wish to be able to will their interest in the property to another, they need a co-tenancy that does not have a right of survivorship. The only concurrent tenancy that does not have a right of survivorship in Oregon is the tenancy in common.

96. **D** Either party to a marriage may own property in his or her own name in severalty. Severalty ownership means only one person or entity owns the property, as opposed to concurrent tenancy (co-tenancy). Getting married in Oregon does not vest the new spouse with any interest in the property of the other. Therefore, upon the death of the spouse who owned property in severalty, that property simply passes to his or her heirs. A surviving spouse is a potential heir.

97. **C** Either party to a marriage may own property in his or her own name as a severalty estate. Severalty ownership means only one person or legal entity owns the property, as opposed to concurrent tenancy (co-tenancy). Getting married in Oregon does not vest the new spouse with any interest in the property of the other (although it does do so in most states). The spouse who owns the property may voluntarily convey any interest he or she wishes to the new spouse, but has no obligation to do so.

98. **A** If there is a right of survivorship it takes precedence over a will. All concurrent tenancies have a right of survivorship except the tenancy in common. Tenancy in partnership is not a recognized form of concurrent tenancy, as a partnership is not a separate legal entity, but rather, the individuals acting in concert.

99. **B** Any tenancy in common is the only co-tenancy where the interests can be unequal. This is because there is no right of survivorship. However, like all concurrent tenancies, a tenancy in common has an equal and undivided right of possession to the entire property, regardless of the quantity of each co-tenant's interest.

100. **C** Any natural person, married or not, or legal entity can be a tenant in common with any other entity. To be tenants by the entirety requires that the parties be married to each other at the time they take title. If a married couple own property as tenants by the entirety, but later become divorced, yet continue to own the property together, the tenancy by the entirety becomes a tenancy in common.

101. **B** All concurrent tenancies have a right of survivorship except the tenancy in common. All concurrent tenancies also have an undivided right of possession, including the tenancy in common. So tenancy in common is the only possibility that fits the description. There is no such thing as "estate of survivorship," unless it should be construed as a synonym for "right of survivorship."

102. **B** There are four types of concurrent tenancies in Oregon: Tenancy in common, joint tenancy (rarely used for real property), tenancy by the entirety, and survivorship estate for unmarried grantees (Erickson case). All contain a right of survivorship except the tenancy in common.

103. **D** All concurrent tenancies have a right of survivorship except the tenancy in common. Severalty is single ownership, not concurrent, so the right of survivorship is irrelevant. A life estate is a freehold estate, not a description of the manner of holding title.

104. **D** In a tenancy in common any co-tenant may also will his or her interest separately, as there is no right of survivorship. A joint tenancy is similar to a tenancy in common, except that there is a right of survivorship and it requires the four unities of time, title, possession and interest. An estate for life (life estate) is a freehold estate, not a description of the manner of holding title.

105. **C** Since both parties signed the lease, then the lessee's interest would survive the death of either spouse. A lease is an encumbrance, and would have been extinguished if it had been signed only by the spouse who died.

106. **D** Oregon does not follow community property laws, nor are the laws of dower and curtesy

followed in Oregon. Therefore, the fact that a person is married does not mean that he or she cannot own property in severalty. If a married person owns property in severalty, his or her spouse has no interest in the property whatsoever, so the only signature needed to buy, encumber or sell the property is that of the spouse who owns it.

107. **C** A married couple may be tenants by the entirety (the presumption, unless otherwise stipulated), or tenants in common (if so stated). A tenancy in common does not have a right of survivorship, but a tenancy by the entirety does. Any natural person, married or not, or legal entity can be a tenant in common with any other entity. To be tenants by the entirety requires that the parties be married to each other at the time they take title and remain so. If a married couple own property as tenants by the entirety, but later become divorced, yet continue to own the property together, the tenancy by the entirety becomes a tenancy in common.

108. **D** There are four types of concurrent tenancies in Oregon: Tenancy in common, joint tenancy (rarely used for real property), tenancy by the entirety, and survivorship estate for unmarried grantees (Erickson case). Community property is a concept that applies to property held in severalty by a married person in some states. Oregon does not recognize community property laws.

109. **D** Cities, counties, and other government agencies are legal entities which enjoy the same rights to own, use, rent, sell or otherwise deal in real property in much the same manner as natural persons. Therefore, when such a government agency owns property it is typically held in severalty.

110. **C** The word "tenancy" legally means "party in possession," and as such, is frequently used to refer to an owner, as well as a renter or lessee. However, this sometimes creates confusion, because we have two separate issues, less than freehold estates, and concurrent tenancies. There are four less than freehold estates, tenancy for years, periodic tenancy, tenancy at will, and tenancy at sufferance. There are four types of concurrent tenancy, tenancy in common, joint tenancy, tenancy by the entirety, and survivorship tenancy for unmarried grantees.

111. **D** A married couple may be tenants by the entirety (the presumption, unless otherwise stipulated), or tenants in common (if so stated). A tenancy in common does not have a right of survivorship, but a tenancy by the entirety does. Any natural person, married or not, or legal entity can be a tenant in common with any other entity. To be tenants by the entirety requires that the parties be married to each other at the time they take title. If a married couple own property as tenants by the entirety, but later become divorced, yet continue to own the property together, the tenancy by the entirety becomes a tenancy in common.

BUSINESS ORGANIZATIONS

Real estate agents frequently encounter business organizations which need to buy or sell real property. Understanding the basics about these entities and how they take title to real estate is essential.

Of all the ways in which a business can be organized, the simplest is the ***sole proprietorship***. A sole proprietorship is an individual operating on his or her own in business. The business is the person and the person is the business – they are legally indistinguishable. Needless to say, the sole proprietor has complete liability for the activity of the business because the actions of the business are the actions of the individual. In spite of this drawback, the sole proprietorship is a very popular form of organization because it is easy to form – you just put your name on a sign and you are in business. Many large corporations started as sole proprietorships.

Suppose you wanted to form a real estate brokerage firm as a sole proprietorship, and suppose further that you wanted to call it "Aardvark Realty." Unless your name happens to be Aardvark, this is called an ***assumed business name***. The term "assumed business name" is usually abbreviated "ABN." You also frequently hear people refer to it as a "DBA." which stands for "doing business as."

When you use an assumed business name Oregon law requires that you register it with the Corporation Commissioner in the Office of the Secretary of State. Registration is on a county-by-county basis, so you could register for all Oregon counties or just the one(s) where you plan to do business. The fee for registration is small and the only requirement is that you not use a name already registered to someone else in the same counties where you will be doing business. If you fail to register an assumed business name you could be subject to a fine and you also lose your right to sue others.

NOTES

Since a sole proprietorship is the same as the individual, when a sole proprietor owns real estate, the title is usually just vested in the personal name of the proprietor. However, it is also possible to vest title in the assumed business name, if the owner desires.

Partnerships

A ***partnership*** form of organization comes about when there are two or more persons (or other legal entities) who desire to engage in business together. Partnerships are categorized as ***general partnerships*** and ***limited partnerships***.

At common law, general partners of a partnership are all agents of each other and can bind the partnership to contracts with third parties with their signature alone. Of course, when they do, they have a fiduciary obligation of good faith and loyalty to their partners. Also, in a general partnership, all the general partners have the same liability as if they were sole proprietors. For example, if a customer suffers a personal injury and sues, the customer can reach not only the partnership's assets, but all the personal assets of each general partner as well.

A ***limited partnership*** offers a way around the liability problem. In a limited partnership, most of the partners are usually ***limited partners***, that is, their liability is limited to the amount they have invested, the same as stockholders in a corporation. Creditors of a limited partnership cannot generally reach the personal assets of the limited partners. However, a limited partnership must have at least one ***general partner***. The general partner can be held personally liable. The general partner is also responsible for management of partnership affairs.

Of course there is a trade-off. In order to have the benefits of limited liability, the limited partners must give up the right to manage the affairs of the partnership. If a limited partner steps in and starts running things, the limited partner might be deemed to have become a general partner, and therefore personally liable.

Limited partnerships can only be created by registering with the Office of the Secretary of State. The process is similar to the creation of a corporation. A limited partnership is a type of legal entity, so when a limited partnership is created a ***registered agent*** must be appointed to receive service of legal process on the partnership.

Whether the partnership is general or limited, real property can be held in the name of the partnership or it can also be held in the name of one or more of the general partners. If it is held in the name of the partnership, then the signature of any one general partner is sufficient to convey it. If it is vested in the personal names of the partners, then the entire interest in the property cannot be conveyed without the signatures of all the partners in whose name the title is vested.

Exercise 6a

When an someone goes into business alone without creating any artificial legal entities, this is called a __________ ____________________. In this case, the owner has full _______________ for the business. An _______________ _______________ __________ (DBA) must be filed with the ____________________ ____________________ when the owner engages in business under a name other than his or her own name.

A ____________________ can be ____________________, in which case all the partners have unlimited personal liability, or it can be ____________________, in which case the liability of the ____________________ partners extends only to the amount they have invested. If a ____________________ partner engages in management, he or she may he held to have become a ____________________ partner. A limited partnership must have at least one ____________________ partner and a ____________________ ____________________ to receive service on the partnership.

Corporations

Corporations are the subject of a great body of law. A corporation is said to be a "creature of the state," that is, it is created by the Oregon Corporation Commissioner when a citizen files ***articles of incorporation***. Upon receipt of proper articles of incorporation and the required fee, the Corporation Commissioner issues a ***certificate of incorporation***, and the corporation has been created. The articles and certificate of incorporation are sometimes referred to as the corporate ***charter***.

Once created, the corporation may conduct any business the charter allows – and corporate charters typically contain a clause authorizing "any lawful activity." Corporations filed in Oregon are called ***domestic corporations*** and are authorized to conduct business only in Oregon. If an Oregon corporation wishes to conduct business by maintaining a physical presence in another state (i.e., a corporate office), then it must first become registered as a ***foreign corporation*** in that state and receive a ***certificate of authority*** or ***certificate of qualification*** from the appropriate officials in that state.

The interesting thing about corporations and limited partnerships is that they are legal entities. General partnerships and sole proprietorships are not legal entities, so any act of the business is an act of the individuals. When it comes to ownership of real estate, unlike partnerships, a corporation may only hold title in the name of the corporation.

A corporation or a limited partnership may sue or be sued in its own name the same as a natural person. And since corporations are legal entities, they must also designate a natural person as the ***registered agent*** upon whom demands and legal papers can be served, the same as a limited partnership. The registered agent does not have any legal liability with respect to such demands or service, except the obligation to forward them to the appropriate corporate officials or general partners.

Corporations are run by a ***board of directors*** who are elected by the stockholders. The board of directors also creates ***bylaws*** for the corporation. The bylaws set forth the duties and powers of the officers, when directors and stockholder's meetings will be held, how votes will be cast, and so forth. The stockholders must elect the board of directors and approve the bylaws.

A corporation cannot act except through authority of the board of directors – that is, during its meetings the board must authorize everything the corporation does. And, since a corporation does not have a physical existence, it can only act through agents. That is, eventually, all contracts the corporation enters into have to be signed by a natural person and this person must be authorized as an agent of the corporation by the board of directors.

NOTES

Of course, in the bylaws various officers will be granted authority to sign documents for day-to-day functions. However, special authority is frequently required in order to buy or sell real estate. When conducting business with a corporation, it is common business practice to ask for a special ***resolution*** to be made by the board. The resolution is an excerpt from the minutes of a board meeting during which the board authorized someone to sign a document on behalf of the corporation. Typically, the resolution must be signed by the president and the secretary.

If someone signs a contract on behalf of a corporation, but was not authorized, the corporation cannot generally be held to the contract. However, the person who signed the contract as agent of the corporation did so wrongfully, and is therefore generally liable personally for any damages suffered by the other party to the contract. To avoid such a legal tangle, real estate agents should always insist on a corporate resolution signed by the president and secretary and authorizing the signer to sign the specific contract on behalf of the corporation.

Warning: Many persons believe that if you incorporate you will shield yourself from legal liability. While generally true, this may not always be so. In *Rice vs. Oriental Fireworks* the Oregon court of Appeals found the officers of a corporation personally responsible when it was determined the corporation did not have sufficient assets to meet its obligations which were reasonably foreseeable from the nature of the business. Specifically, the officers of the corporation failed to purchase a large enough liability insurance policy to cover the damages from a subsequent personal injury case.

Corporations are sometimes organized as ***non-profit corporations***. Such corporations follow the same general rules as ordinary for-profit corporations, except that there are no stockholders. The purpose of having stockholders is to divide up the profits pro-rata according to the number of shares of stock held by each stockholder. If there is to be no profit, then there will be no need for stockholders. There are also other special rules for non-profit corporations, but the rules for ownership of real estate and entering into contracts remain the same – all authority must come from the board of directors and the usual procedure is to obtain a resolution authorizing someone to sign the agreement on behalf of the corporation.

Another special kind of corporation is the ***Subchapter S corporation***. A Subchapter S corporation can be created in order to avoid taxation of corporate profits. Ordinary for-profit corporations must file income tax returns and pay tax on their profits. Subchapter S corporations file "informational returns" only – telling the Internal Revenue Service how much was paid to each stockholder during the year. Each stockholder is responsible for his or her own taxes on the corporate income that was distributed during the year. Subchapter S corporations are subject to a number of other regulations, including a limitation on the number of stockholders.

Note that a Subchapter S corporation takes on many of the aspects of a limited partnership. Assuming that investors wish to limit their liability to the amount of their investment, this can be accomplished with either a limited partnership or a corporation. But the ordinary corporation suffers the disadvantage of double taxation – corporate profits are subject to corporation income taxes, and then when the after-tax profits are distributed to the stockholders as dividends, they become taxable again as income to the stockholders. Limited partnerships are not subject to income taxes, so double taxation is avoided. But if the investors really want the corporate form of ownership, they can have the best of both worlds by creating a Subchapter S corporation. Another advantage of the Subchapter S corporation over the limited partnership is that the Subchapter S corporation can have a perpetual life, where the limited partnership must be created with a finite life.

Exercise 6b

Corporations are created by filing ________ ____ ________ *with the Oregon Corporation Commissioner. In a corporation, the authority to sign documents on behalf of the corporation is derived from the* ________ ____ ________. *To be sure the person signing on behalf of the corporation is authorized, you should always obtain a corporate* ________ *signed by the president and secretary. Corporations must also name someone to be the* ________ ________ *for the corporation, on whom demands and legal process can be served. In order to avoid double taxation, a corporation can elect to become a* ________ ____ *corporation.*

Business trusts

Although not commonly encountered, the ***business trust*** has special significance in the field of real estate. A business trust has many of the same characteristics as a corporation, yet it is legally constituted in a completely different way. All trusts involve three parties, a ***trustor,*** a ***trustee***, and a ***beneficiary***. The trustor entrusts some asset to a trustee, who holds it for the benefit of the beneficiary. It is possible for the trustor and beneficiary to be the same person – that is, you could give your own assets to a trustee to manage them for yourself, thus making yourself both the trustor and the beneficiary. This is precisely what happens in a business trust. The investors (trustors) turn over their assets (e.g., cash) to a trustee, who manages the asset for the benefit of the investors (beneficiaries of the trust).

In a business trust the trustee is normally composed of a ***board of trustees*** who are usually elected by the investors. The investors are said to hold ***shares of beneficial interest***, and are therefore commonly called beneficiaries or shareholders. Business trusts are usually taxed the same way as corporations. Business trusts also conduct business the same way as corporations also – by granting authority to agents to act for the trust through resolutions issued by the board of trustees.

However, when business trusts take title to real estate, the title may be vested in the name of the trust, or may be vested in the names of the trustees as joint tenants with right of survivorship. Note that this is an exception to the rule that joint tenancy as to real property has been abolished in Oregon (see the preceding section on co-ownership of real estate).

Because there is little advantage to a business trust over a corporation the corporation is more popular. Corporations are better understood by the public, so it is easier to raise capital for a corporation than for a business trust. However, there is one kind of organization which uses the business trust exclusively – the ***Real Estate Investment Trust*** (REIT), which was authorized by revisions made in 1960 to the Internal Revenue Code. The essential advantage of a REIT is that it can avoid paying income tax on its income provided that it is created as a business trust and not as a corporation, that it pays substantially all its income to its beneficiaries, and that certain other investment criteria are met. In effect,

Notes

REITS function the same as mutual funds, except that where mutual funds invest in stocks and other securities, REITS invest in mortgages and real estate equities.

Limited liability companies

In the early 1990's various states began to enact legislation to create a new type of business entity, the ***limited liability company***. Limited liability companies combine the benefits of the limited partnership with the flexibility of the corporation. As in a partnership, the limited liability company pays no taxes itself. Tax liabilities and benefits are passed directly through to the shareholders. But like the corporation, the limited liability company can have any number of shareholders, all of whom are shielded from liability. There does not need to be a general partner to take liability.

Limited liability companies are formed through the Office of the Secretary of State. The process is similar to a corporation, including the appointment of a registered agent. Although the limited liability company appears to be a special type of corporation, it is unrelated to the corporation form of business. Limited liability companies should be considered a completely separate type of business entity.

In the few years since limited liability companies have become available in Oregon, they have become very popular as the vehicle for ownership of investment real estate. However, there are a few drawbacks to limited liability companies. For one, not all states have enacted legislation to recognize limited liability companies. If an Oregon limited liability company were to attempt to conduct business in such a state, there would be a question whether the company's actions would be legal. Another problem is that, even in Oregon, there are frequently legal questions about limited liability companies which cannot be answered due to lack of precedent.

Joint ventures and syndicates

Any time two or more persons or other legal entities get together in a business enterprise, this can be called a ***joint venture***. Joint ventures are frequently formed for just one single purpose. For example, suppose you own some land whose highest and best use is for development as a subdivision. Although you own the land, perhaps you know little about how to go about subdividing it. A developer makes an arrangement with you to use the developer's knowledge and experience to develop your land to its maximum potential as a subdivision, in exchange for a portion of the profits. This is a classic example of a joint venture.

Notice that a joint venture could be formed by two investors simply to acquire real estate as an investment. The term "joint venture" is a loose term used to describe many kinds of enterprises. Joint ventures can be complex, or can be nothing more complicated than a couple of investors buying property as tenants in common.

When a business venture takes on the aspect of an ongoing enterprise, we usually refer to it as a ***syndicate***. The word "syndicate" just means a group of persons or entities who have pooled their resources in a common enterprise. Investing in real estate is a popular purpose for a syndication. Note that a syndicate could take any form of business organization. Syndicates are commonly created to invest in large properties. Real estate agents frequently find that it is easier to find several small investors for such properties than to look for one investor who could swing the deal alone.

A principal benefit of investing in real estate is the potential for tax shelter. Because of this, the corporate or business trust form of organization is rarely used, since the tax benefits cannot usually be passed through to the investors. General partnerships involve too much personal liability, so the favored form of organization is the limited partnership or the limited liability company. For small investment properties, a simple tenancy in common is also frequently encountered.

Caution: If you should be involved in a transaction where the promoter of the investment (possibly yourself) will control and direct the passive investment of another (such as where you agree to manage the real estate for the investors after they buy it), you may be involved with a ***security***. Securities must usually be registered with the Oregon Corporation Commissioner or the Securities and Exchange Commission (SEC).

NOTES

Exercise 6c

A ____________ ____________ has a board of ____________ instead of a board of directors. The investors hold shares of ____________ ____________, rather than shares of stock. A common form of business trust is the REIT, which stands for ____________ ____________ ____________ ____________.

A new type of organization which combines the benefits of the limited partnership with the benefits of the corporation is the ____________ ____________ ____________.

When two or more parties get together to accomplish a business goal, this is called a ____________ ____________. When the enterprise is ongoing, we call it a ____________. Large commercial properties are frequently sold by creating a ____________ ____________ or a ____________ ____________ ____________. If an investment will be passive to the investors, it could be a ____________, which must be registered.

KEY TERMS

The key to understanding any new field is the vocabulary used in that field. To maximize your comprehension of the material presented in this chapter, be sure you know the meaning and significance of the following terms. Remember that the majority of test questions primarily test knowledge of vocabulary.

Articles of incorporation
Assumed business name
Beneficiary
Board of directors
Board of trustees
Business trust
Bylaws
Certificate of incorporation
Certificate of authority
Certificate of qualification
Charter
Corporation
Corporate resolution
Domestic corporation
Foreign corporation
General partner
General partnership
Joint venture

Limited liability company
Limited partner
Limited partnership
Non-profit corporation
Partnership
Real Estate Investment Trust
Registered agent
Resolution
Sole proprietorship

ANSWERS

To chapter exercises. If you couldn't figure out what to put in the blanks, find the answer here!

Exercise 6a

When an someone goes into business alone without creating any artificial legal entities, this is called a SOLE PROPRIETORSHIP*. In this case, the owner has full* LIABILITY *for the business. An* ASSUMED BUSINESS NAME *(*DBA*) must be filed with the* CORPORATION COMMISSIONER *when the owner engages in business under a name other than his or her own name.*

A PARTNERSHIP *can be* GENERAL*, in which case all the partners have unlimited personal liability, or it can be* LIMITED*, in which case the liability of the* LIMITED *partners extends only to the amount they have invested. If a* LIMITED *partner engages in management, he or she may he held to have become a* GENERAL *partner. A limited partnership must have at least one* GENERAL *partner and a* REGISTERED AGENT *to receive service on the partnership.*

Exercise 6b

Corporations are created by filing ARTICLES OF INCORPORATION *with the Oregon Corporation Commissioner. In a corporation, the authority to sign documents on behalf of the corporation is derived from the* BOARD OF DIRECTORS*. To be sure the person signing on behalf of the corporation is authorized, you should always obtain a corporate* RESOLUTION *signed by the president and secretary. Corporations must also name someone to be the* REGISTERED AGENT *for the corporation, on whom demands and legal process can be served. In order to avoid double taxation, a corporation can elect to become a* SUBCHAPTER S *corporation.*

Exercise 6c

A BUSINESS TRUST *has a board of* TRUSTEES *instead of a board of directors. The investors hold shares of* BENEFICIAL INTEREST*, rather than shares of stock. A common form of business trust is the REIT, which stands for* REAL ESTATE INVESTMENT TRUST*.*

A new type of organization which combines the benefits of the limited partnership with the benefits of the corporation is the LIMITED LIABILITY COMPANY*.*

When two or more parties get together to accomplish a business goal, this is called a JOINT VENTURE*. When the enterprise is ongoing, we call it a* SYNDICATE*. Large commercial properties are frequently sold by creating a* LIMITED PARTNERSHIP *or a* LIMITED LIABILITY COMPANY*. If an investment will be passive to the investors, it could be a* SECURITY*, which must be registered.*

PRACTICE QUESTIONS

The following practice questions are representative of the questions you will find on the final examination and on the licensing examinations given by the Oregon Real Estate Agency.

1. In a corporation, management policies are set directly by the
(A) corporate officers.
(B) stockholders.
(C) board of directors.
(D) corporate agents.

2. When a legal paper is signed by an officer on behalf of a corporation, this
(A) makes the paper eligible for recording.
(B) shows that consideration has been received by the corporation.
(C) implies the authority of the person signing.
(D) does all of the above.

3. When a corporation takes title to real property, the title is held
(A) by the board of directors as tenants in common.
(B) by the stockholders as tenants in common.
(C) as a severalty estate by the corporation.
(D) by the board of trustees as joint tenants in trust for the corporation.

4. If a real estate firm incorporates, it enjoys
(A) property tax advantages.
(B) limited liability for the stockholders.
(C) the opportunity to raise capital for expansion by selling stock.
(D) both B and C above.

5. A private corporation wants to sell its real estate. Who may sign the listing?
(A) The president of the corporation
(B) The president and the chairman of the board of directors
(C) Any person authorized by the board of directors
(D) Any officer of the corporation

6. In a limited partnership,
I. management can only be carried out by the general partner(s).
II. only the general partners have unlimited liability.
(A) I only
(B) II only
(C) Both I and II
(D) Neither I nor II

7. City owned buildings such as schools, office buildings and the like are held as
(A) severalty estates.
(B) tenancies in common.
(C) community property.
(D) survivorship estates.

8. In real estate investing, a syndicate could take the form of a
(A) corporation.
(B) general partnership.
(C) limited partnership.
(D) any of the above.

9. When the ownership of real estate is syndicated, creditors of the syndicate can reach the personal assets of the investors in the event the syndication is formed as a
(A) tenancy in common.
(B) Subchapter S corporation.
(C) regular business corporation.
(D) limited partnership.

10. When forming a syndicate the investors wanted to limit their personal liability. They could accomplish this with a
I. limited partnership.
II. corporate form of ownership.
III. real estate investment trust (REIT).
(A) I only
(B) I and II only
(C) I, II and III
(D) III only

11. The most popular form of ownership for a real estate syndication is a
(A) corporation.
(B) limited partnership.
(C) general partnership.
(D) joint venture.

ANSWERS

To practice questions. If you chose the wrong letter, here's the right one! The explanations are designed to clarify your understanding.

1. **C** In a corporation, the stockholders clearly have the last say, because it is the stockholders who elect the board of directors. It is the board, however, which directly runs the corporation, setting all policies. The voice of the board of directors is, effectively, the voice of management.

2. **C** In general, if a corporation is to be bound by a document, the document must be signed by someone authorized to sign it by the board of directors. Whether the party signing the document was authorized or not, when someone signs a document on behalf of a corporation, he or she is implying authority to do so.

3. **C** Since a corporation is a legal entity, it takes title in its name in severalty, just as you would take title yourself if you purchased a property alone. Corporations can hold title to real estate with other corporations or with natural persons, or even with government agencies as tenants in common. But even if title is vested as tenants in common, the interest of the corporation is vested in the name of the corporation, not the board of directors or stockholders.

4. **D** The corporate form of ownership has no property tax advantages because property taxes are levied according to value. However, the possibility of shelter from legal liability and the greater ease with which capital can be raised by selling stock, are definite advantages of the corporate form of ownership.

5. **C** A corporation cannot generally be bound by an agreement unless the agreement was signed by someone authorized by the board of directors. The board may (and frequently does) give blanket authority to certain officers in the bylaws. The board may also give special authority by a resolution. In any event, just being the president, the chairman of the board, or other official in the corporation, does not guarantee authority.

6. **C** Limited partnerships are created by registration with the state. The advantage of a limited partnership is that it pays no income taxes itself, so double taxation (as in the corporation) is avoided. Nevertheless, the limited partnership creates a shelter from legal liability for the limited partners. So that someone can be held responsible for the actions of the partnership, each limited partnership must have at least one general partner. The general partner is fully liable personally for the partnership. The general partner is also responsible for management. If a limited partner engages in management, he or she may be deemed to have become a general partner, and may therefore become personally liable for liabilities of the partnership.

7. **A** The key to this question is understanding that cities and towns are municipal corporations. Thus, when a city owns real estate, it is normally in severalty.

8. **D** The term "syndicate" just means that a group has been formed for a business purpose. It can be any form of legal entity.

9. **A** Only limited partners of a limited partnership, stockholders in a corporation or holders of beneficial interests in a business trust are immune from legal liability. Even then, it may be possible to make them personally liable for obligations of the organization under the right legal circumstances.

10. **C** In a limited partnership the limited partners have no liability, although all limited partnerships must have at least one general partner, who will be liable. Stockholders in a corporation are generally liable only in that their stock may become worthless if the corporation cannot pay its obligations. A real estate investment trust is a type of business trust. Investors in a business trust have no liability for obligations of the trust, the same as shareholders in a corporation.

11. **B** Corporations shield the stockholders to some extent from legal liability, but are subject to double taxation and cannot pass tax shelter benefits to the stockholders. General partnerships avoid double taxation and can pass through tax shelter benefits, but have complete liability. Only the limited partnership and the limited liability company enjoy the benefits of both with none of the drawbacks.

TITLE ENCUMBRANCES

A MAJOR AREA OF CONCERN TO REAL ESTATE AGENTS IS THE CONDITION OF THE title to the property being sold. When we talk of the condition of the title, we are generally referring to whether or not there are any ***encumbrances*** on the title. As you recall, encumbrances are things which burden the title. There are countless ways in which real estate can be encumbered. In this chapter we will explore some of the more common encumbrances that real estate agents must deal with on an everyday basis.

An important consideration about encumbrances is that if the property is encumbered, then the owner cannot convey the title to another unless it is conveyed subject to the encumbrance. In other words, selling the property does not extinguish the encumbrance – the new owner must take the title subject to all the encumbrances which existed at the time of the conveyance. Therefore, part of the definition of an encumbrance is that it survives a sale of the property. If an interest would be extinguished by a sale of the property, then the interest was not an encumbrance. There are numerous such interests which are not encumbrances and we will discuss them in this section as well.

There are so many kinds of encumbrances that it is difficult to discuss them without some kind of categorization. Most beginning real estate texts start out by categorizing encumbrances as ***financial encumbrances*** and ***non-financial encumbrances***. Financial encumbrances (technically referred to as ***liens***) include interests such as mortgages, judgments, property taxes, income tax levies, and other matters which make the real property collateral for a debt. Non-financial encumbrances include easements, leases and rental agreements, private land use restrictions, and many other interests which are not financial in nature.

Encumbrances are interests held by others which burden the title. The definition of an encumbrance is that it survives a sale of the property. It an interest would be extinguished by a sale, then it is not an encumbrance. We categorize encumbrances as financial and non-financial. Clouds are defined as possible interests, and can ripen into either a financial or a non-financial encumbrance.

Encumbrances

Financial (Liens)
- Mortgages
- Property Taxes
- Special Assessments
- Income Tax Levies
- Judgments
- Attachments
- Notices of Pendency
- Construction Liens
- Clouds

Non-Financial
- Easements
- Profits
- Covenants
- Tenancies for Years
- Periodic Tenancies
- Clouds

Easements

If your neighbor needed to use your property on a continual basis for some purpose, he or she would normally need an ***easement***. When we think of easements the purpose that comes most quickly to mind is a driveway – legally referred to as an ***easement for ingress and egress***. While this is certainly a very ordinary kind of easement, easements are also commonly created for virtually every conceivable use that someone might make of another's land. For example, easements can be created for utility lines (electric, water, sewer, gas, etc.), for public roads, for use of air space, and even to keep a neighbor from blocking sunlight (solar easement) or a view (scenic easement).

An important concept to remember about an easement is that it is a ***right of use***, not a right of possession. A right of possession is an estate.

Before we can go any deeper into the subject of easements, we need to define some terms. In the drawing below, the property over which the easement runs is called the ***servient tenement*** or ***servient estate***. The land which has the right to use the easement is called the ***dominant tenement*** or ***dominant estate***. The owners are referred to as the ***servient tenant*** and ***dominant tenant***, respectively.

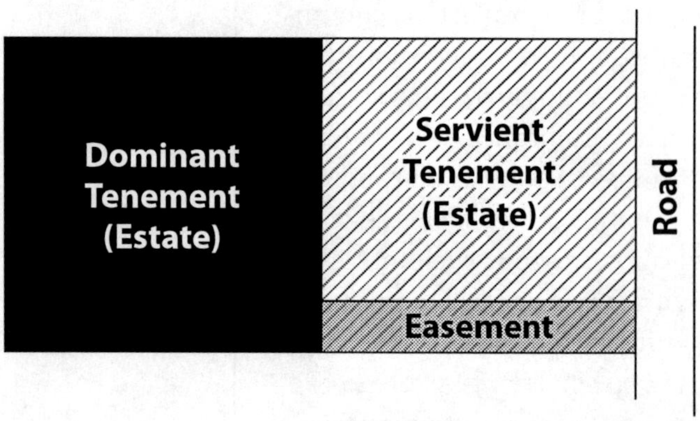

Easements are a common way of granting access to land which would otherwise have no access. An easement appurtenant is a title right which runs with the dominant tenement and is an encumbrance on the servient tenement. A buyer of the dominant tenement automatically receives an existing easement whether it is mentioned in the deed or not. Similarly, a buyer of the servient tenement takes title subject to the easement

Appurtenant and indestructible An easement is normally an appurtenance to the dominant tenement and simultaneously an encumbrance on the servient tenement. Therefore, when the dominant tenement is sold, the buyer will gain title to the easement as well – even if it is not mentioned in the deed. Similarly, when the servient tenement is sold, the buyer will take title subject to the easement.

NOTES

An easement appurtenant to one property can be appurtenant to others as well, such as where one driveway serves two or more properties. In this situation, it is not uncommon for the easement to be appurtenant to properties to which it is not physically adjacent. This might occur if, for example, the dominant tenement is divided.

Easements are normally perpetual and indestructible unless terminated voluntarily or involuntarily (see "Termination of easements" below). Although easements are normally indestructible, it is possible to create a defeasible easement which can be terminated if the dominant tenant violates a condition imposed when the easement was created. Easements are also frequently created with a time limit.

Sometimes an easement is created which is an encumbrance on the servient tenement, but is not simultaneously an appurtenance to another property. Such easements are called ***easements in gross***. For example, suppose you grant to a friend an easement for ingress and egress across your land. But suppose your friend does not own any real estate. Obviously, the easement cannot be appurtenant, since there is no land to which it can be appurtenant. Therefore, we call this an easement in gross instead of an easement appurtenant. Note that, while the easement in gross is not appurtenant to a parcel of real estate, it is nevertheless an encumbrance on the servient tenement.

Even if the easement holder does own real estate, an easement in gross can be granted just by granting the easement to the individual, rather than specifying the property to which it is appurtenant. Easements in favor of utility companies are almost always easements in gross. Utility easements are also sometimes referred to as ***commercial easements***.

Maintenance Whenever an easement exists, a question arises as to who is responsible for the maintenance of the easement. The general rule is that the person receiving the benefit of the easement has the right and the responsibility to maintain the easement. The servient tenant cannot normally interfere with this right. However, easements can be contractual, so if the document creating the easement stipulates a different arrangement, the courts will generally hold the parties to their bargain. When the easement benefits more than one property, there are statutory provisions for sharing of maintenance expense fairly among the dominant tenants.

Exclusivity Whether or not the servient tenant can use the easement as well is a question which commonly arises. The general rule is that, unless there is a specific agreement to the contrary, the easement is non-exclusive and the servient tenant may use the easement as well. Of course, the rights of the dominant tenant are paramount, so use of the easement by the servient tenant must be in a manner which does not interfere with the rights of the dominant tenant.

Community drives In urban areas it is not uncommon to encounter ***community drives***. A community drive is created where each lot has an easement along the adjacent lot for one-half the width of the driveway which runs between the lots.

Creation of easements

There are many ways that easements can come about, but the most common is where an owner simply grants the easement to another, either as an appurtenance or in gross. Oregon law requires that the grant be in writing. And since the easement is a right of use, the use(s) for which the easement is granted should be specified. If the easement is less than perpetual, then its duration, as well as any other provisions and conditions should be listed. Such an easement is said to have been created by ***express grant***.

At common law, Oregon courts also recognize that an easement is created when a developer records a plat map and then sells the lots. The legal concept is that the plat

NOTES

map itself expresses the grant of an easement to the buyers in the common areas such as streets, parks and the like. There are now strict requirements that plat maps be recorded in Oregon and that common areas be formally conveyed to the city or county. This subject will be covered in more detail in later sections.

Easements are also commonly created when an owner sells off the frontage, but retains an easement over it in order not to become landlocked. This is commonly referred to as an ***easement by reservation***. Again, the reservation should stipulate the uses to which the easement can be put and any other desired provisions.

Easements created by express grants or by reservation are considered to have been created by agreement of the parties. But easements can also be created involuntarily by a process called ***prescription***. An ***easement by prescription*** (***prescriptive easement***) can be created when someone uses another's land for ten uninterrupted years. The use must be with the knowledge but without the permission of the owner. It is important to note that the use must be without permission. If the servient tenant can demonstrate that permission was granted, then the claim for a prescriptive easement will be denied.

Note that the unauthorized use of the property is only a claim until the ten years have elapsed and the claim has been perfected. The claim is a ***cloud on the title*** (see "Clouds" later), and must be perfected by court action.

Easements by prescription frequently are created in the public when the public makes use of property for the required ten years. Roads and other rights of way have been created by prescription many times. However, ORS 105.677 provides that an easement in the public by prescription cannot be created if the use was recreational.

Even where there is no agreement the law implies the creation of an easement under certain circumstances. Such easements are called ***easement by implication of law***.

One such circumstance occurs when a parcel of land is severed into two parcels. For example, suppose you purchase the frontage to a parcel of land and the seller retains the back portion. At the time of your purchase, the seller had already been driving across the frontage and a driveway was clearly evident and visible, yet your deed made no mention of an easement by reservation. Will the seller be able to deny the existence of the easement? Probably not, although this is an unsettled area of law in Oregon, so the case could go either way. If allowed, such an easement would be called an ***easement by prior use***.

Another case where implication of law would create an easement is an ***easement by way of necessity***. At common law, an owner of a landlocked parcel can demand an easement for ingress and egress over adjacent land. To be fair, the landlocked owner would have to pay the servient tenant just compensation for loss of market value, to be determined by an appraiser if necessary. The principle of law is that, while it is unfair to the servient tenant to have to allow an easement, the alternative is even more unfair – the landlocked owner would have to forfeit all use of the landlocked parcel.

In Oregon a special statutory means exists for creating an easement by way of necessity (ORS 376.150 – 200). According to statute, the landlocked owner may petition the county to create a ***way of necessity***. Upon approval of the petition, the county will order the creation of an easement from the servient tenant(s). The dominant (landlocked) owner will be required to reimburse the county for the actual costs incurred in creation of the easement and will be ordered to pay just compensation to the affected servient tenant(s). An easement by way of necessity cannot be granted if the landlocked owner had any other legal remedy or if the property is landlocked as a result of the actions of the landlocked owner.

Creation of Easements

Agreement
Express Grant
Reservation

Prescription

Implication
By Prior Use
By Way of Necessity

Termination of easements

Probably the simplest way to terminate an easement is for the holder of the easement to relinquish it to the owner of the servient tenement. This is normally accomplished by a quitclaim deed.

There are a few other simple ways to terminate easements. For example, easements sometimes have expiration dates, in which case they are obviously terminated when the expiration date arrives. Easements created by way of necessity are generally terminated if the need for the easement ceases to exist. Even if the easement was an express grant, it may be terminated by lack of further need, depending on the exact language used in the grant.

One of the more interesting ways an easement can be terminated is by ***merger***. This is best explained by an example. Suppose you own a parcel of real estate and you enjoy access to the road via an easement across another parcel which lies between your property and the road. Now suppose further that you purchase the property through which your easement runs, so now you own both properties. By the principle of merger, you now own all the rights to both properties, but the rights have merged into *one* set of rights. In other words, the easement rights were merged into the entire estate, and therefore *it no longer exists*. Now suppose you decide to sell the frontage parcel. You had better reserve an easement to yourself, or you will leave yourself landlocked.

Easements can also be terminated by ***abandonment***. As a general rule, abandonment can only occur if there was a clear intent by the dominant tenant to abandon the easement. Mere non-use alone is not ordinarily evidence of an intent to abandon, although the circumstances surrounding the non-use can lead a court to conclude that there was an intent to abandon.

As previously noted, an easement can be created by ***prescription***, but it can also be terminated by prescription. As you recall, an easement is created by prescription when someone uses another's land for ten years, adverse to their interests, with their knowledge and without their permission. Then, if you held a valid easement across your neighbor's land, yet your neighbor blocked your use of it continuously for ten years, with your knowledge and without your permission, the easement would be extinguished by prescription.

Termination of Easements

Agreement (Quitclaim)
Expiration
Lack of Further Need
Merger
Abandonment
Prescription

NOTES

Profits, licenses and permits

A ***profit*** (more formally called a ***profit à prendre***) is the right to severance of a benefit from another's land. The profit usually involves crops, timber or minerals. The existence of the profit is an encumbrance on the land and the owner cannot convey the land except subject to the profit.

A ***license*** is created when someone grants to another a personal privilege or right to use land. Unlike easements, however, licenses are revocable. The hallmark of the license is "revocable permission" – in fact ***permit*** is frequently used as a synonym for license. Of course, since a license can be terminated at will, it is not considered an encumbrance on the title – a sale of the land extinguishes the license.

Sometimes people will attempt to create an "irrevocable license." In fact, the licensee may expend substantial money and effort in the belief that his or her license was irrevocable. Depending on the circumstances, a court may agree that the license is not revocable. Technically, this is a contradiction in terms so, depending on the circumstances, a court would likely interpret it as an easement. Many times owners grant "permits" – "hunting permits," "grazing permits," "wood permits" and the like. Such permits may be interpreted as easements or even profits, depending on the exact language used.

Exercise a

An easement is a right of ______, not a right of ____________________. A driveway is an example of an easement for ______________ and ______________. The party who benefits from the easement is called the ________________ tenant and the party over whose property the easement runs is called the ________________ tenant. In most cases, easements are ____________________, that is, they are a title right and run with the land. However, they can be personal, in which case we call them ________________ _____ ____________. Utility company easements are sometimes called ____________________ easements.

Easements can be created by an ______________ ____________, by ____________________ (selling the frontage and holding back an easement), by ____________________ (long and continued use), and easements by implication of law. Implication of law includes easements created by ________ _____ ________________, as where property is landlocked, or by ____________ ______.

Easements can be terminated by agreement, in which case the legal document normally used is a ________________ ____________, by ________________ (running of a time limit), or by lack of further need. When the holder of the easement purchases the property over which the easement runs, the principle of ______________ causes the easement to be extinguished. Intent and non-use of the easement can sometimes result in termination of the easement by ____________________. Not only can ____________________ result in the creation of an easement, but it can also result in the termination of an easement.

The right to severance of a benefit from another's land is called a ____________. A right to use another's property which is personal and revocable is a ______________. These are also sometimes called ______________.

NOTES

Covenants and other restrictions

There are countless ways in which an owner's use of the property can be restricted. Chief among these, of course, are zoning ordinances, building codes, and other ***public restrictions***. However, it is possible to create ***private restrictions*** as well. Private restrictions are commonly created in the deed, so they are sometimes also called ***deed restrictions***. You frequently hear people refer to "covenants, conditions and restrictions," or "CC & Rs" as a catch-phrase to summarize these private restrictions.

The term "restriction" is a generic term which applies to anything which lessens the owner's unfettered right to use the property, including both public and private controls. In the private sector, restrictions are further categorized as ***conditions, covenants*** and ***equitable servitudes***.

A condition is a serious matter which occurs only rarely. A condition creates a defeasible fee title – e.g., "I, the grantor, hereby convey this property provided you never build over thirty feet high at any point on the premises, and if you should ever do so, the fee shall automatically revert and revest in me." As you should recall, this is a determinable fee title. The penalty for violation is loss of title. Since the penalty is so severe, they are not commonly created.

Covenants and equitable servitudes, however, are very common. Both are mere restrictions on the use of a fee title which is vested absolutely – in other words, the title is not defeasible. The distinction between a covenant and an equitable servitude is technical and beyond what ordinary real estate agents need to understand. They go by numerous synonymous terms – ***covenants running with the land, covenants for the benefit of adjacent land, negative easements, real covenants, general plan restrictions, subdivision covenants***, and so on. Usually the reason for the different terms is that there is a slight difference in the desired effect.

Unlike conditions, covenants and servitudes cannot be enforced by taking back the fee title. Instead, covenants and servitudes are enforced by a suit for damages, a suit to enjoin the offending action, or occasionally a suit for specific performance. A suit for damages seeks a monetary award, a suit to enjoin is a suit which seeks an injunction, and a suit for specific performance is a suit which asks the court to compel the other party to comply with an agreement.

When we discuss covenants and servitudes, we must remember that there is a distinction between the burden on one party and the benefit to the other. Covenants and servitudes can be created so the burden is personal, or they can be created so the burden is an encumbrance and runs with the land. Similarly, the benefit to the other party can be personal, or it can be created as an appurtenance which runs with the land. Notice that these concepts are similar to the differences among an easement appurtenant, an easement in gross and a license.

Frequently a subdivider will wish to create a set of covenants for a subdivision. The concepts are still the same, the only difference is that the subdivider will want to create dozens of restrictions instead of just one. In other words, instead of a "covenant for the benefit of adjacent land" we have a "declaration of subdivision covenants," or other similar term.

Because a declaration of subdivision covenants could run to many pages, it would be inconvenient to reproduce them inside the deeds to the individual lots. To keep the deeds simple, it is common practice to record the subdivision covenants. Recording a document means that it has been placed in the public records and therefore everyone is deemed to be given notice of it. When a document is recorded, it is given a number

Notes

by which it can be referenced in the future. Therefore, when the subdivider sells a lot, the deed can be made subject to the recorded covenants just by referring to the number where they were recorded. Such deeds are commonly called ***covenant deeds***.

This leads to an interesting dilemma. By state law, every city and county in Oregon is required to zone their entire jurisdiction – there is no such thing as "unzoned land" in Oregon. Therefore, if a subdivider creates a set of subdivision covenants, there is the possibility of a conflict between the covenants and the zoning. The resolution to such a dilemma is simple. Clearly, the owner must follow both the private covenants and the zoning ordinances. Violation of the subdivision covenants will invite legal action by other homeowners, and violation of zoning ordinances will result in local government action. Logically, if the owner were to follow the more restrictive of the two, this would normally ensure compliance with both the zoning and the covenants. For example, if the zoning says "minimum five feet side yard setback" and the covenant says "minimum ten foot side yard setback," then building no closer than ten feet from the side lot line will satisfy both requirements.

Less than freehold estates

A tenancy for years (lease) and a periodic tenancy are encumbrances. Therefore, if an owner leases the property to a tenant, and then sells the property, the buyer will take title subject to the lease. Similarly, a periodic rental of the property creates an encumbrance which the buyer must take the title subject to. However, tenancy at will and tenancy at sufferance are not encumbrances.

Leases and periodic tenancies are rights of possession without ownership. They are considered less than freehold estates (leaseholds), as contrasted with freeholds (ownerships). For further discussion of less than freehold estates see "Leasehold Estates" starting on page 50.

Clouds

A title problem which (fortunately) occurs only occasionally is the existence of a ***cloud***. Clouds are defined as "possible interests" in the property. In other words, if someone has a cloud on your title, it means that the person has a claim which is uncertain, as yet unproved. Eventually, the cloud could ripen into title, or into a lien – or it could simply be extinguished. Until its status becomes certain, it remains an encumbrance on the title.

Clouds can arise through a variety of circumstances. They are typically caused by errors, defects in legal documents, and even as a result of fraud and misrepresentation. For example, suppose your neighbor builds a fence which is placed one foot over the lot line onto your land. This is called an ***encroachment***. After a period of time your neighbor may actually gain title to the extra one-foot wide strip of land. In the meantime, however, the existence of the encroaching fence is a cloud. (The exact rules of law for turning this encroachment into ownership of the strip of land will be covered in detail in the following section on conveyances.)

An owner's normal protection against a cloud is the title insurance policy. But what could be done if a cloud does show up? The normal remedy is to obtain a ***quitclaim deed*** from the party claiming the interest. On the other hand, if the claimant will not voluntarily relinquish the claim, you can force the issue by filing a ***suit to quiet title (quiet title action)*** or a ***suit for slander of title***. The suit for slander of title would normally be used if you wished to assert that the claimant deliberately and maliciously clouded your title, in which case you may also plead for punitive damages. Note that a ***quiet title*** is a title which is free of clouds.

Exercise b

Restrictions on the use of property can be __________ restrictions (zoning ordinances), or private. When violation of a private restriction could result in loss of the title, the restriction is called a __________. Less serious restrictions such as __________ and __________ __________ are enforced by remedies such as a suit to __________ the offending action, a suit for __________ __________, or a suit for damages. When a subdivider records a set of restrictive covenants for the entire subdivision, this is probably done so that the lots can be sold using deeds which reference to the covenants. Such deeds are called __________ deeds. If there is a conflict between the zoning and the private covenants, then the owner must usually follow __________.

Tenancies at will and tenancies at sufferance (choose one) ❑ *ARE* ❑ *ARE NOT encumbrances.*

A cloud is a __________ interest in another's real property. Clouds are normally removed by obtaining a __________ deed from the claimant. As an alternative, the owner can file a suit to __________ title or a suit for slander of title. A __________ title is a title without clouds.

Financial encumbrances (liens)

While real property can be subject to many kinds of non-financial encumbrances, it is the financial encumbrances which can be more problematical in a real estate transaction. Financial encumbrances include liens such as mortgages and trust deeds, property tax liens and special assessments, income tax levies, judgments, construction liens, and many more.

It is important to understand the difference between a ***lien*** and an obligation to pay (debt). A lien makes the real property collateral for a debt, but a debt can exist unsecured. In other words, you can borrow money as a personal obligation without giving the lender any collateral. Or you could borrow money and give the lender collateral. When you use your property as collateral, you have allowed it to be liened. And since liens are encumbrances on the real estate, if you sell the real estate, your buyer will take the title subject to the lien. If the debt was personal (without collateral), then it could not affect your real estate, so you can sell the real estate any time without having to pay off the personal obligation. When property has been pledged as collateral, we say it has been ***hypothecated***.

Priority of encumbrances

Another important issue which real estate agents must understand about encumbrances is the matter of ***priority***. Priority affects all kinds of encumbrances, both financial and non-financial, although it is of greater importance when dealing with financial matters. The issue of priority relates to the order in which rights in the event there should be a forced sale of the property, i.e., a foreclosure sale.

NOTES

The issue of priority is very complex with many exceptions. The general rule, however, is that rights are apportioned in date order. The date is generally the date when documents were recorded in the public records. In other words, a "first mortgage" means that it was recorded before the "second mortgage," and so forth. Notice that the date the parties signed the mortgage is irrelevant as to the issue of priority – only the date it was recorded matters. Similarly, it doesn't matter what is written in the document – it may say "first mortgage" at the top of the page, but if another mortgage was recorded first, it is a second mortgage.

The issue of priority has two important impacts in real estate. First, the holder of a prior lien has first claim on the proceeds of the sale, and holders of subsequent liens have subsequent claims, in order of their priority. So if the property is sold at a forced sale, the holder of the first mortgage gets paid first, if there is anything left, the holder of the second mortgage gets paid next, and so on until the funds are exhausted.

The second impact is that whenever a lienholder forces the sale of the property by foreclosure, subsequent liens are extinguished, although sometimes the lienholders have a right of redemption. (Redemption rights are explained below under "Mortgages.") This is true, not just of liens, but of non-financial encumbrances as well. For example, suppose you mortgage your property to the bank, and then lease it to a tenant. If the bank forecloses its mortgage, the foreclosure will extinguish the lease. But if the order were reversed and you leased it first and then mortgaged it, the bank will have to take the title subject to the lease, since the lease enjoyed priority.

There are numerous exceptions to the "date rule" above, some of which are significant to real estate agents. The first exception is property taxes and special assessments. As a rule, unpaid property taxes and special assessments are a prior lien ahead of all others, regardless of when the other liens were recorded or the year(s) for which the taxes are due. This is the reason most lenders insist that the borrower establish a reserve account so the taxes will be collected along with the monthly principal and interest payment. This allows the bank to ensure that the taxes were paid so their mortgage lien will not be in second position.

Another exception is the possibility of a voluntary ***subordination***. This is a simple agreement where one lienholder, who currently enjoys priority, agrees to step down in favor of another lienholder. This frequently happens in construction financing. A builder may ask the seller of a lot to finance the sale. Yet the builder also wants to obtain construction financing from a bank for the improvements. The bank will want a first lien, yet their lien will be recorded after the seller's lien. The solution is to put a subordination clause in the seller's lien, making it subordinate (junior) to the bank's lien which will be created later.

Real estate agents should also be aware of the special priority of ***construction liens***. Construction liens frequently enjoy a priority which is ahead of other recorded liens. Construction liens will be discussed in more detail later in this section.

Categories of liens

Liens are categorized as ***voluntary liens*** and ***involuntary liens***. A voluntary lien is a lien which the debtor agreed to, such as a mortgage, trust deed, and the like. An involuntary lien occurred without the debtor's agreement, such as an Internal Revenue Service lien, property taxes, special assessments, judgments and construction liens.

Liens are also categorized as ***general liens*** and ***specific liens***. A general lien reaches everything the debtor owns. Judgments and income tax levies are examples of general liens. A specific lien reaches only the property specified in the document. Examples of specific liens include mortgages and trust deeds, construction liens, and property tax liens.

Exercise c

A __________ makes real property collateral for a debt. The priority of encumbrances is normally determined by the __________ of the encumbrance. However, __________________ ______________ are always in first position. A holder of an encumbrance can voluntarily step aside in favor of another. This is called a __________________ .

Liens are categorized as ____________________ liens (such as a mortgage) and as ____________________ liens, (such as a judgment). Liens which reach only one property are called __________________ liens. But if a lien reaches all property the debtor's property, then it is a __________________ lien.

Mortgages

There are three instruments (legal documents) used to make real property collateral for a loan – the mortgage, the trust deed, and the land sales contract. A promissory note is also involved as the evidence of the debt when the lien instrument is a mortgage or a trust deed. These documents are covered in great detail in courses on real estate finance, however, they merit at least a general discussion here.

Of the three lien instruments, the ***mortgage*** is the oldest. The mortgage dates back to the earliest beginnings of English law. At one time in England (and still today in some states) the mortgage was considered a conveyance of fee title to the lender. States which follow this concept are called ***title theory states***. However, Oregon is a ***lien theory state***, which means that the mortgage is considered a lien against the property, but not a conveyance.

In a mortgage transaction, the borrower gives a mortgage to the lender in order to create the lien on the property. Thus, we call the borrower the ***mortgagor*** and we call the lender the ***mortgagee***. (In law, the –or is the giver of a thing and the –ee is the receiver.) Many times you might hear people say they "got a mortgage from the bank." This is exactly backwards – the bank got the mortgage, the borrowers got the money.

Simultaneously with the mortgage, the mortgagor gives a note to the mortgagee. The note is the evidence of the debt, just as the mortgage is the evidence of the lien. The mortgagee records the mortgage immediately in order to establish the priority date.

If the mortgagor does not pay the debt as agreed, the mortgagee can foreclose the mortgage. The procedure is to file a suit to foreclose and obtain a judgment. The judgment will include all the lender's costs, unpaid interest, late charges, attorney's fees – everything that the lender has asked for in the complaint. The judgment allows the lender to ask the court to order a ***sheriff's sale*** (also called an ***execution sale***) of the property.

Anyone can bid at the sheriff's sale. All bidders have to pay all cash, except the mortgagee. The mortgagee already spent the cash when it was lent to the borrower. If the property sells for more than the amount of the judgment, the surplus is turned over to the borrower.

Following the foreclosure sale, the successful bidder gets a ***sheriff's certificate*** (***certificate of sale***), which entitles the holder to a sheriff's deed in 180 days, provided

NOTES

the mortgagor does not redeem. The mortgagor has a 180-day ***statutory right of redemption***. To "redeem" means buying the property for cash from the successful bidder. Junior liens are extinguished, although junior lienholders have 60 days to protect their position by redeeming.

If the property sells for less than the judgment at the sheriff's sale, then the mortgagee can apply to the court for a ***deficiency judgment***. A deficiency judgment can be enforced the same as any ordinary judgment. This means that the lender can use the deficiency judgment to force a sheriff's sale of all other assets of the debtor until the debt is satisfied in full.

When a mortgage is carried by the seller of the property (as opposed to a third-party lender such as a bank), it is called a ***purchase money mortgage***, because the buyer gave it to the seller as part of the "purchase money." If the lender is a third party lender, then it is called a ***hard money mortgage*** because the lender lent hard cash, not equity in a property.

In the foreclosure of a hard money mortgage, the courts feel that the lender lent hard cash, so the lender is entitled to whatever remedies are necessary in order to recover the cash – including a deficiency judgment to allow the lender to reach the borrower's other assets. But if the lender was the seller (purchase money mortgagee), then the lender lent the equity in the property, not hard cash. Therefore the lender should be satisfied to accept the property back, and is therefore not entitled to a deficiency judgment.

The Oregon Legislature has expanded the above common-law definition of a purchase money mortgage. In order to protect small borrowers from deficiency judgments, a mortgage is considered a purchase money mortgage in Oregon if the original balance was $50,000 or less and the loan is on the borrower's primary or secondary personal residence. (Consider a second home at the beach an example of a "secondary personal residence.") It does not matter if the loan is from a third party lender or not. If the mortgage meets these criteria, it is defined as a purchase money mortgage and therefore deficiency judgments will be barred.

Trust deeds

A ***trust deed*** (***deed of trust***) is a modern replacement for the mortgage. Mortgages take a long time to foreclose, the mortgagee incurs a great deal of expense, and the successful bidder has to wait 180 days to get clear title. As a result, properties tend to sell at sheriff's sales for prices well below market value – which makes the mortgage unpopular with lenders. The Oregon Trust Deed Act was created to make trust deeds an attractive alternative to mortgages.

A trust deed uses the concept of a ***trust*** to create a lien on real property. Suppose you own some property and you wish to borrow from the bank, pledging the property as collateral using a trust deed. The first step is to give your note to the bank in exchange for the cash, the same as if the lien were a mortgage. At the same time, you take a deed and use it to grant one stick from your bundle of rights to a trustee. The trustee is a third party, and must be someone other than the lender. The stick you grant to the trustee is the right to sell the property at public auction to satisfy the note in the event you default on the payments. This stick is called a ***limited power of sale***, or sometimes just ***power of sale***.

The terms of the deed give the trustee the right to hold the power of sale until such time as the lender agrees that the note has been paid in full. The trustee holds the limited power of sale in trust for the lender during the term of the loan. The lender is the ***beneficiary*** of the trust. The borrower is the ***trustor***.

To foreclose, the lender merely instructs the trustee to exercise the power of sale. To protect borrowers, the statutes set forth strict requirements for foreclosure by trustee's sale. Nevertheless, because a lawsuit is not required, it is considerably less ex-

NOTES

pensive than a judicial foreclosure of a mortgage. In addition, the borrower has no right of redemption following the trustee's sale. The successful bidder at the trustee's sale is entitled to a ***trustee's deed*** to the property within ten days of the sale. Because the bidders know they do not have to wait 180 days for the statutory right of redemption, they are willing to pay more for the property.

The trustor gets some benefits also. A trustee's foreclosure sale of the property cannot result in a deficiency judgment – the beneficiary is limited to just what the property can be sold for at the trustee's sale.

Another benefit to the borrower is that the lender cannot exercise the right to ***accelerate*** until the fifth day before the date set for the sale. Acceleration means demanding the entire remaining principal balance in full. Since the lender cannot accelerate, the borrower is free to ***reinstate*** the loan just by bringing it current. In mortgages and land sales contracts, the lender can normally accelerate at any time when the borrower is in default.

While most lenders view the trust deed as an improvement over the mortgage, there may be times the lender would like to be able to accelerate and demand the entire remaining principal balance. The Oregon Trust Deed Act provides that the beneficiary of a trust deed may file suit and foreclose a trust deed as though it were a mortgage. Of course, while this gives the lender the right to accelerate, it also means the borrower will have a statutory 180-day right of redemption. Nevertheless, since the trust deed gives the lender the option of foreclosing as though it were a mortgage, the mortgage is now seldom used in Oregon.

Note that in both the mortgage and trust deed transactions, the note is the evidence of the debt. Oregon law provides that the lender may elect to sue on the note alone, ignoring the mortgage or trust deed. This will result in a judgment against the borrower which the lender can then use to execute upon all the borrower's assets.

Land sales contracts

As a financing instrument, the ***land sales contract*** is fundamentally different from either the mortgage or the trust deed. In fact, technically speaking, the land sales contract is not even a lien, as we shall see below.

Land sales contracts go by a number of synonyms – ***conditional sales agreement for real estate, real estate installment sales agreement, contract for a deed*** – the list is endless. The last mentioned of these terms "contract for a deed," is an excellent description of what the land sales contract really is. It is an agreement where the seller agrees to give the buyer a deed when and if the buyer finishes making all the payments. Until the buyer finishes making the payments and the seller gives the deed to the buyer, the title remains legally vested with the seller. In fact, the existence of the land sales contract is considered to be a cloud on the seller's title. After all, there is no guarantee that the buyer will make all the payments, so the buyer really has a possible interest or claim on the seller's title – exactly the definition of a cloud.

Modern attorneys just call the parties the "seller" and the "buyer," but they are also sometimes referred to by the older terms ***vendor*** and ***vendee***. Since the vendor retains legal title, it is the vendor who remains vested with all the rights and responsibilities of ownership. These rights and responsibilities include the right of possession and the responsibility to pay the taxes. Since the buyer wants possession and the seller wants the buyer to be responsible for the property, normal land sales contracts contain clauses granting the buyer the right of possession, but making the buyer responsible for the property as well. When the contract grants all the rights and responsibilities of ownership to the buyer, the seller's interest is commonly referred to as ***naked title***.

If you think about the nature of the land sales contract, you will realize that the only way it can be created is if it is carried by the seller. If you have a transaction in

NOTES

which the lender is a third party lender, and you wish to use a land sales contract as the financing instrument, then you would have to sell the property to the lender first, and then have the lender resell the property to the buyer.

Typical land sales contracts contain various remedies the seller can use in the event of the buyer's default. The most common remedy is a suit for ***strict foreclosure***. In a suit for strict foreclosure, the seller asks the court to extinguish the buyer's rights (remove the cloud from the seller's title) and restore the seller to possession of the property. There is no public sale of the property and no deficiency judgment, although the seller is normally entitled to a separate judgment against the buyer for attorney's fees.

Another possible remedy is a suit for ***specific performance*** of the ***covenant of indebtedness*** (promise to pay). Specific performance is a suit which asks the court to compel performance of a contract. This can result in a sheriff's sale of the property and deficiency judgment against the buyer if the property does not sell for enough to cover the balance owing and costs.

Land sales contracts also commonly allow the seller the remedy of ***forfeiture***. Forfeiture is a non-judicial remedy where the seller can simply declare the buyer to be in default. After proper notice as required by statute, the seller can cause the buyer's interest in the property to be extinguished without having to file a suit.

Deeds as security

Sometimes you might hear someone say "I borrowed $5,000 from my neighbor, but I had to give the deed to my house." What if the borrower did, in fact, give the neighbor a deed to the house in exchange for the $5,000? Can the neighbor now just legally demand possession of the property?

The courts normally look at such a transaction and attempt to determine the intent of the parties. If the court can find an intent to create an absolute conveyance, then the neighbor will own the house. But if the intent was to make the house collateral for a loan, then the court will require the lender to treat the deed as a mortgage.

Chattel mortgage

Sometimes a debtor wishes to pledge personal property as collateral for an obligation. To secure the interest of the creditor, the debtor may give the creditor a ***chattel mortgage***. The chattel mortgage creates a lien against the personal property, the same as a mortgage creates a lien against real property. If you think about the term "chattel mortgage," it makes sense. As we learned earlier, "chattel" is a synonym for "personal property, so "chattel mortgage" is a mortgage on chattels.

Under the Uniform Commercial Code, the term "chattel mortgage" is now called a ***security agreement***. It is still legal to call the document a chattel mortgage, but the newer term is now far more common.

Release of liens

When a mortgage is paid off, we record a ***satisfaction of mortgage***. This serves to extinguish the lien from the title. The term "satisfaction" is also used to describe the document which extinguishes judgments, construction liens, and other miscellaneous liens.

When a trust deed is paid off, a different situation prevails. The trust deed was created when the borrower deeded a limited power of sale to the trustee. Therefore, to extinguish the trust deed, the trustee should deed the power of sale back to the borrower. Such a deed is called a ***deed of reconveyance***.

When a land sales contract is paid off, the release instrument is simply the deed (***fulfillment deed***) which the seller promised to the buyer.

Exercise d

The oldest financing document is the __________. In a mortgage transaction, the borrower is called the __________ and the lender is the __________. Oregon is a __________ theory state, which means that the mortgage is not a conveyance of the title. To foreclose a mortgage the lender files a suit which results in a __________. The lender then files a writ of __________, a document which asks the court to order the sheriff to sell the property at public auction. The successful bidder at the sheriff's sale receives a sheriff's __________ of __________. This entitles the successful bidder to a sheriff's __________ if the property is not redeemed. The borrower has a statutory right to redeem the property for ______ days from the sheriff's sale. If the property sold for less than the debt, the lender can get a __________ __________. However, the lender will not be entitled to this if the mortgage was a __________ __________ mortgage.

In a trust deed transaction, the borrower gives a __________ of __________ to a trustee. The trustee holds this in trust for the __________ (lender). If the lender wishes to foreclose, the lender can just ask the __________ to exercise the __________ of __________. The __________ will hold the public auction sale. The successful bidder will receive a __________ __________ within ten days following the sale. The borrower has no right of __________ following the sale, although the buyer does have the right of __________ until the fifth day before the date set for the sale. Lenders cannot obtain a __________ judgment on a trustee's sale.

In a land sales contract, the __________ (seller) agrees to give a deed to the property to the __________ (buyer), when the property has been paid for. The most common foreclosure remedy is a suit for __________ __________.

When a mortgage is paid off, the release instrument is called a __________. When a trust deed is paid off, the borrower gets a deed of __________. When a land sales contract is paid off the release instrument is the __________ the seller promised to the buyer at the beginning of the contract.

Judgments

Whenever you are owed money and the other party fails to pay, you are entitled to file a suit to compel them to pay. There are innumerable ways in which an obligation to pay can arise – services rendered, goods purchased, money borrowed, damages for wrongful acts – the list is endless. In this section we will not dwell on the means by which the obligation to pay is created. However, since a judgment is a lien against the debtor's real property, real estate agents should know the procedures by which a forced sale can occur and the effects of a judgment on a sale of the property.

NOTES

The first step the creditor takes is to file a suit against the debtor. Assuming the creditor wins, this will result in a judgment in favor of the creditor and against the debtor. From this point on, we refer to the parties as the ***judgment creditor*** and the ***judgment debtor***. The judgment will be entered on the court records (court docket).

Judgments properly docketed become liens against all real and personal property owned by the judgment debtor in the county where docketed. Each county has its own courts, so if you obtain a judgment in one county, but the judgment debtor owns property in another county, you must have your judgment transcribed into the county where the property is located before it will be a lien against that property.

A judgment is normally good for ten years and, upon motion to the court, can be renewed for ten additional years. Therefore, one approach to collection of the debt is just to wait. Once your judgment has become a lien on the debtor's property, the debtor will probably have to deal with you in order to sell the property. A judgment debtor may always sell property, but once the judgment has reached the property, the property can only be sold subject to the judgment. Most buyers will have nothing to do with this, so it forces the judgment debtor to pay off the judgment in order to give clear title to the buyer.

Of course, a judgment creditor is frequently at the mercy of senior lienholders. For example, suppose you obtain a judgment against someone who owns property, but at the time your judgment is docketed there is already a first mortgage and perhaps several other judgment creditors ahead of you. Foreclosure by any of the senior lienholders will extinguish your judgment as to the property in question, so a judgment creditor has to be careful of his or her position in the property.

An alternative approach to collection is to force the sale of the property. The judgment creditor is free to proceed against any or all property of the judgment debtor. The procedure is to file a ***writ of execution*** with the court. When signed by the judge, the writ becomes a court order directed to the sheriff to sell the property described in the writ at public auction. If there is more than one property listed, the sheriff will sell them in order until the judgment is satisfied or the properties exhausted.

In order to sell the property, the sheriff must advertise the sale. The judgment creditor must advance the funds to pay all costs, but the costs are then added to the total judgment. At the auction sale anyone may bid, including the judgment creditor, the judgment debtor, and any member of the public. All bids must be all cash, except that the judgment creditor can bid up to the amount of the judgment without paying anything at all, since that amount is already owed to the judgment creditor. Frequently the judgment creditor merely gives this bid to the sheriff in advance and then does not bother to appear.

If the property sells for more than the amount of the judgment, the surplus is turned over to the judgment debtor. The judgment, of course, is then satisfied in full. If the property does not sell for enough at the sheriff's sale, then there will be a ***partial satisfaction*** of the judgment.

Regardless of who is the high bidder at the sheriff's sale, upon proper payment, the sheriff will issue to the high bidder a sheriff's certificate, or certificate of sale. The certificate of sale entitles the holder to a sheriff's deed unless the judgment debtor or a junior lienholder redeems within the statutory period. The judgment debtor has a 180-day ***statutory right of redemption***. Junior lienholders have 60 days in which to redeem (unless the junior lienholder is the federal government, in which case the right of redemption is 120 days). Any person redeeming must do so by paying back the successful bidder whatever the successful bidder paid for the property, plus anything the successful bidder paid on unpaid property taxes or to prevent waste, plus 9% interest. During the redemption period, the successful bidder is entitled to possession of the property, however any benefits of ownership, such as rents received, are credited to the debtor if the debtor redeems.

Notice that the above procedures are essentially the same as for foreclosure of a mortgage. In fact, the only benefit of having a mortgage over an unsecured debt is that the mortgage gives the creditor a voluntary lien against the property prior to the judgment.

Oregon law provides for certain protections for homeowners when a judgment has been entered against the homeowner. One of these protections is the ***homestead exemption***. A ***homestead*** is simply defined as your place of personal residence. The homestead exemption provides that the homeowner is entitled to save up to $33,000 of the equity in a homestead ($25,000 if single) from an execution sale arising out of a judgment. The homestead exemption is generally only applicable to judgments and specifically does not apply to mortgages, trust deeds, construction liens or government liens.

The judgment debtor may claim any ownership interest in any personal residence as a homestead, including manufactured housing (mobile homes). The maximum size property that can be claimed is one city block (if located within a city), or 160 acres (if located outside a city). The normal maximum amount of the exemption is $33,000 ($25,000 for a single owner). If the homestead is a manufactured dwelling the maximum is $30,000 ($23,000 for a single person) if located on land owned by the judgment debtor. However, the amount drops to $27,000 ($20,000 if single) if the homestead is manufactured housing and the judgment debtor does not own the land it is situated on.

When the execution sale takes place, the sheriff must place the homestead claim ($33,000, $30,000, $27,000, $25,000 or $20,000, as the case may be) immediately prior to the claim of the judgment creditor. In other words, just before the judgment creditor gets any of the sales proceeds, the sheriff must hold out the homestead claim. The funds will be turned over to the judgment debtor who must have the intent to reinvest them in a new personal residence. If the judgment debtor does not do so within one year, the funds can be reached by the judgment creditor, assuming the judgment has not otherwise been satisfied by then. If the amount bid at the sheriff's sale is not high enough to cover the homestead exemption, so the judgment creditor would receive nothing from the sale, the sheriff must cancel the sale altogether.

Notices of pendency and attachments

When a suit is filed, the plaintiff does not have judgment against the defendant until the case is decided. Meanwhile, the defendant's assets are free of the plaintiff's claims. To prevent a debtor from liquidating and wasting his or her assets, the law provides two potential remedies for the plaintiff.

Sometimes the suit involves real property, such as a divorce case where one party is requesting that the decree grant him or her exclusive ownership of certain real property. In this case, to prevent the other party from selling the property prior to finalization of the case, the party claiming the property can file a ***notice of pendency***, also called a ***notice of lis pendens***. ("Lis pendens" means "litigation pending.") When the notice of pendency has been properly filed, it constitutes a cloud on the title. Any buyer of the property will take title subject to the claims of the party who filed the notice.

In other cases, the plaintiff just wants to be sure that the defendant does not liquidate his or her assets. In this case, the plaintiff can apply to the court for permission to file an ***attachment*** against the defendant's assets. The effect is the same as a notice of pendency, that is, any buyer of the property will take title subject to the claims of the party who filed the attachment.

Exercise e

The winner of a suit where a judgment was awarded is called the judgment creditor and the loser is called the ____________ ____________. The judgment constitutes a ________ against all real property of the ____________ ____________ located in the county where the judgment has been ____________. The judgment is initially good for _____ years. To enforce a judgment, the judgment creditor can simply wait, since the judgment will likely have to be paid upon a sale of the property. Or the judgment creditor can file a ________ of ____________ with the court, which becomes a court order directing the ____________ to sell the property at public auction. The successful bidder at the sale will receive a ____________ ____________ of sale. This will entitle the holder to a ____________ ________ if the property is not redeemed within the statutory _____ -day right of redemption. If the property does not sell for enough to satisfy the judgment, then the sale will create a ________ ____________ of the judgment. If the property sells for more than enough to satisfy the judgment, then the surplus is turned over to the ____________ ____________.

If a judgment creditor executes upon the debtor's personal residence, the debtor can claim protection under the ____________ ____________ . The amount of the exemption is normally $ ________, or $ ________ if the debtor is single. The maximum property which can be claimed is ______ ______ ________, if the property is located inside an incorporated city, or otherwise _____ acres.

To prevent one of the parties to a suit from selling his or her property, the other party could file an ____________ or a ____________ of ____________ .

Construction liens

Real estate agents who deal with new construction, or even property which has recently been remodeled, frequently find that the property is subject to a ***construction lien***. The laws relating to construction liens are complex, but real estate agents should have a basic understanding of the subject.

Construction liens (formerly referred to as ***mechanic's liens***) are special liens which can be claimed by certain individuals who supply labor or materials for improvements on another person's real estate. Notice that a construction lien is a claim – and should be considered a cloud until perfected by a suit to foreclose it. Nevertheless, the cloud is normally sufficient to block a sale of the property until the claimant gets paid.

Construction liens can be claimed by anyone who supplies labor or materials for improvements. While this obviously includes carpenters, bricklayers, roofers, and the like, the statute specifically includes architects, engineers, surveyors, landscapers, rental equipment dealers and materials suppliers, to remove any doubt that they should be included in the list.

To claim a construction lien, the claimant merely records a claim of lien. Although some claimants may be required to file a claim even earlier, no claims

NOTES

are valid unless recorded within 75 days of substantial completion of the construction project. The claimant must also deliver a notice to the property owner prior to recording the claim of lien. The claim of lien is normally valid for 120 days. If the claimant wishes to continue the claim after that time, a suit to foreclose must be filed within the 120-day time limit.

The priority of a construction lien is one of the more complex areas of the law. Most construction liens are prior in right to all other recorded liens, regardless of when the other liens were recorded. A notable exception is that the priority of a construction lien arising from alterations to an existing structure is normally just the date the claim of lien is recorded.

Many times an owner wishes to dispute a construction lien. In order to gain clear title immediately, the owner can post a surety bond (or post cash with the county treasurer) for 150% of the claim, but not less than $1,000. And to prevent a construction lien claim in the first place, Oregon statutes provides that an owner can post a ***notice of non-responsibility*** on the premises within three days after learning the construction has begun.

Powers of the government

Although not technically encumbrances, certain rights in real property are reserved to the government. The exercise of these powers by the government must be within constitutional limits. These rights include police power, eminent domain, taxation and escheat.

Police power One of the most commonly exercised of these powers is ***police power***. Police power is the right of the government to maintain public order and to protect the public health, safety, morals and general welfare. While police power obviously includes everything from police forces to traffic control, its particular impact on real estate is the area of zoning and land use laws. These laws include comprehensive planning, building codes, subdivision control laws, condominium regulations and environmental restrictions, to specify just a few. Note that it is constitutional for a government to exercise police power without paying any compensation.

Eminent domain When the government takes privately owned property it is exercising ***eminent domain***. The process is called ***condemnation***. In order to exercise eminent domain, the government must be able to demonstrate that the use they will make of the property is a public purpose and that they are paying the owner just compensation. Note that even utility companies and quasi-utilities such as railroads can exercise eminent domain.

Many times the government wants only a portion of the owner's property. If the taking of the portion results in a loss in value to the remainder of the property, the owner may be entitled to ***severance damages***.

Sometimes the actions of the government will cause loss to an owner, even without taking any part of the owner's land. An example might be the construction of a freeway which causes noise and air pollution on nearby properties. In this case, the owners of the affected properties may be entitled to ***consequential damages***.

If the government zones an owner's land with such severe restrictions that they leave the owner with little or no economic benefit to be made of the land the owner could claim damages by filing a suit for ***inverse condemnation***.

Escheat When a property owner dies without natural heirs capable of inheriting and without a will, we say that the property ***escheats*** to the state. In Oregon it will be vested in the Division of State Lands and managed by the Oregon State Land Board.

Exercise f

Anyone who supplies ____________ or __________________ for improvements on another person's real estate may file a _____________________ lien. The claim must generally be filed within ______ days of substantial completion of the project. The claim is good for only ______ days, unless the claimant initiates a suit to _________________ it. The priority of most construction liens is prior to all other __________________ liens, unless the lien results from _______________________ to an existing property. A property owner can protect himself or herself from a construction lien by posting a ________________ of ________________________.

The right to maintain public order is called ____________ ____________. When the government takes privately owned property it is called _______________________ and the right to do so is called ________________ ________________. In addition to the government, this right can also be exercised by _______________ companies and quasi-utilities such as railroads. When the government destroys the economic benefit of an owner, this could result in severance damages, __________________ damages or inverse condemnation.

KEY TERMS

The key to understanding any new field is the vocabulary used in that field. To maximize your comprehension of the material presented in this chapter, be sure you know the meaning and significance of the following terms. Remember that the majority of test questions primarily test knowledge of vocabulary.

Abandonment
Accelerate
Attachment
Beneficiary
Certificate of sale
Cloud on the title
Commercial easement
Community drive
Condemnation
Condition
Consequential damages
Construction lien
Contract for a deed
Covenant
Covenant deed
Covenant for the benefit of adjacent land
Covenant of indebtedness
Covenant running with the land
Deed restriction
Deed of reconveyance
Deed of trust
Deficiency judgment
Dominant estate
Dominant tenant
Dominant tenement
Easement by implication of law
Easement by prescription
Easement by prior use
Easement by reservation
Easement by way of necessity
Easement for ingress and egress
Easement in gross

Eminent domain
Encroachment
Equitable servitude
Escheat
Execution sale
Express grant
Financial encumbrance
Forfeiture
General lien
General plan restriction
Hard money mortgage
Homestead
Homestead exemption
Hypothecate
Inverse condemnation
Involuntary lien
Judgment creditor
Judgment debtor
Land sales contract
License
Lien
Lien theory state
Limited power of sale
Mechanic's liens
Merger
Mortgage
Mortgagee
Mortgagor
Naked title
Negative easement
Non-financial encumbrance
Notice of lis pendens
Notice of non-responsibility
Notice of pendency
Partial satisfaction
Permit
Police power
Power of sale
Prescription
Prescriptive easement
Priority
Private restriction
Profit à prendre
Public restriction
Purchase money mortgage
Quiet title
Quiet title action
Quitclaim deed
Real covenant
Real estate sales agreement
Reinstate
Right of use
Satisfaction of mortgage
Servient estate
Servient tenant
Servient tenement
Severance damages
Sheriff's certificate
Sheriff's deed
Sheriff's sale
Specific performance
Specific lien
Statutory right of redemption
Strict foreclosure
Subdivision covenant
Subordination
Suit for slander of title
Suit to quiet title
Title theory state
Trust deed
Trust
Trustee's deed
Trustor
Vendee
Vendor
Voluntary lien
Way of necessity
Writ of execution

ANSWERS

To chapter exercises. If you couldn't figure out what to put in the blanks, find the answer here!

Exercise a

An easement is a right of USE *, not a right of* POSSESSION *. A driveway is an example of an easement for* INGRESS *and* EGRESS *. The party who benefits from the easement is called the* DOMINANT *tenant and the party over whose property the easement runs is called the* SERVIENT *tenant. In most cases, easements are* APPURTENANT *, that is, they are a title right and run with the land. However, they can be personal, in which case we call them* EASEMENTS IN GROSS *. Utility company easements are sometimes called* COMMERCIAL *easements.*

Easements can be created by an EXPRESS GRANT *, by* RESERVATION *(selling the frontage and holding back an easement), by* PRESCRIPTION *(long and continued use), and easements by implication of law. Implication of law includes easements created by* WAY OF NECESSITY *, as where property is landlocked, or by* PRIOR USE *.*

Easements can be terminated by agreement, in which case the legal document normally used is a QUITCLAIM DEED *, by* EXPIRATION *(running of a time limit), or by lack of further need. When the holder of the easement purchases the property over which the easement runs, the principle of* MERGER *causes the easement to be extinguished. Intent and non-use of the easement can sometimes result in termination of the easement by* ABANDONMENT *. Not only can* PRESCRIPTION *result in the creation of an easement, but it can also result in the termination of an easement.*

The right to severance of a benefit from another's land is called a PROFIT *. A right to use another's property which is personal and revocable is a* LICENSE *. These are also sometimes called* PERMITS *.*

Exercise b

Restrictions on the use of property can be PUBLIC *restrictions (zoning ordinances), or private. When violation of a private restriction could result in loss of the title, the restriction is called a* CONDITION *. Less serious restrictions such as* COVENANTS *and* EQUITABLE SERVITUDE *are enforced by remedies such as a suit to* ENJOIN *the offending action, a suit for* SPECIFIC PERFORMANCE *, or a suit for damages. When a subdivider records a set of restrictive covenants for the entire subdivision, this is probably done so that the lots can be sold using deeds which reference to the covenants. Such deeds are called* COVENANT *deeds. If there is a conflict between the zoning and the private covenants, then the owner must usually follow* THE MORE RESTRICTIVE OF THE TWO *.*

Tenancies at will and tenancies at sufferance (choose one) ■ ARE ❑ ARE NOT *encumbrances.*

A cloud is a POSSIBLE *interest in another's real property. Clouds are normally removed by obtaining a* QUITCLAIM *deed from the claimant. As an alternative, the owner can file a suit to* QUIET *title or a suit for slander of title. A* QUIET *title is a title without clouds.*

Exercise c

A LIEN *makes real property collateral for a debt. The priority of encumbrances is normally determined by the* DATE *of the encumbrance. However,* PROPERTY TAXES *are always in first position. A holder of an encumbrance can voluntarily step aside in favor of another. This is called a* SUBORDINATION *.*

Liens are categorized as VOLUNTARY *liens (such as a mortgage) and as* INVOLUNTARY *liens, (such as a judgment). Liens which reach only one property are called* SPECIFIC *liens. But if a lien reaches all property the debtor's property, then it is a* GENERAL *lien.*

Exercise d

The oldest financing document is the MORTGAGE *. In a mortgage transaction, the borrower is called the* MORTGAGOR *and the lender is the* MORTGAGEE *. Oregon is a* TITLE *theory state, which means that the mortgage is not a conveyance of the title. To foreclose a mortgage the lender files a suit which results in a* JUDGMENT *. The lender then files a writ of* EXECUTION *, a docu-*

ment which asks the court to order the sheriff to sell the property at public auction. The successful bidder at the sheriff's sale receives a sheriff's ___CERTIFICATE___ *of* ___SALE___. *This entitles the successful bidder to a sheriff's* ___DEED___ *if the property is not redeemed. The borrower has a statutory right to redeem the property for* ___180___ *days from the sheriff's sale. If the property sold for less than the debt, the lender can get a* ___DEFICIENCY___ ___JUDGMENT___. *However, the lender will not be entitled to this if the mortgage was a* ___PURCHASE___ ___MONEY___ *mortgage.*

In a trust deed transaction, the borrower gives a ___DEED___ *of* ___TRUST___ *to a trustee. The trustee holds this in trust for the* ___BENEFICIARY___ *(lender). If the lender wishes to foreclose, the lender can just ask the* ___TRUSTEE___ *to exercise the* ___POWER___ *of* ___SALE___. *The* ___TRUSTEE___ *will hold the public auction sale. The successful bidder will receive a* ___TRUSTEE'S___ ___DEED___ *within ten days following the sale. The borrower has no right of* ___REDEMPTION___ *following the sale, although the buyer does have the right of* ___REINSTATEMENT___ *until the fifth day before the date set for the sale. Lenders cannot obtain a* ___DEFICIENCY___ *judgment on a trustee's sale.*

In a land sales contract, the ___VENDOR___ *(seller) agrees to give a deed to the property to the* ___VENDEE___ *(buyer), when the property has been paid for. The most common foreclosure remedy is a suit for* ___STRICT___ ___FORECLOSURE___.

When a mortgage is paid off, the release instrument is called a ___SATISFACTION___. *When a trust deed is paid off, the borrower gets a deed of* ___RECONVEYANCE___. *When a land sales contract is paid off the release instrument is the* ___DEED___ *the seller promised to the buyer at the beginning of the contract.*

Exercise e

The winner of a suit where a judgment was awarded is called the judgment creditor and the loser is called the ___JUDGMENT___ ___DEBTOR___. *The judgment constitutes a* ___LIEN___ *against all real property of the* ___JUDGMENT___ ___DEBTOR___ *located in the county where the judgment has been* ___DOCKETED___. *The judgment is initially good for* ___10___ *years. To enforce a judgment, the judgment creditor can simply wait, since the judgment will likely have to be paid upon a sale of the property. Or the judgment creditor can file a* ___WRIT___ *of* ___EXECUTION___ *with the court, which becomes a court order directing the* ___SHERIFF___ *to sell the property at public auction. The successful bidder at the sale will receive a* ___SHERIFF'S___ ___CERTIFICATE___ *of sale. This will entitle the holder to a* ___SHERIFF'S___ ___DEED___ *if the property is not redeemed within the statutory* ___180___ *-day right of redemption. If the property does not sell for enough to satisfy the judgment, then the sale will create a* ___PARTIAL___ ___SATISFACTION___ *of the judgment. If the property sells for more than enough to satisfy the judgment, then the surplus is turned over to the* ___JUDGMENT___ ___DEBTOR___.

If a judgment creditor executes upon the debtor's personal residence, the debtor can claim protection under the ___HOMESTEAD___ ___EXEMPTION___. *The amount of the exemption is normally* $ ___33,000___, *or* $ ___25,000___ *if the debtor is single. The maximum property which can be claimed is* ___ONE___ ___CITY___ ___BLOCK___, *if the property is located inside an incorporated city, or otherwise* ___160___ *acres.*

To prevent one of the parties to a suit from selling his or her property, the other party could file an ___ATTACHMENT___ *or a* ___NOTICE___ *of* ___PENDENCY___.

Exercise f

Anyone who supplies ___LABOR___ *or* ___MATERIALS___ *for improvements on another person's real estate may file a* ___CONSTRUCTION___ *lien. The claim must generally be filed within* ___75___ *days of substantial completion of the project. The claim is good for only* ___120___ *days, unless the claimant initiates a suit to* ___FORECLOSE___ *it. The priority of most construction liens is prior to all other* ___RECORDED___ *liens, unless the lien results from* ___IMPROVEMENTS___ *to an existing property. A property owner can protect himself or herself from a construction lien by posting a* ___NOTICE___ *of* ___NON-RESPONSIBILITY___.

The right to maintain public order is called ___POLICE___ ___POWER___. *When the government takes privately owned property it is called* ___CONDEMNATION___ *and the right to do so is called* ___EMINENT___ ___DOMAIN___. *In addition to the government, this right can also be exercised by* ___UTILITY___ *companies and quasi-utilities such as railroads. When the government destroys the economic benefit of an owner, this could result in severance damages,* ___CONSEQUENTIAL___ *damages or inverse condemnation.*

PRACTICE QUESTIONS

The following practice questions are representative of the questions you will find on the final examination and on the licensing examinations given by the Oregon Real Estate Agency.

1. Any interest in or right to land held by third persons, which adversely affects the title or value of the property, is
   (A) an encumbrance.
   (B) an encroachment.
   (C) an appurtenance.
   (D) a subordination agreement.

2. A claim that one person has on the property of another to secure payment of a debt is
   (A) an encroachment. (C) a title right.
   (B) a lien. (D) any of the above.

3. An acquired privilege or right to use or enjoyment falling short of ownership which one may have in the land of another is known as
   (A) a devise. (C) an easement.
   (B) an abstract. (D) a riparian right.

4. A person has legal rights in another's real property. These rights are short of an estate therein and would be called
   (A) a remainder. (C) an easement.
   (B) a lease. (D) a reversion.

5. The right to limited use, but not to the possession of the real property of someone else, is
   (A) a deed restriction. (C) a mortgage.
   (B) an easement. (D) a lease.

6. The right to use another's land for a specific purpose is
   (A) prescription. (C) an easement.
   (B) adverse possession. (D) a trespass.

7. Which of the following encumbrances affects the physical use of property?
   (A) An easement (C) A money judgment
   (B) A trust deed (D) Delinquent taxes

8. An easement is
   (A) an estate in land.
   (B) an encumbrance, but not a lien.
   (C) a lien.
   (D) both a lien and an encumbrance.

9. An owner who has a permanent right to cross over an adjoining owner's land has
   (A) an easement. (C) a party wall.
   (B) a license. (D) a riparian right.

10. An easement is
    (A) a general lien on real property.
    (B) a specific lien on real property.
    (C) an encumbrance on real property.
    (D) an equitable restriction on real property ownership.

11. An easement of passage across Smith's property would be
    (A) a license.
    (B) a lien.
    (C) an appurtenance to Smith's property.
    (D) an encumbrance.

12. If a property is said to be subject to an easement, then it has
    (A) an encumbrance. (C) a lien.
    (B) an appurtenance. (D) a restriction.

13. Regarding easements,
    I. all easements are encumbrances, but not all encumbrances are easements.
    II. an easement may be appurtenant to one parcel of land and a burden to another.
    (A) I only (C) Both I and II
    (B) II only (D) Neither I nor II

14. When a grantor creates an expressed easement, it
I. must be in writing.
II. is an interest in real property.
III. is an estate.
(A) I only
(B) I and II only
(C) I, II and III
(D) II and III only

15. Susan records a document given to her by Thomas in the county clerk's office. The document states that: "I, Thomas, grant to Susan a right of way for persons and vehicles along and upon the easterly 30 feet of the southerly 64 feet of Lot l, Block 2, Smith's Addition to the City of Ontario, in order to give access to Susan's restaurant." The interest intended to be granted in the document is
(A) a restrictive covenant.
(B) an easement.
(C) a license.
(D) a lease.

16. To the owner of the servient estate, an easement is
(A) a lien.
(B) an encumbrance.
(C) an appurtenance.
(D) a fixture.

17. An easement exists across a property which benefits another property. We would say that the
(A) burdened property is the dominant tenement.
(B) servient tenant cannot use the easement.
(C) easement must have been created by prescription.
(D) easement would be eliminated if the owner of one property buys the other property.

18. The servient estate in regard to an easement appurtenant is the property
(A) owned by the landlord.
(B) upon which the easement is placed.
(C) that benefits from the easement.
(D) owned by the tenant.

19. A right of way over parcel A to parcel B identifies parcel B as the
(A) dominant tenement.
(B) servient tenement.
(C) encroaching estate.
(D) appurtenant estate.

20. When there is an easement appurtenant, the servient tenant
I. owns the property which is burdened by the easement.
II. can terminate the easement if the burden is so great as to deprive the owner of reasonable use of the property.
(A) I only
(B) II only
(C) Both I and II
(D) Neither I nor II

21. Regarding an easement appurtenant, which of the following is not true?
(A) An easement appurtenant must be a burden on one property and a benefit to another.
(B) An easement appurtenant must be transferable.
(C) An easement appurtenant must run with the land.
(D) For an easement appurtenant to exist, the properties must be adjacent.

22. An easement appurtenant
(A) can normally only be created by a written agreement.
(B) cannot be canceled by the owner of the benefited land.
(C) is of temporary duration.
(D) is a purely personal right which does not run with the land.

23. An easement for ingress and egress means an easement
(A) for a right of way.
(B) for the lifetime of the owner of the land benefited by the easement.
(C) for any lawful purpose.
(D) by way of necessity.

24. An easement appurtenant
I. runs with the dominant estate as a property right.
II. involves a dominant and a servient estate.
(A) I only
(B) II only
(C) Both I and II
(D) Neither I nor II

25. An appurtenant easement
(A) has no dominant estate.
(B) is personal to the holder and cannot be transferred.
(C) is a possessory interest in another's real estate.
(D) is an interest in land which can be transferred.

26. Which of the following is true concerning an easement appurtenant?
    I. It is an interest that may be terminated at will by the possessor of the servient estate.
    II. It is considered to be a non-possessory interest.
    (A) I only (C) Both I and II
    (B) II only (D) Neither I nor II

27. When an easement appurtenant exists between two parcels of land that are separately owned
    (A) the dominant tenement has use of this easement only for ingress and egress.
    (B) the servient tenement must have created the easement in writing.
    (C) the dominant tenement is benefited.
    (D) the servient tenement may revoke the use of the easement by giving proper notice.

28. Ward owned two acres of land. He sold one acre to Taylor and reserved an easement appurtenant for ingress and egress over it in order for Ward to reach the public road. Taylor's land
    (A) is called the dominant tenement.
    (B) is subject to an easement in gross.
    (C) is called the servient tenement.
    (D) can be cleared of the easement when Ward sells the adjacent acre to a third party.

29. Two adjoining lots have an easement between them with one owner holding a dominant tenement and the other a servient tenement. Under these circumstances
    (A) the holder of the dominant tenement cannot use the easement for ingress and egress, regardless of the type held.
    (B) the burdened property is owned by the holder of the dominant tenement.
    (C) the easement can be eliminated by merging the two properties under one owner.
    (D) this type of easement can only be created by prescription.

30. Abel owned a lot which had an appurtenant easement over neighboring property belonging to Baker, which gave Abel the right to run a sewer line across Baker's property. If Abel sells his property to Charlie, but does not mention the easement in the deed, the easement
    (A) remains with Abel. (C) reverts to Baker.
    (B) goes to Charlie. (D) is lost by merger.

31. Adams owned a lot with an easement across an abutting lot owned by Sampson. Adams sold the lot to Johnson, but the easement which was appurtenant to Adams' property was not recited in the deed. The easement
    (A) passed to Johnson.
    (B) was eliminated.
    (C) does not run with the land.
    (D) reverted to Sampson.

32. Mr. Ward who owns a parcel of land also has an easement for ingress and egress to get to his property. He sells that land to Mr. Danner, but the deed makes no mention of the easement. Mr. Danner would receive
    (A) property with a clouded title.
    (B) property with the same right to the easement as the seller had.
    (C) a landlocked parcel.
    (D) the parcel, but without the easement.

33. Reed sold his land, which included an easement appurtenant for a road, to Simmons. The deed Reed gave to Simmons had a valid legal description, but did not include a reference to the easement. Which of the following is true about this situation?
    (A) Simmons would take title to landlocked property.
    (B) Simmons' title is clouded.
    (C) The easement would be forfeited to the servient tenement.
    (D) Simmons would possess the same rights as Reed.

34. An easement appurtenant
    (A) is limited to one year by federal regulation.
    (B) runs with the land.
    (C) is a personal right of the grantee.
    (D) is removed when the holder of the servient tenement sells the property.

35. When Madeline Carson bought a property, she received with it the right to cross over her neighbor's land. This is an easement right and will
    (A) be terminated if she sells her property.
    (B) be terminated if the other owner sells the other property.
    (C) be terminated upon the sale of either property.
    (D) not be terminated by the sale of either property.

36. An easement appurtenant is
    I. an interest in real property which can be transferred to another.
    II. extinguished if the property to which it is appurtenant is sold to another.
    (A) I only
    (B) II only
    (C) Both I and II
    (D) Neither I nor II

37. Mr. Michaels granted an easement appurtenant to Mr. Baldwin. Mr. Baldwin recorded the easement. Mr. Baldwin later sold his property to Mr. Charles but failed to mention the easement to him. Which of the following is true?
    (A) The easement was automatically removed from Mr. Michaels' property at the time of the sale.
    (B) If Mr. Charles desired an easement across Mr. Michaels' property, he would have to negotiate it personally.
    (C) Even though he sold the property, Mr. Baldwin retained the easement.
    (D) Mr. Charles would receive the rights of the easement upon the purchase of the property from Mr. Baldwin.

38. An easement in gross is an
    I. encumbrance on the title of the servient tenement.
    II. appurtenance to the title of the dominant tenement.
    (A) I only
    (B) II only
    (C) Both I and II
    (D) Neither I nor II

39. Telephone, electricity and gas line easements are examples of
    (A) commercial easements in gross.
    (B) easements by prescription.
    (C) dominant tenements.
    (D) servient tenements.

40. The right granted by an owner of real property to a telephone company for the purpose of erecting poles to support telephone wires over the property creates
    (A) an exclusive easement.
    (B) a specific lien.
    (C) a commercial easement in gross.
    (D) a declaration of restrictions.

41. An electric company acquired the right to erect its poles and run its lines along the rear five feet of a lot. This property right is referred to as an easement
    (A) appurtenant.
    (B) by necessity.
    (C) by prescription.
    (D) in gross.

42. Which of the following statements concerning easements is true?
    I. An easement in gross is usually used by a utility company to install its lines under or over a privately owned property.
    II. An easement in gross does not have a dominant estate.
    (A) I only
    (B) II only
    (C) Both I and II
    (D) Neither I nor II

43. The electric company and the telephone company ran their lines across the back of Smith's lot. These companies most likely own
    (A) a dominant tenement.
    (B) a servient tenement.
    (C) an easement in gross.
    (D) an easement appurtenant.

44. A telephone company was given the non-revocable use of land across the rear of lots in a subdivision. This is known as
    (A) a prescriptive easement.
    (B) an easement in gross.
    (C) a license.
    (D) an easement appurtenant.

45. The rights of a water company to lay and maintain water mains along the rear of a lot is called
    (A) an appurtenance.
    (B) an easement in gross.
    (C) a right of encroachment.
    (D) a riparian right.

46. Right of way easements, such as those acquired by public utilities, are usually called
    (A) easements of necessity.
    (B) easements in gross.
    (C) easements by prescription.
    (D) implied easements.

47. An easement appurtenant
    I. is the usual type of easement granted to utility companies to permit them to run electric lines across the property.
    II. runs with the land.
    (A) I only (C) Both I and II
    (B) II only (D) Neither I nor II

48. Two residential lots are next to each other in a subdivision. On the side they share in common, each has a ten-foot easement on the other lot for access to a garage so the driveway is 20 feet wide and the use is shared. This arrangement is called
    (A) an easement in gross.
    (B) a license.
    (C) a community drive.
    (D) a party line.

49. Two neighbors share a community drive. If one of them dies, the easement will
    (A) automatically go to the heirs of the deceased neighbor.
    (B) automatically go to the surviving neighbor.
    (C) pass with the title.
    (D) be extinguished.

50. An easement created by a process similar to adverse possession is known as an
    (A) easement in gross.
    (B) easement by prescription.
    (C) easement by necessity.
    (D) implied easement.

51. If an owner does not evict an encroacher in time, then the encroacher may acquire
    I. an easement by way of necessity.
    II. a license to use the property.
    (A) I only (C) Both I and II
    (B) II only (D) Neither I nor II

52. All of the following are essential to prevail in a claim for an easement by prescription, except
    (A) the use must be hostile to the interests of the servient tenant.
    (B) the claimant must pay the taxes on the easement.
    (C) the claimant must use the property under a claim of right.
    (D) open and notorious use for at least ten years.

53. Dottie O'Day owns a parcel of land. If she feels someone may be claiming an easement across her land by prescription, which of the following would be a way for her to defeat the claim?
    (A) Not set foot on the land herself for ten years
    (B) Give the claimant permission to use the land
    (C) Wait ten years and then file a suit to quiet title
    (D) Publish an notice in the paper that she is the true owner

54. Mr. Parker granted permission to Mrs. Adams to use his land for access. Mrs. Adams is not required to pay him any compensation. After ten years, Mrs. Adams may claim an easement
    (A) by way of necessity.
    (B) in gross.
    (C) by prescription.
    (D) under no circumstances.

55. Mr. Farmer had a property on which he posted "no trespassing" signs. In spite of the signs, his neighbor cultivated a garden in one corner of the property. Since Mr. Farmer was not using that corner, he granted the neighbor permission for the garden until such time as he needed the property back. Seventeen years later Mr. Farmer notified the neighbor that he needed the corner and asked him to quit. The neighbor refused. In this case, the neighbor
    (A) acquired title by prescription and need not move.
    (B) has a tenancy in common and need not move.
    (C) has a tenancy at will and need not move.
    (D) must move.

56. Permissive use of a road across another's land would create an easement by prescription in
    (A) five years. (C) 20 years.
    (B) ten years. (D) no case.

57. An easement which was acquired by constant use is called an easement by
    (A) reservation. (C) way of necessity.
    (B) prescription. (D) eminent domain.

58. An easement created when there is no access to a street is
    (A) an easement by prescription.
    (B) an easement in gross.
    (C) an easement by necessity.
    (D) a negative easement.

59. Bill Schwarz owns landlocked land and wishes to acquire an easement over adjoining land for ingress and egress. If the owner of the other land refuses to give him the easement, he can acquire the easement if he
    (A) applies to the county for an easement by way of necessity.
    (B) brings a suit for private condemnation.
    (C) just uses the right of way, as his right of entry is guaranteed by common law.
    (D) He cannot acquire the easement without the voluntary agreement of the other owner.

60. When a party owns landlocked property and requires access over the land of an adjacent owner to reach the owner's property he or she would likely be entitled to
    (A) a prescriptive easement.
    (B) an easement in gross.
    (C) an easement by necessity.
    (D) an adverse claim.

61. Easements are generally created in all but which one of the following methods?
    (A) Express grant (C) Assignment
    (B) Prescription (D) Implied grant

62. Bill O'Wright wishes to give an adjacent owner the right to place a power line across his land. This could be accomplished with
    (A) a transitory right. (C) a contract of sale.
    (B) a deed. (D) an option.

63. Which of the following is the legal right to use land which belongs to someone else?
    I. Easement appurtenant
    II. License
    III. Easement in gross
    (A) I and II only (C) II and III only
    (B) I and III only (D) I, II and III

64. The act of entering upon another person's real estate without authority or permission of the owner is called
    (A) an easement. (C) a trespass.
    (B) a license. (D) an encroachment.

65. Grant DeLande sells off the front part of his land. The deed recites the legal description of the frontage and then adds "excluding therefrom an easement over the east 20 feet for right of way purposes." In this case, an easement can be said to have been created by
    (A) express grant. (C) reservation.
    (B) way of necessity. (D) none of the above.

66. An easement appurtenant
    (A) may be terminated by the dominant tenement.
    (B) may be terminated by the servient tenement.
    (C) will be terminated if abandoned by the servient tenement.
    (D) cannot be terminated.

67. An easement appurtenant to real estate can be terminated by all of the following except
    (A) merger of the dominant and servient parcels.
    (B) revocation by the owner of the servient parcel.
    (C) prescription by the owner of the servient parcel.
    (D) release by the owner of the dominant tenement.

68. Who has the right to terminate an easement appurtenant?
    (A) The owner of the servient tenement.
    (B) The owner of the dominant tenement.
    (C) It can only be terminated by the mutual consent of the dominant and servient tenants.
    (D) It cannot be terminated by either the dominant or servient tenants.

69. A man sold his frontage, but reserved an easement across it to serve the back portion which he retained. If he does not use the easement at all for five years
    (A) he would lose the easement due to abandonment.
    (B) the easement would probably continue to be valid.
    (C) since five years have elapsed, a sale of the front parcel would extinguish his easement.
    (D) since five years have elapsed, a sale of his property would extinguish his easement.

70. Arthur Sullivan sold a property to Charles McHarris. After taking possession McHarris found a road across the property that provided ingress and egress to a property owned by Edward Elgar. If Elgar's easement was not recorded,
   I. his easement is nevertheless probably valid.
   II. he will probably have to pay McHarris for continued use of the easement.
   (A) I only (C) Both I and II
   (B) II only (D) Neither I nor II

71. An easement is said to terminate by "merger" when the
   (A) owner of the easement becomes the owner of the land that is subject to the easement.
   (B) purpose ceases for which the easement was created.
   (C) owner of an easement releases his or her right to the owner.
   (D) easement is abandoned.

72. Merger is a legal way of terminating an easement. In which of the following cases would an easement be extinguished by merger?
   I. The owner of the servient tenement acquires title to the dominant tenement.
   II. The owner of the dominant tenement acquires title to the servient tenement.
   (A) I only (C) Both I and II
   (B) II only (D) Neither I nor II

73. An easement is terminated
   I. when the dominant and servient tenements merge.
   II. if the easement causes an inconvenience to the servient tenement that impinges on the quiet enjoyment of that property.
   (A) I only (C) Both I and II
   (B) II only (D) Neither I nor II

74. Which of the following actions would terminate an easement?
   (A) A release signed by the holder of the dominant tenement
   (B) A revocation granted by the grantor of the easement
   (C) A full conveyance signed by the servient tenement
   (D) An express release granted by the holder of the servient tenement

75. An easement can be terminated by
   (A) satisfaction. (C) quitclaim deed.
   (B) trust deed. (D) deed of reconveyance.

76. An easement on real property could be extinguished by
   (A) foreclosure by underlying mortgagee.
   (B) suit to quiet title.
   (C) quitclaim deed.
   (D) any of the above.

77. Which of the following would terminate an easement?
   (A) Release signed by the holder of the dominant tenement
   (B) Revocation by the grantor of the easement
   (C) Full conveyance of the servient tenement to a third party
   (D) An express release of the easement by the servient tenant

78. The owner of a lakefront property granted the right to cross over the property to several friends to fish from the lake. The owner most likely created
   (A) a grant of adverse use.
   (B) an implied easement.
   (C) a license.
   (D) an easement appurtenant.

79. When one has permission to use land for some limited, specific purpose, but has no other rights, one has a
   (A) tenancy in common.
   (B) leasehold estate.
   (C) tenancy at sufferance.
   (D) license.

80. To grant permission to use a property during hunting season only would create
   (A) an easement. (C) an encroachment.
   (B) a license. (D) a right of way.

81. Samuel Adams gave an adjacent landowner permission to use his property, but reserved the right to revoke the permission at any time. This could ripen into an easement
   (A) immediately.
   (B) after five years of use.
   (C) after ten years of use.
   (D) never.

82. A personal, revocable, non-assignable right to use the property of another is called
(A) an option.
(B) a lease.
(C) an easement.
(D) a license.

83. A license usually differs from an easement in that a license
(A) can be revoked.
(B) may be assigned.
(C) is a permanent right.
(D) must be in writing.

84. A license is
I. assignable by the holder of the license.
II. revocable by the landowner.
(A) I only
(B) II only
(C) Both I and II
(D) Neither I nor II

85. A factor that distinguishes a license from an easement is that a license
(A) must be contained in a deed.
(B) is a permanent right.
(C) may be revoked.
(D) can be assigned.

86. A farmer placed a sign stating that permission to pass over the land was granted, but was revocable at any time. The purpose of the sign was probably to prevent someone from obtaining
(A) a use permit.
(B) an easement by prescription.
(C) a profit for severance of minerals.
(D) a license.

87. The right to enter upon the property of another and fish in a pond on the property is called
(A) an encroachment.
(B) a license.
(C) a riparian right.
(D) a trespass.

88. A license is
(A) revocable.
(B) an appurtenance to the title of the holder.
(C) created by mutual agreement between two landowners.
(D) an interest which runs with the land.

89. A license to cross a private property would
I. expire upon the death of either party to a license.
II. be revoked by sale of the property.
(A) I only
(B) II only
(C) Both I and II
(D) Neither I nor II

90. The right to remove topsoil, minerals or crops from the land of another is called
(A) an easement in gross.
(B) a license.
(C) a right of emblement.
(D) a profit.

91. The right to enter upon the property of another and to take from it sand, gravel, or the like is called a
(A) trespass.
(B) nuisance.
(C) license.
(D) profit.

92. Ingmar gave Dagmar the irrevocable right to use her property, but the right was granted to Dagmar only and not to any future owners. This was probably
(A) an easement appurtenant.
(B) an easement in gross.
(C) a license.
(D) a profit.

93. When a title right runs with the land, it could be
(A) an easement appurtenant.
(B) an easement in gross.
(C) a license.
(D) a profit.

94. Which of the following is a legal right to use land which belongs to another?
I. An easement appurtenant
II. An easement in gross
III. A license
(A) I only
(B) I and II only
(C) I, II and III
(D) III only

95. If I have a permanent right to cross your land to get to my house, my property has
(A) a dominant tenement.
(B) a servient tenement.
(C) an easement in gross.
(D) a license.

96. Mr. Johnson used a roadway over land owned by Mr. Jimson for ingress and egress to his land for a period of 13 years, with Jimson's permission. Jimson then sold his land to Mr. Jackson, who promptly erected a barricade to prevent Johnson's continued use of the roadway. In a suit by Johnson to enjoin Jackson's interference with his use,
    (A) Johnson will win.
    (B) Jackson will win.
    (C) Johnson could be required to pay compensation to Jackson for the use of the easement.
    (D) Jackson could be required to pay damages to Jimson.

97. Mrs. Black owns a parcel of land over which an easement runs which benefits adjacent land owned by Mrs. White. If both parcels are of equal size and value, then the tax bill
    (A) should be higher for Mrs. Black's land.
    (B) should be higher for Mrs. White's land.
    (C) is probably the same for both parcels of land.
    (D) will be determined by some method other than basing it on the real market value.

98. The inclusion of a restriction in a deed which limits the future use of a property creates
    (A) an unmarketable title.
    (B) a cloud on the title.
    (C) a covenant that runs with the land.
    (D) an unconstitutional deprivation of property rights.

99. Restrictions on property owners in a subdivision development are sometimes called
    (A) covenants.
    (B) encroachments.
    (C) easements appurtenant.
    (D) zoning constraints.

100. Private restrictions placed on a landowner may be in the form of covenants or conditions which restrict or limit the use of the land. Private restrictions may be created by
    I. deeds.
    II. written agreements.
    III. zoning ordinances.
    (A) I only
    (B) II only
    (C) I and II only
    (D) I and III only

101. Deed restrictions on real property are created by
    (A) local building commissions.
    (B) local zoning commissions.
    (C) developers and subdividers.
    (D) all of the above.

102. Deed restrictions are created by
    (A) the grantee.
    (B) the planning commission.
    (C) city ordinance.
    (D) the grantor.

103. Deed restrictions are considered to be
    (A) encumbrances.
    (B) general liens.
    (C) constructive notice.
    (D) enforceable only by the property's owner.

104. Regarding deed restrictions,
    (A) restrictions which are beneficial to the grantee are still considered encumbrances.
    (B) they must be recorded by the original developer to be enforceable.
    (C) both A and B are correct.
    (D) neither A nor B is correct.

105. Mrs. Hamilton wants to restrict the height of any building on a lot she wants to sell. She can best accomplish this by
    (A) seeking a zoning restriction.
    (B) placing the restriction in the earnest money agreement.
    (C) expressing her restriction to the purchaser.
    (D) placing the restriction in the deed.

106. Restrictive covenants that run with the land
    (A) expire when the property is sold.
    (B) are enforceable only against past owners.
    (C) apply only to the first owner of the property.
    (D) are applicable to all owners of the property.

107. Deed restrictions are a means whereby
    (A) villages and cities can control construction details.
    (B) the seller can limit or control the buyer's use.
    (C) the local zoning laws are enforced.
    (D) the planning commission's work is made effective.

108. Which of the following statements concerning deed restrictions placed on all of the lots in a subdivision is true?
    I. The restrictions run with the land.
    II. To enforce a restriction a neighboring lot owner has the right to apply to the court for an injunction.
    (A) I only (C) Both I and II
    (B) II only (D) Neither I nor II

109. The customary procedure used to enforce private property restrictions on real property is
    (A) a judgment. (C) an indictment.
    (B) an injunction. (D) a writ of assistance.

110. A developer is creating a subdivision. Which of the following restrictions would the developer be least likely to be able to enforce?
    (A) Minimum lot sizes
    (B) Minimum dollar value of improvements on each lot
    (C) Maximum height restrictions on each lot
    (D) Minimum square footage for each structure

111. Upon complaint of a benefiting owner, a deed restriction or restrictive covenant is enforced by
    (A) the county commissioners.
    (B) the state land use planning agency.
    (C) court injunction.
    (D) the local zoning board.

112. A developer created a subdivision with typical covenants restricting use of the lots to residential purposes. After all the lots have been sold, the covenants can be enforced by
    (A) the developer.
    (B) any lot owner, by filing a suit for an injunction.
    (C) the local planning and zoning commission.
    (D) any of the above.

113. A remedy to enforce a deed covenant might be
    (A) writ of mandamus. (C) equitable estoppel.
    (B) suit for damages. (D) an indictment.

114. Private deed restrictions are allowed only when they
    (A) will not be an undue burden on subsequent owners.
    (B) are based on esthetic values.
    (C) promote health, safety, morals or welfare.
    (D) None of the above is correct.

115. Deed restrictions can be used to
    I. limit the number and type of pets in the neighborhood.
    II. require any television antennas to be located in the attic.
    III. control the size and style of home built in the area.
    IV. limit the purchase of homes to Protestant families only.
    (A) III only (C) II and III only
    (B) IV only (D) I, II and III

116. When a deed contains a clause that prohibits the future sale of a property to persons of a minority race, that clause will
    (A) allow the grantor the right to enforce that restriction.
    (B) create a cloud on the title.
    (C) invalidate the conveyance.
    (D) have no effect on the conveyance, and the clause will be unenforceable.

117. A restrictive covenant in a deed may
    I. enforceably limit the sale of a property to a specific religious group.
    II. introduce restrictions concerning the use to which the property may be put.
    (A) I only (C) Both I and II
    (B) II only (D) Neither I nor II

118. Johnson's neighbor, Jackson, recently began keeping goats. Thirty years earlier, when the area was subdivided, covenants were created which prohibit keeping goats. Johnson may
    (A) take Jackson's property as the penalty for Jackson's violation of the covenants.
    (B) begin to keep goats as well.
    (C) sue to force Jackson to get rid of the goats.
    (D) do nothing, as the covenants have expired.

119. The normal process to enforce a deed covenant is to seek
    (A) an injunction.
    (B) a cease and desist order.
    (C) a lis pendens (notice of pendency).
    (D) recovery of the title.

120. A restriction in a deed states that if the buyer breaches the restriction the title will revert to the seller. This restriction is a
(A) condition subsequent.
(B) covenant for the benefit of adjacent land.
(C) personal restriction.
(D) general plan restriction.

121. Deed restrictions are said to be in the form of a covenant or a condition. Regarding covenants and conditions, the penalty for violation of a
I. condition might be the loss of the entire title.
II. covenant is that an affected owner who is benefited by the covenant could file a suit to enjoin the action which violates the covenant.
(A) I only (C) Both I and II
(B) II only (D) Neither I nor II

122. Regarding deed covenants and deed conditions,
I. covenants are encumbrances on the title.
II. conditions are encumbrances on the title.
(A) I only (C) Both I and II
(B) II only (D) Neither I nor II

123. The penalty for violation of a deed covenant is
(A) harsher than the penalty for violation of a condition.
(B) the same as the penalty for violation of a condition.
(C) less harsh than the penalty for violation of a condition.
(D) Deed covenants are generally unenforceable.

124. Private land use controls include which of the following?
I. Restrictive covenants contained in a subdivision plat map
II. Deed restrictions
(A) I only (C) Both I and II
(B) II only (D) Neither I nor II

125. Deed covenants can be terminated by all of the following except
(A) the local planning and zoning commission.
(B) expiration of a time limit stated in the covenant.
(C) merger of ownership.
(D) voluntary cancellation by the party benefited by the covenant.

126. Deed restrictions may be removed by
(A) quitclaim deed. (C) eviction.
(B) writ of attachment. (D) any of the above.

127. Mira LaVista wishes to sell her adjacent lot, but protect the view from her home in the process. The easiest way for her to accomplish this is to
(A) seek a zoning order restricting the height of structures in the area.
(B) enter into a side contract with the buyer.
(C) insist on a restriction in the earnest money agreement.
(D) place a covenant in the deed.

128. When deed covenants have been created, they normally
(A) expire when the property is sold.
(B) are only enforceable on the first buyer following their creation.
(C) are enforceable indefinitely and run with the land.
(D) are enforceable on all adjacent property owners.

129. Enna Croacher bought a lot and built a house within ten feet of the side property line. Her neighbors sued because there was a subdivision plan that had been recorded 30 years earlier which prohibited building within 20 feet of the side lot line. The plan was not mentioned in Enna's deed. Enna claimed they were not enforceable on her. She was
(A) correct, because the plan was not mentioned in her deed.
(B) correct, because the plan expired after thirty years.
(C) correct, because only the original subdivider can enforce the restrictions.
(D) incorrect, because the covenants run with the land.

130. If a property is covered by both deed restrictions and zoning ordinances, which has priority?
(A) Zoning ordinances
(B) Deed restrictions
(C) Whichever is the more restrictive as to any given prohibited act
(D) Whichever is the less restrictive as to any given prohibited act

131. A right in real estate which has not yet been determined to be a definite right would be
(A) a lien.
(B) a cloud.
(C) an easement in gross.
(D) any of the above.

132. Quieting a title means to
(A) remove a cloud on the title by court action.
(B) obtain title by adverse possession.
(C) mortgage the property.
(D) partition property owned by tenants in common who cannot agree to sell the property.

133. A quitclaim deed would be filed when
(A) questions arise regarding the validity of a title.
(B) the purchaser buys a property with tenants already in possession.
(C) family members purchase a property together.
(D) a tenant in common conveys his or her interest to a co-tenant.

134. If an owner brings a successful quiet title action against someone, it
I. would have the same effect as recording a quitclaim deed from the person.
II. was probably brought because the owner wanted to remove a cloud from his or her title.
(A) I only
(B) II only
(C) Both I and II
(D) Neither I nor II

135. To remove a cloud from the title of a property an owner would most likely obtain
(A) an assessment.
(B) a quitclaim deed.
(C) a trust deed.
(D) an option.

136. Quieting a title can be accomplished by
(A) purchase of title insurance.
(B) providing the purchaser with an affidavit of title.
(C) either A or B.
(D) neither A nor B.

137. An unintentional but illegal intrusion onto the property of another is known as
(A) an encroachment.
(B) a prescription.
(C) an easement.
(D) adverse possession.

138. When the owner of real estate erects improvements that extend onto adjoining property, there exists
(A) a license.
(B) a profit.
(C) a certificate of claim.
(D) an encroachment.

139. After Charlie purchased a property, he had a survey made and found that his neighbor, through error, had recently built an ornamental fence extending two feet into Charlie's land. This is an example of
(A) a party wall.
(B) an encroachment.
(C) an appurtenance.
(D) adverse possession.

140. When Smith's recently constructed patio is found to extend two feet into Brown's property, the inference may properly be made that this trespass has created
I. an encumbrance.
II. a cloud on the title.
(A) I only
(B) II only
(C) Both I and II
(D) Neither I nor II

141. Walker built a fence that extended onto Scott's land. This is an example of
(A) an easement by necessity.
(B) an encroachment.
(C) a license.
(D) an easement in gross.

142. Frick bought a home and moved into it. Soon thereafter, he discovered that his neighbor, Frack, had built a fence which encroached on his land by six feet. If Frick and Frack cannot reach agreement,
(A) Frick can sue Frack for trespass.
(B) Frick can sue Frack to quiet title.
(C) Frack has already gained an easement by prescription.
(D) both A and B are correct.

143. Jess Miller built a fence by mistake on the property of his neighbor, Ruth Yoder. The fence
I. is considered personal property.
II. belongs to Ruth Yoder.
III. can only be removed if Ruth Yoder consents.
(A) I only
(B) III only
(C) Both I and II
(D) Both II and III

144. Kirschbaum owns a lot which has a cherry tree growing on the side of the lot. The tree overhangs the driveway of his neighbor, Baumschneider. Baumschneider can
I. remove branches which overhang his driveway.
II. cut the tree down.
III. pick the fruit which grows on his side of the property line.
(A) I only (C) I, II and III
(B) I and III only (D) II and III only

145. To ensure that there are no encroachments, a purchaser should obtain
(A) a standard form title insurance policy.
(B) a certification of boundary lines from a surveyor.
(C) a statement of no encroachments from the seller.
(D) all of the above.

146. The priority of liens is determined mostly by
(A) whether it is a government lien or a private lien.
(B) whether the lien is voluntary or involuntary.
(C) the date of recording or docketing.
(D) whether the lien derives from statutory law or common law.

147. The priority of a trust deed is affected by
(A) the date it was recorded.
(B) the existence of a subordination clause in the document.
(C) both A and B.
(D) neither A nor B.

148. Which of the following would have priority over a trust deed which had been recorded earlier?
(A) A special assessment for street repairs
(B) A general judgment
(C) Both A and B
(D) Neither A nor B

149. Which of the following liens normally takes priority over all other liens?
(A) Judgment liens
(B) Mortgage liens
(C) Mechanics liens
(D) Real property tax liens

150. A lien for real property taxes
(A) has the same priority as a construction lien.
(B) is subsequent in priority to a construction lien.
(C) has priority over judgment liens only.
(D) normally has priority over all liens.

151. The priority of a lien for real property taxes is
(A) before a first mortgage lien.
(B) subordinate to a mortgage lien.
(C) subordinate to first and second mortgages.
(D) none of the above.

152. First liens that take priority over all other liens are
(A) mortgages. (C) judgments.
(B) tax liens. (D) construction liens.

153. A property tax lien has priority against other interests in property
(A) according to the date the lien was recorded.
(B) regardless of when it becomes a lien of record.
(C) on the basis of when the tax law passes.
(D) only if the owner agrees to assume the debt.

154. A property is subject to a first and a second mortgage. The first mortgage is in default and the lender elects to foreclose. Following the auction sale of the property, the proceeds of the sale will be disbursed in the following order:
(A) First mortgage, second mortgage, balance to the borrower.
(B) First mortgage, balance to the borrower, second mortgagee gets nothing.
(C) First mortgage, balance up to the appraised value of the property to the borrower, balance to the second mortgagee.
(D) First mortgage, balance up to the appraised value of the property to the borrower, remainder to the holder of the second mortgage.

155. Which of the following has priority of claim over a previously recorded trust deed?
(A) Divorce decree (C) Unpaid property taxes
(B) Judgment lien (D) None of the above

156. When a lienholder forces the sale of a property, which of the following would normally be paid first from the proceeds of the sale of the property?
(A) Property taxes due (C) Income tax levies
(B) A first mortgage (D) A first trust deed

157. In discussing real estate liens, the term "subordinate" is most nearly the opposite of
(A) inferior. (C) subrogation.
(B) senior. (D) substituted.

158. A lien covering all property of a debtor would be
(A) an equitable lien.
(B) a property tax lien.
(C) a mechanic's or laborer's lien.
(D) a general lien.

159. A lien which affects only one parcel of property belonging to the debtor is known as a
(A) designated lien. (C) judgment lien.
(B) special lien. (D) general lien.

160. A lien which burdens all of the property of the owner is known as a
I. judgment lien. III. general lien.
II. specific lien.
(A) I only (C) I and II only
(B) II only (D) I and III only

161. When a judgment lien reaches all the property of a judgment debtor in a county, this is called
(A) a blanket lien. (C) a specific lien.
(B) a general lien. (D) a government lien.

162. A federal income tax lien is
(A) a general lien. (C) a voluntary lien.
(B) a specific lien. (D) a judgment lien.

163. Real property taxes that are not paid are
(A) general, involuntary liens.
(B) general, voluntary liens.
(C) specific, voluntary liens.
(D) specific, involuntary liens.

164. Mr. and Mrs. Biondi hired the Blue Water Pool Company to install a swimming pool at their home. If the Pool company needs to file a lien to enforce collection from Mr. and Mrs. Biondi, the lien would be
(A) a specific, or special lien.
(B) a general lien.
(C) a voluntary, or elective lien.
(D) illegal.

165. A real estate agent failed to report income and as a result the Internal Revenue Service filed a tax lien. As to the agent's real property, the income tax lien is
(A) a general lien. (C) an involuntary lien.
(B) a specific lien. (D) both A and C.

166. A lien created by court action which covers all the property of a debtor in the county where it is located is called a
(A) blanket mortgage. (C) general lien.
(B) specific lien. (D) lis pendens.

167. Which of the following is considered to be a voluntary lien?
I. Ad valorem tax
II. Special assessment
III. Mortgage on real property
IV. Mechanic's lien
(A) I only (C) II and III only
(B) III only (D) III and IV only

168. Which of the following statements about liens is not true?
(A) A judgment is a voluntary lien.
(B) A trust deed is a voluntary lien.
(C) A general lien reaches all the property of the debtor.
(D) A specific lien reaches only specified property of the debtor.

169. A court decree determining that one individual is indebted to another and fixing the amount of indebtedness is called
(A) an injunction. (C) an executive decree.
(B) a judgment. (D) an assignment of debt.

170. A money judgment of the court, when recorded, always becomes
(A) an involuntary lien. (C) a superior lien.
(B) a special lien. (D) an equitable lien.

171. If a debtor owns three pieces of real estate in the same county and a judgment is entered against the debtor in that county, it will be a lien against
(A) the property first acquired by the debtor.
(B) the property last acquired by the debtor.
(C) non-homestead property only.
(D) all three properties.

172. When a creditor has obtained a judgment, it creates a security interest in all the
   (A) real property owned by the debtor in the county where obtained.
   (B) personal property owned by the debtor in the county where obtained.
   (C) real property to which the debtor is the only person in title and located in the county where the judgment was obtained.
   (D) Both A and B are correct.

173. For maximum benefit, you should be sure that a judgment is of record in
   (A) the county where the debtor resides.
   (B) the county where the judgment was rendered.
   (C) every county where the judgment debtor owns property.
   (D) the office of the Oregon Secretary of State.

174. What is the court order called directing the sheriff to sell real property to satisfy a judgment?
   (A) Writ of execution (C) Writ of attachment
   (B) Foreclosure (D) Default order

175. When a court orders a person to sell property it issues
   (A) an attachment. (C) a writ of execution.
   (B) a foreclosure. (D) a deficiency judgment.

176. The sale by court order of a debtor's property to satisfy a judgment is accomplished by a court issuing
   (A) an injunction.
   (B) a deficiency judgment.
   (C) an attachment.
   (D) a writ of execution.

177. The document given to the high bidder when property is sold at public auction to satisfy a debt is a
   (A) writ of attachment. (C) certificate of sale.
   (B) writ of execution. (D) sheriff's deed.

178. When a judgment lien has been paid in full, which of the following does the debtor receive as evidence that the debt has been paid in full?
   (A) Abstract of judgment
   (B) Writ of execution
   (C) Satisfaction of judgment
   (D) Docket of judgment

179. A legal procedure which depends on obtaining a judgment would be
   (A) a writ of execution. (C) both A and B.
   (B) a sheriff's certificate. (D) neither A nor B.

180. Regarding judgments, which of the following statements is true?
   (A) A judgment is only effective against property which the debtor already owned at the time the suit was filed.
   (B) A judgment lien is a voluntary lien.
   (C) A judgment imposes a lien on all the real and personal property of the judgment debtor in the county where the judgment is of public record.
   (D) A judgment takes priority over all previous liens except property taxes and construction liens.

181. Regarding judgment liens, which of the following is true?
   (A) A judgment lien reaches only personal property.
   (B) A judgment lien is usually a specific lien.
   (C) A judgment is subject to the protection of the Oregon Homestead Act.
   (D) All of the above statements about judgments are true.

182. The Oregon Homestead Act can provide a homeowner
   (A) some protection against the forced sale of a personal residence.
   (B) a life estate in a personal residence for a surviving spouse.
   (C) a guarantee that a personal residence cannot be sold to satisfy a judgment.
   (D) the right to use a personal residence free from private restrictions.

183. Which of the following statements regarding the Oregon Homestead Act is true?
   I. If a judgment lien is filed against a property owner, the owner may claim a homestead exemption for any property he or she owns.
   II. The Oregon Homestead Act provides Protection against foreclosure of mortgages and trust deeds.
   (A) I only (C) Both I and II
   (B) II only (D) Neither I nor II

184. A homestead exemption has no effect on
(A) a mortgage loan. (C) a construction lien.
(B) a trust deed loan. (D) any of the above.

185. An Oregon Homestead exemption will not prevent foreclosure for satisfaction of
I. a construction lien. II. real property taxes.
(A) I only (C) Both I and II
(B) II only (D) Neither I nor II

186. Under Oregon law, a homestead exemption can be claimed by
(A) a judgment debtor.
(B) an attorney for a judgment debtor.
(C) either A or B.
(D) neither A nor B.

187. According to the Oregon Homestead Act, farm property on which a debtor lives may be exempt from a judgment sale if it does not exceed
(A) 160 acres. (C) 320 acres.
(B) 200 acres. (D) 640 acres.

188. Which of the following is/are the maximum amount of property that can be claimed as a homestead under the Oregon Homestead Act?
I. One city block
II. 300 acres of farmland
(A) I only (C) Both I and II
(B) II only (D) Neither I nor II

189. A judgment lien was placed on all real property belonging to Kenneth Peterson, an Oregon resident. He may lose his right to claim a homestead exemption if he
I. sells his home and invests the proceeds in an out of state business.
II. is absent from his home as a result of being jailed on another judgment against his person.
(A) I only (C) Both I and II
(B) II only (D) Neither I nor II

190. The Oregon Homestead Act will protect up to how much of the equity in a home?
(A) $33,000, or $25,000 if single
(B) $50,000
(C) $100,000
(D) 100% of the equity.

191. If a judgment debtor wishes to take advantage of the protection of the Oregon Homestead Act, who should be informed that the property is a homestead?
(A) The county tax assessor
(B) The clerk of the court where the judgment was rendered
(C) The sheriff who will be responsible for holding the sheriff's sale
(D) The judgment creditor or the attorney for the judgment creditor

192. If a creditor obtains a judgment against a homeowner, the owner may
I. claim the homestead exemption for property actually occupied as a personal residence.
II. continue the homestead if the owner sells the homestead with the intention of getting another homestead within one year.
(A) I only (C) Both I and II
(B) II only (D) Neither I nor II

193. A homestead exemption may be lost by
(A) encroachments. (C) abandonment.
(B) easements. (D) survivorship.

194. What is the name of the document of record that is used to show that a court suit is pending?
(A) Attachment
(B) Construction lien
(C) Lis pendens (notice of pendency)
(D) Judgment

195. A form of public notice filed against certain lands setting forth that court action is about to be instituted is known as
(A) a construction lien.
(B) an attachment.
(C) a lis pendens (notice of pendency).
(D) a judgment.

196. When a claim against a parcel of real estate may result from a pending law suit, a person examining the public records would look for a
(A) forcible entry.
(B) constructive notice.
(C) caveat emptor notice.
(D) notice of pendency (lis pendens).

197. The document allowing for the legal seizure of property for debt before a judgment is called
(A) a writ of execution.
(B) a writ of attachment.
(C) lis pendens (notice of pendency).
(D) habendum terminatis.

198. Legal seizure of property for payment of money before judgment is
(A) a writ of execution.
(B) an attachment.
(C) a condemnation.
(D) a lis pendens (notice of pendency).

199. An attachment is
(A) an encroachment on the title.
(B) a fixture.
(C) an appurtenance to the title.
(D) a lien.

200. In distinguishing between a judgment lien and an attachment, the
(A) attachment covers all property owned by the debtor.
(B) attachment is filed after a court decision has been rendered.
(C) judgment lien is recorded prior to and while awaiting a court decision.
(D) attachment reaches the property before the judgment has been rendered.

201. An attachment may be released by all of the following except
(A) a court order.
(B) a release of attachment signed by the plaintiff.
(C) a judgment in favor of the plaintiff.
(D) the death of the defendant.

202. In order to assist contractors who have not been paid, the law allows the filing of
(A) a subordination lien. (C) either A or B.
(B) a construction lien. (D) neither A nor B.

203. When a firm furnishes materials for the construction of a house and is not paid, it may file
(A) a construction lien.
(B) an estoppel certificate.
(C) a deficiency judgment.
(D) a lis pendens (notice of pendency).

204. A contractor provided labor and material in constructing a new house. To ensure collection of the charges, the contractor may file a
(A) judgment lien. (C) chattel mortgage.
(B) construction lien. (D) labor lien.

205. A construction lien claim arises when a contractor has performed work or provided material to improve a parcel of real estate on the order of the owner and the work has not been paid for. Such contractor has a right to
(A) tear out his or her work.
(B) equitable title.
(C) record a notice of lien and file a court suit within the time required by state law.
(D) have personal property of the owner sold to satisfy the lien.

206. A construction lien can be filed against an owner by
(A) an employee broker against a principal broker.
(B) the building superintendent after completion of building.
(C) an abstractor.
(D) a lumber company furnishing materials.

207. A construction lien can be claimed by
(A) an architect for landscape plans.
(B) a worker performing labor for wages.
(C) either A or B.
(D) neither A nor B.

208. Which of the following would be entitled to claim a construction lien in Oregon?
(A) A surveyor
(B) A real estate appraiser
(C) A real estate broker
(D) All of the above

209. A rental equipment dealer has not been paid for equipment which was used in construction of a property. The dealer may
(A) file a construction lien against the property where the equipment was used.
(B) sue the person who rented the equipment and obtain a general judgment.
(C) do either A or B.
(D) not do either A or B.

210. A homeowner who had owned a home for 20 years decided to have the kitchen remodeled. After the contractor finished the project, the contractor filed a construction lien. In the event a foreclosure of the construction lien should become necessary, the priority of the lien would be
(A) ahead of all other liens except property tax liens.
(B) ahead of all other liens except property tax liens and income tax levies.
(C) in order by date along with all other liens except property taxes.
(D) in order by date along with all other liens except property taxes and income tax levies.

211. The Hometown Savings and Loan Association made a construction loan to a builder to build a home. One of the builder's subcontractors filed a construction lien. The priority of this lien would be
(A) immediately preceding Hometown's construction loan.
(B) senior to all other liens including Hometown's construction loan, but not senior to property taxes and special assessments.
(C) junior to all liens recorded before it.
(D) senior to all liens recorded before it.

212. A worker who wishes to place a construction lien against a property would be affected by
(A) a certificate of completion.
(B) a notice of non-responsibility posted on the premises.
(C) the filing of a suit to foreclose a previously recorded mortgage.
(D) both A and B.

213. To protect your property from liens, you would post a notice of non-responsibility if
(A) your tenant has repairs made to the premises.
(B) you no longer wish to be obligated on a recorded mortgage or trust deed.
(C) there are trespassers on the premises.
(D) your spouse files for divorce.

214. Landscrapers, Inc., a subcontractor on the construction of a house was not satisfied, so they filed a construction lien. When the general contractor went to sell the house, the construction lien was discovered. The general contractor disputed the claim of Landscapers, Inc. In order to obtain clear title to the house, the general contractor could
(A) deposit at least 150% of the claim in cash with the county treasurer.
(B) record a surety bond in an amount equal to at least 150% of the claim.
(C) file a suit to quiet title or a suit for slander of title.
(D) do any of the above.

215. A man who owned his home free and clear hired a contractor to build an addition. The contractor hired several subcontractors to assist. Upon completion, the man paid the contractor in full, but the contractor failed to pay one of the subcontractors. In this case, the
(A) subcontractors can file construction liens and the owner must pay them.
(B) owner could have protected himself by filing a notice of non-responsibility.
(C) owner has recourse against the contractor if the owner has to pay the subcontractors.
(D) all of the above are possible.

216. Mr. and Mrs. Gottrocks bought a new luxury home from a builder. At closing, the Gottrocks will sign a new conventional trust deed loan to obtain the funds to pay for the house. Closing of the transaction will take place upon substantial completion. In this case,
(A) Mr. and Mrs. Gottrocks will have to assume liability for future construction liens.
(B) a portion of the builder's sales proceeds may have to be withheld for up to 75 days after closing.
(C) there can be no further construction liens after Mr. and Mrs. Gottrocks take title.
(D) both A and B are correct.

217. A lien filed by a contractor to enforce payment for a roof which he installed would be a
I. specific lien.
II. general lien.
III. voluntary lien.
(A) I only
(B) II only
(C) I and III only
(D) II and III only

218. Which of the following are rights of the government which would affect privately owned real estate?
(A) Escheat
(B) Police power
(C) Taxation
(D) All of the above

219. Public powers in private property include which of the following?
I. The right to tax
II. Zoning codes
III. Deed restrictions in a subdivision
IV. Eminent domain
(A) I and II only
(B) II and III only
(C) I, II and IV only
(D) II, III and IV only

220. There are four governmental limitations to the private rights of ownership of real property. Which of the following does not belong in the group?
(A) Taxes
(B) Police power
(C) Escheat
(D) Deed restrictions

221. Samuel Farmer was required to sell his land to the county for its appraised value so a dam could be built. The legal principle which gives the county the right to force him to sell is known as
(A) lis pendens (notice of pendency).
(B) escheat.
(C) eminent domain.
(D) police power.

222. The right of government to acquire ownership of privately held real estate regardless of the owner's wishes is called
(A) easement by necessity.
(B) easement by prescription.
(C) eminent domain.
(D) covenant of seizin.

223. The power or right of governmental bodies to take real estate for public use is called
(A) lis pendens (notice of pendency).
(B) ad valorem.
(C) eminent domain.
(D) estate.

224. A governmental agency may acquire a certain property for public use by utilizing
(A) an attachment.
(B) the right of eminent domain.
(C) a suit to quiet title.
(D) a claim of adverse possession.

225. When the city wants to widen the street, it can acquire additional width from the private owners of the abutting property under the exercise of
(A) partition.
(B) right of way.
(C) eminent domain.
(D) severance.

226. The right of eminent domain refers to
(A) the fact that every American has the right to own real property.
(B) the right of the government to condemn property.
(C) a private individual or entity acquiring land by grant from the government.
(D) the right of the government to post a property as uninhabitable.

227. Eminent domain
I. may be exercised by a school district to obtain property for a public school.
II. requires that just compensation be paid to the landowner when exercised.
(A) I only
(B) II only
(C) Both I and II
(D) Neither I nor II

228. If the city wishes to take property for public improvements, it may acquire title by action based on
(A) attachment proceedings.
(B) right of eminent domain.
(C) suit to quiet title.
(D) adverse possession rights.

229. When the government acquires privately-owned real estate through a condemnation suit it is exercising the power of
(A) reversion.
(B) eminent domain.
(C) escheat.
(D) license.

230. Eminent domain is the right of the government to
(A) take privately owned property without just compensation.
(B) sell private property on which taxes have not been paid.
(C) take title to privately owned real property when the owner dies without heirs.
(D) take private property upon payment of just compensation.

231. Condemnation proceedings in Oregon may be used to acquire real property
   I. by a governmental body for a stated public use.
   II. as a right of way for a privately owned public utility company.
   III. only if just compensation is paid to the property owner.
   (A) I and II only (C) I and III only
   (B) I, II and III (D) III only

232. The process under eminent domain by which property is taken for public use is
   (A) lis pendens (notice of pendency).
   (B) judgment.
   (C) condemnation.
   (D) abstract of judgment.

233. Harry O'Hara refused to sell property he owned in Deschutes, Oregon to the school district because he felt the price the district was offering was insufficient. What proceeding would the school board file if it wished to pursue the matter in court?
   (A) Foreclosure
   (B) Easement by way of necessity
   (C) Escheat
   (D) Condemnation

234. When an owner of land refuses to sell his or her land to the government or any governmental agency under the right of eminent domain, the name of the proceeding to require the owner to sell the land is
   (A) escheat. (C) condemnation.
   (B) estoppel. (D) constructive eviction.

235. In a widely publicized dispute, William Shea refused to sell his land in Willamette County to the local school board. Shea believed that the price the school board offered for the land was not sufficient. If the school board wanted to pursue the matter in court, what proceeding would it institute to attempt to force Shea to sell the land?
   (A) Foreclosure (C) Escheat
   (B) Condemnation (D) None of the above

236. A power company has the right to string power lines across private property by exercising
   (A) police power.
   (B) eminent domain.
   (C) prescription.
   (D) the right to an easement by necessity.

237. A landowner is advised that a railroad company plans to cross the landowner's property with a railroad line. If the landowner refuses, the railroad company can proceed by the use of
   (A) eminent domain. (C) partition action.
   (B) accretion. (D) none of the above.

238. When a public railroad needs a specific piece of land and the owner does not want to sell, the railroad may attempt to exercise the right of
   (A) eminent domain. (C) injunction.
   (B) alienation. (D) replevin.

239. A landowner can expect to receive compensation from the government for
   I. land use restrictions caused by zoning.
   II. the physical taking of the land.
   (A) I only (C) Both I and II
   (B) II only (D) Neither I nor II

240. Beau Gentry owned a tract of land on which he operated a golf course. The state decided to place a freeway next to his property, although they did not take any of his land. As a result of the noise from the freeway, Beau's business fell off and he was forced to sell the golf course business at a loss. He might be entitled to
   (A) consequential damages.
   (B) damages for inverse condemnation.
   (C) related damages.
   (D) severance damages.

241. Jim Brown owned a large farm. The government placed a limited access highway through the farm, leaving a small strip of land on one side. As a result, the strip of land became worth less per acre than before. Jim's relief might be a suit for
   (A) eminent domain of government land.
   (B) inverse condemnation.
   (C) an equitable servitude.
   (D) severance damages.

242. A legal proceeding by an owner demanding that the government buy his or her land is a suit for
(A) inverse condemnation.
(B) consequential damages.
(C) either A or B.
(D) neither A nor B.

243. When a person dies intestate and no heirs can be found for intestate succession, the real property will revert to the government through a process known as
(A) reconveyance.
(B) reversion.
(C) escheat.
(D) eminent domain.

244. The term "escheat" means that
(A) a fraud has been committed.
(B) real property has been acquired by the State of Oregon.
(C) a real estate agent's license has been revoked.
(D) property encumbered by a trust deed has been sold.

245. The reversion of property to the sovereign state, owing to lack of any heirs capable of inheriting, is known as
(A) reversionary interest.
(B) sovereign immunity.
(C) escheat.
(D) eminent domain.

246. The word "escheat" refers to
(A) the feudal custom of the king's seizure of land.
(B) the right of the government to take private property for a public purpose upon payment.
(C) the acquisition of title by adverse possession.
(D) the right of the government to acquire title where the owner dies without a will and without heirs.

247. Mr. Smith died leaving no will or natural heirs. His property will
(A) go to the county for the school fund.
(B) go to the State of Oregon
(C) be held in probate for five years and then escheat to the state.
(D) be held in probate for six months and then escheat to the state.

248. Eminent domain is the right of the state to
(A) take private property without compensation.
(B) sell property on which taxes have not been paid.
(C) take title to property when there are no heirs.
(D) take private property with just compensation.

249. An owner wished to build a high fence around the back yard so that cows could be kept there without getting out. Before doing so, the owner should check
(A) the local building codes.
(B) local zoning ordinances.
(C) deed restrictions to the property.
(D) all of the above.

250. The government's right of police power means that the government can
(A) regulate the use of real property in the public interest.
(B) acquire privately held real estate for public use.
(C) levy taxes on real property.
(D) take privately held real property without court action in an emergency.

251. To avoid having to pay just compensation to affected owners, a zoning ordinance cannot
(A) be capricious and arbitrary.
(B) exceed constitutional limits.
(C) take all the rights in the properties affected by the ordinance.
(D) do any of the above.

252. An owner can expect to receive compensation from the government
I. if the government enacts zoning laws which detract from the value of his or her property.
II. in the event the government takes the owner's real estate.
(A) I only
(B) II only
(C) Both I and II
(D) Neither I nor II

253. Which of the following would require the government to pay just compensation?
(A) Requiring that no buildings be placed on the front ten feet of a lot
(B) Condemnation of an easement for a road right of way
(C) Both A and B
(D) Neither A nor B

254. In which of the following pairs does the second phrase relate to the first?
(A) Eminent domain — Zoning laws
(B) Police power — Just compensation
(C) Eminent domain — Just compensation
(D) Escheat — Zoning laws

255. The Northern and Pacific Telephone and Telegraph Company has an easement on real property listed by Broker Root. This easement is
(A) a general lien on the property.
(B) a specific lien on the property.
(C) an encumbrance on the property.
(D) a declaration of restriction on the property.

256. Harry Scairy owns a house which has a mortgage. His property is
(A) subordinated.
(B) restricted.
(C) encumbered.
(D) subject to an execution.

257. Which of the following is not an encumbrance on real estate?
(A) An easement (C) A judgment
(B) A deed (D) A mortgage

258. Encumbrances of record that run with the land would usually include which of the following?
I. Easements III. Licenses
II. Restrictions
(A) II only (C) I and III only
(B) I and II only (D) I, II and III

259. Which of the following is not an encumbrance?
(A) A judgment (C) A mortgage
(B) An easement (D) A covenant of seizin

260. Which of the following is an encumbrance?
(A) Lien (C) Deed restriction
(B) Easement (D) All of the above

261. Which of the following would not be considered an encumbrance?
(A) Unpaid real property taxes
(B) An easement appurtenant to the property
(C) A special assessment levied for street improvements
(D) A recorded abstract of judgment

262. All of the following are encumbrances, except
(A) homesteads. (C) encroachments.
(B) private restrictions. (D) easements.

263. An encumbrance could be a
I. private limitation on the use of land.
II. claim against clear title.
(A) I only (C) Both I and II
(B) II only (D) Neither I nor II

264. Select from the following the one that is not an encumbrance against real property.
(A) Construction lien (C) Attachment
(B) Judgment (D) Covenant of seizin

265. A deed to real property has the statement "subject to an easement." The term "subject to" would mean the burdened land is
(A) appurtenant. (C) encumbered.
(B) a liability. (D) restricted.

266. Permission to use property by the giving of an easement creates
(A) a license. (C) an encumbrance.
(B) a lien. (D) a prescription.

267. Which of the following is an encumbrance, yet not a lien?
(A) A mortgage
(B) A deed restriction
(C) A trust deed
(D) Unpaid property taxes

268. There are two types of encumbrances. One type involves money; the other type affects the use of the property. Which one of the following affects the use of the property?
(A) Easement (C) Tax lien
(B) Trust deed (D) Mechanic's lien

269. Which of the following statements about encumbrances is true?
(A) An income tax levy may become a lien, but is not an encumbrance.
(B) Title insurance is not generally available for encumbered property.
(C) All specific liens are voluntary liens.
(D) Buyers commonly accept deeds to property which is encumbered.

270. Unpaid real property taxes are described as being
(A) a lien.
(B) an encroachment.
(C) a judgment.
(D) an assessment.

271. Which of the following is created when real estate is pledged as security for a loan?
(A) An easement
(B) A restriction
(C) A lien
(D) An encroachment

272. A lien can be created by
(A) posting a notice of non-responsibility.
(B) filing a trust deed of record.
(C) creating a deed restriction when selling a property.
(D) all of the above.

273. Which of the following statements regarding encumbrances is not true?
(A) All encumbrances are liens.
(B) All liens are encumbrances.
(C) Deed restrictions are a form of encumbrance.
(D) Encroachments may properly be regarded as encumbrances.

274. Which of the following may be a lien against real property?
(A) A condition
(B) A judgment
(C) An easement
(D) A covenant

275. Which of the following is a lien?
(A) Easement
(B) Zoning regulation
(C) Attachment
(D) All of the above

276. Which of the following encumbrances would constitute a lien on real property?
(A) Mortgage
(B) Easement
(C) Encroachment
(D) Restriction

277. Which of the following is not a lien on real property?
(A) Charges for street improvements
(B) Unpaid telephone bill
(C) Special assessment
(D) Unpaid property taxes

278. Which of the following is a lien?
(A) An encroachment
(B) An easement
(C) A quiet title action
(D) An attachment

279. Which of the following encumbrances must be filed of record to be effective?
(A) An easement
(B) A construction lien
(C) A lease
(D) All of the above

280. Which of the following statements regarding encumbrances is true?
I. An encumbrance may diminish the value of a piece of property.
II. A specific lien is an encumbrance against a particular parcel of real estate.
III. Encumbrances are always liens.
(A) I only
(B) III only
(C) I and II only
(D) I, II and III

281. A restriction is considered to be which of the following?
(A) An abstract
(B) A color of title
(C) An encumbrance
(D) A lien

282. In the language of real estate, which of the following terms does not belong with the others?
(A) Tenancy in common
(B) Hypothecation
(C) Second mortgage
(D) Subordination

283. Under the Uniform Commercial Code, the document used to create a lien against articles of personal property is a
(A) chattel mortgage.
(B) financial statement.
(C) security agreement.
(D) bill of sale.

ANSWERS

To practice questions. If you chose the wrong letter, here's the right one! The explanations are designed to clarify your understanding.

1. **A** Regardless of the type of estate the owner has (absolutely vested, defeasible fee, or life estate), it can be free and clear or it can be subject to interests which burden it. Such interests are called encumbrances. An encumbrance is the opposite of an appurtenance, i.e., something that benefits the title. Encroachments are a type of encumbrance. A subordination occurs when one encumbrancer gives up priority in favor of another encumbrancer.
2. **B** An encroachment occurs when improvements on neighboring property cross over the lot line. Encroachments are encumbrances, but not liens. A lien is an encumbrance which makes the property collateral for a debt, such as a mortgage, trust deed, tax, etc. The term "title right" is frequently used to describe an appurtenance, but not an encumbrance.
3. **C** An easement is a right of use of another's property. A devise is a gift of real property in a will. An abstract is a summary of the chain of title to a property. A riparian right is any right to a stream enjoyed by an owner whose property lies along the stream.
4. **C** An estate and an easement are both interests in property. An estate is a right of possession. A remainder and a reversionary interest are both estates (right to future possession). A lease is also an estate. An easement, however is a right of use, rather than a right of possession, so it is not an estate.
5. **B** A lease is a right of possession, unlike an easement, which is a right of use. A deed restriction is a covenant in a deed where the buyer agrees to do, or not to do, certain things with the property in the future. A mortgage is a lien on property to make it collateral for a debt.
6. **C** An easement appurtenant is a right of use appurtenant to the property which benefits from it, while simultaneously being an encumbrance on the property over which it runs. Although rare, an easement can be created by prescription, which is when someone uses another's land for a long time with the intent to claim an easement over it. Adverse possession is similar to prescription, except that, instead of using the other's land, the claimant possesses it, with the intent to claim ownership instead of an easement. Trespass is using or possessing another's land without any legal right to do so.
7. **A** An encumbrance is anything which burdens the title. Trust deeds, judgments, and property taxes are liens, that is, encumbrances created to enforce the collection of money. An easement, however is a right of use.
8. **B** An estate and an easement are both interests in property. An estate is a right of possession, where an easement is a right of use. The property which benefits from the easement is the dominant estate or tenement, and the property over which it runs is the servient estate or tenement. An easement is normally appurtenant to the dominant estate and an encumbrance on the servient. A lien is an encumbrance where money is owed, such as a mortgage.
9. **A** An easement is a right of use. An easement is normally appurtenant to the dominant estate and an encumbrance on the servient. An appurtenance runs with the land, so an easement appurtenant could be said to be permanent. A license is also permission to use another's land, but the right is revocable. A party wall separates apartments, condominiums, and other areas from each other. A riparian right is any right to a stream enjoyed by an owner whose property lies along the stream.
10. **C** The term "encumbrance" refers to any interest which burdens the estate held by the owner. Therefore, it includes mortgages and other liens, easements, restrictive covenants, profits, and many other interests. An easement is a right of use, while a lien is an interest which makes the property collateral for a debt. Liens are classed as specific (reach only one property) or general (reach all property owned by the debtor). Restrictions are encumbrances if they are covenants prohibiting certain uses. Restrictions are not the same as easements.
11. **D** The property which benefits from the easement is the dominant estate or tenement, and the property over which it runs is the servient estate or tenement. An easement appurtenant is appurtenant to the dominant estate and an encumbrance on the servient. A lien is an encumbrance where money is owed, such as a mortgage. A license is permission to use another's property but, unlike an easement, is personal, not appurtenant, and is revocable.

12. **A** The question refers only to the property over which the easement runs, which is the property burdened (encumbered), i.e., the servient tenement. The dominant tenement benefits from an appurtenance.

13. **C** The term "encumbrance" refers to any interest which burdens the estate held by the owner. Therefore, it includes mortgages and other liens, easements, restrictive covenants, profits, and many other interests. Normally an easement is an "easement appurtenant," meaning that it is simultaneously an appurtenance to one property, and an encumbrance on another.

14. **B** An easement is a right of use, not a right of possession. A right of possession is an estate, and is either an ownership interest (freehold) or tenancy without ownership (less than freehold). Nevertheless, an easement is an encumbrance on the property over which it runs, so it is an interest in that property. The creation of an easement is in the nature of a contract, and all contracts involving real property in Oregon must usually be in writing.

15. **B** Since the document creates a right of use, it is either an easement or a license. An easement is granted to a person (easement in gross), or as an appurtenance to a person's real estate (easement appurtenant). A license is also granted to a person, but is revocable. In this case, it is most likely an easement in gross rather than a license, because, by recording the document it appears that the grantor wishes to make it permanent. If it were a right of possession, it could be a lease.

16. **B** An easement benefits one property and burdens another. It continues regardless if either property is sold, so it is an encumbrance on the burdened property (servient tenement) and an appurtenance to the property it benefits (dominant tenement). A fixture is personal property which has be come involved with the real estate so it is now considered part of the real estate. A lien makes the real estate collateral for a debt.

17. **D** Usually, when an easement exists it is simultaneously an encumbrance on the property over which it runs, and an appurtenance to the property which it benefits. The property benefited is called the "dominant tenement" (dominant estate) and the property burdened is the "servient tenement" (servient estate). Unless the easement was specifically created to be exclusive, then the owner of the servient tenement (servient tenant) may use the it also. Prescription is only one of many ways easements can be created. Any type of easement can be created by any of the legal ways that easements can be formed. Easements can be terminated in many ways, one of which is merger. Merger occurs when both properties are merged into one ownership.

18. **B** When there is an easement, the property over which the easement runs is called the servient estate or servient tenement. The property which benefits from the easement is the dominant estate or tenement. The easement is normally appurtenant to the dominant tenement and an encumbrance on the servient.

19. **A** An easement always benefits one property, which is called the dominant tenement (estate), and burdens the property over which it runs, which is called the servient tenement (estate).

20. **A** When an easement has been created there are a limited number of ways in which it can be terminated. None of them allow the servient tenant to take back any of the rights held by the dominant tenant without the dominant tenant's voluntary agreement.

21. **D** This question refers only to an easement appurtenant, not an easement in gross. When the easement is appurtenant, all items are required except that there need not be a common border.

22. **A** The creation of an easement is in the nature of a contract, and all contracts involving real property in Oregon must usually be in writing. An easement cannot be unilaterally canceled by the servient tenant, but the dominant tenant may relinquish it at any time. Since an easement appurtenant is a title right, it is of indefinite duration and runs with the land.

23. **A** The terms "ingress" and "egress" mean "entrance" and "exit." An easement could be granted for a person's lifetime or with some expiration date, but is normally granted indefinitely. Easements are not usually created for just any lawful purpose, but rather for some specific use(s). An easement by way of necessity is used when the dominant tenement is landlocked.

24. **C** Appurtenances are items which are considered to be part of the land, and can be physical, such as a structure, or intangible, such as an easement. Encumbrances are matters which burden the title and, like appurtenances, they run with the land also. When an easement appurtenant is created, it is appurtenant to the dominant tenement (the property which benefits from it, and an encumbrance on the servient (the property over which the easement runs).

25. **D** Since this is an easement appurtenant, it does have a dominant estate and is an interest in land which can be transferred with the land or separately.

Easements are rights of use, not of possession. A right of possession is an estate.

26. **B** When an easement appurtenant is created, it is appurtenant to the dominant tenement (the property which benefits from it), and simultaneously an encumbrance on the servient tenement (the property over which the easement runs). An encumbrance cannot be terminated by the owner of the encumbered property. The encumbrance must be released by the party holding the encumbrance, in this case, the dominant tenant. An estate is a possessory interest, where an easement is a right of use.

27. **C** Ingress and egress mean going in and coming out. An easement is typically created for specific use(s), but not always. If the type is not specified, the easement probably allows any reasonable use. When an easement appurtenant is created, it is appurtenant to the dominant tenement (the property which benefits from it), and an encumbrance on the servient tenement (the property over which the land runs). Both appurtenances and encumbrances remain on the title following a sale. The buyer receives the property and enjoys the appurtenance, but takes title subject to all encumbrances.

28. **C** When an easement appurtenant is created, it is appurtenant to the dominant tenement (the property which benefits from it), and simultaneously an encumbrance on the servient tenement (the property over which the easement runs). An easement in gross is where the easement is granted to an individual, or company instead of as an appurtenance to a parcel of land. An appurtenance runs with the land, so if the owner of the dominant tenement sells it, the buyer continues to enjoy the easement.

29. **C** An easement is frequently created for ingress and egress (meaning going in and coming out), but it can be created for any other use(s). It is an appurtenance to the dominant tenement (the property which is benefited by the easement), and an encumbrance on the servient tenement (the property over which the easement runs). An easement can be terminated by merger, that is, if either party purchases the other's property, or if a third party buys both properties. When both parcels are owned by the same person, all rights become one set of rights to one unified parcel, and the lines dividing the interests are erased, including the easement. An easement appurtenant can be created by any number of methods, only one of which is prescription.

30. **B** Since the easement is appurtenant to the one parcel and an encumbrance on the other, it need not be mentioned in the deed when either parcel is sold. Failing to mention it in the deed cannot extinguish it because both appurtenances and encumbrances run with the land.

31. **A** When an easement appurtenant is created, it is appurtenant to the dominant tenement (the property which benefits from it). Appurtenances are items which are considered to be part of the land, and can be physical, such as a structure, or intangible, such as an easement. Since they are part of the land, they pass to a new owner, whether recited in the deed or not.

32. **B** Ingress and egress mean going in and coming out. When an easement appurtenant is created, it is appurtenant to the dominant tenement (the property which benefits from it). Appurtenances are items which are considered to be part of the land, and can be physical, such as a structure, or intangible, such as an easement. Since they are part of the land, they pass to a new owner, whether recited in the deed or not.

33. **D** When an easement appurtenant is created, it is appurtenant to the dominant tenement (the property which benefits from it). Appurtenances are items which are considered to be part of the land, and can be physical, such as a structure, or intangible, such as an easement. Since they are part of the land, they pass to a new owner, whether recited in the deed or not.

34. **B** There is no federal law relating to easements; they are governed solely by state law. When an easement appurtenant is created, it is appurtenant to the dominant tenement (the property which benefits from it), and simultaneously an encumbrance on the servient tenement (the property over which the easement runs). An encumbrance cannot be terminated by the owner of the encumbered property, even by selling the property. The new owner must take title subject to the easement. It is possible to create an easement that is an encumbrance on the servient tenement, but granted to an individual or a company, rather than as an appurtenance to a parcel of real estate. Such easements are called easements in gross.

35. **D** Since an easement is normally appurtenant to one parcel and an encumbrance on the other, it survives a sale of either parcel.

36. **A** Normally an easement is an encumbrance on the servient tenement and an appurtenance to the dominant tenement, thus a sale of either parcel does not affect the easement. Any owner can convey any or all of the sticks in the bundle of rights to another, thus the dominant tenant could convey the easement back to the owner of the dominant tenement.

37. **D** When an easement appurtenant is created, it is appurtenant to the dominant tenement (the property which benefits from it), and simultaneously an encumbrance on the servient tenement (the property over which the easement runs). An appurtenance runs with the land, whether mentioned in the deed, or not.

38. **A** An easement in gross (as opposed to an easement appurtenant) is an easement where there is no dominant tenement. Therefore, while it is an encumbrance on the servient tenement, it cannot be an appurtenance to the dominant tenement.

39. **A** An easement appurtenant is a right of use which is appurtenant to the property which benefits from it (the dominant tenement), while simultaneously being an encumbrance on the property over which it runs (the servient tenement). An easement in gross is also an encumbrance, but is not appurtenant to another property. Instead, an easement in gross is granted to a person or company. Utility company easements are almost always easements in gross. An easement by prescription is created when someone uses another's land for the statutory time period with the intent to claim an easement.

40. **C** An easement appurtenant is a right of use which is appurtenant to the property which benefits from it, while simultaneously being an encumbrance on the property over which it runs. An easement in gross is also an encumbrance, but is not appurtenant to another property. Instead, an easement in gross is granted to a person or company. Utility company easements are almost always easements in gross. An exclusive easement is one where the servient tenant may not also use the easement; it is for the exclusive use of the dominant tenant. A specific lien makes a specific parcel of real property collateral for a debt. A declaration of restrictions is a list of restrictive covenants in a subdivision.

41. **D** An easement appurtenant is a right of use which is appurtenant to the property which benefits from it, while simultaneously being an encumbrance on the property over which it runs. An easement in gross is also an encumbrance on a servient tenement, but is not appurtenant to another property. Instead, an easement in gross is granted to a person or company. Utility company easements are almost always easements in gross. An easement by way of necessity occurs when an owner is landlocked and asks the county to create a right of way across adjacent land to gain access. An easement by prescription is created when someone uses another's land for the statutory time period with the intent to claim an easement.

42. **C** An easement appurtenant is a right of use which is appurtenant to the property which benefits from it, while simultaneously being an encumbrance on the property over which it runs. An easement in gross is also an encumbrance on a servient tenement, but is not appurtenant to another property. Instead, an easement in gross is granted to a person or company. Utility company easements are almost always easements in gross.

43. **C** An easement appurtenant is a right of use which is appurtenant to the property which benefits from it, while simultaneously being an encumbrance on the property over which it runs. An easement in gross is also an encumbrance, but is not appurtenant to another property. Instead, an easement in gross is granted to a person or company. Utility company easements are almost always easements in gross.

44. **B** An easement appurtenant is a right of use which is appurtenant to the property which benefits from it, while simultaneously being an encumbrance on the property over which it runs. An easement in gross is also an encumbrance on the servient tenement, but is not appurtenant to another property. Instead, an easement in gross is granted to a person or company. Utility company easements are almost always easements in gross. An easement by prescription is created when someone uses another's land for the statutory time period with the intent to claim an easement. A license is revocable permission to use another's land.

45. **B** An easement appurtenant is a right of use which is appurtenant to the property which benefits from it, while simultaneously being an encumbrance on the property over which it runs. An easement in gross is also an encumbrance on a servient tenement, but is not appurtenant to another property. Instead, an easement in gross is granted to a person or company. Utility company easements are almost always easements in gross. An encroachment is when someone constructs improvements that cross over onto a neighbor's land. A riparian right is any of several rights that an owner has to a stream when the owner's property lies along the stream.

46. **B** An easement appurtenant is a right of use which is appurtenant to the property which benefits from it, while simultaneously being an encumbrance on the property over which it runs. An easement in gross is also an encumbrance over the servient tenement, but is not appurtenant to another property. Instead, an easement in gross is granted to a person or company. Utility company easements are almost

always easements in gross. An easement by way of necessity occurs when an owner is landlocked and asks the county to create a right of way across adjacent land to gain access. A license is revocable permission, not an easement. An easement by prescription is created when someone uses another's land for the statutory time period with the intent to claim an easement.

47. **B** Normally, an easement is appurtenant to a parcel (easement appurtenant). An easement in gross is where the easement is granted to an individual, or company, instead of as an appurtenance to a parcel of land. An easement in gross, while not appurtenant to a parcel of land, is nevertheless an encumbrance on the property over which it runs. Encumbrances, the same as appurtenances, run with the land, so the easement in gross survives a sale.

48. **C** A community drive is commonly created to afford better use of land when the lots are narrow. Each lot enjoys an easement appurtenant on the other side of the common boundary, so that both owners have joint use of the driveway. Note that the easements must be appurtenant, rather than in gross, since the easements must be transferable with the title.

49. **C** A community drive allows adjacent owners to share a driveway. Each has an easement appurtenant over a strip of the other's land. As with any easement appurtenant, the easements run with the land. If either owner dies, whoever inherits the land will automatically get the easement, since it is an appurtenance.

50. **B** An easement by prescription is created in much the same way as ownership is gained by adverse possession. The main difference is that in creating an easement by prescription the claimant used the property, where in creating ownership by adverse possession, the claimant possessed the property. An easement by way of necessity occurs when an owner is landlocked and asks the county to order a right of way across adjacent land to gain access. An easement in gross is an easement which is an encumbrance on the servient tenement, but granted to an individual or company, rather than as an appurtenance to a parcel of land.

51. **D** An encroachment occurs when improvements intrude on adjacent property, so if the elements required for prescription are met, the encroachment could ripen into an easement by prescription. An easement of necessity is created through government action for an owner who is landlocked. A license, however, is revocable permission. Since there was no permission, the encroachment cannot become a license.

52. **B** An easement by prescription occurs when someone uses land without the owner's permission. the legal requirements are that the use must have been continuous for at least ten years, with the knowledge of the owner but without the owner's permission (hostile), open and notorious (not covert) and under claim of right. There is no tax bill for the easement as such, but even if there were, there is no requirement that the claimant pay the taxes.

53. **B** A claim of an easement by prescription is a cloud on the title, so it could be removed by a suit to quiet title. However, after ten years the claimant will have perfected the claim, so the suit to quiet title would be ineffective. Permission, however, destroys the element of hostility which is one of the elements required to perfect a claim of an easement by prescription.

54. **D** Since there was permission, there cannot be an easement by prescription. Using the land with permission destroys the element of hostility. An easement by necessity occurs when an owner is landlocked.

55. **D** To acquire an easement by prescription (or title by adverse possession) requires the element of hostility. Hostility cannot exist when the claimant has permission to use the land.

56. **D** To create an easement by prescription requires the element of hostility. There is no hostility when using another's land with permission.

57. **B** Using another's property without the owner's permission for ten years creates the right to demand an easement by prescription if the use was with the owner's knowledge and without the owner's permission, and if the use was hostile, actual and notorious.

58. **C** An easement by way of necessity occurs when an owner is landlocked and asks the county to order a right of way across adjacent land to gain access. An easement by prescription is created when someone uses another's land for the statutory time period with the intent to claim an easement. An easement in gross is an easement which is an encumbrance on the servient tenement, but granted to an individual or company, rather than as an appurtenance to a parcel of land. A negative easement is a term used to describe a restrictive covenant in a deed. A negative easement is not really an easement at all.

59. **A** Easements by way of necessity are provided for in Oregon Revised Statutes. The procedure is to apply to the county for a "way of necessity." The county then orders the creation of an easement as required to provide access. The landlocked owner must

pay just compensation to the owner of the servient tenement in an amount as directed by the county.

60. **C** An easement by way of necessity occurs when an owner is landlocked and asks the county to order a right of way across adjacent land to gain access. An easement by prescription is created when someone uses another's land for the statutory time period with the intent to claim an easement. Utility company easements are almost always easements in gross, which is to say, easements which are encumbrances on the servient tenement, but granted to the company, rather than as an appurtenance to a parcel of land. An adverse claim is any claim of a party in possession other than the owner.

61. **C** Easments are normally created by an agreement, in which case the document is an expressed grant. There are cases where the grant of an easement could be implied as well. Prescription is a method of acquiring an easement by long and continued use. However, assignment means placing someone else in your shoes in a contract, and has little to do with easements.

62. **B** There are numerous ways in which easements can be created. Most easements are expressed grants, which could be in any written document, including a deed. A contract of sale would normally be with a third party, other than the dominant tenement, so it would not be likely to be a document in which an easement would be created. The word "transitory" means "of short duration."

63. **D** An easement appurtenant is a right of use which is appurtenant to the property which benefits from it, while simultaneously being an encumbrance on the property over which it runs. An easement in gross is also an encumbrance, but is not appurtenant to another property. Instead, an easement in gross is granted to a person or company. A license is revocable permission.

64. **C** Both an easement and a license are a legal right to use another's land. A trespass is being on another's land without a legal right, and without ever having had a legal right. An encroachment is constructing improvements on another's land.

65. **C** When an owner sells his or her land, but retains some rights in the land, this is called a "reservation." In this case the owner reserved an easement across the land.

66. **A** Appurtenances are items which are considered to be part of the land, and can be physical or intangible, such as an easement. Encumbrances are matters which burden the title and, like encumbrances, they run with the land also. When an easement appurtenant is created, it is appurtenant to the dominant tenement, and an encumbrance on the servient. The easement cannot be terminated by the servient tenant. The dominant tenant, since he or she is the one receiving the benefit of the easement, may terminate it in various ways, one of which is abandonment.

67. **B** Easements can be terminated voluntarily (normally a quitclaim deed), or involuntarily by various means. Easements are lost by intentional waiver (abandonment), expiration of a time limit, lack of further need (if created by way of necessity), or if the servient tenant blocks the use of the easement with the knowledge and without the permission of the dominant tenant for ten years (prescription). And if both the dominant and servient tenements become owned by the same person or entity, the principle of merger will extinguish the easement.

68. **B** The easement is a title right of the dominant tenement, so the dominant tenant is in control and can do with it as he or she wishes, including reconveying it to the servient tenant. It is an encumbrance on the servient tenement, so the servient tenant cannot terminate it without action by the dominant tenant.

69. **B** Since the easement is appurtenant to the dominant tenement and an encumbrance on the servient tenement, a sale of either property would not affect the easement. Mere non-use of the easement does not constitute abandonment.

70. **A** This is an example of an easement created by prior use. Note that, since the easement exists legally, there is no requirement for the dominant tenant to pay the servient for using the easement.

71. **A** An easement can be terminated by merger, that is, if either party purchases the other's property, or if a third party buys both properties. When both parcels are owned by the same person, all rights become one set of rights to one unified parcel, and the lines dividing the original rights are erased, including the easement.

72. **C** Merger occurs whenever both properties are owned by the same person or legal entity. It does not matter which one buys the other's property, or if a third party buys them both.

73. **A** An easement can be terminated by merger, that is, if either party purchases the other's property, or if a third party buys both properties. When both parcels are owned by the same person, all rights become one set of rights to one unified parcel, and

the lines dividing the interests are erased, including the easement. An easement appurtenant is an appurtenance to the dominant tenement and simultaneously an encumbrance on the servient. The owner of an encumbered property normally can do nothing about the encumbrance; the holder of the encumbrance is the one who must release it.

74. **A** An easement is normally terminated by the dominant tenant voluntary releasing it. It must be released, not revoked; revocation is for a license. An easement is not revocable. Since the easement is an encumbrance on the servient tenement, the servient tenant has no right to terminate it.

75. **C** A satisfaction is used to extinguish a lien such as a mortgage or judgment. A trust deed is a financing document, used in modern transactions as a substitute for a mortgage. A deed of reconveyance is a release instrument used by a trustee in a trust deed to extinguish the lien of the trust deed from the borrower's title. The usual way to extinguish an easement is for the dominant tenant to convey the easement right to the servient tenant. This can be done with any kind of written expression of the intent to terminate the easement, but a quitclaim deed is commonly used for this purpose. A quitclaim deed conveys all the grantor's right, title and interest in the property at the time of the conveyance.

76. **D** Easements and mortgages are both encumbrances on the servient tenement. If the dominant tenant accepts an easement over property already mortgaged at the time of the creation of the easement, then the mortgage is prior in right, so a foreclosure of the mortgage would extinguish the easement. A voluntary release, such as by quitclaim deed signed by the dominant tenant, would extinguish the easement. A court order, such as would result from a suit to quiet title, would also extinguish an easement.

77. **A** The grantor of the easement must be the servient tenant. Note that the easement is a title right held by the dominant tenant, so the dominant tenant can release it. However, the servient tenant does not have the right to terminate the easement. An easement is an encumbrance on the servient tenement, so it survives a sale of the servient tenement.

78. **C** Since the permission was a grant, it was expressed, not implied. It cannot be appurtenant, since the owner did not specify any property to which it would be an appurtenance. The implication is that the grant was a revocable privilege, and is therefore a license.

79. **D** A tenancy in common is ownership by more than one party at the same time. A leasehold estate is held by a renter or lessee, as opposed to a freehold, which is an ownership. A tenancy at sufferance is a type of leasehold estate, characterized by a situation where the tenant originally had a legal right to possession, but it has ended, and the tenant has held over wrongfully. A license is considered continuing permission to use another's land. "Permission to use land for some limited, specific purpose" could also describe an easement, but that is not a choice.

80. **B** A license is considered continuing permission, which probably best describes permission to use property only during hunting season. An owner might also create an easement which permits the holder to use the easement only during specified times, but it is less likely. An encroachment is when someone constructs improvements that cross over the lot line onto a neighbor's land. A right of way is any access route, whether an easement or deeded.

81. **D** Since permission was given, an easement by prescription is not possible. Easements are not revocable, so a mere license has been created.

82. **D** Unlike an easement appurtenant, an easement in gross, or a profit, a license is not an encumbrance on the property which serves it. Therefore, it is extinguished by a sale, is revocable by the grantor, and cannot be assigned. It is considered continuing permission, and therefore is also extinguished by the death or future incompetence of the grantor. It can even be created verbally. A lease is a right of possession, unlike an easement or a license, which are rights of use.

83. **A** A license is considered continuing permission, as opposed to an easement, which is a right of use. Unlike an easement, a license is not appurtenant to another property, and is extinguished by death or incompetence of the grantor, or if the grantor sells the property. A license is also revocable and cannot be assigned.

84. **B** Unlike an easement appurtenant, an easement in gross, or a profit, a license is not an encumbrance on the property which serves it. Therefore, it is revocable by the grantor and cannot be assigned. It is considered continuing permission.

85. **C** Unlike an easement appurtenant, an easement in gross, or a profit, a license is not an encumbrance on the property which serves it. Therefore, it is extinguished by a sale, is revocable by the grantor, and cannot be assigned. It is considered continuing permission, and therefore is also extinguished by the

death or future incompetence of either party. It can even be created verbally.

86. **B** An easement is created by prescription as a result of continuous use for ten or more years with the knowledge of the servient tenant. Creating an easement by prescription also requires that the use have been actual, notorious and open and hostile. "Hostile" means that the claimant must act as though he or she has a legal right to use the property and defend that right if challenged. By granting permission, the owner ensures that the claimant could never win on the hostility issue, so the public could never gain an easement across the land. The only interest the public could gain is a license, which is revocable and not an encumbrance on the property.

87. **B** A license is considered continuing permission, which probably best describes permission to use property only for fishing. An encroachment is when someone constructs improvements that cross over the lot line onto a neighbor's land. A riparian right is any of several rights of an owner to a stream when the owner's property lies along the stream. A trespass is use or possession of another's land without a legal right to do so.

88. **A** A license, unlike an easement, is not a title right, does not run with the land, is personal to the individual and is revocable.

89. **C** Unlike an easement appurtenant, an easement in gross, or a profit, a license is not an encumbrance on the property which serves it. Therefore, it is extinguished by a sale, is revocable by the grantor, and cannot be assigned. It is considered continuing permission, and therefore is also extinguished by the death or future incompetence of either party.

90. **D** A profit (profit à prendre) is the right to severance of a benefit from another's land. The benefit is usually minerals or crops. A right of emblement is the right of a tenant to harvest crops after the termination of a tenancy.

91. **D** A trespass is use or possession of another's land without a legal right to do so. A license is considered continuing permission to use another's property, usually for a specific purpose. A profit is a right to severance of a benefit from another's land, usually crops or minerals.

92. **B** Since it was a personal right, then it cannot be an easement appurtenant. Personal rights must be either easements in gross, licenses or profits. An easement in gross and a profit are not revocable, whereas a license can be revoked at any time.

93. **A** A profit is personal to the individual, not a title right. At the same time it is an encumbrance on the property from which the benefit is to be severed. An easement in gross is also personal. A license is extinguished upon a sale, so not only is it not a title right, it is not even an encumbrance on the servient tenement. An easement, however, is normally an appurtenance to one parcel while being an encumbrance on the other.

94. **C** All easements and licenses are rights to use land owned by another. The difference is whether they are title rights, encumbrances and revocable or irrevocable.

95. **A** The property which benefits from the easement is the dominant estate or tenement, and the property over which it runs is the servient estate or tenement. An easement is normally appurtenant to the dominant estate and an encumbrance on the servient. An easement in gross is granted to an individual, rather than as an appurtenance to the individual's real estate. A license is also a personal right to use another's land, but it is revocable.

96. **B** At first glance it appears that there was an easement by prescription. However, since the use was with permission, there was no hostility, so no easement was created.

97. **B** There is no tax bill for the easement as such. Taxes are levied according to value, so the more valuable the property, the higher the bill. When there is an easement, one property gains in value and the other loses, so the tax bills are theoretically apportioned accordingly.

98. **C** Normally, the way the seller restricts the grantee's future use of the property is with a covenant. The covenant is typically created as an encumbrance on the grantee's title.

99. **A** Private restrictions can be many pages long, as where a developer of a subdivision creates a set of restrictions for the entire subdivision, which also normally provide that any lot owner can enforce any of the provisions against any other lot owner. Such restrictions are commonly called covenants, or sometimes other expressions such as "general plan restrictions (covenants)," declaration of subdivision covenants," and so on.

100. **C** Restrictions can be created by governmental action, such as zoning and building codes, or they can be created by private contract, usually between a buyer and a seller. Such private restrictions are almost always stipulated in the deed,

which is an agreement and must be in writing. However, they could also be created in a separate contract.

101. **C** Deed covenants are normally created in a deed, although they can be created by a separate agreement. In a subdivision, a developer will commonly create a long set of covenants, record it once, and then refer to it in each deed. Deeds with covenants, or references to covenants are called covenant deeds. Only private parties create deed covenants. Public land use restrictions include zoning and building codes, among others.

102. **D** Land use restrictions are either public (city or county), such as zoning and building codes, or private. In a deed, the seller is the grantor and the buyer is the grantee. Therefore, deed restrictions would be created by the grantor, not the grantee.

103. **A** Private, contractual restrictions are encumbrances on the title, but not liens. A lien is a type of encumbrance which makes the property collateral for a debt. Constructive notice is that notice given to the world of one's rights in a contract when the contract has been recorded in the public records, or that the notice of his or her rights that an owner in possession gives to the world by the fact of being in possession.

104. **A** Deed restrictions in a subdivision are commonly a two-way street. While an individual owner is restricted (encumbered), the same restriction is applied to other owners, in which case it is a benefit because it enforces conformity and enhances property values. Therefore, subdivision covenants are considered encumbrances, even though they may actually be benefits at the same time. Covenants are usually created in a deed, but can be created any time by mutual agreement.

105. **D** Restrictions can be created by governmental action, such as zoning and building codes, or they can be created by private contract, usually between a buyer and a seller. Such private restrictions are almost always stipulated in the deed. The earnest money agreement should also state the restrictions, but as a means of creating an agreement for the language the deed will eventually contain.

106. **D** Deed restrictions (covenants) are private contractual agreements. Although not always, they are normally created as an encumbrance on the property which is restricted. The nature of an encumbrance is that it survives a transfer of the title, so it runs with the land.

107. **B** Land use restrictions can be public, such as zoning codes created by cities and counties, or private, created by contract between a buyer and a seller. The seller normally states the restriction in the deed when conveying title to the buyer.

108. **C** Deed restrictions (covenants) are private contractual agreements. Although not always, they are normally created as an encumbrance on the property which is restricted. The nature of an encumbrance is that it survives a transfer of the title, so it runs with the land. The party with the right to enforce the covenant may sue for damages, but the usual remedy is to seek an injunction.

109. **B** Privately created covenants could be enforced by a suit for damages, resulting in a money judgment against the party violating the covenant. However, the customary remedy is a suit to enjoin the offending action. A suit to enjoin is a suit which seeks an injunction.

110. **B** Minimum dollar value of improvements is difficult to enforce because the courts may hold the dollar amount to be an absolute figure. Even tying the figure to an index depends on the validity of the index in the future.

111. **C** Privately created covenants could be enforced by a suit for damages, resulting in a money judgment against the party violating the covenant. However, the customary remedy is a suit to enjoin the offending action. A suit to enjoin is a suit which seeks an injunction. The government has no authority to enforce private restrictions.

112. **B** Subdivision covenants benefit every owner of a lot in the subdivision, so they are normally drafted so that they can be enforced by any owner on any other owner. Originally the developer would have had the right to enforce the covenants also, but once all the lots have been sold the developer is no longer an owner in the subdivision. Planning and zoning commissions have no authority to enforce private agreements.

113. **B** A writ of mandamus is a court order compelling someone to perform some action. Equitable estoppel occurs when justice demands that someone be barred from asserting a right. An indictment is an accusation of criminal wrongdoing. The normal remedies to enforce a deed covenant are suit to enjoin or a suit for damages.

114. **D** Private parties are free to enter into any contract they desire, regardless of the burden or benefit to the parties. Therefore, if the covenants are a great burden, it is irrelevant. Nor need covenants be based on general welfare or esthetic values. However,

zoning ordinances and other exercises of police power by the government must be based on the general health, safety, morals or welfare.

115. **D** Deed restrictions (covenants) are private encumbrances, typically created by a seller and stated in the deed. They can be any legal restriction the parties agree to. ORS 93.270 (1) provides "No person conveying … fee title to real property shall include in an instrument for such purpose a provision … restricting the use of the real property by any person or group of persons by reason of color, race, religion, national origin or physical or mental handicap." Otherwise, a deed restriction can be anything the seller wants it to be.

116. **D** Oregon Revised Statutes 93.270 provides "No person conveying … fee title to real property shall include in an instrument for such purpose a provision … restricting the use of the real property by any person or group of persons by reason of color, race, religion, national origin or physical or mental handicap … ," and "any such provision … is void and unenforceable."

117. **B** Oregon Revised Statutes 93.270 provides "No person conveying … fee title to real property shall include in an instrument for such purpose a provision … restricting the use of the real property by any person or group of persons by reason of color, race, religion, national origin or physical or mental handicap … ," and "any such provision … is void and unenforceable." Otherwise, a deed restriction may be anything that the parties agree to.

118. **C** Since the restriction is a covenant, rather than a condition, the only remedies are damages, specific performance or suit to enjoin the offending action. The fact that one owner has violated the covenants does not give others the right to do so as well. It is possible, that the covenants have expired, although in 30 years it is not likely.

119. **A** An injunction results from a suit to enjoin. Recovery of the title is possible only if it is a condition, not a covenant. "Lis pendens" means "pending litigation."

120. **A** A common estate created when a right of reverter is reserved by the grantor is an estate subject to a condition subsequent. In contrast, covenants are mere encumbrances on the title which can be enforced by a suit to enjoin or a suit for damages. Covenants can be a title right or merely a personal obligation. General plan restrictions consist of many individual covenants applied to all the lots in a subdivision.

121. **C** Deed conditions contain a right of reverter (estate in reversion), so the penalty for violation by the grantee is forfeiture of the title back to the grantor. Deed covenants, on the other hand, contain no reversionary rights, and are considered encumbrances on the title. Covenants can be enforced by suit for damages, suit for specific performance, or by a suit to enjoin the offending action.

122. **A** A condition creates a free and clear fee title with a right of reverter. A covenant creates an encumbrance on a fee title absolutely vested.

123. **C** Deed covenants are encumbrances on the title, and are generally enforced by a suit to enjoin the offending action or a suit for damages. A condition creates a defeasible fee, so violating the condition can result in forfeiture of title.

124. **C** Private restrictions on an owner's use of the property are typically created by a seller, and reference to them is usually in the deed. They can be as simple as one single restriction on one buyer for the benefit of the seller, or they can be many pages long, as where a developer of a subdivision creates a set of restrictions for the entire subdivision, which also normally provide that any lot owner can enforce any of the provisions against any other lot owner. In either case, they are called covenants.

125. **A** A deed covenant benefits one person or property, so the person benefited by the covenant can always release it. Covenants are contractual, so a stated time limit would normally be enforceable as well. When two separate properties merge into one ownership, all rights pertaining to both properties are merged into one title. In the merger, any divisions are erased. Thus merger of a dominant and servient tenement extinguishes an easement. And here, merger of the property burdened and the property benefited by the covenant extinguishes the covenant. Public agencies do not generally have the authority to set aside private contracts.

126. **A** A deed covenant benefits one person or property, so the person or property owner benefited by the covenant can always agree to release it. Normally this would be accomplished by a quitclaim deed. A writ of attachment is a provisional lien. Evicting a tenant extinguishes the leasehold rights, but would not necessarily extinguish other rights the tenant may hold in the property.

127. **D** Zoning ordinances are a legal use of police power, but are only constitutional if they are not capricious and arbitrary and promote the general health, safety, morals and welfare. Creating a special right for one owner would likely be considered capricious and arbitrary, and certainly does not promote

the general health, safety, morals or welfare. The earnest money agreement is likely extinguished by the later contract at closing, so the earnest money agreement would be a poor place to create such an agreement, although the nature of the restriction should be stated there. Similarly, a side contract with the buyer is less secure than a deed covenant.

128. **C** Deed covenants can be created with any time limit the grantor desires. They can also be personal to the owner or created as a title right to one property and an encumbrance on the other. Normally, they are created as an encumbrance on one property and an appurtenance to another. They can be enforceable on all property owners (as in a subdivision), but they can also be created to benefit just one property. Since they are normally created as a title right, they typically run with the land and impact all future owners of the property.

129. **D** Even though the restriction was not mentioned in the deed, the fact that it was recorded means that the encumbrance survived from owner to owner. A sale of a property does not extinguish a properly created encumbrance. Buyers always take title to all encumbrances existing at the time of the conveyance, whether the encumbrance was mentioned in the deed or not.

130. **C** A deed restriction is created and enforced by private parties. Zoning ordinances are created and enforced by public agencies. If both are in force, then an owner must comply with both. Logically, if the owner complies with the more restrictive of the two, the owner will normally have complied with both.

131. **B** A cloud is defined as a possible interest in property, as yet unproved; a claim. An easement in gross is an irrevocable personal right to use another's land. A lien makes a property collateral for a debt.

132. **A** A quiet title is a title with no clouds. A cloud is a claim or possible interest. Therefore, a quiet title action (suit to quiet title) is a suit asking for a court order extinguishing any claims.

133. **A** A quitclaim deed conveys all the grantor's right, title and interest in the property, so it could conceivably be used in any of the cases listed. However, it is normally only used to convey a possible interest, i.e., remove a cloud.

134. **C** There are only two ways to remove a cloud from a title – voluntarily, or involuntarily. If the claimant will release the claim voluntarily, any deed will accomplish the desired result, but the most common deed to use is the quitclaim deed. A quitclaim deed contains no warranty of title, so the grantor is not promising that he or she actually has an interest in the property. Involuntary removal of a cloud is accomplished by successfully bringing a suit to quiet title or a suit for slander of title (if the cloud was created deliberately).

135. **B** A cloud is a claim or possible interest. Clouds are frequently caused by errors, such as, for example an incorrect legal description in a deed. To remove the cloud, we simply correct the error. When someone has a claim or interest in your property, having them give you a quitclaim deed would convey all their interest to you without creating any warranty that they did, indeed, have an interest to convey. However, to correct an error in a legal description, we commonly just correct the error on the original deed and re-record it. Although a quitclaim deed is commonly used, it is not the only way to remove a cloud.

136. **D** Purchasing title insurance has no effect on the condition of the title. Title insurance is not even likely to be enforceable, since title insurance policies normally exclude from coverage any defects which the insured party already knew about. An affidavit of title is a warranty which, the same as title insurance, does not change the condition of the title. An affidavit of title is not a conveyance, so it does not operate to convey the claimant's interest.

137. **A** A cloud is a type of encumbrance characterized as a claim or a possible interest. An encroachment clouds the property being encroached on, because the encroaching party may be doing so with the intent to claim ownership. Prescription and adverse possession refer (respectively) to long and continued use or long and continued possession of another's property, with the intent to claim an easement thereon or title thereto.

138. **D** Improvements built on another's land are encroachments, whether deliberate or inadvertent. A license is revocable permission, and is extinguished by a sale, therefore is not considered an encumbrance. A profit is the right to severance of a benefit from another's land.

139. **B** Improvements built on another's land are encroachments, whether deliberate or inadvertent. A party wall is the wall dividing units in a condominium or cooperative. An appurtenance is any right or improvement which runs with the land. Adverse possession means occupying another's land with the intent to obtain title.

140. **C** An encumbrance is anything which burdens the title and is not extinguished by a sale. There

are various kinds of encumbrances, including financial encumbrances (liens), such as mortgages, judgments, property taxes, etc. There are also encumbrances which affect the use, such as easements, deed restrictions, etc. A cloud is a type of encumbrance characterized as a claim or a possible interest. An encroachment clouds the property being encroached on, because the encroaching party may be doing so with the intent to claim ownership.

141. **B** Improvements built on another's land are encroachments, whether deliberate or inadvertent. An easement by necessity can be obtained when an owner is landlocked. An easement in gross is an easement the runs to the individual, rather than being created as an appurtenance to real estate. A license is revocable permission, and is extinguished by a sale, therefore is not considered an encumbrance.

142. **D** Entering another's land without legal right to do so is trespass. The fence constitutes an encroachment. Encroachments are clouds (a possible interest) until the issue is resolved. A cloud can be released by the claimant voluntarily, or by the affected property owner filing a suit to quiet title or a suit for slander of title.

143. **D** When improvements encroach on another's land, they become the property of the other owner, as an appurtenance to the land. Appurtenances are considered real property, not personal property.

144. **B** An owner is entitled to free use of his or her property, including the air space. The tree is an encroachment, so the owner is entitled to do as he or she pleases with the parts which encroach. Presumably, the main trunk does not encroach, so the owner is not permitted to cut the tree down. Even though an owner may remove the branches, an owner cannot cut the tree so severely as to cause the tree permanent harm without prior notice to the neighbor.

145. **B** Standard title insurance policies usually exclude encroachments from the coverage. Obtaining a certification from the seller would not prevent the encroachment from existing nor would it prevent a neighbor from presenting a successful claim for a prescriptive easement. All it would do is make the seller liable to the buyer for damages the buyer might suffer. The proper person to ask about property boundaries is a surveyor.

146. **C** The basic rule of priority for encumbrances is the date the encumbrance was recorded. As to judgments, it is the date the judgment was docketed in the records of the appropriate court. Property taxes and special assessments are common exceptions, since they are always first in priority. Construction liens are frequently ahead of all liens (except property taxes), depending on the nature of the construction lien. And voluntary subordination agreements can alter the normal order of priority.

147. **C** Priority of encumbrances is normally set by recording date. The holder of a senior (prior) encumbrance can voluntarily agree to become junior (subordinate) to another lienholder.

148. **A** Special assessments and property taxes are ahead of all other encumbrances, regardless of their recording date. The priority date of judgments is usually the date the judge entered the judgment on the court docket.

149. **D** The priority of liens is generally in date order. The date is the recording date for liens that are recorded, or the docket date for judgments. Exceptions include property taxes and some city liens, which are ahead of all other liens; construction liens (formerly called mechanics liens), which are immediately prior to all other recorded liens; or the possibility that a senior lienholder has agreed to subordinate to another.

150. **D** The recording date sets the priority for most encumbrances, although for judgments it is usually the docket date (the date the judge granted the judgment). Property taxes, however, are ahead of all other encumbrances, regardless of their recording date. Construction liens arising from primary construction projects are ahead of all other recorded liens. Property taxes are not recorded liens, so a construction lien will not be ahead of the tax bill.

151. **A** The priority of liens is generally in date order. The date is the recording date for liens that are recorded, or the docket date for judgments. Exceptions include property taxes and some city liens, which are ahead of all other liens; construction liens (formerly called mechanics liens), which are immediately prior to all other recorded liens; or the possibility that a senior lienholder has agreed to subordinate to another.

152. **B** The priority of liens is generally in date order. The date is the recording date for liens that are recorded, or the docket date for judgments. Exceptions include property taxes and some city liens, which are ahead of all other liens; construction liens, which are immediately prior to all other recorded liens (note that property taxes are not recorded); or the possibility that a senior lienholder has agreed to subordinate to another.

153. **B** The priority of liens is generally in date order. The date is the recording date for liens that are recorded, or the docket date for judgments. Exceptions include property taxes and some city liens, which are ahead of all other liens; construction liens (formerly called mechanics liens), which are immediately prior to all other recorded liens; or the possibility that a senior lienholder has agreed to subordinate to another.
154. **B** If there is a surplus of funds after the foreclosing mortgagee is paid, the surplus is turned over to the borrower. All liens junior to the foreclosing mortgagee are extinguished. However, junior lienholders have a 60-day right of redemption (120 days if the junior lienholder is the federal government).
155. **C** The priority of liens is generally in date order. The date is the recording date for liens that are recorded, or the docket date for judgments. Exceptions include property taxes and some city liens, which are ahead of all other liens; construction liens (formerly called mechanics liens), which are immediately prior to all other recorded liens; or the possibility that a senior lienholder has agreed to subordinate to another.
156. **A** Tax levies for income tax (both state and federal) follow the normal date rule. Only property taxes and special assessments enjoy first priority.
157. **B** Subrogation occurs most commonly in insurance policies where it means that the insured party grants to his or her insurance company the right to sue a third party who caused the loss. A subordination occurs when a senior lienholder agrees voluntarily to become junior to another lienholder. "Senior" and "junior" refer to the priority of liens, which is normally established by the recording date.
158. **D** Liens can be classed as general (reaching all the property of the debtor), or specific (reaching only the property or properties listed in the document creating the lien). An equitable lien would be a lien granted by a court where there is no formal agreement, but justice demands that a lien be created. "Mechanic's lien" and "laborer's lien" are older terms for "construction lien."
159. **B** Liens can be general (reaching all the property of the debtor), or specific (reaching only the property or properties listed in the document creating the lien). Some textbooks use the term "special" instead of "specific." A judgment is an example of a general lien.
160. **D** Liens can be classed as general (reaching all the property of the debtor), or specific (reaching only the property or properties listed in the document creating the lien). A judgment is an example of a general lien.
161. **B** Judgment liens are normally between private parties, not instituted by the government. Liens which reach all property of the debtor are said to be general, as opposed to liens which reach only a specific property, e.g., a mortgage. A blanket lien is a lien which reaches more than one parcel, but it is still considered specific because it reaches only the properties listed in the lien instrument; it doesn't reach all property owned by the debtor.
162. **A** Income tax liens, both state and federal, are general, since they allow the government to reach all the property of the taxpayer.
163. **D** Liens can be classed as general (reaching all the property of the debtor), or specific (reaching only the property or properties listed in the document creating the lien). Liens can also be categorized as voluntary and involuntary, that is, authorized by the owner or not.
164. **A** Construction liens are specific, since they reach only the property the contractor worked on. They are also involuntary, since they are filed against the owner's wishes.
165. **D** All tax liens are involuntary. Income tax liens reach all the taxpayer's property, so they are also general.
166. **C** If a lien reaches everything the debtor owns, i.e. a judgment, then it is a general lien. If it reaches only specified property i.e., property taxes, then it is specific. A blanket mortgage reaches more than one property, but does not indiscriminately reach all the property of the debtor, so it is still considered a specific lien. A lis pendens (notice of lis pendens) is notice that a suit is pending against a property owner. A lis pendens must list the property it intends to reach, so it is also specific.
167. **B** Liens are voluntary or involuntary. Voluntary liens are those which the debtor agreed to and signed. Involuntary liens are liens allowed or imposed by law, such as property taxes, construction liens, judgments, and the like. "Mechanic's lien" is an older term for "construction lien." "Ad valorem" means "according to value," a term used in relation to property taxes. A special assessment is a one-time charge for public improvements, such as street paving, sewer connection, etc.
168. **A** Liens such as mortgages and trust deeds are considered voluntary because the borrower signed the lien instrument as a voluntary act. However, judg-

ments are involuntary, since they result from an adverse court decision.

169. **B** The most common civil lawsuits are suits for damages or to collect a debt. If successful, the judge enters judgment against the debtor. The judgment is a lien against all property of the debtor in the county where the judgment is entered in the appropriate court docket. An injunction is a court order to cease and desist some activity. An executive decree is a court order to the sheriff, usually ordering the sheriff to sell a property at public auction to satisfy a judgment. Assignment is a procedure to transfer contract rights to another.

170. **A** Liens can be general (reaching all the property of the debtor), or specific (reaching only the property or properties listed in the document creating the lien). Some textbooks use the term "special" instead of "specific." A judgment is usually a general lien, because it reaches all the property of the debtor. "Superior" is an alternative term for "senior," as distinguished from an encumbrance that is "junior" in priority. An equitable lien would be a lien granted by a court where there is no formal agreement, but justice demands that a lien be created.

171. **D** A judgment reaches all the property owned by the judgment debtor in the county where the judgment was obtained. A judgment can be transcribed to any other county in the United States, but until it is so transcribed, the debtor's property in other counties remains free of the judgment. Whether the property is the debtor's homestead or not is irrelevant as to whether the judgment reaches the property. The homestead exemption only becomes an issue if the creditor attempts to have the homestead sold at a sheriff's sale.

172. **D** Judgments are normally general liens, so they reach all property, both real and personal, owned by the debtor in the county where the suit occurred and the judgment is docketed in the records of the court. The function of a judgment is to allow the creditor to collect, so judgments reach all assets of the debtor. Therefore, a judgment reaches not only is every piece of real estate owned by the debtor, it even reaches every interest in real estate held by the debtor as well.

173. **C** A judgment immediately reaches all the property of the debtor in the county where it was entered. Until it is transcribed to other counties, the property of the debtor in other counties is still free and clear of the judgment.

174. **A** When a court has entered a judgment against a person and the judgment creditor wishes to proceed against the debtor's real estate, the first step is to file a writ of execution with the court. The writ lists the property to be sold, and becomes the order from the court to the sheriff to sell the property at auction.

175. **C** When a court has entered a judgment against a person and the judgment creditor wishes to proceed against the debtor's real estate, the first step is to file a writ of execution with the court. The writ lists the property to be sold, and becomes the order from the court to the sheriff to sell the property at auction.

176. **D** When a creditor sues to recover a debt the suit seeks a judgment. Once the creditor gains the judgment, if the creditor wishes to force the sale of real estate, the creditor must file a writ of execution with the court, which must identify the property. The court then orders the sheriff to sell the property identified in the writ at public auction to satisfy the judgment. An attachment liens the property of a defendant prior to the issuance of the judgment so the defendant cannot sell it, thus making the asset available to the judgment creditor.

177. **C** When a creditor has file a suit to collect a debt the first step is to obtain judgment. The szecond step is to file a writ of execution with the court. This becomes the order from the judge to the sheriff to sell the property listed in the writ at public auction. When the sheriff sells the property, the successful bidder gets a certificate of sale (sheriff's certificate), which entitles the successful bidder to a sheriff's deed if the property is not redeemed within the statutory time period.

178. **C** A satisfaction is a document signed by a creditor used as evidence that a debt has been paid.

179. **C** When a creditor has file a suit to collect a debt the first step is to obtain judgment. The szecond step is to file a writ of execution with the court. This becomes the order from the judge to the sheriff to sell the property listed in the writ at public auction. When the sheriff sells the property, the successful bidder gets a certificate of sale (sheriff's certificate), which entitles the successful bidder to a sheriff's deed if the property is not redeemed within the statutory time period.

180. **C** A judgment not only reaches all the debtor's property in the county where it is of record, it even reaches all property the debtor should acquire in the future instantly at the moment of taking title. The priority of a judgment is normally the date the judge granted it. Voluntary liens are those which the debtor agreed to, such as a mortgage, trust deed, etc.

A judgment is an involuntary lien because it is imposed on the debtor by the court.

181. **C** Judgments reach all of the real and personal property of the debtor located in the county or counties where it is of record, which means judgments are classed as general liens. The debtor may claim a homestead exemption to protect his or her personal residence from a judgment lien up to the maximum allowed by the Homestead Act.

182. **A** The creditor can usually proceed with the sale, the homestead exemption merely means that the judgment debtor is entitled to a portion of the proceeds to reinvest in a new homestead. If the debtor can demonstrate to the court that the judgment creditor would receive nothing from the sale because the equity is too low, it is possible that the court would not allow the sale.

183. **D** The Homestead Act provides for exemption from execution by a judgment creditor against a personal residence in the maximum amount of $25,000 for a single owner and $33,000 for married owners. It is effective solely against judgment creditors, and not against any other kind of lien.

184. **D** By statute, a homestead exemption is of no force and effect against voluntary liens, government liens such as property taxes and income tax levies, or construction liens. Its usual use is to afford protection of the homestead against judgments.

185. **C** The Homestead Act provides for exemption from execution by a judgment creditor against a personal residence in the maximum amount of $25,000 for a single owner and $33,000 for married owners. It is effective solely against judgment creditors, not against any other kind of lien.

186. **C** The homestead exemption does not exist until a judgment has been entered against the debtor, a writ of execution has been issued against the debtor's homestead, and the debtor has notified the sheriff that the property to be sold is a homestead. The notice can be made by the debtor or by the debtor's attorney.

187. **A** For homesteads located outside an incorporated city, the maximum size that can be claimed as exempt from execution and sale is 160 acres.

188. **A** The maximum size property which can be declared to be a homestead in Oregon is one city block for homesteads lying within an incorporated city, or otherwise 160 acres.

189. **A** The Homestead Act provides for exemption from execution by a judgment creditor against a personal residence. The exemption is lost if the judgment debtor no longer resides on the property. However, being jailed does not mean one has lost one's residence status.

190. **A** The maximum amount of the homestead exemption is $33,000 or $25,000 if single, with lesser amounts for manufactured dwellings.

191. **C** The homestead exemption can be claimed by the debtor, any co-tenant of the debtor, or the attorney for either. The procedure is to notify the sheriff any time after the judgment has been entered, but prior to the date of the sheriff's sale.

192. **C** A homestead exemption is valid only if the debtor takes the exempted funds from the sales proceeds with the intent to reinvest them in a new personal residence. Not doing so within one year will subject the funds to further seizure by creditors.

193. **C** The Homestead Act provides for exemption from execution by a judgment creditor against a personal residence. The exemption is lost if the judgment debtor no longer resides on the property.

194. **C** The term "lis pendens" is Latin for "pending litigation." It is also called a notice of pendency or notice of lis pendens. An attachment is related to a lis pendens. If either an attachment or a notice of pendency is recorded by a plaintiff to a lawsuit, it clouds the defendant's title. Any buyer will take title subject to the plaintiff's eventual judgment. As a technicality, an attachment can be recorded before even filing the suit. The lis pendens is a "notice of pending litigation," so it can be recorded only after the suit has been filed.

195. **C** "Lis pendens" is Latin for "pending lawsuit." A lis pendens (today more commonly called a notice of lis pendens or notice of pendency) is a claim against the defendant's real estate by a plaintiff to a lawsuit. An attachment is similar, but can be recorded before the suit is filed. A judgment is a final judicial order that money is owed to another. A construction lien may be filed by anyone who supplies labor or materials for improvements on another's property.

196. **D** "Lis pendens" is Latin for "pending lawsuit." A lis pendens (today more commonly called a notice of lis pendens or notice of pendency) is a claim against the defendant's real estate by a plaintiff to a lawsuit. Forcible entry is part of the expression "forcible entry and detainer," the term for a suit to evict a tenant. Constructive notice is notice deemed to have been given to the whole world when a document has been recorded, or when a party has taken possession of real estate. "Caveat emptor" is Latin for "let the buyer beware," but there is no such thing as "caveat emptor notice."

197. **B** Both an attachment and a notice of pendency (lis pendens) are devices used by a creditor prior to obtaining judgment, in order to make sure that the debtor does not liquidate assets to avoid later execution. The attachment asks the court to take possession of the property. The notice of pendency provides that a buyer of the asset will take title subject to the eventual claims of the creditor, once judgment is obtained.

198. **B** Both an attachment and a notice of pendency (lis pendens) are devices used by a creditor prior to obtaining judgment in order to make sure that the debtor does not liquidate assets to avoid later execution. The attachment asks the court to take possession of the property. The notice of pendency (notice of lis pendens) provides that a buyer of the asset will take title subject to the eventual claims of the creditor once judgment is obtained.

199. **D** When a suit seeking a judgment is filed, the debtor's property may be free and clear until the judgment is docketed. An attachment is filed to keep the other party from disposing of his or her assets before the judgment is obtained. It must be ordered by the court, but when so ordered is considered a lien against the property listed in the attachment.

200. **D** The purpose of an attachment is to stop a defendant in a lawsuit from selling his or her assets prior to the plaintiff obtaining a judgment. An attachment is a specific lien, since it must list the property to be attached.

201. **D** Death of one or both of the parties in a lawsuit does not normally terminate the suit – their respective estates become the substitute parties. The purpose of an attachment is to stop a defendant in a lawsuit from selling his or her assets prior to the plaintiff obtaining a judgment. Once the judgment is issued it reaches all the defendant's property so the attachment is extinguished as unnecessary.

202. **B** To assist them in collecting for improvements made or materials used on another person's real estate, certain individuals are entitled to file a construction lien against the property. These include laborers, contractors and subcontractors and materials suppliers.

203. **A** A construction may be filed by anyone who supplies labor or materials for improvements on another's property. An estoppel certificate is a statement from a lender declaring the remaining principal balance. Once given to the borrower, the lender is estopped (barred) from demanding any higher amount. A deficiency judgment occurs when a mortgage lender forecloses, a sheriff's sale of the property is held, but the property did not sell for enough to cover the entire debt and costs. A lis pendens (today more commonly called a notice of lis pendens or notice of pendency) is a claim against the defendant's real estate by a plaintiff to a lawsuit to stop the defendant from selling the property so the plaintiff will be able to reach it when a judgment is finally granted.

204. **B** A construction lien is a claim from someone who supplied labor or improvements on someone else's real property. It clouds the title, as a mechanism to assist in collection. Within certain deadlines, the claimant can file suit on the claim and obtain a judgment. In the past, construction liens were called "mechanics' liens." In other states they are called "workers' liens," "labor liens," and other similar terms.

205. **C** A construction may be filed by anyone who supplies labor or materials for improvements on another's property. The claimant must file a claim within a statutory period after substantial completion. The claim of lien should be viewed as a cloud, since it is based merely the word of the claimant that the money is owed. The claimant cannot reach more than the property on which the labor or materials were used. Equitable title refers to the interest of a buyer under a land sales contract.

206. **D** A construction may be filed by anyone who supplies labor or materials for improvements on another's property. Oregon statutes specifically include architects, rental equipment dealers, engineers and landscapers, but do not include real estate agents, building superintendents or others who do not specifically supply labor or materials.

207. **C** Anyone who supplies labor or materials for improvements to real estate is entitled to claim a construction lien if not paid. The statute specifically includes architects and landscape architects, engineers and surveyors.

208. **A** Real estate brokers, appraisers and property managers are not included under the construction lien laws. However, real estate brokers can serve an escrow with a "notice of demand for commission," which requires the escrow to withhold the commission.

209. **C** The construction lien law allows anyone who supplies labor or materials, including rental equipment dealers, to claim a lien against the property if not paid. As an alternative to a construction lien, a claimant may always file a suit directly. The purpose of the con-

struction lien is to allow the claimant to lien the property immediately and without needing to file a suit.

210. **A** The priority of a construction lien for primary construction projects is prior to all other liens except property taxes and special assessments. However, the priority date for construction liens arising from alterations to existing properties is the date the claim of lien was filed.

211. **B** Do not confuse construction loan with a construction lien. The purpose of the construction loan is to provide the builder with the funds to construct the improvements. A construction lien for primary construction projects is immediately prior to all other liens except property taxes and special assessments, even if another lien was recorded before the claim of lien was filed.

212. **D** A certificate of completion would affect a potential construction lien claimant because the deadline for filing the claim is generally 75 days from substantial completion. A notice of non-responsibility means that the property cannot be liened for subsequent labor or materials charges, so this would also affect a potential claimant. Since construction liens are generally ahead of all other recorded liens, a suit to foreclose a previously recorded mortgage would not normally impact the construction lien claimant.

213. **A** A notice of non-responsibility means that the premises cannot be liened for labor or materials charges occurring after its posting. The usual case where an owner would use a notice of non-responsibility is when a tenant orders work done without the owner's authorization.

214. **D** Construction liens are normally extinguished by payment in full and satisfaction or by a suit to quiet title resulting in a court order. The owner can also gain clear title without paying the claim by posting a bond with the court equal to 150% of the amount of the claim, or by posting 150% of the amount of the claim in cash with the county treasurer.

215. **D** A common problem occurs when an owner hires a general contractor who, in turn, hires subcontractors and other workers. If the subcontractors and other workers do not get paid, they are entitled to claim a lien against the owner's property, even though the owner paid the general contractor in full. The owner can gain protection by posting a notice of non-responsibility or by obtaining a release from the subcontractors and workers. Of course, the owner has recourse against the general contractor who failed to pay the subcontractors and workers, so the owner could also gain protection by insisting that the general contractor be bonded in an amount sufficient to cover possible liens.

216. **D** The buyers never know if some subcontractor or worker will file a construction lien. Since the deadline is 75 days after completion, a claim could be filed even after the buyers take title. Lenders insist on special lender's title insurance policies which cover construction liens. Since this shifts the burden onto the title insurance company, the title insurer will normally require that the builder leave a portion of the builder's sale proceeds with the escrow for 75 days with an indemnification agreement in favor of the title insurance company.

217. **A** Liens are general (reaching all the property of the debtor), or specific (reaching only the property or properties listed in the document creating the lien). Liens can also be voluntary or involuntary, that is, authorized by the owner or not. A construction lien reaches only the property where the labor or materials were supplied, so it is a specific lien and not a general lien. Since the property owner did not authorize it, the construction lien is an involuntary lien.

218. **D** There are four generally recognized rights the government has in all privately owned real estate. These include police power (right to regulate for public order), eminent domain (right to take property for a public purpose by paying just compensation), taxation, and escheat (right to take property when the owner dies intestate and leaves no natural heirs).

219. **C** The Oregon and federal constitutions grant to the government police power (to maintain public order), eminent domain (taking privately owned property for the public good upon payment of just compensation), taxation, and escheat (taking property of a decedent who left no will or other heirs). Zoning is considered an exercise of police power, as long as it promotes the general health, safety and welfare. Deed restrictions in a subdivision (covenants) are created by the developer, not by the government.

220. **D** The Oregon and federal constitutions grant to the government police power (to maintain public order), eminent domain (taking privately owned property for the public good upon payment of just compensation), taxation, and escheat (taking property of a decedent who left no will or other heirs). Deed restrictions in a subdivision (covenants) are created by the developer, not by the government.

221. **C** The U.S. and Oregon Constitutions reserve the power of eminent domain to the government. Eminent domain is the right of the government

to take privately owned property for the public good, upon payment of just compensation.

222. **C** The Oregon and federal constitutions grant to the government police power (to maintain public order), eminent domain (to take private property), taxation, and escheat (to take property of a decedent who dies without a will and no natural heirs). An easement by way of necessity is when the county takes an easement at the request of a landlocked owner. An easement by prescription can occur when an owner uses another's property for ten years. The covenant of seizin is a warranty in a deed that the seller owns the property and has the right to sell it.

223. **C** Eminent domain is a right reserved in the federal and Oregon constitutions where the government can take privately owned property for the public good upon payment of just compensation. A lis pendens (notice of lis pendens or notice of pendency) is a claim against the defendant's real estate by a plaintiff to a lawsuit. Ad valorem means "according to value," a term used in property taxation. An estate is a right of possession.

224. **B** The Oregon and federal constitutions grant to the government the power of eminent domain, which is the right of the government to take privately owned property for the public good upon payment of just compensation. An attachment is a claim against the defendant's real estate by a plaintiff to a lawsuit. A suit to quiet title is a legal action asking the court to extinguish an encumbrance. Adverse possession can result in gaining title to another's land by possessing it for ten years.

225. **C** Eminent domain is a right reserved in the federal and Oregon constitutions where the government can take privately owned property for the public good upon payment of just compensation. A partition action is a suit by a co-tenant to divide the property. A right of way is usually used as a synonym for easement. Severance occurs whenever property or rights in property are divided.

226. **B** Eminent domain is the right of the government to take privately owned property for the public good. Exercising eminent domain is called condemnation.

227. **C** The right of the government to take privately owned property for the public good is called eminent domain. It extends to the states and local jurisdictions, as well as the federal government. The constitution requires payment of just compensation.

228. **B** Eminent domain is a right reserved in the federal and Oregon constitutions where the government can take privately owned property for the public good upon payment of just compensation. An attachment is a claim against the defendant's real estate by a plaintiff to a lawsuit. A suit to quiet title is a legal action asking the court to extinguish an encumbrance. Adverse possession can result in gaining title to another's land by possessing it for ten years.

229. **B** Eminent domain is a right reserved in the federal and Oregon constitutions where the government can take privately owned property for the public good upon payment of just compensation. The exercise of eminent domain is called condemnation. Reversion (right of reversion or estate in reversion) is a future estate, specifically, the right to regain title at some future time. Escheat is taking property of a decedent who dies without a will and no natural heirs. A license is revocable permission to use another's land.

230. **D** The right of eminent domain as specified in the U.S. and Oregon Constitutions provides specifically for the taking of privately owned property upon the payment of just compensation. The power to tax and the power of escheat are separate powers. Escheat is the power to take privately owned property when the owner dies without a will and no natural heirs.

231. **B** Eminent domain is the right of the government to take privately owned property for the public good upon payment of just compensation. The process is called condemnation. Utility companies and quasi-utilities, such as railroads, also have the right of eminent domain.

232. **C** Eminent domain is a right reserved in the federal and Oregon constitutions where the government can take privately owned property for the public good upon payment of just compensation. The process is called condemnation. A lis pendens (notice of lis pendens or notice of pendency) is a claim against the defendant's real estate by a plaintiff to a lawsuit. A judgment is a judicial order that money is owed to another. An abstract of judgment is a summary of the judgment.

233. **D** An easement by way of necessity is an easement granted to a landlocked owner. Escheat refers to the right of the government to take privately owned property when the owner dies without a will or natural heirs. Condemnation is the exercise of eminent domain, which is the right of the government to take privately owned property upon the payment of just compensation.

234. **C** Eminent domain is a right reserved in the federal and Oregon constitutions where the government can take privately owned property for the public good upon payment of just compensation. The exercise of eminent domain is called condemnation. Escheat is taking property of a decedent who left no will or other heirs. Estoppel is said to occur when someone is barred from asserting a right. Constructive eviction is where a landlord forces a tenant out by making the premises uninhabitable.

235. **B** Eminent domain is a right reserved in the federal and Oregon constitutions where the government can take privately owned property for the public good upon payment of just compensation. The exercise of eminent domain is called condemnation. Escheat is taking property of a decedent who dies without a will and no natural heirs.

236. **B** The right of eminent domain extends to utility companies and quasi-utilities such as railroads, etc. If it did not, one single owner could refuse to sell and hold up an entire project.

237. **A** The Oregon and federal constitutions grant to the government the power of eminent domain, which is the right to take privately owned property for a public purpose upon payment of just compensation. The power of eminent domain also extends to utility companies and quasi-utilities, such as railroads. Accretion occurs when soil builds up along the bank of a stream, thus enlarging the size of the adjacent property. A partition action is a suit by a co-tenant to divide the property.

238. **A** The Oregon and federal constitutions grant to the government the power of eminent domain, which is the right of the government to take privately owned property for the public good upon payment of just compensation. The power of eminent domain also extends to utility companies and quasi-utilities, such as railroads. Alienation is a synonym for conveyance of title, as by a deed. An injunction is an order from a court to cease and desist some action. Replevin is an action to recover possession of personal property, as where a tenant sues a landlord to recover property the landlord has wrongfully retained.

239. **B** The government may take privately owned property for the public good under eminent domain, provided just compensation is paid. However, land use restrictions such as zoning, building codes, and the like, are considered exercises of police power, not eminent domain. The constitution does not require the payment of just compensation for an exercise of police power.

240. **A** When the government takes only a portion of the property, but the remainder loses market value because it is now smaller, the owner can claim severance damages. When the government does not take any of the owner's land, but nearby activity of the government causes a loss of market value, this is called consequential damages. When a government agency restricts an owner so severely as to deprive the owner of any effective use of the property, the owner is entitled to demand that the government buy the property because the restrictions constitute inverse condemnation.

241. **D** Severance damages occur when a portion of the property is taken and the remainder loses value because it is smaller. An equitable servitude is a private restriction on land. Inverse condemnation occurs when the government restricts the use of the property so as to deny the owner any marketable use of the property.

242. **A** If zoning or other government restrictions are so severe as to deny the owner any economically viable use of the property, the government can be compelled to pay the owner just compensation for the property. This is called inverse condemnation. If government activity near an owner's land causes a loss of market value (e.g., the government builds a noisy freeway alongside a property), the affected owner can claim consequential damages.

243. **C** When a person dies intestate, the Oregon laws of descent and distribution apply. These laws provide that the estate of the decedent is distributed among the next of kin according to a statutory formula. If there are no heirs capable of inheriting, the property escheats to the state. Eminent domain is the right of the government to take privately owned property for the public good, provided just compensation is paid.

244. **B** The power of escheat is the right of the government to take private property when the owner dies without a will or natural heirs. Escheat is reserved to the states.

245. **C** When a person dies intestate, and there are no heirs capable of inheriting, the property escheats to the state. A reversionary interest is a future estate which frequently follows a life estate. Sovereign immunity refers to the fact that citizens are not permitted to sue the government. Eminent domain is the right of the government to take privately owned property for the public good upon payment of just compensation.

246. **D** When a person dies intestate, and there are no heirs capable of inheriting, the property escheats to the state. Adverse possession is long and continued

possession of another's property with the intent to claim ownership. Eminent domain is the right of the government to take privately owned property for the public good, provided just compensation is paid.

247. **B** Escheat is the power of the government to take private property when the owner dies without a will or natural heirs. The power is reserved to the states. In Oregon the agency in charge of such property is the State Land Board.

248. **D** Eminent domain is a right reserved in the federal and Oregon constitutions where the government can take privately owned property for the public good upon payment of just compensation. When the government sells property on which the taxes have not been paid it is called tax foreclosure. Taking private property when there are no heirs is a description of escheat.

249. **D** Building codes would impact the height and manner in which the fence could be constructed. Zoning ordinances commonly prohibit keeping certain animals in certain areas. Privately created deed restrictions also sometimes prohibit keeping livestock.

250. **A** Police power is the right of the government to maintain public order. The courts have held that zoning and other land use regulations are derived from this power. The government can also acquire privately owned property but doing so would be an exercise of eminent domain, not police power.

251. **D** The exercise of eminent domain requires the government pay the owner just compensation. However, exercising police power does not require payment. To qualify as police power, a regulating must be within constitutional limits, which means that it must be for the general health, safety, or welfare and it cannot be capricious and arbitrary. If it takes so many of the owner's rights in the property that the owner is left with no economically feasible use of the property it is called a taking and falls under eminent domain.

252. **B** The distinction between "taking," for which just compensation must be paid, and "regulating," for which no payment is required, is sometimes arguable. The courts have generally held that, as long as the owner has at least one economic use to make of the property, it is not a "taking."

253. **B** As long as the owner can still make an economic use of the property, it is not condemnation (taking). When a road is placed over the property, the owner can no longer do anything with it. A setback requirement, however, still leaves the owner with uses to make of the land.

254. **C** The exercise of eminent domain requires the payment of just compensation. Police power is the right of the government to regulate private uses of land and does not require just compensation.

255. **C** An encumbrance is anything which burdens the title and is not extinguished by a sale. There are various kinds of encumbrances, including financial encumbrances (liens), such as mortgages, judgments, property taxes, etc. A lien which reaches only specified property is said to be specific, while a lien which reaches everything the debtor owns is general. There are also encumbrances which affect the use, such as easements, deed restrictions, etc.

256. **C** A mortgage is a lien, a special type of encumbrance which makes the property collateral for a debt. Subordinated refers to the priority of liens, not the condition of the title. A writ of execution is the request of a judgment creditor that the judge order the sheriff to sell a property at public auction to satisfy the judgment.

257. **B** An encumbrance is anything which burdens the title and survives a conveyance. A deed is a paper which conveys the title, so it is not an encumbrance.

258. **B** An encumbrance is any interest held by another which burdens the owner's title and survives a sale. If your neighbor has an easement across your property, and you sell your property, your buyer takes title subject to the easement, so the easement is an encumbrance. Restrictions are generally covenants, which the buyer must also take title subject to. A license, however, is continuing permission, and is extinguished by a sale, therefore, it is not an encumbrance.

259. **D** An encumbrance is anything which burdens the title. There are various kinds of encumbrances, including financial encumbrances (liens), as well as encumbrances which affect the use, such as easements, etc. A judgment is a lien because if the judgment debtor sells the property, it is still subject to the judgment. The covenant of seizin is a warranty in a deed.

260. **D** An encumbrance is anything which burdens the title and is not extinguished by a sale. A lien is a type of encumbrance which makes the property collateral for a debt, and would include mortgages, trust deeds, property taxes, construction (mechanic's) liens, judgments, etc. In contrast, a restriction or an easement affect the use of the property. Nevertheless, all are considered encumbrances because they burden the title and are not extinguished by a sale.

261. **B** An easement appurtenant to the property is a benefit, and therefore an appurtenance, not an encumbrance. The fact that it is also an encumbrance on another piece of property is irrelevant to the property in question.

262. **A** An encumbrance is any interest which limits or burdens the title. Private restrictions fall into this category, as do easements. Encroachments are clouds, which are also considered encumbrances, since they potentially limit or burden the title. The term "homestead" means the place of personal residence. The homestead exemption is not a lien, but rather is a means of protecting property from a lien.

263. **C** An encumbrance is anything which burdens the title. Restrictive covenants (as in a deed) would be an example. A cloud (possible interest or claim) is also an encumbrance.

264. **D** An encumbrance is anything which burdens the title and survives a sale. There are various kinds of encumbrances, including financial encumbrances (liens), easements, deed restrictions, etc. A judgment is a lien because if the judgment debtor sells the property it is still subject to the judgment. An attachment is a claim against the defendant's real estate by a plaintiff to a lawsuit and is an encumbrance because if the judgment debtor sells the property, it is still subject to the claim. The covenant of seizin is a warranty in a deed.

265. **C** An encumbrance is anything which burdens the title and is not extinguished by a sale. If a neighbor has an easement across your property, your sale of the property would not extinguish your neighbor's easement, so the easement is an encumbrance on your title. Note that the easement is usually also appurtenant to your neighbor's parcel, while simultaneously being an encumbrance on yours.

266. **C** An encumbrance is anything which burdens the title and is not extinguished by a sale. If a neighbor has an easement across your property, your sale of the property would not extinguish your neighbor's easement, so the easement is an encumbrance on your title. Note that the easement is usually also appurtenant to your neighbor's parcel, while simultaneously being an encumbrance on yours. A license is similar to an easement, but would be extinguished by a sale, so it is not an encumbrance. A lien is an encumbrance which makes the property collateral for a debt. Prescription is a procedure to gain an easement by long and continued use.

267. **B** An encumbrance is anything which burdens the title. A lien is a special type of encumbrances which makes the property collateral for a debt. The most common lien instrument today is the trust deed, used in place of the older mortgage. A deed restriction is used to limit a buyer's use of the property, not to enforce collection of a debt, so it is an encumbrance, but not a lien.

268. **A** An encumbrance is anything which burdens the title and is not extinguished by a sale. A lien is an encumbrance which makes the property collateral for a debt, and would include mortgages, trust deeds, property taxes, construction (mechanic's) liens, judgments, etc. An easement, while also an encumbrance, is a right of use.

269. **D** All liens are encumbrances. Title insurers will issue title insurance for any property, but if they discover encumbrances against the title, they will exclude the encumbrances from the coverage. If the parties agree, property can always be sold subject to whatever encumbrances existed at the time of the conveyance. Liens can be specific (reach just specified property) or general (reach everything the debtor owns). At the same time, they can be voluntary (such as a mortgage), or involuntary (such as a judgment). This creates four possibilities – voluntary and general, voluntary and specific, involuntary and general, or involuntary and specific.

270. **A** A lien is an encumbrance which makes the real property collateral for a debt. An assessment is the determination of the real market value for property tax purposes. An encroachment occurs when improvements are placed on another's land. A judgment is an order of the court that money is owed.

271. **C** Encumbrances are classed as liens (making the real property collateral for a debt), and matters affecting the use of the property. An encroachment is where improvements are placed on another's land.

272. **B** A lien is a special type of encumbrance which makes the property collateral for a debt. Trust deeds are liens, used today as a modern replacement for the mortgage. A notice of non-responsibility is used by an owner to protect the property from construction liens.

273. **A** Liens are a special type of encumbrance which make the property collateral for a debt, so all liens are encumbrances, but not all encumbrances are liens. Deed restrictions are usually covenants, which are classed as encumbrances. A cloud is a possible interest or claim by a third party and is also considered an encumbrance.

274. **B** An encumbrance is anything which burdens the title and is not extinguished by a sale. A lien is a type of encumbrance which makes the property collateral for a debt. Encumbrances may also be things which restrict the use of the property. Conditions, covenants and easements affect the use, but do not make the property collateral for a debt, so they are not liens.

275. **C** Encumbrances are classed as liens (making the real property collateral for a debt), and matters affecting the use of the property. An attachment is a claim recorded by a party to a lawsuit to prevent a property owner from selling the property during the pendency of the suit. The goal of an attachment is to stop the owner from selling it so it will be reached by a judgment which the plaintiff hopes to gain.

276. **A** A lien is any encumbrance which makes the property collateral for a financial obligation. Easements and restrictions affect the use of the property and are not financial in nature. An encroachment clouds the title of the property encroached upon, but also has nothing to do with financial matters.

277. **B** An encumbrance is anything which burdens the title and is not extinguished by a sale. A lien is a type of encumbrance which makes the property collateral for a debt. When a lien is not paid, the property can be sold to satisfy it (foreclosure sale). The telephone company cannot force the sale of the property, so the telephone bill is not a lien.

278. **D** A lien is an interest which makes the real property collateral for a debt. An encroachment and an easement have to do with adverse possession or use of the property. A suit to quiet title is a suit to remove an interest claimed by other(s). An attachment liens the property of a defendant to a lawsuit so the defendant cannot sell it, thus making the asset available to the judgment creditor.

279. **B** The rights of an easement holder or of a lessee are evident because of their physical possession or use of the land. Buyers and others dealing in another's real estate have an obligation to inspect the premises to observe if anyone is in possession or using the property. A construction lien, however, could not be ascertained from a physical inspection of the premises, so it would be unenforceable on a subsequent buyer or lender if not recorded.

280. **C** An encumbrance is anything which burdens the title and is not extinguished by a sale. Since it burdens the title, it would diminish the market value. A lien is a type of encumbrance which makes the property collateral for a debt. Encumbrances do not have to be liens, however. For example, an easement or a deed restriction affect the use of the property, rather than make it collateral for a debt. If a lien reaches everything the debtor owns, i.e. a judgment, then it is a general lien. If it reaches only specified property i.e., property taxes, then it is specific.

281. **C** An encumbrance is anything which burdens the title and is not extinguished by a sale. There are various kinds of encumbrances, including financial encumbrances (liens), such as mortgages, judgments, property taxes, etc. There are also encumbrances which affect the use, such as easements, deed restrictions, etc. An abstract (abstract of title) is a summary of all matters affecting the title. If someone is claiming ownership of another's land, we say he or she is claiming color of title.

282. **A** All the terms relate to liens except tenancy in common. Tenancy in common is a type of concurrent tenancy (co-ownership).

283. **C** Real property is conveyed by a deed, and liened by a note and mortgage or note and trust deed. Title to personal property is transferred by a bill of sale and liened with a note and chattel mortgage. The Uniform Commercial Code defines a chattel mortgage as a "security agreement." It is still legal in Oregon to use the older term "chattel mortgage," although it is seldom heard any more. To give the world notice of the existence of a security agreement, the creditor can file a UCC financing statement in the office of the Oregon Secretary of State.

DEEDS AND OTHER CONVEYANCES

Although Oregon real estate agents do not often draft documents such as deeds, a basic understanding of these documents is nevertheless essential background. Real estate agents frequently encounter deeds in their daily practice and they must be able to read and understand them. And real estate agents must be able to converse with escrow agents and others who do draft deeds in the course of closing real estate transactions.

A transfer of real estate is called a ***conveyance***, or sometimes an ***alienation***. Conveyances are categorized as ***voluntary conveyances*** and ***involuntary conveyances***. For example, selling your property is a voluntary conveyance, but losing it to the bank in a foreclosure is involuntary. When the conveyance is voluntary you sometimes hear people call it a ***grant***. The party conveying the property is called the ***grantor***, and the party receiving it is the ***grantee***.

While voluntary conveyances are far more common in a normal real estate practice, let us turn our attention first to involuntary conveyances. As noted above, a foreclosure is an involuntary conveyance. Involuntary conveyances also result from a many other situations – divorce decrees, bankruptcy, condemnation, suits for partition, even conceivably the forfeiture of a defeasible title – all are examples of involuntary conveyances. In most of these cases (although not all) the actual conveyance is a deed which the grantor is forced to sign under court order. Most of these involuntary conveyances have been, or will be, covered elsewhere in this text. However, there are two possible involuntary conveyances that can happen without a deed. Although sufficiently infrequent that few real estate agents encounter them, they deserve a special discussion.

NOTES

Riparian right of accession

When property along a stream is increased in size as a result of the addition of soil deposited by the stream, the owner is said to have a right of ***accession*** to the additional land area. Accession is the legal right of an owner to that which is incidental to the item owned.

The process of building up soil along a riparian property is called ***accretion***, that is, the silt and other solids "accrete" to the riparian property. The soil itself is called ***alluvium***, or occasionally ***alluvion***.

However, the accretion will result in gaining title to new land only if it is a gradual addition. If the accretion is the result of a sudden flood, then no title changes. A sudden or violent tearing away is called ***avulsion***.

Adverse possession

Gaining title to property by ***adverse possession*** occurs when someone possesses another's property without permission for at least the statutory time period. In this respect it is essentially the same process as obtaining an easement by prescription (discussed in the preceding section). The main difference is that in obtaining an easement by prescription the claimant *used* the property, but in gaining title by adverse possession, the claimant *possessed* the property. Note the distinction between a right of possession (estate), and a right of use (easement).

Various common-law and statutory rules govern a successful claim of adverse possession. The obvious first rule is that the claimant must have been in possession of the property. Under Oregon law, the possession must have been for at least ten years, and in rare cases, even longer is required. Being in possession does not necessarily mean the claimant never left the premises. Being in possession merely means that the claimant possessed the property in the normal way as any owner of the property would.

Adverse possession cannot result in gaining title if the possession was secret. The possession must have been ***open and notorious***. The test of whether or not the possession was sufficiently open and notorious is fairly rigorous. The possession must have been of such character that it left no doubt in the true owner's mind that the party in possession intended to claim the property.

Another rule is that the adverse possession must have been ***hostile***. Hostility means that the claimant possessed the property with the intent to claim it or with ***color of title***. Color of title means that the claim arises from a written conveyance which purports to convey title to the claimant, but was somehow defective and failed to convey the title.

A fundamental element of hostility is that it cannot co-exist with permission. That is, if the true owner gives the adverse possessor permission to occupy the property, then the hostility is extinguished. Without hostility, the claimant cannot prevail. Therefore, a defense commonly asserted by an owner whose land is adversely claimed, is that the claimant had permission.

The adverse claimant must also demonstrate that the possession was ***exclusive***. This does not mean that the adverse claimant may not allow others on the land. It does mean that the claimant must exclude other potential adverse claimants. Invitees and guests are not potential adverse claimants, so an adverse possessor does not diminish his or her claim by allowing ordinary visitors on the property.

The adverse possession must be ***continuous*** for the statutory time period. The statutory time period in Oregon is normally ten years. This means that you cannot adversely claim the property for a couple of years, move away, then return and possess it again for another eight years, and still maintain your claim of title. The ten year require-

NOTES

ment must be met by continuous possession. Note, however, that the continuity can be met by more than one claimant through a process known as ***tacking***. For example, you could adversely claim the property for a couple of years, and then deed your interest to another. Your grantee could continue the possession for another eight years, and then successfully claim the title adversely.

Another requirement is that the property must have been privately owned. Although the government, acting on behalf of the public, can gain title to privately owned property by adverse possession, a claim of title by adverse possession cannot normally be asserted by private parties against property owned by the government.

The final requirement is that the possession must have been under ***claim of right***. Oregon statutes require the claim of right to stem from an honest belief that the claimant was the actual owner of the property and that the belief had "an objective basis" and was "reasonable under the circumstances" (ORS 105.620).

A common question which arises is whether or not the adverse claimant must pay the taxes on the property. Paying the taxes is required in some states, however, in Oregon it is not essential. Of course, if the adverse claimant has paid the taxes continuously for the statutory period of time, his or her claim is no doubt strengthened.

For real estate agents, claims of adverse possession are unusual events. After all, owners of land usually notice someone in possession of their land and take measures to prevent the adverse possession from ripening into a legally enforceable claim. When a claim of adverse possession does occur, the most common case involves a fence or other encroachment. Even then, the owner can usually assert the defense of permission.

Exercise a

A transfer of title is called a ____________________ or an ____________________ and it can be voluntary or ____________________. When it is voluntary, it is frequently called a __________. The party giving up ownership is called the ______________ and the receiving party is the ______________.

When soil is gradually deposited by a stream along a riparian property, the owner of the property may gain title because the owner has a right of ______________. The process of adding soil is called ______________. The soil itself is called ______________.

Gaining title by adverse possession is similar to gaining an easement by ______________. The possession must be __________ and ______________, that is, it cannot be in secret. The possession must also be continuous, normally for at least ____ years. In addition, the possession must be ______________, that is, the claimant must be the only claimant. If the true owner gives the claimant ______________ to occupy the property, this would destroy the element of ______________, which defeats the claim. If the owner believes that he or she is the owner and the belief is based on a written document, then we say the adverse possessor has __________ of __________.

NOTES

Essential elements of deeds

The instrument used in almost all voluntary conveyances is a ***deed***. The parties are called the ***grantor*** (seller) and the ***grantee*** (buyer). There are numerous kind of deeds, each with its own special legal effects, which we will discuss later.

There are various legal requirements for the creation of a valid and enforceable deed. Primary of these is that the deed must be ***in writing***.

In addition to being in writing, a deed must be ***signed by the grantor(s)***. All parties who are in title to the property must sign it. If a party with an ownership interest fails to sign the deed, then his or her interest is not conveyed. In the event one or more of the parties cannot sign the deed it is common practice for the deed to be signed by an authorized representative, such as an attorney in fact (acting under recorded power of attorney), a conservator or a legal guardian. The grantor or the grantor's authorized representative must also be ***competent***.

Note that it is not usually required for the grantee to sign the deed. It logically follows then that the grantee need not necessarily be competent. Therefore, it is possible to deed property to minors and others without legal competence. Of course, such persons are limited in their ability to deal with the real estate, since they must convey it through the signature of a conservator or guardian.

Although the grantee need not ordinarily be competent, the deed must at least state an ***identifiable grantee***. Technically, this does not have to be by name, but if the name is not used, later title problems may result. For example, it may create a legal conveyance to deed property to someone's "first-born daughter," but when that first-born daughter goes to sell the property, she will have to prove that she was indeed the individual named as grantee. It is also not required to spell the name of either the grantor or the grantee correctly. The law follows the principle of ***idem sonans***, that is, if it sounds the same then it is the same, regardless of the spelling.

A related problem occurs when the grantee's name changes. For example, suppose Mary Smith takes title to property while a single woman. Later she gets married to Bob Jones and decides to call herself Mary Jones from then on. When she sells the property, how should she sign the deed? That answer is that it doesn't matter as long as it is clear that the person signing the deed is the same person who was listed as grantee in the previous deed. As a courtesy to title examiners it is customary for her to sign her name "Mary Jones, who took title as Mary Smith." This makes it clear to all that she is the same person.

There must also be ***acceptance*** of the conveyance by the grantee. The evidence of the grantee's acceptance normally occurs when the grantee pays money for the property. Even if the grantee paid nothing for the property, the grantee's acceptance is evidenced by moving into the property or accepting the benefits of ownership, such as rental income. Note that the acceptance is the last requirement to be met.

Deeds must also contain an ***adequate description of the premises*** being conveyed, sufficient to permit the location of the property to be determined with certainty. The description of the real estate is normally a formal description, although an informal description is adequate as long as it is sufficient to leave no doubt as to the boundaries.

A deed must contain ***words of conveyance***, also sometimes referred to as a ***granting clause***. In many states there is a specific word or phrase which is required. In Oregon, however, there is no particular wording required unless the deed is a statutory form deed (see "Types of deeds" below).

One of the more interesting requirements is ***delivery***. Although volumes have been written about the issue of delivery, it can be stated succinctly as "the intent of the grantor to convey." It is conceivable that the grantor could physically hand the deed to

NOTES

the grantee intending some purpose other than to convey the title, in which case there would be no conveyance. Of course, proving that the grantor did not intend delivery would be difficult. To avoid disputes over delivery, in modern real estate practice it is customary for the grantor to hand the deed to a neutral escrow agent with instructions to record it when the buyer has complied with the terms of the sale. Once handed to the escrow, the grantor cannot ordinarily withdraw the deed unless the buyer breaches the terms of the escrow.

A fundamental principal of delivery is that it must generally occur within the lifetime of the grantor. After all, consider the impossibility of a dead person forming the intent to convey title. A technical exception occurs if the deed is delivered to a neutral escrow agent with irrevocable instructions to deliver it to the buyer upon the grantor's death. Since the instructions are irrevocable, it is generally held that the grantor has relinquished dominion and control over the title, therefore there is a valid conveyance at the time of handing the deed to the escrow. The grantee's right of possession is just deferred until the death of the grantor.

There are certain matters which are not required. For example, a deed does not require a date to be enforceable. Although the date is evidence of the time when the seller's warranties take effect, there is no legal requirement to place a date on a deed. Consideration is also not normally required, unless it is needed as the evidence of acceptance. And deeds from corporations do not require a seal in Oregon, although a corporate seal is required in some states.

The preceding has been a discussion of what is required to make the deed valid and enforceable as a conveyance of the property. However, deeds should also be recorded for the protection of the buyer. To record a deed the signature(s) of the grantor(s) must be ***acknowledged***. This means that someone has witnessed the grantor's signature. The witness is normally a notary public. In addition, deeds cannot be accepted for recording unless they state the name and address of the party to whom the tax bill should be sent in the future. And, with some exceptions, deeds must also state the true and actual consideration in dollars. The exceptions include gift deeds, deeds from a personal representative of an estate, and exchanges. Stating a false consideration can subject the grantor to a fine.

In addition, to the above recording requirements, ORS 93.040 requires that deeds (and land sales contracts) contain a land-use disclosure. The disclosure must state "*This instrument will not allow use of the property described in this instrument in violation of applicable land use laws and regulations. Before signing or accepting this instrument, the person acquiring fee title to the property should check with the appropriate city or county planning department to verify approved uses and to determine any limits on lawsuits against farming or forest practices as defined in ORS 30.930.*" The penalty for failure to include the disclosure is merely civil liability to the buyer if the buyer is harmed.

Persons reading textbooks published in other states may find reference to a ***habendum clause***. The habendum clause starts with the words "to have and to hold" and proceeds to describe the quantity or extent of the estate being granted. It is commonly required in some states, but although it can be used, the habendum clause is not required for a valid conveyance in Oregon and its use is increasingly rare.

It must always be remembered that a deed is a contract that lasts for a brief instant at the moment of conveyance, and then has no further effect. Its only function is to convey the title and (possibly) create warranties. Therefore, the grantee cannot further convey the title by endorsing the deed or by delivering it to another person. A new deed must be used each time the property is conveyed, even if the conveyance is back to the original grantor.

NOTES

Types of deeds

There are many, many types of deeds – sheriff's deeds, trust deeds, conservators deeds, deeds in lieu of foreclosure, gift deeds – the list is long. Each of these deeds is a deed which has been specially printed for certain uses. For example, a sheriff's deed is designed to be used by a sheriff when deeding property which has been sold at a foreclosure sale. However, all deeds fall into one of four categories based on the warranties they contain. These four categories will be discussed in detail later.

Real estate agents occasionally run into a ***reformation deed***, also sometimes called a ***correction deed***. A reformation deed is used to correct an error in an already executed deed. For example, the original deed may have misstated the legal description. The usual practice is to obtain the original incorrect deed, type the correction on it, have the grantor sign it a second time with a note that it is being re-signed to correct the error, and then re-record the deed.

Deeds are very important documents, but at the same time, an ordinary deed is a very simple document. Nevertheless, over the centuries numerous extra phrases were added to deeds (such as the habendum clause above). Preprinted deed forms eventually came to the point where no one but attorneys could understand their language.

In 1973, in an effort to simplify deed forms, the Oregon Legislature enacted statutes creating ***statutory form deeds***. The statutory deeds are created by copying the statutory language exactly (ORS 93.850 to 93.870, on facing page). The statutes then prescribe the precise legal effect of each form. Since there was already a great body of law regarding the four categories of deeds, the Legislature created a statutory form for each.

Because the legal effect of the simple statutory form deeds is very similar to the old-fashioned deeds which they were designed to replace, they have become practically the only deeds in common use today. Therefore, we will confine our discussion of the various deed formats to their statutory forms.

The deed which gives the buyer the best protection is the ***warranty deed***, also sometimes referred to as a ***full warranty deed*** or ***general warranty deed***. As the name would imply, it contains warranties for the grantee's protection.

The statutory warranty deed contains three warranties, generally referred to as ***covenants***. We encountered covenants previously where we discovered that they can be used in the deed to restrict the grantee's use of the property. In that sense, they were encumbrances. Now we find the term used in a somewhat opposite sense. The covenants of a warranty deed are promises that the grantor makes to the grantee regarding the condition of the title. The three covenants are

Covenant of seizin By the covenant of seizin the grantor warrants that he or she actually has the estate which the deed purports to convey and the right to convey it.

Covenant against encumbrances As the term would imply, the covenant against encumbrances is the seller's promise that the property is free and clear. Many times the property is to be conveyed subject to an encumbrance, such as where the buyer is buying the property subject to the seller's old loan. In this case, standard preprinted forms provide a place for the seller to exclude such encumbrances from the warranty.

Covenant of quiet enjoyment The covenant of quiet enjoyment obligates the seller to defend against any claims as of the moment of the conveyance.

The statutory ***special warranty deed*** is similar to the warranty deed. The covenants are identical except that the grantor does not warrant that the title is completely free of encumbrances. The grantor warrants only that the title is free of encumbrances

DEED FORMS

93.850 Warranty deed form; effect. (1) Warranty deeds may be in the following form:

______, Grantor, conveys and warrants to ______, Grantee, the following described real property free of encumbrances except as specifically set forth herein: (Describe the property conveyed.)

(If there are to be exceptions to the covenants described in ORS 93.850 (2)(c), here insert such exceptions.)

(Following statement of exceptions, here insert statement required under ORS 93.040 (1).)

The true consideration for this conveyance is $______.

(Here comply with the requirements of ORS 93.030.)

Dated this ______ day of ______, 2 ______.

(2) A deed in the form of subsection (1) of this section shall have the following effect:

(a) It shall convey the entire interest in the described property at the date of the deed which the deed purports to convey.

(b) The grantor, the heirs, successors and assigns of the grantor, shall be forever estopped from asserting that the grantor had, at the date of the deed, an estate or interest in the land less than that estate or interest which the deed purported to convey and the deed shall pass any and all after acquired title.

(c) It shall include the following covenants, each of which shall run in favor of the grantee and the successors in title of the grantee as if written in the deed:

(A) That at the time of the delivery of the deed the grantor is seized of the estate in the property which the grantor purports to convey and that the grantor has good right to convey the same.

(B) That at the time of the delivery of the deed the property is free from encumbrances except as specifically set forth on the deed.

(C) That the grantor warrants and will defend the title to the property against all persons who may lawfully claim the same.

(3) If the grantor desires to exclude any encumbrances or other interests from the scope of the covenants of the grantor, such exclusions must be expressly set forth on the deed.

93.855 Special warranty deed form; effect. (1) Special warranty deeds may be in the following form:

______, Grantor, conveys and specially warrants to ______, Grantee, the following described real property free of encumbrances created or suffered by the grantor except as specifically set forth herein: (Describe the property conveyed.)

(If there are to be exceptions to the covenants described in ORS 93.855 (2), here insert such exceptions.)

(Following statement of exceptions, here insert statement required under ORS 93.040 (1).)

The true consideration for this conveyance is $______.

(Here comply with the requirements of ORS 93.030.)

Dated this ______ day of ______, 2 ______.

(2) A deed in the form of subsection (1) of this section shall have the same effect as a warranty deed as described in ORS 93.850, except that the covenant of freedom from encumbrances shall be limited to those encumbrances created or suffered by the grantor and the covenant of warranty shall be limited to read: "That the grantor warrants and will defend the title to the property against all persons who may lawfully claim the same by, through or under the grantor."

(3) If the grantor desires to exclude any encumbrances or other interests from the scope of the covenants of the grantor, such exclusions must be expressly set forth on the deed.

93.860 Bargain and sale deed form; effect. (1) Bargain and sale deeds may be in the following form:

______, Grantor, conveys to ______, Grantee, the following described real property: (Describe the property conveyed.)

(Following description of property, here insert statement required under ORS 93.040 (1).)

The true consideration for this conveyance is $_____.

(Here comply with the requirements of ORS 93.030.)

Dated this ______ day of ______, 2 ______.

(2) A deed in the form of subsection (1) of this section shall have the following effect:

(a) It shall convey the entire interest in the described property at the date of the deed which the deed purports to convey.

(b) The grantor, the heirs, successors and assigns of the grantor, shall be forever estopped from asserting that the grantor had, at the date of the deed, an estate or interest in the land less than that estate or interest which the deed purported to convey and the deed shall pass any and all after acquired title.

(3) A bargain and sale deed shall not operate to provide any covenants of title in the grantee and the successors of the grantee.

93.865 Quitclaim deed form; effect. (1) Quitclaim deeds may be in the following form:

______, Grantor, releases and quitclaims to ______, Grantee, all right, title and interest in and to the following described real property: (Describe the property conveyed.)

(Following description of property, here insert statement required under ORS 93.040 (1).)

The true consideration for this conveyance is $ ______.

(Here comply with the requirements of ORS 93.030.)

Dated this ______ day of ______, 2 ______.

(2) A deed in the form of subsection (1) of this section shall have the effect of conveying whatever title or interest, legal or equitable, the grantor may have in the described property at the date of the deed but shall not transfer any title or interest which the grantor may thereafter obtain nor shall it operate as an estoppel.

(3) A grantee taking title by way of a quitclaim deed shall not, merely because of receipt of title by or through such a deed, be denied the status of a good faith purchaser for value.

93.870 Statutory deed forms optional. The form of deeds set forth in ORS 93.850 to 93.865 are permissive and not mandatory. Other forms of deeds may be used for the conveyance of real property.

Excerpt from Oregon Revised Statutes, Chapter 93

NOTES

created or suffered by the grantor. A common use of the special warranty deed is in fulfillment of a land sales contract where the seller has not been in possession of the property for years and does not wish to warrant any actions but his or her own.

The statutory ***bargain and sale deed*** specifies that the grantor gives none of the above three covenants. The seller is under no obligation to defend the title. Bargain and sale deeds are also commonly used in fulfillment of land sales contracts. Sheriff's deeds are also normally bargain and sale deeds in format.

In addition, using any of the three statutory deeds above creates two presumptions – that the grantor had a fee title absolutely vested (unless the deed states a lesser interest), and that the deed not only conveys all the grantor's present interest, but any interest the grantor might acquire in the future.

The fact that the above deeds contain these presumptions creates the need for the ***quitclaim deed***. A statutory quitclaim deed not only contains none of the above warranties of title, but also creates no presumption that the grantor had any interest at all. Furthermore, using a quitclaim deed conveys only the interest the grantor had at the time of the conveyance. Any interest acquired by the grantor in the future (***after-acquired title***) is not conveyed.

This makes the quitclaim deed the ideal deed when the grantor wishes to release a possible interest (cloud), without promising that the interest being conveyed is genuine. Remember that using even a bargain and sale deed creates the presumption that the grantor had the interest stated in the deed. If the grantee can later demonstrate that the grantor had no interest at all, the grantor could conceivably be found guilty of fraud. By using the quitclaim deed, the grantor conveys all his or her present interest in the property, but does not promise that anything at all was conveyed, thus gaining protection from a claim of fraud.

Note that it does not matter what kind of deed was used, the grantee gets all the grantor's right, title and interest in the property unless, of course, the grantor stipulates a lesser estate. The differences among the four deed forms is not the quantity of interest conveyed, but rather the extent to which the grantor will stand behind the conveyance and defend the title in the future.

In today's world of real estate, it is an unusual transaction where the buyer does not obtain title insurance. As a result, buyers today are less concerned about the kind of deed they receive, as long as the title insurance policy reflects that the buyer is getting the interest bargained for. Note however, that title insurance policies are limited in the scope of their coverage. The covenants of a warranty deed are broader than the coverage of typical title insurance policies. Nevertheless, the chances of recovering from a financially secure title insurance company are probably greater than from the seller.

It is not unusual in a real estate transaction for the seller to retain some rights in the property being conveyed. For example, the seller may wish to retain an easement. Retaining rights in the property being conveyed is called a ***reservation***. Other times the seller may wish to retain complete ownership of a portion of the property. This is commonly referred to as an ***exception***.

Real estate agents should take special note of the role of the attorney in drafting documents used in a real estate transaction. Obviously, real estate agents should be sure their clients see their attorneys when a legal question comes up. Trying to give legal advice yourself might result in being guilty of unauthorized practice of law, not to mention the legal liability if you are wrong.

Nevertheless, you should remember that it is never unauthorized practice of law to draft documents to which you are a party personally. Of course, be sure the old adage does not apply – "when you represent yourself you have a fool for a client."

NOTES

It is also not considered unauthorized practice of law for agents to fill in the blanks on attorney-prepared standard form contracts such as listings and earnest money agreements, provided no special fee is charged. A special exception is the land sales contract, which real estate agents are not permitted to draft. And whenever you draft documents for your clients, the courts have made it clear that you will be held to the same standard of care as an attorney.

When it comes to deeds, real estate agents (as well as escrow and other closing agents) may fill in the blanks on the statutory forms, but not an old fashioned form. However, the clients must select which form to use, real estate agents cannot advise the clients to use a warranty deed or some other form. And real estate agents would be on dangerous ground indeed if they alter the prescribed language of the statutory form.

Patents

Title to all real estate in Oregon which is currently in private ownership was originally conveyed by the federal government to a private individual at some time. The instrument used was called a ***federal patent***, or just ***patent***. Actually, this is just a modern use of the term. Even in early England, a grant of land from the sovereign to a subject was called a patent. Patents are seldom used in Oregon today, except when the federal government grants just the mineral rights. Note that the patent is the original conveyance of the land. Subsequent conveyances, even when the grantor is the federal government, are by deed.

Starting in the 1850s, federal patents were granted to settlers in the Oregon Territory (what is now Oregon and Washington). The grants were made under the provisions of the federal Donation Land Law of 1850. Settlers would first file a ***Donation Land Claim***. After living on the land and making improvements, they would be granted a federal patent to their claims. Many modern surveys continue to refer to the corners of these donation land claims as starting points for property boundaries. Many times these patents reserved the mineral rights to the federal government.

Dedications

A ***dedication*** is a grant of land to the public. Most commonly, it occurs when a developer conveys property to a city or a county for the roads and streets in a new subdivision. Occasionally other common areas, such as parks, school sites, and so on are included. The instrument is normally a deed, although the conveyance can also be made by recording a plat map showing the areas to be dedicated and containing formal language conveying them to the city or county.

In the early days, developers would simply record the plat map without making any formal dedication. Even though there was never a formal conveyance, by long and continued use, the public has gained at least an easement for the common areas. Such a conveyance is called a ***common-law dedication***. Today, developers are not permitted to do things in such a sloppy manner. By statute, it is illegal to divide land without recording the plat map and making a formal conveyance to the city or county of any roads or streets. In addition, the city or county must formally accept the dedication. The city or county is prohibited by law from accepting the dedication unless the plat map is created and recorded. Since such dedications today are required by statute, they are called ***statutory dedications***. Usually the actual conveyance is done by stating the dedication right on the plat map instead of using a separate deed.

FORM No. 633 – WARRANTY DEED (Individual or Corporate).

NN

Grantor's Name and Address

Grantee's Name and Address

After recording, return to (Name, Address, Zip):

Until requested otherwise, send all tax statements to (Name, Address, Zip):

SPACE RESERVED FOR RECORDER'S USE

STATE OF OREGON,
County of ____________ } ss.

I certify that the within instrument was received for recording on ____________, at ______ o'clock ____ M., and recorded in book/reel/volume No. ______, on page ______ and/or as fee/file/instrument/microfilm/reception No. ______, Records of this County.

Witness my hand and seal of County affixed.

NAME TITLE

By ____________________, Deputy.

WARRANTY DEED

KNOW ALL MEN BY THESE PRESENTS that ____, hereinafter called grantor, for the consideration hereinafter stated, to grantor paid by ____, hereinafter called grantee, does hereby grant, bargain, sell and convey unto the grantee and the grantee's heirs, successors and assigns, that certain real property, with the tenements, hereditaments and appurtenances thereunto belonging or in any way appertaining, situated in ____________________ County, State of Oregon, described as follows, to-wit:

(IF SPACE INSUFFICIENT, CONTINUE DESCRIPTION ON REVERSE SIDE)

To Have and to Hold the same unto grantee and grantee's heirs, successors and assigns forever.

And grantot hereby covenants to and with grantee and grantee's heirs, successors and assigns, that grantor is lawfully seized in fee simple of the above granted premises, free from all encumbrances except (if no exceptions, so state): ____, and that grantor will warrant and forever defend the premises and every part and parcel thereof against the lawful claims and demands of all persons whomsoever, except those claiming under the above described encumbrances.

The true and actual consideration paid for this transfer, stated in terms of dollars, is $ __________. ① However, the actual consideration consists of or includes other property or value given or promised which is ☐ the whole ☐ part of the (indicate which) consideration. ① (The sentence between the symbols ①, if not applicable, should be deleted. See ORS 93.030)

In construing this deed, where the context so requires, the singular includes the plural, and all grammatical changes shall be made so that this deed shall apply equally to corporations and to individuals.

In witness whereof, the grantor has executed this instrument on ____________________; if grantor is a corporation, it has caused its name to be signed and it seal, if any, affixed by an officer or other person duly authorized to do so by order of its board of directors.

THIS INSTRUMENT WILL NOT ALLOW USE OF THE PROPERTY DESCRIBED IN THIS INSTRUMENT IN VIOLATION OF APPLICABLE LAND USE LAWS AND REGULATIONS. BEFORE SIGNING OR ACCEPTING THIS INSTRUMENT, THE PERSON ACQUIRING FEE TITLE TO THE PROPERTY SHOULD CHECK WITH THE APPROPRIATE CITY OR COUNTY PLANNING DEPARTMENT TO VERIFY APPROVED USES AND TO DETERMINE ANY LIMITS ON LAWSUITS AGAINST FARMING OR FOREST PRACTICES AS DEFINED IN ORS 30.930.

State of Oregon, County of ____________________) ss.
This instrument was acknowledged before my on ____________________,
by ____________________.
This instrument was acknowledged before me on ____________________,
by ____________________
as ____________________
of ____________________.

Notary Public for Oregon.
My commission expires ____________________

Old form warranty deed. Use of this form through the kind permission of Stevens-Ness Law Publishing Company, Portland, Oregon

FORM No. 963 – WARRANTY DEED – STATUTORY FORM (Individual or Corporate).

NN

Grantor's Name and Address

Grantee's Name and Address

After recording, return to (Name, Address, Zip):

Until requested otherwise, send all tax statements to (Name, Address, Zip):

SPACE RESERVED FOR RECORDER'S USE

STATE OF OREGON,
County of ____________ } ss.

I certify that the within instrument was received for recording on ____________, at ________ o'clock ____ M., and recorded in book/reel/volume No. ________, on page ________ and/or as fee/file/instrument/microfilm/reception No. ________, Records of this County.

Witness my hand and seal of County affixed.

NAME TITLE

By ______________________________, Deputy.

WARRANTY DEED – STATUTORY FORM
(INDIVIDUAL GRANTOR)

____, Grantor,

conveys and warrants to ____, Grantee,

the following described real property free of encumbrances, except as specifically set forth herein, situated in ____________ County, Oregon, to-wit:

(IF SPACE INSUFFICIENT, CONTINUE DESCRIPTION ON REVERSE SIDE)

The property is free of encumbrances, except (if none, so state):

The true consideration for this conveyance is $ ____________ . (Here, comply with the requirements of ORS 93.030.)

DATED ______________________________

THIS INSTRUMENT WILL NOT ALLOW USE OF THE PROPERTY DESCRIBED IN THIS INSTRUMENT IN VIOLATION OF APPLICABLE LAND USE LAWS AND REGULATIONS. BEFORE SIGNING OR ACCEPTING THIS INSTRUMENT, THE PERSON ACQUIRING FEE TITLE TO THE PROPERTY SHOULD CHECK WITH THE APPROPRIATE CITY OR COUNTY PLANNING DEPARTMENT TO VERIFY APPROVED USES AND TO DETERMINE ANY LIMITS ON LAWSUITS AGAINST FARMING OR FOREST PRACTICES AS DEFINED IN ORS 30.930.

STATE OF OREGON, County of ______________________) ss.

This instrument was acknowledged before me on ______________________________,

by ____.

Notary Public for Oregon.
My commission expires ______________________

Statutory form warranty deed. Note the simplified language. This statutory form relies on the statute to provide essentially the same warranties as the old form on the preceding page.

FORM No. 967 – SPECIAL WARRANTY DEED – STATUTORY FORM (Individual or Corporate).

NN

Grantor's Name and Address

Grantee's Name and Address

After recording, return to (Name, Address, Zip):

Until requested otherwise, send all tax statements to (Name, Address, Zip):

SPACE RESERVED FOR RECORDER'S USE

STATE OF OREGON,
County of ________ } ss.

I certify that the within instrument was received for recording on ________, at ________ o'clock ____ M., and recorded in book/reel/volume No. ________, on page ________ and/or as fee/file/instrument/microfilm/reception No. ________, Records of this County.

Witness my hand and seal of County affixed.

NAME TITLE

By ________, Deputy.

SPECIAL WARRANTY DEED – STATUTORY FORM
(INDIVIDUAL GRANTOR)

________, Grantor, conveys and warrants to ________, Grantee, the following described real property free of encumbrances created or suffered by the Grantor, except as specifically set forth herein, situated in ________ County, Oregon, to-wit:

(IF SPACE INSUFFICIENT, CONTINUE DESCRIPTION ON REVERSE SIDE)

The property is free of encumbrances, except (if none, so state):

The true consideration for this conveyance is $ ________. (Here, comply with the requirements of ORS 93.030.)

DATED ________

THIS INSTRUMENT WILL NOT ALLOW USE OF THE PROPERTY DESCRIBED IN THIS INSTRUMENT IN VIOLATION OF APPLICABLE LAND USE LAWS AND REGULATIONS. BEFORE SIGNING OR ACCEPTING THIS INSTRUMENT, THE PERSON ACQUIRING FEE TITLE TO THE PROPERTY SHOULD CHECK WITH THE APPROPRIATE CITY OR COUNTY PLANNING DEPARTMENT TO VERIFY APPROVED USES AND TO DETERMINE ANY LIMITS ON LAWSUITS AGAINST FARMING OR FOREST PRACTICES AS DEFINED IN ORS 30.930.

STATE OF OREGON, County of ________) ss.

This instrument was acknowledged before me on ________,

by ________.

Notary Public for Oregon.
My commission expires ________

Statutory form special warranty deed. Note the change from "conveys and warrants" in the warranty deed to "conveys and specially warrants." Note also the limitation on the grantor's liability.

FORM No. 961 – BARGAIN AND SALE DEED – STATUTORY FORM (Individual or Corporate).

NN

Grantor's Name and Address

Grantee's Name and Address

After recording, return to (Name, Address, Zip):

Until requested otherwise, send all tax statements to (Name, Address, Zip):

SPACE RESERVED FOR RECORDER'S USE

STATE OF OREGON,
County of ________ } ss.

I certify that the within instrument was received for recording on ________, at ______ o'clock ____ M., and recorded in book/reel/volume No. ______, on page ______ and/or as fee/file/instrument/microfilm/reception No. ______, Records of this County.

Witness my hand and seal of County affixed.

NAME TITLE

By ________________, Deputy.

BARGAIN AND SALE DEED – STATUTORY FORM
(INDIVIDUAL GRANTOR)

________________, Grantor,

conveys to ________________, Grantee,

the following described real property situated in ____________ County, Oregon, to-wit:

(IF SPACE INSUFFICIENT, CONTINUE DESCRIPTION ON REVERSE SIDE)

The property is free of encumbrances, except (if none, so state):

The true consideration for this conveyance is $ ________. (Here, comply with the requirements of ORS 93.030.)

DATED ________________

THIS INSTRUMENT WILL NOT ALLOW USE OF THE PROPERTY DESCRIBED IN THIS INSTRUMENT IN VIOLATION OF APPLICABLE LAND USE LAWS AND REGULATIONS. BEFORE SIGNING OR ACCEPTING THIS INSTRUMENT, THE PERSON ACQUIRING FEE TITLE TO THE PROPERTY SHOULD CHECK WITH THE APPROPRIATE CITY OR COUNTY PLANNING DEPARTMENT TO VERIFY APPROVED USES AND TO DETERMINE ANY LIMITS ON LAWSUITS AGAINST FARMING OR FOREST PRACTICES AS DEFINED IN ORS 30.930.

STATE OF OREGON, County of ________________) ss.

This instrument was acknowledged before me on ________________,

by ________________.

Notary Public for Oregon.
My commission expires ________________

Statutory form bargain and sale deed. Note the lack of a place to state encumbrances which the grantee will take the title subject to. This is because there is no covenant against encumbrances in the bargain and sale deed.

FORM No. 969 – QUITCLAIM DEED – STATUTORY FORM (Individual or Corporate).

NN

Grantor's Name and Address

Grantee's Name and Address

After recording, return to (Name, Address, Zip):

Until requested otherwise, send all tax statements to (Name, Address, Zip):

SPACE RESERVED FOR RECORDER'S USE

STATE OF OREGON,
County of ______ } ss.

I certify that the within instrument was received for recording on ______, at ______ o'clock ____ M., and recorded in book/reel/volume No. ______, on page ______ and/or as fee/file/instrument/microfilm/reception No. ______, Records of this County.

Witness my hand and seal of County affixed.

NAME TITLE

By ______, Deputy.

QUITCLAIM DEED – STATUTORY FORM
(INDIVIDUAL GRANTOR)

______, Grantor,
releases and quitclaims to ______, Grantee,
all right, title and interest in and to the following described real property situated in ______ County, Oregon, to-wit:

(IF SPACE INSUFFICIENT, CONTINUE DESCRIPTION ON REVERSE SIDE)

The property is free of encumbrances, except (if none, so state):

The true consideration for this conveyance is $ ______. (Here, comply with the requirements of ORS 93.030.)

DATED ______

THIS INSTRUMENT WILL NOT ALLOW USE OF THE PROPERTY DESCRIBED IN THIS INSTRUMENT IN VIOLATION OF APPLICABLE LAND USE LAWS AND REGULATIONS. BEFORE SIGNING OR ACCEPTING THIS INSTRUMENT, THE PERSON ACQUIRING FEE TITLE TO THE PROPERTY SHOULD CHECK WITH THE APPROPRIATE CITY OR COUNTY PLANNING DEPARTMENT TO VERIFY APPROVED USES AND TO DETERMINE ANY LIMITS ON LAWSUITS AGAINST FARMING OR FOREST PRACTICES AS DEFINED IN ORS 30.930.

STATE OF OREGON, County of ______) ss.

This instrument was acknowledged before me on ______,
by ______.

Notary Public for Oregon.
My commission expires ______

Statutory form quitclaim deed. Note the change in the language from "conveys" to "releases and quitclaims." This is because "conveys" implies a warranty of fee title, and the grantor here may have no interest at all.

NOTES

Transfer of personal property

Where deeds are the normal instrument used to convey real property, we transfer personal property by a ***bill of sale***. A bill of sale is to personal property what a deed is to real property. Many real estate transactions involve personal property as well as the real estate – e.g., a range and a refrigerator included in the sale price. Therefore it is not uncommon to find a bill of sale in a real estate transaction as well as a deed.

While deeds are very important documents and real estate agents usually avoid being involved in drafting them, the bill of sale usually involves far less liability. Even so, in most places in Oregon today transactions are closed in escrow and the escrow closing agent prepares the bill of sale as well as the deed.

Exercise b

To be valid and enforceable a deed must be in writing and signed by the ______________ who must be ______________. The signature of the ______________ is not required, nor need the ______________ be competent. Nevertheless, a deed must state an identifiable ______________. The deed must recite an ______________ ______________ of the premises and must contain words of conveyance, also called a ______________ clause. To finalize the deed the seller must ______________ it to the buyer, and the buyer must ______________ the conveyance. Although not required for validity, deeds must contain a land use ______________ statement. Deeds do not need a consideration, a date or a ______________ clause.

The best deed for the buyer is a ______________ deed. A similar deed, but where the grantor's liability is limited is the ______________ ______________ deed. These deeds contain three covenants, which are:

1. ______________________________

2. ______________________________

3. ______________________________

The ______________ and ______________ deed contains no warranties of title, but its use creates a presumption that the grantor has a fee title. The ______________ deed does not even contain a presumption that the grantor has a fee title, so it is commonly used in order to release a ______________ from the title. The most common versions of these deeds in use today are the ______________ formats. Real estate agents should not ______________ the language of these forms, nor should agents select which form to use.

A ______________ is a grant of land from the federal government to the first settler. The settler's claims were commonly called ______________ ______________ Claims.

A conveyance to the public, such as for roads and streets in a subdivision, is called a ______________, which formerly was a ______________ - ______________ dedication, but today would be a ______________ dedication.

The transfer of personal property is accomplished with a ______________ of ______________.

NOTES

Oregon inheritance laws

At one time or another, most real estate agents become involved in the sale of property in an estate. Inheritance laws are complex, but a knowledge of at least the terminology can be useful in these situations.

A deceased person is called the ***decedent***. When the decedent leaves a will, we say that he or she died ***testate***. A decedent who died without leaving a valid will is said to have died ***intestate***. Ordinarily, the only wills recognized in Oregon are formal, written, witnessed wills.

A gift of real property by will is called a ***devise*** and the recipient (heir) is the ***devisee***. A gift of personal property in a will is called a ***bequest*** or a ***legacy*** and the recipient is called the ***legatee***.

When the decedent dies intestate there is a question of the disposition of the estate. Of course, if there are no heirs, the estate will escheat to the state. If there is a spouse, and no other heirs, the spouse will take all. If there is a spouse and children, the spouse will take one-half and the children will share the other half. If a married couple are divorced, then the spouse is entitled to nothing. If the spouse and children have died, their children, if any, will share the estate. There are also provisions for further distribution which are too involved for our discussion here.

Although there are ways to avoid it, the estate of a decedent must usually go through ***probate***. Probate is the process of submitting the estate to the scrutiny of the probate court for final distribution of the decedent's assets.

A decedent who died testate may have named a ***personal representative*** in his or her will. If not, or if the decedent died intestate, the probate court will appoint a personal representative. Personal representative is the modern term for "executor" and "administrator." The personal representative has broad powers in Oregon, including the right to list property for sale, accept offers, sign deeds, contracts, leases, etc. – as long as the action is consistent with the provisions of the will.

KEY TERMS

The key to understanding any new field is the vocabulary used in that field. To maximize your comprehension of the material presented in this chapter, be sure you know the meaning and significance of the following terms. Remember that the majority of test questions primarily test knowledge of vocabulary.

Acceptance
Accession
Accretion
Acknowledgment
Adequate description of the premises
Adverse possession
After-acquired title
Alienation
Alluvium (or alluvion)
Avulsion
Bargain and sale deed
Bequest
Bill of sale
Claim of right
Color of title
Common-law dedication
Competence
Continuous possession
Conveyance
Covenant against encumbrances
Covenant of quiet enjoyment
Covenant of seizin

Decedent
Dedication
Deed
Delivery
Devise
Devisee
Donation Land Claim
Exception
Exclusive possession
Full warranty deed
General warranty deed
Grant
Grantee
Granting clause
Grantor
Habendum clause
Hostile
Idem sonans
Identifiable grantee
In writing
Intestate
Involuntary conveyances
Legacy
Legatee
Open and notorious
Patent
Personal representative
Probate
Reservation
Quitclaim deed
Signature of the grantor(s)
Special warranty deed
Statutory dedications
Statutory form deeds
Tacking
Testate
Voluntary conveyances
Warranty deed
Words of conveyance

ANSWERS

To chapter exercises. If you couldn't figure out what to put in the blanks, find the answer here!

Exercise a

A transfer of title is called a CONVEYANCE *or an* ALIENATION *and it can be voluntary or* INVOLUNTARY. *When it is voluntary, it is frequently called a* GRANT. *The party giving up ownership is called the* GRANTOR *and the receiving party is the* GRANTEE. *When soil is gradually deposited by a stream along a riparian property, the owner of the property may gain title because the owner has a right of* ACCESSION. *The process of adding soil is called* ACCRETION. *The soil itself is called* ALLUVIUM.

Gaining title by adverse possession is similar to gaining an easement by PRESCRIPTION. *The possession must be* OPEN *and* NOTORIOUS, *that is, it cannot be in secret. The possession must also be continuous, normally for at least* 10 *years. In addition, the possession must be* EXCLUSIVE, *that is, the claimant must be the only claimant. If the true owner gives the claimant* PERMISSION *to occupy the property, this would destroy the element of* HOSTILITY, *which defeats the claim. If the owner believes that he or she is the owner and the belief is based on a written document, then we say the adverse possessor has* COLOR *of* TITLE.

Exercise b

To be valid and enforceable a deed must be in writing and signed by the GRANTOR *who must be* COMPETENT. *The signature of the* GRANTEE *is not required, nor need the* GRANTEE *be competent. Nevertheless, a deed must state an identifiable* GRANTEE. *The deed must recite an* ADEQUATE DESCRIPTION *of the premises and must contain words of conveyance, also called a* ___GRANTING___ *clause. To finalize the deed the seller must* ___DELIVER___ *it to the buyer, and the buyer must* ___ACCEPT___ *the conveyance. Although not required for validity, deeds must contain a land use* ___DISCLOSURE___ *statement. Deeds do not need a consideration, a date or a* ___HABENDUM___ *clause.*

The best deed for the buyer is a ___WARRANTY___ *deed. A similar deed, but where the grantor's liability is limited is the* ___SPECIAL___ ___WARRANTY___ *deed. These deeds contain three covenants, which are:*

1. ___COVENANT OF SEIZEN___
2. ___COVENANT OF QUIET ENJOYMENT___
3. ___COVENANT AGAINST ENCUMBRANCES___

The ___BARGAIN___ *and* ___SALE___ *deed contains no warranties of title, but its use creates a presumption that the grantor has a fee title. The* ___QUITCLAIM___ *deed does not even contain a presumption that the grantor has a fee title, so it is commonly used in order to release a* ___CLOUD___ *from the title. The most common versions of these deeds in use today are the* ___STATUTORY___ *formats. Real estate agents should not* ___ALTER___ *the language of these forms, nor should agents select which form to use.*

A ___PATENT___ *is a grant of land from the federal government to the first settler. The settler's claims were commonly called* ___DONATION___ ___LAND___ *Claims.*

A conveyance to the public, such as for roads and streets in a subdivision, is called a ___DEDICATION___*, which formerly was a* ___COMMON___ - ___LAW___ *dedication, but today would be a* ___STATUTORY___ *dedication.*

The transfer of personal property is accomplished with a ___BILL___ *of* ___SALE___ .

PRACTICE QUESTIONS

The following practice questions are representative of the questions you will find on the final examination and on the licensing examinations given by the Oregon Real Estate Agency.

1. The transferring of title to real property to another is defined as
(A) proration.
(B) alienation.
(C) prescription.
(D) consideration.

2. Voluntary alienation refers to
(A) sale or gift.
(B) adverse possession.
(C) eminent domain.
(D) descent.

3. Alienation means
(A) a conveyance.
(B) adverse possession.
(C) prescription.
(D) accession.

4. Alienation is a term which is most nearly the opposite of
(A) acquisition.
(B) sale.
(C) conveyance.
(D) accession.

5. Alienation in real estate could result from which of the following?
(A) Adverse possession
(B) Delivery of a deed
(C) Eminent domain proceedings
(D) Any of the above

6. An alienation can occur by
(A) creating a cloud on the title.
(B) conveying the title.
(C) filing a declaration of homestead.
(D) creating a lien on the title.

7. Which of the following would not be a way in which title can be conveyed?
(A) Accession
(B) Forfeiture
(C) Sufferance
(D) Dedication

8. Title to real property can be obtained as a result of
(A) accretion.
(B) hypothecation.
(C) either A or B.
(D) neither A nor B.

9. Real estate can be conveyed by
(A) intestate succession.
(B) devise.
(C) voluntary alienation.
(D) any of the above.

10. Which of the following is a document which transfers possession for a consideration, but does not transfer ownership?
(A) A special warranty deed
(B) A deed containing a restriction
(C) A last will and testament
(D) Lease

11. Involuntary alienation of an estate means
(A) an estate cannot be transferred without the consent of the owner.
(B) aliens are forbidden ownership in fee simple.
(C) ownership of estates may be transferred by operation of law.
(D) no one can be compelled to relinquish title without giving consent.

12. The right of alienation is defined as
(A) the right to execute and deliver a deed.
(B) the right to transfer an interest in real property.
(C) the right to make a will.
(D) statutes of descent and distribution.

13. The purchaser of real property, who acquires clear title from the seller, is the
(A) grantor.
(B) beneficiary.
(C) grantee.
(D) vendor.

14. The addition to one's land by the gradual deposit of soil through natural causes is
(A) annulation.
(B) avulsion.
(C) accretion.
(D) ademption.

15. Gaining land by any natural or man-made cause is
(A) accretion.
(B) accession.
(C) avulsion.
(D) reliction.

16. Soil added through accretion is called
(A) accession.
(B) alluvium.
(C) gneiss.
(D) backfill.

17. When land is acquired by accretion it is called ownership by
(A) annexation. (C) eminent domain.
(B) accession. (D) adverse possession.

18. The sudden tearing away or removal of land by action of water is
(A) accretion. (C) adversion.
(B) erosion. (D) avulsion.

19. Avulsion is a term which would be best described as
(A) the gradual lowering of the water level leaving dry land.
(B) the sudden tearing away of land by water action.
(C) the gradual addition of land by water action.
(D) what happens when a surveyor moves a monument.

20. Which of the following statements concerning the addition or subtraction of land is correct?
I. Accretion is the gradual deposit of soil through natural causes.
II. The sudden tearing away of land by action of water is called avulsion.
III. Erosion is the gradual loss of soil due to currents, tides, or winds.
(A) I only (C) II and III only
(B) II only (D) I, II and III

21. The removal of land when a stream suddenly changes its channel is
(A) adverse possession. (C) avulsion.
(B) accretion. (D) breach.

22. When accretion occurs, title to extra land created becomes vested in
(A) the State of Oregon.
(B) the city or county.
(C) the owner of the adjacent land.
(D) the federal government.

23. A means of acquiring title where the occupant has been in actual, open, notorious, exclusive and continuous occupation of property under a claim of right for the statutory period of time is known as
(A) eminent domain. (C) prescription.
(B) escheat. (D) adverse possession.

24. Under certain circumstances, an encroachment on another's land may ripen into
(A) an easement by prescription.
(B) title by adverse possession.
(C) either A or B.
(D) neither A nor B.

25. In order to perfect a claim of adverse possession, the claimant must do all of the following except
(A) maintain possession under claim of right at all times.
(B) pay the taxes on the land.
(C) exhibit open and notorious possession of the land.
(D) The claimant must do all of the above.

26. In Oregon, the time period of adverse possession is generally
(A) five years. (C) fifteen years.
(B) ten years. (D) twenty years.

27. One of the requirements for perfecting a claim of adverse possession is that the claimant's occupancy must have been continuous. In Oregon this means that the claimant
I. must have used the premises for at least ten years.
II. cannot leave the property for more than one month.
(A) I only (C) Both I and II
(B) II only (D) Neither I nor II

28. A claim based upon adverse possession of property must be
I. open. III. hostile.
II. notorious.
(A) I and II (C) II and III
(B) I and III (D) I, II and III

29. In order to receive a title by adverse possession, the claimant must do which of the following?
I. Be open and notorious
II. Have actual possession
III. Register with public agencies at the time of first possession
(A) I only (C) I and II only
(B) III only (D) I, II and III

30. The word hostile as applied to adverse possession means
    (A) the tenant hates the landlord.
    (B) the possessor claims ownership, rejecting other claims.
    (C) the possessor will defend the land by force if necessary.
    (D) the possessor has fenced off the land.

31. An owner can defeat a potential claim of adverse possession by
    (A) ejecting the adverse claimant before the claimant has been in possession for ten years.
    (B) giving the adverse claimant permission to occupy the property for ten years.
    (C) either A or B.
    (D) neither A nor B.

32. An owner can defeat an adverse possession claim by
    I. evicting the adverse claimant within the statutory time period.
    II. resuming actual possession within the statutory time period.
    (A) I only (C) Both I and II
    (B) II only (D) Neither I nor II

33. An unmarried man claims to own land which he has occupied for the past eighteen years. His claim will probably be worthless if he
    (A) pays rent to the person named in the most recent deed of record.
    (B) fails to pay the taxes on the property each year.
    (C) should marry.
    (D) cannot obtain a quitclaim deed from adjacent property owners.

34. Mr. Sams owns a lot and in addition occupies a strip ten feet wide on Mr. Alberts' land in the mistaken belief that this was the boundary. During the period of possession, Mr. Alberts notifies Mr. Sams of Mr. Sams' encroachment. Nevertheless, Mr. Sams continues to occupy the strip for ten years. If Mr. Sams sues Mr. Alberts to get title to the property, the court will most likely
    (A) find that Mr. Sams now owns the ten-foot strip.
    (B) find that Mr. Alberts owns the ten-foot strip.
    (C) require that Mr. Sams pay Mr. Alberts for the fair market value of the ten-foot strip.
    (D) require that Mr. Alberts pay Mr. Sams the fair market value of the ten-foot strip.

35. Barbara Barbells received permission from her neighbor to occupy a portion of the neighbor's land and occupied it under this permission for over twenty years. She could acquire title to the land by
    (A) adverse possession. (C) eminent domain.
    (B) prescription. (D) none of the above.

36. That which gives the appearance of title, but which really is not title, is called
    (A) an easement. (C) color of title.
    (B) a subordination. (D) prescription.

37. All but one of the following terms describe the type of occupancy needed for adverse possession.
    (A) Continuous (C) Lawful
    (B) Exclusive (D) Open and notorious

38. Occupation of real property may ripen into legal title by adverse possession. The adverse possessor must in all cases
    I. be in actual possession of the subject property for the statutory period of time.
    II. show in his or her manner of possession that it is hostile to the true owner's title.
    III. obtain a judicial decree quieting the title or obtain a quitclaim deed from the ousted owner in order to have marketable title.
    (A) II only (C) I and III only
    (B) I and II only (D) I, II and III

39. To acquire title by adverse possession, the adverse claimant
    I. must maintain actual, open, hostile and continuous possession for the statutory time period set by the state.
    II. may tack the time of possession to that of a previous adverse possessor if the two were successors in interest.
    (A) I only (C) Both I and II
    (B) II only (D) Neither I nor II

40. Which of the following statements concerning adverse possession is correct?
    I. A license usually cannot be converted into adverse possession.
    II. Adverse possession generally cannot be perfected over land held by the state.
    (A) I only (C) Both I and II
    (B) II only (D) Neither I nor II

41. Adverse possession and prescription could be terminated by all of the following except
    (A) asserting ownership rights after nine years.
    (B) giving the adverse possessor permission to trespass after five years.
    (C) taking legal steps to remove the adverse possessor after ten years.
    (D) taking legal steps to remove the adverse possessor after three years.

42. Title acquired through adverse possession can be perfected by
    (A) recording a claim of right within ten years of the start of the possession.
    (B) filing a suit to quiet title after the statutory time period.
    (C) either A or B.
    (D) neither A nor B.

43. The boundary line of your property can be changed by
    (A) accretion.
    (B) adverse possession.
    (C) both A or B.
    (D) neither A nor B.

44. In order to convey title to real property, a deed must contain which of the following?
    I. Words of conveyance
    II. An offer and acceptance
    (A) I only
    (B) II only
    (C) Both I and II
    (D) Neither I nor II

45. In order to be valid a deed must
    (A) be in writing.
    (B) be recorded.
    (C) be signed by both the grantor and grantee.
    (D) have all of the above.

46. To be legal, a deed must have
    (A) acknowledgment.
    (B) verification.
    (C) the grantee's signature.
    (D) a granting clause.

47. Every valid deed must contain
    I. words of conveyance.
    II. the name of the grantee.
    III. the name of the grantor.
    (A) I only
    (B) III only
    (C) II and III only
    (D) I, II and III

48. Which of the following is not necessary to the validity of a deed?
    (A) Grantor execution
    (B) Delivery to grantee
    (C) Recording the deed
    (D) Designating the grantee

49. A valid deed must have which of the following?
    I. Description of the property
    II. Grantor's signature
    III. Tax assessed value of the property
    IV. Words of conveyance
    (A) I and II only
    (B) II and III only
    (C) I, II and IV only
    (D) I, III and IV only

50. Which of the following is not a requirement of a valid deed?
    (A) A written form
    (B) Signed by the grantor
    (C) A good legal description of the property being conveyed
    (D) Acknowledgment by the grantor

51. Which of the following are essential elements of a valid deed?
    I. Grantee's signature
    II. Adequate legal description
    III. Acknowledgment
    IV. Grantor's signature
    (A) I and II only
    (B) II and III only
    (C) II and IV only
    (D) I, II and IV only

52. Which of the following is required for a deed to be valid in Oregon?
    (A) Recording within 15 days of the delivery
    (B) A legal description of the property written by a surveyor
    (C) A granting or releasing clause
    (D) The name and address where the tax bill is to be sent

53. Mr. Black made out a proper deed intending to deed property to one of several friends. Not having finalized the decision, he left the grantee's name out temporarily. Later he decided who to convey the property to so he delivered the deed to the person, but never filled in the name. The friend will receive
    (A) full title regardless.
    (B) full title by writing his or her name in the proper place in the deed.
    (C) full title, but with the restriction that it cannot be conveyed to anyone by Mr. Black.
    (D) nothing.

54. Which of the following is required for a deed to be valid?
    I. A witness to the signature of the grantee
    II. An adequate description of the property
    III. Acknowledgment of the grantor's signature
    (A) I only (C) I and II only
    (B) II only (D) II and III only

55. Which of the following is a requirement for a valid deed?
    I. Acknowledgment by the grantee
    II. Recordation
    III. Granting clause
    (A) II only (C) I and III only
    (B) III only (D) I, II and III

56. In order to be valid a deed must
    (A) contain the street address identification.
    (B) state nature of the improvements on the land (dwellings).
    (C) contain adequate description to identify the property being conveyed.
    (D) state the total area in the tract.

57. Which of the following affects the validity of a deed?
    (A) Illiteracy
    (B) Omission of the habendum clause
    (C) Error in stating the true amount of consideration
    (D) Insufficient description of the land to be conveyed

58. Which of the following is essential for a deed to be legally effective?
    I. The parties must be properly identified.
    II. It must be in writing.
    III. The property conveyed must be adequately described.
    IV. There must be a breach of contract clause.
    (A) II only (C) I, II and III only
    (B) I and II only (D) II, III and IV only

59. A deed fails to state an adequate description of the property being conveyed unless it
    (A) states the property tax account number of the property.
    (B) describes the improvements on the land.
    (C) contains a description adequate to identify the property with certainty.
    (D) states the area in square feet or acres.

60. Which of these is not essential to the validity of a deed?
    (A) Competent grantor
    (B) Monetary consideration
    (C) Description
    (D) Delivery

61. A deed which does not include a date, an acknowledgment and which is not recorded is
    (A) nevertheless valid between the parties.
    (B) unenforceable on the grantor.
    (C) revocable by the grantee.
    (D) void.

62. If consideration is not stated in a deed, it
    I. is still valid.
    II. can still be recorded provided that it is an exchange, gift or conveyance from an estate.
    (A) I only (C) Both I and II
    (B) II only (D) Neither I nor II

63. A gift deed can be set aside
    I. if it is revoked by the grantor.
    II. by a creditor of the grantor.
    (A) I only (C) Both I and II
    (B) II only (D) Neither I nor II

64. If only air rights are being conveyed by a deed, the
(A) words of conveyance can be omitted.
(B) phrase "to have and to hold" must be omitted.
(C) property description will be in three dimensions.
(D) signature of the grantee will be required.

65. The words "grant" and "release"
I. are not required for a valid deed in Oregon.
II. are examples of words of conveyance.
(A) I only (C) Both I and II
(B) II only (D) Neither I nor II

66. The words of conveyance in a deed
I. state that the grantor is making a transfer of the title to the grantee.
II. grant the grantee the covenant against encumbrances.
(A) I only (C) Both I and II
(B) II only (D) Neither I nor II

67. Which of the following must always sign a deed for it to be valid?
(A) The grantor
(B) The grantee
(C) The recording officer
(D) All of the above

68. A deed conveying the title to a parcel of real estate must be signed by the
(A) grantor and grantee.
(B) grantee.
(C) grantor.
(D) grantee and, if married, his or her spouse.

69. In order to transfer title to real estate, a deed must be
(A) signed by the grantor.
(B) acknowledged.
(C) recorded.
(D) signed by the grantee.

70. The absence of which of the following would invalidate a deed?
(A) Signature of the grantee
(B) Delivery
(C) Capacity of the grantee
(D) Recordation

71. In order to be valid in Oregon a deed must contain
(A) the expression "to have and to hold."
(B) words of conveyance.
(C) both A and B.
(D) neither A nor B.

72. The clause that defines or limits the quantity of the estate being conveyed is the
(A) partition clause. (C) reversion clause.
(B) revocation clause. (D) habendum clause.

73. When a long form deed states "to have and to hold forever," these words indicate that the estate being conveyed is
(A) an estate for years. (C) a tenancy at will.
(B) a fee simple estate. (D) a life estate.

74. With the words of conveyance in a deed, the grantor
I. makes a transfer of the title to the grantee.
II. identifies the type of estate that is being transferred.
(A) I only (C) Both I and II
(B) II only (D) Neither I nor II

75. Which of the following would cause a deed to be invalid in its inception?
(A) Legal incompetence of the grantor
(B) The deed was signed and dated on a legal holiday
(C) Failure to insert the clause "to heirs and assigns" following the name of the grantee
(D) Legal incompetence of the grantee

76. A deed may be invalidated by which of the following actions?
(A) Failure to insert the clause "to successors in interest" following the name of the grantee
(B) Legal incompetence of the grantor
(C) Executing and dating the deed on a legal holiday
(D) Any of the above actions would invalidate a deed

77. A deed would be void if the
I. grantee was incompetent.
II. deed failed to state the manner in which the title was to be taken by the grantee.
(A) I only (C) Both I and II
(B) II only (D) Neither I nor II

78. A deed was made out and signed by the grantor who was incompetent at the time. The deed
   I. cannot be recorded.
   II. can be set aside at the option of the grantor.
   (A) I only
   (B) II only
   (C) Both I and II
   (D) Neither I nor II

79. All of the following would have capacity to execute a valid deed except
   (A) a minor.
   (B) a convicted felon who is incarcerated.
   (C) a person who is not a citizen of the United States.
   (D) the husband acting alone when the property is owned as tenants by the entirety.

80. A father, deeded some property to his son. Which of the following is correct?
   (A) The deed is ineffective because the son is a minor.
   (B) The deed is ineffective because, since the father is the guardian, the conveyance is actually from the father to himself.
   (C) The deed is ineffective until the son's 18th birthday.
   (D) The deed is valid and enforceable.

81. A deed would be void if it
   I. failed to state the estate being conveyed to the grantee.
   II. purported to convey title to a grantee who was incompetent at the time of the conveyance.
   III. failed to state the manner in which two or more grantees are to take title.
   (A) I only
   (B) I and III only
   (C) II and III only
   (D) None of the above

82. A deed would be unenforceable if the
   I. spelling of the grantor's name is wrong.
   II. spelling of the grantee's name is wrong.
   III. grantee takes title in an assumed name.
   (A) I only
   (B) I and II only
   (C) I, II and III
   (D) None of the above

83. Which of the following would render a deed invalid?
   (A) Failing to insert the phrase "and successors in interest" after the grantee's name
   (B) Incapacity of the grantor
   (C) Grantor signing the deed on a Sunday
   (D) Any of the above

84. A deed would be rendered invalid if
   (A) the space for the grantee's name was made out to "bearer."
   (B) the grantor's signature was not acknowledged.
   (C) the deed is not recorded.
   (D) any of the above defects exist.

85. A deed may be
   (A) assigned to another.
   (B) endorsed to another.
   (C) signed with the grantor's mark.
   (D) any of the above.

86. Ted Mahoney gave a general warranty deed to his nephew John when John bought the apartment building Ted owned. John had the deed recorded. Later John decided to convey the property back to Ted. How could this best be accomplished?
   (A) John must give Ted a reconveyance deed.
   (B) John must make a new deed to Ted and Ted should record it.
   (C) John must endorse the deed and return it to Ted.
   (D) John must do either A or B above.

87. Paulson deeds property to Samuelson. Later Samuelson desires to convey the property back to Paulson. In this case
   (A) the original conveyance can be voided by a mutual agreement to rescind.
   (B) Samuelson must make out a new deed and deliver it to Paulson.
   (C) it is sufficient for Samuelson simply to hand the deed back to Paulson.
   (D) Samuelson must deliver a special deed of reconveyance to Paulson.

88. Bebe Rebozo deeds property to Richard Nixon who has the deed recorded. Later, for political reasons, they want to undo the transaction. They should
   (A) have Nixon give a new deed back to Rebozo.
   (B) have Nixon endorse the deed back to Rebozo.
   (C) pay hush money to the recorder of deeds so the existence of the deed will not be revealed.
   (D) hire someone to break into the recorder's office and steal the deed.

89. Wolf Panter gives a deed to property he owns to his friend Bambi LaTush, but asks her not to record it until after his death. Title is conveyed
(A) upon Panter's death. (C) never.
(B) upon recording. (D) immediately.

90. Harry hands Charlie a deed with the intent to pass title and asks Charlie not to record the deed until Harry dies. When does title transfer?
(A) Upon Harry's death
(B) When Charlie records the deed
(C) Never
(D) Immediately

91. A woman delivered a deed to an escrow with instructions that it be delivered to the grantee when the grantee turned 21 years of age. Before the grantee turned 21, the woman died. In this case,
(A) the grantee will receive title upon turning 21 years of age.
(B) the woman's estate will have the use of the property until the grantee turns 21.
(C) the grantee will take title immediately upon the woman's death.
(D) both B and C are correct.

92. A man made out a deed naming his cousin as the grantee and placed it in his safe deposit box. When the man died, the deed was discovered. In this case, the
(A) cousin came into title immediately upon finalization of probate.
(B) cousin came into title as of the date the deed was signed and placed in the box.
(C) property went immediately to the man's heirs upon his death.
(D) property escheated to the state.

93. Which of the following could be used to convey property after the grantor's death?
(A) Warranty deed (C) Bargain and sale deed
(B) Quitclaim deed (D) None of the above

94. Effective delivery of a deed depends upon the
(A) physical transfer of the deed to the grantee.
(B) intention of the grantor.
(C) notarization of the grantor's signature.
(D) recording of the deed by the grantor.

95. Ownership of property is transferred when the
(A) delivery of the deed is made.
(B) grantor signs the deed.
(C) grantee pays the balance owing on the mortgage.
(D) grantor's signature has been notarized.

96. In a real estate sale transaction title to the real estate passes from seller to buyer when
(A) the buyer takes possession of the property.
(B) the seller executes and delivers the deed, and the buyer accepts the deed.
(C) the buyer records the deed.
(D) all of the above have happened.

97. Of the following, the most important act towards the effective conveyance of real property would be
(A) recording the deed.
(B) buyer's possession of the property.
(C) issuance of a policy of title insurance.
(D) delivery of a deed to the buyer.

98. When does legal title to real property pass from the seller to the buyer?
(A) On the date of recording of the deed
(B) When the closing statement has been signed
(C) When the deed is placed in escrow
(D) When the deed is delivered

99. Which of the following is necessary for a valid transfer of title to real estate?
I. Delivery of the deed III. A competent grantee
II. Recording of the deed
(A) I only (C) I and III only
(B) I and II only (D) II and III only

100. A deed is signed and delivered by the
(A) grantee. (C) broker.
(B) notary public. (D) grantor.

101. A covenant in a deed is
(A) a promise to do or not to do something.
(B) a privilege granted to the buyer.
(C) the same as a defeasance clause.
(D) a condition subsequent to the vesting of title.

102. A covenant in a special warranty deed which guarantees the owner the right to uninterrupted possession of the property is called the covenant
(A) of quiet enjoyment.
(B) of seizin.
(C) against encumbrances.
(D) of title insurance.

103. The covenant whereby the grantor warrants that he or she is the owner and the possessor of the property being conveyed is called the covenant of
(A) seizin.
(B) quiet enjoyment.
(C) habendum.
(D) quantum.

104. The covenant in a deed which states that the grantor is the owner and has the right to convey title is called the covenant
(A) of warranty of title.
(B) of seizin.
(C) against encumbrances.
(D) of further assurance.

105. The covenant in a deed stating that the grantor has full possession of the premises in fee simple, or any other estate the grantor purports to convey, is called the covenant of
(A) seizin.
(B) habendum.
(C) quiet enjoyment.
(D) further assurance.

106. The covenant of quiet enjoyment in a deed
(A) gives the grantee assurance of ownership uninterrupted by claims of others.
(B) warrants that the property is free and clear.
(C) obligates the grantee to adhere to all public land use laws.
(D) requires the seller to provide the buyer with a title insurance policy.

107. The expression "quiet enjoyment" means most nearly the same as
(A) no interruption from a claimant with paramount title.
(B) no interference from adjacent landowners.
(C) no interruption from a landlord.
(D) the covenant of seizin.

108. The covenant whereby the grantor guarantees that there are no tax liens, mortgages or assessments, except as stated in the deed, is called the covenant
(A) of seizin.
(B) against encumbrances.
(C) of warranty of title.
(D) against grantor's acts.

109. Which of the following is not considered a separate covenant in an Oregon statutory warranty deed?
(A) Covenant against encumbrances
(B) Covenant of seizin
(C) Covenant of quantum
(D) Covenant against encumbrances

110. A short form deed with special wording would be
(A) a special warranty deed.
(B) a statutory dedication.
(C) a statutory form deed.
(D) a patent.

111. Since the 1973 Oregon Legislature established statutory deed forms for the voluntary conveyance of real property, the real estate licensee should
(A) help his or her clients choose the deed form.
(B) have his or her clients hire an attorney to make any needed deviations from the statutory forms.
(C) make sure that only an attorney fills in the blank spaces on the forms.
(D) do all of the above.

112. In handling a real estate transaction, a licensee may
I. help a client fill in the blanks on a statutory deed form.
II. advise a client on the selection of a statutory deed form.
(A) I only
(B) II only
(C) Both I and II
(D) Neither I nor II

113. An Oregon statutory deed
I. is mandatory in order to record the deed in the county clerk's office.
II. requires the services of an attorney to fill in the blank spaces on the form.
(A) I only
(B) II only
(C) Both I and II
(D) Neither I nor II

114. The Oregon statutory special warranty deed
I. gives the purchaser the highest form of protection against claims on the property.
II. conveys any interest the grantor may receive after the deed is signed.
(A) I only
(B) II only
(C) Both I and II
(D) Neither I nor II

115. Which of the following are differences between an Oregon statutory bargain and sale deed and an Oregon statutory quitclaim deed?
   I. The Oregon statutory bargain and sale deed conveys any title acquired by the grantor after the deed is signed.
   II. The Oregon statutory bargain and sale deed contains several warranties concerning the quality of title conveyed by the grantor.
   (A) I only
   (B) II only
   (C) Both I and II
   (D) Neither I nor II

116. In Oregon, the statutory quitclaim deed
   (A) is the only quitclaim deed accepted for recordation.
   (B) has the effect of conveying title the grantor may have at the date of the deed.
   (C) has the effect of conveying title the grantor may have at the date of the deed and transfers any title which the grantor may thereafter obtain.
   (D) is the same as the bargain and sale deed.

117. The main difference among the different deed forms is in the
   (A) manner of delivery.
   (B) manner of execution.
   (C) recording requirements.
   (D) warranty of title.

118. From the grantee's point of view, which of the following deeds would be most desirable?
   (A) Special warranty deed
   (B) General warranty deed
   (C) Bargain and sale deed
   (D) Quitclaim deed

119. The best deed a grantee can receive is ordinarily the
   (A) special warranty deed.
   (B) general warranty deed.
   (C) grant deed.
   (D) quitclaim deed.

120. The deed form that creates the greatest potential liability to the grantor is the
   (A) general warranty deed.
   (B) administrator's deed.
   (C) executor's deed.
   (D) sheriff's deed.

121. Which of the following covenants would be contained in a warranty deed?
   I. Warranty forever
   II. Quiet enjoyment
   III. Seizin (or seizin)
   IV. Against encumbrances
   (A) I and III
   (B) II and III
   (C) III and IV
   (D) I, II, III and IV

122. A grantee who obtains a warranty deed receives all of the following warranties except that the
   (A) grantor will defend the title against all claims except as stated in the deed.
   (B) grantor will reimburse the grantee if the structure is defective.
   (C) identified estate is free of all encumbrances except as stated in the deed.
   (D) grantor is the owner of the property.

123. An undisclosed encumbrance placed on the property by the seller would be warranted under a
   I. general warranty deed.
   II. special warranty deed.
   (A) I only
   (B) II only
   (C) Both I and II
   (D) Neither I nor II

124. Under a general warranty deed, the
   I. grantor will defend the property if a structural defect is discovered.
   II. grantor's promise to defend the title expires with the death of the grantee.
   (A) I only
   (B) II only
   (C) Both I and II
   (D) Neither I nor II

125. Which of the following types of deeds is generally required of an individual seller?
   (A) Special warranty deed
   (B) Quitclaim deed
   (C) General warranty deed
   (D) Bargain and sale deed

126. Which type of deed limits the covenants made by the grantor when real estate is conveyed?
   I. General warranty deed
   II. Special warranty deed
   III. Bargain and sale deed
   (A) I only
   (B) II only
   (C) I and II only
   (D) II and III only

127. Compared to a warranty deed, the covenants in a special warranty deed are
(A) fewer in number.
(B) narrower in coverage.
(C) both A and B.
(D) neither A nor B.

128. George McGraw sold his house to Sylvia White. In the form of deed that was used in the transaction, McGraw's only warranty was that the property was not encumbered during the time he held title as noted in the deed. The type of deed McGraw gave to White was a
(A) special warranty deed.
(B) bargain and sale deed.
(C) trust deed.
(D) quitclaim deed.

129. Susan is not certain that the property she is selling is completely unencumbered, but she is willing to guarantee the title against defects arising from any action by, through or under herself, the grantor. The deed that she would offer in this real estate transfer would be a
(A) general warranty deed.
(B) quitclaim deed.
(C) bargain and sale deed.
(D) special warranty deed.

130. Which of the following deed types would have the least number of warranties and covenants?
(A) Quitclaim deed
(B) Special warranty deed
(C) General warranty deed
(D) Bargain and sale deed

131. Which of the following deeds contain no warranty of title?
I. Quitclaim deed
II. Bargain and sale deed
III. Sheriff's deed
(A) I only
(B) I and II only
(C) I, II and III
(D) II only

132. A quitclaim deed transfers all rights the grantor may
I. hold when the deed is delivered.
II. acquire in the future.
(A) I only
(B) II only
(C) Both I and II
(D) Neither I nor II

133. The difference between a bargain and sale deed and a quitclaim deed is that the
(A) quitclaim deed does not convey after-acquired title.
(B) words of conveyance in a quitclaim deed contain the word "convey."
(C) bargain and sale deed conveys a greater title than the quitclaim deed.
(D) quitclaim deed contains warranty of title.

134. The type of deed which creates the least protection to the grantee is a
(A) quitclaim deed.
(B) general warranty deed.
(C) special warranty deed.
(D) bargain and sale deed.

135. A deed that passes any interest the signer may have, but does not tie the signer to any warranty, is called a
(A) trust deed.
(B) quitclaim deed.
(C) warranty deed.
(D) grant deed.

136. Which of the following deeds entails the least liability to the grantor?
(A) Special warranty deed
(B) Quitclaim deed
(C) General warranty deed
(D) Bargain and sale deed

137. A properly executed quitclaim deed should always convey
(A) a fee title to the property.
(B) a first lien on the property.
(C) an after-acquired interest in the property.
(D) an existing interest in the property.

138. Which of the following deed forms may convey no ownership rights at all?
(A) Quitclaim deed
(B) Sheriff's deed
(C) Special warranty deed
(D) General warranty deed

139. When would a quitclaim deed generally be used?
(A) To transfer a warranted title
(B) To remove a defect in title
(C) If grantor is financially unable to guarantee title
(D) If grantee has lost the recorded deed to the property

140. A properly executed quitclaim deed will always convey
(A) a fee title to the property.
(B) an existing interest in the property.
(C) a first lien on the property.
(D) an after-acquired interest in the property.

141. A quitclaim deed is frequently used to
(A) remove a cloud on a title.
(B) remove an escrow.
(C) terminate a power of attorney.
(D) evict a tenant.

142. Which of the following deeds would most commonly be used to remove a cloud from a title?
(A) Bargain and sale deed
(B) Quitclaim deed
(C) Special warranty deed
(D) General warranty deed

143. A quitclaim deed is most commonly used to
(A) cure title defects.
(B) give notice to the world that an owner has rights in the property.
(C) deed any future rights in a certain piece of property.
(D) convey fee simple title.

144. Which of the following statements about Oregon quitclaim deeds is true?
I. The Oregon quitclaim deed conveys any title or interest the grantor may have in the property.
II. A quitclaim deed must be completed by an attorney.
(A) I only
(B) II only
(C) Both I and II
(D) Neither I nor II

145. The words of conveyance are fundamentally different in which of the following deeds?
(A) Warranty deed
(B) Special warranty deed
(C) Bargain and sale deed
(D) Quitclaim deed

146. All of the following types of deeds are used in Oregon for voluntary conveyance of real property except the
(A) grant deed.
(B) full warranty deed.
(C) bargain and sale deed.
(D) quitclaim deed.

147. A deed used to convey a minor's interest in real property could be
(A) a gift deed.
(B) a sheriff's deed.
(C) a guardian's deed.
(D) a trustee's deed.

148. Vulture Enterprises, Inc. bought a property at a foreclosure sale. After the borrower's statutory right of redemption is over, they are entitled to a
(A) deed in lieu of foreclosure.
(B) trustee's deed.
(C) referee's deed.
(D) sheriff's deed.

149. When a land sales contract has been paid off, the seller must deliver a deed to the buyer. This deed is sometimes called
(A) a trust deed.
(B) a fulfillment deed.
(C) a deed of reconveyance.
(D) an installment deed.

150. A seller sold property to a buyer on a land sales contract. The buyer wished to give the property back to the seller. The usual deed to accomplish this would be
(A) a trust deed.
(B) a quitclaim deed.
(C) a deed of reconveyance.
(D) a sheriff's deed.

151. A quitclaim deed can be used to convey title
I. at the conclusion of a suit to quiet title.
II. when a sales transaction is being closed.
(A) I only
(B) II only
(C) Both I and II
(D) Neither I nor II

152. An "exception" in a deed
(A) reduces the rights conveyed in a fee simple estate.
(B) excepts part of the real property in the deed.
(C) is the same as a "subject to" clause.
(D) is an error in the deed.

153. An "exception" in a deed is a clause which
(A) provides that the grantor retains a portion of the property.
(B) allows the grantor to retain a lien on the property being conveyed.
(C) does both A and B.
(D) does neither A nor B.

154. A seller deeded property to a buyer but stipulated that the conveyance excluded a strip of land along the edge. This clause was
(A) an exception.
(B) a reservation.
(C) both A and B.
(D) neither A nor B.

155. Regarding deeds, which of the following statements is true?
(A) When a deed is delivered to the grantee, this is the same as recording.
(B) A reservation in a deed occurs when a portion of the property is withheld.
(C) A reservation in a deed occurs when some of the rights in the property are withheld.
(D) An exception is the same as a reservation.

156. A deed contains the statement "subject to an easement." This means the land
(A) has an appurtenance.
(B) is restricted.
(C) is encumbered.
(D) is subject to an exception.

157. A patent is
(A) the result which occurs when the government exercises its right of eminent domain.
(B) a grant of land from the federal government to a citizen.
(C) the right to the benefits and profits from an invention which has been affixed to real property.
(D) a legal term for an obvious fact.

158. A patent issued by government would involve
(A) an easement.
(B) dedication.
(C) a gradient.
(D) a conveyance.

159. First grant or patent in a chain of title is issued by
(A) a sovereign power.
(B) U.S. Government Patent office.
(C) the Recorder.
(D) the Recorder of Deeds.

160. When the state of Oregon today wishes to convey land to a citizen, the instrument used is
(A) a deed.
(B) a public land grant.
(C) a patent.
(D) a dedication.

161. A voluntary grant of land to the public is known as
(A) a patent.
(B) annexation.
(C) a dedication.
(D) condemnation.

162. The turning over of land by a developer to a public use is called
(A) subordination.
(B) dedication.
(C) condemnation.
(D) escalation.

163. When an owner, by act or by word, shows intent that land be conveyed to the public, even though no formal conveyance has been made, this is called
I. a common-law dedication.
II. a statutory dedication.
(A) I only
(B) II only
(C) Both I and II
(D) Neither I nor II

164. In order for a statutory dedication of land to be effective today, the
I. government agency acquiring title must formally accept the conveyance.
II. land must be properly platted and the plat recorded.
(A) I only
(B) II only
(C) Both I and II
(D) Neither I nor II

165. Personal property is conveyed using
(A) a bill of sale.
(B) a deed.
(C) a partial release for blanket encumbrances.
(D) an encumbrance.

166. Which of the following instruments would not transfer an interest in real property?
(A) Option
(B) Lease
(C) Bill of sale
(D) Agreement of sale

167. A person who dies without a will is said to have died
(A) testate.
(B) intestate.
(C) in succession.
(D) by devise.

168. If you acquire property by intestate succession, you received it
(A) by being a natural heir of a decedent.
(B) as a grant in a will.
(C) Both A and B are true.
(D) Neither A nor B is correct.

169. A devise is
 (A) a sum of money paid for real estate.
 (B) a gift of real property in a will.
 (C) a method of obtaining title to property without court action.
 (D) the creation of a less than freehold estate in real property.

170. The term "demise" means
 (A) a gift of real property to an heir.
 (B) the conveyance of an estate for years.
 (C) the creation of a life estate.
 (D) the death of a life tenant.

171. In Oregon, a person named to wind up the affairs of a decedent is called
 (A) an executor.
 (B) an executrix.
 (C) a personal representative.
 (D) either A or B.

172. When a person dies testate, the real property
 (A) escheats and is sold at an auction by the state.
 (B) goes to the next of kin.
 (C) passes by devise.
 (D) goes to the administrator.

173. If no heirs or devisees are in existence, a deceased person's estate
 (A) passes to the county by prescription.
 (B) passes to the state by escheat.
 (C) passes to the deceased person's church by mains froides, or to the state if the deceased is unaffiliated.
 (D) passes to the federal government by Title VII of the FICA.

174. If an Oregon resident owns property in severalty and dies intestate, leaving a widow and their child as survivors, the estate passes to the
 (A) widow alone. (C) child alone.
 (B) widow and child. (D) state of Oregon.

175. The transfer of title by descent means the owner
 (A) died testate, and property passes to the owner's heirs.
 (B) transferred a property interest by gift.
 (C) died intestate and property passes to the owner's heirs.
 (D) transferred the owner's property interest by sale.

176. A person receiving ownership of real property through a valid will is called the
 (A) testator or testatrix. (C) executor or executrix.
 (B) legatee. (D) devisee.

177. Conveyance of real property by escheat means that the owner has died
 (A) intestate without heirs.
 (B) with heirs and testate.
 (C) with unpaid real property taxes.
 (D) owing bills.

178. The power whereby property reverts to the state for lack of heirs is known as
 (A) escheat. (C) patented.
 (B) intestate property. (D) defaulted property.

179. Which of the following government rights permits the state to take ownership to land left by a person with no devisees or heirs?
 (A) Eminent domain (C) Escheat
 (B) Police power (D) Estoppel

180. A deed limitation on the use or enjoyment of real property is
 (A) an option. (C) an easement.
 (B) a restriction. (D) a license.

181. A condition which passes with the title could be created by
 I. written agreement. II. deed.
 (A) I only (C) Both I and II
 (B) II only (D) Neither I nor II

182. The main purpose of a deed is to
 (A) provide a written instrument suitable for recordation.
 (B) identify the party to whom the tax statement should be sent.
 (C) evidence the terms of a real estate transaction.
 (D) evidence the change in title or transfer of an interest in real property.

183. Which of the following statements about conveyances is true?
 (A) A deed is used to convey a freehold estate.
 (B) A lease is used to convey an estate for years.
 (C) A bill of sale is used to convey chattels.
 (D) All of the above are correct.

ANSWERS

To practice questions. If you chose the wrong letter, here's the right one! The explanations are designed to clarify your understanding.

1. **B** The terms "alienation" and "conveyance" are synonyms. Proration occurs in real estate transactions where we adjust at closing the amount the buyer and seller should each pay for the expenses attributable to the property. Prescription is long and continued use of the property, with the intent to gain an easement thereby. Consideration is what is given in exchange in a contract.

2. **A** The term "alienation" is a synonym for conveyance, or transfer. If voluntary, it would be by way of deed. Adverse possession is long and continued possession of another's property with the intent to claim ownership. Eminent domain is when the government takes privately owned property for the public good.

3. **A** Adverse possession and prescription are claims, the actual conveyance normally occurs by court order after the claim is perfected. Accession is the right of an owner to those things which are incidental to the thing owned. "Alienation" is a synonym for "conveyance."

4. **A** Accession is the right of an owner to those things which are incidental to the thing owned. A conveyance (also called an alienation) is a transfer of title to another.

5. **D** The term "alienation" is a synonym for conveyance, or transfer. Adverse possession is long and continuous possession of another's real estate with the intent to claim ownership. Once the claim is perfected, title changes hands. The final act to convey title by deed is to deliver the deed to the buyer and for the buyer to evidence acceptance. Eminent domain is when the government takes privately owned property for the public good.

6. **B** An alienation is a conveyance of title. Clouds and liens are encumbrances, not title. A declaration of homestead is used to protect a personal residence from execution sale by a judgment creditor.

7. **C** Accession occurs when an owner gains title to those things which are incidental to a thing owned. Forfeiture occurs when a right is lost by breaching a contractual obligation, such as violating a condition clause in a deed, which could result in transfer of title by reversion. A dedication is a conveyance to the public, usually by a developer for roads and streets in a subdivision. Sufferance is doing something without permission, such as being a tenant at sufferance in real property.

8. **A** Accretion is the building up of soil which is gradually deposited along a bank of a stream. If gradual, it can result in the upland owner gaining title to it. Hypothecation occurs when property is pledged as collateral for a loan. Hypothecating real estate results in a lien on the real estate. Liens are encumbrances, not title.

9. **D** Intestate succession refers to gaining title by being the natural heir of someone who died without a will. A gift of real property in a will is a devise.

10. **D** Estates are rights of possession, which can be ownerships (freeholds) or non-ownerships (leaseholds). A freehold is transferred by a deed. A leasehold is transferred by a lease.

11. **C** The term "alienation" means "conveyance." Title can be conveyed voluntarily (i.e., a deed, a will, etc.), or involuntarily (i.e., foreclosure, condemnation, divorce decree, etc.). In an involuntary conveyance the law gives someone the right to take the property away from the owner, so the conveyance could be said to be "by operation of law."

12. **B** The term "alienation" is a synonym for "conveyance," i.e., transfer of ownership. Technically, delivering a deed is an act of conveyance, and a will is instructions to the personal representative to convey title. However, "transfer an interest" is more all-encompassing as a definition.

13. **C** The parties to a deed are the grantor (seller) and the grantee (buyer). One could argue that the seller is a vendor, but the terms ordinarily used to describe the parties to a deed are grantor and grantee.

14. **C** Accretion is the action of water to deposit soil and thereby add to the land. The term "avulsion" means a sudden tearing away, usually by action of water. Ademption is the revocation of a grant. Annulation is not a legal term.

15. **B** Accretion is the process whereby soil is deposited and builds up along the bank of a stream. Avulsion is a sudden tearing away, as where a flood rips out the bank. Reliction is where the waters of a lake or sea recede, leaving dry land. Accession is

when one gains title, usually used in the context of natural causes.

16. **B** Soil gradually deposited along the bank of a stream is called alluvium. The act of building up alluvium is called accretion. Gneiss is a type of rock.

17. **B** Eminent domain is the right of the government to take private property by condemnation. Adverse possession occurs through long and continued use of another's land resulting in a claim of ownership. Accession is gaining ownership of things incidental to the land, such as title to land which is added along the bank of a stream.

18. **D** The term "avulsion" means a sudden tearing away, usually by action of water. When gradual, it is called erosion. Accretion is the action of water to deposit soil and thereby add to the land. There is no such thing as adversion.

19. **B** Avulsion is a sudden tearing away. When water recedes leaving dry land, it is called reliction. The addition of land is accretion.

20. **D** Accretion is the action of soil building up along the bank of a stream. Erosion and avulsion are the opposite of accretion; they are the removal of soil. Avulsion is sudden and erosion is gradual.

21. **C** The term "avulsion" means a sudden tearing away, usually by action of water. Accretion is the action of water to deposit soil and thereby add to the land. Adverse possession occurs when someone other than the owner possesses the land with the intent to gain title. A breach occurs when someone defaults on a promise in a contract.

22. **C** Accretion is the building up of soil which is gradually deposited along a bank of a stream. If gradual, it can result in the upland owner gaining title to it.

23. **D** Adverse possession requires ten years of possession which was actual, under claim of right, open and notorious, exclusive and hostile. Prescription is the same, except that the claimant used the property instead of possessing it, and therefore claims an easement instead of title. Eminent domain is the right of the government to take private property for the public good upon payment of just compensation. When a person dies intestate and has no heirs who can inherit, the estate escheats to the state.

24. **C** Whether the encroachment was a possession or a use of the land is a question which a court would decide based on the particulars of the case. Long and continued use of another's land can ripen into an easement by prescription. Long and continued possession can ripen into an estate by adverse possession. Other than the fact that one is a use and the other is a possession, there is little difference in the requirements for prescription and adverse possession.

25. **B** To perfect a claim of adverse possession requires continuous possession of the land for at least ten years under claim of right. The claimant's possession must have been based on the belief that he or she was the owner. Possession must have been in the usual manner of an owner, i.e., the owner can leave the premises to go shopping, etc. The possessor must be willing at all times to defend the claim and cannot claim property for which permission to occupy was granted by the true owner. The possession must also be open and notorious to the extent that the true owner could not have mistaken the fact that the claimant intended to claim the property. Paying the taxes on the land is not required in Oregon, although it may strengthen the claim.

26. **B** To perfect a claim of adverse possession requires ten years of possession which was actual, under claim of right, open and notorious, exclusive and hostile.

27. **D** Continuous possession for at least ten years is required by statute. The term "continuous" does not mean that the claimant can never leave the premises. It means that the claimant must possess the property in the manner in which it would normally be used. Merely using the property for ten years may result in an easement by prescription, but cannot ripen into title by adverse possession.

28. **D** To perfect a claim of adverse possession requires ten years of possession which was actual, under claim of right, open and notorious, exclusive and hostile.

29. **C** To perfect a claim of adverse possession requires ten years of possession which was actual, under claim of right, open and notorious, exclusive and hostile. There is no requirement that the claimant make any public registration of his or her intentions.

30. **B** When we way that an adverse claimant must be hostile, we mean that the claimant must have defended his or her claim against any other claims, including the claims of the owner.

31. **C** Adverse possession requires continuous possession for ten years in the normal manner in which the land in question would be occupied. It must also be adverse to the interests of the true owner and the claimant must defend his or her claim of ownership (hostile), which would be destroyed if the claimant's possession was with permission.

32. **C** Adverse possession requires, among other things, that the possession was hostile. When we way that an adverse claimant must be hostile, we mean that the claimant must have defended his or her claim against any other claims, including the claims of the owner. If the true owner is successful in evicting the tenant before the statutory time period has run, then the claimant was not successful in defending his or her claim. The adverse possession must also have been exclusive, which is inconsistent with someone else other than the claimant being in possession at the same time.

33. **A** Paying rent to the true owner would be construed as acknowledgment of the true owner's paramount title, therefore the claimant did not possess the property under claim of right and did not defend his or her claim. Some states require that the claimant have paid the taxes on the land, but Oregon does not.

34. **A** The adverse claimant in this case has complied with all the requirements. His possession was actual, notorious and open, hostile (without permission), continuous, exclusive and under claim of right.

35. **D** Title by adverse possession is blocked because the claimant accepted the permission of the true owner to occupy the property, hence lack of hostility. Hostility means the claimant must defend his or her claim.

36. **C** A claim of right is required to perfect a claim of adverse possession. Color of title occurs when the claim of right derives from a written instrument which purports to convey title, but which does not, such as a deed which appears to be good but, in fact, is unenforceable.

37. **C** To perfect a claim of adverse possession requires ten years of possession which was actual, under claim of right, open and notorious, exclusive and hostile. By definition, adverse possession is adverse to the interests of the owner, so it is a wrongful possession, not lawful.

38. **D** To perfect a claim of adverse possession requires ten continuous years of possession which was actual, under claim of right, open and notorious, exclusive and hostile. Actual possession still allows the possessor to leave the property for normal purposes. Having performed everything necessary to perfect the claim of adverse possession does not make the new ownership a matter of public record. In order to finalize the matter, the adverse possessor usually has to file a suit to quiet title, in which all the elements must be proved. The court will then issue an order confirming the adverse claimant's title. As an alternative to the suit to quiet title the adverse claimant may be able to get the original owner to give a voluntary deed.

39. **C** To perfect a claim of adverse possession requires ten years of possession which was actual, under claim of right, open and notorious, exclusive and hostile. Tacking means that one adverse claimant can start the possession period and it can be completed by a successor in interest as long as the possession was continuous. Some states do not allow tacking, but Oregon does.

40. **C** Adverse possession requires, among other things, that the possession was hostile. When we way that an adverse claimant must be hostile, we mean that the claimant must have defended his or her claim against any other claims, including the claims of the owner. If the true owner gave permission and the adverse possessor accepted it, as in the case of a license, then the adverse possessor has taken a position inconsistent with a claim of ownership. You cannot, on the one hand, accept permission to use another's land, and yet maintain you own it. The principle of nullum tempus occurrit regi means "no time runs to the king," in other words, you cannot adversely claim property owned by the government.

41. **C** Adverse possession requires, among other things, that the possession was hostile. When we way that an adverse claimant must be hostile, we mean that the claimant must have defended his or her claim against any other claims, including the claims of the owner. If the true owner is successful in evicting the adverse claimant or resuming his or her own possession before the statutory time limit has run (ten years, normally), the owner can defeat the adverse possessor's claim. Even giving the adverse possessor permission can defeat the possessor's hostility, if the adverse claimant accepts the permission.

42. **B** Once the requirements have been met, the title must be made a matter of public record. The usual way this is done is by a suit to quiet title, although the issue can be decided in the course of any lawsuit.

43. **C** Accretion is the building up of soil which is gradually deposited along a bank of a stream. If gradual, it can result in the upland owner gaining title to it. Adverse possession can ripen into ownership if continuous for ten years and other requirements are met.

44. **A** To be valid and enforceable, a deed must be in writing and signed by the grantor, the grantor must be competent, there must be words of conveyance (usually a granting clause), an adequate descrip-

tion, and an identifiable grantee. And finally, the deed must be delivered to and accepted by the grantee. A deed is a contract, so by stretching, it could be argued that there is an offer and an acceptance buried in its creation. However, if there is an offer and acceptance in a deed, it is certainly not a formal offer and acceptance.

45. **A** To be valid and enforceable, a deed must be in writing and signed by the grantor, the grantor must be competent, there must be words of conveyance, an adequate description, and an identifiable grantee. And finally, the deed must be delivered to and accepted by the grantee. While a buyer would be foolish not to record, a deed is still valid even if not recorded. A deed need not be signed by the grantee, as the grantee indicates acceptance by moving in.

46. **D** To be valid and enforceable, a deed must be in writing and signed by the grantor, the grantor must be competent, there must be words of conveyance (usually a granting clause), an adequate description, and an identifiable grantee. And finally, the deed must be delivered to and accepted by the grantee. The grantee would be foolish not to record a deed, but recording is not required for it to be valid and enforceable. Acknowledgment is a recording requirement, not a requirement for the deed to be valid and enforceable.

47. **D** To be valid and enforceable between the parties, a deed must be in writing and signed by the grantor, the grantor must be competent, there must be words of conveyance, an adequate description, and an identifiable grantee. And finally, the deed must be delivered to and accepted by the grantee.

48. **C** A deed must be in writing and signed by the grantor, the grantor must be competent, there must be words of conveyance (usually a granting clause), an adequate description, and an identifiable grantee. And finally, the deed must be delivered to and accepted by the grantee. The grantee would be foolish not to record a deed, but recording is not required for it to be valid and enforceable.

49. **C** A deed must be in writing and signed by the grantor, the grantor must be competent, there must be words of conveyance (also called the granting clause), an adequate description, and an identifiable grantee. And finally, the deed must be delivered to and accepted by the grantee. The tax assessor will take care of making sure the property has a tax assessed value.

50. **D** To be valid and enforceable between the parties, a deed must be in writing and signed by the grantor, the grantor must be competent, there must be words of conveyance, an adequate description, and an identifiable grantee. And finally, the deed must be delivered to and accepted by the grantee. The grantee would be foolish not to record a deed, but recording is not required for it to be valid and enforceable. Acknowledgment is a recording requirement, not a requirement for the deed to be valid and enforceable.

51. **C** To be valid and enforceable, a deed must be in writing and signed by the grantor, the grantor must be competent, there must be words of conveyance (usually a granting clause), an adequate description, and an identifiable grantee. And finally, the deed must be delivered to and accepted by the grantee. The grantee does not need to sign the deed indicating acceptance, as the grantee normally evidences the acceptance by moving in. Acknowledgment is required for recording, but neither acknowledgment nor recording are required for a deed to be valid between the parties.

52. **C** The essential elements of a valid and enforceable deed are a grantee entity identified, words of conveyance, an adequate description of the property, a sufficient writing, signature of a competent grantor, delivery by the grantor and acceptance by the grantee. Recording, acknowledgment and specifying the name and address for the tax bill are not required for the deed to be valid and enforceable.

53. **D** A valid and enforceable deed in Oregon requires a sufficient writing, signature of a competent grantor, words of conveyance, an adequate description of the premises, an identifiable grantee, delivery by the grantor and acceptance by the grantee. Since the grantee was not identified, the deed is void.

54. **B** A deed must be in writing and signed by the grantor, the grantor must be competent, there must be words of conveyance, an adequate description, and an identifiable grantee. And finally, the deed must be delivered to and accepted by the grantee. Since the grantee does not ordinarily need to sign the deed, a witness to the grantee's signature is also unnecessary. Acknowledgment of the grantor's signature is required for recording, but not in order to make the deed valid between the parties.

55. **B** Deeds must be in writing and signed by the grantor, the grantor must be competent, there must be words of conveyance (usually a granting clause), an adequate description, and an identifiable grantee. And finally, the deed must be delivered to and accepted by the grantee. A buyer would be foolish not to record, but recording is not required for the deed to be valid between the buyer and seller.

56. **C** A deed must stipulate the description of the property with certainty. The description must be by metes and bounds, government survey, or lot and block. These are methods for describing the boundaries of the land. Stating the area is not required because anyone could calculate the area from the dimensions. Everything else that is appurtenant (such as the improvements), runs with the land without needing to be described.

57. **D** Illiteracy is not incompetence. If one of the parties is illiterate, all that is necessary is for the document to be read aloud and a separate statement made and signed by the person who read it to the illiterate person. The habendum clause limits the amount of the estate being conveyed, but if it is left out, it is presumed that it conveys all the grantor's interest in the property. Consideration must be stated for the deed to be recorded, but a deed does not require a consideration to be valid between the parties.

58. **C** To be valid and enforceable, a deed must be in writing and signed by the grantor, the grantor must be competent, there must be words of conveyance (usually a granting clause), an adequate description, and an identifiable grantee. And finally, the deed must be delivered to and accepted by the grantee. A breach of contract clause is not required.

59. **C** An adequate legal description must identify the boundaries of the property sufficient to segregate the property from all other property with certainty. Stating the dimensions is required, although stating the area is not. The improvements and other appurtenances which run with the land need not be described, since they are conveyed automatically. By statute, property tax accounts are not adequate for a valid and enforceable deed.

60. **B** Oregon deeds must be in writing and signed by the grantor, the grantor must be competent, there must be words of conveyance, an adequate description, and an identifiable grantee. And finally, the deed must be delivered to and accepted by the grantee. Consideration must usually be stated for recording, but not for the deed to be valid between the parties.

61. **A** Deeds need not be recorded in order to be valid and enforceable between the grantor and the grantee. However, recording a deed gives the grantee protection against some potential claims fom third parties. To be recorded a deed must state the true and actual consideration (except gift deeds, personal representative's deeds and exchanges), must state the name and address for the tax bill in the future, and the signature of the grantor must be acknowledged. A date on a deed means that the grantor's warranties (if any) become effective on that date, but otherwise, a deed without a date is still an enforceable conveyance.

62. **C** A deed need not state the consideration to be valid. However, the consideration must be stated in order to record a deed, except a gift deed, personal representative's deed, or in the event of an exchange purely for other property.

63. **B** Once a deed has been properly made out, delivered and accepted the title has been conveyed. The grantor could only revoke the conveyance in the event the buyer could be found guilty of fraud or misrepresentation, undue influence, duress, or some other matter which would render the deed unenforceable. However, creditors of a bankrupt seller can have transactions set aside if they can demonstrate that the conveyance favored the interests of one creditor over another or was an attempt to hide assets from the creditors.

64. **C** Air rights are an interest in real property, so there is no difference in the requirements for their conveyance than for any other type of property, except that the description will have to be in three dimensions to qualify as a description sufficient to identify the property with certainty.

65. **C** No particular language is required to create a valid Oregon deed as long as the intent to convey is clear. Use of the word "convey" in a statutory deed creates the presumption that the grantor is conveying a fee title, unless additional language to the contrary is used.

66. **A** The words of conveyance are the most important words in a deed, since they are the words whereby the grantor states that the title is being transferred. The usual word in Oregon is "convey," but other terms are also acceptable. The covenant against encumbrances is a warranty, and is stated separately.

67. **A** The grantor must sign the deed (or the grantor's authorized representative), but the grantee need not. The grantee evidences acceptance by moving in. The recording officer never signs anything.

68. **C** Only the grantor's signature is required on a deed. The buyer normally evidences acceptance by moving in. There are occasional circumstances where the buyer should sign the deed, but rarely is the buyer's signature required for the deed to be valid. The grantor's spouse needs to sign the deed in most states, but not Oregon.

69. **A** To be valid and enforceable between the parties, a deed must be in writing and signed by the

grantor, the grantor must be competent, there must be words of conveyance, an adequate description, and an identifiable grantee. And finally, the deed must be delivered to and accepted by the grantee. There are occasions where the grantee's signature of acceptance is required, but normally we rely on the fact that the grantee moved into the property as evidence of acceptance. The grantee would be foolish not to record a deed, but recording is not required for it to be valid and enforceable. Acknowledgment is a recording requirement, not a requirement for the deed to be valid and enforceable.

70. **B** A deed must be in writing and signed by the grantor, the grantor must be competent, there must be words of conveyance (also called the granting clause), an adequate description, and an identifiable grantee. And finally, the deed must be delivered to and accepted by the grantee. While the grantor must be competent, the grantee need not be. A buyer would be foolish not to record the deed, but it is not required for the deed to be valid and enforceable on the seller.

71. **B** The phrase "to have and to hold" is part of the habendum clause, which is not required in Oregon. However, all deeds must contain a clause conveying the title, called the "words of conveyance."

72. **D** The habendum clause limits the extent or quantity of the estate being conveyed, and starts with the words "to have and to hold." If left out, the deed conveys all of the grantor's interest in the property. Since that is what the parties generally want, it is rarely used.

73. **B** An estate for years and a tenancy at will are less than freehold estates. A life estate and a fee simple estate are freeholds, but the life estate is for the life of the person named as the governing life. Only the fee simple can be said to be perpetual (forever). Oregon deeds are presumed to convey a fee estate, so the phrase "to have and to hold forever" is unnecessary.

74. **C** The words of conveyance are typically words such as "convey," "grant," "quitclaim," and the like. The words can also include limitations such as "convey for life," in which case the title being conveyed is a life estate rather than a fee. If no special words are used, the presumption in a statutory deed in Oregon is that a fee title is conveyed.

75. **A** The grantee need not be competent, but a deed fails if the grantor was not competent. Laws prohibiting transactions on Sundays and holidays are no longer in force. The grantee must be identified but, unless there is language to the contrary, it is presumed that the grantee is free to convey the title to successors in interest.

76. **B** To be valid and enforceable, a deed must be in writing and signed by the grantor, the grantor must be competent, there must be words of conveyance (usually a granting clause), an adequate description, and an identifiable grantee. And finally, the deed must be delivered to and accepted by the grantee. Sunday blue laws are no longer in force, nor are there any restrictions regarding holidays. Oregon deeds require only that the grantee be identified with certainty; the grantee need not be competent.

77. **D** While the grantor of a deed must be competent, the grantee need not be. If the manner in which the grantee takes title (i.e., in common, by the entirety, etc.) is not stated, the deed is still valid. The law presumes that, when there are more than one grantee, the interests are equal, husband and wife take as tenants by the entirety, and unmarried persons take as tenants in common.

78. **B** Recording has nothing to do with validity, so an unenforceable deed can still be recorded. Any contract entered into by one who is incompetent is voidable by the incompetent (after regaining competence) or completely void if the incompetence was permanent.

79. **A** The grantor must be competent, or if incompetent, the deed must be signed by someone authorized to act on behalf of the incompetent. Being a minor or mentally incapable of entering into a contract is sufficient to render the deed unenforceable. However, being convicted of a felony or being a citizen of another country, does not create lack of competence. When property is held as tenants by the entirety, either spouse may convey the entire estate by his or her signature alone, although the other spouse's right of survivorship would not be conveyed without the other spouse's signature as well.

80. **D** The grantor must be competent, but the grantee need not be. Therefore, a deed to a minor is valid and enforceable. When a minor child owns property the title is vested in the child, not in the child's guardian.

81. **D** There is a presumption in all deeds that it conveys all the grantor's right, title and interest, unless the grantor specifies some lesser interest. Therefore it is not necessary to state the interest being conveyed. The grantor of a deed must be competent at the time of the conveyance, but the grantee need not. The rules for co-tenancy provide a presumption that married co-tenants take as tenants by the entirety and unmarried co-tenants take as tenants in common, unless some

contrary intent is expressed. Therefore it is not necessary for a deed to state how co-tenants take title.

82. **D** Even the law recognizes that many people cannot spell, especially names. Therefore, the law follows the sound of the name rather than the spelling. Assumed names are completely legal as long as they are not used to commit fraud or deceitful acts.

83. **B** The phrase "and successors in interest" is unnecessary since Oregon deeds, including the statutory form warranty, special warranty, and bargain and sale deeds, contain a presumption that the estate being conveyed is a fee title. The grantor of a deed must be competent, but the grantee need not be. There are no laws in Oregon banning any activity on Sunday.

84. **A** The essential elements of a valid and enforceable deed are a grantee entity identified, words of conveyance, an adequate description of the property, a sufficient writing, signature of a competent grantor, delivery by the grantor and acceptance by the grantee. Recording and acknowledgment are not required to be valid and enforceable.

85. **C** Deeds last only for the brief moment when the title is conveyed and then cease to exist. Therefore they cannot be assigned or endorsed to another. The signature of the grantor can be any mark. To be recorded the mark must be acknowledged.

86. **B** A deed conveys title to the grantee, and then is finished. It cannot be used further. It can be neither assigned nor endorsed. Tearing it up also has no effect. The only way to transfer the title further is to use a new deed.

87. **B** A deed exists merely for the instant it conveys title. It cannot be assigned or further performed because it is of no further force and effect. To reconvey the property requires a new deed.

88. **A** A deed exists merely for the instant it conveys title. It cannot be assigned or further performed because it is of no further force and effect. To convey property back to the grantor the grantee must become the grantor of a new deed and reconvey the title back to the original grantor.

89. **D** Recording protects the buyer from certain possible claims by third parties, but it has nothing to do with the actual conveyance. A properly drafted deed, signed by the grantor is effective at the moment of delivery and acceptance, whether recorded or not.

90. **D** Title passes to the buyer upon delivery and acceptance of the deed. Delivery is the intent of the grantor to convey, therefore, it must be within the lifetime of the grantor. Since the seller in this case delivered the deed with the intent to convey, title passed immediately.

91. **B** While delivery must normally be within the lifetime of the grantor, the exception is an irrevocable delivery to an escrow with instructions to deliver it to the grantee upon the happening of some future event, such as the death of the grantor. The law says that such delivery to an escrow creates delivery to the grantee at the moment the deed is handed to the escrow, with possession deferred until the future event.

92. **C** Delivery is an essential element of a valid deed, and must be within the lifetime of the grantor. It would go to the state by escheat, except that in this case we know the man had at least one heir (the cousin).

93. **D** Delivery is essential to form a valid deed. Since there can be no delivery after the death of the grantor, none of the deeds will be effective.

94. **B** Delivery is the intent of the grantor to convey. Even if the deed has been handed to the buyer or recorded, there is no conveyance if the grantor did not yet intend to convey.

95. **A** Delivery is the intent of the grantor to convey, and is the point at which the conveyance is deemed to be effective.

96. **B** The final act in a deed is delivery to and acceptance by the grantee. Delivery is the intent of the grantor to convey. Although normally delivery has already happened by the time the deed is recorded, it is possible to record even though the grantor has not yet agreed to the conveyance.

97. **D** Delivery is the intent of the grantor to convey, and is the point at which the conveyance is deemed to be effective. Deeds have a number of other essential elements, but the buyer being in possession, recording, and title insurance are not among the list.

98. **D** Title passes to the buyer upon delivery and acceptance of the deed. Recording establishes the priority date as of which the buyer is protected against f third parties claiming to have had an interest prior to the conveyance.

99. **A** Delivery is the intent of the grantor to convey, and is the point at which the conveyance is deemed to be effective. Recording protects the buyer by giving constructive notice, but is not required for the deed to be valid. The grantor must be competent, but not the grantee.

100. **D** Delivery is the intent of the grantor to convey, and is the point at which the conveyance is deemed to be effective. While the grantor may delegate the duty to deliver to another, i.e., a broker or

an escrow agent, it is nevertheless the grantor who is deemed to be the one who delivers the deed.

101. **A** A covenant in a deed could take the form of a restriction on the grantee's use of the property, or it could be a warranty of title made by the grantor. Covenants which are restrictions should be carefully contrasted with conditions. Conditions create defeasible fees, such as a fee simple determinable or fee title subject to a condition subsequent. The penalty for violation of a condition could be forfeiture of the title through the reverter. The penalty for violating a restrictive covenant is generally a suit for damages or a suit to enjoin.

102. **A** The covenant of quiet enjoyment is a warranty from the seller that the grantee's possession of the property will be uninterrupted. The covenant of seizin is a warranty that the grantor owns the property and has the right to convey it. The covenant against encumbrances guarantees that the property is free and clear. There is no such thing as a covenant of title insurance.

103. **A** The habendum clause (not required in an Oregon deed) says "to have and to hold" and then proceeds to define or limit the quantity or extent of the estate being granted. The quantum is sometimes included as a part of the habendum clause, when the grantor wishes to define a time limit for the estate. The covenant of quiet enjoyment is the grantor's warranty that the grantee's use and enjoyment of the property will be uninterrupted. The covenant of seizin is the grantor's warranty that the grantor owns the property and has the right to sell it.

104. **B** Both the warranty and the special warranty deed contains the covenant of seizin (that the grantor owns the property and has the right to convey it), the covenant of quiet enjoyment (that the grantee's possession of the property will be uninterrupted by adverse claimants, the covenant against encumbrances (that the property is free and clear) and the covenant of warranty forever (that the grantor will take any action necessary to correct any defects).

105. **A** Both the warranty and the special warranty deed contains the covenant of seizin (that the grantor owns the property and has the right to convey it), the covenant of quiet enjoyment (that the grantee's possession of the property will be uninterrupted by adverse claimants, the covenant against encumbrances (that the property is free and clear) and the covenant of warranty forever (that the grantor will take any action necessary to correct any defects).

106. **A** Warranty deed contain three covenants – the covenant of seizin, the covenant of quiet enjoyment and the covenant against encumbrances. The covenant of seizin warrants that the grantor has good title and the right to convey it. The covenant of quiet enjoyment warrants that no one with paramount title will interfere with the grantee's right of possession and enjoyment of the property. The covenant against encumbrances warrants that the property is free of encumbrances (except those stated).

107. **A** The covenant of seizin is a warranty that the grantor owns the property and has the right to convey it. The covenant of quiet enjoyment is a warranty from the seller that the grantee's possession of the property will be uninterrupted by anyone asserting a paramount title.

108. **B** Both the warranty and the special warranty deed contains the covenant of seizin (that the grantor owns the property and has the right to convey it), the covenant of quiet enjoyment (that the grantee's possession of the property will be uninterrupted by adverse claimants, the covenant against encumbrances (that the property is free and clear) and the covenant of warranty forever (that the grantor will take any action necessary to correct any defects).

109. **C** There is no such thing as a covenant of quantum.

110. **C** In order to make deeds easier to use, the Oregon Legislature enacted special statutes creating short deed forms. The statute further spells out the legal effect of each form so everyone will know exactly what to expect. These are called statutory form deeds.

111. **B** Statutory form deeds are simplified deeds that have more or less the same legal effect as the older non-standard deeds that were in common use. One of the reasons for creating statutory forms was so that non-professionals could fill them out. It is not considered unauthorized practice of law for a real estate or escrow licensee to fill in the blanks for the client, although the licensee should not make the decision as to whether it should be a warranty, special warranty, bargain and sale, or quitclaim deed. Since the format was specified by the statute, under no circumstances should a licensee alter the language of the statutory form.

112. **A** Statutory form deeds are simplified deeds that have more or less the same legal effect as the older non-standard deeds that were in common use. One of the reasons for creating statutory forms was so that non-professionals could fill them out. It is not considered unauthorized practice of law for a real estate or escrow licensee to fill in the blanks for the

client, although the licensee should not make the decision as to whether it should be a warranty, special warranty, bargain and sale, or quitclaim deed.

113. **D** Statutory form deeds are simplified deeds that have more or less the same legal effect as the older non-standard deeds that were in common use. One of the reasons for creating statutory forms was so that non-professionals could fill them out. Any document may be recorded, provided the signatures are acknowledged and, if a deed or contract, it states the consideration and the name and address for the tax bill. A deed does not have to be in statutory format to be recorded.

114. **B** The statutory form special warranty deed is essentially the same as the special warranty deed that was in common use before the statutory deeds were created. It is shorter and the language is simpler. The best deed for the buyer is a warranty deed, because the grantor is obligated to defend any claims under its warranties. The special warranty deed has the same warranties, but the grantor is obligated to defend only those claims arising through or under the grantor. All deeds, except the quitclaim deed, convey after-acquired title.

115. **A** All deeds, except the quitclaim deed, convey after-acquired title. The bargain and sale deed contains only the warranty that the buyer is getting a fee title, or such other interest as the deed may state by special language. The quitclaim deed contains no warranties at all.

116. **B** Any document may be recorded, as long as the signatures are acknowledged and, in the case of deeds, it contains the consideration and the name and address for the tax bill. The date on a deed has little practical effect; the time of the conveyance is the moment of delivery and acceptance, regardless of when the deed was dated or signed. All deeds, except the quitclaim deed, convey after-acquired title. The quitclaim deed contains no warranties at all. The bargain and sale deed contains only the warranty that the buyer is getting a fee title, or such other interest as the deed may state by special language.

117. **D** All deeds have the same requirements to be valid and enforceable and all deeds can be recorded, but need not be to be valid. It also makes no difference what form deed is used, the grantee gets all the grantor's right, title and interest (unless a lesser interest is stipulated). The differences are, therefore, not in what is conveyed, but rather the extent to which the grantor will stand behind the conveyance, i.e., the warranties.

118. **B** There are four formats for deeds. The best for the grantee is the warranty deed, also sometimes called the full warranty, or general warranty deed. It contains the greatest number of warranties.

119. **B** There are four formats for deeds. The best for the grantee is the warranty deed, also sometimes called the full warranty, or general warranty deed. It contains the greatest number of warranties.

120. **A** In the warranty deed, the grantor promises to defend the title against all claims. An administrator's or executor's deed is given by the person authorized to wind up the affairs of a decedent. Administrators and executors are now referred to as personal representatives in Oregon, and the deed they give is a personal representative's deed. A sheriff's deed is given by the sheriff to the successful bidder at a foreclosure sale. Sheriff's deeds are usually bargain and sale in format. Personal representative's deeds are usually special warranty deeds. The general warranty deed creates more liability for the grantor than either of these.

121. **D** The warranty deed contains the covenant of seizin (that the grantor owns the property and has the right to convey it), the covenant of quiet enjoyment (that the grantee's possession of the property will be uninterrupted by adverse claimants, the covenant against encumbrances (that the property is free and clear) and the covenant of warranty forever (that the grantor will take any action necessary to correct any defects).

122. **B** The covenant of seizin warrants that the grantor owns the property and has the right to sell it. The covenant against encumbrances warrants that the property is free and clear. The covenant of further assurance warrants that the grantor will defend the title against all claims. However, the covenants in deeds warrant the title only; none of them have anything to do with the condition of the property.

123. **C** In the warranty deed, the grantor promises to defend the title against all claims. In the language of the special warranty deed it states that the grantor will defend the title against all claims arising through or under the grantor only.

124. **D** The covenants in deeds warrant the title only; none of them have anything to do with the condition of the property. One of the covenants in a warranty deed is the covenant of warranty forever, which requires the grantor (and the grantor's estate) to defend the title forever.

125. **C** The most commonly used deed is the warranty deed. Most standard earnest money contracts

require the seller to deliver a warranty deed to the buyer. Although the parties could modify the form, they generally are not aware that they even have the option. Once the earnest money agreement is signed, the escrow agent closing the transaction has no choice but to follow the terms of the earnest money contract.

126. **D** In the warranty deed, the grantor promises to defend the title against all claims. In the language of the special warranty deed it states that the grantor will defend the title against all claims arising through or under the grantor only. In the bargain and sale deed, the only warranty is that the grantor has a fee title.

127. **B** Both warranty deeds have the same covenants, but the special warranty deed limits the grantor's liability to his or her acts only.

128. **A** In the warranty deed, the grantor promises to defend the title against all claims. In the language of the special warranty deed it states that the grantor will defend the title against all claims arising through or under the grantor only.

129. **D** The covenants of the warranty deed require the grantor to defend the title against all claims. In the language of the special warranty deed it states that the grantor will defend the title against all claims arising through or under the grantor only.

130. **A** In the warranty deed, the grantor promises to defend the title against all claims arising under the covenant of seizin, the covenant against encumbrances, the covenant of quiet enjoyment, and the covenant of warranty forever. In the language of the special warranty deed, which has the same covenants, it states that the grantor will defend the title against all claims arising through or under the grantor only. In the bargain and sale deed, the only warranty is that the grantor has a fee title. The quitclaim deed has no warranties at all.

131. **C** When a sheriff issues a deed following a foreclosure sale the sheriff is acting merely in an administrative manner and has no way to guarantee that the original borrower or some other party might not present some claim that the foreclosure sale should be set aside. Therefore, the sheriff does not wish to create any liability by using a deed which would create a warranty, so a "sheriff's deed" is normally a bargain and sale deed in form. A quitclaim deed also contains no warranties of title, but should be used only when there is a possibility that the grantor has no title at all.

132. **A** A quitclaim deed, the same as any deed, conveys all the grantor's interest at the time of the conveyance. All deeds except the quitclaim deed convey after-acquired title. After-acquired title is any interest the grantor obtains after the conveyance.

133. **A** Since the quitclaim deed is used when the grantor is not sure that he or she has any title at all, it uses words such as "quitclaim," "release" or "remise" to avoid the word "convey," which implies that the grantor does have a title. Warranty, special warranty and bargain and sale deeds also convey after-acquired title. All Oregon deeds will convey all the right, title and interest in the property the grantor has at the time of the conveyance.

134. **A** In the warranty deed, the grantor promises to defend the title against all claims arising under the four warranties it contains. The special warranty deed has the same warranties but it states that the grantor will defend the title against all claims arising through or under the grantor only. The bargain and sale deed has only a warranty that the grantor has a fee title. The quitclaim deed has no warranties at all.

135. **B** All deeds convey all the interest the grantor has at the time of the conveyance. All deeds contain any of various warranties and covenants, except the quitclaim deed. The quitclaim deed contains no warranties of any kind.

136. **B** The warranty deed contains the covenant of seizin, the covenant of quiet enjoyment, the covenant against encumbrances and the covenant of warranty forever. The grantor is obligated to defend any claims under these warranties. The special warranty deed has the same covenants, but the grantor's liability is limited to claims arising through or under the grantor only. The bargain and sale deed contains only a covenant that the grantor has a fee title. The quitclaim deed has no covenants at all.

137. **D** A quitclaim deed, the same as any deed, conveys all the grantor's interest at the time of the conveyance. However, it is usually used when the grantor is not sure of the interest held and does not wish to warrant that a fee title is being conveyed. All deeds except the quitclaim deed convey after-acquired title. After-acquired title is any interest the grantor obtains after the conveyance.

138. **A** All deeds convey all the grantor's interest in the property at the time of the conveyance. However, only the quitclaim deed completely lacks warranties. If a grantor is unsure of the interest held, to avoid a possible misrepresentation or fraud, the appropriate deed to use is the quitclaim deed. Of all the deed forms, the quitclaim is by far the most likely to result in no interest being transferred.

139. **B** Since the quitclaim deed does not warrant that the grantor has any interest at all, it is popular to use it to release a cloud or defect on the title. The quitclaim deed has no warranties at all. Losing a deed is irrelevant. Once the conveyance has been effected, the conveyance is complete and the grantee has become the owner. At that point the deed is merely a piece of paper.

140. **B** A quitclaim deed, the same as any deed, conveys all the grantor's interest at the time of the conveyance. However, if the grantor does not have a fee title, then it will not convey a fee title, so it can't be said that it will always convey a fee title. A quitclaim deed would extinguish a lien, if signed by the lienholder and given to the borrower. However, as a technicality, we do not "convey" liens, they are "released." After-acquired title is any interest the grantor obtains after the conveyance. All deeds except the quitclaim deed convey after-acquired title.

141. **A** A cloud is a possible interest or a claim. Since all deeds except the quitclaim deed contain a covenant that the grantor has a fee title, the grantor could be held liable for fraud or misrepresentation if it is discovered that the interest or claim was groundless. To prevent this we commonly use the quitclaim deed to release a cloud, which does not promise the grantor has anything at all, yet conveys any interest the grantor may have.

142. **B** All deeds contain an implied covenant that the grantor has a fee title, except the quitclaim deed, which has no warranties at all. If the grantor gave any deed other than a quitclaim deed, and it was later discovered that the grantor had no interest in the property at all at the time of the conveyance, then the grantor could be held liable for fraud or misrepresentation. A cloud is a possible interest, something not certain. To convey such an interest, the grantor would be best advised to use the quitclaim deed.

143. **A** A quitclaim deed, the same as any deed, conveys all the grantor's interest at the time of the conveyance. However, if the grantor does not have a fee title, then it will not convey a fee title. All deeds except the quitclaim deed convey after-acquired title. After-acquired title is any interest the grantor obtains after the conveyance. If the grantor is not sure of the interest held, then the quitclaim deed is the best to use. The other three all contain an implied covenant that the grantor has a fee title, which could be a fraud or misrepresentation if the interest turns out not to be a fee title.

144. **A** All deeds convey all the interest the grantor has at the time of the conveyance. It is not unauthorized practice of law for the parties to complete legal documents themselves. It is also acceptable for a real estate licensee to assist the parties by filling in the blanks on a statutory form deed according to the instructions of the clients.

145. **D** Statutory form deeds generally use the word "convey" which entails the implication that the grantor has a fee title. Since the quitclaim deed is used when the grantor is not sure that he or she has any title at all, it uses words such as "quitclaim," "release" or "remise" to avoid the implications of the word "convey."

146. **A** In Oregon there are four formats for deeds, the warranty deed, the special warranty deed, the bargain and sale deed, and the quitclaim deed. A grant deed is a deed used in California, similar to the Oregon special warranty deed.

147. **C** There are four deed formats – warranty, special warranty, bargain and sale and quitclaim. However, there are an endless number of special purpose deeds, all of which fall into one of the four formats. A "guardian's deed" would be used by a legal guardian. Its distinction is that it contains language referring to the ward and that the guardian is legally empowered to sign on behalf of the ward, usually a minor child. A minor can be the grantee of a deed because competence is not required for the grantee. But the grantor must be competent, so the minor cannot further convey the title. Therefore, if the minor is to convey title the deed must be executed by the minor's guardian. A gift deed is an ordinary deed which deletes the place to state a dollar amount of consideration and a sheriff's deed recites the fact that the grantor is the sheriff and the circumstances of the transaction, i.e., that the sheriff acquired title in a foreclosure sale. A trustee's deed is used by a trustee who is holding property for another.

148. **D** A deed in lieu of foreclosure is used by the borrower. A trust deed is a financing instrument, akin to a mortgage. A referee's deed would be used by a referee in bankruptcy. A foreclosure sale in which there is a right of redemption would have been held by the sheriff, so the deed conveying title to the successful bidder would be a sheriff's deed.

149. **B** Since the buyer under the land sales contract has probably been in possession of the property for a considerable time, there is a very real possibility that the buyer's actions could have created

encumbrances against the title. Therefore, the seller would not want to give a general warranty deed to the buyer. The usual form is a special warranty deed or bargain and sale deed. Regardless of the form, it is also commonly referred to as a fulfillment deed, since it fulfills the seller's obligation to the buyer.

150. **B** A deed in lieu of foreclosure is exactly what it sounds like – a deed from the borrower to the lender to shortcut the legal travails of a foreclosure. When the borrower has fee title, the deed should be a bargain and sale deed or better. But when the instrument used to finance the property is a land sales contract, the buyer does not obtain legal title. In fact, the land sales contract is a cloud on the seller's title. The normal deed used to remove a cloud is a quitclaim deed. Thus the customary deed in lieu of foreclosure of a land sales contract is a quitclaim deed.

151. **C** All deeds convey all the right, title and interest held by the grantor at the time of the conveyance. Therefore, any deed can be used in any setting. But there may be times when after-acquired title and warranties of title are desirable, in which case there are specific deeds to accomplish exactly what the parties desire. The fact that a grantee or a title insurance company might object to a quitclaim deed does not mean that it does not convey all the grantor's interest in the property at the time of the conveyance.

152. **B** When an owner sells property, but retains an interest in the property being sold (e.g., an easement), then we say the interest was reserved (a reservation). When a deed states that the owner conveys the property except a portion thereof, the excluded portion was not conveyed at all. The latter is an exception.

153. **A** A reservation in a deed occurs when the grantor conveys an entire property, but holds back (reserves) some rights in the property conveyed, such as an easement or other interest. An exception is a modification to the legal description so the grantor simply retains title to a portion of the property.

154. **A** When title is conveyed but the grantor retains an interest in the property being conveyed, the deed is said to have a reservation. When title is conveyed, but the grantor retains full ownership of a portion (i.e., not all the property is conveyed), this is called an exception.

155. **C** Delivery is the intent of the grantor to convey. Recording makes a public record of the conveyance, but is not delivery. Delivery is the intent of the grantor to convey. When title is conveyed but the grantor retains an interest in the property being conveyed, the deed is said to have a reservation. When title is conveyed, but the grantor retains full ownership of a portion (i.e., not all the property is conveyed), this is called an exception.

156. **C** To the land conveyed it is an encumbrance. To another parcel (perhaps a parcel the grantor retained) it is an appurtenance. This is a reservation, not an exception.

157. **B** All land in Oregon was originally owned by the federal government. Much of this land was subsequently granted by the federal government to the state of Oregon and to private individuals under the provision of the Donation Land Law of 1850. This law provided that a settler who lived on and made improvements to a homestead claim would receive a federal patent to the land. The federal patent is essentially a deed from the federal government.

158. **D** A patent is the original conveyance by the federal government to a homesteader. There is only one patent in the chain of title. Once the homesteader owns the land all future conveyances will be by deed. Even if the federal government should reacquire the land and then resell it, the resale will be by deed.

159. **A** In real estate law, a patent is the original grant from the sovereign to a citizen. In the U.S. the sovereign became the federal government. After the federal patent, all voluntary conveyances, including any conveyances from the federal government, will be by deed. The patent office issues patents for inventions only.

160. **A** The use of the patent is restricted to the federal government and only to the first homestead conveyance. Subsequent conveyances of property is normally by deed. State owned land is also conveyed by deed.

161. **C** When a conveyance is made to the public it is called a dedication. Normally this occurs as a conveyance of roads, streets, parks, etc. in a subdivision by the developer to the city or county.

162. **B** A conveyance by a developer for roads and streets or other public purposes is called a dedication. It can be by deed, or simply stated on the recorded plat map. A subordination is when one lienholder who enjoys a senior position, agrees to become junior to another lienholder. Condemnation is the process by which the government takes private property; the exercise of eminent domain. Escalation is a clause in a lease allowing the rent to increase.

163. **A** In the early days the dedication was created just by recording a plat map showing the roads and

streets. After long and continued use the public gained a right to the roads and streets. This is called a common-law dedication. Today statutes require a formal conveyance to the city or county and acceptance by the city or county. Since the formal conveyance is required by statute, we call these statutory dedications.

164. **C** Oregon law states that the city or county cannot accept the dedication until a formal plat map has been recorded.

165. **A** Real property is normally conveyed by a deed, and usually liened by a note and mortgage or note and trust deed. Title to personal property is transferred by a bill of sale and liened with a note and chattel mortgage, or as it is called today, a security agreement.

166. **C** While an option, agreement of sale or lease could involve personal property, they ordinarily just convey an interest in real property. A bill of sale, however, is used only for personal property.

167. **B** A last will and testament is the deceased person's final request. The deceased person who dies having left a will is called the testator and is said to have died testate. Dying without a will is dying intestate.

168. **A** Succession means gaining title to property as an heir. If the deceased person left a will (died testate), then the property was gained by testate succession according to the wishes expressed in the will. If an heir gains title from an estate of a person who died without a will, then it is called intestate succession.

169. **B** A devise is a gift of real property in a will. The creation of a less than freehold estate is a demise.

170. **B** A devise is a gift of real property in a will, not to be confused with a "demise," which is the creation of a less than freehold estate (rental or lease).

171. **C** Formerly in Oregon, and still in many other states, a person named in a will to wind up the affairs of a deceased person was called an executor (executrix if female). A person named by a court was called an administrator (administratrix if female). Today all of these are called personal representatives in Oregon.

172. **C** To have died "testate" is to have died with a will; "intestate" means without a will. When a person dies intestate, the Oregon laws of descent and distribution apply. These laws provide that the estate of the decedent is distributed among the next of kin according to a statutory formula. If there is no one capable of inheriting, the property escheats to the state. However, if one dies testate, the chance of escheat is minimal, since the purpose of a will is to specify heirs. A devise is a gift of real property in a will.

173. **B** When a person dies intestate, the Oregon laws of descent and distribution apply. These laws provide that the estate of the decedent is distributed among the next of kin according to a statutory formula. If there are no heirs capable of inheriting, the property escheats to the state. "Mains froides" is French for "cold hands," and refers to attempts to control future ownership of property after one's death, usually by stringing together lengthy life estates.

174. **B** To have died "testate" is to have died with a will; "intestate" means without a will. When a person dies intestate, the Oregon laws of descent and distribution apply. These laws provide that the estate of the decedent is distributed among the next of kin according to a statutory formula. When the heirs are a wife, the wife takes all, but if there is a wife and children, the wife takes one half and the children share the other half.

175. **C** "Testate" means to have died with a will and "intestate" means without a will. When a person dies intestate, the Oregon laws of descent and distribution apply. These laws provide that the estate of the decedent is distributed among the next of kin according to a statutory formula.

176. **D** In a will, a bequest is a gift of money, a legacy is a gift of jewelry, and a devise is a gift of real property, so the person receiving real property in a will is a devisee. The testator is a male person making a will, and testatrix is a female person making a will. An executor or executrix is the male or female (respectively) who handles the affairs of a deceased person. The terms executor and executrix have been replaced in Oregon with "personal representative."

177. **A** When a person dies intestate (without a will) and there are no natural heirs capable of inheriting, the property escheats to the state.

178. **A** When a person dies intestate (without a will) and there are no natural heirs capable of inheriting, the property escheats to the state.

179. **C** When a person dies intestate, but there are no heirs capable of inheriting, the property escheats to the state. Eminent domain is the right of the government to take privately owned property for the public good, provided just compensation is paid. Police power is the right of the government to maintain public order, which includes the right to regulate owners' use of their property. An estoppel occurs when someone is barred from asserting contract rights.

180. **B** Normally, the way the seller restricts the grantee's future use of the property is with a cov-

enant. The covenant is typically created as an encumbrance on the grantee's title. A restriction could also be a condition. If a condition is created, it creates a possibility of reverter; that is, the grantor can take the title back if the grantee violates the condition. Both would ordinarily be created in the deed.

181. **C** If a condition is created, it creates a possibility of reverter; that is, the grantor can take the title back if the grantee violates the condition. This would have to be stated in writing. While it is commonly done in the deed, it is possible to do it after the fact. The deed, of course, is also a written agreement itself.

182. **D** A deed conveys title to real property. It is valid without being recorded, without identifying the party to whom the tax bill is to be sent, and without stating the price or other terms. Note that recording is essential to protect the buyer so it is almost always done. And a deed cannot be recorded unless it states the name and address for the tax bill in the future and the consideration paid. But the deed is still valid between the parties without those items.

183. **D** Personal property (chattels) are transferred by bill of sale, the same as real property is conveyed by deed. An estate for years is a lease of real property.

ACKNOWLEDGMENT, NOTICE AND RECORDING

THERE ARE MANY TIMES IN THE COURSE OF BUSINESS TRANSACTIONS WHEN IT is desirable to have a signature on a legal document verified by another person. This is usually done by an ***acknowledgment***. It is called an acknowledgment because the party signing the document acknowledges before an official that it was a voluntary act. The party who witnesses or verifies the signature is said to "take an acknowledgment."

We have signatures acknowledged for a variety of reasons, but the most important is that a document ordinarily cannot be recorded in Oregon unless it has been acknowledged. Acknowledgment also creates prima facie evidence that the signature on the instrument was a voluntary act (not under duress). And it is also prima facie evidence that the official taking the acknowledgment verified the identity of the signer, so we know the signature was not a forgery. Today, most persons taking an acknowledgment are required to maintain a log and records of what identification was given by the person signing a document.

An acknowledgment is most commonly taken by a ***notary public***. You can usually find notaries in banks, escrow offices, title insurance companies and attorneys' offices, since such people constantly deal with instruments which must be acknowledged and recorded. The maximum fee for a notarization is a nominal amount and many notaries perform the service at no charge. Many real estate agents find it is convenient to become notaries since documents needed in closing real estate transactions usually must be acknowledged. Oregon law also permits judges, including justices of the peace, to take acknowledgments. Acknowledgments properly taken by officials in other states are also generally accepted in Oregon.

State of Oregon, County of ____________________) ss.
Be it remembered that on this ______ day of ______________, 20 ______, before me, the undersigned, a notary public in and for said County and State, personally appeared the within named ______________________________

____

____

known to me to be the identical individual described in and who executed the within instrument and acknowledged to me that executed the same freely and voluntarily.
In testimony whereof, I have hereunto set my hand and affixed my official seal the day and year last above written.

____

Notary Public for Oregon
My commission expires ________________________

Documents which need to be acknowledged are usually printed with language similar to the above for the notary's use.

Notice

At its simplest, ***notice*** is the concept that people should not be held responsible for things that were unknown to them or, to put it in legal terms, of which they had no notice. While this may seem fair and just, it raises a problem. You could easily escape legal responsibility just by saying "I didn't know." To prevent this, there are various situations where the law provides that you are deemed to have been given notice, whether you actually knew it or not.

One simple concept is that everyone is deemed to have notice of the law, therefore ignorance of the law is no excuse. While a court might be sympathetic to a lay person who was unaware of the law, everyone has access to attorneys, so everyone will be held responsible for their actions, whether they knew the law or not.

In other circumstances, it is often necessary to be able to prove that you gave someone notice. For example, if you sue someone, you cannot prevail in court unless the defendant was properly served with the complaint. The service puts the defendant on notice of the pending suit and the process server files papers with the court attesting to the service. And in civil contracts it is also often necessary for one party to give notice to the other. Certified mail is a common device to demonstrate proof that notice was given.

When it comes to real estate transactions, the issue of notice becomes crucial because of the doctrine of the ***bonafide purchaser*** (also sometimes called an ***innocent purchaser***). When a bonafide purchaser buys property ***in good faith, for value***, and ***without notice of defect***, the bonafide purchaser will be held safe from any claims against the title. For example, if you buy a parcel of real estate without any notice that there is a mortgage on the title, the mortgagee may find that your purchase caused their mortgage to be extinguished. Any person who holds an interest in another's real estate has a duty to give notice to the world of the interest, lest it be extinguished when the property is sold.

Of course, this is impossible. There is no way a lender or other party with an interest in another's real estate can actually notify the entire world. Therefore, in matters involving title to real estate, the law imposes a duty on anyone dealing in the real estate to make certain inquiries, and the party is deemed to have been given notice of anything which would be revealed thereby.

One matter which the buyer is required to investigate is the rights of any parties in possession. A party in possession of real estate is deemed to have given the entire world notice of his or her rights by the mere act of being in possession.

Notes

Another matter which must be investigated is the ***public record***. The public record consists of all documents which have been recorded and which affect the property (see "Recording" later). In other words, if a lessee is in possession, the buyer takes title subject to the lease, whether the buyer knew of it or not, because being in possession gave the buyer notice. Or the lessee could simply record the lease, in which case the buyer would also be given notice of it. Either notice is sufficient to protect the lessee from having his or her lease extinguished by a sale of the property.

Notice given by being possession or notice given by recording is called ***constructive notice***. Notice can also be given by personally informing someone of a fact, verbally, in writing or by actions. This is called ***actual notice***. Again, it makes no difference if the notice was constructive or actual – the interest is protected as long as the buyer was given notice.

Notice can also arise when a buyer had a duty to inquire about a suspicious situation. Suppose, for example, that a seller sold a property to a buyer, but the buyer did not record the deed. Subsequently, the seller sold the property to you. If you record your deed, then normally you would be held to be the "innocent purchaser in good faith for value without notice of the defect," so your title would be good. But suppose the first buyer ordered improvements to be made. When you inspect the premises, you notice the improvements being made and there is further evidence that the improvements were not being made by the seller. Nevertheless, you do nothing. Because the situation was suspicious, you had an obligation to investigate. Such investigation would have revealed the truth, so your title is not good. The duty to investigate suspicious situations is called ***inquiry notice***.

The doctrine of the bonafide purchaser also extends to encumbrances, particularly as to priority. If a lender takes a mortgage on property, but does not record it, is not in possession, and gives no actual notice, then a subsequent lender who does record is deemed to have the first mortgage. The subsequent lender who recorded is an innocent party in good faith for value without notice of the defect. An unrecorded encumbrance is always last in priority.

Exercise a

When a party verifies before an official that he or she actually signed a document, this is called an ____________________, and is evidence that the signature was not a ____________________ and that it was a ____________________ act. In most cases the official who verifies the signature is a ____________________ ____________________.

To protect themselves, buyers, lenders and others dealing in real estate should be sure to give notice to the world of their interest in the property. When you tell someone of your interest, this is ____________________ notice. When you give notice by being in possession or by recording, this is called ____________________ notice. When someone has a duty to inquire, we say that they have been given ____________________ notice. If you fail to give notice of your interest in the property, the interest could be extinguished by a sale to a bonafide ____________________ in good faith for value with no ____________________ of the defect.

NOTES

It is important to understand that neither recording nor acknowledgment make a document legally enforceable. Acknowledgment merely creates evidence that the signatures were legitimate and voluntary. Recording gives constructive notice. But a neither a notary nor a recording officer has the authority to pass judgment as to the legal enforceability or effect of a contract.

Recording

In early England the concept did not exist that a bonafide purchaser in good faith for value should be held safe from claims of which he or she had no notice. The idea did not become law until 1640 in the Massachusetts Bay Colony. But from that beginning, modern recording statutes have spread throughout the United States, and in much the same format.

In the early days of recording, an exact copy of the document to be recorded would literally be bound in a book. As it was bound into the book it was given a page number. Thus, it became possible to refer to the document by the "book and page number" where it was recorded.

Today, each county has its own system for recording documents. However, a common thread runs throughout, so most things are very similar, if not identical, from one county to the next. In some counties, for example, deeds are recorded in one set of books, while mortgages and other liens are recorded in another set of books. In other counties, there is just one set of books for all real estate records. In some counties they use the Latin terms for book and page, "liber and folio." In other counties they have adopted the nomenclature of modern microphotography, so documents are referred to by the "reel and instrument number" where they can be found on the microfilm. It is also common to find counties where each document is just given a sequential "file" or "document" number. As long as the document can be found in readable format in the location where it belongs, proper notice is given.

Of course, in order to find anything in the public records, there must be an index. In those counties where deeds are recorded in one set of books and mortgages in another, you will typically find the deed records indexed by last name of the grantor and grantee, and mortgages indexed by last name of the mortgagor and mortgagee. In other counties, the grantors and mortgagors are in one index (called the "direct" index), and grantees and mortgagees are in the other (called the "indirect" or "invert" index).

Fortunately, Oregon real estate agents rarely find it necessary to deal with the recorder's office. The vast majority of transactions today are handled by escrow agents (or the escrow department of a title insurance company). These professionals close hundreds of real estate transactions every day and are experts at recording requirements. Most will record any document as a courtesy if you just reimburse them the recording fee.

Nevertheless, real estate agents should be familiar with some of the requirements for recording documents. Of course, we have already noted that most documents must be acknowledged to be recorded. And there are statutory as well as local ordinances which set the fees charged for the service. The fees vary according to the type of document and the number of pages.

In addition, certain documents create additional requirements. For example, deeds and land sales contracts must state the true and actual consideration in dollars (exception – gift deeds, personal representative's deeds and exchanges). Failure to state the consideration means the recording clerk cannot accept it for recording. Stating a false consideration does not invalidate the document, but subjects the seller to a fine. In addition, deeds and land sales contracts must state the name and address where the tax bill is to be sent in the future.

NOTES

As we have seen, a buyer would be foolish not to record his or her deed or land sales contract. However, there are times when the parties wish to keep their transaction from the public. There are other times when the document (especially a land sales contract) may be many pages in length and the recording charges could be avoided by not recording. For these situations, the law permits the recording of a ***memorandum*** of the document. The memorandum must meet the same requirements as the original – that is, it must have the signature(s) of the parties, which must be acknowledged, and it must state the true and actual consideration and the name and address for the tax bill. Once recorded, it gives the same notice as recording the entire original would.

In the past it was not unusual for a sophisticated property owner to sell property on a land sales contract with a provision that it not be recorded. By not recording the contract a title search would not show the cloud of the contract on the seller's title. Then, if the buyer defaulted, the seller would simply resell the property to another. This seems like a simple solution to the problem, but even worse problems might occur if the first buyer should reappear and claim that only a proper foreclosure could have extinguished his or her contract rights.

To prevent these problems, Oregon law requires the recording of a land sales contract (or a memorandum thereof) within fifteen days of the date the parties are bound by the instrument. Furthermore, any provision in a land sales contract which prohibits its recording is void. The exception is a land sales contract which is to be fully performed within twelve months. Options and earnest money agreements are also specifically excluded and need not be recorded.

Exercise b

Recording a document does not make it any more or less legally enforceable as between the parties, but it does serve to give ______________ ______________ to the world of the existence of the document. To record a document requires that the signatures of the parties be ______________, and if it is a deed or land sales contract, it must state the name and address where the ______ ________ is to be sent in the future, as well as the true and actual ______________ paid for the property. Although failing to record is generally foolish, it is nevertheless optional for all documents except a ________ ________ ______________, which must be recorded within ____ days of the date the parties are bound, unless it is a short term agreement to be fully performed within _____ months. In lieu of recording the entire document, it is permitted to record just a ______________ of a document. This gives the same notice as recording the entire document.

KEY TERMS

The key to understanding any new field is the vocabulary used in that field. To maximize your comprehension of the material presented in this chapter, be sure you know the meaning and significance of the following terms. Remember that the majority of test questions primarily test knowledge of vocabulary.

Acknowledgment
Actual notice
Bonafide purchaser
Constructive notice
For value
In good faith
Innocent purchaser
Inquiry notice
Memorandum
Notary public
Notice
Public record
Without notice of defect

ANSWERS

To chapter exercises. If you couldn't figure out what to put in the blanks, find the answer here!

Exercise a

When a party verifies before an official that he or she actually signed a document, this is called an ACKNOWLEDGMENT*, and is evidence that the signature was not a* FORGERY *and that it was a* VOLUNTARY *act. In most cases the official who verifies the signature is a* NOTARY PUBLIC.

To protect themselves, buyers, lenders and others dealing in real estate should be sure to give notice to the world of their interest in the property. When you tell someone of your interest, this is ACTUAL *notice. When you give notice by being in possession or by recording, this is called* CONSTRUCTIVE *notice. When someone has a duty to inquire, we say that they have been given* INQUIRY *notice. If you fail to give notice of your interest in the property, the interest could be extinguished by a sale to a bonafide* PURCHASER *in good faith for value with no* NOTICE *of the defect.*

Exercise b

Recording a document does not make it any more or less legally enforceable as between the parties, but it does serve to give CONSTRUCTIVE NOTICE *to the world of the existence of the document.*

To record a document requires that the signatures of the parties be ACKNOWLEDGED*, and if it is a deed or land sales contract, it must state the name and address where the* TAX BILL *is to be sent in the future, as well as the true and actual* CONSIDERATION *paid for the property.*

Although failing to record is generally foolish, it is nevertheless optional for all documents except a LAND SALES CONTRACT*, which must be recorded within* 15 *days of the date the parties are bound, unless it is a short term agreement to be fully performed within* 12 *months. In lieu of recording the entire document, it is permitted to record just a* MEMORANDUM *of a document. This gives the same notice as recording the entire document.*

PRACTICE QUESTIONS

The following practice questions are representative of the questions you will find on the final examination and on the licensing examinations given by the Oregon Real Estate Agency.

1. A declaration made by a person to an official stating that a deed has been freely and voluntarily executed is called
   (A) an acknowledgment.
   (B) an authorization.
   (C) an authentication.
   (D) an execution.

2. An acknowledgment is
   I. proof of execution of a deed by a grantor.
   II. necessary to make a deed valid.
   (A) I only (C) Both I and II
   (B) II only (D) Neither I nor II

3. The term "acknowledgment" means most nearly the same as
   (A) witnessing. (C) recording.
   (B) notice. (D) recognizance.

4. A deed must be acknowledged before it can be recorded. To acknowledge means to
   (A) admit before a witness that you signed the document.
   (B) make an affidavit.
   (C) authenticate the contents of a contract.
   (D) give notice to the world of the existence of the document.

5. Having an instrument acknowledged
   (A) creates a presumption of the legitimacy of the signatures.
   (B) creates a presumption that the signature was a voluntary act.
   (C) makes it possible to have the instrument recorded.
   (D) does all of the above.

6. Acknowledgment is necessary on a legal document
   (A) if you want to record it.
   (B) to make it legally enforceable.
   (C) only if the document is a deed.
   (D) only if the document is a lease.

7. It is considered proper acknowledgment for a deed if it is
   I. sworn to by the person taking the acknowledgment.
   II. witnessed by a notary public in another state.
   (A) I only (C) Both I and II
   (B) II only (D) Neither I nor II

8. In order to record a deed, whose signature must be acknowledged?
   (A) Grantor (C) Both A and B
   (B) Grantee (D) Neither A nor B

9. In order to record a lease, whose signature must be acknowledged?
   (A) Lessor (C) Both A and B
   (B) Lessee (D) Neither A nor B

10. Whose signature must be acknowledged on a land sales contract in order to record it?
    (A) Vendor (C) Both A and B
    (B) Vendee (D) Neither A nor B

11. Which of the following documents are commonly recorded?
    I. Deeds III. Listing agreements
    II. Trust deeds
    (A) I only (C) I, II and III
    (B) I and II only (D) III only

12. The recording system is designed to
    I. require acknowledgment to prevent forgery in recorded documents.
    II. provide public notice concerning the documents affecting the title of real estate.
    (A) I only (C) Both I and II
    (B) II only (D) Neither I nor II

13. Recording of instruments in the county records protects the
    (A) broker. (C) grantee.
    (B) grantor. (D) lawyer.

14. Recording a document gives
(A) constructive notice. (C) presumptive notice.
(B) actual notice. (D) private notice.

15. Deeds, mortgages, options and other real estate documents are ordinarily recorded in order to
I. give notice of interests in a particular parcel of real estate.
II. establish legal priority for those interests which are recorded first.
(A) I only (C) Both I and II
(B) II only (D) Neither I nor II

16. A person would receive constructive notice by which of the following?
(A) A recorded lease
(B) Tax judgment
(C) A recorded power line easement
(D) All of the above

17. Recording gives constructive notice. Which of the following also gives constructive notice?
(A) Express knowledge of a fact
(B) Possession of land by a person other than the grantor
(C) Knowledge of a deed that has not been delivered
(D) None of the above

18. A prospective buyer of real estate is presumed to have inspected
(A) the land itself.
(B) the public records pertaining to the land.
(C) both A and B.
(D) neither A nor B.

19. Which of the following need not be recorded to be valid against future purchasers?
(A) Property tax lien
(B) Agreement of sale
(C) Installment sale contract
(D) Deed

20. Which of the following needs to be recorded to be valid against subsequent purchasers?
(A) Property tax lien
(B) Properly created prescriptive easement
(C) An option to purchase
(D) None of the above needs to be recorded to be valid against future purchasers

21. It is a common procedure to record which of the following documents?
I. Listing agreement
II. Trust deed
III. Land sale contract or memorandum of the land sale contract
(A) I and II only (C) II and III only
(B) I and III only (D) I, II and III

22. Which of the following statements regarding priority of interests is true?
I. The date a mortgage is executed establishes the priority of that mortgage.
II. The priority of a deed is established by the date the deed was recorded.
(A) I only (C) Both I and II
(B) II only (D) Neither I nor II

23. Instruments are recorded in order to give notice to the world of an interest; this type of notice is
(A) actual. (C) constructive.
(B) hearsay. (D) implied.

24. A person cannot successfully claim lack of knowledge of the content of any recorded document. This is due to the legal principle known as
(A) caveat emptor (let the buyer beware).
(B) actual notice of the facts.
(C) the Statute of Frauds (requiring documents to be in writing).
(D) constructive notice.

25. Which statement below best explains why instruments affecting real estate are recorded with the recorder of deeds of the county where the property is located?
(A) To give constructive notice to the world of the interest in a particular parcel of real estate.
(B) The law requires that they be recorded.
(C) The broker cannot get the commission until they are recorded.
(D) To comply with the terms of the Statute of Frauds.

26. If the deed to a parcel of land in Oregon is properly recorded, the grantee has
    I. furnished constructive notice of his or her interest in the land.
    II. forestalled all actions arising from unrecorded interests in the land.
    (A) I only (C) Both I and II
    (B) II only (D) Neither I nor II

27. Notice of ownership given by a person's presence on the or her land is called
    (A) inquiry notice. (C) constructive notice.
    (B) actual notice. (D) physical notice.

28. Which of the following would provide the least notice to protect a purchaser's interest in a property against subsequent purchasers?
    (A) A person with a recorded warranty deed
    (B) A person with an unrecorded bargain and sale deed who is not in possession of the property
    (C) A lessee who is in possession of the property
    (D) A tenant with an unrecorded warranty deed

29. Which of the following documents can be recorded?
    (A) A deed (C) A lease
    (B) A land sales contract (D) All of the above

30. When the purchaser under a land sales contract records the contract
    I. legal title immediately passes to the purchaser.
    II. all prior encumbrances on the property are rendered invalid.
    (A) I only (C) Both I and II
    (B) II only (D) Neither I nor II

31. Harris sold land to Henderson under a land sales contract which was not recorded. Harris then mortgaged the property and that mortgage was recorded. In the event of foreclosure on the mortgage, who has the best legal claim to the property?
    (A) Harris
    (B) Henderson
    (C) The mortgage holder
    (D) All are equal in precedence.

32. Samuels sold land to White under an installment contract, but did not record the contract. Two days later Samuels mortgaged the property to Peoples Savings and Loan who recorded the mortgage. In the event of foreclosure on the mortgage, who would take precedence?
    (A) Samuels
    (B) Peoples Savings and Loan
    (C) White
    (D) All are equal in precedence

33. Which of the following is normally in the weakest position against loss of property due to a claim of title by an outsider?
    (A) Holder of a recorded sheriff's deed who does not reside on the property
    (B) Holder of an unrecorded special warranty deed who occupies the property
    (C) Holder of an unrecorded quitclaim deed who does not occupy the property
    (D) Holder of a recorded bargain and sale deed who rents the property to a tenant

34. An unrecorded deed to property is
    I. binding on the grantor and grantee of the deed.
    II. not binding on a subsequent purchaser of the land who has no notice of it.
    (A) I only (C) Both I and II
    (B) II only (D) Neither I nor II

35. What effect does an unrecorded quitclaim deed have?
    (A) It is valid between the parties and valid as to subsequent parties who have no notice of it.
    (B) It is invalid between the parties and invalid as to subsequent parties with or without notice.
    (C) It is valid between the parties but invalid as to subsequent parties with or without notice of it.
    (D) It is valid between the parties and valid as to subsequent parties with notice of it.

36. Peters received a deed to some land from Albertson. If Peters does not record the deed, it is
    I. still binding between Peters and Albertson.
    II. potentially invalid as to the rest of the world.
    (A) I only (C) Both I and II
    (B) II only (D) Neither I nor II

37. Adam deeded property to Abel, who took possession of the property but did not record his deed. Adam subsequently deeded the property to Cain who recorded his deed without inspecting the property. The result would be
(A) no title transfer at all.
(B) Abel is the rightful owner of the property.
(C) Cain is the rightful owner of the property.
(D) Cain will be the rightful owner of the property if he files a suit to quiet title.

38. Caesar O'Gustus sold a property to Cassius McMoney on an contract which was not recorded. Shortly thereafter, O'Gustus mortgaged the property to the Second National Bank, which recorded its mortgage. If the bank forecloses,
(A) McMoney's contract will be extinguished.
(B) it must take title subject to McMoney's contract.
(C) its mortgage will be extinguished.
(D) it will have to share the proceeds from the sheriff's sale with McMoney.

39. A deed to property selling for a price of $40,000 meets the consideration tests if it states that the consideration was
I. $10 and other good and valuable consideration, the receipt of which is acknowledged.
II. $40,000, the receipt of which is acknowledged.
(A) I only
(B) II only
(C) Both I and II
(D) Neither I nor II

40. Every deed executed to convey title in Oregon must show which of the following before the document will be accepted for recordation?
(A) Monetary consideration
(B) Acknowledgment of grantor
(C) Acknowledgment of grantee
(D) Whether or not the property is to be encumbered with a purchase money mortgage

41. All of the following are required for recordation of a deed except that
(A) the deed must be properly acknowledged.
(B) consideration must be either stated in dollars or noted on the face of the deed that other property or value was part or the whole consideration.
(C) the deed must include the name and address to where the tax statement should be sent.
(D) the deed must be signed by the grantee.

42. To be recorded a deed must
(A) be signed and acknowledged by the grantee.
(B) be dated.
(C) have consideration stated.
(D) meet all of the above.

43. To record a deed in Oregon, you need
(A) to show the consideration.
(B) the grantee's signature properly notarized.
(C) the date.
(D) all of the above.

44. To be effective, recording of documents affecting title to real estate is performed
(A) in the county where the property is located.
(B) in the county of residence of the seller.
(C) in the county of residence of the purchaser.
(D) at the state capitol building.

45. Consideration in dollars must be stated on the deed
I. in order for the deed to be recorded, except if given by gift or through exchange.
II. in order to have a valid deed.
(A) I only
(B) II only
(C) Both I and II
(D) Neither I nor II

46. Which one of the following is a necessary element to enable you to record a deed?
(A) Acknowledgment
(B) Date
(C) Delivery
(D) None of the above

47. For a bargain and sale deed to be recorded in Oregon
(A) it must state the true and actual consideration paid.
(B) it must be properly acknowledged.
(C) the name and address for the tax bill must be stated.
(D) all of the above are required.

48. To be recorded, a warranty deed in an ordinary transaction must contain
(A) a covenant of seizin.
(B) a covenant against encumbrances.
(C) a statement of the true and actual consideration paid.
(D) all of the above.

49. To be recorded, all deeds require that the true and actual consideration be stated except
I. a personal representative's deed.
II. a gift deed.
(A) I only
(B) II only
(C) Both I and II
(D) Neither I nor II

50. If a mortgage is to be recorded,
I. the signature of the mortgagor must be acknowledged.
II. the amount of the mortgage must be stated.
(A) I only
(B) II only
(C) Both I and II
(D) Neither I nor II

51. Jackson, who lives in Willamette County, Oregon and owns land in Rogue County, Oregon sells the land to Monroe, who lives in Siuslaw County, Oregon. The deed from Jackson to Monroe would be recorded in
(A) Willamette County.
(B) Rogue County.
(C) Siuslaw County.
(D) all three counties.

52. Regarding the recording of land sales contracts,
(A) a land sales contract must contain the name and address where the tax bill is to be sent before it can be accepted for recording.
(B) all land sales contracts must be recorded within 15 days of the date the parties are bound by the agreement if title will be conveyed at a time more than 12 months from the date the contract is executed.
(C) a memorandum of contract is admissible for recording in Oregon.
(D) all of the above are correct.

53. Which of the following is true regarding recording of land sales contracts in Oregon?
(A) A contract for fewer than twelve months need not be recorded.
(B) Most land sales contracts must be recorded within fifteen days.
(C) Contracts cannot be recorded unless they state the true and actual consideration.
(D) All of the above are true.

54. Under Oregon law, land sales contracts in which the buyer has more than one year to pay the purchase price must be recorded
I. by the buyer.
II. by the seller.
III. within 15 days from the effective date.
(A) I only
(B) II only
(C) Both I and III
(D) Both II and III

55. A buyer and a seller enter into a transaction which involves a typical land sales contract. At closing the parties specify to the escrow agent that the contract not be recorded. In this case
(A) the buyer may be subject to a fine.
(B) the seller may be subject to a fine.
(C) the escrow agent may be subject to a fine.
(D) the contract would be unenforceable and all the parties may be subject to a fine.

56. Ownership of real estate is actually transferred from one party to another upon
(A) payment of the stated consideration by the grantee of the deed.
(B) acknowledgment of the deed by the grantor.
(C) delivery and acceptance of the deed.
(D) recording the deed.

57. In the transfer of real property by deed, ownership changes hands when the deed has been
(A) signed.
(B) delivered.
(C) recorded.
(D) notarized.

58. A deed executed and delivered, but not recorded is
(A) void.
(B) voidable.
(C) valid.
(D) unenforceable.

59. The recording of a warranty deed
(A) passes title.
(B) insures the title.
(C) gives constructive notice of ownership.
(D) guarantees the title.

60. An acknowledgment is necessary on a deed
(A) if you want to record it.
(B) if you want to make it legal.
(C) only if it is a general warranty deed.
(D) only if it is a quitclaim deed.

61. Generally, a deed that is not acknowledged
    I. is effective between the parties to transfer title.
    II. will be accepted for recordation by the county clerk.
    (A) I only (C) Both I and II
    (B) II only (D) Neither I nor II

62. As far as its validity between grantor and grantee is concerned, a deed that is not dated, acknowledged, or recorded is
    (A) invalid because of these omissions.
    (B) void.
    (C) revocable by the grantor.
    (D) valid despite these omissions.

63. An unrecorded deed is valid and binding
    I. between parties to the deed.
    II. upon a later bona fide purchaser for value who first records the deed.
    (A) I only (C) Both I and II
    (B) II only (D) Neither I nor II

64. A deed
    (A) cannot be recorded in more than one county.
    (B) does not have to be recorded to transfer title.
    (C) that is recorded will not give the grantee the protection of the recording laws if a quitclaim deed is used.
    (D) that is recorded gives notice of its contents.

65. Written instruments documenting the conveyance of real property are recorded
    I. in the county where the real property is located in order to give constructive notice.
    II. to have the conveyance valid between the parties.
    (A) I only (C) Both I and II
    (B) II only (D) Neither I nor II

66. Recording a deed
    (A) guarantees title.
    (B) insures ownership.
    (C) verifies title.
    (D) constitutes constructive notice of ownership.

67. Recording a deed
    (A) guarantees that no lien will be leveled against the real estate.
    (B) guarantees ownership.
    (C) protects the seller.
    (D) protects the interests of the purchaser.

68. Which of the following statements concerning Oregon deeds is true?
    (A) Real estate licensees may advise their principals as to which type of deed would be best suited for them.
    (B) To be recorded, a deed must contain the name and address of the party to whom the tax statement will be sent.
    (C) Statutory deed forms must be used to convey property within Oregon.
    (D) In Oregon, the bargain and sale deed has the same warranties and covenants as the special warranty deed.

69. The chronological order in which documents are recorded can be ascertained
    I. from the recording officer's date and time stamp on the instrument.
    II. by the last name of the grantee.
    (A) I only (C) Both I and II
    (B) II only (D) Neither I nor II

70. Mrs. Blue says she owns a piece of land. You would expect to find her name listed in
    (A) the grantee, or indirect index.
    (B) the grantor, or direct index.
    (C) both A and B.
    (D) neither A nor B.

71. A deed which is voidable because the grantor is in fact mentally incompetent
    I. cannot be recorded.
    II. may be set aside later by legal proceedings.
    (A) I only (C) Both I and II
    (B) II only (D) Neither I nor II

72. A mechanics lien is usually removed from public record by
    (A) court order.
    (B) payment in full.
    (C) recordation of a release.
    (D) satisfaction of the judgment.

ANSWERS

To practice questions. If you chose the wrong letter, here's the right one! The explanations are designed to clarify your understanding.

1. **A** An acknowledgment is when someone's signature is witnessed. The normal person who witnesses the signature is a notary public. The notarial acknowledgment states that the person appeared before the notary and acknowledged the signature to be his or her voluntary act. The notary then verifies the identification of the person signing.

2. **A** An acknowledgment is a witnessing of the signature, which is normally done by a notary public. The notary laws require the notary to verify the parties identity. In an acknowledgment the notary states that the signature was legitimate (identity verified) and voluntary. A deed is valid between the parties without acknowledgment. We always have the grantor's signature acknowledged, however, because we wish to record the deed, and the recording statutes require all documents to be acknowledged in order to be recorded.

3. **A** The person taking the acknowledgment is attesting that the signatures are genuine and voluntary. Notice is the result of recording. Recording occurs when a document is placed in the public records. Acknowledgment is a prerequisite to recording.

4. **A** Neither acknowledgment nor recording has any effect on the legal enforceability of a document. Acknowledgment creates prima facie evidence that the signature is genuine and a voluntary act. An affidavit is a statement signed under penalty of perjury.

5. **D** The person taking an acknowledgment is veryifying that the signatures are genuine and voluntary. Acknowledgment is a prerequisite to recording in Oregon.

6. **A** Any document must usually be acknowledged in order to be recorded. Acknowledgment merely establishes that the signatures were voluntary and genuine. It does not have any effect on enforceability. It is, however, required for documents to be recorded.

7. **B** Under Oregon law acknowledgments can be taken by notaries public and by judges. Oregon also recognizes acknowledgments sworn to before officials in other states, provided the official is authorized to take acknowledgments in the other state.

8. **A** When an interest in property is being conveyed or created the owner or creator of the interest must sign the contract creating it. Note, however, that grantees of deeds and lessees of leases do not have to sign the deed or lease to evidence their acceptance. Therefore, their signatures need not be acknowledged.

9. **A** A lease need be signed only be the lessor to be valid. The lessee consents to its terms by accepting possession. Therefore, if it is to be recorded only the signature of the lessor must be acknowledged.

10. **C** A contract requires the signatures of both buyer and seller. The buyer's signature is needed because the contract is a future promise. Recording statutes require signatures to be acknowledged, so both signatures will have to be acknowledged.

11. **B** A listing agreement would normally affect the seller, but not a buyer. Therefore, there is no need to give a buyer notice of it. Deeds are recorded to protect the buyer from claims of subsequent parties, and trust deeds protect lenders' liens against claims of subsequent parties.

12. **C** An acknowledgment is a witnessing of the signature, which is normally done by a notary public. Its effect is to create prima facie evidence that the signature was genuine and a voluntary act. The notary laws require the notary to verify the parties identity. Recording gives constructive notice, so future purchasers or encumbrancers cannot say they did not know.

13. **C** The purpose of recording is to give notice to the world and establish priority in the event that should become an issue. If someone did not have notice of something then they are an innocent purchaser in good faith for value with no notice of the defect, and the law holds them harmless. However, the law holds that everyone is deemed to have notice of everything that is of public record. While recording might save the broker or lawyer from a malpractice suit, the primary beneficiaries are usually a buyer (grantee of a deed) or lender (mortgagee or beneficiary).

14. **A** Notice can be actual, as where someone told you or you found out some other way; inquiry, as where something looked dubious and a prudent person would have a duty to inquire; or constructive. Constructive notice is given of anything that

has been recorded, or of any rights of any party when they are in possession. The surest way to prove you gave notice is to record, although any notice is as good as any other, as long as you can prove it. When the circumstances make it obvious that someone had notice, we say it is presumptive.

15. **C** The purpose of recording is to give notice to the world and establish priority in the event that should become an issue. If someone did not have notice of something then they are an innocent purchaser in good faith for value with no notice of the defect, and the law holds them harmless. However, the law holds that everyone is deemed to have notice of everything that is of public record.

16. **D** Everyone is deemed to have notice of the rights of any party in possession of a property. This is one kind of constructive notice. Another kind is that everyone is deemed to have notice of everything in the public records.

17. **B** Notice can be actual, as where someone told you or you found out some other way; inquiry, as where something looked dubious and a prudent person would have a duty to inquire; or constructive. Constructive notice is given of anything that has been recorded, or of any rights of any party when they are in possession.

18. **C** The concept of constructive notice depends on the legal principle that any buyer or encumbrancer of real estate has a duty to inspect and is presumed to know that which would be revealed by an inspection of the premises and of the public record relative to the property.

19. **A** Recording gives constructive notice, so future purchasers or encumbrancers cannot say they did not have notice. If you buy on an unrecorded contract, and the seller later deeds the property to someone else, the new party may not have had notice of your contract. If so, the new party is held harmless and your contract is extinguished. However, everyone is deemed to have notice of property taxes, even without being recorded.

20. **C** Either recording or being in possession gives constructive notice, so future purchasers or encumbrancers cannot say they did not have notice. If you buy on an unrecorded option, or you gain an easement but the easement grant was not recorded, and the seller later deeds the property to someone else, the new party may not have had notice of your interest. If so, the new party is held harmless and your interest is extinguished. However, everyone is deemed to have notice of property taxes, even without being recorded. A prescriptive easement is not created by a written document, but rather, by being in possession. The possession gives notice.

21. **C** Either recording or being in possession give constructive notice, so future purchasers or encumbrancers cannot say they did not know. If you buy on an unrecorded contract, or a lender takes a trust deed from the seller and fails to record it, and the seller later deeds the property to someone else, the new party may not have had notice of your contract or the lender's trust deed. If so, the new party is held harmless and the contract or trust deed would be extinguished. However, brokers do not record their listings because it is not considered necessary, and because it would create a cloud on the seller's title which could be construed as harming the seller, for which the broker might be liable for damages.

22. **B** Recording not only gives constructive notice, it also establishes the date for priority of claims. If a document is not recorded, its priority is always last.

23. **C** Actual notice is when you were told, or found out on your own, inquiry notice is when something looked unusual and a prudent person would have a duty to investigate, and constructive notice is given by recording or by being in possession.

24. **D** Actual notice is when you were told, or found out on your own, inquiry notice is when something looked unusual and a prudent person would have a duty to investigate, and constructive notice is given by recording or by being in possession.

25. **A** Constructive notice is given by recording or by being in possession. Documents are still valid between the parties without being recorded, but giving notice protects the parties to the document from the claims of third parties. It might be argued that the last thing in closing a transaction is to record the documents, therefore the broker does not get the commission until the documents are recorded, however, giving constructive notice is the real reason we record. The Statute of Frauds is the law that requires contracts involving real property to be in writing.

26. **A** When a document is recorded, it gives notice to the world (constructive notice). All subsequent parties are deemed to have been given notice of it, but it does not affect the interests of parties that were of record before it was recorded. Anyone who did not have notice is an innocent party in good faith without notice of the defect, and is held harmless as to the matter of which they had no notice.

27. **C** Constructive notice is given either by recording a document in the public records or by being in possession of the property. Actual notice is when people were told about the matter or learned about it themselves some other way. Inquiry notice is when something looked unusual and a prudent person would have a duty to inquire.

28. **B** Constructive notice is given either by recording a document in the public records or by being in possession of the property. Actual notice is when the person was told about the matter or learned about it themselves some other way. Inquiry notice is when something looked unusual and a prudent person would have a duty to inquire. Any type of notice is as good as any other type. One might argue that recording is more certain to give notice than being in possession, but the person who is not in possession and has not recorded is surely in the weakest position.

29. **D** Practically anything can be recorded.

30. **D** Recording has the effect of giving constructive notice and, as to encumbrances, establishing the priority date. If an instrument creating an encumbrance is not recorded it is always last in priority. In a land sales contract the seller retains legal title until the buyer has finished paying for the property. Encumbrances run with the land, so a buyer always takes title subject to whatever encumbrances were in existence at the time.

31. **C** Recording is optional for all documents except the land sales contract. However, failing to record a land sales contract merely makes the seller subject to a fine; it does not render the contract unenforceable. Nevertheless, recording has the effect of giving constructive notice and, as to encumbrances, establishing the priority date. If an instrument creating an encumbrance is not recorded it is always last in priority. Thus foreclosure by the mortgage holder would extinguish the contract.

32. **B** With some exceptions, the priority of encumbrances is generally in date order. The date is the recording date for matters that are recorded, or the docket date for judgments. An unrecorded lien is always last in priority.

33. **C** If you buy property you take title subject to any encumbrances or other interests that you had notice of. It is the duty of the holder of the encumbrance or other interest to see that you were given notice. Notice can be actual, as where someone told you; inquiry, as where something looked dubious and a prudent person would have a duty to inquire, or constructive. Constructive notice is given of anything that has been recorded, or of any rights of any party when they are in possession. The surest way to prove you gave notice is to record, although any notice is as good as any other as long as you can prove it. A grantee of a deed who does not live on the property and did not record the deed is in grave danger of a third party claiming an interest superior to the interest of the grantee.

34. **C** A contract is valid between the parties, but it is of no effect on third parties unless the third party has notice of it. A deed between a buyer and a seller is valid between them. But if the seller fraudulently deeds the property to another person afterwards, and if the second buyer has no notice of the first deed, the second buyer may ignore the first deed.

35. **D** The fact that the document is a quitclaim deed is irrelevant. Subsequent purchases or encumbrances by parties without notice always take priority over previous unrecorded instruments.

36. **C** Contracts may be valid between the parties, but subsequent partis can ignore contracts of which they had no notice. If a subsequent buyer records his or her deed first, the first buyer's title will be extinguished.

37. **B** Constructive notice is given by recording a document or by being in possession of real estate. If a party has taken possession, subsequent parties take title subject to his or her rights.

38. **A** First to record is first in right, and unrecorded documents are always last. Foreclosure by a senior lienholder extinguishes junior liens. Therfore, failing to record the contract caused it to be junior to the later recording of the mortgage. If the mortgagee forecloses the foreclosure will extinguish the contract.

39. **C** A deed does not have to be supported by consideration to be valid and enforceable. Therefore, it is still valid if a nominal consideration is stated. However, it cannot be accepted for recording unless the true and actual consideration is stated.

40. **B** To be accepted for recording deeds and land sales contracts must show the true and actual consideration and the name and address for the tax bill, in addition to the usual requirement that the signature be acknowledged and the fee paid. However, the consideration does not have to be stated in the event of an exchange, a gift, or if it is a personal representative's deed. The grantor must sign the deed, but not the grantee, so the acknowledgment of the grantee is unnecessary. Whether or not the property is encumbered is also irrelevant to the recording official.

41. **D** To be accepted for recording, deeds and land sales contracts must show the true and actual consideration, and the name and address for the tax bill, in addition to the usual requirement that the signature be acknowledged and the fee paid. The grantor must sign the deed, but not the grantee.

42. **C** To be accepted for recording, deeds and land sales contracts must show the true and actual consideration, and the name and address for the tax bill, in addition to the usual recording requirements. The date is unnecessary, even to be valid and enforceable. The grantor must sign the deed, but not the grantee.

43. **A** For most documents, recording requires only that the appropriate fee be paid and that the signature(s) be acknowledged. Deeds and land sales contracts must also show the true and actual consideration (except for gift deeds, personal representatives' deeds and exchanges), and the name and address for the tax bill.

44. **A** Every county maintains its own recording. Recording a document involving real estate gives constructive notice, but only if recorded properly in the county where the property is located.

45. **A** Deeds and land sales contracts must state the true and actual consideration to be recorded. Exceptions are gifts, personal representatives' deeds, and exchanges (in an exchange where cash is included, the amount of cash must be stated). Consideration is essential for most contracts to be enforceable, but not for deeds. We state the consideration only in order to record.

46. **A** The same as any other document, the signature on a deed must be acknowledged. The date is not required even for a deed to be valid between the parties. Delivery is required, but it would be impossible for the recording officer to know whether a deed had been delivered or not.

47. **D** To be recorded, most documents only need to be acknowledged. Deeds and land sales contracts must also stipulate the true and actual consideration and must contain the name and address where the tax bill is to be sent in the future.

48. **C** To be a warranty deed in the first place a deed must contain a covenant of seizin and a covenant against encumbrances. But recording has no effect on the enforceability of the document being recorded, so whether or not the deed qualifies as a warranty deed has nothing to do with its being recorded.

49. **C** Deeds need not state the true and actual consideration if they are gift deeds, personal representative's deeds, or given in exchange for other property rather than cash because such deeds do not have a dollar amount.

50. **A** Oregon law requires acknowledgment of the signatures on documents prior to recording. Consideration need only be stated on deeds, not liens.

51. **B** Documents affecting the title to real property fail to give constructive notice unless they are recorded in the right place and properly indexed. All real property documents must be recorded in the county where the property is located.

52. **D** Recording is optional for all documents except the land sales contract. A land sales contract must be recorded within fifteen days of the date the parties are bound, unless the term of the contract is less than one year. To be recorded, deeds and land sales contracts must state the name and address where the tax bill is to be sent in the future, as well as the true and actual consideration paid. A memorandum of contract is a short statement as to its existence, and may be recorded in lieu of the entire document provided it contains the name and address for the tax bill and the consideration.

53. **D** Recording is generally permissive, i.e., not required. However, Oregon law does require all land sales contracts to be recorded within fifteen days of the date the parties are bound. Earnest money agreements and contracts to be fully performed within twelve months are exempt.

54. **D** Recording is optional for all documents except the land sales contract. A land sales contract must be recorded within fifteen days of the date the parties are bound, unless the term of the contract is less than one year. If not recorded the seller is subject to a fine.

55. **B** Oregon statutes provide that all land sales contracts must be recorded within fifteen days of the date the parties are bound by the instrument, unless the terms of the contract provide that it is to be fully performed within twelve months. The statute was enacted to protect buyers, so if the seller fails to cause the contract to be recorded, he or she is subject to a fine. Similarly, any provision in a contract that it not be recorded is void and unenforceable on the buyer. However, the only penalty the seller may suffer is a fine – the contract is still valid and enforceable between the buyer and the seller, even if not recorded.

56. **C** A deed is valid between the parties when it has all the essential elements, has been delivered by the seller to the buyer, and the buyer has accepted it.

Recording gives constructive notice and protects the buyer from claims of third parties, but is not required for the deed to be valid and enforceable.

57. **B** Title passes to the buyer upon delivery and acceptance of the deed, not recording, not the date it was signed, and not the date it was notarized. The recording date does provide the priority date as against the interests of future claimants.

58. **C** A deed is valid between the parties when it has all the essential elements, has been delivered by the seller to the buyer, and the buyer has accepted it. Recording gives constructive notice and protects the buyer from claims of third parties, but is not required for the deed to be valid and enforceable.

59. **C** When a document is recorded, it gives constructive notice to the world. All subsequent parties are deemed to have been given notice of it. Anyone who did not have notice is an innocent party in good faith without notice and is held harmless as to the matter of which they had no notice. It cannot guarantee ownership, however, because, even if the deed is recorded, the seller's title may not have been good in the first place. The title passes to the buyer upon delivery and acceptance of the deed, not upon recording.

60. **A** An acknowledgment is a witnessing of a signature, and is normally done by a notary. It has three effects – it creates prima facie evidence that the signature is genuine, prima facie evidence that the signature was voluntary and, the recording statutes require all documents to have been acknowledged in order to be recorded.

61. **A** The purpose of recording is to give constructive notice to the world of the existence of a document. However, even if not recorded, a document is still valid as between the parties. In order to ensure that signatures are legitimate and voluntary, the recording statutes require that the signatures be acknowledged on all documents to be recorded.

62. **D** To be valid and enforceable a deed must be in writing and signed by the grantor, the grantor must be competent, there must be words of conveyance (usually a granting clause), an adequate description, and an identifiable grantee. And finally, the deed must be delivered to and accepted by the grantee. The grantee would be foolish not to record a deed, but recording is not required for it to be valid and enforceable. Acknowledgment is a recording requirement, not a requirement for validity of the deed. A date on a deed establishes the time from which the warranties are effective, but is otherwise unnecessary.

63. **A** Anyone who deals in another's real property is deemed to have notice of certain interests. The law provides that notice can be given personally (actual notice), or because something looked unusual and a prudent person would have investigated (inquiry notice), or because something was recorded or someone was in possession of real property (constructive notice). If someone did not have notice then the law holds that person as innocent with no notice of the defect, and the matter is not effective as against that person. For example, if a buyer fails to give notice of his or her deed, and the original owner later sells the property to a buyer who does not otherwise receive notice of the first sale, then the first deed is extinguished and the new buyer's title is free and clear. Therefore, while the first deed is valid between the parties, and the first buyer can sue the seller for fraud, the first buyer has nevertheless lost the property.

64. **B** Each county maintains its own records. Recording a deed outside of the county other than the county where the property is located would be of no value, but legally allowable, nevertheless. Recording gives constructive notice and is important to protect the buyer's interest, but not necessary to make the deed valid between the seller and buyer. A quitclaim deed conveys all the grantor's interest in the property at the time of the conveyance, and the recording laws make no exceptions or special provisions for it. Actual notice is notice that was given in person, by mail, or which a person otherwise knew of. Constructive notice is the type of notice given by recording.

65. **A** Every county maintains its own recording. Recording a document involving real estate gives constructive notice, but only if recorded in the county where the property is located. Constructive notice means that the parties to the document that was recorded are protected against the claims of third parties. It has no effect, however, on the validity or enforceability of the document between the parties to it.

66. **D** When a document is recorded, it gives notice to the world (constructive notice). All subsequent parties are deemed to have been given notice of it, but it does not affect the interests of parties that were of record before it was recorded. Anyone who did not have notice is an innocent party in good faith without notice, and is held harmless as to the matter of which they had no notice.

67. **D** When a document is recorded, it gives notice to the world (constructive notice). All subsequent parties are deemed to have been given notice

of it. Anyone who did not have notice is an innocent party in good faith without notice of the defect and is held harmless as to the matter of which they had no notice. Therefore, recording a deed protects the buyer by giving constructive notice of his or her ownership. It cannot guarantee ownership, however, because, even if the deed is recorded, the seller's title may not have been good in the first place. It also does not affect any future interests in the property.

68. **B** Real estate and escrow licensees may assist their clients as to filling in the blanks on statutory form deeds, but may not advise as to which form to select. Statutory deeds are optional, short form deeds. The warranty deed contains the covenant of seizin, the covenant of quiet enjoyment, the covenant against encumbrances, the covenant of warranty forever and a covenant that the grantor has a fee title. The bargain and sale deed contains only a covenant that the grantor has a fee title. All deeds and land sales contracts must state the true and actual consideration, as well as the name and address for the tax bill in order to be recorded, but not in order to be valid.

69. **A** Since the first to record is the first in right, the exact time a document is recorded is crucial to the parties. Therefore, the recording clerk assigns a book and page number, or some other file number, to each document in consecutive order as received. In addition, the date and time of day is machine-stamped on each document before it is filmed.

70. **A** All recording clerks are required to keep an index to documents which affect real property titles. The index is normally arranged alphabetically by last names of the parties (grantors and grantees, or mortgagors and mortgagees). In counties where deeds and mortgages are kept in one set of books, the grantors and mortgagors are kept in a "direct" index, while grantees and mortgagees are kept in an "indirect" index. Therefore, the current owner of any property can be ascertained by finding the last grantee for the property.

71. **B** The recording statutes provide that any document can be recorded. The purpose of recording is to give constructive notice to the world of the existence of a document. The recording officer has no way to pass judgment on the validity or legal effect of a document. A deed requires a competent grantor, so if the grantor is incompetent, the deed is void or voidable.

72. **C** Recording a document creates public notice and, as to liens, establishes the priority date. Once it has been recorded, there is no way to "un-record" it, so to remove a lien from the public record it is necessary to record a new document to annul the first one. A mechanic's lien is an older term for "construction lien." In the case of a construction lien, the document is a release or satisfaction of construction lien.

TITLE INSURANCE

As we saw previously, there are many complicated laws which buyers must deal with in a real estate transaction. Yet buyers are typically ill-prepared to ensure that the interest they bargained for is, in fact, the interest the seller is delivering. At the same time, they have to be sure. An error could cost them their ownership in the property.

To assist buyers (as well as lenders, lessees and others) in determining the condition of the seller's title, an entire title insurance industry has arisen. In this section we will explore the origins of this industry and the types of title insurance policies which are commonly available today.

In the early days the seller would provide a buyer with an ***abstract of title***. The abstract would be prepared by an abstract company (commonly called title companies or title and trust companies). The abstract was a bulky document, sometimes containing hundreds of pages, bound together in date order. Each page in the abstract would be a summary of some recorded document which affected the title to the property. Normally, the very first page in an abstract would be a summary of the original federal patent to the first homestead claimant. Subsequent pages would describe everything that followed, right up to the date the abstract was prepared.

Each recorded document is referred to as a ***link*** in the ***chain of title***. Researching the public records relative to a property to determine the current status of the title is called ***chaining the title***, or conducting a ***title search***.

Abstract companies were able to prepare an abstract easily because they had developed their own files of recorded documents. Over the years, the abstract companies would take down a summary of each document recorded at the recorder's office, and

NOTES

re-file these summaries in their own company records. These records are referred to as a ***title plant***.

An interesting feature of the title plant is that it was arranged in a ***tract index*** – property by property, rather than by grantor-grantee and mortgagor-mortgagee. Keeping all the records relating to each property in a single file greatly simplified the creation of the abstract. Even today, modern title insurance records are kept much the same way.

The job of the abstract company was only to provide information about documents in the public records, not to pass judgment on their legal effect or the quality of the title. Therefore, buyers would receive the abstract of title, and would also obtain the opinion of a title attorney as to the condition of the seller's title. For this reason, we usually refer to this system as ***abstract and opinion***.

Torrens title registration

Although abstract and opinion was better than no evidence of the condition of the seller's title, it was expensive and it afforded relatively limited protection. Various alternatives were proposed and, in most parts of the country, the abstract and opinion system has been replaced.

One of the earliest alternative methods was the Torrens system. The Torrens system was created in the mid 1800's by Sir Robert Torrens, a businessman who was experienced in registering ship titles.

Under the Torrens system, an owner would apply to register the title to his or her property with a county registrar of titles. In order to ensure that the title was correctly registered in the beginning, a suit to quiet title would be filed. Once the court decreed the condition of the title, the initial registration was made. In the future, any encumbrances, conveyances, or other matters would be filed with the registrar of titles. Each filing with the registrar would require a fee, and a portion of each fee would be set aside as a recovery fund for losses caused by registration errors.

The Torrens system can be an effective and inexpensive way to assure buyers of the condition of the title. Its major drawback is the time and expense involved in the initial registration. Although it is still used in several other countries and in 19 states, today its use in the United States is limited mostly to Hawaii, Massachusetts and the Chicago area. At one time the Torrens system was used in some Oregon counties, however, the statute permitting its use has been repealed.

Title certificates

In a few parts of the United States a system of ***title certificates*** is used. The title certificates are issued by an attorney who researches the condition of the seller's title. Generally speaking, the certificate is really nothing more than the attorney's opinion as to the condition of the title. Not only is the system expensive, but in the event of an error, the buyer has little recourse other than the attorney's malpractice insurance.

Exercise a

Originally, a buyer could only get an ____________________ *and* ____________________ *as evidence of the condition of the seller's title. It contained a summary of each recorded* ______________ *in the* ______________ *of* ______________ *. Part of this was the* __________________ *of an attorney. When all these summaries are filed in* *a title company it is referred to as a _____________ _____________.*

Title registration under the _________________ system is no longer used in Oregon.

Title insurance

In the western United States today (not including Hawaii), the most common way for the buyer to get evidence of the condition of the seller's title is title insurance. Although the concept of title insurance began much earlier, it was not until the 1920s that it first appeared as a serious alternative to the abstract and opinion.

An interesting footnote in the development of the title insurance industry is that it was the abstract companies which formed the original title insurance companies. After all, you cannot issue title insurance without a title plant, and the abstract companies had the only title plants. So when people started asking for title insurance instead of abstracts, the abstract companies simply became licensed as insurance companies and began issuing title insurance.

Title insurance has a number of advantages over earlier systems. For one thing, a title insurance policy is only a few pages and is reissued anew each time the property is sold. With abstracts, the buyer always had to keep the abstract so it could be updated and turned over to the next buyer. But the biggest advantage is that it is *insurance* – if the buyer suffers a loss covered by the policy, the buyer can simply present a claim. In addition, title insurance companies are regulated by the Oregon Insurance Commissioner, so consumers can be assured that each company will maintain adequate resources to protect their policyholders.

Policy types

Today there are numerous different title insurance policies available, each specifically tailored to a certain situation. For example, you would no doubt be embarrassed if you built a building on a long term leasehold, only to discover that the lessor's title was in question and you were about to be dispossessed at any moment. A wise move would have been to obtain a ***leasehold policy*** to protect your lessee's interest.

In addition to leasehold policies, title insurance companies issue various other policies, but none is more common than the ***owner's policy***. The owner's policy, obviously, insures the interest of an owner. But many times a seller will carry a land sales contract from the buyer. In this case, the seller retains legal title, so the buyer does not become the owner. Yet the buyer needs coverage, so the buyer obtains a ***purchaser's policy***. Except that it is issued to a contract buyer rather than a buyer who receives a deed at closing, the purchaser's policy is essentially the same as the owner's policy.

When property is financed through an outside lender (such as a bank), the lender will normally insist on a ***mortgagee's policy***. The mortgagee's policy insures that the lender has a good lien and the priority of the lien It is issued in the amount of the loan, rather than the purchase price. The coverage declines as the loan balance is paid off and ceases upon full satisfaction.

Although real estate agents seldom have use for them, title insurance companies also issue ***foreclosure guaranties***, ***trustee's sale guaranties*** and ***litigation guaranties***. When a lienholder forecloses, or when other litigation is commenced, all other parties with an interest in the property must be served with notice of the suit. Therefore, the purpose of these policies is so the plaintiff will know all the parties claiming an interest in the property.

NOTES

Coverages

Different title insurance policies offer different coverages, but all insure that the insured's title is a ***marketable title***. Marketable title is sometimes referred to as ***insurable title***. Marketable title does not mean that the property is completely free of encumbrances. Rather, marketable title means that the title is free of financial encumbrances but not other encumbrances which are normal in the area. For example, utility easements are encumbrances, but when they benefit all the properties in the area, the buyer is ordinarily expected to accept the title subject to them.

A common point of confusion for beginners is that, unlike other types of insurance, title insurance only insures the condition of the title at one specific moment in time. Title defects which are created in the future are not covered. Note the difference between a title defect which *occurs* in the future (not covered) and a title defect which *is discovered* in the future, but which existed at the time the policy was issued (covered defect).

While coverage is as of a given point in time, the term of a policy is unlimited. You would be covered even after selling the property, if called upon by your buyer to honor a warranty in the conveyance, for example.

The coverage afforded under the policy depends on the form on which it was issued. Today there are three title insurance forms in general use in Oregon. Two of these are considered ***standard form*** policies – the OLTA policy and the ALTA standard form policy. "OLTA" stands for "Oregon Land Title Association" which is the author of the first of these forms. "ALTA" means "American Land Title Association," which originated the second form. The American Land Title Association has also created an ***extended form*** policy. There is an example of the ALTA standard form policy on pages 266–269.

An owner's, purchaser's or mortgagee's policy could be issued on any one of the three forms. However, it is customary for the owner's or purchaser's policy to be issued on one of the standard forms, while the mortgagee's policy is usually an ALTA extended coverage policy. Nevertheless, buyers of new construction frequently ask for the ALTA extended coverage policy, since it covers construction liens which the standard form does not. And there are a few lenders who are satisfied with a standard form mortgagee's policy.

The ALTA standard form policy insures

- That the title is vested as stated in the policy
- That there are no defects in, or liens on, the title
- Against lack of a right of access
- Against the title not being marketable

However, there are numerous exclusions from coverage. These include

- Government exercise of police power or eminent domain, including environmental protection laws
- Defects of which the insured had actual notice
- Taxes or special assessments not already shown as liens by the taxing authority
- Interests of others which could be ascertained from an inspection of the premises
- Unrecorded easements
- Unpatented mining claims, reservations in federal patents (mineral rights)
- Water rights
- Construction liens
- Encroachments discrepancies or shortages which would be disclosed by a survey

In addition, the title search frequently reveals encumbrances such as mortgages, property taxes and other liens which the buyer is assuming, easements appurtenant to adjacent land, and others. Such defects do not necessarily mean the transaction will fail, if the buyer

NOTES

already knew of them and has agreed to buy the property subject to them. However, they will be excluded from the coverage under an additional schedule appended to the policy.

The OLTA standard form policy is approximately the same as the ALTA form above. There is one significant difference, however. Where the ALTA version insures that the owner will have right of access, the OLTA does not. Since property in urban areas almost always has good access, most title insurance companies in the cities issue the ALTA policy as their standard form. In outlying areas, it is more common to find title insurance companies issuing the OLTA policy.

The American Land Title Association extended coverage form was originally created in response to the needs of the secondary mortgage market. A "secondary lender" is a lender who purchases loans, usually in large "pools" from a "primary" or originating lender. When a primary lender sells a loan to a secondary lender the mortgagee's title insurance policy is assigned to the secondary lender. In the early days of title insurance, policies were not uniform throughout the United States and the coverage was sometimes poor. As a result, secondary lenders developed, jointly with the American Land Title Association, a uniform mortgagee's policy with extended coverage. Originally it was available only for lenders, but today a modified extended coverage policy can also be issued in owner's, purchaser's and lessee's forms.

The ALTA extended coverage mortgagee's policy insures

- That the title is vested as stated in the policy
- That there are no defects in, or liens on, the title
- Against lack of a right of access
- Against the title not being marketable
- Against the unenforceability of the mortgage, including the unenforceability of any assignment of it, listed in the policy, unless unenforceable due to violation of usury or consumer protection or disclosure law
- Against any other encumbrance having priority
- Against construction liens

Exclusions from coverage include

- Government exercise of police power or eminent domain, including environmental protection laws
- Defects of which the insured had actual notice

Note that the number of issues covered is considerably greater under the ALTA extended coverage policy than under either standard form policy. At the same time, the exclusions are far fewer. Additional endorsements are also available for a small additional charge.

Real estate agents usually to refer to the ALTA mortgagee's extended coverage policy as an "ALTA" policy, without stipulating "mortgagee's extended coverage." The buyer may be receiving an ALTA standard form owner's policy in the same transaction, which is commonly just referred to as the "standard form" policy. In other words, when real estate agents speak of an "ALTA" policy they mean "ALTA mortgagee's extended coverage" and when they say "standard form" they mean either the OLTA or ALTA owner's or purchaser's standard form policies.

While it is customary for the seller to pay the premium for the owner's or purchaser's policy, there is no law requiring the premium to be paid by the seller. Similarly, the borrower is the party who is normally responsible for the mortgagee's policy, but the parties can negotiate otherwise if they desire. Oregon real estate agents should be aware that these customs also prevail in most of the rest of the western United States, but not everywhere. In some areas it is customary for the buyer to pay for the owner's policy, and in other areas the normal practice is for the buyer and the seller to split the cost. Clients moving to this area may be surprised by our customs.

NOTES

Preliminary title reports

A problem occurs in the closing of a real estate transaction. The buyer does not want the cash to be released to the seller without first receiving the title insurance policy. The seller, on the other hand, does not want the deed recorded without getting the cash. The title insurance policy insures that the buyer has good title, so it cannot be issued until the seller's deed to the buyer has been recorded. This creates an endless circle with no apparent solution.

The remedy lies in the ***preliminary title report***, sometimes just called a ***title report***, or in common jargon, a "PTR" or "prelim." The preliminary title report is issued prior to closing and is a summary of what the title insurance company found when searching the seller's title. It will show the seller in title, and will report all encumbrances, even those which the seller plans to pay off on closing. The preliminary title report is not insurance and does not create any liability on the part of the company.

When the buyer and the seller sign an earnest money (sales) agreement, there is typically a clause where the buyer agrees to accept the preliminary title report as conclusive evidence of the seller's title and close the transaction if the preliminary title report shows the seller's title to be as the seller represented it. This allows the transaction to close, the seller can receive the cash and the seller's deed can be recorded, all without the actual policy being issued. A short time after closing the title insurance company will issue the owner's or purchaser's policy.

A sample preliminary title report is reproduced on pages 264–265.

Exercise b

A buyer normally receives an ________________ title insurance policy, although if the buyer is buying on a land sales contract, a ____________________ policy is issued instead. Lenders receive assurance through a ____________________ policy.

Title insurance policies insure that the title is ____________________ (insurable) but cover only defects which existed as of the moment the policy is issued. The Oregon Land Title Association and the American Land Title Association both issue ____________________ form policies. The American Land Title Association also issues an ____________________ ____________________ policy. All policies exclude from coverage:

1. ____

2. ____

Prior to closing it is customary to order a ________________________ title report, which shows the condition of the seller's title.

KEY TERMS

The key to understanding any new field is the vocabulary used in that field. To maximize your comprehension of the material presented in this chapter, be sure you know the meaning and significance of the following terms. Remember that the majority of test questions primarily test knowledge of vocabulary.

Owner's policy
Abstract and opinion
Abstract of title
Chain of title
Chaining the title
Extended form
Foreclosure guaranty
Insurable title
Leasehold policy
Link
Litigation guaranty
Marketable title
Mortgagee's policy
Preliminary title report
Purchaser's policy
Standard form
Title search
Title report
Title plant
Title certificate
Tract index
Trustee's sale guaranty

ANSWERS

To chapter exercises. If you couldn't figure out what to put in the blanks, find the answer here!

Exercise a

Originally, a buyer could only get an ABSTRACT *and* OPINION *as evidence of the condition of the seller's title. It contained a summary of each recorded* LINK *in the* CHAIN *of* TITLE*. Part of this was the* OPINION *of an attorney. When all these summaries are filed in a title company it is referred to as a* TITLE PLANT.
Title registration under the TORRENS *system is no longer used in Oregon.*

Exercise b

A buyer normally receives an OWNER'S *title insurance policy, although if the buyer is buying on a land sales contract, a* PURCHASER'S *policy is issued instead. Lenders receive assurance through a* MORTGAGEE'S *policy.*
Title insurance policies insure that the title is MARKETABLE *(insurable) but cover only defects which existed as of the moment the policy is issued. The Oregon Land Title Association and the American Land Title Association both issue* STANDARD *form policies. The American Land Title Association also issues an* EXTENDED COVERAGE *policy. All policies exclude from coverage:*

1. GOVERNMENT EXERCISE OF POLICE POWER OR EMINENT DOMAIN
2. DEFECTS OF WHICH THE INSURED HAD ACTUAL NOTICE

Prior to closing it is customary to order a PRELIMINARY *title report, which shows the condition of the seller's title.*

OREGON TITLE
Insurance Company
DIVISION OF
Lawyers Title Insurance Corporation
A LANDAMERICA COMPANY

Hillsboro Branch
4550 Kruse Way, Ste 175
Lake Oswego, Oregon 97035
(503) 635-8851 FAX 635-9187

Oregon Title Insurance Company
Attn: Carol
4550 Kruse Way, Ste 175
Lake Oswego, Oregon 97035

Date Prepared: September 29, 2002

PRELIMINARY TITLE REPORT
FOR ISSUING TITLE INSURANCE

SAMPLE

ORDER NO : 564321W
PARTY REFERENCE : MOUSE/DUCK
PROPERTY ADDRESS : 12225 N.W. Kearney Street, Portland, Oregon 97225
OTHER REFERENCE : Lot 17, Block 4, Fred & Ethel's Place

Lawyers Title Insurance Corporation is prepared to issue title insurance as of the effective date and in the form and amount shown on Schedule A, subject to the conditions, stipulations and exclusions from coverage appearing in the policy form and subject to the exceptions shown on Schedule B. This report is preliminary to the issuance of a policy of title insurance and shall become null and void unless a policy is issued and the full premium paid.

This report is for the exclusive use of the persons to whom it is addressed. Title insurance is conditioned on recordation of satisfactory instruments that establish the interests of the parties to be insured; until such recordation, the Company may cancel, amend, or supplement this report for any reason.

Thank you for placing the order with us.

If you need assistance with this report, please contact:

Carol at 648-0531

SCHEDULE A, Page No. 1

1. The effective date of this preliminary title report is 5:00 P.M. on

September 22, 2002

2. The policy or policies to be issued:

Policy/Edorsement Description	**Charge**
ALTA Standard Owner's for $160,000.00	605.00
ALTA Extended Lender's for $128,000.00	181.25
Lender Indorsements 100, 116, and 8.1	50.00
Government Service Fee	50.00

3. Title to the land described herein is vested in:

Mickey Mouse and Minnie Mouse, as tenants by the entirety

4. The land referred to in this report is described as follows

Lot 17, Block 4, FRED & ETHEL'S PLACE, in the City of Beaverton, County of Washington and State of Oregon

SCHEDULE B

Except for the items properly cleared through closing, the proposed policy or policies will not insure against loss or damage which may arise by reason of the following:

1. Taxes or assessments which are not shown as existing liens by the records of any taxing authority that levies taxes or assessments on real property or by the public records; proceedings by a public agency which may result uin taxes or assessments, or notice of such proceedings, whether or not shown by the records of such agency or by the public records.
2. Any facts, rights, interests or claims which are not shown by the public reocrds but which could be ascertained by an inspection of said land or by making inquiry of persons in possession thereof.
3. Easements, claims of easements or encumbrances, not shown by the public records reservations or exceptions in patents or in acts authjorizing the issuance thereof; water rights, or claims or title to water.
4. Any lien, or right to a lien, for unemployment taqxes, workman;s compensation, services, labor, equipment rental or material, heretofore or hereafter furnished, imposed by law and not shown by the public records.
5. Discrepancies, conflicts ion boundary lines, shortage in area, encroachments, or any other facts which a correct survey would disclose.

6. 2002-03 taxes, a lien in an amount to be determined, but not yet payable.
7. An easement created by instrument, including the terms and provisions thereof,
   Recorded : July 1, 1956, Book 352, Page 20
   In favor of : Aloha Sanitary District
8. A judgment in the Circuit Court for Washington County,
   Entered : August 8, 1988, Case S1234
   Against : Mickey Mouse
   In favor of : Rita Rat
   Amounts : $300 per month child support
9. Trust deed, including the terms and provisions thereof,
   Recorded : March 3, 1990, Book 1000, Page 111
   Grantor : Mickey Mouse and Minnie Mouse, husband and wife
   Beneficiary : Scrooge Federal Savings and Loan Association
   Amount : $180,000

DOTE 1: We find no unsatisfied judgments, state or federal tax liens against Donald Duck or Daisy Duck

Egghead Pettifogger, Title Officer

ISSUED BY

Lawyers Title Insurance Corporation
A LANDAMERICA COMPANY

OWNER'S POLICY OF TITLE INSURANCE

SUBJECT TO THE EXCLUSIONS FROM COVERAGE, THE EXCEPTIONS FROM COVERAGE CONTAINED IN SCHEDULE B AND THE CONDITIONS AND STIPULATIONS, LAWYERS TITLE INSURANCE CORPORATION, a Virginia corporation, herein called the Company, insures, as of Date of Policy shown in Schedule A, against loss or damage, not exceeding the Amount of Insurance stated in Schedule A, sustained or incurred by the insured by reason of:

1. Title to the estate or interest described in Schedule A being vested other than as stated therein;
2. Any defect in or lien or encumbrance on the title;
3. Unmarketability of the title;
4. Lack of a right of access to and from the land.

The Company will also pay the costs, attorneys' fees and expenses incurred in defense of the title, as insured, but only to the extent provided in the Conditions and Stipulations.

IN WITNESS WHEREOF, LAWYERS TITLE INSURANCE CORPORATION has caused its corporate name and seal to be hereunto affixed by its duly authorized officers, the Policy to become valid when countersigned by an authorized officer or agent of the Company.

LAWYERS TITLE INSURANCE CORPORATION

Attest: [signature] Secretary

LAWYERS TITLE INSURANCE CORPORATION SEAL 1925 RICHMOND, VA

By: [signature] President

EXCLUSIONS FROM COVERAGE

The following matters are expressly excluded from the coverage of this policy and the Company will not pay loss or damage, costs, attorneys' fees or expenses which arise by reason of:

1. (a) Any law, ordinance or governmental regulation (including but not limited to building and zoning laws, ordinances, or regulations) restricting, regulating, prohibiting or relating to (i) the occupancy, use, or enjoyment of the land; (ii) the character, dimensions or location of any improvement now or hereafter erected on the land; (iii) a separation in ownership or a change in the dimensions or area of the land or any parcel of which the land is or was a part; or (iv) environmental protection, or the effect of any violation of these laws, ordinances or governmental regulations, except to the extent that a notice of the enforcement thereof or a notice of a defect, lien or encumbrance resulting from a violation or alleged violation affecting the land has been recorded in the public records at Date of Policy.
   (b) Any governmental police power not excluded by (a) above, except to the extent that a notice of the exercise thereof or a notice of a defect, lien or encumbrance resulting from a violation or alleged violation affecting the land has been recorded in the public records at Date of Policy.

2. Rights of eminent domain unless notice of the exercise thereof has been recorded in the public records at Date of Policy, but not excluding from coverage any taking which has occurred prior to Date of Policy which would be binding on the rights of a purchaser for value without knowledge.

3. Defects, liens, encumbrances, adverse claims or other matters:
   (a) created, suffered, assumed or agreed to by the insured claimant;
   (b) not known to the Company, not recorded in the public records at Date of Policy, but known to the insured claimant and not disclosed in writing to the Company by the insured claimant prior to the date the insured claimant became an insured under this policy;
   (c) resulting in no loss or damage to the insured claimant;
   (d) attaching or created subsequent to Date of Policy; or
   (e) resulting in loss or damage which would not have been sustained if the insured claimant had paid value for the estate or interest insured by this policy.

4. Any claim, which arises out of the transaction vesting in the insured the estate or interest insured by this policy, by reason of the operation of federal bankruptcy, state insolvency, or similar creditors' rights laws, that is based on:
   (a) the transaction creating the estate or interest insured by this policy being deemed a fraudulent conveyance or fraudulent transfer; or
   (b) the transaction creating the estate or interest insured by this policy being deemed a preferential transfer except where the preferential transfer results from the failure:
      (i) to timely record the instrument of transfer; or
      (ii) of such recordation to impart notice to a purchaser for value or a judgment or lien creditor.

NM 1 PA 10
ALTA Owner's Policy (10-17-92)
Face Page
Form 1190-88

ORIGINAL

Valid Only If Schedules A and B Are Attached

ALTA Owner's Policy (10/17/92)

SCHEDULE A

Date of Policy: October 10, 2002
Policy No.: 564321w
Order No.: 564321w
Amount of Insurance: $160,000.00
Premium: $605.00

1. **Name of Insured:**
   Donald Duck and Daisy Duck

2. **The estate or interest in the land which is covered by this policy is:**
   an estate in fee simple

3. **Title to the estate or interest in land is vested in:**
   Donald Duck and Daisy Duck, as tenants by the entirety

4. **The land referred to in this policy is situated in the State of Oregon, County of** Washington **and is described as follows:**

   Lot 17, Block 4, FRED & ETHEL'S PLACE, in the City of Beaverton, County of Washington and State of Oregon.

SCHEDULE B
EXCEPTIONS FROM COVERAGE

This policy does not insure against loss or damage (and the Company will not pay costs, attorneys' fees or expenses) which arise by reason of:

1. Taxes or assessments which are not shown as existing liens by the records of any taxing authority that levies taxes or assessments on real property or by the public records; proceedings by a public agency which may result uin taxes or assessments, or notice of such proceedings, whether or not shown by the records of such agency or by the public records.
2. Any facts, rights, interests or claims which are not shown by the public reocrds but which could be ascertained by an inspection of said land or by making inquiry of persons in possession thereof.
3. Easements, claims of easements or encumbrances, not shown by the public records reservations or exceptions in patents or in acts authjorizing the issuance thereof; water rights, or claims or title to water.
4. Any lien, or right to a lien, for unemployment taqxes, workman;s compensation, services, labor, equipment rental or material, heretofore or hereafter furnished, imposed by law and not shown by the public records.
5. Discrepancies, conflicts ion boundary lines, shortage in area, encroachments, or any other facts which a correct survey would disclose.
6. An easement created by instrument, including the terms and provisions thereof, Recorded July 1, 1956, Book 352, Page 20
7. Trust deed, including the terms and provisions thereof,
   Recorded : October 9, 2002 in Book 1105, Page 243
   Grantors : Donald Duck and Daisy Duck, husband and wife
   Trustee : Oregon Title Insurance Company
   Beneficiary : Perpetual Loan Company, an Oregon Corporation
   Amount : $120,000.00

CONDITIONS AND STIPULATIONS

1. **DEFINITION OF TERMS.**

The following terms when used in this policy mean:

(a) "insured": the insured named in Schedule A, and, subject to any rights or defenses the company would have had against the named insured, those who succeed to the interest of the named insured by operation of law as distinguished from purchase including, but not limited to, heirs, distributees, devisees, survivors, personal representatives, next of kin, or corporate or fiduciary successors.

(b) "insured claimant": an insured claiming loss or damage.

(c) "knowledge" or "known": actual knowledge, not constructive knowledge or notice which may be imputed to an insured by reason of the public records as defined in this policy or any other records which impart constructive notice of matters affecting the land.

(d) "land": the land described or referred to in Schedule (A), and improvements affixed thereto which by law constitute real property. The term "land" does not include any property beyond the lines of the area described or referred to in Schedule (A), nor any right, title, interest, estate or easement in abutting streets, roads, avenues, alleys, lanes, ways or waterways, but nothing herein shall modify or limit the extent to which a right of access to and from the land is insured by this policy.

(e) "mortgage": mortgage, deed of trust, trust deed, or other security instrument.

(f) "public records": records established under state statutes at Date of Policy for the purpose of imparting constructive notice of matters relating to real property to purchasers for value and without knowledge. With respect to Section 1(a)(iv) of the Exclusions From coverage, "public records" shall also include environmental protection liens filed in the records of the clerk of the United States district court for the district in which the land is located.

(g) "unmarketability of the title": an alleged or apparent matter affecting the title to the land, not excluded or excepted from coverage, which would entitle a purchaser of the estate or interest described in Schedule A to be released from the obligation to purchase by virtue of a contractual condition requiring the delivery of marketable title.

2. **CONTINUATION OF INSURANCE AFTER CONVEYANCE OF TITLE.**

The coverage of this policy shall continue in force as of Date of Policy in favor of an insured only so long as the insured retains an estate or interest in the land, or holds an indebtedness secured by a purchase money mortgage given by a purchaser from the insured, or only so long as the insured shall have liability by reason of covenants of warranty made by the insured in any transfer or conveyance of the estate or interest. This policy shall not continue in force in favor of any purchaser from the insured of either (i) an estate or interest in the land, or (ii) an indebtedness secured by a purchase money mortgage given to the insured.

3. **NOTICE OF CLAIM TO BE GIVEN BY INSURED CLAIMANT.**

The insured shall notify the Company promptly in writing (i) in case of any litigation as set forth in Section 4(a) below, (ii) in case knowledge shall come to an insured hereunder of any claim of title or interest which is adverse to the title to the estate or interest, as insured, and which might cause loss or damage for which the Company may be liable by virtue of this policy, or (iii) if title to the estate or interest, as insured, is rejected as unmarketable. If prompt notice shall not be given to the Company, then as to the insured all liability of the Company shall terminate with regard to the matter or matters for which prompt notice is required: provided, however, that failure to notify the Company shall in no case prejudice the rights of any insured under this policy unless the Company shall be prejudiced by the failure and then only to the extent of the prejudice.

4. **DEFENSE AND PROSECUTION OF ACTIONS; DUTY OF INSURED CLAIMANT TO COOPERATE.**

(a) Upon written request by the insured and subject to the options contained in Section 6 of these Conditions and Stipulations, the Company, at its own cost and without unreasonable delay, shall provide for the defense of an insured in litigation in which any third party asserts a claim adverse to the title or interest as insured, but only as to those stated causes of action alleging a defect, lien or encumbrance or other matter insured against by this policy. The Company shall have the right to select counsel of its choice (subject to the right of the insured to object for reasonable cause) to represent the insured as to those stated causes of action and shall not be liable for and will not pay the fees of any other counsel. The Company will not pay any fees, costs or expenses incurred by the insured in the defense of those causes of action which allege matters not insured against by this policy.

(b) The Company shall have the right, at its own cost, to institute and prosecute any action or proceeding or to do any other act which in its opinion may be necessary or desirable to establish the title to the estate or interest, as insured, or to prevent or reduce loss or damage to the insured. The Company may take any appropriate action under the terms of this policy, whether or not it shall be liable hereunder, and shall not thereby concede liability or waive any provision of this policy. If the Company shall exercise its rights under this paragraph, it shall do so diligently.

(c) Whenever the Company shall have brought an action or interposed a defense as required or permitted by the provisions of this policy, the Company may pursue any litigation to final determination by a court of competent jurisdiction and expressly reserves the right, in its sole discretion, to appeal from any adverse judgment or order.

(d) In all cases where this policy permits or requires the Company to prosecute or provide for the defense of any action or proceeding, the insured shall secure to the Company the right to so prosecute or provide defense in the action or proceeding, and all appeals therein, and permit the Company to use, at its option, the name of the insured for this purpose. Whenever requested by the Company, the insured, at the Company's expense, shall give the Company all reasonable aid (i) in any action or proceeding, securing evidence, obtaining witnesses, prosecuting or defending the action or proceeding, or effecting settlement, and (ii) in any other lawful act which in the opinion of the Company may be necessary or desirable to establish the title to the estate or interest as insured. If the Company is prejudiced by the failure of the insured to furnish the required cooperation, the Company's obligations to the insured under the policy shall terminate, including any liability or obligation to defend, prosecute or continue any litigation, with regard to the matter or matters requiring such cooperation.

5. **PROOF OF LOSS OR DAMAGE.**

In addition to and after the notices required under Section 3 of these Conditions and Stipulations have been provided the Company, a proof of loss or damage signed and sworn to by the insured claimant shall be furnished to the Company within 90 days after the insured claimant shall ascertain the facts giving rise to the loss or damage. The proof of loss or damage shall describe the defect in, or lien or encumbrance on the title, or other matter insured against by this policy which constitutes the basis of loss or damage and shall state, to the extent possible, the basis of calculating the amount of the loss or damage. If the Company is prejudiced by the failure of the insured claimant to provide the required proof of loss or damage, the Company's obligations to the insured under the policy shall terminate, including any liability or obligation to defend, prosecute, or continue any litigation, with regard to the matter or matters requiring such proof of loss or damage.

In addition, the insured claimant may reasonably be required to submit to examination under oath by any authorized representative of the Company and shall produce for examination, inspection and copying, at such reasonable times and places as may be designated by any authorized representative of the Company, all records, books, ledgers, checks, correspondence and memoranda, whether bearing a date before or after Date of Policy, which reasonably pertain to the loss or damage. Further, if requested by any authorized representative of the Company, the insured claimant shall grant its permission, in writing, for any authorized representative of the Company to examine, inspect and copy all records, books, ledgers, checks, correspondence and memoranda in the custody or control of a third party, which reasonably pertain to the loss or damage. All information designated as confidential by the insured claimant provided to the Company pursuant to this Section shall not be disclosed to others unless, in the reasonable judgment of the Company, it is necessary in the administration of the claim. Failure of the insured claimant to submit for examination under oath, produce other reasonably requested information or grant permission to secure reasonably necessary information from third parties as required in this paragraph, unless prohibited by law or governmental regulation, shall terminate any liability of the Company under this policy as to that claim.

6. **OPTIONS TO PAY OR OTHERWISE SETTLE CLAIMS: TERMINATION OF LIABILITY.**

In case of a claim under this policy, the Company shall have the following additional options:

(a) **To Pay or Tender Payment of the Amount of Insurance.**

To pay or tender payment of the amount of insurance under this policy together with any costs, attorneys' fees and expenses incurred by the insured claimant, which were authorized by the Company, up to the time of payment or tender of payment and which the Company is obligated to pay.

Upon the exercise by the Company of this option, all liability and obligations to the insured under this policy, other than to make the payment required, shall terminate, including any liability or obligation to defend, prosecute, or continue any litigation, and the policy shall be surrendered to the Company for cancellation.

(b) **To Pay or Otherwise Settle With Parties Other than the Insured or With the Insured Claimant.**

(I) to pay or otherwise settle with other parties for or in the name of an insured claimant any claim insured against under this policy, together with any costs, attorneys' tees and expenses incurred by the insured claimant which were authorized by the Company up to the time of payment and which the Company is obligated to pay; or

(ii) to pay or otherwise settle with the insured claimant the loss or damage provided for under this policy, together with any costs, attorneys' fees and expenses incurred by the insured claimant which were authorized by the Company up to the time of payment and which the Company is obligated to pay.

Upon the exercise by the Company of either of the options provided for in paragraphs (b)(i) or (ii), the Company's obligations to the insured under this policy for the claimed loss or damage, other than the payments required to be made, shall terminate, including any liability or obligation to defend, prosecute or continue any litigation.

CONTROL NO. Z27-9939357

CONDITIONS AND STIPULATIONS – Continued

7. **DETERMINATION, EXTENT OF LIABILITY AND COINSURANCE.**

This policy is a contract of indemnity against actual monetary loss or damage sustained or incurred by the insured claimant who has suffered loss or damage by reason of matters insured against by this policy and only to the extent herein described.

(a) The liability of the Company under this policy shall not exceed the least of:

(i) the Amount of Insurance stated in Schedule A; or

(ii) the difference between the value of the insured estate or interest as insured and the value of the insured estate or interest subject to the defect, lien or encumbrance insured against by this policy.

(b) In the event the Amount of Insurance stated in Schedule A at the Date of Policy is less than 80 percent of the value of the insured estate or interest or the full consideration paid for the land, whichever is less, or if subsequent to the Date of Policy an improvement is erected on the land which increases the value of the insured estate or interest by at least 20 percent over the Amount of Insurance stated in Schedule A, then this Policy is subject to the following:

(i) where no subsequent improvement has been made, as to any partial loss, the Company shall only pay the loss pro rata in the proportion that the Amount of Insurance at Date of Policy bears to the total value of the insured estate or interest at Date of Policy; or

(ii) where a subsequent improvement has been made, as to any partial loss, the Company shall only pay the loss pro rata in the proportion that 120 percent of the Amount of Insurance stated in Schedule A bears to the sum of the Amount of Insurance stated in Schedule A and the amount expended for the improvement.

The provisions of this paragraph shall not apply to costs, attorneys' fees and expenses for which the Company is liable under this policy, and shall only apply to that portion of any loss which exceeds, in the aggregate, 10 percent of the Amount of Insurance stated in Schedule A.

(c) The Company will pay only those costs, attorneys fees and expenses incurred in accordance with Section 4 of these Conditions and Stipulations.

8. **APPORTIONMENT.**

If the land described in Schedule (A) consists of two or more parcels which are not used as a single site, and a loss is established affecting one or more of the parcels but not all, the loss shall be computed and settled on a pro rata basis as if the Amount of Insurance under this policy was divided pro rata as to the value on Date of Policy of each separate parcel to the whole, exclusive of any improvements made subsequent to Date of Policy, unless a liability or value has otherwise been agreed upon as to each parcel by the Company and the insured at the time of the issuance of this policy and shown by an express statement or by an endorsement attached to this policy.

9. **LIMITATION OF LIABILITY.**

(a) If the Company establishes the title, or removes the alleged defect, lien or encumbrance, or cures the claim of unmarketability of title, all as insured, in a reasonably diligent manner by any method, including litigation and the completion of any appeals therefrom, it shall have fully performed its obligations with respect to that matter and shall not be liable for any loss or damage caused thereby

(b) In the event of any litigation, including litigation by the Company or with the Company's consent, the Company shall have no liability for loss or damage until there has been a final determination by a court of competent jurisdiction, and disposition of all appeals therefrom, adverse to the title as insured.

(c) The Company shall not be liable for loss or damage to any insured for liability voluntarily assumed by the insured in settling any claim or suit without the prior written consent of the Company.

10. **REDUCTION OF INSURANCE; REDUCTION OR TERMINATION OF LIABILITY.**

All payments under this policy, except payments made for costs, attorneys' tees and expenses, shall reduce the amount of the insurance pro tanto.

11. **LIABILITY NONCUMULATIVE.**

It is expressly understood that the Amount of Insurance under this policy shall be reduced by any amount the Company may pay under any policy insuring a mortgage to which exception is taken in Schedule B or to which the insured has agreed, assumed, or taken subject, or which is hereafter executed by an insured and which is a charge or lien on the estate or interest described or referred to in Schedule A, and the amount so paid shall be deemed a payment under this policy to the insured owner.

12. **PAYMENT OF LOSS.**

(a) No payment shall be made without producing this policy for endorsement of the payment unless the policy has been lost or destroyed, in which case proof of loss or destruction shall be furnished to the satisfaction of the Company

(b) When liability and the extent of loss or damage has been definitely fixed in accordance with these Conditions and Stipulations, the loss or damage shall be payable within 30 days thereafter.

13. **SUBROGATION UPON PAYMENT OR SETTLEMENT.**

(a) The Company's Right of Subrogation.

Whenever the Company shall have settled and paid a claim under this policy, all right of subrogation shall vest in the Company unaffected by any act of the insured claimant.

The Company shall be subrogated to and be entitled to all rights and remedies which the insured claimant would have had against any person or property in respect to the claim had this policy not been issued. If requested by the Company, the insured claimant shall transfer to the Company all rights and remedies against any person or property necessary in order to perfect this right of subrogation. The insured claimant shall permit the Company to sue, compromise or settle in the name of the insured claimant and to use the name of the insured claimant in any transaction or litigation involving these rights or remedies.

If a payment on account of a claim does not fully cover the loss of the insured claimant, the Company shall be subrogated to these rights and remedies in the proportion which the Company's payment bears to the whole amount of the loss.

If loss should result from any act of the insured claimant, as stated above, that act shall not void this policy, but the Company, in that event, shall be required to pay only that part of any losses insured against by this policy which shall exceed the amount, if any, lost to the Company by reason of the impairment by the insured claimant of the Company's right of subrogation.

(b) The Company's Rights Against non-insured Obligors.

The Company's right of subrogation against non-insured obligors shall exist and shall include, without limitation, the rights of the insured to indemnities, guaranties, other policies of insurance or bonds, notwithstanding any terms or conditions contained in those instruments which provide for subrogation rights by reason of this policy.

14. **ARBITRATION**

Unless prohibited by applicable law, either the Company or the insured may demand arbitration pursuant to the Title Insurance Arbitration Rules of the American Arbitration Association. Arbitrable matters may include, but are not limited to, any controversy or claim between the Company and the insured arising out of or relating to this policy, any service of the Company in connection with its issuance or the breach of a policy provision or other obligation. All arbitrable matters when the Amount of Insurance is $1,000,000 or less shall be arbitrated at the option of either the Company or the insured. All arbitrable matters when the Amount of Insurance is in excess of $1,000,000 shall be arbitrated only when agreed to by both the Company and the insured. Arbitration pursuant to this policy and under the Rules in effect on the date the demand for arbitration is made or, at the option of the insured, the Rules in effect at Date of Policy shall be binding upon the parties. The award may include attorneys' fees only if the laws of the state in which the land is located permit a court to award attorneys' tees to a prevailing party. Judgment upon the award rendered by the Arbitrator(s) may be entered in any court having jurisdiction thereof.

The law of the situs of the land shall apply to an arbitration under the Title Insurance Arbitration Rules.

A copy of the Rules may be obtained from the Company upon request.

15. **LIABILITY LIMITED TO THIS POLICY; POLICY ENTIRE CONTRACT.**

(a) This policy together with all endorsements, if any, attached hereto by the Company is the entire policy and contract between the insured and the Company. In interpreting any provision of this policy, this policy shall be construed as a whole.

(b) Any claim of loss or damage, whether or not based on negligence, and which arises out of the status of the title to the estate or interest covered hereby or by any action asserting such claim, shall be restricted to this policy.

(c) No amendment of or endorsement to this policy can be made except by a writing endorsed hereon or attached hereto signed by either the President, a Vice President, the Secretary, an Assistant Secretary, or validating officer or authorized signatory of the Company.

16. **SEVERABILITY**

In the event any provision of the policy is held invalid or unenforceable under applicable law, the policy shall be deemed not to include that provision and all other provisions shall remain in full force and effect.

17. **NOTICES, WHERE SENT.**

All notices required to be given the Company and any statement in writing required to be furnished the Company shall include the number of this policy and shall be addressed to: Consumer Affairs Department, P.O. Box 27567, Richmond, Virginia 23261-7567.

PRACTICE QUESTIONS

The following practice questions are representative of the questions you will find on the final examination and on the licensing examinations given by the Oregon Real Estate Agency.

1. The first method used to verify the seller's title was called
   (A) title insurance.
   (B) Torrens registration.
   (C) abstract and opinion.
   (D) certificates of title.

2. The term "chain of title" refers to
   (A) a certificate of title.
   (B) a measurement of distance used by a surveyor.
   (C) heirs taking title after the death of the owner.
   (D) all the recorded documents affecting the condition of a title.

3. Chain of title is
   (A) a certificate of title issued under the Torrens system.
   (B) a list of all previous owners.
   (C) the heir named in a will to inherit property after a death of a testator.
   (D) a listing of all recorded instruments affecting the subject property.

4. A summary of the history of all conveyances and legal proceedings affecting a specific parcel of real estate is called
   (A) an affidavit of title.
   (B) a certificate of title.
   (C) a title Insurance policy.
   (D) an abstract of title.

5. The history of the title to a parcel of real estate, including deeds, wills, mortgages, and all items affecting, encumbering, or transferring the title is called the
   (A) opinion of title.
   (B) guaranty policy.
   (C) affidavit of title.
   (D) abstract.

6. An abstract of title is best described as
   (A) a digest of the title history to a particular property.
   (B) a summary of each deed in a title search.
   (C) an appraisal of the lands and the improvements.
   (D) a summary of all the improvements and encroachments on the property.

7. An abstract of title performs which of the following functions?
   I. Guarantees a clear title
   II. Insures the title
   (A) I only
   (B) II only
   (C) Both I and II
   (D) Neither I nor II

8. Abstract of title is a
   (A) contract for a deed.
   (B) history of the title.
   (C) guarantee of title.
   (D) property survey.

9. The abstract of title prepared for a specific parcel of real estate provides a
   I. full historical summary of matters affecting title.
   II. guarantee of title.
   (A) I only
   (B) II only
   (C) Both I and II
   (D) Neither I nor II

10. An abstract of title
    I. shows the history of ownership of the parcel.
    II. guarantees a valid title.
    (A) I only
    (B) II only
    (C) Both I and II
    (D) Neither I nor II

11. In order to determine the condition of the title, a purchaser should secure
    (A) a survey from a licensed surveyor.
    (B) an estoppel statement from the lender.
    (C) a title search from a title insurance company.
    (D) a certificate of no defense from the seller.

12. Tracing the conveyances and encumbrances of real property is known as
    (A) chain of title.
    (B) title search.
    (C) cloud on title.
    (D) recordation of title.

13. The best way to discover a flaw in the recorded title to a piece of real property is by
    (A) calling the county surveyor.
    (B) taking out property insurance.
    (C) a search of title.
    (D) hiring a lawyer.

14. A title insurance company would do which of the following before issuing a standard policy?
    I. Examine the chain of title
    II. Require a surveyor's certification against encroachments
    (A) I only
    (B) II only
    (C) Both I and II
    (D) Neither I nor II

15. Very often a preliminary title report for an owner's title insurance policy states that it is subject to the "rights of the parties in possession" because the party in possession may be an
    I. adverse possessor.
    II. owner of an unrecorded deed.
    (A) I only
    (B) II only
    (C) Both I and II
    (D) Neither I nor II

16. You are buying a house and the preliminary title report shows an encumbrance against the title which the seller finds impossible to remove. This makes your earnest money agreement
    (A) voidable at your option.
    (B) voidable at the seller's option.
    (C) voidable at either party's option.
    (D) It has no effect on your earnest money contract.

17. Bill and Bonnie Harrison own a home in fee simple absolute, although it is mortgaged to the Perpetual Mortgage Company. They agree to sell the home to Harold and Clara Bowe who will obtain a new loan. When the preliminary title report is delivered the Bowe's are upset to discover that there is a mortgage against the title. As the real estate agent you
    (A) explain to the buyers that they must lend the purchase price to the sellers for a few days before closing so the sellers can use the funds to obtain clear title.
    (B) should speak to the sellers immediately to make sure they have adequate funds to pay off the loan before closing.
    (C) explain to the buyers that this is normal and that their deed will be free and clear by closing.
    (D) should tell the buyers that the sellers cannot deliver clear title and refund the buyers' money.

18. Mary Lamb wishes to buy a house from Fleessem & Howe on a land contract. When the title report arrives it shows that title is vested in Constance Trueheart. This may be because Fleessem & Howe
    (A) does not have the right to sell the property since they do not even own it.
    (B) are buying the property on a land sales contract from Constance Trueheart.
    (C) may be buying the property on a mortgage carried by Constance Trueheart.
    (D) may be owned by the sole heirs of Constance Trueheart.

19. When the title insurance policy is delivered, the fee for it
    (A) can be paid by the buyer if the parties so agree.
    (B) is set by the Oregon Real Estate Agency.
    (C) is set by the Oregon Insurance Commissioner.
    (D) is a flat amount regardless of the dollar amount of the coverage.

20. The cost of an owner's title insurance policy is based primarily on
    (A) age of property.
    (B) cost of property.
    (C) the number of covenants in the warranty deed.
    (D) all of the above.

21. An instrument or document which protects the insured parties (subject to specific exceptions) against defects in the examination of the title record and against hidden risks, such as forgeries, is called
    (A) a chain of title.
    (B) certification of title.
    (C) a title insurance policy.
    (D) an abstract of title.

22. Which of the following is true regarding title insurance?
    I. The policy will protect the insured party's interest forever.
    II. Subsequent owners of the property must obtain their own title insurance if they want it.
    (A) I only
    (B) II only
    (C) Both I and II
    (D) Neither I nor II

23. When a property is sold and title insurance is issued, it insures
    (A) against future events which adversely affect the title.
    (B) the purchasers or owners of the property.
    (C) anyone to whom the buyer assigns his or her interest.
    (D) the previous owners of the property.

24. An owner's title insurance policy protects
    I. the owner, his or her heirs and devisees.
    II. all subsequent owners.
    (A) I only (C) Both I and II
    (B) II only (D) Neither I nor II

25. Which of the following statements regarding title insurance is true?
    I. Title insurance coverage passes from seller to buyer with conveyance of title.
    II. Title insurance must be renewed every five years.
    (A) I only (C) Both I and II
    (B) II only (D) Neither I nor II

26. A standard title insurance policy ordinarily
    I. must be renewed every year.
    II. protects only the party named as the insured party in the written policy.
    (A) I only (C) Both I and II
    (B) II only (D) Neither I nor II

27. An owner's policy of title insurance continues in force
    (A) as long as the insured has a liability.
    (B) as long as annual premiums are paid.
    (C) for a maximum of 50 years.
    (D) as long as the buyer resides on the property.

28. Title insurance in Oregon is
    (A) not required by law.
    (B) protection against false impersonations.
    (C) issued to insure the named party only.
    (D) accurately characterized by all of the above.

29. When a title insurance policy is issued
    (A) an inspection of the records has been made.
    (B) premiums are paid on an annual basis.
    (C) Both A and B are correct
    (D) Neither A nor B is correct.

30. For a buyer to be certain the property has no encroachments he or she should obtain
    I. a survey.
    II. a standard title insurance policy.
    (A) I only (C) Both I and II
    (B) II only (D) Neither I nor II

31. In order to determine boundaries of a property, one should obtain
    (A) a title policy. (C) an abstract.
    (B) a survey. (D) a court order.

32. If a buyer desires to be sure there are no encroachments on a property, he or she should obtain a
    (A) standard title insurance policy.
    (B) survey.
    (C) warranty deed from the seller.
    (D) homestead exemption.

33. A purchaser should obtain which of the following to be sure there are no encroachments?
    (A) Power of attorney
    (B) Title insurance policy
    (C) Survey
    (D) Certificate of no set-off

34. A standard form title insurance policy insures that
    (A) there are no tax liens against the property.
    (B) there are no judgment liens against the property.
    (C) the property is free and clear of all encumbrances.
    (D) the title only as it appears of record, subject to printed exceptions.

35. A standard coverage title policy insures against
    (A) building code changes.
    (B) unrecorded easements.
    (C) forged recorded deeds.
    (D) all of the above.

36. A standard title insurance policy would give coverage for which of the following?
   (A) A governmentally imposed restriction on the use of the property
   (B) A claim on the title that the purchaser could have discovered upon a physical inspection of the property
   (C) A missing heir
   (D) All of the above

37. A standard title insurance policy insures against
   (A) prescriptive easements.
   (B) a recorded deed that was forged.
   (C) claims of persons in possession of the property at the time the purchaser takes title.
   (D) all of the above.

38. Title insurance protects the purchaser by providing that
   (A) the mortgage balance will be paid off in case of default.
   (B) there will be protection against adverse claim to the ownership of the property except those exclusions listed in the policy.
   (C) the mortgage balance will be paid off in case of death or disability.
   (D) the property will be restored in the event of any damage covered by the policy.

39. A standard title insurance policy protects the insured against which of the following?
   I. The power of eminent domain
   II. The lack of capacity of a grantor
   III. Unrecorded easements
   (A) I only (C) III only
   (B) II only (D) II and III only

40. An owner's title insurance policy will not provide protection against
   I. expenses incurred in defending a title.
   II. lack of intent to deliver a deed.
   III. governmental regulation.
   (A) I only (C) III only
   (B) II only (D) I and III only

41. A standard form policy of title insurance does not protect against loss resulting from
   (A) encroachments on the property.
   (B) failure to deliver an earlier recorded deed.
   (C) lack of capacity of the grantor.
   (D) forgery in the chain of title.

42. A standard policy of title insurance does not insure against which of the following in the chain of title?
   (A) Matter of record (C) Mining claims
   (B) Forgery (D) Contractual capacity

43. The standard form title insurance policy insures against
   (A) governmental actions.
   (B) forgery of a deed.
   (C) rights of parties in possession.
   (D) water and mineral rights.

44. Which of the following title defects will, if loss results, fall under the coverage of a standard form owner's title insurance policy?
   I. Forged grantor's signature in recorded claim of title
   II. Title lost through adverse possession not yet confirmed by suit
   (A) I only (C) Both I and II
   (B) II only (D) Neither I nor II

45. A standard title insurance policy protects against problems arising from all of the following except
   (A) a prior grantor's lack of legal capacity to convey title.
   (B) governmentally imposed zoning restrictions.
   (C) forgery of documents.
   (D) missing heirs.

46. A standard title insurance policy will protect the insured against all of the following except
   (A) forgery.
   (B) false impersonation.
   (C) government restrictions (zoning).
   (D) missing heirs after probate.

47. Rusty Naylor is a builder who built his own home. At the time he purchased the lot he obtained a standard owner's title insurance policy. Now he has discovered that his eaves overhang his neighbor's lot by several feet and that his house violates the setback requirements in the local zoning ordinance. His title insurance should pay for
(A) the costs of removing the overhang.
(B) the costs of obtaining legal clearance on the setback violation.
(C) both A and B.
(D) neither A nor B.

48. Enid Crowe is a widow lady who has just discovered that her neighbor's fence encroaches on her property. If she cannot reach a settlement with the neighbor, she could sue
(A) the broker who sold her the home, for failing to disclose the encroachment.
(B) the title insurer who issued her standard owner's policy when she bought the place.
(C) her neighbor for trespass.
(D) her neighbor for adverse possession.

49. A buyer was issued a standard form owner's policy on a purchase. Subsequently, a serious title defect of record is discovered. How can the title insurance company get out of paying the claim?
I. If an inspection of the premises would have revealed the defect
II. If the buyer knew personally of the defect
(A) I only
(B) II only
(C) Both I and II
(D) Neither I nor II

50. The ALTA extended policy form protection is normally required by
I. owners of real property.
II. purchasers of real property.
III. lenders secured by real property liens.
(A) I only
(B) II only
(C) III only
(D) Both I and III

51. In the states where it is available, which of the following would not be covered under an extended coverage owner's title insurance policy?
(A) Rights of parties in possession
(B) Unrecorded physical easements
(C) The effect of zoning regulations
(D) Unrecorded mechanics liens

52. An extended coverage title insurance policy provides coverage against which of the following?
I. Unrecorded easements
II. Unrecorded liens
III. Rights of parties in possession
(A) I and II only
(B) II only
(C) II and III only
(D) I, II and III

53. An ALTA extended title insurance policy would not cover
(A) unrecorded deeds.
(B) unrecorded easements.
(C) unrecorded homestead rights.
(D) governments regulating the use of property through zoning ordinances.

54. How can a lender be sure the lien is enforceable?
(A) Mortgagee's title insurance policy
(B) Recordation
(C) Deed
(D) None of the above

55. The mortgagee's title insurance policy terminates when which of the following occurs?
I. The mortgage debt is paid in full
II. The mortgagee dies
(A) I only
(B) II only
(C) Both I and II
(D) Neither I nor II

56. Every possible title problem would be insured by which of the following policies?
(A) an ALTA owner's policy.
(B) a standard form policy.
(C) both A and B.
(D) neither A nor B.

57. Title insurance will give protection against
I. undisclosed heirs.
II. forgery in the chain of title.
III. zoning restrictions.
(A) II only
(B) III only
(C) I and II only
(D) II and III only

58. A loss to the insured that resulted from a forged document is covered by
   I. an extended coverage title insurance policy.
   II. a standard coverage title insurance policy.
   (A) I only (C) Both I and II
   (B) II only (D) Neither I nor II

59. A title insurance company will not insure property against
   I. forged documents. III. a mortgage of record.
   II. zoning restrictions.
   (A) I only (C) I and II only
   (B) II only (D) II and III only

60. A mortgagee's title insurance policy is good until the
   (A) loan is paid in full.
   (B) satisfaction of the mortgage is recorded.
   (C) earlier of A or B occurs.
   (D) loan is paid in full and the satisfaction of it has been recorded.

61. A mortgagee's title insurance policy would be required
   (A) when a seller is carrying a mortgage as part of the purchase price.
   (B) when a buyer obtains a new loan at a bank or savings and loan.
   (C) when a buyer buys from an owner on a land sales contract.
   (D) in any of the above cases.

62. Broker Williamson has taken a listing on a property which is encumbered with a federal tax lien. In this case,
   I. the property cannot be sold until the lien is cleared.
   II. a buyer cannot get title insurance until the lien is cleared.
   (A) I only (C) Both I and II
   (B) II only (D) Neither I nor II

63. When you are getting a land sales contract at closing, you should get
   (A) a purchaser's policy of title insurance.
   (B) an owner's policy of title insurance.
   (C) an ALTA title insurance policy.
   (D) no title insurance until the land sales contract is paid off.

64. A purchaser's title policy normally protects the
   (A) grantor.
   (B) grantee.
   (C) vendor on a land sales contract.
   (D) vendee on a land sales contract.

65. When there is a sale of land on a land sales contract, the seller must have clear title
   (A) before the transaction can close.
   (B) at the time set in the contract for the delivery of the deed.
   (C) at the time the seller accepts the buyer's offer.
   (D) whenever the buyer decides to sell the property.

66. James and Nancy Brown agree to buy a house from Sam Fastpen on a land sales contract. When the preliminary title report is issued it shows that fee title is vested in Faith Trueblood. Which of the following is the most likely explanation for this?
   (A) Sam Fastpen apparently does not have the right to sell the property to the Brown's.
   (B) Sam Fastpen may be buying the property on a mortgage from Faith Trueblood.
   (C) Sam Fastpen may be buying the property on a land sales contract from Faith Trueblood.
   (D) Sam Fastpen has apparently committed a fraud and the Browns are entitled a complete refund.

67. Which of the following interests in property can be insured with title insurance?
   (A) A leasehold
   (B) A life estate
   (C) A fee title absolutely vested
   (D) All of the above

68. All abstract companies and title insurance companies have
   (A) a title plant. (C) an insurance license.
   (B) an escrow division. (D) a real estate license.

69. A "title plant" is a
   (A) collection of real estate records.
   (B) subdivision map.
   (C) corner marker.
   (D) policy of title insurance.

70. When a missing heir is claiming an interest in property, this title defect could be cured by a
(A) special warranty deed.
(B) quiet title proceeding.
(C) partition.
(D) general warranty deed.

71. When a title search reveals that there is a broken chain of title, this is best cured by a
(A) suit for specific performance.
(B) general warranty deed.
(C) partition.
(D) quiet title proceeding.

ANSWERS

To practice questions. If you chose the wrong letter, here's the right one! The explanations are designed to clarify your understanding.

1. **C** Abstract companies came into existence in most parts of the United States in order to give buyers some assurance of the condition of the title. These were replaced in some areas by Torrens registration or certificates of title. In most places abstracts have been replaced with title insurance.

2. **D** The chain of title is the history of all conveyances and encumbrances since the original federal patent.

3. **D** The chain of title is the record of all matters that have affected the title from the original federal patent to the present day. Reviewing the chain of title and reporting the results is called a title search, whichy results in a title report. The Torrens system is a method for governmental registration of land ownership; an alternative to title insurance. An heir designated in a will to receive real property is called a devisee.

4. **D** An abstract of title is a summary of all documents affecting the title, which used to be accompanied by an attorney's opinion and together constituted proof of ownership and the condition of the title. There was no guarantee, however, other than the attorney's opinion, so an abstract and opinion cannot be construed as title insurance. Abstracts are no longer used in Oregon. Certificates of title are used in a few states, but not Oregon. There is no such thing as an affidavit of title.

5. **D** An abstract of title is a summary of all documents affecting the title, which used to be accompanied by an attorney's opinion and together constituted proof of ownership and the condition of the title. There was no guarantee, however, other than the attorney's opinion. Abstracts are no longer used in Oregon.

6. **A** An abstract of title is a summary of all documents affecting the title, which used to be accompanied by an attorney's opinion and together constituted proof of ownership and the condition of the title. There was no guarantee, however, other than the attorney's opinion. Abstracts are no longer used in Oregon.

7. **D** An abstract of title is a summary of all documents affecting the title, which used to be accompanied by an attorney's opinion and together constituted proof of ownership and the condition of the title. There was no guarantee, however, other than the attorney's opinion, so the abstract cannot be construed as insurance. Abstracts are no longer used in Oregon.

8. **B** An abstract of title is a summary of all documents affecting the title, which used to be accompanied by an attorney's opinion and together constituted proof of ownership and the condition of the title. There was no guarantee, however, other than the attorney's opinion. Abstracts are no longer used in Oregon. A contract for a deed is a synonym for land sales contract. A survey determines the physical boundaries of the property.

9. **A** An abstract of title is a summary of all documents affecting the title, which used to be accompanied by an attorney's opinion and together constituted proof of ownership and the condition of the title. There was no guarantee, however, other than the attorney's opinion. Abstracts are no longer used in Oregon.

10. **A** An abstract of title is a summary of all documents affecting the title, which used to be accompanied by an attorney's opinion and together constituted proof of ownership and the condition of the title. There was no guarantee, however, other than the attorney's opinion. Abstracts are no longer used in Oregon.

11. **C** A survey is the process of determining the physical boundaries of the property. An estoppel statement or certificate is the same as a certificate of no defense, i.e., a statement from the lender as to the remaining balance due. The results of a title search are frequently called a preliminary title report, since it is issued preparatory to closing and issuance of title insurance.

12. **B** The chain of title is the record of all matters that have affected the title from the original federal patent to the present day. Reviewing the chain of title and reporting the results is called a title search and results in a title report. A cloud on the title is a possible interest or claim.

13. **C** A survey is the process of determining the physical boundaries of the property. Property insurance (i.e., fire and casualty insurance) does not cover

the condition of the title. If a lawyer is consulted, the lawyer will simply order a title search. A title search is frequently called a preliminary title report, since it is issued preparatory to closing and issuance of title insurance.

14. **A** A standard form policy excludes matters known to the insured, police power, eminent domain, future taxes, rights of others which could be ascertained by an inspection of the premises, unrecorded easements, unpatented mining rights, water rights, reservations in the federal patent, construction liens, and matters which would be disclosed by a survey. Nevertheless, it does insure that the named party is actually vested in title, so a search of the chain of title is required.

15. **C** Adverse possession occurs when someone is in possession of another's land, with the intent to gain ownership. A deed is valid between the parties, even if not recorded.

16. **A** A voidable contract is a contract where one party (but not both parties) can avoid performance. In this case, in a standard form earnest money agreement, the seller agrees to sell the property and deliver good title to the buyer. The buyer would normally (depending on the language in the earnest money agreement) have the right to enforce this on the seller. On the other hand, whether to do so, or to let the seller out of the contract is the buyer's option.

17. **C** Since the buyer is not yet in title. the preliminary title report will always show the condition of the seller's title. Presumably, if the preliminary title report shows that the seller's title is encumbered with a mortgage, the seller will pay the mortgage off at closing so as to deliver clear title to the buyer.

18. **B** Preliminary title reports always show who is currently in title on the face of the report. A party buying on a land sales contract is not in title. The preliminary title report will show further down in the report the existence of the contract, but on the face page it will show the name of the contract seller as the party in title.

19. **A** Title insurance companies determine their own fee structure. Each company must file their proposed fee schedule with the Oregon Insurance Commissioner, who must approve the schedule. The Commissioner does not set the schedule, but rather approves the company's request. Anyone can pay the fee for the title insurance, although it is customary for the seller to pay for the buyer's policy and for the buyer to pay for the mortgagee's policy, if any.

20. **B** A title insurance company must obtain approval from the insurance commissioner for their premiums. The amount is always based on the sales price of the property, except for a mortgagee's policy, which is based on the loan balance.

21. **C** The chain of title is the record of ownerships from deed to deed since the original federal patent. Since an owner's or purchaser's policy insures that the person named in the policy is actually vested in title, the chain of title must be examined before the policy is issued. Certificates of title are used in some states, but not in Oregon. An abstract of title is a summary of all documents affecting the title, which used to be accompanied by an attorney's opinion, and together constituted proof of ownership and the condition of the title. Abstracts are no longer used in Oregon.

22. **C** Title insurance premiums are always a one-time charge and the coverage is good forever, even after the insured has sold the property. The policy names only one party as the insured party. For example, a title insurance policy insuring a lender is no protection to the borrower (buyer). The buyer needs his or her own title insurance policy (owner's policy). And when the buyer sells the property, while his or her policy is still good, it nevertheless only protects the party named in the policy. The new buyer needs a new policy.

23. **B** Title insurance insures the condition of the title as of the moment the policy is issued. It cannot insure that the condition will always remain the same, however. Title insurance only insures the "named insured party" and a title insurance policy cannot be assigned to another (although a mortgagee's policy can). Except for mortgagee's policies, title insurance policies are unlimited in the length of time the coverage lasts. The coverage endures even after the named insured sells the property. Therefore, if the insured party sells the property and a future owner discovers a covered defect which existed at the time the policy was issued, and if the future owner has recourse (e.g., through a warranty deed) to the insured party, then the coverage is still good.

24. **A** The policy names only one party as the insured party, although it does extend to the immediate heirs and devisees of the insured party. For example, a title insurance policy insuring a lender is no protection to the borrower (buyer). The buyer needs his or her own title insurance policy (owner's policy). And when the buyer sells the property, while his or her

policy is still good, it nevertheless only protects the party named in the policy. The new buyer needs a new policy. A devise is a gift of real property in a will.

25. **D** Title insurance premiums are always a one-time charge and the coverage is good forever, even after the insured has sold the property. The policy names only one party as the insured party, although an owner's or purchaser's policy extends to the heirs of the owner or purchaser. When the property is sold, the seller is still covered under the policy he or she originally obtained, but the buyer will need a new policy.

26. **B** Title insurance premiums are always a one-time charge and the coverage is good forever, even after the insured has sold the property. The policy names only one party as the insured party. For example, a title insurance policy insuring a lender is no protection to the borrower (buyer). The buyer needs his or her own title insurance policy (owner's policy).

27. **A** Title insurance premiums are always a one-time charge and the coverage is good forever, even after the insured has sold the property. The policy names only one party as the insured party, although an owner's or purchaser's policy extends to the immediate heirs of the owner or purchaser.

28. **D** Although it is used in practically all transactions between strangers, there is no law requiring title insurance. All title insurance policies protect against false impersonations and forged signatures. The policy names only one party as the insured party. For example, a title insurance policy insuring a lender is no protection to the borrower (buyer). The buyer needs his or her own title insurance policy (owner's policy).

29. **A** Reviewing the records relating to a title and reporting the results is called a title search, and the results are a preliminary title report, so-called because it is most commonly ordered prior to the closing of a sale and issuance of title insurance. Title insurance premiums are always a one-time charge and the coverage is good forever, even after the insured has sold the property.

30. **A** A survey determines the physical boundaries of the property. A standard title insurance policy covers the condition of the title, but excludes matters which would be disclosed by a survey.

31. **B** A survey determines the physical boundaries of the property. A standard title insurance policy covers the condition of the title, but excludes matters which would be disclosed by a survey. An abstract of title is a summary of all documents affecting the title, which used to be accompanied by an attorney's opinion and together constituted proof of ownership and the condition of the title. A court order could, conceivably, set the boundaries of the property, as where the parties had a dispute and the judge entered a ruling, but the normal way to determine the boundaries is to order a survey.

32. **B** An encroachment occurs when improvements are placed on another's land. A standard form title insurance policy excludes matters which would be revealed by a survey. The covenants in a warranty deed also do not cover matters which would be disclosed by a survey. Therefore if a buyer fears there is an encroachment the appropriate action is to order a survey. The homestead exemption sometimes allows a judgment debtor to obtain some of the proceeds from a sale of a personal residence when a judgment creditor has foreclosed.

33. **C** An encroachment occurs when improvements are placed on another's land. A standard form title insurance policy excludes matters which would be revealed by a survey. A power of attorney is authority for another to act in one's place. A certificate of no set-off (usually called a certificate of no defense, or reduction certificate), is a statement from a lender setting forth the remaining balance due.

34. **D** A standard form policy insures that the named party is vested in title, but the printed exceptions exclude matters known to the insured, police power, eminent domain, future taxes, rights of others which could be ascertained by an inspection of the premises, unrecorded easements, unpatented mining rights, water rights, reservations in the federal patent, construction liens, and matters which would be disclosed by a survey. It is possible to issue the policy even if the title search discloses liens or other encumbrances, merely by adding them to the end of the policy as additional excluded items. Therefore, a standard form policy may not cover a tax lien, a judgment lien, or that the property is free of all encumbrances.

35. **C** A standard form policy excludes matters known to the insured, police power (which includes land use laws and regulations), eminent domain, future taxes, rights of others which could be ascertained by an inspection of the premises, unrecorded easements, unpatented mining rights, water rights, reservations in the federal patent, construction liens, and matters which would be disclosed by a survey.

36. **C** A standard form policy covers practically any title defect, but excludes matters known to the insured, police power, eminent domain, future taxes, rights of others which could be ascertained by an inspection of the premises, unrecorded easements, unpatented mining rights, water rights, reservations in the federal patent, construction liens, and matters which would be disclosed by a survey.

37. **B** A standard form policy covers practically any title defect except matters known to the insured, police power, eminent domain, future taxes, rights of others which could be ascertained by an inspection of the premises, unrecorded easements, unpatented mining rights, water rights, reservations in the federal patent, construction liens, and matters which would be disclosed by a survey. Prescription occurs where a party is using another's land with the intent to gain an easement thereby, and adverse possession is where someone is in possession of another's land with the intent to gain title thereby. An inspection of the property would disclose either condition, so neither would be covered.

38. **B** A mortgagee's policy insures that the lender has a good and valid lien, but does not insure against default, death, or disability of the borrower, nor is it casualty insurance. It also provides no title protection to the buyer or anyone else except the mortgagee.

39. **B** A standard form policy insures that the named party is actually vested in title, free of practically any title defect except matters known to the insured, police power, eminent domain, future taxes, rights of others which could be ascertained by an inspection of the premises, unrecorded easements, unpatented mining rights, water rights, reservations in the federal patent, construction liens, and matters which would be disclosed by a survey.

40. **C** The provisions of all title insurance policies give the title insuranace company the right to settle disputes and defend the claim as they see fit, but they must pay the costs of the defense and settlement. Owner's and purchaser's policies also insure that the person named in the policy is actually vested in title. No title insurance policy will cover the government's right of police power, eminent domain, or future property taxes.

41. **A** A standard form policy covers practically any title defect except matters known to the insured, police power, eminent domain, future taxes, rights of others which could be ascertained by an inspection of the premises, unrecorded easements, unpatented mining rights, water rights, reservations in the federal patent, construction liens, and matters which would be disclosed by a survey.

42. **C** A standard form policy covers practically any title defect except matters known to the insured, police power, eminent domain, future taxes, rights of others which could be ascertained by an inspection of the premises, unrecorded easements, unpatented mining rights, water rights, reservations in the federal patent, construction liens, and matters which would be disclosed by a survey.

43. **B** No title insurance policy insures powers of the government, such as police power, eminent domain, future taxation or escheat.

44. **A** All title insurance policies protect against false impersonations and forged signatures. However, a standard form policy excludes interests of others which could be ascertained from an inspection of the premises.

45. **B** No title insurance policy insures powers of the government, such as police power, eminent domain, future taxation or escheat.

46. **C** No title insurance policy insures powers of the government, such as police power, eminent domain, future taxation or escheat.

47. **D** One difference between standard form policies and extended coverage policies is that extended coverage policies cover encroachments and matters which would be disclosed by a survey, but the standard form does not. All title insurance policies exclude land use laws.

48. **C** Standard form policies do not cover defects which would be disclosed by an inspection of the premises and they also exclude defects which would be disclosed by a survey. The neighbor's encroachment constitutes at least trespass and, if it has continued for at least ten years, would be adverse possession.

49. **C** All title insurance policies exclude title defects which could have been ascertained from an inspection of the premises and matters already known to the insured.

50. **C** Standard and extended coverage are the two basic title insurance forms available today. Either can be issued to insure an owner (person who receives a deed at closing), a purchaser (person who receives a land sales contract at closing), or a mortgagee (lender). While owners and purchasers are generally content to accept a standard form policy, practically all lenders today require the extended coverage form.

51. **C** Neither a standard form nor an extended coverage title insurance policy will cover the government's right of police power (which includes zoning and land use laws), eminent domain, or future property taxes.

52. **D** A standard form policy covers practically any title defect except matters known to the insured, police power, escheat, eminent domain, future taxes, rights of others which could be ascertained by an inspection of the premises, unrecorded easements, unpatented mining rights, water rights, reservations in the federal patent, construction liens, and matters which would be disclosed by a survey. The ALTA extended coverage policy adds coverage for rights of others which could be ascertained by an inspection, unrecorded easements, unpatented mining rights, construction liens and matters which would be disclosed by a survey. Mortgagees almost always require an extended coverage policy because it covers unrecorded documents, therefore it insures that their lien is in first position (i.e., no other recorded liens).

53. **D** No title insurance policy insures powers of the government, such as police power, eminent domain, future taxation or escheat. Most matters that are not recorded are not covered in a standard form policy, but the extended coverage policy does cover them.

54. **A** Unlike an owner's or purchaser's policy, the mortgagee's policy does not insure that the lender has title, but rather, that the lender has a good and valid lien, and the priority of the lien. The mortgagee's title insurance policy is the lender's final protection. For example, if the lender's mortgage or trust deed is not recorded, the title insurance company will not issue the mortgagee's policy.

55. **A** Unlike an owner's or purchaser's policy, the mortgagee's policy is issued in the amount of the loan balance (not the amount of the sales price), with a further clause providing for the coverage to be automatically reduced as the loan is paid down. It also does not insure that the lender has title, but rather, that the lender has a good and valid lien, and the priority of the lien. Death of the mortgagee would mean death of the lender (the mortgagee is the lender) and, even if the lender were a person and did die, the loan would not be canceled thereby, so death of the lender would have no effect on the mortgagee's title insurance policy. Neither would death of the borrower, for that matter.

56. **D** No title insurance policy will insure all possible title defects. The best policy is the ALTA extended coverage policy, but it still excludes powers of the government (police power, eminent domain, future taxes) and matters known to the insured.

57. **C** A standard form policy covers practically any title defect except matters known to the insured, police power (which includes zoning and land use laws), eminent domain, future taxes, rights of others which could be ascertained by an inspection of the premises, unrecorded easements, unpatented mining rights, water rights, reservations in the federal patent, construction liens, and matters which would be disclosed by a survey. The coverage extends only to the named insured and his or her immediate heirs. It would also cover a situation where the seller was not really in title because a previously unknown heir of a prior owner presents a claim that he or she is entitled to the property.

58. **C** A standard form policy covers practically any title defect except matters known to the insured, police power, eminent domain, future taxes, rights of others which could be ascertained by an inspection of the premises, unrecorded easements, unpatented mining rights, water rights, reservations in the federal patent, construction liens, and matters which would be disclosed by a survey. Therefore, it covers forged signatures on prior instruments. The ALTA extended coverage policy includes the same coverages and adds additional coverages.

59. **B** Neither a standard form nor an extended coverage title insurance policy will cover the government's right of police power, eminent domain, escheat, or future property taxes.

60. **C** Mortgagee's policies insure that the lender has a good lien on the property and are valid until loan payoff or recording of a satisfaction of mortgage, whichever occurs first. The satisfaction extinguishes the lien, whether the loan is paid off or not.

61. **B** Mortgagee's title insurance policies are almost never issued when the loan is carried by the seller of the property. This is true regardless of whether the instrument used is a land sales contract, mortgage or trust deed. This is because the seller presumably already knows the condition of the title.

62. **D** Title insurance is always available for all properties, regardless of how encumbered. However, the title insurance company will exclude the encumbrances from the coverage. If the buyer is willing to accept the property as encumbered, there is nothing to stop the sale.

63. **A** Both owner's and purchaser's policies are normally issued in standard form, although either

can be issued in ALTA extended coverage form upon request. A contract buyer definitely needs title insurance at the beginning of the contract. Discovering that the seller did not have good title and can't deliver the promised deed is of little use after the contract has been paid in full.

64. **D** When a sale is closed, the buyer must receive from the seller either a deed or a promise of a deed in the future. A "promise of a deed in the future" is really a land sales contract. In other words, all sales must be closed by the buyer getting a deed or a contract. If the buyer gets a deed, the buyer is an owner, so the policy to be issued will be an owner's policy. If the buyer gets a contract at closing, the buyer is not technically an owner. But the buyer under a land sales contract needs title insurance just as much as one who receives a deed at closing. For the contract buyer we call the policy a "purchaser's policy." In a deed, the grantor is the seller and the grantee is the buyer. In a land sales contract, the vendor is the seller and the vendee is the buyer.

65. **B** It is common practice for the seller to sell a property on a land sales contract even though there is still a balance owing on the seller's old loan. As the buyer pays off the contract, the seller pays off the underlying loan. Since the contract typically calls for the seller to deliver a free and clear deed when the buyer finishes paying off the contract, the seller must have clear title at least by then.

66. **C** Preliminary title reports always show who is in fee title. If the seller is a contract purchaser, fee title will still be shown as vested in the name of the contract vendor.

67. **D** Most title insurance companies will insure any interest in real property. The most commonly issued policy is the owner's policy insuring that a buyer is vested absolutely with a fee title. While many lessees do not bother with title insurance, it is essential if the lease is long term or if the lessee plans to make improvements to the land.

68. **A** Abstract companies obtained information regarding the condition of property titles in their county from the county recorder's office. This information was transferred to their own offices. These records are called a "title plant." Title plants continue to be maintained today by title insurance companies, who were the successors to the abstract companies. Abstract and title insurance companies commonly have an escrow department, but there is no requirement to do so. Abstract companies do not need insurance licenses and neither abstract companies nor title insurance companies need real estate licenses.

69. **A** The title insurance company (who originally was an abstract company), maintains its own independent records of every document ever recorded that affects titles to real estate. These records are referred to as its title plant.

70. **B** A cloud on the title is a possible interest or claim. Clouds are removed by whatever is the most appropriate method to clarify the issue. Frequently a quitclaim deed is used or, if the claimant refuses to grant a quitclaim deed or the claimant cannot be found, a suit to quiet title is used. A partition is a division of land into two or three new parcels.

71. **D** A broken chain of title means there is a missing deed. Presuming that the parties who need to sign the deed are not available, the only choice is to file a suit to quiet title, at the conclusion of which which the judge will enter an order stating who is the owner.

DESCRIPTIONS OF REAL ESTATE

AN ESSENTIAL ELEMENT OF ANY CONTRACT IS A CLEAR MEETING OF THE MINDS of the contracting parties. If the parties to a real estate transaction have differing ideas as to the boundaries and location of a property, then the contract could well be unenforceable. And if the failure to agree was caused by the negligence of the agent, then the agent could be held liable for damages as well. Fortunately for real estate agents, getting an accurate, enforceable legal description of the property is usually a simple matter. If the owner does not have an accurate description of the property, you can generally get one from the customer service department of any title insurance company.

To be adequate, a description of the property must describe the property sufficiently that a disinterested third party could locate the property, find the boundaries of the property, and clearly segregate it from all other property of its type. As a general rule, there is no requirement that any particular system for creating legal descriptions be used. Meeting the foregoing test is all that is necessary, and how you do it is not legally significant.

There are numerous ways to describe property adequately. Three of these are called ***legal descriptions*** because their methodology is considered to be part of the law. These include the ***government*** or ***rectangular survey***, ***metes and bounds***, and ***lot and block*** descriptions.

In addition, Oregon recognizes the ***grid coordinate system***. The grid coordinate system is used by government agencies to describe very large tracts of land using computer programs. Since real estate agents rarely encounter it, its inclusion here is unnecessary.

Real estate agents sometimes use other methods, such as giving constructive notice by referring to the description in a recorded deed. These methods may be adequate

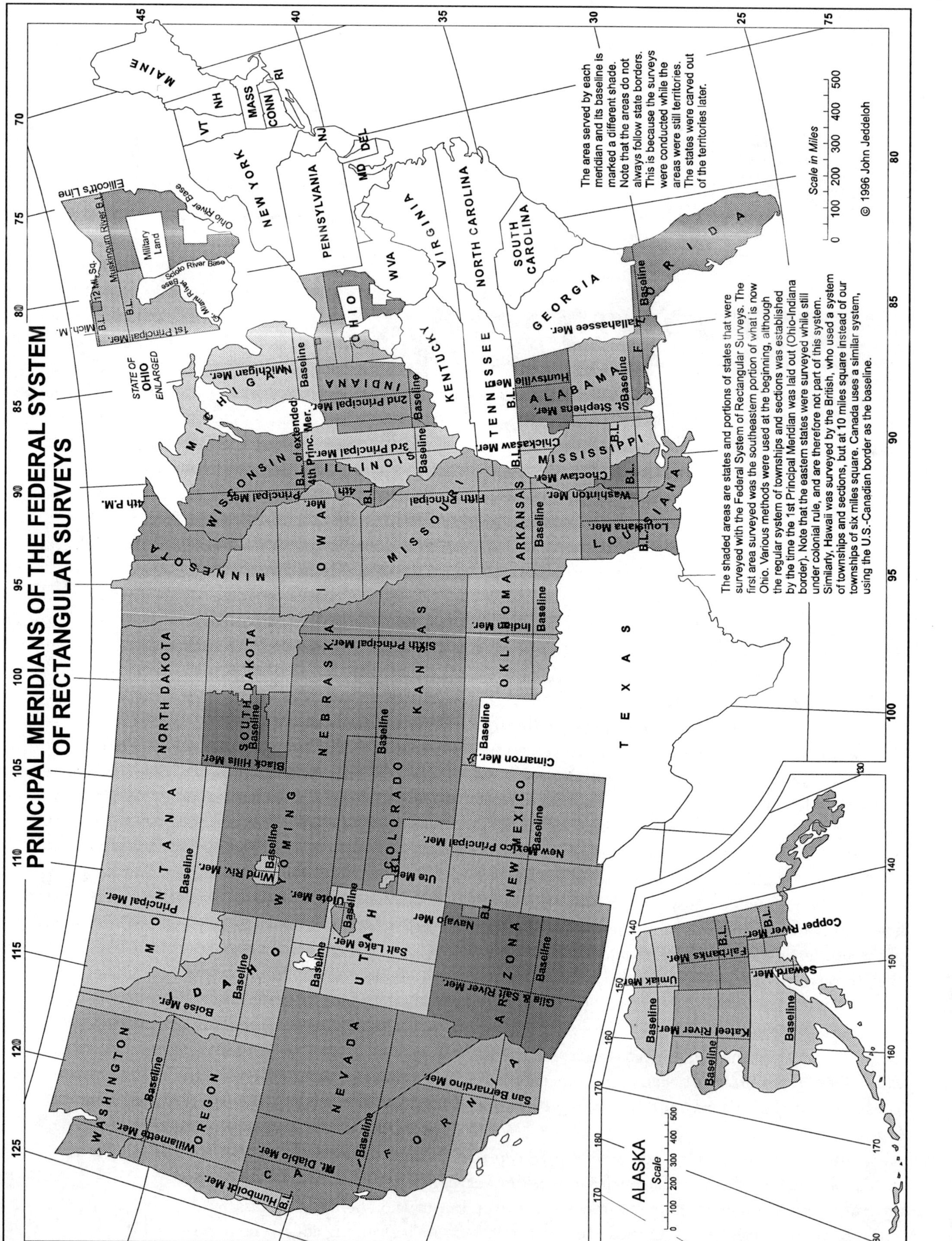
PRINCIPAL MERIDIANS OF THE FEDERAL SYSTEM
OF RECTANGULAR SURVEYS
The area served by each meridian and its baseline is marked a different shade. Note that the areas do not always follow state borders. This is because the surveys were conducted while the areas were still territories. The states were carved out of the territories later.
The shaded areas are states and portions of states that were surveyed with the Federal System of Rectangular Surveys. The first area surveyed was the southeastern portion of what is now Ohio. Various methods were used at the beginning, although the regular system of townships and sections was established by the time the 1st Principal Meridian was laid out (Ohio-Indiana border). Note that the eastern states were surveyed while still under colonial rule, and are therefore not part of this system. Similarly, Hawaii was surveyed by the British, who used a system of townships and sections, but at 10 miles square instead of our townships of six miles square. Canada uses a similar system, using the U.S.-Canadian border as the baseline.
Scale in Miles
0 100 200 300 400 500
© 1996 John Jeddeloh
STATE OF OHIO ENLARGED
Ellicott's Line
Ohio River Base
Military Land
Muskingum River B.L.
Scioto River Base
12 Mi. Sq.
Gr. Miami River Base
1st Principal Mer.
Mich. M.
MAINE
VT
NH
MASS
CONN
RI
NEW YORK
NJ
PENNSYLVANIA
MD
DEL
WVA
VIRGINIA
NORTH CAROLINA
SOUTH CAROLINA
GEORGIA
FLORIDA
Tallahassee Mer.
OHIO
MICHIGAN
Michigan Mer.
INDIANA
2nd Principal Mer.
KENTUCKY
TENNESSEE
ALABAMA
Huntsville Mer.
St. Stephens Mer.
MISSISSIPPI
Chickasaw Mer.
Choctaw Mer.
Washington Mer.
LOUISIANA
Louisiana Mer.
ILLINOIS
3rd Principal Mer.
B.L. of extended 4th Princ. Mer.
4th P.M.
4th Principal Mer.
WISCONSIN
IOWA
MISSOURI
Fifth Principal Mer.
ARKANSAS
MINNESOTA
NORTH DAKOTA
SOUTH DAKOTA
Black Hills Mer.
NEBRASKA
KANSAS
Sixth Principal Mer.
OKLAHOMA
Indian Mer.
Cimarron Mer.
TEXAS
MONTANA
Principal Mer.
WYOMING
Wind Riv. Mer.
COLORADO
Ute Mer.
Uinta Mer.
NEW MEXICO
New Mexico Principal Mer.
Navajo Mer.
UTAH
Salt Lake Mer.
ARIZONA
Gila & Salt River Mer.
IDAHO
Boise Mer.
NEVADA
CALIFORNIA
Mt. Diablo Mer.
San Bernardino Mer.
Humboldt Mer.
OREGON
WASHINGTON
Willamette Mer.
Baseline
B.L.
ALASKA
Scale
0 100 200 300 400 500
Copper River Mer.
Fairbanks Mer.
Seward Mer.
Umiak Mer.
Kateel River Mer.

Notes

to meet the requirements of contract law, but are not considered legal descriptions. Real estate agents should also be aware that the law holds different standards for different types of contracts. An accurate, but informal, description may be acceptable in a listing agreement or month-to-month rental agreement, but might fail if used in a deed.

Government survey

Although the oldest method of creating legal descriptions is by metes and bounds, all property in Oregon (and most of the rest of the western United States) was originally surveyed by the government. These government surveys form the base from which all subsequent private surveys are made. Therefore, we must understand the government survey system before turning to other methods.

Prior to independence, the English colonies in America were surveyed by metes and bounds in much the same way that England had been surveyed. Metes and bounds is simply a description of the monuments and boundary lines for a property. But after the new United States government was formed, Congress looked westward. Lands lying west of the original thirteen colonies were called the "Wilderness." That these lands should be settled was inevitable, and to facilitate settlement, surveys were essential.

In 1785 Congress passed the first law for surveying this new territory. The initial part of the Wilderness to be surveyed was the eastern portion of what is now Ohio. Each time new areas were surveyed, the law was amended, with the result that the government surveys of Ohio were not done with exactly the same system as was used in the rest of the country. The final format was adopted in 1796, essentially the same format which would be used eventually in the Oregon Territory.

The official name of this system is the ***Federal System of Rectangular Surveys***. As you can see from the map of the United States on the opposite page, it covers several states east of the Mississippi and all western states (except Texas and Hawaii).

As each area was surveyed, the first step was to select a beginning point. In Oregon, this point is called the ***Willamette Stone***. It is located just off Northwest Skyline Blvd., not far from the intersection with West Burnside in Portland. After the beginning point was selected, a ***principal meridian*** (sometimes called a ***prime meridian***) was surveyed straight north and south through the beginning point. There are 31 such principal meridians throughout the United States, each with a unique name. Ours is called the ***Willamette Meridian***, and runs from the Willamette Stone north to Canada and south to the California border.

An east-west line, called the ***baseline*** was also surveyed through the beginning point for each territory surveyed. Our baseline runs from the Willamette Stone west to the ocean and east to the Idaho border. The field notes from the early surveyors tell us that the site for the Willamette Stone was selected so that the Willamette Meridian would avoid major mountains of the Coast and Cascade Ranges, and so that the baseline would run through the narrow strip of flat land between Mt. Hood and the Columbia River. Thus the Willamette Meridian and its baseline formed the north-south and east-west coordinates from which all further surveys in Oregon and Washington would be made.

As you can see by looking at the map on the preceding page, all of Oregon and Washington (and only the states of Oregon and Washington) were surveyed from the Willamette Stone and its baseline. The historical reason is quite simple. Oregon and Washington were originally the Oregon Territory. Oregon, in its present form, became a separate state in 1859, and the remainder of the original Oregon Territory became the State of Washington in 1889. At the time of the first surveys, no one had any idea that the territory would later be divided into two separate states, so one survey for the entire Territory seemed logical.

NOTES

Following the establishment of the Willamette Stone, the surveyors moved out to survey the rest of the Oregon Territory, using the same grid system which had been used previously in other territories. The drawing below shows the Willamette Meridian and its baseline, and the Willamette Stone.

The Willamette Stone forms the point through which the baseline and Willamette Meridian were surveyed (the black dot in the center of the drawing). The baseline and parallels are continuous arcs, following the curvature of the earth. Guide meridians and rangelines were surveyed toward true north.

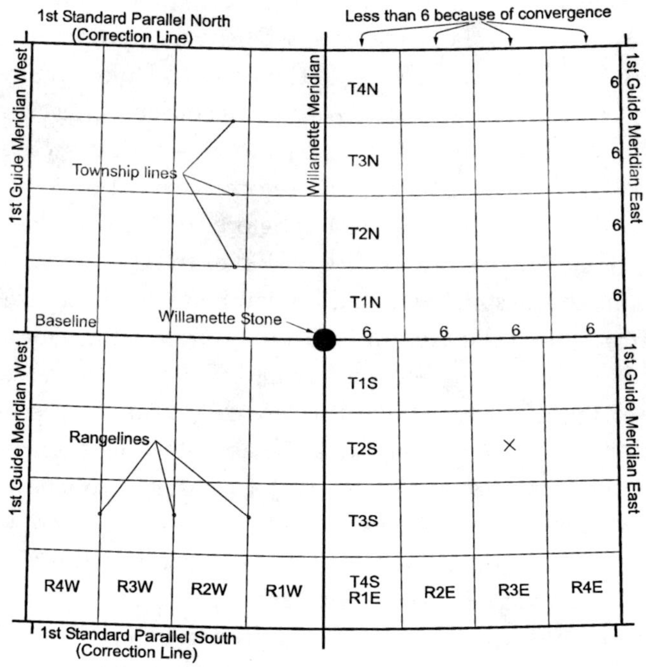

Referring to the drawing, notice that at a distance of 24 miles east and west the baseline is intersected by a major north-south line called a ***guide meridian***. The guide meridians are numbered consecutively, so the first ones shown in the drawing are the "First Guide Meridian East" and the "First Guide Meridian West." Guide meridians were laid out to make sure that the curvature of the earth was properly adjusted for.

Between each guide meridian you will find three additional north-south lines called ***rangelines***. The rangelines are six miles apart, except at the top where they converge due to the curvature of the earth.

In similar fashion, there are ***standard parallels***, also called ***correction lines*** laid out at distances of 24 miles north and south along the Willamette Meridian. The same as the guide meridians, their purpose was to ensure that the curvature of the earth was properly adjusted for. They are also numbered, the same as the guide meridians. The drawing shows the First Standard Parallel South and the First Standard Parallel North.

Just as there are three rangelines between each guide meridian, so there are three ***township lines*** between each standard parallel. Notice that this system creates a regular grid of large, more or less square blocks which are 24 miles on a side, each of which is further divided into 16 smaller squares. Each of the smaller squares is approximately six miles by six miles, and is called a ***township***.

Townships are referred to by their distance north or south of the baseline and their distance east or west of the Willamette Meridian. In the drawing you will notice the first range of townships east of the Willamette Meridian has been labeled. The numbering to the north starts at T1N (read as "township one north"), and continues until you reach the Canadian border. To the south the number starts with T1S (read as "township one south") and continues until the California border. Each township line or standard parallel creates a ***tier of townships***. In similar fashion the rangelines form ***ranges*** which are numbered consecutively east and west of the Willamette Meridian. In the drawing the first four to the east and west have been labeled.

NOTES

By numbering the tiers of townships and the ranges we can identify any given township very easily. For example, locate the small × in the township which is the second township south of the baseline and third east of the Willamette Meridian. Since it is the second south and the third east, it would be referred to as "T2S, R3E, W.M." (read as "township two south, range three east of the Willamette Meridian"). It is customary to state the "township" first and the "range" second, followed by reference to the principal meridian. Notice also that "Willamette Meridian" is usually abbreviated "W.M."

Townships, in turn, are divided into smaller pieces called ***sections***. (See the drawing below.) Each township is more or less six miles on each side, so each township contains approximately 36 square miles (6 miles × 6 miles = 36 square miles). Therefore, we simply divide each township into 36 regular sections, each of which is approximately one square mile.

So that we can identify any given section easily, sections are numbered consecutively 1 through 36. The numbering starts in the northeast corner and zigzags back and forth until the last section is found in the southeast corner of the township. Much has been written about the reason for this numbering system, all of which is speculation since the records surrounding its creation have been lost. The section numbering system in the early Ohio surveys was different and this arrangement did not appear until 1796, although it has been used consistently ever since.

In order to describe a given square mile, it is only necessary to state the section number, followed by the township in which it is located and a reference to the principal meridian. For example, suppose the drawing below represents Township 2 South, Range 3 East of the Willamette Meridian (the township with the × in it on the previous drawing). Now suppose that Section 15 is for sale and you want to take the listing on it. You could describe it simply as "Section 15, T2S, R3E, W.M." Note that it is customary to state the section first, followed by the township, range, and principal meridian.

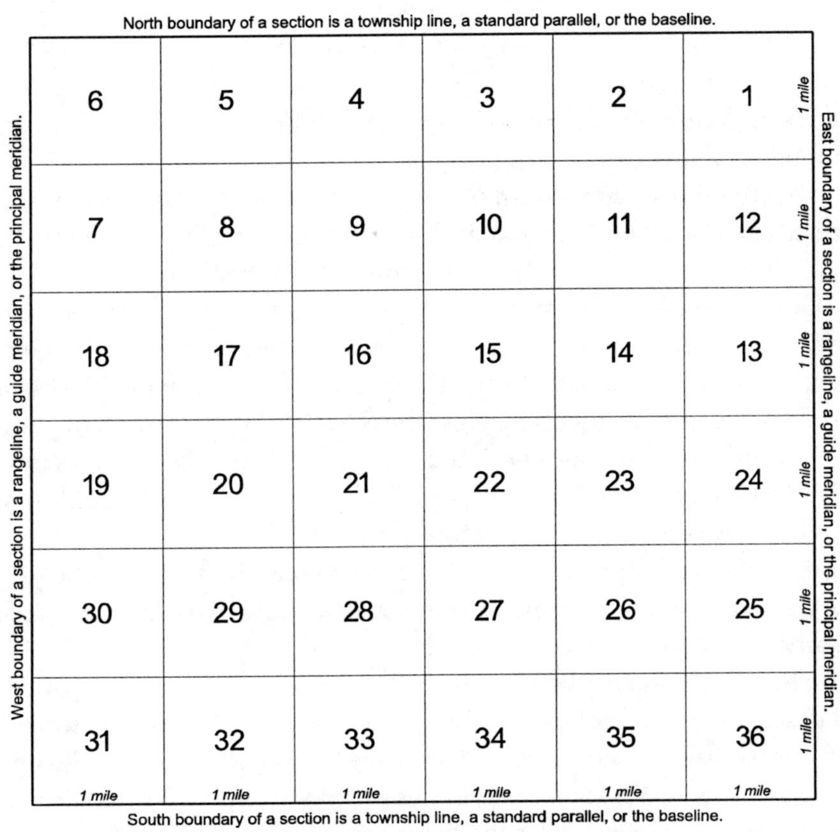

Representation of a typical township, divided into 36 sections of more or less one square mile. Adjustment for the curvature of the earth and for accumulated errors were thrown into the northernmost and westernmost sections of each township, leaving as many full sections as possible.

NOTES

At one square mile, a section is a lot of area, so sections are divided into even smaller pieces. See the drawing below –

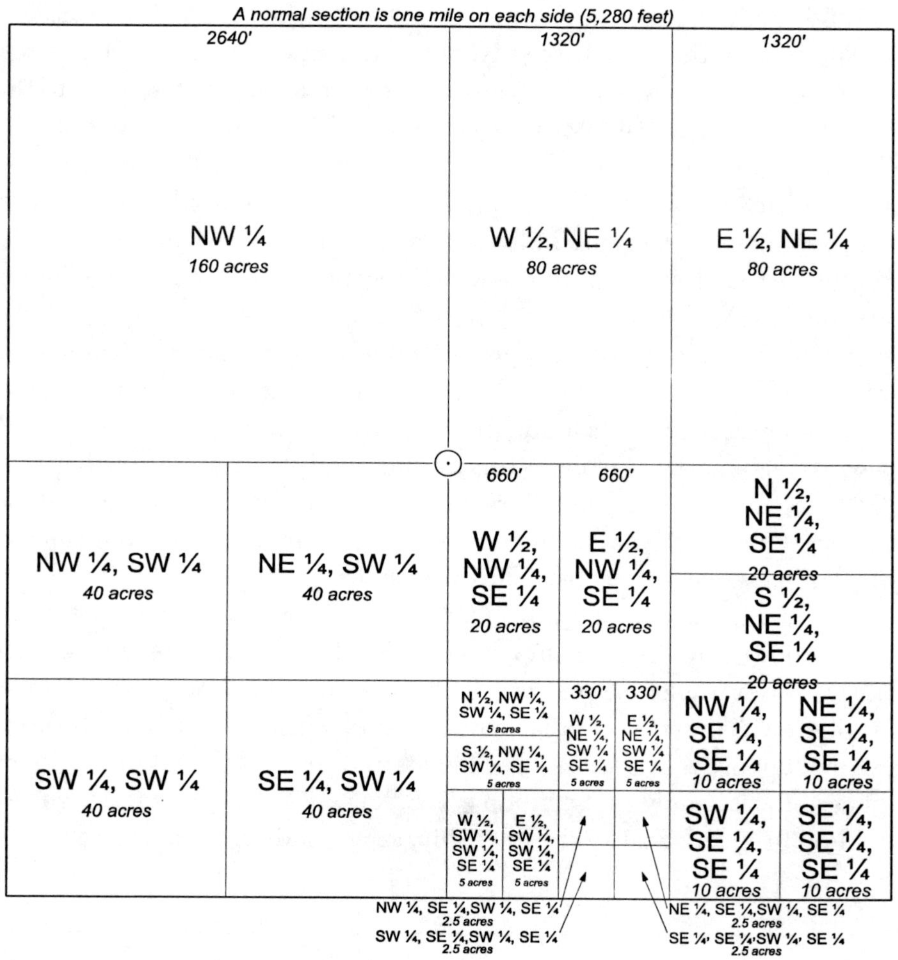

Drawing of a regular section containing 640 acres. A normal 40-acre parcel (quarter of a quarter section) is called a "lot." Most of Oregon has been surveyed by the government surveyors down to the quarter section corners.

There are an unlimited number of ways this can be done, but there are certain rules which must be followed –

- The only fractions that you can use are quarters and halves. If you want to make one sixteenth, you have to say it as "a quarter of a quarter." If you want to make one-eighth, you have to say "a half of a quarter," and so on.
- You can have halves of halves or halves of quarters, but you cannot have quarters of halves. If there are any "one-half's" in the description, they have to come first.
- If you are describing a half of something, then the word "half" must be preceded by only one compass direction, e.g., "the *S* ½," "the *W* ½," and so on. You cannot use two compass directions with the fraction ½. Similarly, quarters must be preceded by two compass directions, e.g., "the *SW* ¼," "the *NE* ¼," and so on. You can never say "the SW ½" or "the S ¼."
- Commas are read "of the," or just "of." Semicolons are read "and the." If you mistake a semicolon for a comma or vice-versa, it could make a drastic difference in the amount of property being described.

As a further tip, if you are having difficulty interpreting a complex government survey legal description, try working the description backwards from the word "Section" toward the front. Written descriptions always place the smallest piece at the beginning, but in locating a property it is sometimes easier to work from the largest piece down to the smallest. For example, consider the description "the S ½, NE ¼, SW ¼, NW ¼,

NOTES

Section 27, T2S, R3E, W.M." The first piece immediately before the word "Section" is the NW ¼, so put your finger on the NW ¼ of a section. The next piece is the SW ¼, so find the SW ¼ of the piece your finger is on. Repeat the process until you get it down to the smallest piece in the description.

Notice the dimensions on the drawing on the preceding page. A normal section is exactly one mile square (5,280 feet on a side). Therefore, a regular quarter section will be one-half mile (2,640 feet) on a side, a quarter of a quarter section will be one-quarter mile (1,320 feet), and so on.

A regular section is 640 acres. Real estate agents find it useful to remember the areas of certain configurations. For example, a quarter section is 160 acres, a quarter of a quarter is 40 acres, and so on. By knowing the dimensions of standard parcels you can save yourself a lot of time in making calculations.

In the original surveys the survey lines would run into lakes, rivers and the ocean. In addition, some sections were less than full size because of the curvature of the earth. The parcels left over are commonly called ***fractional sections***. In fractional sections the odd portion would be taken up in the "quarter-quarters" (40 acre parcels) along the north and west of the section. A quarter of a quarter is commonly referred to as a "lot" in early surveys. It was not uncommon for title to these odd parcels to be vested in the state or federal government, so these odd quarter-quarters are also sometimes called ***government lots***.

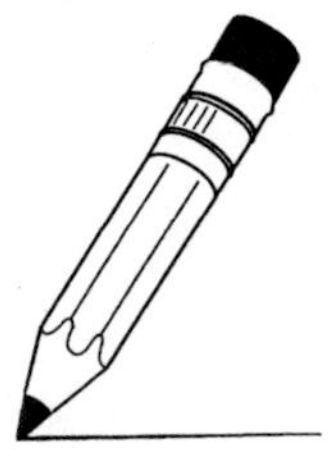

Exercise a

The government survey in Oregon started at the ____________________ ____________. The main north-south line is called the ____________________ ____________________ and runs from the beginning point north to the ____________________ border and south to the California border. A ____________________ was surveyed west from the beginning point to the ocean and east to the ____________ border. North-south lines called ____________ ____________________ were surveyed every ____ miles along the baseline. A ____________________ ____________________ was surveyed to intersect the principal meridian every ____ miles from the baseline. Between each guide meridian there were three ____________________ surveyed to run in a north-south direction. Between each standard parallel three ____________________ lines running east and west were surveyed. The result is a grid of large blocks 24 miles square, each containing ____ townships. Townships are located by the number north or south of the ____________________ and the number east or west of the ____________________ ____________________.

A township is divided into ____ sections which are numbered consecutively back and forth starting in the ____________________ corner of the township. Each section can be further divided into halves and quarters.

Describe the following drawings and give the area in acres:

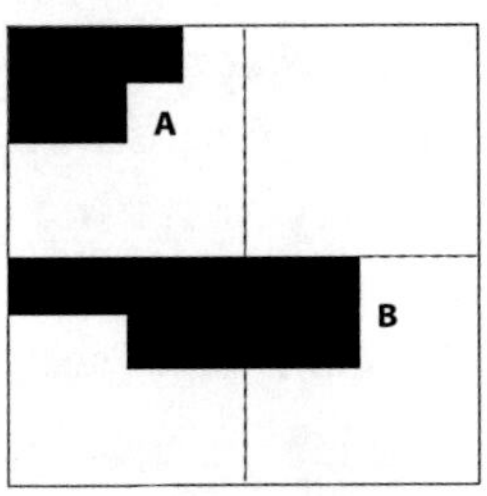

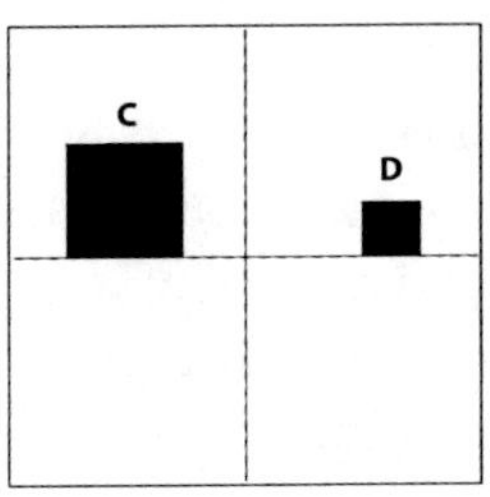

Using the blank sections below, draw these legal descriptions. (Pretend that the blank sections on the following page could be any section in any township and range.)

1. *SE ¼, Section 5, T1S, R8W, W.M.*
2. *NW ¼, SW ¼, Section 10, T23S, R10E, W.M.*
3. *NE ¼, SE ¼, SW ¼, Section 32, T2S, R40E, W.M.*
4. *N ½, NW ¼, SE ¼ and the SE ¼, NW ¼, SE ¼, Section 1, T6S, R42E, W.M.*

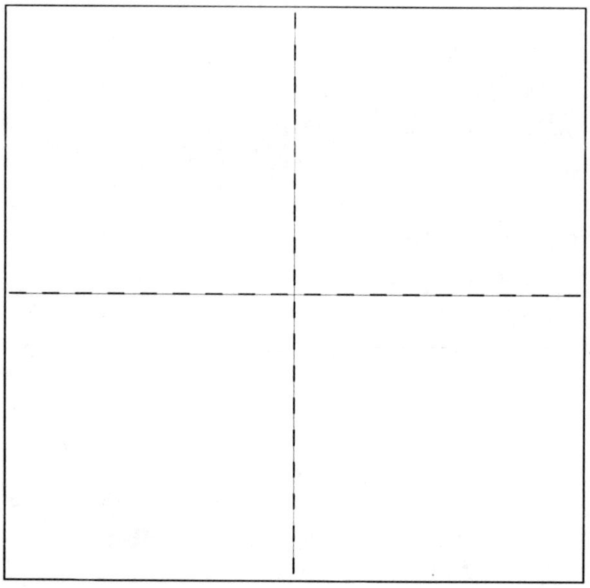

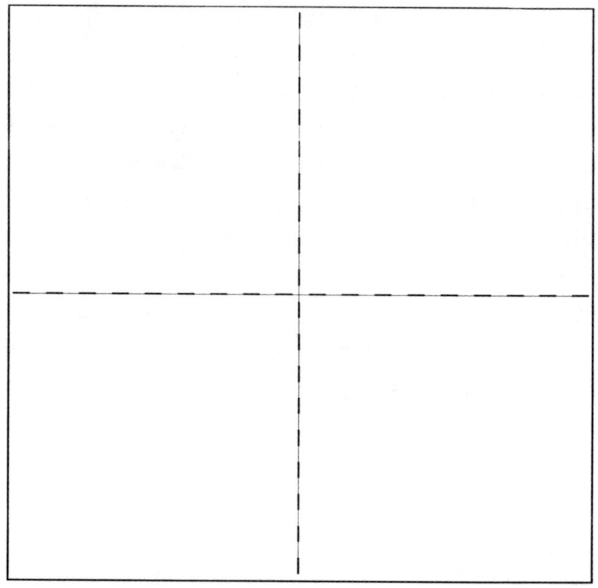

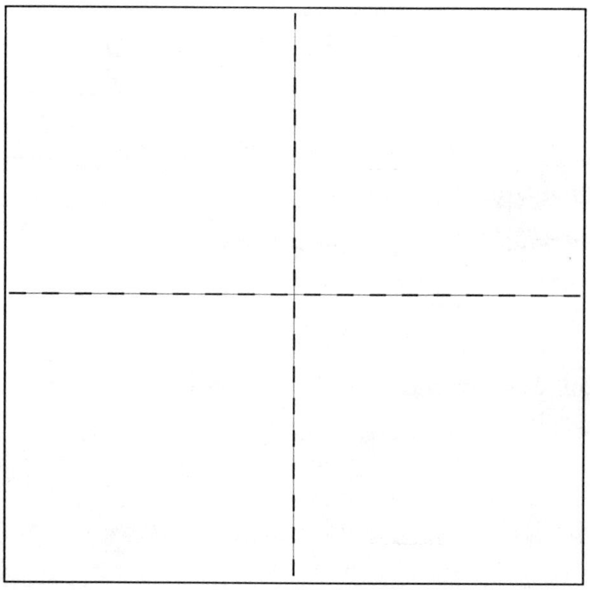

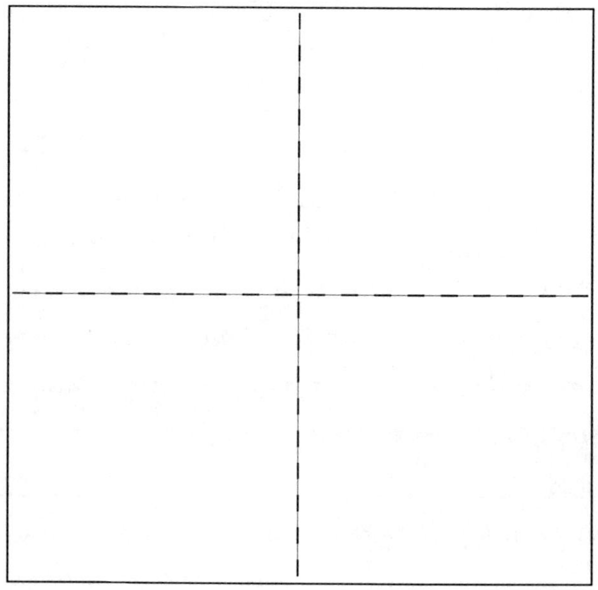

Metes and bounds surveys

Metes and bounds is the oldest and most direct method for describing land. To survey by metes and bounds a surveyor just describes the boundaries of the property by stating the distance and direction from one corner to the next. The drawing on the next page is an example of a typical simple metes and bounds description.

NOTES

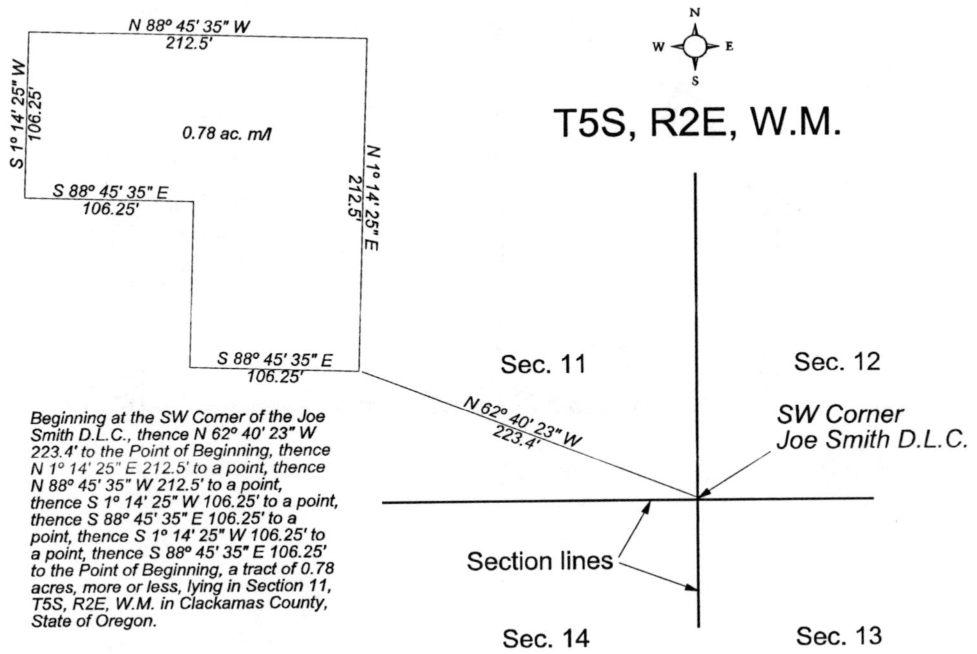

Example of a metes and bounds description for a property which lies slightly askew of true compass directions. It is customary, although not required, to survey the distances counterclockwise around the parcel. For practice, read the written description in the lower left corner and trace the boundaries in the drawing as you do so. Real estate agents frequently have to trace the boundaries to make sure the written description matches the map of the property.

Notice that the description of the property above actually starts in the corner of the section. In the description above it is referred to as the "SW Corner of the Joe Smith D.L.C." The Donation Land Law of 1850 allowed each married settler to claim 640 acres (one section), or a half-section if single. The claims were called ***donation land claims***. Therefore a section corner is probably also the corner of some early settler's donation land claim. Since these land claims were recorded, it is common practice to refer to the section corner by reference to the corner of the donation land claim, although reference to the section corner is also commonly encountered. The term "donation land claim" is usually abbreviated "D.L.C."

In describing a property by metes and bounds, a surveyor frequently starts the survey at some point other than the boundary of the property. The drawing of a metes and bounds description above is a typical example of this. The description of the property itself starts at a point called the ***point of beginning***, frequently abbreviated just "POB." Whenever you read the phrase "point of beginning" in a metes and bounds description, it means that you are now reading the description of the actual property boundaries. Everything before the words "point of beginning" was just a reference to where the land lies on the earth.

Direction is given in ***quadrant bearings***. The drawing on the next page shows a circle divided into four quadrants of 90° each. To describe any direction, start in the center of the circle and draw an imaginary line through the edge of the circle in the direction of travel. For example, direction *A* in the drawing runs from the center of the circle through the edge of the circle at exactly 73°, so it is written "N 73° W" (read as "north 73 degrees west"). Similarly, direction *B* is "N 45° E" because it is north, deflected 45 degrees toward the east. Direction *C* travels south from the center, deflected 24° toward the east, so it is "S 24° E."

All bearings start with either north or south, followed by the number of degrees of deflection toward the east or west. When the direction is absolutely north, south, east or west, we just say the direction without any number of degrees of deflection. That is, "North" is the same as saying "North 00° East (or West), so we just say "North."

NOTES

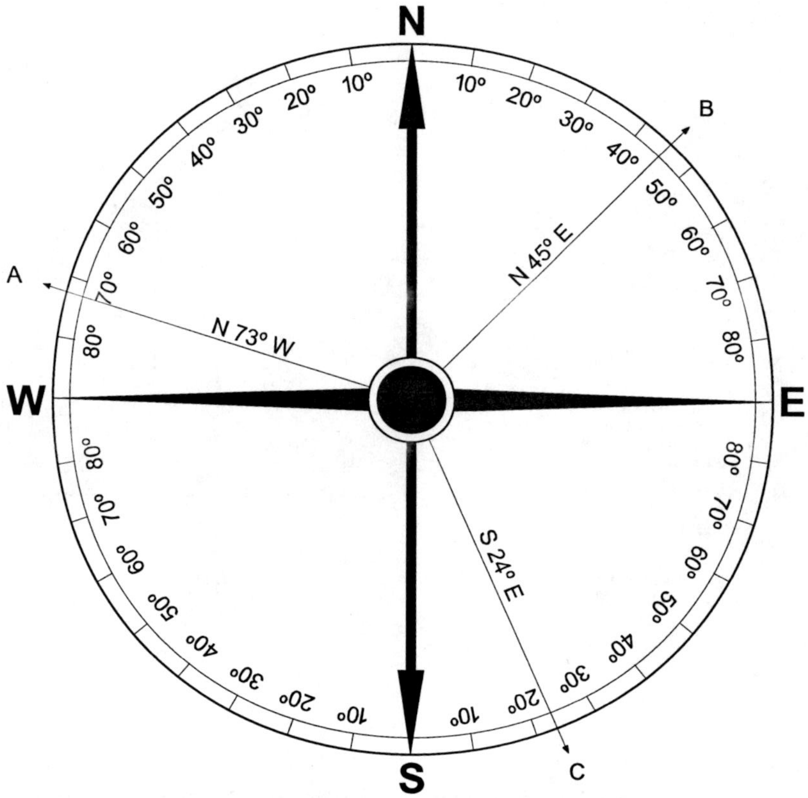

Circle showing the four quadrants of 90 degrees each. Each degree is divided into 60' (minutes) and each minute is divided into 60" (seconds). By using degrees, minutes and seconds surveyors can pinpoint direction very accurately.

In the real world, surveyors divide each degree into 60 minutes and each minute into 60 seconds. Thus, a direction stated as "N 23° 29' 15" W" would be about midway between 23° and 24°. Using degrees, minutes and seconds allows surveyors to state a direction with great precision. Notice that there can never be a quadrant bearing greater than 89° 59' 59". One more second of arc would be just "East" or "West."

Real estate agents find it is useful to understand quadrant bearings because it helps them locate property. For example, if you were reading a legal description which contained the direction "S 88° 45' 22" E," it would be helpful to know that this describes a direction which is almost due east.

In the past, surveyors would sometimes describe a compass direction by ***azimuth bearing***. Azimuth bearings are the same as quadrant bearings except that the circle is not divided into quadrants. Instead, north is 0°, east is 90°, south is 180° and west is 270°. The circle is just continuously numbered with degrees starting with north (0°) through 359° 59' 59". A quadrant bearing of S 1° W would be stated as Azimuth Bearing 181°.

Exercise b

In the Oregon Territory a settler would receive a ________________ ____________ Claim which is frequently referred to as an anchor point for a private survey by metes and bounds.

Directions in metes and bounds surveys are usually by ________________ ________________, although older surveys may use ____________ ______________. State the opposite of the following bearings:

S 45° E ______________ *N 10° 30′ E* ______________

S 23° E ______________ *S 22° 25′ 30″ W* ______________

Lot and block descriptions

When a subdivision is created, Oregon law requires the developer to record a ***plat map*** showing how the land has been divided. The plat map must be drawn by a surveyor and must meet statutory drafting standards. An example of an actual plat map is reproduced on the following pages (Bertha Crossing Addition).

To record a subdivision plat map, the subdivision must be given a unique name, not used on any other subdivision in the county. Each lot must be numbered or otherwise given a unique designation. Of course, since the plat map was drawn by metes and bounds, all the distances and bearings of each lot will be shown. In fact, anyone who was looking at the map would know the dimensions of each lot. And since the map is recorded, the result is that we can now legally refer to any given lot by the designation on the map. In other words, if you wanted to sell the lot on the northwest corner of S.W. Karla Court and Bertha Boulevard, you could describe it in your documents as "Lot 1, Bertha Crossing Addition to the City of Portland, Multnomah County, Oregon." This description will be legally enforceable because the world was given constructive notice of the dimensions of the lot when the plat map was recorded.

We call such a description a ***lot and block*** legal description, or sometimes a description by ***recorded plat***. Notice that the lots in Bertha Crossing are numbered from one to sixteen. Most subdivisions are considerably larger, so it is customary to divide the subdivision into blocks, and then divide the blocks into lots (hence "lot and block" legal description). But there is no legal requirement to create blocks and divide the blocks into lots. And it is also possible to use other nomenclature, such as "tracts," "divisions," "parcels" and the like. The following examples will give you a feel for how lot and block descriptions are used.

"Lot 8, Block 12, Gray's Addition to the City of Benton, Idaho County, Oregon"

"Tract 2, Division 3, The King Ranch, Rogue County, Oregon"

"Parcel 3, Yamhill Heights Addition to the City of Polk, Salem County, Oregon"

As you can see, lot and block legal descriptions are simple and easy to use. Typically, you will find that large tracts of land, such as ranches, timberland, and the like, will be described with government survey descriptions. Suburban land which was not part of a formal subdivision is more commonly described by metes and bounds. And the more populated the area, the more likely the land will be described by lot and block.

Tax lot numbers and other methods

Metes and bounds descriptions, as we have seen, tend to be lengthy and difficult to copy accurately. This is a problem not only for real estate agents, but also for the tax assessor and the tax collector, as well as many others who must deal in real property descriptions.

To avoid having to include lengthy legal descriptions on tax bills, the tax assessor in each county creates large quarter-section maps of the county which are maintained on public display. Each map is given a unique number. Then the assessor assigns a tax

BERTHA CROSSING

SOUTHEAST QUARTER, SECTION 17, T. 1S., R.1E., W.M.
CITY OF PORTLAND, MULTNOMAH COUNTY, OREGON

AUGUST, 1985 BY R.A. WRIGHT ENGINEERING, INC.
1340 SW BERTHA BOULEVARD
PORTLAND, OREGON 97219
PHONE (503) 246-4293

SURVEYOR'S CERTIFICATE

I, Robert A. Wright, being first duly sworn, depose and say that I have correctly surveyed and marked with proper monuments the lands represented on the attached map of **BERTHA CROSSING**, that for the initial point of said plat I set a 2" x 36" galvanized iron pipe 6" below the surface of the ground, over a 5/8" x 30" iron rod found at the southwesterly corner thereof as set by P.S. 45577. The location of said iron pipe being S00°27'25"E, 8.16 feet along the southerly extension of the easterly line of Knollwood Manor, an Oregon condominium, recorded in Plat Book 1213, Page 20, said point and southeasterly corner of Knollwood Manor being marked by a 5/8" x 30" iron rod set by P.S. 43994. From said initial point of **BERTHA CROSSING** I ran S68°42'05"E, 416.22 feet along the northerly line of S.W. Bertha Boulevard as described in Deed Book 807, Pages 1216 through 1219, to a point of curvature; thence along the arc of a 10.00 foot radius curve to the left 19.46 feet, through a central angle of 111°29'55", the chord of which bears N55°32'57"E, 16.53 feet to a point of tangency in the westerly line of S.W. 30th Avenue (50 feet wide); thence along said westerly line of S.W. 30th Avenue N00°12'00"W, 250.23 feet to the southeasterly corner of the Mary Flora tract as described in Deed Book 825, Page 183; thence N78°51'20"W along the southerly line of the Mary Flora tract, 409.77 feet to the southwesterly corner thereof; thence S00°27'25"E along the southerly extension of the westerly line of said Mary Flora tract and the easterly line of Knollwood Manor, 187.61 feet to the **initial point**. Containing 90,711 square feet, more or less. I hereby certify that the accompanying tracings for sides 1 and 2 are exact copies of the original plat.

Subscribed and Sworn To Before Me

This 2nd day of August, 1985

REGISTERED PROFESSIONAL LAND SURVEYOR
OREGON
ROBERT A. WRIGHT
1544

JUDITH A. GRAM
NOTARY PUBLIC - OREGON
My Commission Expires 4-7-89

DEDICATION

Know all men by these presents, that I, Herbert Hoffart, the owner of the lands shown on the annexed map and particularly described in the accompanying Surveyor's Certificate do hereby declare the annexed map to be a true and correct map of the land laid out as **BERTHA CROSSING**, and that all lots, tracts, streets and easements are of the dimensions hereon set forth. I do hereby dedicate all streets as shown hereon to the public as public ways forever.

Herbert Hoffart

ACKNOWLEDGEMENT

State of Oregon)
) S.S.
County of Multnomah)

BE IT REMEMBERED THAT on this 5th day of August, 1985, before me, a notary public in and for said state and county personally appeared **HERBERT HOFFART** who duly sworn did say that he is the identical person named and described in the foregoing instrument and who acknowledged to me that he executed said instrument free and voluntarily.

In testimony whereof, I have hereunto set my hand and my official seal the day and year last above written.

INTERIOR CORNER MONUMENTATION

I, Robert A. Wright, first being duly sworn say that in accordance with ORS 92.070, have correctly surveyed and marked with proper monuments the interior corners as indicated on the attached plat of **BERTHA CROSSING**, as originally recorded in Plat Book ______, Page ______, Multnomah County Plat Records.

Subscribed and Sworn To Before Me

This ______ day of ______________, 1985

REGISTERED PROFESSIONAL LAND SURVEYOR
OREGON
ROBERT A. WRIGHT
1544

JUDITH A. GRAM
NOTARY PUBLIC OREGON
My Commission Expires

Approved this ______ day of ______________, 198___, pursuant to ORS 92.070 (4)
Multnomah County Surveyor

By ______________________

APPROVALS

APPROVED ______________, 1985
PLANNING DIRECTOR
MULTNOMAH COUNTY, OREGON

BY ______________________
DELEGATE

APPROVED November 4, 1985
COUNTY SURVEYOR
MULTNOMAH COUNTY, OREGON

BY ______________________

APPROVED November '85, 1985

____

BOARD OF COUNTY COMMISSIONERS
MULTNOMAH COUNTY, OREGON

APPROVED Sept. 24, 1985
CITY OF PORTLAND
CITY ENGINEER

BY ______________________

APPROVED October 2nd, 1985
CITY OF PORTLAND
PLANNING DIRECTOR

BY ______________________

ALL TAXES, FEES, ASSESSMENTS OR OTHER CHARGES AS PROVIDED BY O.R.S. 92:095 HAVE BEEN PAID AS OF Nov. 5, 1985
1985
DIRECTOR, DIV. OF ASSESSMENT & TAXATION, MULTNOMAH COUNTY, OREGON

BY ______________________
DEPUTY

ATTEST
RECORDED Nov 5, 1985
COUNTY RECORDING OFFICE
MULTNOMAH COUNTY, OREGON

BY ______________________
DEPUTY

APPROVED Oct 2, 1985
CITY OF PORTLAND
HEARINGS OFFICER

BY ______________________

1218
31-32
11.5.85

SIDE 1 OF 2

BERTHA CROSSING

SOUTHEAST QUARTER, SECTION 17, T. 1S., R.1E., W.M.
CITY OF PORTLAND, MULTNOMAH COUNTY, OREGON

AUGUST, 1985 BY R.A. WRIGHT ENGINEERING, INC.
1340 SW BERTHA BOULEVARD
PORTLAND, OREGON 97219
PHONE (503) 246-4293

1" = 30' -N-

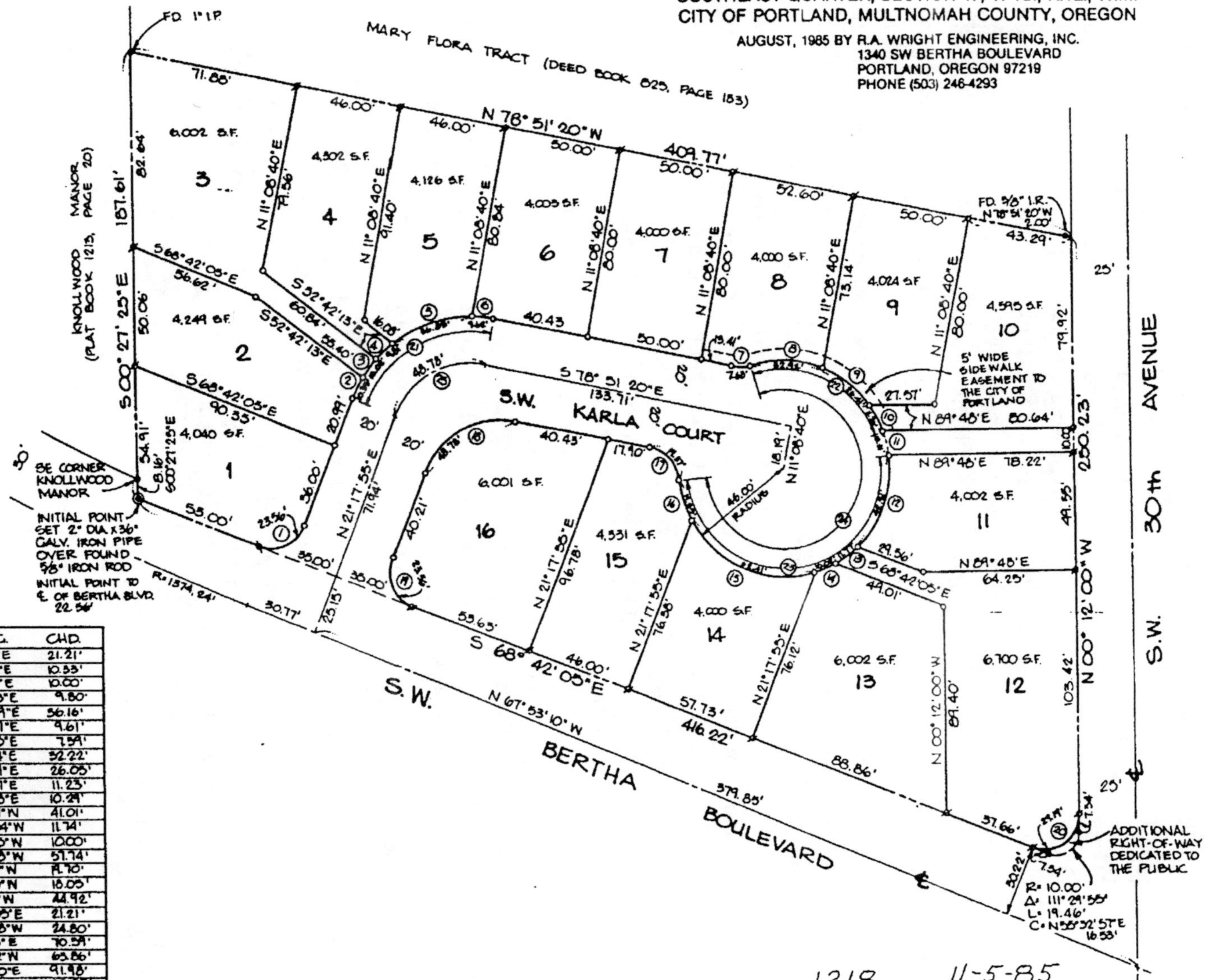

NOTES

- ● INDICATES FOUND 5/8" IRON ROD UNLESS OTHERWISE NOTED.
- ⌀ INDICATES SET 5/8" DIA X 30" LONG IRON ROD WITH YELLOW PLASTIC CAP STAMPED "WRIGHT L.S. 1544".

EXTERIOR BOUNDARY BASED ON COUNTY SURVEY No. 48,467.

BEARINGS BASED ON S.W. 30th AVENUE FROM COUNTY SURVEY No. 46,577.

- ○ INDICATES SET 5/8" DIA. X 30" LONG IRON ROD WITH YELLOW PLASTIC CAP STAMPED "WRIGHT L.S. 1544", SET ________ (DATE)

CURVE DATA

No.	R	Δ	L.	CHD. BRG.	CHD.
1	15.00'	90°00'00"	23.56'	N66°17'56"E	21.21'
2	55.00'	10°46'54"	10.35'	N 26°41'22"E	10.33'
3	55.00'	10°25'54"	10.02'	N37°17'45"E	10.00'
4	55.00'	10°13'19"	9.81'	N47°37'25"E	9.80'
5	55.00'	38°23'13"	36.85'	N 71°55'39"E	36.16'
6	55.00'	10°01'25"	9.62'	N96°07'51"E	9.61'
7	15.00'	29°19'08"	7.68'	N86°29'05"E	7.59'
8	46.00'	41°00'06"	32.92'	S87°40'24"E	32.22'
9	46.00'	32°53'45"	26.41'	S50°43'29"E	26.05'
10	46.00'	14°01'21"	11.26'	S27°15'57"E	11.23'
11	46.00'	12°50'37"	10.31'	S 13°49'58"E	10.29'
12	46.00'	52°56'56"	42.51'	S 19°03'49"N	41.01'
13	46.00'	14°39'32"	11.77'	S 52°52'04"W	11.74'
14	46.00'	12°28'49"	10.02'	S 66°26'15"W	10.00'
15	46.00'	77°44'26"	62.41'	N 68°27'08"W	57.74'
16	46.00'	24°43'35"	19.85'	N 17°13'08"W	19.70'
17	15.00'	73°59'59"	19.37'	N 41°51'20"W	18.05'
18	35.00'	79°50'45"	48.78'	S 61°13'18"W	44.92'
19	15.00'	90°00'00"	23.56'	S 23°42'05"E	21.21'
20	15.00'	111°29'55"	29.19'	S 55°32'58"W	24.80'
21	55.00'	79°50'45"	76.65'	N 61°13'18"E	70.59'
22	46.00'	87°58'12"	70.59'	N64°12'52"W	63.86'
23	46.00'	182°33'18"	146.56'	N83°52'00"E	91.98'
24	46.00'	283°19'07"	227.46'	S 33°29'06"W	57.07'
25	35.00'	79°50'45"	48.78'	N61°13'18"E	44.92'

1218
31-32

11-5-85

SIDE 2 OF 2

NOTES

lot number to a property that has a long legal description and marks it on the map. The maps are part of the public records, so everyone has constructive notice of the dimensions and location of the properties on them.

However, there are pitfalls in using tax lot numbers. The biggest danger is that the numbers can be repeated on various quarter-section maps. Therefore, to use a tax lot number correctly, you must not only note the tax lot number, but the number of the map on which it appears. A further danger is that the assessor may change tax lot numbers without warning, so the number you use may be out of date and actually refer to a completely different property. Because of these problems the Legislature enacted a statute declaring that a tax lot number in a contract involving real property is not adequate for the contract to be enforceable.

Reference legal descriptions Real estate agents occasionally make use of a previously recorded document as a reference for a legal description. For example, if you take a listing, the seller's deed is recorded, and you know the deed is an excellent source of an accurate description of the property. Every recorded document gives constructive notice of its contents, so you could create an enforceable description of the property in your listing or earnest money agreement just by making reference to the seller's recorded deed and where it is recorded. Reference descriptions in this fashion are not acceptable for the final closing documents such as deeds and mortgages, but they are adequate to meet the test of contract law for listing and earnest money agreements.

Street addresses Street addresses should be used only when no alternative is available. There is no way to tell the dimensions of the land or its location on the surface of the earth from a street address. Nevertheless, real estate agents sometimes use addresses when there is no other choice. If you use a street address you should consider that the contract is not legally enforceable until you have the parties sign an addendum clarifying the legal description. An exception might be an informal contract such as a month-to-month rental agreement.

Personal property Personal property is quite commonly included with the sale of real estate. Describing the personal property properly is frequently overlooked, even by experienced agents. To make sure that you will not have to spend your commission buying a new range or refrigerator for the buyer, be sure to identify all personal property sufficiently so the seller cannot switch one item for another of lesser quality or remove the item altogether.

Exercise c

Lot and block legal descriptions are created by recording a ________ ________ of a subdivision. The individual ________ in the subdivision are numbered and the subdivision is given a ____________ name. Recording creates ________________ notice, so now we can refer to any lot by the lot number, block number, and name of the subdivision.

Large tracts of rural land tend to be described by government survey, suburban property is mostly described by __________ and ____________, and urban property is mostly described by ________ and __________.

Tax lot numbers are assigned by the county ________ ______________ and posted on maps which are maintained on public display. Tax lot numbers (choose one) ❑ ARE ❑ ARE NOT acceptable as a legal description in a contract involving real property.

A legal description can be created by referring to a previously ____________________ document such as a deed, land sales contract, or the like.

One section	=	One mile square*
	=	One square mile*
	=	640 acres
One acre	=	43,560 square feet
	=	208.71 feet square
One mile	=	5,280 feet
One township	=	36 sections
	=	6 miles square*
One hectare	=	10,000 square meters
	=	2.47 acres

* Note that "miles square" means "miles on a side," so "two miles square" is a square whose sides are two miles long and which contains four square miles. The expression "two square miles" describes a property (of any shape) which contains two square miles, and is not at all the same thing as "two miles square."

One chain contains 100 links, or four rods, and is equal to 66 feet. A rod is 16½ feet. Real estate agents today rarely encounter rods, chains and links.

KEY TERMS

The key to understanding any new field is the vocabulary used in that field. To maximize your comprehension of the material presented in this chapter, be sure you know the meaning and significance of the following terms. Remember that the majority of test questions primarily test knowledge of vocabulary.

Azimuth bearing
Baseline
Correction line
Donation land claim
Federal System of Rectangular Surveys
Fractional section
Government survey
Government lot
Grid coordinate system
Guide meridian
Legal description
Lot and block
Metes and bounds
Plat map
Point of beginning
Prime meridian
Principal meridian
Quadrant bearing
Range
Rangeline
Recorded plat
Rectangular survey
Section
Standard parallel
Tax lot number
Tier of townships
Township
Township line
Willamette Meridian
Willamette Stone

ANSWERS

To chapter exercises. If you couldn't figure out what to put in the blanks, find the answer here!

Exercise a

The government survey in Oregon started at the WILLAMETTE STONE. *The main north-south line is called the* WILLAMETTE MERIDIAN *and runs from the beginning point north to the* CANADIAN *border and south to the California border. A* BASELINE *was surveyed west from the beginning point to the ocean and east to the* IDAHO *border. North-south lines called* GUIDE MERIDIANS *were surveyed every* 24 *miles along the baseline. A* STANDARD PARALLEL *was surveyed to intersect the principal meridian every* 24 *miles from the baseline. Between each guide meridian there were three* RANGELINES *surveyed to run in a north-south direction. Between each standard parallel three* TOWNSHIP *lines running east and west were surveyed. The result is a grid of large blocks 24 miles square, each containing* 16 *townships. Townships are located by the number north or south of the* BASELINE *and the number east or west of the* WILLAMETTE MERIDIAN.

A township is divided into 36 *sections which are numbered consecutively back and forth starting in the* NORTHEAST *corner of the township. Each section can be further divided into halves and quarters.*

Describe the following drawings and give the area in acres:

A. NW ¼ AND THE NW ¼ OF THE NE ¼

B. N ½ OF THE NW ¼ OF THE SW ¼ AND THE NE ¼ OF THE SW ¼ AND THE W ½ OF THE NW ¼ OF THE SE ¼

C. E ½ OF THE SW ¼ OF THE NW ¼ AND THE W ½ OF THE SE ¼ OF THE NW ¼

D. SW ¼ OF THE SE ¼ OF THE NE ¼

Using the blank sections below, draw these legal descriptions. (Pretend that the blank sections on the following page could be any section in any township and range.)

1. SE ¼, Section 5, T1S, R8W, W.M.
2. NW ¼, SW ¼, Section 10, T23S, R10E, W.M.
3. NE ¼, SE ¼, SW ¼, Section 32, T2S, R40E, W.M.
4. N ½, NW ¼, SE ¼ and the SE ¼, NW ¼, SE ¼, Section 1, T6S, R42E, W.M.

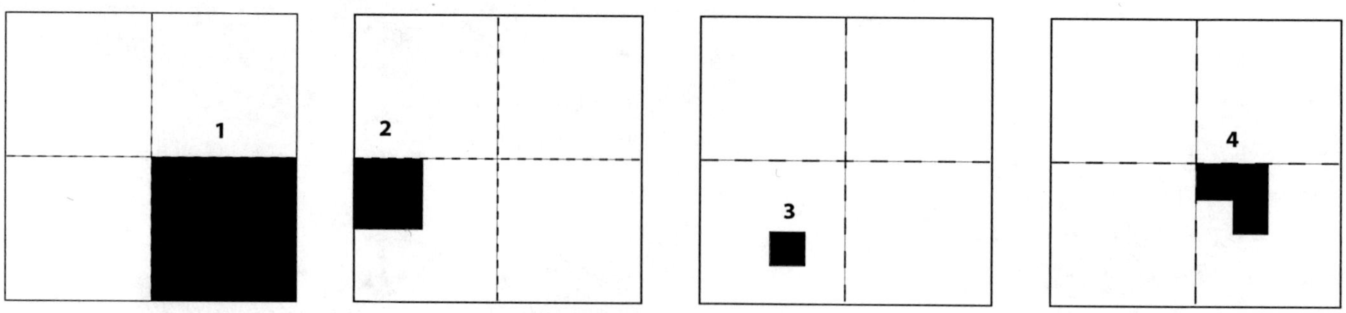

Exercise b

In the Oregon Territory a settler would receive a DONATION LAND *Claim which is frequently referred to as an anchor point for a private survey by metes and bounds.*

Directions in metes and bounds surveys are usually by QUADRANT BEARINGS, *although older surveys may use* AZIMUTH BEARINGS. *State the opposite of the following bearings:*

S 45° E	N 45° W	N 10° 30′ E	S 10° 30′ W
S 23° E	N 23° W	S 22° 25′ 30″ W	N 22° 25′ 30″ E

Exercise c

Lot and block legal descriptions are created by recording a __PLAT__ __MAP__ *of a subdivision. The individual* __LOTS__ *in the subdivision are numbered and the subdivision is given a* __UNIQUE__ *name. Recording creates* __CONSTRUCTIVE__ *notice, so now we can refer to any lot by the lot number, block number, and name of the subdivision.*

Large tracts of rural land tend to be described by government survey, suburban property is mostly described by __METES__ *and* __BOUNDS__ *, and urban property is mostly described by* __LOT__ *and* __BLOCK__ .

Tax lot numbers are assigned by the county __TAX__ __ASSESSOR__ *and posted on maps which are maintained on public display. Tax lot numbers (choose one)* ❑ *ARE* ■ *ARE NOT acceptable as a legal description in a contract involving real property.*

A legal description can be created by referring to a previously __RECORDED__ *document such as a deed, land sales contract, or the like.*

PRACTICE QUESTIONS

The following practice questions are representative of the questions you will find on the final examination and on the licensing examinations given by the Oregon Real Estate Agency.

1. All of the following are types of property descriptions except
   (A) lot and block.
   (B) allodial system.
   (C) metes and bounds.
   (D) rectangular survey.

2. Which of the following legal descriptions typically uses a principal meridian?
   (A) Metes and bounds
   (B) Lot and block
   (C) Government survey
   (D) All of the above

3. A description which reads "The SW ¼ of the NW ¼ and the S ½ of the NW ¼ of Section 9, T3S, R14E, W.M." is an example of a legal description by
   (A) surveyed metes and bounds.
   (B) federal rectangular survey.
   (C) lot and block.
   (D) tax lot number.

4. Townships, ranges, meridians and the like may be found in
   (A) lot and block legal descriptions.
   (B) metes and bounds legal descriptions.
   (C) government surveys.
   (D) all of the above.

5. Land description by measure and direction is known as description by
   (A) lot and block.
   (B) metes and bounds.
   (C) government survey.
   (D) courses and monuments.

6. All of the following are commonly used methods of describing the location of land except
   (A) the allodial system.
   (B) metes and bounds.
   (C) the rectangular survey system.
   (D) the recorded plat (lot and block system).

7. The legal description method that uses angles, terminal points, and established lines is the
   (A) government survey.
   (B) metes and bounds description.
   (C) lot and block description.
   (D) rectangular survey.

8. A metes and bounds description must
   (A) cover an area larger than ten acres.
   (B) only be made in areas not included in the Rectangular Survey System.
   (C) commence and finish at the same identifiable point.
   (D) always use north as the basis for directions.

9. The phrase "metes and bounds" refers to
   (A) compass directions.
   (B) distance and direction.
   (C) justice and the law.
   (D) punishment and criminal justice.

10. Which of the following would be considered man-made monuments?
    I. Canals
    II. Trees and rivers
    III. Boundary fences
    (A) I only
    (B) I and III only
    (C) I, II and III
    (D) II only

11. Metes and bounds
    I. is a good method for describing irregularly shaped parcels of land.
    II. makes use of distances and direction points.
    (A) I only
    (B) II only
    (C) Both I and II
    (D) Neither I nor II

12. Metes and bounds
    I. uses an anchor point which is ultimately described in terms of the government survey.
    II. is the oldest method used to describe real estate.
    (A) I only
    (B) II only
    (C) Both I and II
    (D) Neither I nor II

13. Metes and bounds descriptions measure boundaries from
(A) north or south points to east or west points.
(B) east or west points to north or south points.
(C) any point to any other point according to compass direction and distance of travel.
(D) the center point of the section in which the property is located.

14. The term "point of beginning" refers to
(A) the intersection of the baseline and Willamette Meridian.
(B) the first corner of the parcel to be surveyed.
(C) the anchor point from which the entire legal description is begun.
(D) any of the above.

15. In surveying, a monument is
(A) always the true point of beginning for the description of property.
(B) a landmark established as a permanent point of reference in a legal description.
(C) always tangible and visibly identifiable.
(D) never a natural feature such as a river or a stream.

16. Which of the following is correct about metes and bounds surveys?
(A) Metes and bounds is a good way to describe irregularly shaped parcels.
(B) Metes and bounds descriptions use terminal points and compass directions.
(C) Metes and bounds descriptions are not generally brief or simple.
(D) All of the above are correct.

17. Which of the following statements about metes and bounds descriptions is not correct?
(A) A river can be used as a property boundary.
(B) Artificial monuments such as the corners of buildings can be used to mark property corners.
(C) "metes" are measurements and "bounds" are boundaries.
(D) Metes and bounds descriptions cannot be used in conjunction with other methods.

18. When a metes and bounds legal description is used, it must
I. have a clearly defined point of beginning.
II. completely enclose the property described.
(A) I only (C) Both I and II
(B) II only (D) Neither I nor II

19. Using the hour hands of a clock as a guide, the direction S 30° 00' 00" W would most closely correspond to
(A) one o'clock. (C) seven o'clock.
(B) five o'clock. (D) eleven o'clock.

20. A bearing of N 45° E would be the same as
(A) north by southwest. (C) north by northeast.
(B) northwest. (D) northeast.

21. "South fifty-one degrees, twenty-three minutes, forty-five seconds west" would be abbreviated
(A) W 51° 23' 45" S (C) SW 51° 23' 45"
(B) S 45° 23' 51" W (D) S 51° 23' 45" W

22. Which of the following is the opposite of a bearing N 30° 14' 26" W?
(A) S 30° 14' 26" W (C) S 60° 46' 24" E
(B) S 30° 14' 26" E (D) S 59° 46' 24" E

23. The description "East 300', thence south 300', thence N 45° W 425.25' more or less" would describe
(A) a square. (C) a triangle.
(B) a rectangle. (D) a polygon.

24. "Due east 300', then due south 500', then due west 300', then due north 400', then due west 100', then due north 200', then due east 100', then due south 100' to the POB" would describe
(A) a rectangle.
(B) a rectangle and a triangle.
(C) an irregularly shaped parcel.
(D) two rectangles adjacent to each other.

25. A map or survey drawing showing how a parcel has been divided into smaller lots and blocks is
(A) an abstract. (C) a plat map.
(B) a section map. (D) a township map.

26. A lot and block legal description
    I. is the easiest and simplest method to describe real property.
    II. uses street addresses.
    (A) I only (C) Both I and II
    (B) II only (D) Neither I nor II

27. A plat map is used in which type of legal description?
    (A) Metes and bounds (C) Street and number
    (B) Lot and block (D) Rectangular survey

28. When a lot and block legal description is created, the
    I. developer of a subdivision records a plat map of the subdivision.
    II. compass bearings and distances are contained on a plat map.
    (A) I only (C) Both I and II
    (B) II only (D) Neither I nor II

29. If a lot and block description is used in a deed, the description must also
    I. describe the metes and bounds distances and directions of the boundaries of the property.
    II. refer to the distance and direction from the nearest monument in the government survey.
    (A) I only (C) Both I and II
    (B) II only (D) Neither I nor II

30. A township is
    (A) one mile square, 640 acres.
    (B) six miles square, 640 acres.
    (C) approximately 36 square miles.
    (D) equal to one section.

31. A township contains
    (A) six square miles. (C) 36 sections.
    (B) eighteen sections. (D) 640 acres.

32. A township contains
    (A) 36 square miles.
    (B) 640 acres.
    (C) 640 sections.
    (D) more than 10,000 hectares.

33. A road built completely around a township would be
    (A) 18 miles long. (C) 32 miles long.
    (B) 24 miles long. (D) 36 miles long.

34. In a township, there are
    I. approximately 23,040 acres.
    II. 36 sections.
    (A) I only (C) Both I and II
    (B) II only (D) Neither I nor II

35. One section of land is established by
    (A) staking the boundaries of any 640 acre tract.
    (B) government survey.
    (C) filing a plat with the county.
    (D) grid coordinates.

36. A normal size section in the Government Rectangular Survey System contains
    (A) 160 acres. (C) six square miles.
    (B) one square mile. (D) 36 square miles.

37. A standard section of land
    I. is one mile wide. II. contains 640 acres.
    (A) I only (C) Both I and II
    (B) II only (D) Neither I nor II

38. In the rectangular survey method, units of one square mile are called
    (A) townships. (C) sections.
    (B) ranges. (D) quarter sections.

39. A section of land, as used in the government survey method, may be described as
    (A) 56,340 square feet.
    (B) 1,760 yards × 1,760 yards.
    (C) 160 square rods.
    (D) six square miles.

40. Which of the following is larger than a standard section?
    (A) sixteen parcels, 40 acres each
    (B) 5,000 feet by 6,000 feet
    (C) 1/36 of a township
    (D) 5,280 feet by 5,280 feet

41. Which of the following is the largest?
    (A) A parcel which is two miles square
    (B) Two sections
    (C) 5,280 feet by 10,560 feet
    (D) 10% of a township

42. Which of the following is the largest parcel?
(A) Four square miles
(B) Two sections
(C) 10% of a township
(D) 43,560 feet by 43,560 feet

43. Which of the following contains the smallest parcel of land?
(A) 640 acres
(B) Nine square miles
(C) One-half of a township
(D) 36 sections

44. A property was described as the NW ¼, SW ¼, NE ¼, Section 22, T30S, R3E, W.M. The distance around this property is
(A) 1,980 feet.
(B) 2,640 feet.
(C) 3,960 feet.
(D) 4,620 feet.

45. The total distance in feet around the W ½, NW ¼, NW ¼, SW ¼ of Section 12, Township 12 North, Range 2 East of the Willamette Meridian is
(A) 1,320 feet.
(B) 1,980 feet.
(C) 3,760 feet.
(D) 3,980 feet.

46. How many yards of fencing would be needed to enclose the area described as E ½ of the SE ¼ of the NW ¼ and the N ½ of the SW ¼ of the NE ¼ of Section 24?
(A) 950 yards
(B) 2,200 yards
(C) 2,640 yards
(D) 3,800 yards

47. Which of the following statements of land measurement is an error?
(A) A section is a mile square.
(B) A section contains 640 acres.
(C) A quarter section is half a mile square.
(D) An eighth section is a quarter of a mile square.

48. A square parcel of property contains 160 acres. What is the distance along each side?
(A) ⅛ mile
(B) ¼ mile
(C) ½ mile
(D) ¾ mile

49. If you own a square parcel which contains exactly 40 acres, its sides are
(A) one-eighth of a mile long.
(B) one-quarter of a mile long.
(C) three-eighths of a mile long.
(D) one-half of a mile long.

50. If a 160-acre parcel of land is square, the length of one side would be
(A) ⅛ mile.
(B) ¼ mile.
(C) ⅜ mile.
(D) ½ mile.

51. In a description of land based on the rectangular survey system, the SE ¼ of the SE ¼ of the SE ¼ of Section 1 contains
(A) 10 acres.
(B) 20 acres.
(C) 30 acres.
(D) 40 acres.

52. If a quarter-section of land is divided into four equal parcels, each parcel will contain
(A) 10 acres.
(B) 30 acres.
(C) 40 acres.
(D) 60 acres.

53. How many acres are contained in a rectangular tract of land which measures ¼ mile by ½ mile?
(A) 10 acres
(B) 20 acres
(C) 40 acres
(D) 80 acres

54. How many acres are in the W ½ and the NE ¼ of Section 10?
(A) One square mile
(B) 144 acres
(C) 240 acres
(D) 480 acres

55. How many acres are in the following description? "E ½ of SW ¼ of NE ¼ of section 23"
(A) 10 acres
(B) 20 acres
(C) 40 acres
(D) 160 acres

56. How many acres are contained in the S ½ of the SE ¼ of the NE ¼ of Section 20?
(A) 5 acres
(B) 12½ acres
(C) 10 acres
(D) 20 acres

57. The E ½ of the E ½ of the E ½ of the SW ¼ of the SW ¼ of Section 32, T2N, R3E would contain how many acres?
(A) 5
(B) 20
(C) 40
(D) 80

58. What is the acreage in the parcel of land described as SE ¼ of the NW ¼ and the N ½ of the SW ¼ of the NE ¼ of Section 24?
(A) 50 acres
(B) 60 acres
(C) 70 acres
(D) 80 acres

59. How many acres are contained in the S ½ of the SE ¼ of the NW ¼ of the NE ¼ of Section 29?
(A) 5 acres (C) 12½ acres
(B) 10 acres (D) 15 acres

60. How many acres are there in the W ½ of the NW ¼ of the NE ¼ of the SW ¼ of Section 10, Township 12N, Range 4E, less the south 165' thereof?
(A) 3.25 acres (C) 5.0 acres
(B) 3.75 acres (D) 18.75 acres

61. How many acres are contained in the following legal description? "The N ½ of the E ½ of the E ½ of the NW ¼ of Section 4 and the W ½ of the NW ¼ of the NE ¼ of Section 5."
(A) 20 acres (C) 50 acres
(B) 40 acres (D) 60 acres

62. You are asked to shade in the S ½ of the SE ¼ of Section 15 and the NE ¼ of the NE ¼ of Section 22 and the W ½ of the NW ¼ of Section 23. You would shade in
(A) 160 acres. (C) 220 acres.
(B) 200 acres. (D) 240 acres.

63. In which of the following do the two sets of parcels contain the same number of acres?
I. The east 10 acres of the NW ¼ — The SW ¼, SW ¼, SW ¼
II. The SE ¼, NE ¼ — The NE ¼, SE ¼
(A) I only (C) Both I and II
(B) II only (D) Neither I nor II

64. A 330' by 330' tract of land is bisected diagonally by a stream, leaving two equally sized triangular lots. How many acres does each lot contain?
(A) 1.25 acres (C) five acres
(B) 2.5 acres (D) ten acres

65. Farmer Jones' daughter owns the following described property: SW ¼, NW ¼ and the E ½, NW ¼, SW ¼ and the S ½, NE ¼. What is the total acreage of her land?
(A) Less than one acre (C) 120 acres
(B) 2.5 acres (D) 140 acres

66. How many acres in Section 27 are included in the following description? "Beginning at the NE corner of Section 17; thence southeasterly to the SE corner of Section 22; thence southwesterly to the SW corner of Section 33, thence northwesterly to the NW corner of Section 30; thence northeasterly to the true point of beginning."
(A) None (C) 320
(B) 145.7 (D) 640

67. The description of a property reads "From the NW corner of Section 30, T2S, R40E, W.M., thence west 1,320 feet to a point, thence south 660 feet to a point, thence east 1,320 feet to a point, thence north 660 feet to the point of beginning." This parcel contains
(A) five acres. (C) 20 acres.
(B) ten acres. (D) 40 acres.

68. How many acres are in the following description? "Beginning at the NW corner of the SW ¼, thence south along the west line to the SW corner of the section, then east along the south line of the section 2,640 feet to the SE corner of the said SW ¼, thence in a straight line to the point of beginning."
(A) 80 acres (C) 100 acres
(B) 90 acres (D) 110 acres

69. How many acres are contained in the following description? "Beginning at the SW corner of the NE ¼ of Section 26, thence north 1 mile to the NW corner of the SE ¼ of Section 23; thence southwesterly to the SE corner of the NW ¼ of Section 27; thence east 1 mile to the point of beginning."
(A) 80 acres (C) 260 acres
(B) 160 acres (D) 320 acres

70. A square parcel 1,320 feet on a side would contain
(A) 10 acres. (C) 40 acres.
(B) 20 acres. (D) 80 acres.

71. Sir Grant Conveyer owned the S ½ of the NE ¼ of the SE ¼ of Section 7. If he sold this property for $2,000 per acre, at closing he should receive
(A) $20,000. (C) $160,000.
(B) $40,000. (D) $320,000.

72. Land sells for $1,200 per acre. What is the price of the E ½ of the NE ¼ of the SW ¼ of Section 7?
(A) $ 9,000 (C) $24,000
(B) $12,000 (D) $48,000

73. Rusty Boltz bought the S ½ of the SW ¼ of the SE ¼ of the NE ¼ of a section. The sales price was a total of $52,500. What was the cost per acre?
(A) $5,250 (C) $21,000
(B) $10,500 (D) $42,000

74. A farm, described as the "NW ¼ of the SE ¼ of Section 10, Township 4N, Range 4W of the Gila and Salt River Baseline and Meridian" sold for $500 per acre. The sale price would be
(A) $10,000. (C) $25,000.
(B) $20,000. (D) $40,000.

75. If a parcel described as the W ½, NE ¼, NW ¼, Section 8, T40S, R7W, WM is sold at a price of $1,200 per acre the total sales price would be
(A) $6,000. (C) $24,000.
(B) $12,000. (D) $48,000.

76. You listed the N ½ of NE ¼ of SW ¼ of Section 10 at $2,400 an acre. Your brokerage fee is 8%. Your commission will be
(A) $1,920.00. (C) $3,840.00.
(B) $3,480.00. (D) $4,830.00.

77. Broker Dean has an agreement with his broker whereby he gets 60% of the commission on each property sold. He sells the W ½ of the SE ¼ of a section for $2,100 per acre. The office receives a commission that is 11% of the first $8,000 and 7% of the balance of the selling price. Dean must pay 9% of his share of the commission to Broker Whitmire, who listed the acreage. How much does Dean net?
(A) $6,420.96 (C) $10,992.80
(B) $6,595.68 (D) $12,080.00

78. Mrs. Carlson bought the S ½ of the SW ¼ of the SE ¼ of the NW ¼ of a section. If the sale price was $52,410 what was the cost per acre?
(A) $10,482.00 (C) $22,796.90
(B) $13,363.33 (D) $23,263.90

79. The Pacific Railroad Company owns three sections of land. They sold the land in 20-acre parcels in the following manner: Sixteen parcels at $4,000 each; the remainder at $5,000 each. About how much in all did the company receive from the sale?
(A) $90,000 (C) $480,000
(B) $464,000 (D) $500,000

80. The northeast quarter of Section 10 is priced at $400 per acre, while the southeast quarter is priced at $200 per acre more. How much money would be required to purchase the northeast quarter and one quarter of the southeast quarter of this section?
(A) $24,000 (C) $88,000
(B) $64,000 (D) $128,000

81. In what corner of a township would you find Section 1?
(A) Northeast corner (C) Southeast corner
(B) Northwest corner (D) Southwest corner

82. In the Government Rectangular Survey System Section 12 is located due
(A) north of Section 1. (C) east of section 11.
(B) south of section 6. (D) west of section 13.

83. How would the section directly south of section 16 be numbered?
(A) 15 (C) 21
(B) 17 (D) 22

84. In a regular township, the shortest distance between Section 4 and Section 34 is
(A) 4 miles. (C) 12 miles.
(B) 6 miles. (D) 24 miles.

85. Under a government rectangular survey, a correction line is required because of
(A) errors made by surveyors.
(B) the monument being in the wrong place.
(C) the curvature of the earth.
(D) an error in legal description.

86. The primary survey line running East and West in the rectangular survey is a
(A) township line. (C) range line.
(B) base line. (D) principal meridian.

87. Section 32, T2N, R3E, W.M. would be ______ of Section 32, T2S, R3W, W.M.
(A) north (C) northeast
(B) south (D) southwest

88. North and south boundaries of townships are created by
(A) township lines.
(B) range lines.
(C) metes and bounds description.
(D) plat numbers.

89. What are the east-west rows of townships called?
(A) Ranges (C) Sections
(B) Tiers (D) Parallels

90. The column of townships running north and south is numbered according to its distance from the principal meridian and is referred to as a
(A) check. (C) range.
(B) tract. (D) tier.

91. Land in Township 12 South, Range 6 East of the Willamette Meridian is located how many miles east of the Principal Meridian?
(A) Between 5 and 6 (C) Between 30 and 36
(B) Between 15 and 18 (D) 72

92. The number of townships in an area 24 miles square is
(A) 32. (C) 8.
(B) 16. (D) 4.

93. Under the rectangular survey system, the legal description of a particular land unit is based on
(A) one township line.
(B) one range.
(C) one meridian and one base line.
(D) metes and bounds.

94. The main north and south line in a government survey from which townships are located is called a
(A) principal meridian. (C) monument.
(B) township line. (D) range line.

95. An acre contains
(A) 26,650 square feet. (C) 43,560 square feet.
(B) 34,780 square feet. (D) 54,670 square feet.

96. Which of the following contain just one acre?
(A) A parcel 66' by 660'
(B) A parcel 200' by 217.8'
(C) Both A and B
(D) Neither A nor B

97. An acre could be
(A) 43,560 square feet.
(B) 25 feet by 1,742.4 feet.
(C) 50 feet by 871.2 feet.
(D) any of the above.

98. A parcel of land measuring 220 yards by 220 yards contains
(A) 1.1 acres. (C) 10.0 acres.
(B) 5.0 acres. (D) 302.5 acres.

99. If a tract of land is 264 feet wide by 660 feet deep, the value of the land at $1,600 per acre is
(A) $5,800. (C) $7,200.
(B) $6,400. (D) $7,600.

100. How many acres are contained within an area measuring 220 yards by 220 yards?
(A) 1.1 (C) 7
(B) 5 (D) 10

101. A rectangular tract of land is divided diagonally by a stream, leaving two lots in the shape of right triangles. One lot has a street frontage of 400 feet and a depth of 680 feet. How many acres does this lot contain?
(A) 1.56 (C) 6.24
(B) 3.12 (D) 7.30

102. If an acre of land has four sides of equal length, the length of each side would be approximately
(A) 150 feet. (C) 330 feet.
(B) 210 feet. (D) 435 feet.

103. How many 30-foot by 120-foot lots can be extracted from an acre of land?
(A) 1.31 (C) 12.1
(B) 4.35 (D) 14.52

104. A parcel of land which is 720 feet square contains
(A) 10 acres. (C) 40 acres.
(B) 11.9 acres. (D) 40.08 acres.

105. Which of the following methods of describing property is not considered to be sufficient as a legal description in a deed?
(A) Metes and bounds
(B) Street name and number
(C) Recorded plat map
(D) Government survey

106. Ben Baker's home address is: 2055 Keen Street, Warm Springs, Oregon 97761. This description of Baker's property is adequate for
I. preparing a valid deed.
II. informal reference on a listing agreement.
(A) I only (C) Both I and II
(B) II only (D) Neither I nor II

107. A legal description
I. is valid if it is sufficient for a disinterested third party to segregate the property being described from all other property of its type.
II. must be adequate if the agreement in which it is found is to be enforceable.
(A) I only (C) Both I and II
(B) II only (D) Neither I nor II

108. An inventory of the buildings which exist on a parcel of property must be included in
(A) a deed to the property.
(B) a land sales contract.
(C) an ALTA title insurance policy.
(D) none of the above.

109. A deed stated that the description of the property was "the N ½, SE ¼, NW ¼, Section 36, T18S, R2E." This description is
(A) a metes and bounds description.
(B) by reference to latitude and longitude.
(C) an example of a lot and block description.
(D) inadequate.

110. Of the following descriptions, which would be the most likely to be unenforceable?
(A) "All of Tax Lot 150 as found on Curry County Assessor's 1990 map #2362 as it existed this day"
(B) "642 S. Ocean Breeze Way, Brookings, Oregon 97415"
(C) "The S ½, NE ¼, NE ¼, SW ¼, Section 13, T45S, R8W, W.M."
(D) "Lot 16, Ocean Breeze Ranchettes Addition to Curry County, Oregon"

111. The street address of a property may be legally acceptable for
I. preparing a valid and enforceable deed.
II. reference on a month-to-month rental agreement.
(A) I only (C) Both I and II
(B) II only (D) Neither I nor II

112. Which of the following would be an adequate description of real estate?
I. The NE ¼, NW ¼, SW ¼, Section 23, T2S, R23E, W.M.
II. Starting at the SW corner of the NW ¼ of Section 23, T2S, R23E, W.M., then east 660' to the Point of Beginning, then east 660', then south 660', then north 660' to the Point of Beginning
(A) I only (C) Both I and II
(B) II only (D) Neither I nor II

113. The legal description "the Northwest ¼ of the Southwest ¼ of Section 6, Township 2N, Range 3 West" is defective because there is no reference to
(A) lot number. (C) meridian.
(B) boundary line. (D) record of survey.

114. To be valid a deed which contains a lot and block description must also
I. describe the metes and bounds distances and angles of the perimeter lines of the parcel conveyed.
II. contain references to the nearest section corner of the Government Rectangular Survey System.
(A) I only (C) Both I and II
(B) II only (D) Neither I nor II

115. A property described as "NW ¼, SW ½, Sec. 7, WM" is
(A) a lot and block legal description.
(B) adequately described.
(C) a metes and bounds description.
(D) incompletely described.

116. When a legal description is created, the
   I. surface boundaries are laid out according to the number of feet of actual distance in a horizontal plane, regardless of whether the land slopes uphill or downhill.
   II. quantity of property described by the surface boundaries extends to the depth necessary for the ordinary beneficial use of the property.
   (A) I only
   (B) II only
   (C) Both I and II
   (D) Neither I nor II

117. When making a legal description of an air lot, a surveyor must
   (A) make a description in three dimensions.
   (B) describe the surface boundaries of the land under the air lot.
   (C) indicate the elevation of the air space.
   (D) do all of the above.

118. In heavily populated areas, legal descriptions are most commonly created by
   (A) local government survey.
   (B) lot and block.
   (C) metes and bounds.
   (D) reference to recorded deeds.

119. In which of the following would you be least likely to find a full legal description of the property?
   (A) Preliminary title report
   (B) Policy of title insurance
   (C) Deed
   (D) Real property tax statement

120. Which of the following would not be a way to measure commercial land area?
   (A) Hectare
   (B) Front foot
   (C) Metes and bounds
   (D) Square foot

121. The existence of an encroachment is best determined by
   (A) a survey.
   (B) a quitclaim deed.
   (C) a title insurance policy.
   (D) an appraisal.

ANSWERS

To practice questions. If you chose the wrong letter, here's the right one! The explanations are designed to clarify your understanding.

1. **B** Lot and block descriptions are created by drawing a plat map of a subdivision. The individual lots in the subdivision are shown with their boundaries on the map, which is then recorded to give constructive notice. "Allodial" is a term which means "pertaining to others," originally used to mean "not of the king," in reference to the fact that ownership of land today is vested in the individual citizen owners, not in the government. The term has nothing directly to do with legal descriptions. Metes and bounds means describing a property by tracing the distances and directions around the sides. Rectangular survey is the government survey.

2. **C** The government survey for a region starts with a principal meridian that runs north and south. The principal meridian from which the Oregon Territory was surveyed is the Willamette Meridian.

3. **B** The Federal System of Rectangular Surveys makes use of all the elements of this description, so it would be called a government survey description rather than metes and bounds or lot and block.

4. **D** While these terms appear in government survey descriptions, they are not found exclusively in such descriptions. Metes and bounds descriptions and even plat maps make reference to monuments in the government survey. Government surveys were the original surveys of the Oregon Territory, and therefore provide the anchor points for all subsequent surveys.

5. **B** Individual irregular parcels are usually described by noting the location of monuments on the corners and the distances and directions from one monument to the next. This is called a metes and bounds description.

6. **A** Before the federal system of rectangular surveys, land was divided either by metes and bounds (describing the distance and compass direction for each border around the property), or by platting a parcel into lots. When the plat is recorded, it creates constructive notice of the dimensions as shown on the map, thus the property can be described merely by the lot and block numbers, together with the name of the subdivision in which it is located. The allodial system refers to land tenure, and is contrasted with the feudal system. Under the feudal system of land tenure, the sovereign owned all the land, and individuals held their land at the pleasure of the sovereign. Under the allodial system of land tenure, the individual owns the land, and the government has the right to regulate its use or take it under condemnation for the common good upon payment of just compensation.

7. **B** "Metes and bounds" is the official name of the method for creating legal descriptions by following around the perimeter of the parcel from monument to monument, writing down the distance of each boundary and the compass direction of travel.

8. **C** A metes and bounds description consists of the directions and distances around a parcel from one monument to the next. Directions are generally stated in quadrant bearings, which are the degrees of deflection from north or south. It is defective if it fails to close. Metes and bounds was the original system for describing land. The government survey is the basis for all descriptions in Oregon, and provides the beginning anchor points for private surveys, including metes and bounds descriptions.

9. **B** The phrase "metes and bounds" originally meant "measurements and boundaries," but now people take it to mean the compass directions as well as the distances of travel along a property boundary.

10. **B** Trees and rivers are natural in origin, not artificial.

11. **C** "Metes and bounds" is the name given to the method of describing a property by placing monuments on the corners and describing the distance and compass direction from one monument to the next. It is ideally suited to individual lots of irregular shapes.

12. **C** The Federal System of Rectangular Surveys (government survey) was started in 1785. Prior to that time property was generally surveyed by metes and bounds. In states such as Oregon, where the government survey was used, the section corners and other government monuments form the anchor points to which most other surveys are referenced.

13. **C** Metes and bounds is a system of describing property by noting the location of monument points (corners) and the distance and compass direc-

tion from one monument to the next. The distances and directions can travel in any direction, but it is customary to travel counterclockwise around the parcel being described.

14. **B** Metes and bounds descriptions frequently start at a point other than one of the corners or boundaries of the property. Such a point is called a reference point, initial point or monument. This point is frequently a monument of the government surveys. The purpose of the reference point is to fix the location of the property on the earth. The phrase "point of beginning" is not the same as the reference point. The point of beginning is the actual point where the property itself starts.

15. **B** Any feature of the land, whether man-made or natural, can be used as a monument. Over time, monuments are frequently covered over or destroyed. Frequently we start a description at some monument that is a short distance from the property itself. We describe the distance and direction from this starting point to a location on the property boundary. The location on the property boundary is then called the "point of beginning," because it starts the actual description of the parcel.

16. **D** Metes and bounds is a method of describing land by noting the position of monuments and the distance and direction from one monument to the next around the parcel. Because these descriptions tend to be lengthy and contain language which is difficult to copy correctly, most people consider them to be the most complex way of describing land. However, for single irregular parcels, there is sometimes little choice.

17. **D** Most property boundaries are man-made because the location of natural monuments such as rivers, etc. can change. However, the law requires only that the description located the property with certainty, so any monument can be acceptable. "Metes and bounds" comes from the French "mete" (measurement) and the Anglo-Saxon "bounds" (boundaries). Any method of creating legal descriptions can be used in conjunction with any other method. For example, "the south 200', SW ¼, SW ¼ Section 22, T3S, R4W, W.M." is a metes and bounds ("the south 200') and a government survey description used together.

18. **C** Failing to close (failing to return to the point of beginning) is a fatal flaw in a legal description. It happens when one side of a metes and bounds description is inadvertently left out, usually by copying the description incorrectly.

19. **C** Directions were formerly described by azimuth bearings, but today quadrant bearings are used almost exclusively. Quadrant bearings use a 360° circle divided into four 90 quadrants. By placing the center of the circle on the monument and lining it up with true north, a surveyor can read off the number of degrees of deflection from north (0°) toward the east or west. Thus, S 30° 00' 00" W would be south but deflected 30° toward the west. On a clock, south would be 6:00, west would be 9:00. There are 90 between due south and due west, so 30° would be about one-third of the way between 6: 00 and 9:00, or about 7:00.

20. **D** In quadrant bearings, there are 90° between north and east, so N 45° E would be halfway between north and east, or due northeast.

21. **D** In quadrant bearings a circle (360°) is divided into four quadrants of 90° each. Each degree is divided into 60 minutes (abbreviated with a single quote), and each minute is divided into 60 seconds (abbreviated with a double quote).

22. **B** A feature of quadrant bearings is that you can always create the opposite of any direction by using the same number of degrees, minutes and seconds, but changing the compass directions. Thus, the opposite of "N 45° W" is "S 45° E."

23. **C** Since there are three boundary lines described, the parcel must be a triangle. The direction N 45° W is due northwest.

24. **D** The letters "POB" are a standard abbreviation for "point of beginning." By tracing the distances and directions you will find that "due east 300', then due south 500', then due west 300', then due north 400'" falls 100 feet short of describing a rectangle which is 300 feet wide and 500 feet high. (Draw this out to see how it looks.) The balance of the description, "then due west 100', then due north 200', then due east 100', then due south 100' to the POB" describes a second rectangle which is 100 feet wide and 200 feet high and which lies adjacent to the first rectangle. The 100 feet of shortage in the description of the first rectangle is actually the common boundary and need not be included in the description of the total property.

25. **C** A township is divided into smaller parcels (halves and quarters), but not into lots and blocks. Only a subdivision can result in the creation of lots and blocks. The final step in the creation of a subdivision is to record a plat map showing the lots, blocks, roads and other land divisions.

26. **A** The final step in the creation of a subdivision is to record a plat map showing the lots, blocks, roads and other land divisions. Each lot is marked with a unique designation on the map so that it can be identified by that designation in the future. The street addresses are not listed on the plat map, since they are assigned later by the post office after structures have been built.
27. **B** Lot and block descriptions are created by recording a plat map of a new subdivision. The map shows all the distances, directions and lot lines. Each lot is numbered so it can be referred to easily in the future. Recording the map creates constructive notice of the description of each lot.
28. **C** The subdivision is normally surveyed by metes and bounds, so the map will show all the distances and compass directions. Each lot will be marked on the map and its boundary lines shown with the distances and compass directions. By recording the map we give constructive notice of the dimensions of each lot, so in the future each lot can be referred to just by its lot and block number.
29. **D** The distances and directions are contained on the recorded map, so constructive notice of them has been given. Therefore, it is not necessary to repeat them in the deed. Plat maps, as well as other descriptions, are quite commonly anchored to other surveys and monuments besides monuments of the government survey.
30. **C** A section is one mile square, containing 640 acres. A township is 36 sections, each one mile square, i.e., 36 square miles, and six miles on a side.
31. **C** A township is six miles square, not six square miles. "Six miles square" is 36 square miles. Each township is divided into 36 sections, of 640 acres each.
32. **A** Townships are six miles on a side, therefore 36 square miles, each of which is a section. A section is 640 acres, so there are 23,040 acres in a township (36 sections × 640 acres = 23,040 acres). A hectare is 10,000 square meters, or 2.47 acres, so 10,000 hectares would be 24,700 acres.
33. **B** A township is six miles square, so its perimeter would be 24 miles (4 sides × 6 miles = 24 miles).
34. **C** A township is six miles by six miles (36 square miles), and contains 36 sections, each of which is one square mile. Each section is 640 acres, so a township would contain 23,040 acres (36 sections × 640 acres = 23,040 acres).
35. **B** A section is 640 acres, but not just any parcel of 640 acres. Sections are surveyed out in the government survey, 36 sections to each township.
36. **B** A township is six miles by six miles, or 36 square miles, and contains 36 sections.
37. **C** A township is six miles on a side, or 36 square miles. Each square mile is a section, so a standard section is one mile on each side. There are 640 acres in each section.
38. **C** In the federal system of rectangular surveys, meridians (north-south lines) are laid out six miles apart. Similarly, township lines (east-west lines) are also laid out six miles apart. This creates a grid of squares, each of which is six miles on a side (six miles square). These squares are called townships. Each township, in turn, is further divided into sections. Since the township is six miles on each side, it is logical to make 36 divisions of one square mile each in each township. Each of these square miles is called a section.
39. **B** A section is one mile square and contains 640 acres. A mile is 5,280 feet, which is 1,760 yards (5,280 ÷ 3 feet = 1,760 yards). The total square footage is 27,878,400 (5,280 × 5,280 = 27,878,400). A rod is 16½ feet, so each side would be 320 rods (5,280 ÷ 16.5 = 320).
40. **B** There are 36 sections in a regular township, so a section is the same as one thirty-sixth of a township. A section is 640 acres. Sixteen 40-acre parcels would be the same size (16 × 40 acres = 640 acres). An acre is 43,560 square feet, so a section is also 27,848,400 square feet (640 acres × 43,560 square feet = 27,848,400 square feet). A parcel 5,000 by 6,000 feet would be 30,000,000 square feet (5,000 × 6,000 = 30,000,000). A parcel 5,280 feet by 5,280 feet would be the same size as a section (5,280 feet × 5,280 feet = 27,848,400 square feet).
41. **A** There are 36 sections in a regular township. A section is one square mile and one mile (5,280 feet) on a side. A parcel which is "two miles square" means a parcel which is two miles on a side, or four square miles, or four sections.
42. **D** A township contains 36 sections, so 10% of it would be 3.6 sections. Each section is one square mile, so four square miles is the same as four sections. However (D) is by far the largest, as it is 43,560 acres, or 68.06 sections. To calculate, 43,560 × 43,560 = 1,897,473,600 square feet, divided by the number of square feet in an acre (43,560) gives us 43,560 acres (1,897,473,600 ÷ 43,560 = 43,560). If a section has 640 acres, then 43,560 acres is 68.06 sections (43,560 acres ÷ 640 acres = 68.0625 sections).

43. **A** A section is 640 acres. A section is one square mile, so nine square miles is nine sections. There are 36 sections in a township, so one-half of a township is 18 sections.

44. **B** The NW ¼, SW ¼, NE ¼ is a quarter of a quarter of a quarter. All the parcels are square. A section is one mile (5,280 feet) on a side. If you visualize a quarter of a section you will realize that it is one-half of a mile (2,640 feet) on a side. A quarter of a quarter would cut the length in half again, or one-quarter mile (1,320 feet). And a quarter of a quarter of a quarter would cut the distance in half one more time, or one-eighth mile (660 feet). Since the parcel is square, just multiply 660 feet by 4 to find its perimeter. This comes to 2,640 feet (660 feet × 4 = 2,640 feet). It is easiest to see this if you draw a section and divide it into quarters, then into quarters of quarters.

45. **B** The entire section is one mile on a side (5.280 feet). Work backwards from the end of the description, so first take the SW ¼, which is one-half mile (2,640 feet) on each side. The NW ¼ of this will be half the width, or one-quarter mile (1,320 feet) on a side. The NW ¼ of this will be half the width again, or one-eighth mile (660 feet). The W ½ of this will be the same height (660 feet) but half the width, or one-sixteenth of a mile (330 feet). Therefore, the dimensions will be 330 feet wide and 660 feet high. The perimeter will be 330 feet + 330 feet + 660 feet + 660 feet, or 1,980 feet total. It is easiest to do this by drawing the parcels.

46. **B** There are two parcels in this problem, divided by the word "and." You must draw the parcels in order to visualize the answer. Always draw the largest parcel first, working down in successively smaller portions. Therefore, first draw the NW ¼ then, within the NW ¼ draw the SE ¼ of it, and finally, within the SE ¼ of the NW ¼, draw the E ½ of it. To find the dimensions, start with the side of the entire section, which you know is one mile, or 5,280 feet. Halfway across the section, is therefore 2,640 feet, one-quarter will be 1,320 feet, one-eighth will be 660 feet, and one-sixteenth will be 330 feet. By visualizing the drawing, you can see that the dimensions of the E ½, SE ¼, NW ¼ are 660 feet wide by 1,320 feet tall. Now draw the other parcel (the N ½ of the SW ¼ of the NE ¼) in the same manner. Again, by looking at it, you can see that its dimensions are 660 feet high and 1,320 feet wide. You can also see that it shares one 660 foot end with the first parcel. Bear in mind that this shared boundary will not be fenced. Now add up all the sides of the combined parcel. This should come to 6,600 feet, total. We know there are three feet to a yard, so 6,600 feet is the same as 2,200 yards.

47. **D** In the government survey, a section is one mile square and contains 640 acres. If you draw a section and divide it into quarters, you will see that the side of a quarter section is actually one-half mile. An eighth of a section would have to be one-half of one-quarter, so it could not be square.

48. **C** A section is 640 acres, so 160 acres would be a quarter section. The distance of the side of a quarter section is easiest to see by drawing a section and dividing it into quarters. Remember that the side of a section is one full mile.

49. **B** A section contains 640 acres, a quarter section contains 160 acres, and a quarter of a quarter section contains 40 acres. Therefore, a square parcel containing 40 acres is a quarter of a quarter section. The side of a section is one mile (5,280 feet), so the side of a quarter section is one-half mile (2,640 feet), and the side of a quarter of a quarter section is one-quarter mile (1,320 feet). To see this visually, draw a section and divide it into quarters, then each quarter again into quarters.

50. **D** The federal system of rectangular surveys consists of a grid of squares, each of which is six miles on a side (six miles square). These squares are called townships. Each township, in turn, is further divided into 36 square sections, each of which is one square mile. The distance along each side of the section is, therefore, one mile. Each section consists of 640 acres. Therefore, a square parcel of 160 acres, must be one-quarter of some section. If it is one quarter of a section, then its boundaries are one-half mile long. If you don't believe this, draw a square, then divide it neatly into quarters. Note that the boundary lines for each quarter goes to the midpoint of the larger square – one half mile.

51. **A** Work backwards from the largest to the smallest piece. A section is 640 acres, so the SE ¼ contains 160 acres, the SE ¼ of this is 40 acres, and the SE ¼ of that is 10 acres.

52. **C** A section is 640 acres, a quarter section is 160 acres, so dividing a quarter section into four gives four parcels of 40 acres each.

53. **D** Draw a section and divide it into quarters. Divide one of the quarters in half. Bearing in mind that the side of a section is one mile, you can see that the half of a quarter is ¼ mile by ½ mile, which matches the dimensions of the subject property. A quarter section is 160 acres, and half of that is 80 acres.

54. **D** These are two separate parcels. A section is 640 acres, so the W ½ would be 320 acres. The NE ¼ would be 160 acres. Therefore, the total would be 480 acres (320 acres + 160 acres = 480 acres).

55. **B** To calculate acreage in government survey descriptions, work backwards from the largest piece to the smallest. The NE ¼ contains 160 acres, the SW ¼ of this is 40 acres, and the E ½ of that is 20 acres.

56. **D** Calculate acreage by working backwards from the largest parcel to the smallest. The NE ¼ is 160 acres, the SE ¼ of this is 40 acres, and the S ½ of this is 20 acres.

57. **A** Work the problem backwards from the largest parcel to the smallest. The SW ¼ is 160 acres, the SW ¼ of this is 40 acres, the E ½ of this is 20 acres, the E ½ of this is 10 acres, and the E ½ of this is a skinny piece of five acres.

58. **B** To find acreage, work the property backwards from the largest piece. The NW ¼ is 160 acres, and the SE ¼ of it would be 40 acres. For the second parcel, the NE ¼ is 160 acres, the SW ½ of it is 40 acres, and the N ½ of that would be 20 acres. Therefore, the two parcels are 40 and 20 acres, or a total of 60 acres.

59. **A** Work backwards from the largest to the smallest piece. The NE ¼ contains 160 acres, the NW ¼ of it contains 40 acres, the SE ¼ of that contains 10 acres, and the S ½ of that contains 5 acres.

60. **B** It is easier to solve this problem by visualizing it, so you must draw this parcel first. Draw a section and start by outlining the largest parcel (the SW ¼). Within the SW ¼, outline the NE ¼. Within the NE ¼, outline the NW ¼. And finally, within the NW ¼, outline the W ½. You know that the whole section has 640 acres, so the SW ¼ has 160 acres, the NE ¼ of the SW ¼ has 40 acres, the NW ¼ of the NE ¼ of the SW ¼ has 10 acres, and the E ½ of it must have 5 acres. However, the problem states "less the south 165' thereof." To calculate the number of acres in the south 165 feet, you must calculate how wide the E ½ of the NW ¼ of the NE ¼ of the SW ¼ is. You know that an entire section is one mile (5,280 feet) on a side, so by dividing down, you find that the parcel is 330 feet wide by 660 feet tall. Therefore, the south portion that we must subtract is 330 feet wide by 165 feet high. This is a total of 54,450 square feet (330 × 165 = 54,450). You also know that an acre is 43,560. Therefore, to find how many acres this portion is, divide it size (54,450) by the number of square feet in an acre (43,560). The result is 1.25 acres (54,450 ÷ 43,560 = 1.25). In conclusion, the entire parcel was 5 acres, but the bottom portion we are to subtract is 1.25 acres, so the answer is 3.75 acres (5 – 1.25 = 3.75).

61. **B** There are two parcels in this description. Work backwards from the largest piece of each. Starting with the first one, the NW ¼ is 160 acres, the E ½ of it is 80 acres, the E ½ of that is 40 acres, and the N ½ of that is 20 acres. The largest piece in the second parcel is the NE ¼, which is 160 acres. The NW ¼ of this is 40 acres, and the W ½ of that is 20 acres. Therefore, we have two 20-acre parcels, for a total of 40 acres.

62. **B** Calculate area by working backwards from the largest piece to the smallest for each of the three parcels here. The SE ¼ is 160 acres, so the S ¼ of it is 80 acres. The NE ¼ is 160 acres, so the NE ¼ of it is 40 acres. The NW ¼ is 160 acres, so the W ½ of it would be 80 acres. Therefore, there is a parcel of 80 acres, one of 40 acres, and a third of 80 acres. This totals 200 acres.

63. **C** First, consider the first description of (I). Whatever it is part of, if it is "the east 10 acres," then it is always 10 acres. The rest of the description is irrelevant. The second description of (I) is the "SW ¼, SW ¼, SW ¼," which is a quarter of a quarter of a quarter, or 10 acres (640 acres ÷ 4 ÷ 4 = 10 acres). The first description of (II) is the "SE ¼, NE ¼," which is a quarter of a quarter, or 40 acres. The second part of (II) is the "NE ¼, SE ¼," which is also a quarter of a quarter, or 40 acres. Therefore, both descriptions in (I) are ten acres, and both descriptions in (II) are 40 acres.

64. **A** A section is 5,280 feet on a side, therefore a quarter section (160 acres) is 2,640 feet on a side. A quarter of that (40 acres) is 1,320 feet on a side. And a quarter of that (10 acres) is 660 feet on a side. Thus a parcel which is 330 feet on a side must be one-fourth of 10 acres, or 2½ acres. Bisecting it means each parcel must be 1¼ acres. You can also calculate by square footage. Multiply 330 feet by 330 feet to get the total square footage (330 feet × 330 feet = 108,900 square feet). Because the stream bisects the parcel, divide this in two to find the square footage in each triangle – 54,450 square feet (108,900 square feet ÷ 2 = 54,450 square feet). Divide this by the number of square feet in one acre (43,560) to find the number of acres, which is 1¼ acres (54,450 ÷ 43,560 = 1.25).

65. **D** There are three parcels. The SW ¼, NW ¼ is a quarter of a quarter. The whole section is 640 acres, so a quarter section is 160 acres, and a quarter of that is 40 acres. The second parcel, the E ½, NW ¼,

SW ¼, is a half of a quarter of a quarter. If the whole section is 640 acres, one quarter is 160, and a quarter of that is 40 acres and a half of that is 20 acres. The third parcel, the S ½, NE ¼ is a half of a quarter. The whole section is 640 acres, so a quarter is 160 acres and half of that is 80 acres. Therefore the total is 40 acres + 20 acres + 80 acres, which equals 140 acres.

66. **C** You must draw this parcel, tracing it out on a drawing of a township. First, draw a township and divide it into its 36 sections, and number each section. (Remember to start in the upper-right corner and zigzag.) Now look for the NE corner of section 17 and put your pencil on that point. With your pencil on that point, look for the SE corner of section 22. When you have identified the SE corner of section 22, draw a line to it. In similar fashion, while holding your pencil on the SE corner of section 22, identify the SW corner of section 33, then draw a line to it. And finally, while holding your pencil in the SW corner of section 33, identify the NW corner of section 30, and draw a line to it. The result is that you should have drawn a diamond-shaped parcel toward the left and bottom of the township. Looking at the lines you drew, focus on section 17. You will see that one of the lines runs diagonally through it. Obviously, the description includes half of section 27. A section is 640 acres, so the answer is 320 acres.

67. **C** The entire section is 640 acres in area and 5,280 feet on a side. Therefore, a quarter section is 160 acres and one-half mile (2,640 feet) on a side. And a quarter of a quarter section is 40 acres and one-quarter mile (1,320 feet) on a side. However, this parcel is 1,320 feet by 660 feet, so it is one half of the quarter of a quarter. Since the quarter of a quarter is 40 acres, this parcel must be 20 acres. You can also calculate by square footage. Multiply 1,320 feet by 660 feet to find the total square footage, then divide by 43,560 (the number of square feet in one acre). The result is 20 acres (1,320' × 660' = 871,200 square feet; 871,200 square feet ÷ 43,560 square feet = 20 acres).

68. **A** Draw a section and divide it into quarters. Locate the NW corner of the SW ¼, which will be midway along the west side, and label it "POB" (point of beginning). Next locate the SW corner of the section, and draw a line from the POB south to it. Next locate the SE corner of the SW ¼, which will be midway along the south side, and draw a line to it. Now just complete the parcel by drawing a line diagonally back to the POB. This will create a triangle. The triangle will be one-half of the SW ¼. A quarter-section is 160 acres, so the triangle must be 80 acres.

69. **D** Start by drawing four squares adjacent to each other to represent four sections. Label the two top ones 23 and 24, and the bottom two 27 and 26 (27 is below 23 and 26 is below 24). Divide them into quarters and locate the SW corner of the NE ¼ in Section 26 (which will be in the middle of the section. A section is one mile, so to go one mile north from this point would take you to the center of the Section 23. Notice that this is correctly the "NW corner of the SE ¼ of Section 23." The next direction is a 45 direction (southwesterly). Draw a line in this direction down to the SE corner of the NW ¼ of Section 27. Then complete the final direction by drawing a line back to the starting point. You will have drawn a triangle. Part of the triangle will be a whole quarter section (the NW ¼ of Section 26), and the other two will be triangles each representing one-half of a quarter section. The two triangles will, therefore, also total one quarter section, so you have an area equal to two quarter sections. A quarter section is 160 acres, so this parcel is 320 acres total.

70. **C** The easiest way to do this problem is to apply knowledge of the government survey. In the government survey, a section is 640 acres, a quarter section is 160 acres, and a quarter of a quarter section is 40 acres, and so on. In linear measure, a section is one mile (5,280 feet) on a side. Therefore a quarter section is one-half mile on a side. (Draw it if you don't believe it.) And a quarter of a quarter section is 1,320 feet on a side. Therefore, a parcel that is 1,320 feet square must be a quarter of a quarter section, or 40 acres. As an alternative method to solve the problem, if you remember that one acre is 43,560 square feet, you can divide it into the total square footage of the parcel. The square footage of a parcel 1,320 feet on a side will be 1,742,400 (1,320 × 1,320 = 1,742,400). Dividing this by the number of square feet in an acre (43,560) gives us 40 acres (1,742,400 ÷ 43,560 = 40).

71. **B** First find the acreage. The S ½ of the NE ¼ of the SE ¼ is a half of a quarter of a quarter. The entire section is 640 acres, so one quarter is 160 acres, a quarter of that is 40 acres, and half of that is 20 acres. Now multiply by the price per acre ($2,000). The result is $40,000 (20 acres × $2,000 = $40,000).

72. **C** First, find the acreage by working the descriptions backwards from the largest parcel. The SW ¼ is 160 acres, the NE ¼ of it would be 40 acres, and the E ½ of that would be 20 acres. If the price is $1,200 per acre, then the total price is $24,000 (20 × $1,200 = $24,000).

73. **B** First find the acreage. The S ½ of the SW ¼ of the SE ¼ of the NE ¼ is a half of a quarter of a quarter of a quarter. The whole section is 640 acres, so one quarter is 160 acres, a quarter of that is 40 acres, a quarter of that is 10 acres, and a half of that is 5 acres (note you must divide them backwards from the end of the description). If the total price paid was $52,500, then the price was $10,500 per acre ($52,500 ÷ 5 acres = $10,500 per acre).

74. **B** To calculate the acreage, work backwards from the largest piece toward the smallest. The SE ¼ is 160 acres, and the NW ¼ of this would be 40 acres. If the sales price is $500 per acre, then the total sales price would be $20,000 (40 acres × $500 = $20,000).

75. **C** We must find the number of acres in this parcel. To do so, the easiest method is to draw the parcel. Always start with the largest parcel, working down to the smallest, so start by drawing the NW ¼. Within the NW ¼, mark out the NE ¼, and within the NE ¼, mark out the W ½. We know the entire section has 640 acres, so the NW ¼ has 160 acres, the NE ¼ of the NW ¼ has 40 acres, and the W ½ has 20 acres. If the price is $1,200 per acre, we just multiply this amount by 20 to get the total price, which comes to $24,000 ($1,200 × 20 = $24,000).

76. **C** First you must find out how many acres this parcel is. To do so, it is easiest if you draw the parcel. Draw a section, then outline the SW ¼. (Always start with the largest parcel and work down to successively smaller pieces.) Within the SW ¼, outline the NE ¼. And finally, within the NE ¼ of the SW ¼, outline the N ½. You know that the entire section has 640 acres, so the SW ¼ has 160, the NE ¼ of the SW ¼ has 40, and the N ½ of the NE ¼ of the SW ¼ must have 20. If the sales price is $2,400 per acre, then it must be $48,000 (20 × $2,400 = $48,000). And if your commission is 8%, then the total commission is $3,840 ($48,000 × 0.08 = $3,840.00).

77. **B** First, find out how may acres there are in the parcel. An entire section has 640 acres, so the SE ¼ of the section has 160 acres, and the W ½ of the SE ¼ has 80 acres. If the selling price is $2,100 per acre, then the total selling price is $168,000 (80 × $2,100 = $168,000). The first $8,000 is at 11% commission, so the commission on the first $8,000 is $880 ($8,000 × 0.11 = $880). This leaves $160,000 of the sales price on which we apply the 7% commission rate. This comes to $11,200 ($160,000 × 0.07 = $11,200). Adding the commission on the first $8,000, we find that the total commission is $12,080 ($11,200 + $880 = $12,080). The broker's share is 60%, which comes to $7,248 ($12,080 × 0.60 = $7,248). However, we must subtract 9% of this which goes to the other broker. The amount to subtract is $652.32. Subtracting this amount leaves a net of 6,595.68 ($7,248 – 652.32 = $6,595.68).

78. **A** A section contains 640 acres. Working the description backwards, the NW ¼ is 160 acres, the SE ¼ of this is 40 acres, the SW ¼ of this is 10 acres, and the S ½ of this is 5 acres. If the sales price was $52,410, then the per-acre price was $10,482.00 ($52,410.00 ÷ 5 = $10,482.00).

79. **B** A section is 640 acres, so three sections is 1,920 acres (640 acres × 3 = 1,920 acres). If they sold 16 parcels at $4,000 each, then they sold 320 acres (16 × 20 acres = 320 acres) for a total of $64,000 (16 × $4,000 = $64,000). This leaves 1,600 acres (1,920 acres – 320 acres = 1,600 acres) which they sold in 20-acre parcels for $5,000 each. The 1,600 acres will make 80 parcels of 20 acres each (1,600 acres ÷ 20 acres = 80 parcels). Multiplying by $5,000 per parcel, means that the remaining parcels were sold for a total of $400,000 (80 parcels × $5,000 = $400,000). Adding the two sales together means that the total price realized was $464,000 ($64,000 + $400,000 = $464,000).

80. **C** If the NE ¼ is priced at $400 per acre and the SE ¼ is priced at $200 more, then the SE ¼ is priced at $600 per acre. Each quarter section is 160 acres, so the NE ¼ would cost $64,000 (160 acres × $400 = $64,000). The SE ¼ of the SE ¼ is 40 acres, so this parcel would cost an additional $24,000 (40 acres × $600 = $24,000). Adding the cost of the two parcels together, means the total cost would be $88,000 ($64,000 + $24,000 = $88,000).

81. **A** Sections are numbered starting in the northeast corner, proceeding west across the top six sections and then zigzagging down to the southeast corner.

82. **C** Sections are numbered starting in the northeast corner and zigzagging down to the southeast corner. Draw the township and number the sections to see the answer easily.

83. **C** Sections are numbered starting in the northeast corner and zigzagging down to the southeast corner. Draw the township and number the sections to see the answer easily.

84. **A** Sections are numbered starting in the northeast corner and zigzagging back and forth so number 36 will be in the southeast corner. Draw a township and divide it into 36 equal sections of one

mile each and number them correctly. Section 4 will lie in the top row just to the left of the center line and Section 34 will lie in the bottom row just to the right of the center line. The closest points will be the SE corner of Section 4 and the NW corner of Section 34. Since each section is one mile, there will be four miles of distance between the two section corners.

85. **C** Correction lines are placed every 24 miles to adjust for the curvature of the earth.

86. **B** In the government survey (Federal System of Rectangular Surveys), for each region there is a principal meridian running north and south, intersected by a baseline running east and west.

87. **C** Sections are numbered zigzagging from the northeast corner (section 1) to the southeast corner (section 36). Draw the township and number the sections to see the answer easily.

88. **A** East-west lines (forming the north and south boundaries of townships) are township lines or parallels. Similarly, north-south lines are rangelines or guide meridians.

89. **B** Between each standard parallel there are three township lines which run east-west and create four tiers of townships.

90. **C** Between each guide meridian there are three rangelines, which divide the area into four ranges. A range is row of townships running from north to south.

91. **C** Townships are numbered conscutively north and south from the baseline and east and west from the principal meridian. Each township is six miles, so a township in Range 6 would be start 30 miles from the principal meridian and extend another six miles. Range 7 would start at mile 36.

92. **B** In the goverenment survey there are guide meridians every 24 miles east and west, and standard parallels every 24 miles north and south. In between townships are marked out by three township lines running east and west, and three rangelines running north and south. Therefore, the area between each 24 mile square contains 16 townships.

93. **C** In the government survey (Federal System of Rectangular Surveys), for each region there is a principal meridian running north and south, intersected by a baseline running east and west. These two lines form the coordinates for the entire grid.

94. **A** In the government survey (Federal System of Rectangular Surveys), for each region there is a principal meridian running north and south, intersected by a baseline running east and west.

95. **C** An acre is 43,560 square feet, which can be derived from a section, which is 5,280 feet on a side, or 27,878,400 square feet (5,280 × 5,280 = 27,878,400). Dividing this by the number of acres in a section (640) gives us the number of square feet in an acre (27,878,400 ÷ 640 = 43,560).

96. **C** An acre is 43,560 square feet. A parcel 66' by 660' is 43,560 square feet (66' × 660' = 43,560 square feet.). A parcel 200' by 217.8' is 43,560 square feet (200' × 217.8' = 43,560 square feet.

97. **D** An acre is 43,560 square feet. A parcel 25' by 1,742.4' is 43,560 square feet (25' × 1,742.4' = 43,560 square feet). A parcel 50' × 871.2' is also 43,560 square feet (50' × 871.2' = 43,560 square feet.

98. **C** A pacel 220 yards by 220 yards is 660 feet by 660 feet, which is 435,600 square feet (660 × 660 = 435,600). An acre is 43,560 square feet, so 435,600 square feet would be 10 acres (435,600 ÷ 43,560 = 10).

99. **B** First, find the total square footage by multiplying one side times the other. This gives us 174,240 square feet (264 × 660 = 174,240). Next, we must find how many acres this is. We know there are 43,560 square feet in an acre, so divide the total square footage by 43,560 to get the number of acres. This comes to 4 (174,240 ÷ 43,560 = 4). If the land sells for $1,600 per acre, then multiply by the number of acres (4) to get the total value. This comes to $6,400 ($1,600 × 4 = $6,400).

100. **D** First, convert to feet, which means the parcel is 660 feet by 660 feet. (One yard = three feet, so 220 × 3 = 660.) To find the total square footage, multiply the sides, which gives us 435,600 (660 × 660 = 435,600). There are 43,560 square feet in an acre, so divide the total square footage by 43,560 to get the number of acres. This comes to 10 acres (435,600 ÷ 43,560 = 10).

101. **B** The area of a triangle is one-half the base times the height (A = ½ bh). The base and the height are 400 and 680, respectively, so the total square footage is 136,000 (400 × 680 ÷ 2 = 136,000). We know that an acre is 43,560 square feet, so the total acreage is 3.12 acres (136,000 ÷ 43,560 = 3.1221303).

102. **B** An acre could be many shapes. However, if the sides are of equal length, it must be square. You know an acre is 43,560 square feet, so to find the side of a square acre, take the square root of 43,560. This comes to 208.71 feet. If you don't have a square root button on your calculator, just experiment. You know, for example, that 200 times 200 is 40,000, and that is a little less than 43,560. So try 201 times 201,

then 202 times 202, until you find a number that is too much (which will be 209). Then you know that the square root of 43,560 is somewhere between 208 (which was not quite enough) and 209 (which was a little too much). This is close enough to answer the question correctly.

103. **C** A parcel 30' × 120' is 3,600 square feet. Dividing this into 43,560 square feet gives us 12.1 lots (43,560 square feet ÷ 3,600 square feet = 12.1).

104. **B** A parcel "720 feet square" is 720 feet on each side, and therefore contains 518,400 square feet (720' × 720' = 518,400 square feet). Divide this by 43,560 to find that the number of acres is 11.9 (518,400 square feet ÷ 43,560 square feet = 11.9 acres).

105. **B** All contracts involving real property must have an adequate description of the property. To be adequate, a description of real property must segregate the property from all other property with certainty. Therefore, the boundaries and location must be specified accurately. A street address alone does not accomplish this. There are three official ways of creating legal descriptions – metes and bounds, lot and block, and government survey.

106. **D** All contracts involving real property must have an adequate description of the property. To be adequate, a description of real property must segregate the property from all other property with certainty. Therefore, the boundaries and location must be specified accurately. A street address alone does not accomplish this.

107. **C** Any contract concerning real property is normally considered void for lack of a meeting of the minds if either party entered into the contract without a clear understanding of the dimension of the property and its location.

108. **D** Buildings and other improvements are usually appurtenances and fixtures which run with the land. Therefore, it is not necessary to describe them in any contract. Describing the boundaries of the land creates a presumption that the description includes all rights to the center of the earth and above the land to a height necessary for the ordinary and reasonable use and enjoyment of the land.

109. **D** This is an example of a government survey description, but it is inadequate because it fails to make reference to the principal meridian or give some other indication of the location of the property. There are many principal meridians in the Federal System of Rectangular Surveys, so this description could be any of numerous properties around the United States.

110. **A** A street address is usually the least acceptable way to describe property because there is no guarantee the parties to have constructive notice of the boundaries and location. However, by statute in Oregon, a tax lot number is inadequate as a legal description, without exception.

111. **B** Informal contracts such as listing agreements and rental agreements creating periodic tenancies are routinely acceptable with a street address. Of course, when there is any doubt, care should be taken that the parties have notice of the quantity and location of property which is the subject of the contract.

112. **A** The second description fails because a boundary line was left out. It should probably have read "starting at the SW corner of the NW ¼ of Section 23, T2S, R23E, W.M., then east 660' to the Point of Beginning, then east 660', then south 660', then west 660', then north 660'."

113. **C** The Willamette Meridian is only one of many principal meridians throughout the United States. Each area uses the same system of meridians, ranges, townships and sections, so failing to state "Willamette Meridian" is a potentially fatal flaw in a legal description, unless the county or state is designated, or some other means is used is used to clarify that is the Willamette Meridian.

114. **D** A contract involving real property is unenforceable on any party who did not have notice of the dimensions of the property and where it is located. When a plat map showing the lots and blocks, together with all the dimensions, has been recorded it gives constructive notice of the dimensions of each lot and where it is located. Therefore, the lot and block description is all that is necessary.

115. **D** The problem with this description is that you cannot have the "SW ½." In the government survey, you can have the N ½, the S ½, the E ½ or the W ½, but you cannot have the fraction "½" preceded by two compass points.

116. **A** Ownership of real property extends from the surface boundaries to the center of the earth and to a height above the land necessary for the ordinary and reasonable use and enjoyment of the property. Unless the property is an air lot, surface boundaries are in a level plane and topography must be ignored.

117. **D** Real property is a volume of space, any portion of which can be sold separately from the land. In order to do so the volume of space must be described with certainty. All of the choices would be required to do this accurately.

118. **B** Large land areas, such as forest and farm land, is most easily described by government survey. Subdivisions are best described by recording a plat map containing the directions and distances around each lot, which are then numbered for easy future reference. Individual small parcels are usually described by metes and bounds. Therefore, property in a city will be generally lot and block, while suburban and close-in rural land will be mostly metes and bounds.

119. **D** Title insurance companies can generally be counted on to take great care in preparing title reports and title insurance policies, since they have a potential financial exposure for any errors they create. Similarly, deeds are routinely scrutinized for accuracy before recording, so they are considered a good source for a legal description. Tax records are generally acceptable, but are more prone to error, and not at all acceptable if the description is a tax lot number.

120. **A** Commercially, land is frequently marketed by square foot, front foot or acreage. A hectare is 10,000 square meters (2.47 acres), a measurement not commonly used in this country.

121. **A** An encroachment occurs when improvements have been built on adjacent land. The best way to determine if there is an encroachment is to hire a surveyor.

REAL AND PERSONAL PROPERTY TAXATION

Real property is permanent, indestructible and immovable. Because of this we say that real estate has fixity. And because of its fixity, governments have always enjoyed a reasonable degree of certainty that they would be able to collect taxes levied on real property. After all, the owner can't just pick up the real estate and leave town.

We have had real property taxes since feudal times, although in early England taxes were levied in very different ways. Lands held by tenant farmers were taxed a portion of the production of the land. Property owned by knights was taxed in the form of a certain number of days of military service, and so forth. Today we have reduced this system to just a monetary tax, yet the operation of today's property tax system is far more complex than the feudal system from which it is derived.

Most property taxation today is a function of county government and other local taxing districts. There are no federal property taxes and real property taxation by the State of Oregon is minimal.

Within each county there are many small and some large political units which depend primarily on property taxes for their source of revenue. School districts come foremost to mind as examples of such districts, since school districts are typically the largest property tax district on the tax bill. Other examples include city governments, port authorities, public library districts, community college districts, and even the county itself. Regardless of its size or purpose, each local government unit which levies property taxes is called a ***tax levy district***.

Every year each tax levy district creates a budget for its operations during the coming year. This process takes place in the spring of each year and results in a prop-

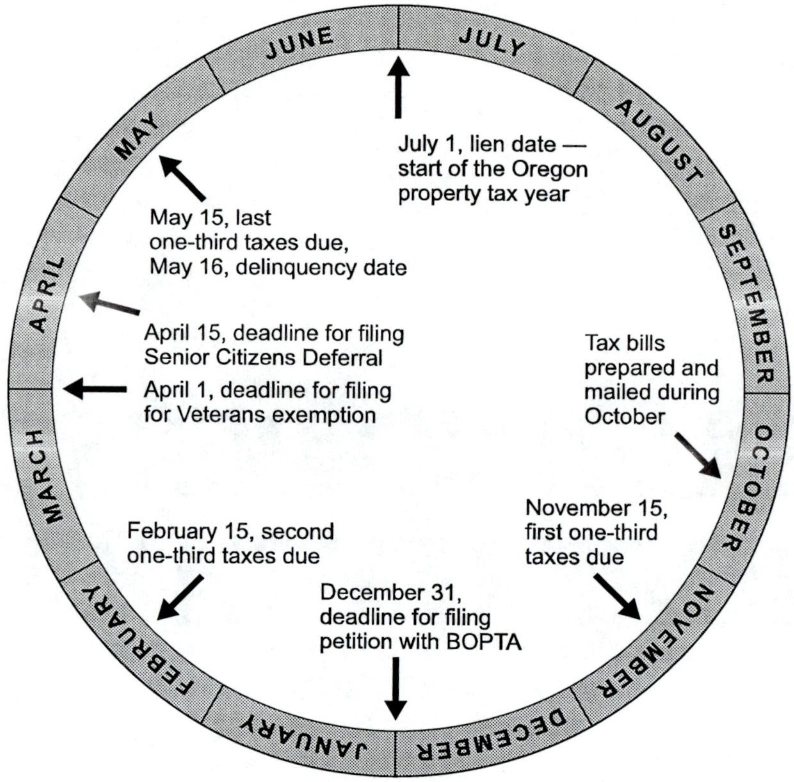

The Oregon real property tax year. Each property is valued for its real market value as of January 1. The tax levy becomes a lien on all taxable property within each tax levy district on July 1. The first one-third of the property tax bill is due on November 15. The second third is due February 15, and the final third is due May 15. Payment in full pays the taxes for the period from the preceding July 1 through the coming June 30. This fact is very important when prorating the tax liability between a buyer and a seller. If any portion of the tax or interest remains unpaid on May 16 it is delinquent.

erty tax ***levy***. There are limits on the amount each district may levy, set by the Oregon Constitution. On July 1 the levy becomes a lien on all taxable property in the district. Each owner will pay his or her share of the levy ***ad valorem***, that is, according to the value the property.

Someone must determine the values of all the properties in each tax levy district, and this person is the ***tax assessor***. The process of appraising all taxable properties each year is called ***assessment***. The tax assessor's job is endless. No sooner than one year's valuations are finished and it's time to start on the next year. The important thing to remember about assessment is that its sole function is to apportion the tax burden fairly according to value among all property within each tax levy district. Although today we have constitutional limits on increases in valuation, the concept of assessment is still to apportion the tax load according to value.

In the summer the tax assessor determines the tax rate for each tax levy district. The tax rate is calculated from the amount of each district's levy and the total value of all property from which the levy must be raised. The amount due each tax levy district is then adjusted to comply with Measure 5 and Measure 50, Oregon's property tax limitation laws. Once the levies have been approved and the valuations have been determined, the collection process begins. This job falls to the county ***tax collector***. In some counties, the tax collector is a separate official and in other counties, the sheriff serves as the tax collector.

Tax bills are sent in October. Property owners can pay their bills one-third at a time, or all at once. At least the first third is due on November 15. If the taxes are not paid, ultimately the tax collector will foreclose on the property.

The foregoing has been a brief overview of real property taxation in Oregon. You should note that there are three separate entities which are responsible for our property tax bills. The tax levy districts determine how much they are going to spend. This, more than any other single factor, determines how much our property tax bills will be. Next

NOTES

comes the tax assessor. The job of the tax assessor is to value every taxable property so that each owner can be billed for his or her share of the total levy according to the value of the property. And finally comes the tax collector. The tax collector programs the computers with the tax rates for each tax levy district and sends out the bills. The tax collector also enforces collection of the tax by foreclosure, if necessary.

Many people mistakenly blame the tax collector or the tax assessor when they feel their bills are too high. This is usually incorrect. The tax collector's function is merely to collect the taxes. The amount of an owner's tax bill is determined by the amount of the levy and the amount of the owner's assessment. If the assessment is too high, then the owner is paying more than his or her share of the total tax burden. But if the property is valued at its market value, then the owner's real complaint is that the tax levy districts are spending too much.

In the following pages we will discuss the details of the levy process, tax assessment, and collection procedures. We will also discuss exemptions and deferrals and taxation of personal property, among other matters.

Tax levies

Creating a tax levy is a complicated affair, not made easier by the fact that it is a purely political process. Each duly constituted tax levy district is run by a group of elected officials. For example, school districts are run by a school board, county commissioners run the county government, cities are run by council members, and so forth. These are all elected positions, so each member is sensitive to the fact that voters wish the budgets to be kept low. Nevertheless, voters also want more and better services, so the job of the politician is always a balancing act.

Oregon voters approved Measure 50 in 1997, the most recent of various tax limitation measures. Under Measure 50, the maximum amount of the levy is set by law. It can be either a flat dollar amount or a rate per $1,000 of total assessed valuation in the district. The maximum amounts were established during the 1997-98 tax year. This is called the district's ***permanent rate authority***. However, the permanent rate authority is still subject to the limits of Measure 5, which sets the maximum tax rates. This may result in a district not receiving all of their levy, even though it is under their permanent rate authority.

Sometimes there are special undertakings, especially temporary projects that local officials wish to fund separately. A common way to do this is to ask the voters to approve a ***serial levy***, a special annual levy, for a specified number of years only. The district will automatically lose funding at the end of the serial levy unless the voters approve a new levy. Under Measure 50, serial levies are now known officially as ***local option levies***. They may run for a maximum of five years for operations and ten years for capital improvements. Voter approval must have been at an election in which at least 50% of registered voters voted, or in a November election of an even-numbered year.

Although capital improvements are frequently funded by local option levies, sometimes the project must be paid for at once. Raising the funds with a local option levy would take too long. Local governments solve this problem with a ***bond issue***. The local government issues bonds to raise the capital to pay for the project. The bonds are bought by investors, who are repaid from future taxes – in fact, sometimes by a local option levy. Sometimes the bonds are to be paid off from the income produced by the improvement. For example, the local government may decide that a bridge is needed. By making it a toll bridge, the income generated from the tollgate can be used to pay off the bonds which were sold to finance its construction. Bonds which are to

NOTES

be paid off from the profits generated by the improvement are called ***revenue bonds***. Under Measure 50, voter approval for bond issues is subject to the same 50% rule requirements as local option taxes.

When local improvements are desired which will serve only certain properties, a ***special assessment*** is used. Special assessments are used to fund improvements such as street paving, curbs, gutters and sidewalks, sewer systems, street lighting, and so on. Special assessments are apportioned to the owners in various ways. For example, the total cost of a street improvement project may be allocated to adjacent property owners on a front-foot basis. The cost of a sewer system may be based on the number of bedrooms per house, etc. Special assessments are a lien against the property, the same as property taxes and can usually be assumed by a buyer.

Sometimes special assessments must be paid at once. However, since the assessment can easily run to thousands of dollars per property, the Oregon Legislature passed the ***Bancroft Bonding Act***. The Bancroft Bonding Act allows the owners to elect to pay for the improvements in installments. The city or county sells tax-exempt bonds to raise the cash to pay for the improvements. The bonds are paid off as each owner pays his or her share of the total. The city or county may set the repayment term as long as they wish, up to a maximum of 30 years. Property owners make periodic payments (usually semi-annually) which include interest. The city or county sets the interest rate as necessary to cover the interest paid on the bonds, plus costs associated with the assessment, collection, and the bond sales. In order to pay in installments the owner must make an election to do so within ten days of receiving notice of the assessment, although the city or county may waive this deadline. At the election of the city or county the assessments may be second liens to existing mortgages. Buyers may assume special assessments which are being paid under the Bancroft Bonding Act.

Exercise a

A government unit which levies property taxes is called a tax ____________ ______________. Each year the elected officials of each district create a tax ____________, which must be within their ________________ ____________ ______________. A ____________ levy is an example of a temporary tax levy to fund a special project. Today, these are called ____________ ____________ ____________. Capital improvements are frequently paid for by a ____________ issue. When the income from the project will be used to pay off the ____________, they are called ______________ ____________.

When improvements benefit only specific properties, it is common for the city or county to levy a ______________ ________________ against the affected properties. The owner can elect to pay this in installments under the provisions of the ______________ Bonding Act.

NOTES

Assessment

As noted previously, property taxes are levied according to value (ad valorem). Therefore, accurate valuation of each property is important if the total tax burden is to be distributed fairly among all property owners.

We must distinguish between the market value and the ***assessed value*** Taxes are levied on the assessed value, which is a percentage of the market value. The percentage is called the ***assessment ratio***. By basing the tax on the assessed value, we can shift the tax burden from one class of property onto another class, if we wish. For example, if we make a law which assesses personal residences at half their real market value, this would significantly lower the tax bills for personal residences, but at the same time shift a higher portion of the overall burden to other classes of property (e.g., business and industrial property). In the past this has been done numerous times. Of course, lowering taxes on homes at the expense of business and industrial property is popular, but in reality may be a bad idea. Businesses must cover their costs, which means charging more for their products. But if their competition is located in a region with lower costs, local businesses will have no choice but to move or go out of business. Having a lower property tax bill may be desirable for a homeowner, but not if the homeowner becomes unemployed as a result.

The tax assessor is required by law to appraise all taxable property according to the value of the property on January 1, which is called the ***assessment date***. This is called the ***real market value***.

Some counties have as many as hundreds of thousands of property tax accounts. To appraise each of these properties every year would cost an enormous amount. To maintain accurate values, yet keep the costs down, each county uses a process called ***trending***. Oregon law requires each county assessor to visit each property at least once every six years. Thus, each county is divided into six ***tax maintenance districts***. Staff from the assessor's office visit each property in one district every year, on a rotating basis ensuring that each property will be visited within the statutory requirements.

Because six years is a long time to go between appraisals, a computer generated adjustment is made every year for the five intervening years. The tax assessor simply programs the computer to change the values of all properties in each district by a certain percentage. The percentages are different for each district, and are determined primarily from the values stated on recorded deeds and land sales contracts. Value changes from physically visiting the property during the maintenance year are called ***maintenance changes***. Adjustments for the five years between maintenance changes are called ***trending changes***.

The tax assessor must send notice of any significant assessed value change to the property owner. The notice is included on the bill which is sent in October. If the owner wishes to appeal, he or she may file a petition with the ***Board of Property Tax Appeals*** (formerly called the Board of Equalization). The deadline is December 31. Most petitioners receive at least some of the relief they ask for. A personal appearance is not required and the forms and procedures are designed so the average owner can state his or her case without professional representation.

In all property valuation appeals the property owner must prove by preponderance of the evidence that the assessor's valuation of the property was too high. There are various types of evidence which an owner can use toward this end. An independent appraisal is certainly admissible as evidence, but may not be cost-effective. Comparable sales are considered valid evidence, whether contained in an appraisal report or not. A recent purchase of the property at a price under the assessed value is also excellent evidence. After all, a sale of the property itself is the very best comparable sale, provided, of course, that it was an open market, arms-length transaction. The best argument occurs

NOTES

when the property has been listed for sale in the open market for a reasonable period of time and has not sold.

Many times property owners will attempt to argue that the assessor has valued their property higher than other similar property, and therefore their valuation should be lowered. This argument will usually fail, since it only demonstrates that the valuations are unequal. It does not prove the value of the owner's property is less than what the assessor says it is.

If the owner is dissatisfied with the results of the petition to the Board of Property Tax Appeals, a further appeal can be taken to the ***Magistrate Division of the Oregon Tax Court***. Decisions of the Magistrate Division of the Oregon Tax Court can be further appealed to the regular session of the Oregon Tax Court, unless the appeal was filed under the small claims procedure. Small claims election is limited to properties with valuations of $250,000 or less. Both Magistrate and small claims hearings are usually conducted via conference telephone calls. Decisions of the Tax Court can be appealed to the Oregon Supreme Court.

In 1997 Oregon voters passed Measure 50, which rolled back assessed values to 90% of their 1995-96 amounts (called the ***maximum assessed value***), and put a 3% annual cap on increases in the maximum assessed values. It further defined the ***assessed value*** as the lower of real market value or maximum assessed value. Remember that the tax bill is based on assessed value, so this means the tax bill will be based on the lower of the real market value, or the "90% of 1995-96 value plus 3% per year amount." Since the maximum assessed value is now lower than real market value for the vast majority of properties, the need to appeal real market values has diminished dramatically.

There is a statutory provision for a ***proration of tax*** in the event the property is damaged or destroyed after the January 1 assessment date. The loss must be by act of God or fire. The amount of the loss will be subtracted from the real market value, not the maximum assessed value. Since the tax bill is based on the lower of the two figures, the loss would make no change in the tax bill unless it was enough to lower the real market value to below the maximum assessed value. The amount of the loss is applied on a per-month basis from the time the loss occurred, not for the entire tax year.

Measure 50 contains a special provision for increasing the maximum assessed value if an ***exception*** occurs. An exception means a change to the property that increases the value more than $10,000 in one year, or $25,000 over five assessment years (e.g., remodeling, additions, rezoning, and so on). In order to determine if the $25,000 limit is reached the tax assessor maintains a ledger for each property on which changes that raised the value under $10,000 are recorded.

Exercise b

When we say that property taxes are levied ______ ____________ we mean that they are levied according to value. Tax bills are based on the ____________ __________, which is the lower of the ________________ ______________ __________ and the __________ ____________ __________. The assessor appraises all property as of ______________, which is called the __________________ __________. A ____________________ adjustment is made once every ____ years to the value of all taxable property in Oregon. In the intervening five years, values are maintained by ____________________ . Property value appeals must be filed first with the ______________ of ____________________ __________ __________________ . Further appeals can be made to the ________________________ _____________________ of the Oregon __________ _____________ or to the Small Claims Division. If the property is damaged during the tax year, the owner may be eligible for a _____________________ of the tax due for the year. If the property is improved, there may be an _____________________, which can raise the assessed value.

Tax collection

Tax levy districts are required to complete their levies by July 15. When the tax collector has the levy for each district and the total amount of the assessed values for all property in each district, the ***tax rate*** for each district can be calculated. The tax rate in Oregon is expressed in dollars of tax per thousand dollars of assessed valuation. In the past, the tax rate was computed using ***mills***. A mill is one-thousandth of a dollar (one-tenth of a cent). For example, a typical overall tax rate in Oregon today would be about $15.00 per thousand. A $200,000 house taxed at this rate would have a tax bill of $3,000 each year (200 × $15 = $3,000). The same rate expressed in mills would be "15 mills," or 15 thousandths of a dollar per one dollar of value. Because people have difficulty with the mathematics of mills, we now state the tax rate in terms of dollars of tax per thousand dollars of value rather than mills of tax per dollar of value. Still, it is not uncommon to hear the term "***millage rate***."

Calculating a tax rate is very simple, but is easier to see if we use an example. Let us assume that the tax collector is determining the tax rate for a very small fire protection district. The district has a levy of $500,000 to fund operations in the coming year. The total assessed values of all property lying within the boundaries of the district is $1 billion. The calculation is to divide the total assessed values into the amount of the levy –

$$\frac{500{,}000}{1{,}000{,}000{,}000} = \frac{.5}{1{,}000}$$

In other words, the tax rate for this district will be 50¢ per thousand dollars of property value. Translated into real world terms, the tax bill for a $200,000 house will include $100 per year for fire protection (200 × $ .50 = $100.00).

Now the tax collector can calculate the rates for all the other districts in the county in the same way. Before Measure 5, these rates were entered into the computer. The computer had been programmed earlier with all the assessed values. And years earlier each property was coded in the computer for the property tax levy districts within whose boundaries it lay. Thus it was a simple matter to turn on the computer and start producing tax bills. The computer would automatically charge each owner for the districts in which the property was located.

However, today another calculation must be made. Ballot Measure 5 limits the total amount the county can collect each year. That is, it sets a cap on the tax rate. The cap is $5 per thousand for education taxes, and $10 per thousand for general government operations. All levies subject to the education limit must be added up. If the total exceeds the $5 limit, then the levies are "compressed," that is, each district will receive less than

NOTES

its total levy. Similarly, all levies for general government operations must be added up. If they exceed the $10 limit, then they are also compressed.

If compression occurs, the amount lost to the district is taken first from any local option levies, and thereafter out of operating levies. However, levies for bonded debt are not subject to Measure 5, therefore they will not be compressed. Measure 5 excludes bonded debt because the investors who bought the bonds must be paid. If there was a chance that the government might not collect enough tax to pay the bondholders then investors would refuse to buy the bonds.

Measure 5 also mandates that all revenue lost by the schools must be made up by legislative appropriations from the state general fund. Since the largest source of general fund monies is state income taxes, Measure 5 should be seen less as a tax limitation measure, than as a tax shift measure, at least as far as schools are concerned. It shifts a large part of the burden of funding schools from local property taxes to state income taxes. It is important to note, however, that the replacement funds are apportioned to all districts throughout the state. The result is that some of the richer school districts lost funds, at the expense of poorer districts, which gained.

Tax bills are mailed during October in most counties. The bill is sent to the owner of record. It is important for real estate agents to realize that the bill does not arrive until October, but there has been a lien against the property since July 1. The Oregon tax year runs from July 1 through the following June 30, so if the owner pays the bill in full on the due date, the taxes will be paid for the period from the preceding July 1 through the coming June 30. The fact that the due dates do not coincide with the tax year is important when prorating property taxes between a buyer and a seller.

Property taxes in Oregon can be paid one-third at a time. The first third is due on or before November 15. You may pay more than one-third if you wish. If you pay at least two-thirds or more of the bill on or before November 15 you will earn a discount. For example, if you pay

All three thirds	*your discount is*	3% of the amount you pay
Two thirds	*your discount is*	2% of the amount you pay.
One third	*your discount is*	nothing

Unless prepaid, the second one third becomes due on February 15 and the last one third is due on May 15. There are no discounts after November 15, even if taxes are prepaid.

If taxes remain unpaid past November 15 they are considered ***past due***. If they remain past due, on May 16, they become ***delinquent***. Both past due and delinquent taxes accrue an interest penalty. The penalty is 1.33% per month (16% per annum) on the amount that is past due. The interest rate is the same whether the taxes are merely past due or whether they are delinquent.

When calculating an interest penalty, the interest is calculated at 1.33% per month or fraction of a month. One day is a fraction of a month, so taxes late by one day incur the same penalty as if they were late by a whole month. Take careful note that the interest penalty is charged only on the amount that is past due, not the entire bill. If an owner pays nothing on November 15, until February 15 the interest will accrue only on the first one-third of the bill. The other two thirds are not yet past due.

Becoming delinquent means that the clock starts running for foreclosure. By law, the county cannot foreclose on your property until the tax has been delinquent for three full years. Being past due does not count toward the three years, so an owner has three years from May 16 before foreclosure can commence. Even when the taxes have been delinquent for three years, the owner can rescue the property from foreclosure by paying just the oldest year's taxes and all the interest that has accrued for that year.

NOTES

If the taxes remain unpaid three years after delinquency, the tax collector will add the property to the list of properties to be foreclosed on. The following October the circuit court will enter a decree of foreclosure for non-payment of taxes. Following the decree, the owner remains vested in title and also retains a right of possession and a ***statutory right of redemption*** for two additional years. If the property is not redeemed by the end of the two-year statutory right of redemption, the sheriff will deed the property to the county. Once ownership is vested in the county, the county is free to keep the property or dispose of it, including selling it back to the former owner.

Property taxes are generally prior to all other liens, regardless of when the other liens were recorded. This means that a property tax foreclosure will extinguish any mortgage, trust deed, land sales contract, or other encumbrance on the property. Because of this, mortgage lenders take great care to be sure that the borrower pays the property taxes. A common mechanism to ensure this is to require the borrower to pay one-twelfth the projected annual property taxes along with the principal and interest each month. The lender accumulates these funds in a ***reserve account*** and uses the funds to pay the taxes for the borrower on November 15.

Exercise c

Property tax rates in Oregon are expressed in dollars of tax per ____________ dollars of assessed value. The tax rate for each tax levy district would be ____________ if the total assessed values in the district increases without a corresponding increase in the levy.

The property tax year in Oregon begins on ____________ and runs through ____________ of the following year. However, the due dates are ____________________ for the first one-third of the bill, ____________________ for the second third, and ____________ for the last third. If the bill is paid in full on or before November 15, the owner earns a ____ % discount. If the bill is not paid, then an interest penalty of _____ % per month is charged on the amount that is past due. If the taxes remain unpaid after ____________ they are considered delinquent. Property can be foreclosed on after the unpaid taxes have been delinquent for ____ years. Following foreclosure, the owner has a statutory right of redemption for __________ years, during which time the taxpayer retains ____________________ of the property. If the property is not redeemed, it is deeded to the ______________ for non-payment of taxes.

Unpaid property taxes are a lien which is ____________ to most other liens. To ensure that the property will not be foreclosed on for non-payment of taxes, mortgage lenders typically require that the borrower establish a ______________ ______________.

NOTES

Timber taxation

Timber taxation is an exceptionally complex area of property taxation. Private managed forests in Oregon comprise over 8.5 million acres. Owners of these lands have a unique problem. An owner who plants trees intends to harvest the crop decades in the future. In the meantime, the growing trees increase the value of the property and the resulting tax burden discourages owners from committing their land to tree farming. To alleviate this problem special procedures have been devised for taxation of timber.

Although the exact tax treatment of a given tree farm depends on a multitude of factors, in most cases, the land is taxed separately from the trees. The growing trees are called ***stumpage*** and are taxed at harvest through a ***severance tax***. The severance tax is collected and administered by the Department of Revenue in Salem. The Department of Revenue apportions the severance tax revenues back to the counties.

Senior citizens homestead deferral program

Oregon law provides for the ***deferral*** of taxes on a homestead owned by certain senior citizens. The taxes are deferred, not forgiven. The taxes must be paid eventually. Deferred taxes accrue interest at 6%. In reality, it is not the county which defers payment of the tax and interest. Rather, when a senior citizen elects to defer payment of homestead property taxes the Department of Revenue, using general funds of the State of Oregon, lends the funds to the owner by paying the owner's taxes to the county. When the deferred taxes and accrued interest are repaid, the repayment is to the Department of Revenue.

To qualify, the owner must be 62 years of age by April 15 of the tax year (or be a surviving spouse who will be 62 years of age by the following April 15). The property must be the personal residence of the owner, and the owner must have a fee title or be buying on a land sales contract; a life estate does not qualify. The applicant's total household income (both taxable and nontaxable) cannot exceed $32,000 for the 2001 tax year, and thereafter an amount calculated annually by the Department of Revenue as a consumer price index adjustment to the $32,000 figure. Any year the income exceeds the maximum, the taxes for the following year will not be deferred. The claim for the deferral need be filed only once.

The deferral is lost if the owner dies, sells the property, changes ownership or ceases to live permanently on the property. All deferred taxes and accrued interest must be paid when the deferral is terminated. But if the owner's income exceeds the annual limit it does not cause the entire deferred amount to become due – it just means that the taxes for that year cannot be deferred. Taxes already deferred remain deferred.

The program can be used even if the property is mortgaged or if the owners are buying on a land sales contract. However, this could create a problem, since property taxes are a prior lien. To protect the interests of lenders, the program contains a special provision. Deferred taxes are junior to all mortgages, trust deeds and land sales contracts in existence at the time the senior citizen begins the deferral. If a lien instrument is recorded after the deferral begins, it will be senior at least to the taxes accruing every July 1 thereafter.

In addition to the Senior Citizens' Homestead Deferral program, there is a special provision for deferral of payments on special assessments which are being paid in installments (e.g., Bancrofted assessments). The requirements are similar to the requirements for the deferral of taxes on the homestead, so a senior citizen who qualifies for one can usually qualify for the other as well.

NOTES

Veterans property tax exemption

Oregon law provides for exemption from taxation of part of the real market value on the homestead of an eligible veteran. In order to qualify, the veteran must have been honorably discharged and at least 40% disabled. In addition to the disability, the veteran must have served at least 90 days during World War I, World War II or the Korean War period, or if the time of the service was after 1955, the veteran must have served at least 210 days of continuous active duty. The time period is waived, however, if the veteran was unable to complete the tour of duty due to injury.

Unremarried surviving spouses can also qualify for the exemption. In the event the exemption is claimed by an unremarried surviving spouse, the veteran need not have been disabled while alive.

The amount of the exemption is $8,750 of the assessed value of the homestead. However, if the veteran's disability is service connected, then the amount of the exemption is $11,670. If the claimant is an unremarried surviving spouse, the amount is $8,750 unless the veteran was already receiving the $11,670 exemption while alive. For each tax year after 2000 the amounts of the exemption increase by 3%.

To qualify for the exemption, the veteran, or surviving spouse must file a claim with the county assessor by April 1 of the tax year. The claim must be renewed each year.

Personal property taxation

Certain categories of personal property are subject to taxation in Oregon. These include tangible personal property held for the production of income, floating homes, and certain manufactured housing (mobile homes). Tangible personal property held for the production of income (trade or business property) specifically excludes inventory and materials to be consumed in the course of business as well as certain other categories. Taxable trade or business property usually consists of furniture, fixtures and equipment.

The assessment and taxation of manufactured housing follows the same procedures as for the assessment of real property when it is classified as real property. However, floating homes are taxed as personal property, as are manufactured housing (mobile homes) in some cases. For manufactured housing the distinction lies in ownership of the land. If the owner of the manufactured dwelling also owns the land on which the manufactured dwelling is situated, then the manufactured dwelling and the land are both taxed as real property. If the owner is renting or leasing the land on which the manufactured dwelling is situated, the manufactured dwelling is taxed as personal property. The reason for taxing manufactured housing as personal property when the owner does not own the land on which it is situated is simply because it has no fixity. If the owner of a manufactured dwelling owns land as well, the taxes can always be collected from the land, so we can give the owner the more liberal collection procedures of real property taxation (see below).

Trade or business property is assessed in a different manner than real property. Regardless of the value of the personal property the owner of trade or business personal property is required to file a ***personal property tax return*** in the spring of each year. The return must list all the personal property together with the owner's estimate of its real market value. This amount is then entered on the tax rolls for the tax levy districts in which the ordinary address where the personal property is kept. The assessor can accept the amount on the owner's return, or can change it. If the value of the personal property is determined to be $12,500 or less, it is exempt from taxation. Note that a return must be filed regardless of the owner's estimate of its value.

NOTES

Regardless of how the assessed value is derived, the owner can appeal the value to the Board of Property Tax Appeals, and thereafter all the way to the Oregon Supreme Court, the same as for real property.

Tax collection procedures for personal property taxes are very different from real property. The due dates, discounts for early payment, and interest charges for late payment are the same as for real property taxes. However, the personal property tax year runs from January 1 through December 31. Also, the collection of taxes remaining unpaid after the due date is very different. Unpaid personal property taxes become delinquent on November 16 – there is no "past due" period before delinquency. And when unpaid personal property taxes become delinquent, the personal property becomes subject to immediate seizure and sale. As an alternative to seizure and sale, the tax collector can file suit against the owner of the personal property and obtain a general judgment. Or the tax collector can simply add the bill for the unpaid personal property taxes to the tax bill for any real property owned by the same taxpayer in the same county. Note that collection procedures are faster for personal property taxes than for real property taxes. The reason, of course, lies in the fixity of the real estate compared to the mobility of the personal property.

Exercise d

Growing timber is called ____________________ and usually not taxed until it is harvested at which time a ____________________ tax is levied.

Senior citizens may defer the tax on their ____________________ if they are _____ years of age, or a surviving spouse _____ years of age. Deferred taxes accrue interest at ____ % until paid. The deferred taxes must be paid if the property is ______________, if the owner dies, or if the property ceases to be the owner's ____________________. The owners must have a ________ title or be buying on a land sales contract. A ___________ _______________ does not qualify.

Disabled veterans may qualify for an exemption of a portion of the ________________ value of their home. The amount of the exemption is more if the disability was ________________ - ____________________. The veteran must be at least _____ % disabled and be ____________________ ____________________. An ____________________ ____________________ ______________ of a deceased veteran is also eligible, in which case the veteran need not have been disabled while alive.

Personal property held for the production of __________________ is taxed in Oregon. Manufactured housing and floating homes are also taxed as ____________________ property, although manufactured housing which is situated on land owned by the owner of the manufactured housing is taxed as ______________ property. The personal property lien date is ____________________ and the assessment date is ____________________. The delinquency date for personal property taxes is ______________________.

KEY TERMS

The key to understanding any new field is the vocabulary used in that field. To maximize your comprehension of the material presented in this chapter, be sure you know the meaning and significance of the following terms. Remember that the majority of test questions primarily test knowledge of vocabulary.

Ad valorem
Assessed value
Assessment
Assessment date
Assessment ratio
Bancroft Bonding Act
Board of Property Tax Appeals
Bond issue
Deferral
Delinquent
Exception
Levy
Local option levy
Magistrate Division
Maintenance changes
Maximum assessed value
Millage rate
Mills
Oregon Tax Court
Past due
Permanent rate authority
Personal property tax return
Proration of tax
Real market value
Reserve account
Revenue bonds
Serial levy
Severance tax
Small Claims Division
Special assessment
Statutory right of redemption
Stumpage
Tax collector
Tax levy district
Tax maintenance districts
Tax rate
Trending
Trending changes

ANSWERS

To chapter exercises. If you couldn't figure out what to put in the blanks, find the answer here!

Exercise a

A government unit which levies property taxes is called a tax LEVY DISTRICT. *Each year the elected officials of each district create a tax* LEVY, *which must be within their* PERMANENT RATE AUTHORITY *A* SERIAL *levy is an example of a temporary tax levy to fund a special project. Today, these are called* LOCAL OPTION LEVIES. *Capital improvements are frequently paid for by a* BOND *issue. When the income from the project will be used to pay off the* BONDS, *they are called* REVENUE BONDS.

When improvements benefit only specific properties, it is common for the city or county to levy a SPECIAL ASSESSMENT *against the affected properties. The owner can elect to pay this in installments under the provisions of the* BANCROFT *Bonding Act.*

Exercise b

When we say that property taxes are levied AD VALOREM *we mean that they are levied according to value. Tax bills are based on the* ASSESSED VALUE*, which is the lower of the* MAXIMUM ASSESSED VALUE *and the* REAL MARKET VALUE*. The assessor appraises all property as of* JANUARY 1*, which is called the* ASSESSMENT DATE*. A* MAINTENANCE *adjustment is made once every* 6 *years to the value of all taxable property in Oregon. In the intervening five years, values are maintained by* TRENDING*. Property value appeals must be filed first with the* BOARD *of* PROPERTY TAX APPEALS*. Further appeals can be made to the* MAGISTRATE DIVISION *of the Oregon* TAX COURT *or to the Small Claims Division. If the property is damaged during the tax year, the owner may be eligible for a* PRORATION *of the tax due for the year. If the property is improved, there may be an* EXCEPTION*, which can raise the assessed value.*

Exercise c

Property tax rates in Oregon are expressed in dollars of tax per $1,000 *dollars of assessed value. The tax rate for each tax levy district would be* LOWER *if the total assessed values in the district increases without a corresponding increase in the levy.*

The property tax year in Oregon begins on JULY 1 *and runs through* JUNE 30 *of the following year. However, the due dates are* NOVEMBER 15 *for the first one-third of the bill,* FEBRUARY 15 *for the second third, and* MAY 15 *for the last third. If the bill is paid in full on or before November 15, the owner earns a* 3 *% discount. If the bill is not paid, then an interest penalty of* 1⅓ *% per month is charged on the amount that is past due. If the taxes remain unpaid after* MAY 15 *they are considered delinquent. Property can be foreclosed on after the unpaid taxes have been delinquent for* 3 *years. Following foreclosure, the owner has a statutory right of redemption for* TWO *years, during which time the taxpayer retains* POSSESSION *of the property. If the property is not redeemed, it is deeded to the* COUNTY *for non-payment of taxes.*

Unpaid property taxes are a lien which is PRIOR *to most other liens. To ensure that the property will not be foreclosed on for non-payment of taxes, mortgage lenders typically require that the borrower establish a* RESERVE ACCOUNT.

Exercise d

Growing timber is called STUMPAGE *and usually not taxed until it is harvested at which time a* SEVERANCE *tax is levied.*

Senior citizens may defer the tax on their HOMESTEAD *if they are* 62 *years of age, or a surviving spouse* 62 *years of age. Deferred taxes accrue interest at* 6 *% until paid. The deferred taxes must be paid if the property is* SOLD*, if the owner dies, or if the property ceases to be the owner's* HOMESTEAD*. The owners must have a* FEE *title or be buying on a land sales contract. A* LIFE ESTATE *does not qualify.*

Disabled veterans may qualify for an exemption of a portion of the ASSESSED *value of their home. The amount of the exemption is more if the disability was* SERVICE - CONNECTED*. The veteran must be at least* 40 *% disabled and be* HONORABLY DISCHARGED*. An* UNREMARRIED SURVIVING SPOUSE *of a deceased veteran is also eligible, in which case the veteran need not have been disabled while alive.*

Personal property held for the production of INCOME *is taxed in Oregon. Manufactured housing and floating homes are also taxed as* PERSONAL *property, although manufactured housing which is situated on land owned by the owner of the manufactured housing is taxed as* REAL *property. The personal property lien date is* JANUARY 1 *and the assessment date is* JANUARY 1*. The delinquency date for personal property taxes is* NOVEMBER 16.

PRACTICE QUESTIONS

The following practice questions are representative of the questions you will find on the final examination and on the licensing examinations given by the Oregon Real Estate Agency.

1. Property taxes are the major source of income for
   (A) the federal government.
   (B) state governments.
   (C) local governments.
   (D) public utilities.

2. Which of the following would be primarily funded by property taxes?
   (A) State highways
   (B) Public welfare
   (C) Unemployment compensation
   (D) School districts

3. Property taxes are
   I. levied ad valorem.
   II. a lien against the property until paid.
   (A) I only
   (B) II only
   (C) Both I and II
   (D) Neither I nor II

4. Select from the following the most correct meaning of the phrase "ad valorem."
   (A) A property tax
   (B) According to value
   (C) Value received, as in consideration
   (D) A unit tax

5. A property tax lien is
   (A) a general lien.
   (B) a voluntary lien.
   (C) a government lien.
   (D) all of the above.

6. Taxes on real property in Oregon become a lien on
   (A) January 1, the day of assessment.
   (B) February 15 of the year following assessment.
   (C) July 1 of the year of assessment.
   (D) November 16, the day following the due date of the first installment payment.

7. If taxes on real property in Oregon become delinquent and remain unpaid, they constitute an involuntary lien on the property that is
   (A) inferior to all voluntary liens.
   (B) inferior to a mechanic's lien.
   (C) superior only to liens recorded after the tax lien
   (D) superior to all other liens.

8. With certain exceptions a property tax lien has priority over other interests in real property
   (A) according to the date they were recorded
   (B) regardless of when they were recorded.
   (C) based on when the tax law was passed.
   (D) only if the property owner agrees to assume the obligations.

9. For ad valorem purposes, real property taxes first become a lien as of
   (A) January 1.
   (B) May 16.
   (C) July 1.
   (D) November 15.

10. The tax year for real property in Oregon is from
    (A) January 1 through the following December 31.
    (B) July 1 through the following June 30.
    (C) October 1 through the following September 30.
    (D) November 16 through the following November 15.

11. When a tax district establishes a levy for the year, this becomes
    (A) an immediate levy on all non-exempt property in the district.
    (B) an immediate assessment on all non-exempt property in the district,
    (C) an immediate lien on all non-exempt property in the district.
    (D) a lien as of July 1 of the tax year.

12. Payment of an owner's tax bill is due on or before
    (A) January 1.
    (B) May 15.
    (C) July 1.
    (D) November 15.

13. The first one-third of an annual real property tax bill becomes delinquent on
(A) January 1.
(B) February 16.
(C) May 16.
(D) November 16.

14. The second installment on a property tax bill is due not later than
(A) January 1.
(B) February 15.
(C) May 15.
(D) July 1.

15. If you fail to keep up your real property tax payments,
I. the unpaid amount is delinquent on July 1.
II. two years after the taxes become delinquent, the property is subject to foreclosure.
(A) I only
(B) II only
(C) Both I and II
(D) Neither I nor II

16. Tax foreclosure of real property can occur
(A) three years after the earliest delinquency.
(B) four years after the earliest delinquency.
(C) three years after the lien date.
(D) four years after the lien date.

17. Following foreclosure for non-payment of taxes, there is a statutory right of redemption. The right of redemption is for
(A) ten days.
(B) 180 days.
(C) one year.
(D) two years.

18. In the foreclosure by the county of real property because of non-payment of taxes, who has the right of possession during the statutory period of redemption?
(A) The delinquent taxpayer
(B) The county
(C) The sheriff
(D) The buyer at public auction

19. Following foreclosure of real property due to non-payment of property taxes and during the statutory redemption period, Oregon law
(A) allows the taxpayer to live there for the whole period undisturbed.
(B) requires the taxpayer to vacate the property at the time of the sale.
(C) relieves the taxpayer of the liability for taxes after foreclosure.
(D) provides for none of the above.

20. Upon foreclosure of property by the county for delinquent taxes, there is a statutory period of time during which the delinquent taxpayer
(A) must vacate the property.
(B) must pay rent to the state.
(C) is under no liability for further tax payments if he or she wishes to redeem.
(D) can continue in undisturbed possession of the property.

21. After real estate has been foreclosed on by the county because of a delinquent real estate tax lien, the owner has a right to
(A) set a minimum sales price for the sheriff's sale.
(B) remain in possession indefinitely.
(C) redeem the property within the statutory redemption period.
(D) have the sale canceled.

22. If foreclosure proceedings are begun because of delinquent taxes, the taxpayer's real property can be removed from the foreclosure list by
I. filing reasons within 60 days why this property should not be on the list.
II. paying full tax and interest for the year causing foreclosure.
(A) I only
(B) II only
(C) Both I and II
(D) Neither I nor II

23. Lotta Thunderham bought a house and the taxes were paid in full through June 30, 2003 at closing. If she never pays any taxes, on what date can the county commence foreclosure proceedings?
(A) May 16 one year later
(B) May 16 two years later
(C) May 16 three years later
(D) May 16 four years later

24. Ida Padit owned a house on which she did not pay any taxes until eventually a foreclosure order was entered. Following the foreclosure there is a statutory right of redemption. During this time, who is entitled to possession?
(A) Ida Padit
(B) The county
(C) The buyer at the public auction sale
(D) The sheriff

25. If the county has already begun foreclosure proceedings, the owner can halt the proceedings by
    I. filing a hardship claim with the tax collector within 60 days.
    II. paying the oldest year's taxes and all the interest which has accrued for it.
    (A) I only
    (B) II only
    (C) Both I and II
    (D) Neither I nor II

26. Each year the county tax assessor determines the
    I. portion of the total tax levy that will be paid by each property owner.
    II. tax rate for each tax levy district.
    (A) I only
    (B) II only
    (C) Both I and II
    (D) Neither I nor II

27. A valuation of property by a local official for tax purposes is best described as
    (A) an assessment.
    (B) an appraisal of land only.
    (C) a market appraisal.
    (D) a reproduction cost appraisal.

28. According to Oregon law, the assessed valuation of real property is based upon the
    (A) cash value less encumbrances.
    (B) real market value of the property.
    (C) front footage plus cost of improvements.
    (D) square footage of the land.

29. The property tax bill the owner receives in October is based on the value of the property
    (A) as of January 1.
    (B) as of May 15.
    (C) during the tax year.
    (D) as of July 1.

30. In Oregon an ad valorem tax is based on the
    (A) real market value.
    (B) assessed value.
    (C) most recent sales price.
    (D) amount of the levy.

31. Property tax assessments are based on the
    (A) purchase price.
    (B) real market value.
    (C) intrinsic value of the property.
    (D) average value in the neighborhood.

32. Local assessment of property for tax purposes must be at
    (A) loan value plus down payment.
    (B) market value.
    (C) 90% of real market value.
    (D) the value of the land only.

33. Property tax appraisals must be made at least once every
    (A) year.
    (B) three years.
    (C) four years.
    (D) six years.

34. Real property in Oregon must be reappraised for tax purposes
    (A) every year.
    (B) if it goes up in value more than 5%.
    (C) whenever it is sold.
    (D) at least every six years.

35. All property in the county is reassessed every year. Usually the assessment is changed by computer analysis. This process is called
    (A) the tax levy.
    (B) trending.
    (C) assessment.
    (D) revenue sharing.

36. Taxes on personal residences in Oregon are calculated by assessing the land and improvements
    (A) separately, then applying a different tax rate to each.
    (B) separately, then applying the same tax rate to each.
    (C) together, then applying one tax rate to the entire valuation.
    (D) separately, then applying the same or a different rate to each depending on whether the home is a condominium or not.

37. If there is a disagreement concerning the assessed value of real property, the burden of proof is upon the
    (A) assessor.
    (B) taxpayer.
    (C) Board of Property Tax Appeals.
    (D) State.

38. If you are not satisfied with the amount of your property tax assessment, what recourse do you have?
(A) Appeal to the county Board of Property Tax Appeals
(B) Appeal to the Superior Court
(C) Appeal to the County Commissioners
(D) None

39. If an owner of real property in Oregon believes the real market value placed on his or her property by the county assessor is too high, the owner should be aware that the burden of proof in determining the valuation of the property rests on the
(A) fee appraiser appointed by the Oregon tax court.
(B) taxpayer alone.
(C) Oregon Department of Revenue.
(D) county Board of Property Tax Appeals.

40. When a taxpayer appeals a property tax assessment, the burden of proof falls on the
(A) county tax collector.
(B) county tax assessor.
(C) property owner.
(D) Department of Revenue.

41. Sally Saltz owned a house near the docks in Sailor Flats, Oregon. She appealed her tax assessment to the Magistrate Division of the Oregon Tax Court and lost. She may
(A) appeal the decision to the Oregon Department of Revenue.
(B) appeal the decision to the county Board of Property Tax Appeals.
(C) appeal the decision to the regular session of the Oregon Tax Court.
(D) do nothing.

42. Violet Rose is a senior citizen who owns her own home. She may defer her property taxes
(A) if she has a fee title or life estate in the property.
(B) only if she was at one time married.
(C) if she is 62 years old or older by March 15 of the year in which she files for the deferral.
(D) even though she takes in paying boarders. Renters Roommates

43. The property taxes of an Oregon homeowner aged 62 or over who lives on the property may be
(A) deferred until the owner dies, or sells the property.
(B) reduced by 25% if the owner or spouse sustains physical disability rated in excess of 50%.
(C) reduced by 50% if the owner or spouse is blind.
(D) canceled altogether if the breadwinner is blind or has sustained a physical disability rated in excess of 50 percent.

44. In order to qualify for the Senior Citizens Homestead Property Tax Deferral Program, you must be
(A) 62 years of age.
(B) 63 years of age.
(C) 65 years of age.
(D) 70 years of age.

45. A man and wife own their home and have deferred the property taxes under the Senior Citizens Property Tax Deferral Program. If either should die, how old would the survivor have to be in order to continue the deferral?
(A) 55 years old
(B) 59½ years old
(C) 62 years old
(D) There is no age requirement for surviving spouses to continue the deferral.

46. Under Oregon's Senior Citizen Tax Deferral Program, Beverly Poole may defer payment of her property taxes on her homestead
(A) if she has a freehold interest or life estate in the property.
(B) only if her husband is 65 years old by April 15 of the year in which she files application for the deferral.
(C) if she is 62 years old by April 15 of the year in which she files application.
(D) regardless of the amount of her household income.

47. Senior citizen's property tax deferral comes to an end and the deferred taxes plus 6% interest must be paid
I. when the taxpayer receiving the deferral dies unless the surviving spouse continues the deferral.
II. upon ownership change or residence change.
(A) I only
(B) II only
(C) Both I and II
(D) Neither I nor II

48. The property taxes on the homestead of an Oregon senior citizen can be
(A) deferred until the owner's death or sale of the property.
(B) reduced by 30% if the owner suffers a physical disability in excess of 30%.
(C) reduced by 50% if the owner is legally deaf or blind.
(D) canceled if the owner is both legally deaf and legally blind.

49. A widow is 70 years old and owns her own home. She can qualify for the Senior Citizens Property Tax Deferral Program if she
(A) has a fee title to the property.
(B) is buying on a recorded land sales contract.
(C) has a recorded life estate in the property.
(D) has either a fee title or is buying on a recorded land sales contract.

50. To qualify for a veteran's property tax exemption, a veteran
I. must own the property free and clear of any encumbrance.
II. must reside on the property.
(A) I only
(B) II only
(C) Both I and II
(D) Neither I nor II

51. To establish eligibility for the Veterans Property Tax Exemption, the claimant must be
(A) certified as being at least 40% or more disabled.
(B) honorably discharged.
(C) an unremarried surviving spouse of a deceased veteran.
(D) either both A and B, or C only.

52. To qualify for the Veterans Property Tax Exemption, a veteran in Oregon must
I. obtain proof of his or her age.
II. reside on the property.
III. be 40% or more disabled.
(A) I and II only
(B) I, II and III
(C) I and III only
(D) II and III only

53. The last day a veteran can file for a property tax exemption is
(A) January 1.
(B) April 1.
(C) May 16.
(D) November 15.

54. Eligible veterans and their surviving spouses are entitled to exempt a certain portion of their homestead property's real market value from property taxation. Under this law a disabled veteran may exempt
(A) the first $5,000 or $7,000 of real market value.
(B) the first $8,750 of assessed value, or $11,670 if 40% or more disabled, plus 3% from the 2000 tax year.
(C) 55% of real market value.
(D) 89% of real market value.

55. Deferral of property taxes is possible for
(A) a home owned by an eligible veteran.
(B) a home owned by a senior citizen.
(C) low-income housing.
(D) all of the above.

56. A charge against a property owner to cover the proportionate cost of a street paving is referred to as
(A) an ad valorem tax.
(B) a special assessment.
(C) a county tax.
(D) an equitable obligation.

57. Charges levied by a local government to finance street paving are
(A) excess condemnations.
(B) ad valorem taxes.
(C) zoning charges.
(D) assessments.

58. The charge imposed for paving of a road is called
(A) an assignment.
(B) a special assessment.
(C) an encroachment.
(D) a mortgage.

59. What is the usual way to finance a new sewer line installation in a neighborhood?
(A) Excise tax
(B) Special assessment
(C) Real property tax
(D) Utility charge

60. A special assessment becomes a lien on real property
(A) whenever payments are two or more installments in arrears.
(B) at the time the improvement is completed.
(C) at the time the amount is determined and set.
(D) 60 days after completion of the work.

61. Oregon law permits property owners to pay special assessments for local improvements, such as sidewalks, in
I. a lump sum.
II. payments plus interest on the unpaid balance.
(A) I only
(B) II only
(C) Both I and II
(D) Neither I nor II

62. The Bancroft Bonding Act provides that payments for special assessments
(A) are not due until the property is sold.
(B) may be made in installments.
(C) must be made prior to completion of the improvement.
(D) None of the above is correct.

63. Which of the following concerning assessments covered by the Bancroft Bonding Act is true?
I. Property owners must make an application to take advantage of the Act.
II. The assessment will not appear as a lien against the property if the owner takes advantage of the Act.
(A) I only
(B) II only
(C) Both I and II
(D) Neither I nor II

64. The Bancroft Bonding Act which allows property owners to pay assessment in installments covers which of the following improvements?
I. Sidewalks
II. Curbs
III. Sewers
(A) I only
(B) I and II only
(C) II and III only
(D) I, II and III

65. A Bancrofted special assessment can be amortized over as long as
(A) ten years.
(B) 15 years.
(C) 20 years.
(D) 30 years.

66. The lien date for personal property taxes is
(A) January 1.
(B) May 15.
(C) July 1.
(D) November 15.

67. Personal property taxes become delinquent on
(A) January 1.
(B) May 16.
(C) July 1.
(D) November 16.

68. Personal property taxes are due on
(A) receipt of the bill.
(B) January 1.
(C) August 15.
(D) November 15.

69. A mobile home used as a residence is assessed as personal property when the land under it is owned by
I. the owner of the mobile home.
II. someone other than the owner of the mobile home.
(A) I only
(B) II only
(C) Both I and II
(D) Neither I nor II

70. Which of the following would be considered real property for purposes of property taxes?
I. A mobile home on land rented by the owner of the mobile home
II. A mobile home on land owned by the owner of the mobile home
(A) I only
(B) II only
(C) Both I and II
(D) Neither I nor II

71. If an owner of personal property which is subject to taxation does not pay the tax, the county can
(A) seize the personal property.
(B) obtain a judgment against the owner.
(C) place a lien for the unpaid taxes against any real property in the same county owned by the owner of the personal property.
(D) do any of the above.

72. Fritz Futzputtle owns taxable personal property. The property may be seized and sold
(A) immediately after the tax due on it becomes delinquent.
(B) three years after the tax due on it becomes delinquent.
(C) any time after the January 1st next following the due date of the unpaid taxes.
(D) any time after the lien date had passed and the taxes remain unpaid.

73. Which of the following would be subject to property taxes?
(A) Desks and chairs in a real estate office
(B) Ranges and refrigerators in an apartment building
(C) Shares of stock in a real estate investment company
(D) Both A and B

74. Property owners who complain that property taxes are generally too high should take a look at the
(A) real market values of all property.
(B) budgets.
(C) property tax assessments.
(D) tax collection procedures.

75. The city of Cascade, Oregon has a total income from property taxes of $3,692,000 and two cents of every dollar is spent on libraries and museums. The amount spent for libraries and museums would be
(A) $73,840.
(B) $110,760.
(C) $369,200.
(D) $738,400.

76. The tax rate for each tax levy district is determined by dividing the
(A) total number of properties in the district by the amount of tax money needed.
(B) amount of tax money needed by the number of properties in the district.
(C) total of all assessed values in the district by the amount of the district's levy.
(D) amount of tax money needed by the total of all assessed values in the district.

77. Tax rates are determined by the
(A) county commissioners.
(B) tax collector.
(C) tax assessor.
(D) Board of Property Tax Appeals.

78. You own property in National City, Oregon which is assessed at $180,000. The assessed value of all property in National City is $45 billion. If the annual tax levy for National City is $28.125 million, how much will your tax bill be?
(A) $1,100
(B) $1,125
(C) $1,800
(D) $2,250

79. The community of Rogueville Heights, Oregon has tax rates per thousand dollars of value of $2 for police and fire protection, $0.50 for the community college and $4.50 for the public schools. The county also charges a tax rate of $7 per thousand. What would be the tax bill for a property valued at $200,000 if the assessment is 180,000?
(A) $2,444
(B) $2,520
(C) $2,716
(D) $2,800

80. Jim Dan Dee received a notice that his tax assessment would remain unchanged. Shortly thereafter he read in the paper that the local tax rate would go up by 50¢ per thousand because of a bond issue. He can expect that his total bill would be
(A) unaffected.
(B) lowered.
(C) raised.
(D) exempted.

81. Nancy Drew owns a condominium which is assessed at $135,000. The tax rate is $15 per thousand. To the nearest dollar, what will she have to pay if she pays in full on November 15?
(A) $1,964
(B) $2,025
(C) $4,050
(D) The amount cannot be calculated without the real market value.

82. Joe Hardy owns a house whose real market value is $220,000. The tax rate in his area is $14 per thousand. If he pays the bill in full on February 16, how much will he pay?
(A) $2,987.60
(B) $3,055.97
(C) $3,080.00
(D) $3,148.37

83. The property tax bill on a property is $1,850. If paid in full on November 12, the owner will pay
(A) $598.
(B) $1,795.
(C) $1,850.
(D) $1,906.

84. A property had a tax assessment of $264,000. The tax rate is $16.50 per thousand, including local bonded debt. If the taxes are paid in full before the due date, the owner will pay
(A) $1,408.
(B) $4,225.
(C) $4,356.
(D) $4,487.

85. An industrial property had a real market value according to the tax assessor of $855,000. It was assessed at $598,500 and the tax rate was $14 per thousand. The tax bill was
(A) $8,128.
(B) $8,379.
(C) $11,611.
(D) $11,970.

86. A property was assessed at $240,000. The tax rate was $14 per thousand and there was a 3% discount for promptness. What was the amount paid if the taxes were paid in full three months after the due date and there is an interest penalty of 16% per annum?
(A) $3,259 (C) $3,390
(B) $3,360 (D) $3,405

87. Percy Hockfarthing owned a parcel whose tax bill last year was $1,505. His tax rate was $14.75 per thousand. The assessment is 72% of the real market value. What was the real market value?
(A) $88,795 (C) $141,700
(B) $102,000 (D) $216,720

88. Ima Thrumpmorton's home was valued at $224,000 for ad valorem tax purposes. The assessment rate was 90%. If she paid monthly taxes of $240, her tax rate per thousand of assessed value was
(A) $10.72. (C) $14.29.
(B) $11.90. (D) $21.00.

89. When prorating real property taxes between a buyer and a seller we use the date of
(A) January 1. (C) July 1.
(B) May 16. (D) November 15.

90. When prorating taxes in a sale, you should remember that
I. the tax year for real property taxes runs from July 1 through June 30 of the following year.
II. the tax year for personal property taxes runs from July 1 through June 30 of the following year.
III. taxes are prorated using November 15 as the start of the tax year.
(A) I only (C) I and III only
(B) I and II only (D) II and III only

91. Frank Scott owed $1,600 in property taxes on his home for the fiscal. If Scott paid his tax bill in full on November 12, he would have paid
(A) $1,552. (C) $1,600.
(B) $1,568. (D) $1,616.

92. The assessed value of all property in Wheeler County is $34 billion. The county tax levy is $455 million. Your property in Wheeler County is assessed at $270,000. What taxes will you pay?
(A) $655.10 (C) $2,597.00
(B) $2,151.00 (D) $3,613.24

93. If a property is assessed at $174,000 and the tax rate is $14 per $1,000 of assessed value, how much will the taxes be to the nearest dollar?
(A) $805 (C) $2,139
(B) $1,243 (D) $2,436

94. In the town of Wilderville, the tax rates per $1,000 of assessed value are: Schools , $4.75; community college, $1.50; city, $4.00 and county $3.00. How much are the taxes on a property worth $111,000, assessed at 80% of its real market value?
(A) $556.40 (C) $1,176.60
(B) $865.20 (D) $1,694.00

95. A property is assessed at $192,000. The tax rate is $13 per $1,000 with a 3% discount for promptness and a 12% per annum charge for delinquency. Determine the amount owed if taxes are paid three months after the due date.
(A) $2,520.96 (C) $3,520.83
(B) $3,193.05 (D) $3,620.96

96. The taxes on a property were $2,305.50. The tax rate is $14.50 per $1,000 of assessed value. Property is assessed at 75% of the real market value. The real market value of the property is approximately
(A) $159,000. (C) $209,500.
(B) $200,000. (D) $212,000.

97. The total tax on a home was $2,268.50, and the tax rate was $13.90 per $1,000 of assessed valuation. Taxes are assessed at 96% of appraised value. What is the appraised value of the home?
(A) $131,200 (C) $163,200
(B) $144,800 (D) $170,000

98. The assessed value of all property in Smithville is $12 billion. The city budget is $156 million. Your property is assessed at $160,000. How much do you have to pay in property taxes, if you are taxed on a pro-rata basis?
(A) $1,662.50 (C) $2,080.00
(B) $1,997.50 (D) $2,262.50

ANSWERS

To practice questions. If you chose the wrong letter, here's the right one! The explanations are designed to clarify your understanding.

1. **C** Property taxes are reserved to the states. In Oregon, property taxes have always been used strictly for city and county purposes, especially school districts, for whom they are the single largest source of revenue.
2. **D** Schools account for approximately one-third to one-half the total property tax levy. The rest of the tax bill is used for city and county operations.
3. **C** Property is taxed according to the assessed value. "Ad valorem" is Latin for "according to value." The purpose of levying taxes ad valorem is to apportion the total levy among all property owners in the district. Real property taxes become a lien as of July 1 each year.
4. **B** "Ad valorem" is Latin for "according to value."
5. **C** General liens are liens which reach all property owned by the debtor, such as a judgment. Property tax liens are not general liens because failure to pay real property taxes cannot affect any property other than the property on which the taxes were not paid. Voluntary liens are liens which the debtor agreed to, such as a mortgage.
6. **C** The lien date for real property taxes in Oregon is July 1, and the tax year runs from July 1 through June 30 of the following year. November 15 is the due date for the first one-third, and May 16 is the delinquency date.
7. **D** The normal priority date of an encumbrance is the date it was created, which is generally the recording date. With a few exceptions, property tax liens are ahead of all other liens, including IRS levies, construction liens, judgments and all private financing, regardless of the date when the other lien was created. "Mechanic's lien" is an older term for "construction lien."
8. **B** The normal priority date of an encumbrance is the date it was created, which is generally the recording date. With a few exceptions, property tax liens are ahead of all other liens, including IRS levies, construction liens, judgments and all private financing, regardless of the date when the other lien was created.
9. **C** The lien date for real property taxes in Oregon is July 1, and the tax year runs from July 1 through June 30 of the following year. November 15 is the due date for the first one-third, and May 16 is the delinquency date.
10. **B** The lien date for real property taxes in Oregon is July 1, and the tax year runs from July 1 through June 30 of the following year. November 15 is the due date for the first one-third of the tax bill, and the last day on which to earn a discount.
11. **D** Each tax levy district prepares a budget for its operations during the coming year. The budget is prepared in the spring. When the budget has been approved, it is called a levy. As of July 1, the levy becomes a lien on each property in the district.
12. **D** July 1 is the lien date. The first one-third of the bill is due on November 15, the second one-third is due on February 15, and the final one-third is due on May 15. Taxes unpaid after May 15 are delinquent.
13. **C** The first one-third of the tax bill is due on November 15 and thereafter becomes past due, not delinquent. The same is true for the second third, which is due by February 15. The final third is due May 15 and any portion of the unpaid bill becomes delinquent thereafter. Therefore we say the delinquency date is May 16.
14. **B** The first one-third of the bill is due on November 15, the second one-third is due on February 15, and the final one-third is due on May 15. Taxes unpaid after May 15 are delinquent.
15. **D** The lien date for real property taxes is July 1, and the tax year runs from July 1 through June 30 of the following year. November 15 is the due date for the first one-third of the tax bill, and the last day on which to earn a discount. If the first one-third is not paid by November 15, it becomes past due. The due date for the second one-third is February 15, and for the last one-third is May 15. After May 15, the entire bill is now due, and is considered delinquent, not merely past due. Unpaid taxes make the property subject to foreclosure after they have been delinquent for three years.
16. **A** Oregon law provides that foreclosure cannot begin until the property taxes are delinquent for

three years. This will occur on a May 16, because that is the delinquency date (the date unpaid taxes first became delinquent).

17. **D** Foreclosure follows three years of delinquency. The owner (taxpayer) has the right to redeem the property if the tax bill is paid in full, even after foreclosure. This is called the statutory right of redemption. In Oregon it is two years from the date the foreclosure is entered.

18. **A** Oregon law provides a two-year statutory right of redemption following order of foreclosure for non-payment of property taxes, during which time the taxpayer is entitled to retain possession.

19. **A** Oregon law provides that foreclosure cannot begin until the property taxes are delinquent for three years. This will occur on a May 16, because that is the delinquency date (the date unpaid taxes first became delinquent). Following the three years of delinquency, the notice of foreclosure will be published, and a few months later the county circuit court will enter an order of foreclosure for non-payment of taxes. From the time of foreclosure, the taxpayer has a two-year statutory right of redemption, during which time the taxpayer is entitled to retain possession. In order to redeem, the taxpayer must pay up all the unpaid taxes and interest, including all taxes that have accrued after foreclosure. Taxes are a lien on the real property only, not a personal obligation of the owner.

20. **D** Foreclosure cannot begin until the property taxes are delinquent for three years. This will occur on a May 16, because that is the delinquency date (the date unpaid taxes first became delinquent). Following the three years of delinquency, the notice of foreclosure will be published, and a few months later the county circuit court will enter an order of foreclosure for non-payment of taxes. From the time of foreclosure, the taxpayer has a two-year statutory right of redemption, during which time the taxpayer is entitled to retain possession. In order to redeem, the taxpayer must pay up all the unpaid taxes and interest, including all taxes that have accrued after foreclosure.

21. **C** Following three years of delinquency, a notice of foreclosure will be published, and a few months later the county circuit court will enter an order of foreclosure for non-payment of taxes. From the time of foreclosure, the taxpayer has a two-year statutory right of redemption, during which time the taxpayer is entitled to retain possession. In order to redeem, the taxpayer must pay up all the unpaid taxes and interest, including all taxes that have accrued after foreclosure. If the taxpayer does not redeem within the two years, the sheriff deeds the property to the county. Once the county owns the property it can do anything it wishes with it. There is no automatic sheriff's sale, as there would be with a mortgage foreclosure.

22. **B** Property can be foreclosed on for non-payment of property taxes after they have been delinquent for three years. Oregon statutes do not give the government authority to grant exceptions because of the taxpayer's personal problems and there are no provisions for filing reasons to remove the property from the list. However, if all the tax and interest for the oldest year is paid before the foreclosure, then there will be only two years of delinquent taxes and they cannot foreclose for another year.

23. **D** The property taxes that were paid through June 30 were due on November 15 of the previous year. Therefore, the next due date will be November 15 of the year in which the purchase occurred. These taxes will become delinquent on May 16 of the following year. They will be subject to foreclosure on May 16 three years later.

24. **A** In most foreclosure cases, the foreclosure is followed by a public auction of the property. The successful bidder at the auction sale is entitled to possession of the property immediately, even if there is a redemption period. In real property tax foreclosures, however, the taxpayer retains the right of possession during the redemption period.

25. **D** Since foreclosure cannot begin until the property taxes have been delinquent for three years, a taxpayer can keep the property off the foreclosure rolls just by paying the oldest year and all the interest which has accrued for it not later than May 15 of the third year following delinquency. There are no provisions in property tax laws for deferral of foreclosure proceedings because of hardship. However, once the county owns the property they can do with it as they will, including selling the property back to the owner, in which case, the terms can be as liberal as the county wishes.

26. **C** The amount of any given tax bill is determined by the assessed value of the property and by the amounts of the levies of all the tax levy districts in which the property lies, although the final bill may be lowered in some areas by the effects of Measures 5 and 50. The assessment process is to apportion the total tax burden for each tax levy district fairly among all property owners in the district according

to the value of their properties. Therefore, the tax assessor determines the amount of each owner's share of the total levy. The tax assessor also determines the tax rate by making sure the total of the rates for all districts on a given tax bill do not exceed the limits of Measure 5, and compressing the rates if they do.

27. **A** There are many kinds of value. Even the term "market value" has various meanings. All taxable real property in Oregon must be appraised for its "real market value." The owner pays taxes on the lower of the real market value or the maximum assessed value. The portion which is taxed is called the "assessed value." Therefore, it would be most appropriate to call a property tax valuation an "assessment." To reflect this fact, the official in each county who values property for tax purposes is called the "tax assessor."

28. **B** To find the tax bill we multiply the tax rate by the real market value of the property. The real market value is the lowest value the property will have during the tax year. The real market value cannot increase more than 3% per year.

29. **A** While the taxes become a lien on July 1 and are due on November 15, the amount of the tax is determined by the assessed value and the tax rate. State law defines the assessed value as the lower of the "real market value," which is defined as the value of the property as of January 1, and the "maximum assessed value," which is determined by a formula based on past real market value.

30. **B** Tax is levied on the assessed value. The assessed value is the lower of the real market value as of January 1, or 90% of the assessed value for the 1995-96 tax year plus 3% annual increase, plus the value of any improvements over $10,000 in any one year or cumulative improvements over $25,000 in any five-year period.

31. **B** Oregon law defines assessed value as the lower of the real market value as of January 1 or the maximum assessed value. The maximum assessed value is 90% of the assessed value for the 1995-96 tax year, plus 3% per annum since then, plus the value of any exceptions (additions, remodeling, etc.)

32. **B** Oregon law defines assessed value as the lower of the real market value as of January 1, and the maximum assessed value. The maximum assessed value is 90% of the assessed value for the 1995-96 tax year, plus 3% per annum, plus the value of any exceptions (improvements, etc.).

33. **D** To appraise each property every year by visiting it would be prohibitive in terms of labor. Therefore, state law requires that a physical inspection and appraisal of the property be made only once every six years. In the intervening five years a statistical adjustment is made.

34. **D** To appraise each property every year by visiting it would be prohibitive in terms of labor. Therefore, state law requires that a physical inspection and appraisal of the property be made only once every six years. In the intervening five years a statistical adjustment is made.

35. **B** To appraise each property every year by visiting it would be prohibitive in terms of labor. Therefore, state law requires that a physical inspection and appraisal of the property be made only once every six years. In the intervening five years a statistical adjustment is made. When an adjustment is made following a physical visit to the property and reappraisal, it is called a "maintenance" adjustment. Statistical adjustments between maintenance adjustments are called "trending" adjustments.

36. **B** Over a historical period of time, appraisers know that land and improvements go up or down in value at different rates. Therefore, each improved property will have two assessed values, one for the land and one for the improvements. However, when calculating the tax bill, the same tax rate is applied to both.

37. **B** Normally you are innocent until the government proves you guilty. However, in matters of taxation, this idea went out the window a long time ago.

38. **A** The immediate appeal is to the county Board of Property Tax Appeals. The decision of the Board can be further appealed to the tax court.

39. **B** Normally you are innocent until the government proves you guilty. However, in matters of taxation, this concept went by the board a long time ago.

40. **C** As a general rule, in criminal law, the citizen is presumed innocent until the state proves him or her guilty. In civil disputes, the case is won by the party in whose favor the preponderance of the evidence lay. In tax matters, the citizen must bear the burden of proving his or her case.

41. **C** Appeals of assessed valuations are made first to the county Board of Property Tax Appeals. From the Board of Property Tax Appeals the taxpayer can appeal to the Magistrate Division of the Oregon Tax Court. Decisions of the Magistrate Division can be appealed to the regular session of the Oregon Tax Court. The final appeal is to the Oregon Supreme Court.

42. **D** The requirements are that she have a fee title or be buying on a contract; a life estate is not eligible. There is no requirement to have been married. The deadline is April 15, not March 15. There is no prohibition on earning income from the property. The only requirement is that she live in it herself as well.

43. **A** Under the Oregon Senior Citizens Homestead Deferral Program, a senior citizen may defer payment of all property taxes on a personal residence. To qualify, the senior citizen must be 62 or over and earn household income of $32,000 or less based on the 2001 tax year, plus an annual cost of living increase. The unpaid taxes accrue interest at 6% and must be paid when the owner dies, or sells the property.

44. **A** The requirement is to be 62 years of age by April 15 of the tax year to be deferred.

45. **B** A surviving spouse may continue the deferment if he or she is 62 years of age or older by April 15 of the tax year. If the surviving spouse is not old enough to continue the deferral, taxes already deferred can still remain deferred.

46. **C** Under the Oregon Senior Citizens Homestead Deferral Program, a senior citizen may defer payment of all property taxes on a personal residence. To qualify, the senior citizen must be 62 or over by April 15 of the year in which they first apply, or a surviving spouse also 62, and earn household income of $32,000 or less based on the 2001 tax year, plus a cost of living increase each year thereafter. The unpaid taxes accrue interest at 6% and must be paid when the owner dies, sells the property, or ceases to reside there. The senior citizen must have a fee title or be buying on a land sales contract; life estates do not qualify.

47. **C** Under the Oregon Senior Citizens Homestead Deferral Program, a senior citizen may defer payment of all property taxes on a personal residence. The unpaid taxes must be paid when the owner dies, sells the property or ceases to reside there other than a temporary absence.

48. **A** Low- and moderate-income senior citizens may be eligible for the Senior Citizens Homestead Property Tax Deferral Program. Payment of the tax is deferred until the home is sold, ceases to be the senior citizen's homestead, or until the death of the owner. To qualify there are maximum income limitations as well as age requirements, but there are no requirements that the senior citizen be disabled or handicapped in any way.

49. **D** To qualify senior citizen must also be 62 years of age. The statute specifically permits the deferral of taxes as long as the senior citizen has a fee title or is buying on a recorded land sales contract. Since the statute does not mention other interests, such as life estates or leaseholds, the deferral cannot apply to anything but a fee title or equitable title under a land sales contract.

50. **B** The Veteran's Homestead Exemption provides an exemption from property taxes for the first $8,750 of real market value for a veteran who is 40% or more disabled. The amount is increased to $11.670 if the disability is service-related. These figures are for the 2000 property tax year and increase by 3% each year thereafter. To qualify the veteran or surviving spouse must reside on the property. The property does not have to be free and clear, however.

51. **D** There are two categories of veterans who are eligible for the Veterans Homestead Property Tax Exemption. Any veteran who served the required minimum number of days of active duty is eligible if the veteran was honorably discharged and is 40% or more disabled. The second category is the unremarried surviving spouse of an honorably discharged deceased veteran who served the required minimum number of days of active duty, in which case the veteran need never have been disabled while alive.

52. **D** The tax exemption is only valid for the veteran's homestead. There are no age requirements to qualify for the Veterans Homestead Property Tax Exemption. The only requirements are to have been honorably discharged and 40% or more disabled, or the unremarried surviving spouse of a deceased veteran, in which case the deceased veteran need not have been disabled while alive.

53. **B** The filing deadline for most exemptions and deferrals is April 15, but for the Veteran's Homestead Property Tax Exemption it is April 1. The claim must be renewed annually.

54. **B** The Veteran's Homestead Exemption provides an exemption from property taxes for the first $8,750 of real market value for a veteran who is 40% or more disabled. The amount is increased to $11.670 if the disability is service-related. These figures are for the 2000 property tax year and increase by 3% each year thereafter.

55. **B** Low- and moderate-income senior citizens may be eligible for the Senior Citizens Homestead Property Tax Deferral Program. Payment of the tax is deferred until the home is sold, ceases to

be the senior citizen's homestead, or until the death of the owner. Veterans are eligible for a property tax exemption, not deferral. Similarly, certain qualifying low-income housing is eligible for property tax exemption, but not deferral.

56. **B** A property tax bill may include a special assessment for local improvements. These typically include paving, sidewalks, street lighting, sewers, etc. The tax is usually levied on a front footage basis or by some method other than the value of the property (ad valorem).

57. **D** A property tax bill may include a special assessment for local improvements. These typically include paving, sidewalks, street lighting, sewers, etc. They are usually levied on the basis of front footage or something other than the value of the property (ad valorem).

58. **B** A property tax bill may include a special assessment for local improvements. These typically include paving, sidewalks, street lighting, sewers, etc. While such special assessments are liens against the property, they are not mortgages.

59. **B** A property tax bill may include a special assessment for local improvements. Such improvements typically include paving, sidewalks, street lighting, sewers, etc. The assessment is not the same as the annual property tax, even though the tax collector includes it on the same bill.

60. **C** Special assessments are government liens for local improvements such as street paving, sewer systems, and the like. The lien reaches the property as soon as the government unit has legally elected to impose the assessment.

61. **C** To encourage public improvements for streets, sidewalks, and the like, the Bancroft Bonding Act allows an owner to elect to pay off the cost in installments of up to 30 years (or as permitted by the local jurisdiction), including interest.

62. **B** To encourage public improvements for streets, sidewalks, and the like, the Bancroft Bonding Act allows an owner to elect to pay off the cost in installments of up to 30 years (or as permitted by the local jurisdiction), including interest at 7%.

63. **A** The Bancroft Bonding Act allows an owner to elect to pay off the cost of local improvements in installments of up to 30 years (or as permitted by the local jurisdiction), including interest at 7%. The owner must make the election by an application no later than ten days after receiving the official notice of the assessment. All special assessments, whether under the Bancroft Bonding Act or otherwise, appear as liens against the title.

64. **D** To encourage public improvements for streets, sidewalks, and other local improvements, the Bancroft Bonding Act allows an owner to elect to pay off the cost in installments of up to 30 years (or as permitted by the local jurisdiction).

65. **D** Any special assessment is automatically due in full unless the owner elects, within ten days of receiving the notice of the assessment, to Bancroft it. If it is Bancrofted, the jurisdiction which made the improvements may set up a repayment schedule for up to 30 years. The term is at the discretion of the local jurisdiction.

66. **A** The real property tax year runs from the lien date of July 1 through the following June 30. The assessment date for real property is January 1. However, the lien date and assessment date for personal property are both January 1. Therefore, the tax year for personal property runs from January 1 through the following December 1.

67. **D** If an owner of real property fails to pay the taxes by the due date, the unpaid taxes are "past due" until the delinquency date, which is May 16. Unlike real property taxes, however, personal property taxes become delinquent immediately if not paid by the due dates.

68. **D** While the lien date is January 1, the due dates for each one-third are November 15, February 15 and May 15, the same as for real property. Therefore, when the taxes are paid on November 15 the owner is paying them 10½ months in arrears and 1½ months in advance.

69. **B** A mobile home (a manufactured dwelling) is considered personal property for property tax purposes unless the owner also owns the land on which it is situated.

70. **B** A mobile home (a manufactured dwelling) is considered personal property for property tax purposes unless the owner also owns the land on which it is situated.

71. **D** Foreclosure is not a remedy which can be used on personal property, so the tax collector has three other remedies instead. First, the personal property can be seized and sold if necessary. Second, the tax collector can sue the owner and obtain a general judgment, which can be used to reach any assets of the owner. And third, the tax collector can add the bill for unpaid personal property taxes to the tax bill for any real property owned by the taxpayer in the same county.

72. **A** Seizure and sale of taxable personal property for failure to pay taxes on it can occur any time after the taxes become delinquent. The delinquency date for personal property taxes is immediately after the due date. There is no "past due" grace period before delinquency as there is with real property taxes.

73. **D** Personal property is subject to taxation if it is tangible and held for the production of income, or if it is manufactured housing or a floating home. Shares of stock are intangible.

74. **B** The purpose of assessment is to apportion the total tax load fairly according to value, therefore, if an owner's assessed valuation is at real market value, the owner is paying his or her fair share. The cause of high taxes in general is that the levy (budget) is too high, causing all property owners to pay more than they wish.

75. **A** "Two cents of every dollar" is the same as saying "2% of the total income." This comes to $73,840 ($3,962,000 × .02 = $73,840).

76. **D** The tax rate is expressed in terms of dollars and cents of tax per thousand dollars of assessed value. For example, a tax rate of $15 per thousand applied to a property assessed at $100,000 would result in a bill of $1,500. To find the tax rate for a tax levy district the assessor divides the district's levy by the total assessed value of all property lying within the district. This rate sometimes must be compressed to comply with the maximum tax rate allowed by Measure 5.

77. **C** Tax rates are established primarily based on the amount of the levy for each district, divided by the total assessed value of all taxable property in the district. However, the assessor must sometimes compress the tax rates if the total rates on an individual bill exceed the limits of Measure 5.

78. **B** The tax rate is found by dividing the total assessed values into the amount of the levy. Therefore the tax rate in this case is found by dividing $28.125 million by $45 billion. This gives a tax rate of $6.25 per thousand ($28,125,000 ÷ $45,000,000,000 = $.000625, or $6.25 per thousand of assessed value. If your property is assessed at $180,000, multiply the rate ($6.25) by the number of thousands (180) to find the bill. The result is $1,125 (180 × $6.25 = $1,125).

79. **B** First, add up all the tax rates to find the total tax rate. This comes to $14.00 ($2.00 + $0.50 + $4.50 + $7.00 = $14.00). Taxes are levied on the assessed value, not the real market value. Find the bill by multiplying the rate ($14.00) by the number of thousands of assessed value (180). The result is $2,520 (180 × $14 = $2,520).

80. **C** The tax bill is calculated by multiplying the assessed value by the total tax rate. Therefore, an increase in the rate will increase the amount of the bill.

81. **A** The tax rate in Oregon is expressed in dollars of tax per thousand dollars of assessed value, so to find a tax bill, multiply the thousands of assessed value by the tax rate. In this case there are 135 thousands, so multiply the rate ($15) times 135. The result is a tax bill of $2,025 (135 × $25 = $3,375). However, taxpayers who pay in full by November 15 are entitled to a discount of 3% of the amount paid. Therefore the amount paid on November 15 was 97% (100% – 3% = 97%) of $2,025, or $1,964 ($2,025 × .97 = $1,964.25, or $1,964 rounded).

82. **D** To find the amount of a tax bill, multiply the thousands of assessed value by the tax rate. In this case there are 220 thousands, so multiply the rate ($14) times 220. The result is a tax bill of $3,080. However, since the bill is not paid until February 16, there will be an interest penalty of 1.33% per month or fraction of a month on the amount which is past due. From November 15 through February 15 one-third is past due, so the total interest charge will be 4% (1.33% × 3 months = 4%). One third of the total bill is $1,026.67 ($3,080 ÷ 3 = $1,026.67). Therefore the interest penalty through February 15 is 4% of $1,026.67, or $41.06 ($1,026.67 × .04 = $41.06). February 16 is only one day, but it is still a fraction of a month, so 1.33% interest will be charged. After February 15, two thirds will be past due, so the interest penalty will be $27.31 ($1,026.67 × 2 × .0133 = $27.3094). Adding the two interest penalties gives a total interest penalty of $68.37 ($41.06 + $27.31 = $68.37). Adding this to the bill gives the total amount of $3,148.37 ($3,080 + $68.37 = $3,148.37).

83. **B** There is a discount of 3% of the amount paid for payment in full on or before November 15. This means the owner only has to pay 97% of the bill. So to find the amount to pay, multiply the bill ($1,850) by .97%. The result is $1,795 ($1,850 × .97 = $1,794.50, or $1,795, rounded.

84. **B** The tax rate in Oregon is expressed in dollars of tax per thousand dollars of value, so to find a tax bill, multiply the of thousands of assessed value by the tax rate. In this case there are 264 thousands, so multiply the rate ($16.50) times 264. The result is a tax bill of $4,356 (132 × $33 = $4,356). There is a discount of 3% if the bill is paid in full on or before November 15. A 3% discount means the owner only has to pay 97% of the bill. So to find the amount,

multiply the bill ($4,356) by 97%. The result is $4,225 ($4,356 × .97 = $4,225.32 ($4,225, rounded.

85. **B** The tax rate in Oregon is expressed in dollars of tax per thousand dollars of value, so to find a tax bill, multiply the thousands of assessed value by the tax rate. The real market value of $855,000 is irrelevant. The assessed value of $598,500 is the basis for the tax bill. Since there are 598.5 thousands, multiply the rate ($14) times 598.5. The result is a tax bill of $8,379 (598.5 × $14 = $8,379).

86. **D** The tax rate in Oregon is expressed in dollars of tax per thousand dollars of assessed value, so to find a tax bill, multiply the thousands of assessed value by the tax rate. In this case there are 240 thousands, so multiply the rate ($14) times 240. The result is a tax bill of $3,360 (240 × $14 = $3,360). There are no discounts after November 15, so the 3% discount for promptness must be ignored. The interest penalty is 16%, or 1.33% per month or fraction of a month. For the first three months (through February 15) only one-third of the bill is past due. One-third of the bill is $1,120 ($3,360 ÷ 3 = $1,120). Multiplying this by 1.33% for each of the three months gives a total interest penalty of $45.00 ($1.120 × .0133 × 3 months = $44.68, or $45, rounded). Adding the penalty of $45 to the bill of $3,360, gives a total to pay of $3,405 ($3,360 + $45 = $3,405).

87. **C** To find a tax bill, multiply the thousands of assessed value by the tax rate. When you know the rate and the amount of the tax, you can reverse this process to find the assessed value by dividing the tax rate into the amount of the tax. In this case, the bill is $1,505 and the rate is $14.75 per thousand, so the assessed value is $102,034 ($1,505 ÷ $14.75 = 102.03389 thousands, or $102,034, rounded). However, $102,034 is the assessed value, not the real market value. The assessed value is a percentage of the real market value, in this case, 72%. Therefore, $102,034 is 72% of the real market value. To find the real market value, divide the assessed value by 72%. The result is $141,700 ($102,034 ÷ .72 = $141,713.88, or $141,700, rounded).

88. **C** To find a tax bill, multiply the thousands of assessed value by the tax rate. When you know the amount of the tax bill and the assessed value, you can reverse this process to find the tax rate by dividing the assessed value into the amount of the tax. In this case, the assessed value is 90% of $224,000, so we must first find the assessed value, which comes to $201,600 ($224,000 × .90 = $201,600). Next we must find the annual bill. The monthly tax bill is $240, so the annual amount is $2,880 ($240 × 12 = $2,880). Now divide the bill ($2,880) by the number of thousands of assessed value ($201,600 = 201.600 thousands) to find the rate. This comes to $14.29 ($2,880 ÷ 201.6 thousands = $14.2857, or $14.29, rounded).

89. **C** The lien date for real property taxes is July 1, which is considered the start of the tax year. The tax year runs through the following June 30. When the tax bill is paid in November, it is paid 4½ months in arrears, and 7½ months in advance.

90. **A** When prorating real property taxes between a buyer and a seller, the lien date is July 1, so if the seller paid the taxes in full, the taxes were paid through the following June 30. Since the lien date for personal property taxes is January 1, when the owner pays personal property taxes in full, they are paid for the period from January 1 through the following December 31. November 15 is the due date, but the start of the tax year is the lien date.

91. **A** By statute in Oregon, a taxpayer is entitled to a 3% discount for paying property taxes in full on or before November 15. Therefore, we must subtract 3% from the original bill of $1,600, which is $48.00 (0.03 × $1,600 = $48.00). Subtracting the $48.00 from the original bill leaves a discounted bill to pay of $1,552.00 ($1,600 – $48 = $1,552).

92. **D** To find the tax rate we must divide the total levy by the total of assessed values. This gives us a tax rate of $13.3823 per thousand. Multiplying the tax rate by the number of thousands of assessed valuation (270 thousands) gives us the total tax bill. This comes to $3,613.24 (270 × $13.3823 = $3,613.24).

93. **D** To find the tax bill, we multiply the assessed value by the tax rate. However, the tax rate is given "per thousand," so we must multiply the tax rate times the number of thousands (174), not the total (174,000). The result is a tax bill of $2,436 (174 × $14 = $2,436).

94. **C** The first thing to notice is that the property is assessed at 80% of its real market value. If the assessment ratio is 80%, then only 80% of the real market value, or $88,800, is subject to taxation ($111,000 × 0.80 = $88,800). To find the tax bill, multiply the assessed value by the tax rate. In this case, the tax rate is a total of 13.25 ($4.75 + $1.50 + $4.00 + $3.00 = $13.25). Multiplying this by the number of thousands of assessed value (88.8) gives us a tax bill of $1,176.60 (88.8 × $13.25 = $1,176.60).

95. **A** First, the discount for promptness is lost if the taxes are paid after November 15. Second, we must calculate the original bill. Tax bills are calcu-

lated by multiplying the number of thousands of real market value (192, in this case), by the tax rate ($13). This gives us a bill of $2,496 (192 × $13 = $2,496). However, the interest can be charged only on the amount that is past due. The second one-third of the bill does not come due until February 15, three months after the initial due date. So, for the entire past due period, the amount that was past due was one-third of the total bill, or $832 ($2,496 ÷ 3 = $832). The interest rate is 12% per annum, which is the same as saying 1% per month. Since we have been past due for three months, the total penalty is 3% (1% for each of the three months). To find the total interest penalty, we multiply this rate times the one-third of the bill that is past due ($832). This comes to $24.96 of interest ($832 × 0.03 = $24.96). Since the question asks what amount is owed, this must be added to the total bill ($2,496), to give us a grand total of $2,520.96 ($2,496 + $24.95 = $2,520.96).

96. **D** Since the tax bill is found by multiplying the number of thousands of assessed value by the tax rate, we can reverse the process (divide) to find the number of thousands of assessed value. If the total bill is $2,305, then the assessed value is $159,000 ($2,305 ÷ $14.50 = $159,000). However, this is not the answer. This is 75% of what the real market value is. To find the real market value, we must divide the assessed value ($159,000) by the assessment ratio (75%). This comes to $212,000 ($159,000 ÷ 0.75 = $212,000).

97. **D** Since the tax bill is found by multiplying the number of thousands of assessed value by the tax rate, we can reverse the process (divide) to find the number of thousands of assessed value. If the total bill is $2,268.50, then the assessed value is $163,200 ($2,268.50 ÷ $13.90 = $163,201.43, which is 163.2 thousands). However, this is not the answer. This is 96% of what the real market value is. To find the real market value, we must divide the assessed value ($163,200) by the assessment ratio (96%). This comes to $170,000 ($163,200 ÷ 0.96 = $170,000).

98. **C** The first problem is to find the tax rate. The tax rate is determined by dividing the amount of the levy ($156 million) by the total assessed value ($12 billion). This comes to $13.00 per thousand ($156,000,000 ÷ $12,000,000,000 = $13.00). Now we find the tax bill by multiplying the number of thousands of assessed value of the property (160 thousands) times the tax rate ($13.00). This comes to $2,080 (160 × $13.00 = $2,080).

LAND USE REGULATIONS

To promote the general health, safety and welfare, federal, state and local governments are empowered to create laws regulating the use of land. While these laws are sometimes highly controversial, there are some issues which are no longer a matter for debate. In this section we will explore the nature of these regulations and their impact on the practice of real estate in Oregon.

As long as a government land use restriction merely ***regulates*** the owner's use of the land, the right to create the restriction is said to be derived from ***police power*** – the right of the government to maintain public order. The majority of such restrictions are ***zoning ordinances***. However, if the restriction is so severe that it deprives the owner of all possible uses of the land, then we say there has been a ***taking***, and the government is exercising its right of ***eminent domain***. The exercise of eminent domain is called ***condemnation***. According to the U.S. Constitution, condemnation requires the government to pay the owner ***just compensation***. The government is also not allowed to condemn property unless it is for a ***public use***. Zoning ordinances are an exercise of police power and not eminent domain according to the decision of the United States Supreme Court in the case of *Village of Euclid v. Amber Realty Company* [272 U.S. 365 (1926)].

However, how far a jurisdiction may regulate before it becomes a taking is sometimes a matter for heated arguments. For example, ***down-zoning*** is not considered a taking. Down-zoning occurs when a local jurisdiction re-zones an owner's property for a use which is of less monetary value to the owner.

To be constitutional, not only must a land use regulation be enacted to promote the general health, safety and welfare, but it must also meet the constitutional requirements of ***due process*** and ***equal protection***. Due process means that the regulations

NOTES

must have been enacted after public debate, deliberation or election, decisions can be appealed, and that each property owner has the right to his or her day in court. Equal protection means that the regulation must be applied equally and fairly to all owners.

Real estate agents should be careful to distinguish between public land use restrictions such as zoning ordinances, building codes, and the like, and restrictions created by private parties. Private restrictions include conditions and covenants, which were discussed previously in the section on Title Encumbrances.

Zoning

Zoning ordinances are created by cities and counties to regulate the way land in their jurisdiction is used. Zoning ordinances create a wide variety of limitations. A zoning ordinance describes a particular land use activity in detail. This is called a ***zone designation***, or sometimes also a ***zone classification***, or just ***zone***.

For convenience, the zone designation is given a short name. For example, a zone designation as "R-7" might mean **R**esidential, 7,000 square feet of lot area required for one single-family dwelling. In similar fashion "M-1" might allow heavy **M**anufacturing, "M-2" might be applied to medium **M**anufacturing, and "M-3" could be reserved for light **M**anufacturing. Each local jurisdiction will create their own unique set of zone classifications. The zoning ordinance will typically go into great detail as to matters such as maximum lot coverage permitted, side, front and back yard setback requirements, height restrictions – even the design of the improvements is sometimes regulated.

Once the zoning designations have been created they are applied to land within the jurisdiction of the city or county. The result of the process is a zoning map of the jurisdiction which shows all the districts in which each zoning designation applies.

When applying the zoning designations to different districts, it is common to create ***buffer zones***. A buffer zone is a zone district placed between two incompatible uses. For example, a zone district designated for apartments may be placed between a commercial district and a single-family residential district. Buffer zones are also used along freeways, airports and other noise-producing uses. Even a park can be used as a buffer zone to keep inharmonious uses apart.

When a zoning ordinance is enacted, particularly when property is down-zoned, a conflict is frequently created between the new ordinance and land uses already in existence. When this happens, we call the conflicting use a ***nonconforming use***, or sometimes a ***pre-existing condition***. In order to be legal, the zoning ordinance must allow these uses to continue, at least for a time. The clause in the zoning ordinance which permits nonconforming uses and pre-existing conditions to continue is called a ***grandfather clause***.

Of course, if an owner changes the use of the land or discontinues the use (abandonment), the right to continue the use will be in jeopardy. However, a temporary discontinuance of the use, such as where an owner is unable to locate a tenant for a period of time, will probably not result in abandonment. Sometimes the local jurisdiction will require an ***abatement*** of a nonconforming use. An abatement requires that the owner discontinue the use over a period of time. An abatement is typically required over the remaining economic life of the improvements, so as to avoid the owner's complaint that anything of value was taken.

When the owner wishes to sell a property that is a nonconforming use the question arises whether the new owner can continue the use. Oregon Revised Statutes 215.130 (5) provides that a new owner must be allowed to continue the existing use when the property is located in the unincorporated area of a county. If the property is located inside an incorporated city, the issue is less clear. Since this is an area of potential for misrepresentation, real estate agents should be careful to insist that buyers and sellers seek proper counsel before assuming that a buyer can continue a nonconforming use.

If an owner wishes to use a property in a manner which does not comply with the zoning, and the desired use is not a legal nonconforming use, the use can be made legal by obtaining a ***zone change***. Obtaining a zone change, however, can be a very expensive and time-consuming process.

Even if the local jurisdiction is willing to grant a zone change, it may not be legal to do so. For example, a ***spot zone*** occurs where a jurisdiction zones just one or two owners' properties, without any apparent justification, in a manner which is inconsistent with the tenor of the neighborhood. If the spot zone results in loss of market value for adjacent owners, the jurisdiction may even be liable for damages.

Another problem with zone changes is that a zone change may require a change to the ***comprehensive plan*** which the jurisdiction has adopted. (See "Planning," later.) This adds another step to the approval process.

Many times what an owner wishes to do with the property does not require a substantive change to the zone, but rather a small exception to the permitted uses. In fact, when zoning ordinances are created, it is customary to anticipate requests for adjustments to prevent a hardship. The permitted adjustments are frequently stipulated in the zoning ordinance itself.

For example, an owner may have a substandard size lot. Since the zoning ordinance is probably specific about the minimum number of square feet required, the property is unbuildable and therefore worthless. To prevent the owner from suffering from such a hardship, the owner could apply for a ***variance*** to permit building on the lot. Variances are typically granted as title rights (appurtenances) and run with the land. A variance would be used to adjust for setback requirements, height restrictions, lot coverage, and so forth.

Another type of exception to the zoning ordinance is a ***use permit***, also sometimes called ***special use permit***. A use permit is usually personal to the owner, and not a title right. Use permits frequently have conditions attached, in which case they are called ***conditional use permits***.

Permits are not typically used for dimension problems, but rather for more serious exceptions, such as where a different use of the property is required. For example, if an owner wishes to run a small business operation out of a personal residence, this would involve a commercial use in a residential zone, so a permit would be appropriate. Note that running a small home based business in a residential zone is an exception which is commonly asked for, so the zoning ordinance creating the residential zone would probably contain precise rules for when and under what conditions such a permit could be granted.

In an active real estate practice, an agent sells many properties, and each property may be located in a different city or county jurisdiction. Since zoning is created at the city or county level in Oregon, there is a great deal of difference in the way terms are used from one jurisdiction to the next. What may be a variance in one jurisdiction becomes a conditional use permit in another. Real estate agents find they must learn a completely different set of rules for each jurisdiction in which they work.

Building and housing codes

While zoning ordinances affect what type of improvements are permitted, ***building codes*** address construction standards. Building codes are adopted by the Oregon Building Codes Agency, but enforced in most areas by cities or counties. In areas where the city or county does not enforce the building codes, the state will take over enforcement.

Many cities in Oregon have also adopted ***housing codes***. A housing code is applied retroactively to existing structures. As a generalization, a housing code will declare

NOTES

that structures meet the requirements of the housing code if they met the building code which was in force at the time they were constructed. From time to time, however, a city will enact ordinances requiring owners to modify certain conditions which were formerly legal.

Exercise a

A zoning ordinance regulates the owner's use of the land and is an exercise of ____________ ____________.
When a law deprives an owner of all economic use of the property, this is a taking and is an exercise of ____________ ____________. The process is called ____________. When there is a taking, the owner is entitled to ____________ ____________ and the taking must be for a ____________ ____________. Zoning ordinances cannot violate the constitutional requirements of ________ ____________ and ____________ ____________.
A zoning district created to keep incompatible uses apart is called a ____________ zone. When a zoning ordinance is enacted which creates a conflict with existing uses, the existing uses can continue as a ____________ ________. To recognize this, the zoning ordinance will contain a ____________ ____________.
To make a use legal the owner could request a ____________ ____________. However, this would be illegal if it created a ____________ ____________. Sometimes a ____________ to the zoning ordinance is granted to prevent a hardship. These are commonly used for dimensional problems. A ____________ is sometimes granted for more serious exceptions to the zoning ordinances.
The State of Oregon creates ____________ ____________ to regulate new construction. Existing structures are sometimes regulated by a ____________ ____________.

Planning

Cities and counties in Oregon have been creating and enforcing zoning ordinances for many decades. In recent years, however, the concept of ***planning*** has become the focus of attention. A zoning ordinance indicates what uses are permitted in an area. Planning, on the other hand, involves decisions about future land use needs.

In theory, planning precedes zoning. For example, we might plan for future economic expansion, resulting in an anticipated number of new jobs, which in turn will result in the need for additional housing, more waste disposal requirements, more transportation corridors, and so forth. Once the plan is determined, then appropriate land areas can be zoned to meet the needs of the plan. Planning impacts more than just zoning, however. Having an effective plan also allows orderly creation of government services at all levels and allows the private sector to plan better as well.

In Oregon, planning begins at the city or county level. Starting in the 1970s, state law required every city and county to create a comprehensive plan which had to be approved by the ***Land Conservation and Development Commission*** (LCDC). The Land

Land Use Goals of the LCDC

1. **Citizen involvement** Goal 1 calls for "the opportunity for citizens tobe involved in all phases of the planning-process." It requires each city and countyto have a citizen involvement programcontaining six components specified in the goal. It also requires local governments to have a committee for citizen involvement (CCI) to monitor and encourage public participation in planning.

2. **Land use planning** Goal 2 outlines the basic procedures of Oregon's statewide planning program. It says that land use decisions are to be made in accordance with a comprehensive plan, and that suitable "implementation ordinances" to put the plan's policies into effect must be adopted. It requires that plans be based on "factual information"; that local plans and ordinances be coordinated with those of other jurisdictions and agencies; and that plans be reviewed periodically and amended as needed. Goal 2 also contains standards for taking exceptions to statewide goals. An exception may be taken when a statewide goal cannot or should not be applied to a particular area or situation.

3. **Agricultural lands** Goal 3 defines "agricultural lands." It then requires counties to inventory such lands and to "preserve and maintain" them through farm zoning. Details on the uses allowed in farm zones are found in ORS Chapter 215 and in Oregon Administrative Rules, Chapter 660, Division 33.

4. **Forest lands** This goal defines forest lands and requires counties to inventory them and adopt policies and ordinances that will "conserve forest lands for forest uses."

5. **Open spaces, scenic and historic areas and natural resources** Goal 5 covers more than a dozen natural and cultural resources such as wildlife habitats and wetlands. It establishes a process for each resource to be inventoried and evaluated. If a resource or site is found to be significant, a local government has three policy choices: preserve the resource, allow proposed uses that conflict with it, or strike some sort of a balance between the resource and the uses that would conflict with it.

6. **Air, water and land resources quality** This goal requires local comprehensive plans and implementing measures to be consistent with state and federal regulations on matters such as groundwater pollution.

7. **Areas subject to natural disasters and hazards** Goal 7 deals with development in places subject to natural hazards such as floods or landslides. It requires that jurisdictions apply "appropriate safeguards" (floodplain zoning, for example) when planning for development there.

8. **Recreation needs** This goal calls for each community to evaluate its areas and facilities for recreation and develop plans to deal with the projected demand for them. It also sets forth detailed standards for expedited siting of destination resorts.

9. **Economy of the state** Goal 9 calls for diversification and improvement of the economy. It asks communities to inventory commercial and industrial lands, project future needs for such lands, and plan and zone enough land to meet those needs.

10. **Housing** This goal specifies that each city must plan for and accommodate needed housing types, such as multifamily and manufactured housing. It requires each city to inventory its buildable residential lands, project future needs for such lands, and plan and zone enough buildable land to meet those needs. It also prohibits local plans from discriminating against needed housing types.

11. **Public facilities and services** Goal 11 calls for efficient planning of public services such as sewers, water, law enforcement, and fire protection. The goal's central concept is that public services should to be planned in accordance with a community's needs and capacities rather than be forced to respond to development as it occurs.

12. **Transportation** The goal aims to provide "a safe, convenient and economic transportation system." It asks for communities to address the needs of the "transportation disadvantaged."

13. **Energy** Goal 13 declares that "land and uses developed on the land shall be managed and controlled so as to maximize the conservation of all forms of energy, based upon sound economic principles."

14. **Urbanization** This goal requires cities to estimate future growth and needs for land and then plan and zone enough land to meet those needs. It calls for each city to establish an "urban growth boundary" (UGB) to "identify and separate urbanizable land from rural land." It specifies seven factors that must be considered in drawing up a UGB. It also lists four criteria to be applied when undeveloped land within a UGB is to be converted to urban uses.

15. **Willamette greenway** Goal 15 sets forth procedures for administering the 300 miles of greenway that protects the Willamette River.

16. **Estuarine resources** Goal 16 requires local governments to classify Oregon's 22 major estuaries in four categories: , natural, conservation, shallow-draft development, and deep-draft development. It then describes types of land uses and activities that are permissible in those "management units."

17. **Coastal shorelands** The goal defines a planning area bounded by the ocean beaches on the west and the coast highway (State Route 101) on the east. It specifies how certain types of land and resources there are to be managed: major marshes, for example, are to be protected. Sites best suited for unique coastal land uses (port facilities, for example) are reserved for "water-dependent" or "water related" uses.

18. **Beaches and dunes** Goal 18 sets planning standards for development on various types of dunes. It prohibits residential development on beaches and active foredunes, but allows some other types of development if they meet key criteria. The goal also deals with dune grading, groundwater drawdown in dunal aquifers, and the breaching of foredunes.

19. **Ocean resources** Goal 19 aims "to conserve the long-term values, benefits, and natural resources of the nearshore ocean and the continental shelf." It deals with matters such as dumping of dredge spoils and discharging of waste products into the open sea. Goal 19's main requirements are for state agencies rather than cities and counties.

NOTES

Conservation and Development Commission was created in 1973 with various missions. Its primary function is to create statewide land use planning. It accomplishes this by creating land use goals (see preceding page) for the state as a whole, and then granting approval to a comprehensive plan if the comprehensive plan is in compliance with the goals. The actual approval is done by the Department of Land Conservation and Development (DLCD), a state agency governed by the LCDC. When a plan has been approved, it is said to be ***acknowledged*** by the DLCD.

The comprehensive plan provides overall guidance for a community's land use, economic development and resource management. One element of the comprehensive plan sets forth the community's long range objectives and the policies by which it intends to achieve them. This portion of the comprehensive plan is adopted by local ordinance and has the force of law.

Local jurisdictions may revise their plan at any time, as long as the revisions are in keeping with the land use goals of the LCDC. State law requires periodic reviews of each community's comprehensive plan in order to ensure continuing compliance and that the plan continues to meet the needs of the community it was designed to serve.

An important fact to bear in mind about the LCDC is that neither it nor any agency of state government creates comprehensive plans, zoning ordinances, variances, use permits, or any other kind of direct land use decision. Its sole function is to implement land use planning by creating land use goals and seeing that local communities create plans which implement the goals.

The LCDC does have one additional responsibility besides creating land use goals for Oregon. Oregon Revised Statutes 197.040 requires the LCDC to review and recommend to the legislature the designation of areas of critical state concern. Note that the LCDC does not have the authority to designate an area as being of critical concern. That power is reserved to the legislative process.

Land Use Board of Appeals In 1979, in response to a need for review of planning issues, the Land Use Board of Appeals (LUBA) was created as a special court. Decisions from the Land Use Board of Appeals can be appealed to the Court of Appeals and thereafter to the Oregon Supreme Court.

Exercise b

A zoning ordinance dictates what a property can be used for, but long range land use decisions are part of the ______________ process. This process is accomplished by requiring each local jurisdiction to create a ______________ ______________, which must be in compliance with the land use ______________ of the LCDC. The "LCDC" stands for the ______________ ______________ ______________ ______________ ______________.

For the following land use issues, choose whether it is a function of the local jurisdiction (city or county) or of the LCDC:

Creating a zoning ordinance	❑ *Local jurisdiction*	❑ *LCDC*
Granting a variance	❑ *Local jurisdiction*	❑ *LCDC*
Creating land use goals	❑ *Local jurisdiction*	❑ *LCDC*
Creating a comprehensive plan	❑ *Local jurisdiction*	❑ *LCDC*

NOTES

Dividing land

Any division of land must be reviewed to ensure that it meets all applicable laws and regulations, including the applicable comprehensive plan. Although a few land divisions must be reviewed by the Oregon Real Estate Agency, most land division approvals are handled by cities and counties. There is also a possibility that a land division must comply with the requirements of federal law, but this is very infrequent.

The first step in dividing land is to file an application with the local jurisdiction (city or county). The application must be accompanied by a ***tentative plan*** (sometimes called a ***preliminary plat***). The tentative plan is a drawing showing the general design of the proposed division. Although the local jurisdiction usually requires that the tentative plan be drawn to certain scale and meet other standards, it does not generally have to be prepared by a surveyor. Ultimately, the division will have to be surveyed, but the expense of a survey can be deferred until such time as the owner knows the division will be approved.

Each local jurisdiction will have its own categories for different types of divisions, but all make use of some statutory terminology. For example, a division of a parcel into four or more lots is called a ***subdivision***. A division into two or three parcels is called a ***partition***. Note that the result of a subdivision is called a ***lot***, but a partition results in ***parcels***.

Regardless of what type of division it is, in most jurisdictions it will be reviewed and approval will be granted only if it meets all applicable laws. State law requires the local jurisdiction to review and approve all subdivisions and partitions.

Matters which the local jurisdiction will take into account include whether the property is served by utilities and the location of the utilities, flood dangers or high water tables in the area, excessive slope to the land, soil conditions not conducive to building, and many other issues. In similar fashion, the proposed division must also be approved by other local officials such as the fire bureau, roads and public works, water agency, sanitation department, and others. And, of course, the proposed division must comply with existing zoning ordinances and the comprehensive plan for the area.

Real estate agents should be aware that the approval of the tentative plan can be relatively simple or it can be very time consuming, depending on the type of division which is being proposed. For example, in a subdivision, road requirements, location of water and sewer lines and other utilities, street lighting, sidewalks, and a host of other issues will demand greater scrutiny. But in a simple partition where there are no new roads to be built (all the parcels have frontage on an existing dedicated street), where there will probably be little need for discussion of utilities and other matters, approval is usually granted with only an informal hearing. Approval of a subdivision, however, will require a formal public hearing.

Assuming the applicant is granted approval, the final step in the process is to create and record a ***final plat*** of the division. The final plat must also be approved, and ultimately recorded. The purpose of recording the final plat is to give constructive notice as to how the land has been divided. If the land is a subdivision, the lots will be designated by number, and sometimes grouped into blocks. Once the map has been recorded, it becomes possible to create an adequate legal description for any particular lot just by referring to the lot and block and the name of the subdivision. In other words, the final act of recording the plat map results in the creation of lot and block legal descriptions. (For further discussion, see the section on Descriptions of Real Property.)

Sell or negotiate When an owner desires to divide land, the usual reason is to sell the resulting lots or parcels. For the protection of the public, it is illegal to sell a lot or parcel until the final plat for the subdivision or partition has been recorded. A buyer who is damaged by such an illegal sale can sue the developer for actual damages and attorney's fees.

NOTES

However, there is a statutory difference between ***selling*** and ***negotiating***. You are selling at the point when you enter into a binding agreement with a buyer. Anything short of this, such as advertising, showing the property, negotiating price and terms, and so forth, is considered negotiating. You cannot negotiate until at least the tentative plan is approved and you cannot sell until the final plat is approved and recorded.

Special requirements for subdivisions In most cases, when the land division is a subdivision, the buyer has a right to cancel the transaction for three business days. The developer must give the buyer a notice of this right at the time of entering into a sales agreement with the buyer. The buyer cannot waive the right to cancel the transaction.

If a developer sells a lot on a land sales contract, there are additional requirements. The developer must establish a ***collection escrow***. A collection escrow is a third party who will collect the payments. The subdivider must deposit certain items prescribed by statute with the escrow. These items include those documents necessary to ensure that when the buyer finishes paying for the property, the buyer will be able to obtain a deed conveying good title.

Subdivisions and Series Partitions

In the past, the Oregon Subdivision and Series Partition Control Law regulated all subdivisions in Oregon. Today it applies to subdivisions located in other states which are offered to Oregon residents but, even then, only if the state where the subdivision is located does not have reciprocity with Oregon. And it also applies to subdivisions which are sales of undivided interests (usually tenancies in common) in a property such as a resort complex.

It defines a ***subdivision*** as "eleven or more undivided interests or four or more other interests," and a ***series partition*** as "a series of partitions of land ... resulting in the creation of four or more parcels over a period of more than one calendar year" (ORS 92.305). It is enforced by the Oregon Real Estate Agency.

From the name of the law, it would appear that the its purpose is to limit the number of subdivisions or control the type and character of subdivisions. Nothing could be further from the truth. In enforcing the law the Real Estate Agency ordinarily has no authority to deny the creation of a subdivision or to regulate the size of lots, character of the development, or use which should be made of the lots. Such decisions are made by local jurisdictions through zoning ordinances and comprehensive plans.

The sole purpose of the Oregon Subdivision and Series Partition Control Law is to protect the public from fraud, deceit and misrepresentation in the sale of subdivided lands. To accomplish this, when the law applies to a subdivision, it requires that the developer make full disclosure of certain facts to buyers of the lots. As a fundamental principle of contract law, fraud, deceit and misrepresentation are eliminated when full disclosure is made.

To ensure that full disclosure is made, the developer must submit the subdivision to the Oregon Real Estate Agency. After investigating the proposed subdivision, the real estate agency will issue a ***public report***. The public report contains all factual matters which the Real Estate Agency wishes to be sure will be disclosed to buyers. It is illegal to sell subdivided lots until the public report is issued.

Developers are required to give a copy of the public report to each buyer prior to entering into a sales agreement with the buyer. As proof that the buyer received a copy of the public report. the developer must keep a receipt from the buyer for the public report. The developer cannot use the public report in advertising unless it is quoted in its entirety. The law also provides that the developer cannot imply that the Real Estate Agency or any other government entity has approved or endorsed the subdivision.

Notes

While the above would appear that every subdivision in the state must be approved by the Real Estate Commissioner and a public report be issued before a lot can be sold, there are numerous exemptions. The biggest exemption is that any subdivision is completely exempt from filing and public report requirements if it is located in a city or county which has an acknowledged comprehensive plan. There are no cities or counties without an acknowledged comprehensive plan, so all subdivisions in the state are exempt. This exemption was added by the 1991 Legislature. At the same time the Legislature added provisions to local platting requirements so that if the divided lot or parcel lacks anything which a buyer might expect (e.g., utility connections, access, adequate drainage, etc.) the local jurisdiction must require that the developer give a property disclosure statement to the buyer. Essentially, the activity of the Real Estate Agency with respect to subdivisions was replaced by the same functions at the city or county level. The Real Estate Agency does still have jurisdiction over sales of subdivided lands located in other states that are being offered to Oregon residents.

Interstate Land Sales Full Disclosure Act

The Interstate Land Sales Full Disclosure Act is a federal law which regulates the sale of certain subdivided lots when the sales are made in interstate commerce or by use of the mails. Developers of subdivisions in Oregon who offer the lots only to Oregon residents are usually exempt from the law. Subdivisions are also exempt if –

- There are fewer than 25 lots, or
- All the lots are twenty acres or more in size, or
- The lots are improved, or the developer has a contract with the buyer to construct a building on the lot within two years, or
- The project is a low-volume operation (no more than 12 lots sold each year)

A developer should be aware that the above exemptions do not apply in every case. And there are also other exemptions available which apply to certain subdivisions and developers. Moreover, even if the property is exempt, it is a violation of federal law to make false statements about the property in interstate commerce.

The Act is administered by the Office of Interstate Land Sales Registration, an agency of the Department of Housing and Urban Development.

When a subdivision is not exempt, to comply with the Act the procedure is to register the subdivision with the Office of Interstate Land Sales Registration and prepare a ***property report*** which makes full disclosure of facts which buyers should know about the lots. The developer must give a copy of the property report to each buyer and the buyer has a seven-day right to cancel the transaction. Note that the purpose of the property report required by the Interstate Land Sales Full Disclosure Act is the same as the public report sometimes required by the Oregon land division laws, that is, to prevent fraud and misrepresentation by requiring full disclosure.

Exercise c

A division of land into two or three pieces is called a ____________ *and the resulting pieces are called* ____________. *A* ____________ *is the division of land into* _____ *or more pieces.*

The first step in gaining approval is to file a ____________ ____________ *with the local jurisdiction.*

Upon approval, a surveyor must create a ____________ ____________, *which must be* ____________.

Until this has been accomplished, the developer cannot __________ a lot or parcel, which means that the developer cannot bind a buyer. Advertising and showing the property would be ____________________.

If the division is a subdivision, the buyer has a ____________ - day right to cancel the transaction, which the buyer cannot ____________. In addition, if the lot is sold on a land sales contract, the developer must establish a ____________________ ______________.

The Oregon Subdivision and Series Partition Control Law is administered by the Oregon __________ ____________ ____________. Its purpose is to protect the public from fraud, deceit and misrepresentation by requiring that the developer give each buyer a copy of a ____________ ______________ on subdivisions to which the law applies.

The Interstate Land Sales Full Disclosure Act requires developers of certain subdivisions to register the subdivision with the federal Office of Interstate Land Sales Registration, and to prepare a ______________ ______________, a copy of which must be given to each buyer.

KEY TERMS

The key to understanding any new field is the vocabulary used in that field. To maximize your comprehension of the material presented in this chapter, be sure you know the meaning and significance of the following terms. Remember that the majority of test questions primarily test knowledge of vocabulary.

Abatement
Acknowledge
Buffer zone
Building code
Collection escrow
Comprehensive plan
Condemnation
Conditional use permit
Down-zoning
Due process
Eminent domain
Equal protection
Final plat
Grandfather clause
Housing code
Just compensation
Land use goals
LCDC
Lot
Negotiate
Nonconforming use
Parcel
Partition
Planning
Police power
Pre-existing condition
Preliminary plat
Property report
Public use
Public report
Regulate
Sell
Series partition
Special use permit
Spot zone
Subdivision
Taking
Tentative plan
Use permit
Variance
Zone designation
Zone change
Zone classification
Zone
Zoning ordinance

ANSWERS

To chapter exercises. If you couldn't figure out what to put in the blanks, find the answer here!

Exercise a

A zoning ordinance regulates the owner's use of the land and is an exercise of POLICE POWER. *When a law deprives an owner of all economic use of the property, this is a taking and is an exercise of* EMINENT DOMAIN. *The process is called* CONDEMNATION. *When there is a taking, the owner is entitled to* JUST COMPENSATION *and the taking must be for a* PUBLIC PURPOSE. *Zoning ordinances cannot violate the constitutional requirements of* DUE PROCESS *and* EQUAL PROTECTION.

A zoning district created to keep incompatible uses apart is called a BUFFER *zone. When a zoning ordinance is enacted which creates a conflict with existing uses, the existing uses can continue as a* NONCONFORMING USE. *To recognize this, the zoning ordinance will contain a* GRANDFATHER CLAUSE.

To make a use legal the owner could request a ZONE CHANGE. *However, this would be illegal if it created a* SPOT ZONE. *Sometimes a* VARIANCE *to the zoning ordinance is granted to prevent a hardship. These are commonly used for dimensional problems. A* PERMIT *is sometimes granted for more serious exceptions to the zoning ordinances.*

The State of Oregon creates BUILDING CODES *to regulate new construction. Existing structures are sometimes regulated by a* HOUSING CODE.

Exercise b

A zoning ordinance dictates what a property can be used for, but long range land use decisions are part of the PLANNING *process. This process is accomplished by requiring each local jurisdiction to create a* COMPREHENSIVE PLAN, *which must be in compliance with the land use* GOALS *of the* LCDC. *The "*LCDC*" stands for the* LAND CONSERVATION AND DEVELOPMENT COMMISSION.

For the following land use issues, choose whether it is a function of the local jurisdiction (city or county) or of the LCDC:

Creating a zoning ordinance	■ *Local jurisdiction*	☐ LCDC
Granting a variance	■ *Local jurisdiction*	☐ LCDC
Creating land use goals	☐ *Local jurisdiction*	■ LCDC
Creating a comprehensive plan	■ *Local jurisdiction*	☐ LCDC

Exercise c

A division of land into two or three pieces is called a PARTITION *and the resulting pieces are called* PARCELS. *A* SUBDIVISION *is the division of land into* 4 *or more pieces.*

The first step in gaining approval is to file a TENTATIVE PLAN *with the local jurisdiction. Upon approval, a surveyor must create a* FINAL PLAT, *which must be* RECORDED. *Until this has been accomplished, the developer cannot* SELL *a lot or parcel, which means that the developer cannot bind a buyer. Advertising and showing the property would be* NEGOTIATING.

If the division is a subdivision, the buyer has a THREE *- day right to cancel the transaction, which the buyer cannot* WAIVE. *In addition, if the lot is sold on a land sales contract, the developer must establish a* COLLECTION ESCROW.

The Oregon Subdivision and Series Partition Control Law is administered by the Oregon REAL ESTATE AGENCY. *Its purpose is to protect the public from fraud, deceit and misrepresentation by requiring that the developer give each buyer a copy of a* PUBLIC REPORT *on subdivisions to which the law applies.*

The Interstate Land Sales Full Disclosure Act requires developers of certain subdivisions to register the subdivision with the federal Office of Interstate Land Sales Registration, and to prepare a PROPERTY REPORT, *a copy of which must be given to each buyer.*

PRACTICE QUESTIONS

The following practice questions are representative of the questions you will find on the final examination and on the licensing examinations given by the Oregon Real Estate Agency.

1. Zoning is done by authority of
   (A) the law of eminent domain.
   (B) the mayor.
   (C) petition.
   (D) police power.

2. Local zoning ordinances are examples of police power and cover such matters as
   (A) setback lines. (C) deed restrictions.
   (B) value of land. (D) all of the above.

3. Which of the following would not be an example of the use of police power?
   (A) A fire department making safety inspections
   (B) Zoning ordinances and planning goals
   (C) County health department regulations
   (D) All of the above are examples of police power.

4. Zoning ordinances usually cover such matters as
   (A) baselines. (C) prescription.
   (B) deed restrictions. (D) setback lines.

5. Zoning regulations frequently limit the
   I. type of use of a building.
   II. height and size of a building.
   III. lot size.
   IV. number of deed restrictions placed on property.
   (A) I and II only (C) III and IV only
   (B) II and III only (D) I, II and III only

6. A zoning ordinance is
   (A) a restriction. (C) a lien.
   (B) an easement. (D) a reservation.

7. Zoning ordinances control the use of privately owned land in several ways. Which of the following is not a zoning control?
   (A) Regulating land use
   (B) Restricting height of buildings
   (C) Providing for control of rentals
   (D) Restricting the area which a building may occupy

8. The primary justification for a zoning ordinance is to
   (A) control the quality of building construction.
   (B) prevent an over-supply of specified types of business enterprises within a zoned area.
   (C) maintain conformity in the physical requirements of a building in a zoned area.
   (D) protect the public health, safety, and general welfare of an area.

9. The main goal of zoning ordinances is to accomplish all of the following except
   (A) promote the general health, safety and welfare of the community.
   (B) separate harmonious uses from each other.
   (C) maintain values of property.
   (D) bring into existence a comprehensive plan for an area.

10. You intend to build a six-foot fence around your property on the property line. You should check
    I. local building codes and zoning restrictions.
    II. deed restrictions.
    (A) I only (C) Both I and II
    (B) II only (D) Neither I nor II

11. An area of land set off by local ordinance for specific use is called a
    (A) subdivision. (C) public improvement.
    (B) zone. (D) cul de sac.

12. Which of the following is not a requirement for a zoning ordinance to be legal?
    (A) It must promote the general health, safety and welfare.
    (B) It must be applied equally to all.
    (C) It must have been created under a democratic process.
    (D) It must have a definite ending date.

13. Which of the following best states the purpose of the building permit?
   I. Method of overriding a deed restriction
   II. Evidence of compliance with municipal rules
   (A) I only (C) Both I and II
   (B) II only (D) Neither I nor II

14. Of the following, which is the greatest effect that the government has on the value of real property?
   (A) Ad valorem taxes
   (B) Declassification
   (C) FHA minimum housing standards
   (D) Zoning

15. Which of the following statements regarding zoning ordinances is correct?
   I. Zoning ordinances do not independently create land value.
   II. Zoning ordinances only regulate types of structures that can be built.
   (A) I only (C) Both I and II
   (B) II only (D) Neither I nor II

16. When legal private restrictions on permissible building uses conflict with public restrictions, the ______________ restrictions prevail. The best words to complete the above sentence are
   (A) legal private (C) public
   (B) less stringent (D) more stringent

17. If there is a difference in the degree of restriction between zoning restrictions and deed restrictions on a property, which has priority?
   (A) Deed restrictions
   (B) Zoning restrictions
   (C) Whichever is more restrictive
   (D) Neither

18. When a zoning regulation permits a specific use of a property, but a private restriction contained in the deed limits that use of the property, the one that would prevail is the
   (A) deed restriction. (C) master plan.
   (B) building restriction. (D) zoning law.

19. The type of structure that an owner can build can be controlled by
   I. zoning. II. deed restrictions.
   (A) I only (C) Both I and II
   (B) II only (D) Neither I nor II

20. Deed restrictions may be created by
   (A) planning commissions.
   (B) the federal Department of Housing and Urban Development.
   (C) the grantor in the deed.
   (D) zoning boards.

21. Conditions, covenants and restrictions may be created by the
   I. seller at the time of sale.
   II. original developer in a master document.
   III. planning commission.
   (A) I only (C) I and II only
   (B) II only (D) II and III only

22. Private restrictions can be placed on real property by
   I. deed. III. zoning ordinance.
   II. written agreement.
   (A) I only (C) I and II only
   (B) II only (D) I, II, and III

23. Who normally puts deed restrictions on property in a subdivision?
   (A) The developer
   (B) The Real Estate Agency
   (C) The purchaser
   (D) The local planning board

24. After a developer has sold all the lots in a subdivision in which deed restriction on the lots to single-family residential use had been established, subsequent action to enforce the restriction must be initiated by
   (A) the developer, exercising rights as a grantor of a quitclaim deed.
   (B) a lot owner looking to a court of equity for an injunction.
   (C) the Land Conservation and Development Commission.
   (D) the County Zoning and Planning Commission.

25. After the developer who has created general plan restrictions on a subdivision has sold all of the lots, enforcement of the restriction must be initiated by
   I. the developer who created the restriction, or the developer's heir.
   II. a lot owner within the subdivision.
   III. the county planning commission.
   (A) I only (B) II only (C) III only (D) Both I and II

26. A nonconforming use of real property is
   I. a pre-existing use under the present zoning that would otherwise be illegal.
   II. illegal under most zoning codes and must be removed or changed.
   (A) I only (B) II only (C) Both I and II (D) Neither I nor II

27. A conflicting land use that predates present zoning and which is allowed to remain is a
   (A) variance. (B) nonconforming use. (C) covenant. (D) permit.

28. An example of a nonconforming use is
   I. A large, new supermarket recently built in an area zoned for small retail shops
   II. An old grocery store located in an area recently rezoned residential
   (A) I only (B) II only (C) Both I and II (D) Neither I nor II

29. A pre-existing condition which is still permitted under a "grandfather clause" in a zoning ordinance would be considered a
   (A) variance. (B) spot zone. (C) nonconforming use. (D) conditional use.

30. The right to continue a nonconforming use would cease if the owner attempts to
   I. enlarge the building or repair extensive structural damage.
   II. repair the building due to general wear and tear.
   (A) I only (B) II only (C) Both I and II (D) Neither I nor II

31. Rezoning often involves ridding the area of nonconforming uses. The means utilized may involve all of the following, except
   (A) retroactive zoning ordinances.
   (B) amortization provision terminating use within reasonable time.
   (C) prohibition against rebuilding.
   (D) prohibition against expanding.

32. Larry Webster constructed a twelve story building. Later a city ordinance was passed prohibiting the construction of buildings over ten stories. This instance represents a
   I. nonconforming use.
   II. situation in which the building would have to be demolished.
   (A) I only (B) II only (C) Both I and II (D) Neither I nor II

33. The Quantity Shoe Shop is an assumed business name of Bill Jones. Bill runs his business on a corner lot which is located in the City of Wonderview, Oregon. If the zoning is changed to residential,
   I. Bill must immediately discontinue the shoe store operation.
   II. the shoe store is now a nonconforming use.
   (A) I only (B) II only (C) Both I and II (D) Neither I nor II

34. As defined in local zoning ordinances, the distance between lot lines and improvements is known as
   (A) frontage. (B) setback. (C) the buffer zone. (D) depth.

35. Charlie wants to extend the side of his house beyond the setback boundary. Which must Charlie obtain?
   (A) A nonconforming use
   (B) A reservation
   (C) A subordination agreement
   (D) A variance

36. A special permit that is issued to allow a land use normally in violation with current zoning is called
   (A) a nonconforming use. (B) an amendment. (C) a variance. (D) a modification.

37. Zoning in an area required that there be ten feet from the edge of a building to the lot line. If approval were to be obtained to build up to seven feet from the lot line, it would be called a
(A) nonconforming use.
(B) spot zone approval.
(C) variance.
(D) conditional use permit.

38. An example of a variance would be
I. a large supermarket located in an area zoned for small shops.
II. an old supermarket located in an area which was recently rezoned residential.
(A) I only (C) Both I and II
(B) II only (D) Neither I nor II

39. A woman owned a house on a lot in the middle of an area zoned exclusively for single-family residences. If she requests a zone change to commercial and it is granted, this could be
I. an illegal act on the part of the jurisdiction granting the zone change.
II. a spot zone change.
(A) I only (C) Both I and II
(B) II only (D) Neither I nor II

40. As part of urban planning, areas are planned to provide separation between residential areas and areas zoned industrial. What are these areas called?
(A) Buffer zones (C) Protective zoning
(B) Spot zoning (D) Setback areas

41. The major purpose of the Land Conservation and Development Commission is to
(A) pass zoning laws for counties and local governments which supersede existing zoning laws.
(B) evaluate local comprehensive plans to ensure compliance with statewide goals and guidelines.
(C) establish wildlife sanctuaries.
(D) administer the sale of federal land within the state.

42. State-wide land use planning in Oregon is administered by
(A) the League of Oregon Cities (LOC).
(B) local governments.
(C) the Land Conservation and Development Commission (LCDC).
(D) the Department of Environmental Quality (DEQ).

43. Oregon's Land Conservation and Development Commission is authorized by law to
I. acknowledge the completed comprehensive land use plans of cities and counties based upon compliance of LCDC statewide planning goals.
II. prepare management plans for geographic areas designated by the Legislative Assembly as areas of critical state concern.
(A) I only (C) Both I and II
(B) II only (D) Neither I nor II

44. The functions of the Land Conservation and Development Commission include
(A) passing zoning ordinances for local jurisdictions.
(B) evaluating comprehensive plans to ensure they comply with statewide land use goals.
(C) establishing wildlife sanctuaries and preserves.
(D) all of the above.

45. A comprehensive plan would be concerned with all of the following except
(A) land use ordinances. (C) sanitation.
(B) flood control. (D) deed covenants.

46. A comprehensive plan would include matters such as
(A) existing streets and roads.
(B) water drainage and flood control.
(C) current traffic flow on arterials.
(D) all of the above.

47. Building codes in Oregon
(A) are uniform throughout the state.
(B) are usually enforced by cities and counties.
(C) are created by the Oregon Builders Board.
(D) follow federal guidelines.

48. A violation of a zoning ordinance can create
I. a lien. II. an unmarketable title.
(A) I only (C) Both I and II
(B) II only (D) Neither I and II

49. Zoning ordinances control the use of private land through several kinds of restrictions. Which of the following is not a zoning restriction?
(A) Building height limitations
(B) Designation of land area which building may occupy
(C) Nonconforming uses
(D) Setback requirements for buildings

50. All of the following are used in municipal planning except
(A) building codes.
(B) housing codes.
(C) subdivision regulations.
(D) subdivision covenants.

51. A Community Planning Board is established to
(A) stimulate wider interest in community problems.
(B) coordinate civic developments.
(C) stabilize property values and city growth.
(D) do all of the above.

52. A partition
(A) is created any time an owner divides land into two or three parcels.
(B) is created when an owner divides land into two or three parcels, provided each parcel has access to an existing road or street.
(C) must always be regulated by the city or county.
(D) Both A and C are correct.

53. Which of the following would be a partition in Oregon?
I. A division of land into four parcels, all of which have frontage on an existing road or street.
II. A division of land into two parcels which did not require the creation of a private road.
(A) I only (C) Both I and II
(B) II only (D) Neither I nor II

54. The regulation of partitions in Oregon is
(A) usually something which local jurisdictions have no authority to do.
(B) normally optional with cities and counties.
(C) required of cities and counties by state law.
(D) carried out directly by the Land Conservation and Development Commission.

55. Partitions must be regulated
(A) in all cases by all cities and counties with planning and zoning authority.
(B) by all counties and cities over 5,000 population.
(C) by all counties and cities over 10,000 population.
(D) by all cities and counties when the partition is in an exclusive farm use zone.

56. Charlie Cheatem owned a parcel of land 660 feet wide by 660 feet deep which fronted on a county road. He divided the property equally into two pieces, each with 330 feet of frontage and 660 feet deep. Then he advertised the property for sale and wrote his ad to say "two five-acre parcels, 330 feet on a county road." Which of the following statements is true?
I. His division is called a partition.
II. His advertising is false because the properties do not each contain five acres.
(A) I only (C) Both I and II
(B) II only (D) Neither I nor II

57. Joe Jones owned a property which had a long frontage on an existing dedicated road. Joe divided the property into three parcels and sold them after going through the requirements of the local jurisdiction for platting a partition. A few months after the sale one of the new owners wished to divide the newly acquired property in two again. Each resulting parcel would have its own frontage on the same road. This activity requires approval as a
(A) partition. (C) subdivision.
(B) lot of record. (D) short plat.

58. Dividing a tract of contiguous land under single ownership at the beginning of a year into four or more lots within that year results in what is defined as a
(A) subdivision. (C) minor partition.
(B) major partition. (D) final plat.

59. In Oregon, to create a subdivision
    (A) means to divide land into two or three lots with a new street to make sure all lots are accessible.
    (B) means to divide land into two or three lots, as long as no new street is created.
    (C) means to divide land into four or more lots within a calendar year.
    (D) depends on whether a new street is created.

60. A man owning an acre of ground with five rental houses on it decides to divide the property and sell the houses to the tenants. He needs to
    (A) file a subdivision plat.
    (B) have a real estate license.
    (C) pay a fine to the Real Estate Commissioner.
    (D) do nothing.

61. The Oregon Subdivision Control Act applies to the sale of
    (A) apartments.
    (B) residential lots.
    (C) commercial property.
    (D) parcels larger than 160 acres.

62. Twenty years ago the Landslide Development Company, Inc. built ten houses on land it owned. The company has now hired a surveyor to set the property boundaries so the houses can be sold separately. Before the houses can be sold, the company must
    (A) plat a subdivision.
    (B) have a real estate license in good standing.
    (C) get approval for a partition.
    (D) Since the houses are over ten years old, nothing need be done in order to sell them.

63. An elderly farmer decided to divide a 640-acre farm into eight equal portions and give one portion to each of eight children. This would be
    (A) a subdivision.
    (B) exempt from local platting requirements.
    (C) a series partition.
    (D) a subdivision which is exempt from local platting requirements.

64. Montana Morales owned a ranch in eastern Oregon. He sold off two lots and created a private driveway to each lot in the process. This is
    (A) a partition which is subject to regulation by the county.
    (B) a partition which is not subject to regulation by the county.
    (C) an unrecorded subdivision.
    (D) a transfer which the county is not required to regulate.

65. Under the Oregon Subdivision Control Law, to qualify for an exemption from the requirement to file for a public report the subdivision must provide which of the following?
    I. Adequate drainage
    II. Power services available and ready for hook-up for each lot at the time of sale or lease
    (A) I only
    (B) II only
    (C) Both I and II
    (D) Neither I nor II

66. The Oregon Subdivision and Series Partition Control Law would regulate the sale to Oregonians of
    (A) subdivision lots located in another state when offered to Oregon buyers.
    (B) commercial property located in a rural area in Oregon.
    (C) all lots located in Oregon which are 160 acres or more.
    (D) condominium units located in Oregon.

67. In a subdivision the units of land are referred to as
    (A) sections.
    (B) parcels.
    (C) lots.
    (D) partitions.

68. In an Oregon subdivision requiring approval, final approval of the plat has not been received. Lots in the subdivision may be sold
    (A) at any time, if the subdivision is the result of a court order.
    (B) after the Real Estate Commissioner authorizes the sale in writing.
    (C) when all requirements are substantially met in good faith and delay of the sale is not in the public interest.
    (D) under none of the above circumstances; final approval must be granted before any sale.

69. Under Oregon law which of the following is the final thing required of a subdivider before a lot in a subdivision can be transferred?
    (A) Approval by the city or county of the preliminary plan for the subdivision
    (B) Acknowledgment and recording of the plat of the subdivision
    (C) Written application for subdivision approval to the city or county having jurisdiction
    (D) Preparation of the subdivision plat

70. A subdivision disclosure statement, when it is required, must be given to the buyer of a lot prior to
    (A) negotiation of the sale.
    (B) execution of the binding sale agreement.
    (C) closing.
    (D) viewing the property.

71. Which of the following statements concerning subdivision public reports is true?
    I. A licensee must give a copy of a public report to a purchaser only after the execution of a binding sales contract.
    II. A licensee may use portions of a public report without using the entire statement in advertising of the subdivision.
    (A) I only (C) Both I and II
    (B) II only (D) Neither I nor II

72. After the Real Estate Commissioner's public report on a subdivision is issued
    (A) it must be displayed in the subdivider's office.
    (B) a prospective buyer must be given a copy of it and sign a receipt for it before buying the property.
    (C) the subdivider must wait at least 10 days after receiving the final public report before selling any lots.
    (D) all of the above are true.

73. The following two statements concern the public report on a subdivision issued by the Real Estate Commissioner.
    I. A copy of the public report must be displayed at all times in the office of the subdivider.
    II. A prospective buyer must be given a copy of the public report and sign a receipt for it before being permitted to purchase the property.
    (A) I only (C) Both I and II
    (B) II only (D) Neither I nor II

74. When a public report for a subdivision has been issued by the Real Estate Agency, it
    I. may be quoted in advertising by the developer, provided that it is quoted in its entirety.
    II. is evidence that the subdivision has the Real Estate Commissioner's recommendation.
    (A) I only (C) Both I and II
    (B) II only (D) Neither I nor II

75. If a vacant lot is purchased on a land sales contract, how many days must the subdivider give the purchaser to cancel the contract?
    (A) Three business days unless the cancellation right is waived by the buyer
    (B) Three calendar days, unless waived by the buyer
    (C) Three business days; no waiver by the buyer permitted
    (D) Three calendar days; no waiver by the buyer permitted

76. Under the Oregon Subdivision and Series Partition Control Law
    I. a buyer has a three-day right of rescission if he or she buys a lot for which a public report has been issued.
    II. there is a provision for a buyer to waive his or her rights under the law, if the buyer signs a written statement to that effect.
    (A) I only (C) Both I and II
    (B) II only (D) Neither I nor II

77. The Oregon Subdivision Control Act is administered by the
    (A) Attorney General.
    (B) State Land Board.
    (C) Real Estate Commissioner.
    (D) Governor.

78. A new subdivision project is subject to many controls requiring approvals which must be obtained before the plat can be recorded. Which one of the following is such a control?
    I. Zoning ordinance restrictions governing use and lot sizes of the land being subdivided
    II. Land for streets, schools, and civic facilities is acceptable and will be dedicated to public use
    (A) I only (C) Both I and II
    (B) II only (D) Neither I nor II

ANSWERS

To practice questions. If you chose the wrong letter, here's the right one! The explanations are designed to clarify your understanding.

1. **D** The constitution reserves to the government the power of eminent domain and police power. Zoning is considered an exercise of police power, for which just compensation does not need to be paid. A taking, on the other hand, is an exercise of eminent domain (condemnation), and requires payment.
2. **A** A zoning ordinance affects the value of the land, but cannot be used to set a value. Deed restrictions (covenants) are private contracts, usually between a seller and a buyer.
3. **D** The full implication of police power is the power of the government to maintain public order and to preserve and protect the public health, safety and welfare. Zoning and other land use regulations are only part of police power.
4. **D** Zoning ordinances frequently require a small amount of space between structures and the lot line. This area is called a setback. Deed restrictions (covenants) also restrict an owner's use of the land, but are created by private parties, not the government. The baseline is the point from which distances are measured north and south in the government survey. Prescription is long and continued use of another's land with the intent to gain an easement thereby.
5. **D** The purpose of zoning is to create value by enforcing conformity and thereby extending the economic life of structures. All of the above would work toward this goal, except limiting the number of deed restrictions. Deed restrictions (covenants) are created as a contractual matter between a buyer and a seller.
6. **A** Zoning ordinances are part of the government's power to maintain public order (police power). The other powers of the government are eminent domain (condemnation), taxation, and escheat. They are considered restrictions, but not encumbrances.
7. **C** Police power is the right of the government to maintain public order, and zoning is considered a part of that power. However, there are limits. Zoning cannot be capricious and arbitrary and must promote the general health, safety and welfare. Making special provisions for owners who rent their property, or restricting the number of rentals, would exceed the authority of the government.
8. **D** Quality of building construction and maintaining conformity in the physical requirements of buildings are enforced by building and housing codes, not zoning ordinances. If the local government attempted to prevent an over-supply of specified types of business enterprises, it would likely be in restraint of trade and in violation of federal law. Zoning is a legal exercise of police power, provided it is not capricious and arbitrary and promotes the general health, safety and welfare.
9. **B** Zoning ordinances are an exercise of police power, which is the power to maintain public order and promote the general health, safety and welfare. Zoning does create and maintain property values, but this is not the central purpose. Zoning ordinances are more a reaction to a comprehensive plan than a cause of it.
10. **C** Zoning ordinances and building codes both regulate the type of structure which can be built and the manner in which it must be constructed. Private covenants (sometimes called deed restrictions) can create the same kind of restrictions as zoning ordinances, if the parties have agreed to them.
11. **B** A subdivision is the act of dividing a large parcel into smaller lots, or it can mean the area so divided. A cul de sac is a short, dead end street, usually with a circular area at the end. A zone area is an area which has been set aside for particular purposes to the exclusion of other uses.
12. **D** Zoning not only must promote the general health, safety and welfare, but must also meet the constitutional tests of due process and equal protection. However, there is no requirement that a land use ordinance have an ending date.
13. **B** The primary purpose of a building permit is to ensure that minimum constructions standards are met. Deed restrictions (covenants) are private contractual agreements, usually between a buyer and a seller. The buyer must comply with all legal deed restrictions, as well as all governmental regulations. Governmental regulations do not override private contracts.
14. **D** Taxes, because they are a burden on the owner, decrease property values. The FHA has in-

creased property values by creating minimum housing standards, and also by making financing readily available. However, zoning has a far greater effect on property values. Properly enforced, zoning enforces conformity, which extends the economic life of a structure (the period of time over which the owner will receive an economic benefit). The longer the benefit period, the greater the present value.

15. **A** Zoning has a great effect on property values. Properly enforced, zoning enforces conformity, which extends the economic life of a structure (the period of time over which the owner will receive an economic benefit). The longer the benefit period, the greater the present value. Zoning ordinances regulate the size of the structure, and also the use to which it can be put, the size of the parcel required for building, and a number of other matters.

16. **D** Private restrictions do not supersede government restrictions, nor do government restrictions nullify private restrictions. The owner must comply with both. Normally, both private and public restrictions provide for minimums or maximums. Therefore, by adhering to the more restrictive of the two, the owner complies with both.

17. **C** As a technicality, neither has priority. Both the zoning and the deed restrictions must be adhered to. However, by conforming to the more restrictive of the two the owner effectively complies with both.

18. **A** Both the zoning and the deed restrictions must be adhered to. The word "permits" implies that the owner may, but does not have to, use the property in the designated manner. If the deed restriction prohibits it, then the deed restriction is what will control.

19. **C** Zoning restricts an owner's use of the property in many ways, one of which is the type of structure that can be built and the use to which it can be put. By contract, private parties can agree to restrictions also. These restrictions are commonly found in the deed, which is why a typical term for them is "deed restrictions" or "deed covenants." As private agreements, deed covenants can be any legal restriction the parties agree to, including limitations on the type of structure to be built and the use to which it can be put.

20. **C** Private covenants (sometimes called deed restrictions) can create the same kind of restrictions as zoning ordinances, if the parties have agreed to them. The government creates land use restrictions by zoning only.

21. **C** The phrase "conditions, covenants and restrictions" refers to a document created by a private party when selling the property, usually a developer. These are in the form of covenants, which are encumbrances on the title. Planning is a broad view of the future of an area, and is not directly a means by which restrictions are created.

22. **C** Private parties can contract to create a restriction on the use of the property. These are typically created in the deed (deed covenants). Zoning ordinances are restrictions also, but not private restrictions.

23. **A** Deed restrictions (covenants) are private contracts, usually between a buyer and a seller. They are frequently used by developers when creating a subdivision. The purpose is to require standards above those which the government has the power to impose, in order to enhance the prestige of the subdivision and create value thereby.

24. **B** Deed restrictions (covenants) are private contracts, usually between a buyer and a seller. They run to the benefit of whatever party is stipulated in the agreement. In a subdivision, this is usually all the other owners of lots in the subdivision. Private covenants can be enforced by a suit for damages, or a suit to enjoin. A suit to enjoin asks the court to enter an injunction.

25. **B** Deed restrictions (covenants) are private contracts, usually between a buyer and a seller. They run to the benefit of whatever party is stipulated in the agreement. In a subdivision, this is usually any of the other owners of lots in the subdivision. Private covenants can be enforced by a suit for damages, or a suit to enjoin. A suit to enjoin asks the court to enter an injunction.

26. **A** Zoning is considered an exercise of police power for which just compensation does not need to be paid. A taking, on the other hand, requires payment. If a local jurisdiction enacts a zoning ordinance which renders an owner's structure useless, they have taken it, and must pay. Therefore, they enact zoning ordinances which exempt existing structures and uses to avoid having to pay. These are called nonconforming uses.

27. **B** Zoning is considered an exercise of police power for which just compensation does not need to be paid. A taking, on the other hand, requires payment. If a local jurisdiction enacts a zoning ordinance which renders an owner's structure useless, they have taken it, and must pay. Therefore, they enact zoning ordinances which exempt existing structures and uses to avoid having to pay. These are called nonconforming uses.

28. **B** Zoning is considered an exercise of police power, for which just compensation does not need

to be paid. A taking, on the other hand, requires payment. If a local jurisdiction enacts a zoning ordinance which renders an owner's structure useless, they have taken it, and must pay. Therefore, they enact zoning ordinances which exempt existing structures and uses to avoid having to pay.

29. **C** Zoning is considered an exercise of police power, for which just compensation does not need to be paid. A taking, on the other hand, requires payment. If a local jurisdiction enacts a zoning ordinance which renders an owner's structure useless, they have taken it, and must pay. Therefore, they enact zoning ordinances which exempt existing structures and uses to avoid having to pay. Such pre-existing uses are called nonconforming uses. A variance and a permit are granted to allow an owner to do something not strictly permitted by the zoning, because not to do so would create a hardship. A spot zone is where only a small property is zoned differently in the middle of an area that is zoned another way, in a manner that is capricious and arbitrary or does not promote the general health, safety and welfare.

30. **A** The concept of a nonconforming use goes to the U.S. and Oregon Constitutions. Zoning is considered an exercise of police power, for which just compensation does not need to be paid. A taking, on the other hand, requires payment. If a local jurisdiction enacts a zoning ordinance which renders an owner's structure useless, they have taken it, and must pay. Therefore, they enact zoning ordinances which exempt existing structures and uses, to avoid having to pay. Exactly what they must permit the owner to do can get to fine points of law. However, it is generally held that the owner has the right to maintain the building, but not to add on or change the use.

31. **A** Zoning is considered an exercise of police power, for which just compensation does not need to be paid. A taking, on the other hand, requires payment. If a local jurisdiction enacts a zoning ordinance which renders an owner's structure useless, they have taken it, and must pay. Therefore, they enact zoning ordinances which exempt existing structures and uses, to avoid having to pay. Exactly what they must permit the owner to do can get to fine points of law. However, it is generally held that the owner has the right to maintain the building, but not to add on or change the use. An abatement is also legal, without having to pay, but they must allow the owner to continue to use the structure to at least the end of its useful economic life. Economic life is an appraisal concept which holds that, when a structure reaches the end of its economic life, it has no further value. Therefore, if they allow the owner to use the structure to the end of its economic life, but not beyond, they have taken nothing, because at that point the structure was worthless anyway.

32. **A** Zoning is considered an exercise of police power, for which just compensation does not need to be paid. A taking, on the other hand, requires payment. If a local jurisdiction enacts a zoning ordinance which renders an owner's structure useless or requires its demolition, they have taken it, and must pay. Therefore, they enact zoning ordinances which exempt existing structures and uses, called a nonconforming use, to avoid having to pay.

33. **B** A pre-existing condition must generally be allowed to continue. Requiring it to cease before the end of the economic life of the structure would be a taking for which the local jurisdiction would have to pay just compensation. A pre-existing condition that is allowed to continue in this way is called a nonconforming use.

34. **B** To ensure light and air, a more healthful environment, and for fire and safety considerations, zoning ordinances frequently require a small amount of space between structures and the lot line. This area is called a setback. A buffer zone is a zone area that is placed between two inharmonious uses.

35. **D** A variance or a permit should be viewed as a bending of the rules in order to prevent a hardship. The legal difference between a variance and a permit is that a permit is not appurtenant to the title. Normally, anything involving distances, arithmetic, or geometry will be a variance. Anything which allows a different use altogether, for example, a store in a residential area, would likely be a permit.

36. **C** A variance or a permit should be viewed as a bending of the rules in order to prevent a hardship. The legal difference between a variance and a permit is that a permit is not appurtenant to the title. Normally, anything involving distances, arithmetic, or geometry will be a variance. Anything which allows a different use altogether, for example, a store in a residential area, would likely be a permit.

37. **C** There are three ways to use a property in a manner that is not consistent with the existing zoning. The easiest is to be a nonconforming use, i.e., the use is grandfathered because it was in existence before the zoning was enacted. The hardest would be a zone change. A variance or a permit should be

viewed as a bending of the rules, in order to prevent a hardship. The legal difference between a variance and a permit is that a permit is not appurtenant to the title. Normally, anything involving distances, arithmetic, or geometry will be a variance. Anything which allows a different use altogether, for example, a store in a residential area, would likely be a permit.

38. **A** Both variances and conditional use permits are used to make exceptions to the zoning. As a rule, variances are used for physical adjustments, and conditional use permits are used when the use does not comply – e.g., a commercial use in a residential area.

39. **C** A spot zone is an illegal action creating a small, isolated area which is inconsistent with the general tenor of the neighborhood.

40. **A** In order to keep inharmonious uses apart, planners frequently allow a buffer zone between them, such as a park between an industrial area and a residential neighborhood. Spot zoning is creating one small parcel zoned differently from its neighbors, in a manner that is capricious and arbitrary and which is not required by the general health, safety and welfare. Spot zoning is unconstitutional. A set-back is a requirement that an owner not build within a certain distance of the property boundaries.

41. **B** The LCDC was established by the legislature to create state-wide land use planning. To accomplish this, the LCDC created land use goals for the state. Every city and county must create a comprehensive plan, which must be in compliance with the goals. To ensure that it does, it must be submitted to the DLCD (Department of Land Conservation and Development) and approved. Zoning and all other land use decisions are still made at the local level.

42. **C** The LCDC was established by the legislature to create state-wide land use planning. To accomplish this, the LCDC created land use goals for the state. Every city and county must create a comprehensive plan, which must be in compliance with the goals. To ensure that it does, it must be submitted to the DLCD (Department of Land Conservation and Development) and approved.

43. **C** The LCDC was originally established by the legislature to create state-wide land use planning. To accomplish this, the LCDC created land use goals for the state. Every city and county must create a comprehensive plan, which must be in compliance with the goals. To ensure that it does, it must be submitted to the DLCD (Department of Land Conservation and Development) and approved. When a comprehensive plan has been approved, it is said to be "acknowledged." Later, the legislature also gave the LCDC the authority to identify and create plans for areas of critical state concern.

44. **B** The Land Conservation and Development Commission has no authority to create zoning ordinances or comprehensive plans, nor can it grant variances, permits or subdivision and partition approvals. These functions are all administered by local jurisdictions.

45. **D** The land use goals of the Land Conservation and Development Commission address all public issues involving land use, but do not address the possibility of private land use restrictions such as deed covenants.

46. **D** The concept of a comprehensive plan is to include more than merely zoning. It encompasses all human activity in the jurisdiction for which it is adopted. It addresses the need for adjustments as anticipated changes occur.

47. **B** The Oregon Building Codes Agency adopts building codes for Oregon, but each local jurisdiction has the option of making local modifications. Major cities and most counties have building code enforcement departments, but if they do not, the Oregon Building Codes Agency will enforce the codes. The majority of such enforcement is local. There are no federal building code guidelines as such.

48. **B** Violation of a zoning ordinance usually results in a fine. However, if an owner sells a property to a buyer which does not conform to the zoning ordinance the buyer might have the right to rescind or seek damages. Thus the title could be considered unmarketable.

49. **C** Zoning is considered an exercise of police power, for which just compensation does not need to be paid. A taking, on the other hand, requires payment. If a local jurisdiction enacts a zoning ordinance which renders an owner's structure useless, they have taken it, and must pay. Therefore, they enact zoning ordinances which exempt existing structures and uses to avoid having to pay. These are called nonconforming uses.

50. **D** Planning involves a broad view of a jurisdiction's future. Therefore, it encompasses all public restrictions on land use, including zoning, subdivision regulations, building and housing codes. Subdivision covenants, however, are private restrictions on land use, usually created by a developer. The government has no control over these agreements.

51. **D** Oregon law requires cities and counties to create community planning boards, whose goal is to assist in the creating comprehensive plans. The goal of comprehensive planning is to stabilize property values and city growth and to coordinate developments. State law requires citizen involvement in this process.

52. **C** There are generally two types of land divisions. Partitions involve the division of land into two or three parcels. If the land is divided into four or more pieces, it is a subdivision. State law requires cities and counties to regulate all partitions and subdivisions by holding a public hearing. If the land is divided into four or more parcels as the result of successive partitions within a calendar year, this is called a series partition. A series partition must be regulated the same as a subdivision.

53. **B** When there are four or more pieces it is no longer a partition; it is a subdivision.

54. **C** State law requires regulation of all partitions and subdivisions by local jurisdictions. The manner in which they must be regulated is spelled out in some detail.

55. **A** Oregon statutes require all local jurisdictions to regulate all subdivisions and partitions. There are no exceptions for jurisdictions with different populations, nor does it matter what the zoning of the property is.

56. **A** Dividing a parcel into two or three parcels is called a partition. Dividing it into four or more is a subdivision. A parcel 660 feet by 660 feet is a quarter of a quarter of a quarter section, or ten acres.

57. **C** Since there are now four pieces out of the original, this is a subdivision. The term "short plat" has no meaning in Oregon. A "lot of record" is a term used to describe a lot which was platted but never built on, and for which the zoning has been changed so that building would now require a larger parcel. In general, a local jurisdiction must permit building on a lot of record, although there are exceptions.

58. **A** Dividing a piece of land into two or three pieces is a partition. If there are four or more, it is a subdivision. Whether a new street or road is created is irrelevant. The final plat is the map drawn by a surveyor and recorded once the subdivision has been approved.

59. **C** Dividing a piece of land into two or three pieces is a partition. If there are four or more, it is a subdivision. Whether a new street or road is created is irrelevant.

60. **A** If you divide a piece of land into four or more pieces within a calendar year, it is legally a subdivision. The fact that there were already more than four structures on the property is irrelevant.

61. **B** The Oregon Subdivision Control Act applies to all sales of subdivided lands where the city or county does not have an approved comprehensive plan and is not regulating the subdivisions at the local level. If all the lots are 160 acres or more, or if the property is commercial or multi-family, the subdivision is exempt from state law (although it may not be exempt under local rules).

62. **A** Since there are more than four lots, this is a subdivision, not a partition. The fact that the properties are ten years old is irrelevant in this case. Note that the original construction did not trigger the subdivision. Only when the houses were sold individually did it become a subdivision. Since the houses will be sold by the owner (the development company), no real estate license will be needed.

63. **A** Any division into two or three parcels is a partition. Dividing into four or more is a subdivision. Local platting requirements apply to all divisions of land, whether regulated or not. There are no exemptions for sale to relatives or heirs.

64. **A** A division into two or three parcels is a partition; four or more is a subdivision. Cities and counties must regulate all divisions of land.

65. **C** Normally, a public report is required. However, if there is nothing to disclose, then there is no need for a public report, so the entire filing is waived. This is done only for "full service" subdivisions, i.e., where all utilities are available at the lot line, roads and other necessary improvements are finished, and the lot is ready to build.

66. **A** All land divisions must be platted and meet platting requirements. The local jurisdiction must review and approve all land divisions as well. Subdivisions must also be reviewed by the Oregon Real Estate Agency when they involve lots located in other states which do not have reciprocity with Oregon, or subdivisions which are "common interests" such as tenancies in common. Developers of subdivisions which must be reviewed by the Oregon Real Estate Agency cannot sell lots until the Agency has issued a public report about the subdivision. In a few cases, subdivisions must also be reviewed by the Office of Interstate Land Sales of the Department of Housing and Urban Development.

67. **C** The result of a subdivision (four or more pieces) is always called a "lot." If it is a partition (two or three pieces), it is called a "parcel."

68. **D** The law distinguishes between "negotiating" and "selling." To sell is to bind the buyer irrevocably. As long as the buyer is not bound, it is negotiating. One can negotiate as soon as the tentative plan has been approved, but a sale requires that the final plat be approved and recorded.

69. **B** Selling is binding the buyer irrevocably. As long as the buyer is not completely bound, it is negotiating. One can negotiate as soon as the tentative plan has been approved, but a sale requires that the final plat be approved and recorded.

70. **B** The law provides that the buyer must be furnished a copy of the public report and the sales agent or seller must obtain a receipt from the buyer for it. The buyer has three business days to cancel the transaction from the date of receiving the public report, therefore, any sales agreement cannot be binding until the buyer receives the copy.

71. **D** The law provides that the buyer must be furnished a copy of the public report and the sales agent or seller must obtain a receipt from the buyer for it. The buyer has three business days to cancel the transaction from the date of receiving the public report. The seller and the seller's agent may use the public report in their advertising, but only if it is quoted in its entirety.

72. **B** The law provides that the buyer must be furnished a copy of the public report and the sales agent or seller must obtain a receipt from the buyer for it. The buyer has three business days to cancel from the date of receiving the public report. There is no requirement that it be displayed or recorded, as a copy is always available from the Real Estate Agency. Although the developer can begin negotiating, it is illegal to sell any lot before the report is issued. However, once it has been issued, the developer may begin sales immediately.

73. **B** The law provides that the buyer must be furnished a copy of the public report and the sales agent or seller must obtain a receipt from the buyer for it. The buyer has three business days to cancel from the date of receiving the public report. There is no requirement that it be displayed or recorded, as a copy is always available from the Real Estate Agency.

74. **A** The Oregon Subdivision Control Act provides that, unless exempt, the Real Estate Agency will issue a public report. Once issued, it can be quoted by the developer in advertising, but only if it is quoted in its entirety. The public report merely states the negative aspects of the property, but passes no judgment otherwise on the merits of the development. Therefore the developer may make no references implying that the public report is an approval or endorsement.

75. **C** The Oregon Subdivision Control Act provides that a buyer must be given three business days to cancel the transaction from receipt of a copy of the sales agreement and the public report. Any attempt to waive the right is void. This is also true of public reports issued by local jurisdictions.

76. **A** The Oregon Subdivision Control Act provides that a buyer must be given three business days to cancel the transaction from receipt of a copy of the sales agreement and the public report. If the subdivision is a exempt as a full-service subdivision and there is no public report, then the buyer does not have the right to cancel the transaction. Any attempt to waive the right is void. This is also true of public reports issued by local jurisdictions.

77. **C** The legislature has appointed the Real Estate Agency as the department to administer all matters relating to the Oregon Subdivision Control Act. However, practically all subdivisions are now exempt, as the law allows individual cities and counties to regulate subdivisions if they have an approved comprehensive plan, which they all do.

78. **C** Today, subdivision approvals are almost always done at the city or county level. The law provides the city or county with the authority to refuse approval of a subdivision if it does not meet all local, state and federal land use laws. In addition, local jurisdictions, within constitutional limitations, may demand that certain areas be set aside and dedicated to the public at no cost for schools, roads, streets, and other necessary public areas.

CONDOMINIUMS AND PLANNED COMMUNITIES

IN WESTERN CIVILIZATION, THE CONDOMINIUM FORM OF OWNERSHIP IS KNOWN to have been used at least as far back as ancient Rome. Of course, today's condominium and cooperative developments are governed by laws and regulations which are vastly more sophisticated than early Roman law. Nevertheless, the basic concept remains the same – ownership of your own unit, while sharing the use and expense of the common areas.

The underlying legal concept of a ***condominium*** today is relatively simple. Each owner owns his or her own unit, and owns the surrounding common areas as a tenant in common with the other unit owners. The percentage of interest in the common areas is usually apportioned according to the square footage of each unit, so the owners of larger units have a larger share than the owners of smaller units, and vice-versa.

Note that the tenancy in common gives each owner has the same undivided right of possession to the common areas, regardless of the percentage interest. Therefore, the amount of interest in the common elements would seem to be unimportant. However, it is not unusual to apportion common expenses, profits and occasionally voting privileges according to the percentage of interest in the common elements.

Each condominium development must have an ***association of unit owners***. In the case of a residential condominium development, the association is commonly referred to as a ***homeowners association***. Of course, condominiums can be created for any type of property – including offices, industrial parks, recreation property, mobile home parks – the list of possibilities is endless. The association is run by board members who are elected by the unit owners. The main function of the association is to manage and maintain the common areas, although it may have other duties as well. To cover the cost

NOTES

of maintenance and other expenses, the association has the right to levy assessments against each unit.

Many times condominiums are built on leased land. Since most buyers need financing, a buyer will have to give the lender a mortgage on the leasehold. While leasehold mortgages are common, a problem will arise if the lessor should evict the unit owner. Eviction extinguishes the leasehold, and thereby the leasehold mortgage as well. This would leave the lender with an unsecured note.

Lenders have several ways to protect themselves from this situation. The most common solution is to insist that the lessor subordinate the lease to the mortgage. This will allow the mortgage to be senior to the lease, even though recorded later. Then, if the lessor evicts a tenant, the lessor must take the unit back subject to the mortgage. It is common to find such a subordination clause in the master lease.

Planned communities

A ***planned community*** (formerly called a ***planned unit development (PUD)***) is a hybrid between a condominium and a subdivision. As in a subdivision, each owner owns an individual lot, separately platted. But, as in the condominium, each owner is a member of a homeowners association. As in the condominium, the association takes care of matters such as exterior maintenance and the like.

In many planned communities, there are also common areas (e.g., a golf course, recreation buildings, and so on) which the owners hold as tenants in common. Instead of tenancy in common, title is sometimes vested in the association. In either case, the association will also manage and maintain the common areas. And, as in a condominium, the association levies assessments against each owner's property to cover the costs of operation.

Planned communities also frequently contain commercial enterprises for the convenience of the lot owners. In creating a planned community it is common to find the concept of ***cluster zoning***. Cluster zoning stipulates a total density for the area, but allows the developer to place all the units compactly in one area and leave other areas as open space.

Cooperatives

A ***cooperative*** is another form of common ownership. In some day-to-day aspects, cooperatives appear very similar to condominiums, but the underlying legal principles are very different. A cooperative is created by forming a corporation (or occasionally a limited partnership or trust), which then sells shares to the unit owners. The organization then uses the funds acquired from sales of shares to purchase a property. Ownership of a share entitles the shareholder to occupy a particular unit.

Note, however, that each owner holds a share – personal property – not title to real property. Title to the real property is vested in the organization. Nevertheless, income tax laws generally treat ownership of cooperative apartments the same ownership of condominiums and ordinary homes.

As in any organization, each shareholder is entitled to vote his or her share in the election of board members. The board, in turn, takes care of the operation of the property. The organization assesses each shareholder for his or her share of the common expenses, such as taxes, insurance, maintenance, and so on.

From a practical standpoint, creating a cooperative would appear to accomplish the same ends as a condominium. But a difficulty arises when the cooperative organization borrows in order to acquire the property. For example, if the organization finances the property, then each owner only needs enough cash to pay his or her share of the down payment. This makes the acquisition easier, but it also means that each owner

NOTES

must be assessed his or her share of the mortgage principal and interest, in addition to the amount needed to cover the taxes, insurance, maintenance and other operating expenses. And if an owner defaults on paying the assessment, then the other owners will have to be assessed additional amounts until the default can be cured.

Timeshares

A ***timeshare*** is a relatively new concept in the real estate marketplace. Any interest in property, whether fee title, leasehold, condominium, cooperative, or otherwise can be marketed as a timeshare. Since the bundle of rights to any property can be divided in any manner, to create a timeshare, a seller simply sells the right of occupancy for a specific time, recurring each year.

Timeshares have been an especially attractive way to market vacation property, where the buyer really only intends to occupy the property for a week or two each year. Timeshare developments usually have a management team to maintain the property. In most cases, the management can also rent the property to others for those times when the owner is unable to use the occupancy period.

Exercise a

In a condominium, each owner has an interest as a ____________ in ____________ to the common areas. This gives each owner an undivided right of ________________ of the common areas together with all other unit owners. To manage the affairs of the condominium, each development must have an ________________ of ____________ ____________. This is called a ________________ ________________ when the development is a residential condominium. The association has the right to levy ________________ against each unit to cover the costs of operation. When a condominium is built on leased land, there must be a ________________ clause in the master lease which provides that, in the event of an ____________, the lessor must take the property back subject to a mortgage on the leasehold. A planned community is like a ________________, in that each owner owns a lot which is separately platted, but like a ________________ because there is a homeowners association which manages and maintains the property.

In a cooperative, owners hold shares which are ____________ property. Share ownership entitles the holder to occupy a particular unit. Title to the property is usually vested in a ________________. A difficulty with cooperative ownership occurs when a shareholder fails to pay the ________________ for maintenance and operational expense. In this case, all other owners must make up the difference.

Timeshares involve a recurring right of ____________ and are a popular way to market vacation property.

NOTES

The Oregon Condominium Act

The ***Oregon Condominium Act**** (ORS 100.005 to 100.910) has been created to answer the many questions involved in the creation and operation of condominiums. The Act also contains regulations to protect the public from fraud, deceit and misrepresentation in the sale of condominiums.

The creation of a condominium starts when the developer records a ***declaration***. The developer is called the ***declarant***, because the developer is declaring that the property described in the declaration is now under the provisions of the Oregon Condominium Act. The declaration must include numerous matters. While not a complete list, the following are the most important –

- A legal description of the entire property
- A listing and legal description of the units and the designation by which each shall be known, to be shown on floorplans for the structure(s)
- The name by which the development will be known, which must be a unique name not used for any other condominium in the county
- The percentage interest in the common elements which appertain to each unit
- Limited common elements (see below) and the unit(s) to which they appertain
- How common expenses, profits and voting rights are to be allocated
- The percentage of voting rights required to amend the declaration, if over 75%

The declaration must be approved by the Real Estate Commissioner, the tax collector, and the tax assessor before it can be recorded. Approval by the Real Estate Commissioner requires that the declaration meet statutory standards. The tax collector will approve the declaration upon receipt of all unpaid taxes, including taxes for the current year. This is to avoid having to decide how to apportion unpaid taxes on the newly created units. The tax assessor is especially interested in the floorplans, since the tax assessor must now place each unit on the tax rolls as a separate account and appraise it for its real market value.

As noted previously, when a condominium is created, each unit owner also owns an undivided interest as a tenant in common to the ***common elements***. The common elements can be thought of as "the entire development, less the units themselves." The majority of the common elements are classed as ***general common elements***. However, the common elements may also include ***limited common elements***. Remember that in a tenancy in common each co-tenant has an undivided right of possession of the entire property. Thus, in a condominium, no unit owner could ever be legally excluded from any portion of the common elements. This would make it impossible to have parking spaces or other portions of the common elements reserved for specific units. The Condominium Act fixes this problem by creating the possibility of limited common elements. Limited common elements are portions of the common areas which are reserved for the exclusive use of a particular unit owner.

Once a condominium has been created, the Oregon Condominium Act provides that the interest in the common elements, both general and limited, becomes an inseparable appurtenance to the unit. This means that a deed conveying the unit will also automatically convey the interest in the common elements. Such deeds are called ***unit deeds***. Were it not for this provision in the Condominium Act owners would be constantly deeding their unit to a buyer and forgetting to include their interest in the common elements, leaving the buyer owning a landlocked property.

At common law, any tenant in common always has the right to partition of the tenancy. This can't be allowed for the common elements in a condominium, so another

* The original name of the Oregon Condominium Act was the "Unit Ownership Act." Many older text materials still refer to the original name of the statute and to "unit ownership."

NOTES

provision of the Condominium Act is that, once a development has been declared to be a condominium, there can be no suit for partition of the common elements.

A question commonly arises as to whether the tax bill for the common elements should be sent to the association of unit owners or not. Property taxes are assessed ad valorem (according to value). This means that the assessor must place a value on each unit. The most direct way to appraise each unit is by a process called "sales comparison," where the unit to be appraised is compared to other similar units which have recently been sold. Note, however, that when each of the other units was sold, the price the buyer paid included the inseparable interest in the common elements which was appurtenant to the unit. Comparable sales prices, therefore, include the common elements, so the tax value of each unit includes the value of the common elements. Now, if the tax collector were to send a bill to the association for the common elements, the common elements would be taxed twice.

Oregon statutes also provide that when a condominium is a leasehold condominium, the tax assessor is to value each unit as though it were a fee title.

Under the Oregon Condominium Act, a developer may create a condominium on which the development is to take place all at once, or in stages. A ***staged condominium*** would be created where a developer had additional adjacent land and desired to build more units later.

Condominiums can also contain ***variable property*** and ***non-withdrawable property***. Variable property occurs in a ***flexible condominium***, where it is defined as land which the developer reserves the right to withdraw from the condominium (for up to seven years) without needing the permission of the unit owners. Property which is non-withdrawable must remain within the condominium unless the unit owners vote to approve its withdrawal.

An important part of the process of creating a condominium is the recording of the ***floorplans*** of the structure(s). The floorplans must be created by an architect, surveyor or engineer, who must certify that they accurately depict the building(s) and the boundaries of the units. The unit designation as listed in the declaration must be shown on the floorplans.

The purpose of recording the floorplans is to create a public record which will give constructive notice of the dimensions of each unit. Once this has been accomplished, the legal description of any given unit can simply be the unit designation. Note that this process is conceptually identical to the creation of a lot and block legal description.

Simultaneous with recording the declaration and the floorplans, the developer must record the initial ***bylaws*** which will govern the operation of the association of unit owners. Of course, once the units have been sold, each owner has the right to vote to amend the bylaws. The bylaws contain matters such as the officers of the association and their duties and powers, calling special meetings, quorums, election of board members, procedures for amending the bylaws, and the like. Operational matters are also included, such as collection of assessments, maintenance of the units, insurance coverage, financial statements, hiring personnel, and so forth. And the initial bylaws will also include procedures for turnover of control from the developer to the unit owners (see below).

The association of unit owners may levy on each unit an assessment for common expenses. The levy is considered a lien on the unit, which can be foreclosed, if necessary. The lien of the association of unit owners is prior to all other liens except property taxes, special assessments and a recorded first trust deed or mortgage.

By stipulation in the declaration, the declarant can retain control of the association of unit owners for a period of time. The maximum time can normally be until the declarant has sold 75% of the units, but in no case longer than three years (seven years if

Notes

it is a flexible condominium). The declarant usually retains control for the period of time needed to finish selling the units, but the statutes do not require the declarant to retain any control at all. If nothing is specified in the declaration, then the presumption is that control must be turned over to the association when 50% of the units have been sold. Of course, regardless of the time when turnover is required, the declarant retains the right to vote as the owner of any units the declarant may still own.

Oregon Revised Statutes 100.485 further prohibits an initial management contract in excess of three years. The purpose of this provision is to prevent a developer from creating an organization to provide management services and then binding the association to use their services for an excessive time. In the past developers used to create a management company and, while still in control of the project, contract with the developer's own management company at abusive rates for many years. The association would be bound by the contract and all unit owners would have to share in the cost.

Conversion Existing structures can be converted to condominiums with little problem in Oregon. However, if the structure is residential, the owner must give 120 days advance notice to each tenant. The notice may be waived if 100% of the tenants agree to do so. The notice does not constitute a notice to terminate the existing tenancy, although an owner can give such notice separately as provided by the Oregon Residential Landlord and Tenant Law.

If the units will not be substantially altered, then the owner must offer to sell each unit to the tenant in the unit. The offer must be left open for 60 days or until the tenant rejects the offer, whichever occurs first. This means that the developer may not be free to sell the units to the public for 60 days after recording the declaration and other documents. Following the offer period, the owner cannot offer the unit to the public on terms more favorable than the terms on which it was offered to the tenant.

These provisions were made a part of the Oregon Condominium Act in order to protect tenants from having their apartments sold out from under them and to ensure that such units would be offered to the tenants at reasonable prices. However, in reality, when apartments are converted to condominiums, the owner usually offers more favorable terms to the tenants since a sale to a tenant can be faster and cheaper.

Note that if all the tenants are on month-to-month tenancies, the owner can simply terminate all tenancies. Once the tenants have all moved out there will be no need to give notice prior to recording the declaration or an offer to sell to the tenant.

Amendments to the declaration Supplemental declarations or amendments to the declaration must be approved by the unit owners. The Oregon Condominium Act requires the vote in favor to be as required in the original declaration, but in no case less than 75% of the unit owners.

Removal from condominium status The unit owners (with the permission of lienholders) may remove a property from the provisions of the Oregon Condominium Act and convert it to a tenancy in common by recording an agreement to that effect. The vote required by the unit owners must be 100%, unless the property is obsolete (90% vote), or damaged (60% vote).

Once removed from the Act, the owners become ordinary tenants in common to the whole property. Each co-tenant has a percentage interest according to the appraised value of his or her unit as a percentage of the appraised value of the entire property. An interest as a tenant in common is separately lienable, so liens previously existing against a unit normally become liens against the unit owner's resulting percentage interest as a tenant in common.

NOTES

Structural warranty As an additional consumer protection, a developer of a condominium which is new construction must give buyers a one-year warranty on the improvements, including the common elements, but not including consumer goods such as appliances. The warranty is in addition any warranties provided by the contractor who constructed the project.

Sales regulations In the event the condominium development is residential, the developer must comply with certain sales regulations. The most significant part of these regulations deals with the creation of a ***condominium disclosure statement***, a copy of which must be given to each buyer. The developer must create the disclosure statement according to statutory requirements and submit it to the Real Estate Commissioner for approval. The Commissioner may inspect the units and require that additional information be included in the disclosure statement.

The developer cannot quote the disclosure statement in advertising unless it is quoted in its entirety. The Commissioner's approval of the disclosure statement is not an endorsement or approval of the units and the developer may not imply that the Commissioner has given such approval.

A developer cannot ***sell*** a unit in a condominium until the developer has given a copy of the approved disclosure statement, the bylaws of the association of unit owners, and the declaration to the buyer. The developer must obtain a receipt from each buyer for the disclosure statement and other documents and keep the receipt on file for at least three years.

However, prior to giving the buyer copies of the documents, the developer can ***negotiate*** for the sale. Selling occurs when the developer enters into a binding agreement with a buyer. Negotiating includes marketing efforts and promotion, including entering into a non-binding sales agreement with a buyer. A sales agreement is non-binding if the buyer is entitled to a full refund of any funds paid to the developer in the event the developer cannot or will not produce a disclosure statement approved by the Real Estate Commissioner. If a developer wishes to enter into a non-binding pre-sale agreement with a buyer, all funds and documents must be deposited with a neutral escrow in Oregon with instructions not to close the transaction until the developer has complied with these sales requirements.

Either in the sales agreement or separately, the developer must give the buyer notice of the buyer's right to cancel the transaction within five business days of signing the sales agreement, the receipt for the disclosure statement, and the receipt for the declaration and bylaws, whichever occurs last. However, the buyer can waive the right to cancel the transaction provided the waiver is on a document separate from the sales contract. The buyer cannot waive any other rights.

Sales on land sales contracts When real estate is sold on a land sales contract, the buyer normally does not receive the deed until the balance is paid in full. To protect buyers and ensure that a deed to their unit will be forthcoming when they have finished paying the balance, the Oregon Condominium Act requires developers who sell condominium units on land sales contracts to establish a collection escrow to receive the buyer's payments. The developer must give the escrow a copy of the sales contract between the developer and the buyer, the deed (or other document as required for a leasehold condominium) conveying title (or other interest) to the buyer, a copy of a title report on the unit, and a commitment, satisfactory to the Real Estate Commissioner, from the holder of any underlying blanket encumbrance to give a partial release of the unit from the blanket encumbrance. This requirement applies only to sales on land sales contracts from the developer to the first consumer; thereafter sales on land sales contracts between ordinary buyers and sellers do not need to meet these provisions.

NOTES

Exercise b

The developer of a condominium project is called the ____________ when he or she records a declaration. The declaration must list all the units, together with the percentage interest in the ____________ common elements as well as any ____________ common elements which will become an inseparable ____________ to each unit. Title to a condominium is transferred by a ____________ deed. In addition to recording the declaration, the developer must record the ____________ for the development, which will assist in creating a legal description for each unit. The developer must also record ____________ for the association of unit owners.

When apartments are converted to condominiums, the developer must give ______ -days advance notice to each tenant prior to recording the declaration, unless all tenants agree to waive the notice. If the units will not be substantially altered, the developer must offer to ________ each unit to the tenant in the unit and the developer must leave the offer open for _____ days. Thereafter, for _____ days the developer cannot offer the unit to the public on terms more favorable than the terms on which the unit was offered to the tenant.

If owners wish to remove their units from condominium status, they can do so if _____ % vote in favor, although only a _____ % vote is required if the property is obsolete and a _____ % vote is required if the property is substantially destroyed. Following removal, each unit owner becomes a ____________ in ____________ to the entire property, with a percentage interest calculated according to the market value of his or her unit in proportion to the market value of the entire project.

When a project is ________ construction, the developer must give buyers a ________ -year warranty.

Prior to selling a condominium unit, the developer must give each buyer a copy of a ____________ ____________ ____________ which has been approved by the Oregon Real Estate Commissioner. The developer cannot quote this document in advertising unless it is quoted in its entirety, nor can the developer imply that the Real Estate Commissioner has ____________ the project. To ________ means to enter in a binding sales agreement. If the sales agreement is non-binding, this is called ____________. In addition, the developer must give the buyer a copy of the ____________ and the bylaws. The developer must obtain a receipt from the buyer for these documents and retain the receipt for ____ years. When a condominium unit is sold on a land sales contract, the developer must establish a ____________ ____________ to ensure that the buyer will be able to obtain the ____________, or other final document, when the contract is paid in full.

NOTES

The Oregon Planned Community Act

Planned communities are regulated by the Oregon Planned Community Act (ORS 94.550 to 94.785). As noted earlier, a planned community is a subdivision, subject to platting and land use regulation the same as any subdivision. However, a planned community also has a homeowners association, like a condominium. Therefore, a planned community will have a declaration and bylaws (but a platted subdivision instead of floorplans). There will also be provisions for the declarant to turn over control; statutory powers of the homeowners association, including meetings and voting procedures and setting lot owners' assessments. Nevertheless, because of the unique nature of a planned community, the details are sometimes different from condominium practices.

The Act defines a class I planned community as one that has thirteen or more lots and has total annual projected assessments of $10,000 or $100 per lot, whichever is greater. A class II planned community is one containing five to twelve lots with projected annual assessments of $1,000 or more for all lots. Planned communities of two to four lots are defined as class III planned communities.

In some planned communities there is no common property, and the sole function of the homeowners association is to provide maintenance and other services to lot owners. But in most planned communities there is common property, the use and enjoyment of which is shared by all lot owners. In a condominium, the common elements are held as tenants in common, and in a planned community, this is also possible. However, planned communities are frequently created where the homeowners association is actually a corporation, and title to common property is vested in the corporation. Each lot owner, therefore, becomes a shareholder in the corporation. In this case, the developer should be sure that each share of stock becomes an inseparable appurtenance to the title to each lot.

Timeshare regulation

Timeshares in Oregon are regulated by ORS 94.803 to 94.945. Timeshares are defined as improved residential property where the buyer receives a right of occupancy in separated periods. However, exemptions include timeshares in a project comprised of timeshares with four or fewer periods over a period of less than five years, or three years or less if the right of occupancy is a license rather than a fee title or leasehold estate.

It should be noted that a timeshare is frequently an interest in a condominium unit, but it could also be a regular house in an ordinary subdivision or planned community, or even a parcel of vacant land. Also, a timeshare can be created out of a leasehold as well as a fee. The timeshare can be deeded or it can be a recurring leasehold, or even a license to occupy a fee or a leasehold.

A timeshare is created when the developer records a ***timeshare instrument*** which sets forth the provisions of the ***timeshare plan***. This is similar to the function of the declaration in the creation of a condominium. Note that, if the property is a condominium, the condominium must first be created in the usual manner, and then the timeshare instrument can create the timeshare plan. The statutes list specific facts which the timeshare instrument must contain, including matters such as voting privileges, who will be the managing entity, and so forth.

As in a condominium, no suit for partition of the timeshare interests is usually permitted as long as the property is subject to a timeshare plan. However, if one timeshare estate is owned by two or more persons as tenants in common, their interests may be partitioned as to each other.

NOTES

Sales regulation A developer of a timeshare plan must submit a notice of intent to sell timeshares to the Real Estate Commissioner. The statutes require the notice to contain information which the Commissioner needs in order to issue a ***timeshare public report***. When the timeshare plan includes the rights of timeshare owners to exchange their timeshare rights for rights of other timeshare owners in other timeshare plans, the Commissioner must also be furnished information on the exchange program. The Commissioner may also examine the timeshare property before or after the issuance of the public report, and may modify the public report, as appropriate.

Note that the function of the timeshare public report is the same as the subdivision public report and the condominium disclosure statement. It should not be surprising then that the developer may not use the public report in advertising unless it is quoted in its entirety, and cannot imply that the Real Estate Commissioner has approved or endorsed the timeshare plan. Negotiation is permitted, but no binding sales can be made until the public report has been issued. Selling and negotiating have the same meaning here as in subdivision and condominium law.

In addition, the developer must give a copy of the public report to each buyer and obtain a receipt from the buyer. The developer must retain the receipt for at least three years. The buyer has the right to cancel the transaction for five calendar days which cannot be waived. Note that this is slightly different from the Oregon Condominium Act which provides for five business days and the right to cancel the transaction can be waived.

When the developer wishes to sell timeshares and carry the financing essentially the same procedures apply as with condominiums. That is, a collection escrow must be established into which the developer must deposit the deed or release instrument and other documents sufficient for the buyer to obtain good title when the obligation has been paid in full. The buyer must make all payments to the escrow, and the escrow is responsible for making all payments on underlying encumbrances owed by the developer.

Property taxes Because there may be multiple owners in a timeshare plan, the statutes provide that the manager of the timeshare plan will be the agent of the owners for property tax purposes, including appeals of valuations as well as payment of the bill. Each unit in a timeshare plan is taxed as one tax account, the cost of which is to be shared by each timeshare owner.

Exercise c

A planned community is essentially a ____________________ which also has a homeowners association in the same manner as a ____________________ development. The association levies ____________________ against each lot in order to collect the funds necessary to pay for maintenance and other community expenses. A timeshare is a right of ____________________ over separated periods. A timeshare is created by recording a ____________________ ____________________ setting forth the details of the timeshare plan. In addition, the developer must obtain a timeshare ______________ ______________ from the Real Estate Commissioner before selling timeshares. The developer must give a copy of it to each buyer and obtain a receipt which must the developer must maintain for ______ years. When timeshares are sold on a land sales contract, the developer must establish a ____________________ ______________ . In a timeshare, the managing entity acts as ______________ of the owners in all property tax matters.

KEY TERMS

The key to understanding any new field is the vocabulary used in that field. To maximize your comprehension of the material presented in this chapter, be sure you know the meaning and significance of the following terms. Remember that the majority of test questions primarily test knowledge of vocabulary.

Association of unit owners
Bylaws
Cluster zoning
Common elements
Condominium
Condominium disclosure statement
Conversion condominium
Cooperative
Declarant
Declaration
Flexible condominium
Floorplans
General common elements
Homeowners association
Limited common elements
Negotiate
Non-withdrawable property
Oregon Condominium Act
Planned community
Planned unit development
Planned community
Sell
Staged condominium
Structural warranty
Timeshare plan
Timeshare public report
Timeshare instrument
Timeshare
Unit deed
Variable property

ANSWERS

To chapter exercises. If you couldn't figure out what to put in the blanks, find the answer here!

Exercise a

In a condominium, each owner has an interest as a TENANT *in* COMMON *to the common areas. This gives each owner an undivided right of* POSSESSION *of the common areas together with all other unit owners. To manage the affairs of the condominium, each development must have an* ASSOCIATION *of* UNIT OWNERS*. This is called a* HOMEOWNERS ASSOCIATION *when the development is a residential condominium. The association has the right to levy* ASSESSMENTS *against each unit to cover the costs of operation. When a condominium is built on leased land, there must be a* SUBORDINATION *clause in the master lease which provides that, in the event of an* EVICTION*, the lessor must take the property back subject to a mortgage on the leasehold. A planned community is like a* SUBDIVISIONS*, in that each owner owns a lot which is separately platted, but like a* CONDOMINIUM *because there is a homeowners association which manages and maintains the property.*

In a cooperative, owners hold shares which are PERSONAL *property. Share ownership entitles the holder to occupy a particular unit. Title to the property is usually vested in a* CORPORATION*. A difficulty with cooperative ownership occurs when a shareholder fails to pay the* ASSESSMENT *for maintenance and operational expense. In this case, all other owners must make up the difference.*

Timeshares involve a recurring right of POSSESSION *and are a popular way to market vacation property.*

Exercise b

The developer of a condominium project is called the ___DECLARANT___ *when he or she records a declaration. The declaration must list all the units, together with the percentage interest in the* ___GENERAL___ *common elements as well as any* ___LIMITED___ *common elements which will become an inseparable* ___APPURTENANCE___ *to each unit. Title to a condominium is transferred by a* ___UNIT___ *deed. In addition to recording the declaration, the developer must record the* ___FLOORPLANS___ *for the development, which will assist in creating a legal description for each unit. The developer must also record* ___BYLAWS___ *for the association of unit owners.*

When apartments are converted to condominiums, the developer must give ___120___ *-days advance notice to each tenant prior to recording the declaration, unless all tenants agree to waive the notice. If the units will not be substantially altered, the developer must offer to* ___SELL___ *each unit to the tenant in the unit and the developer must leave the offer open for* ___60___ *days. Thereafter, for* ___60___ *days the developer cannot offer the unit to the public on terms more favorable than the terms on which the unit was offered to the tenant.*

If owners wish to remove their units from condominium status, they can do so if ___100___ *% vote in favor, although only a* ___90___ *% vote is required if the property is obsolete and a* ___60___ *% vote is required if the property is substantially destroyed. Following removal, each unit owner becomes a* ___TENANT___ *in* ___COMMON___ *to the entire property, with a percentage interest calculated according to the market value of his or her unit in proportion to the market value of the entire project.*

When a project is ___NEW___ *construction, the developer must give buyers a* ___ONE___ *-year warranty. Prior to selling a condominium unit, the developer must give each buyer a copy of a* ___CONDOMINIUM___ ___DISCLOSURE___ ___STATEMENT___ *which has been approved by the Oregon Real Estate Commissioner. The developer cannot quote this document in advertising unless it is quoted in its entirety, nor can the developer imply that the Real Estate Commissioner has* ___APPROVED___ *the project. To* ___SELL___ *means to enter in a binding sales agreement. If the sales agreement is non-binding, this is called* ___NEGOTIATING___ *. In addition, the developer must give the buyer a copy of the* ___DECLARATION___ *and the bylaws. The developer must obtain a receipt from the buyer for these documents and retain the receipt for* ___3___ *years. When a condominium unit is sold on a land sales contract, the developer must establish a* ___COLLECTION___ ___ESCROW___ *to ensure that the buyer will be able to obtain the* ___DEED___ *, or other final document, when the contract is paid in full.*

Exercise c

A planned community is essentially a ___SUBDIVISION___ *which also has a homeowners association in the same manner as a* ___CONDOMINIUM___ *development. The association levies* ___ASSESSMENTS___ *against each lot in order to collect the funds necessary to pay for maintenance and other community expenses.*

A timeshare is a right of ___POSSESSION___ *over separated periods. A timeshare is created by recording a* ___TIMESHARE___ ___INSTRUMENT___ *setting forth the details of the timeshare plan. In addition, the developer must obtain a timeshare* ___PUBLIC___ ___REPORT___ *from the Real Estate Commissioner before selling timeshares. The developer must give a copy of it to each buyer and obtain a receipt which must the developer must maintain for* ___3___ *years. When timeshares are sold on a land sales contract, the developer must establish a* ___COLLECTION___ ___ESCROW___ *. In a timeshare, the managing entity acts as* ___AGENT___ *of the owners in all property tax matters.*

PRACTICE QUESTIONS

The following practice questions are representative of the questions you will find on the final examination and on the licensing examinations given by the Oregon Real Estate Agency.

1. Condominiums may be
   (A) residential property.
   (B) resort property.
   (C) industrial property.
   (D) all of the above.

2. What does an owner who purchases a condominium receive?
   (A) Title in an apartment and tenancy in common of undeveloped land
   (B) Title in airspace and common interest in common areas
   (C) Tenancy in common in the building and common interest in other areas
   (D) Tenancy in common in the building and tenancy in severalty in the common areas

3. Condominium ownership is a
   I. type of space ownership.
   II. form of fee simple ownership of real property.
   (A) I only
   (B) II only
   (C) Both I and II
   (D) Neither I nor II

4. A person who owns fee title to air space within a residential, industrial, or commercial building together with an undivided interest in common in the common areas usually has an interest in a
   (A) community apartment project.
   (B) planned development project.
   (C) condominium project.
   (D) stock cooperative project.

5. The term "common elements" is most often associated with what type of real estate?
   (A) Condominiums
   (B) Cooperatives
   (C) Corporate headquarters
   (D) Leasehold estates

6. Oregon law specifically includes which of the following as "general common elements" of a condominium?
   (A) Parking areas
   (B) Gardens
   (C) Premises for the lodging of caretakers
   (D) All of the above

7. Sarah Miller purchased a condominium which included several common facilities: Swimming pool, tennis courts, and a putting green. Under a typical condominium arrangement, these common elements are owned by
   (A) an association of homeowners in the condominium.
   (B) Miller and the owners of the units in the condominium in the form of undivided percentage interest.
   (C) a corporation in which Miller and the owners of the other units in the condominium own stock.
   (D) Miller and the owners of the other units in the condominium in the form of divided interests.

8. The Westgate condominium has tennis courts, a large parking lot, and a swimming pool. These common elements, under the terms of a typical condominium arrangement, are owned by
   (A) the owners of the units in the condominium in the form of undivided percentage interest.
   (B) the owners of the units in the condominium in the form of divided interest.
   (C) a corporation in which the owners of the units within the condominium own stock.
   (D) an association of homeowners within the condominium.

9. Under the condominium form of ownership, common elements typically include
   I. storage for janitors, exits, and girders.
   II. guest parking stalls.
   (A) I only
   (B) II only
   (C) Both I and II
   (D) Neither I nor II

10. Everett Washington just bought a luxury condominium which included items such as a swimming pool, tennis courts and gym. These common elements can be owned by
(A) the association of unit owners.
(B) Washington and the other unit owners as tenants in common.
(C) a corporate entity, whose stock in turn is owned by the unit owners.
(D) any of the above.

11. Unit owners' fees are typically used to pay for
(A) exterior maintenance.
(B) insurance policy on the structure.
(C) water, sewer and garbage bills.
(D) any of the above.

12. In Oregon, a condominium homeowner's association would normally use the fees it collects to pay which of the following expenses?
I. Insurance premiums for the policy covering common areas
II. Redecorating expenses for the common areas
(A) I only (C) Both I and II
(B) II only (D) Neither I nor II

13. In a fee title condominium taxes on all the common elements are paid by
(A) the association of unit owners.
(B) each individual unit owner.
(C) the declarant, until transfer of control to the association of unit owners.
(D) The condominium can be created so that any of the above is possible.

14. How is title to a condominium unit transferred?
(A) By master deed
(B) By unit deed
(C) Through the declaration
(D) Through the association bylaws

15. Which of the following statements is true regarding condominiums?
I. Each unit owner has a fractional undivided interest in the common areas and facilities.
II. Each unit owner has a separate tax statement.
III. Each unit owner has a proprietary lease with the association covering the owner's unit.
(A) I only (C) I and III only
(B) I and II only (D) I, II and III

16. A condominium is an estate in real property consisting of an undivided interest in common in a portion of the property, together with a separate complete ownership of space. The estate may be
(A) fee simple only.
(B) an estate for life only.
(C) an estate for years only.
(D) any of the above.

17. An owner of a condominium can usually obtain which of the following on an individual unit?
I. Title insurance
II. Homeowner's hazard insurance
(A) I only (C) Both I and II
(B) II only (D) Neither I nor II

18. The owners of an apartment in a condominium can do which of the following?
I. Convey a freehold title to a grantee
II. Hypothecate the apartment as security for a mortgage
(A) I only (C) Both I and II
(B) II only (D) Neither I nor II

19. Which of the following statements does not apply to condominium ownership?
(A) Individuals take title to their units and an interest in commonly held property.
(B) Each owner receives a tax bill which covers the value of his or her unit and his proportionate share of the commonly held property.
(C) Individuals are responsible only for mortgage indebtedness and taxes involving their units and a proportionate share of the property held in common.
(D) Liens against individual units or individual unit owners are liens against the entire property.

20. Gladys Glottis owns fee title to Unit 12 of Excelsior Apartments and a 4.5% interest in the common elements. Gladys
(A) probably has a life estate in her unit.
(B) may mortgage her unit without placing a lien on the title of the other units.
(C) Both A and B are true.
(D) Neither A nor B is true.

21. In a leasehold condominium,
(A) taxes on the common elements are assessed the same as if the units were owned in fee.
(B) the property tax bill can be paid by the owner (lessor) of the land or by each unit owner.
(C) both A and B are correct.
(D) neither A nor B is correct.

22. The lien of a unit owners association for unpaid unit owners fees does not take priority over
(A) a first trust deed.
(B) a second trust deed.
(C) a land sales contract.
(D) either A or B.

23. Which of the following terms does not pertain to the condominium form of ownership?
(A) Fee simple ownership
(B) Homeowner's association
(C) Proprietary lease
(D) Common areas

24. Johnson bought for his use an apartment in a large building and received a deed conveying to him a fee simple estate and also a tax bill on his ownership. His apartment ownership is called a
(A) real estate investment trust.
(B) cooperative.
(C) corporation.
(D) condominium.

25. Henry Kinkaid owns fee simple title of unit 12 of Evergreen Condominiums and 4½% of the common elements. Kinkaid
I. owns a life estate in his unit.
II. may mortgage his unit without placing a lien upon the title of the other unit owners.
(A) I only
(B) II only
(C) Both I and II
(D) Neither I nor II

26. Which of the following is true concerning unit ownership?
I. Ownership in a cooperative usually requires purchase of shares of stock in the cooperative corporation.
II. Individual units in a condominium are conveyed and are financed as if they were single family dwellings on separate pieces of land.
(A) I only
(B) II only
(C) Both I and II
(D) Neither I nor II

27. Mr. Able purchased a two-bedroom condominium. He now holds
I. a freehold interest in his unit.
II. a proprietary lease.
(A) I only
(B) II only
(C) Both I and II
(D) Neither I nor II

28. Schlock & Heistem, Inc. wishes to create a corporation to hold title to a building in which investors have a right of occupancy to a portion of the premises, but can only transfer their right of occupancy by transferring shares of stock. This kind of subdivision is called
(A) a planned community development.
(B) a condominium project.
(C) a stock cooperative development.
(D) a community housing project.

29. The purchaser of which of the following apartment units could have a fee simple interest?
I. Cooperative apartment
II. Condominium apartment
(A) I only
(B) II only
(C) Both I and II
(D) Neither I nor II

30. If the owner of a condominium defaults on the loan payment, the owners of the remaining units
(A) become subject to foreclosure.
(B) must immediately institute a suit to quiet title.
(C) must file an injunction against the defaulting owner.
(D) are not affected.

31. An apartment in which the tenant buys stock in the corporation that owns the building rather than simply renting his apartment is called
(A) a real estate trust.
(B) a condominium.
(C) a cooperative apartment.
(D) none of the above.

32. Joe Patterson occupies an apartment in a multi-unit building. At the time he moved in, Patterson received a proprietary lease as well as stock in the building corporation that holds title to the land and building. Patterson's form of ownership is which of the following?
(A) Cooperative
(B) Townhouse
(C) Planned community
(D) Condominium

33. A purchaser of an apartment in a cooperative apartment building will secure which of the following with his or her purchase?
    I. A deed to the apartment
    II. Shares of stock in the corporation which owns the building
    (A) I only
    (B) II only
    (C) Both I and II
    (D) Neither I nor II

34. An owner of a cooperative apartment has
    (A) an ownership interest in the one entity that must pay taxes, mortgage interest and principal, and operating expenses.
    (B) a proprietary long term lease.
    (C) community property.
    (D) both A and B.

35. Gerald O'Reilly owns an apartment building that he wishes to convert to condominiums. How soon in advance must O'Reilly give notice to his tenants of his intention to declare a conversion?
    (A) 60 days
    (B) 120 days
    (C) six months
    (D) one year

36. Before an existing Oregon apartment building can be converted into a condominium, if there is no substantial alteration in the physical layout, all existing tenants must be given
    I. the right to purchase units.
    II. 120 days' notice of intent to convert.
    III. 90-day termination of tenancy notices.
    (A) I only
    (B) II only
    (C) III only
    (D) Both I and II

37. Which of the following practices are generally true in a conversion of an apartment building to a condominium?
    I. Existing tenants are given at least 120 days' notice of the conversion.
    II. The existing tenants are given the first right to purchase their units if the physical layout of the condominium will not be substantially altered.
    (A) I only
    (B) II only
    (C) Both I and II
    (D) Neither I nor II

38. Which of the following are true when an apartment building is converted to condominiums in Oregon?
    I. The tenant is entitled to a 60-day first right of refusal.
    II. The tenant is entitled to a separate notice from the conversion notice if the tenancy is to be terminated.
    III. The tenant must be notified of the conversion at least 120 days prior to the recording of the declaration, bylaws and floor plans.
    (A) I and II only
    (B) I and III only
    (C) II and III only
    (D) I, II and III

39. In Oregon, when an apartment building is converted to condominiums
    I. tenant must be notified of the conversion at least 120 days prior to the recording of the declaration, bylaws and floor plans.
    II. tenant is entitled to a 60-day first right of refusal.
    (A) I only
    (B) II only
    (C) Both I and II
    (D) Neither I nor II

40. Ernestine LeDoux owns an apartment building which she wishes to convert to condominiums. How much notice must she give to her tenants of her intention to declare a conversion.
    (A) None
    (B) 60 days
    (C) 120 days
    (D) Six months

41. Unit Developers, Inc. converted an apartment building to condominiums. They granted a management agreement on the units to the Ideal Management Company on October 15 and sold the first unit on April 30 the following year. The latest date the service contract could be canceled is
    (A) two years from when the agreement was created.
    (B) one year from the sale of the first unit.
    (C) three years from the date of the management agreement.
    (D) two years from the sale of the first unit.

42. A condominium is created by recording
    (A) a declaration.
    (B) floorplans to the building.
    (C) bylaws of the unit owners association.
    (D) all of the above.

43. Unit Hab Inc. has filed a declaration creating a set of condominiums. What percent of the unit owners are usually needed to approve amendments to the declaration?
(A) A simple majority (50% plus one)
(B) Two-thirds (67%)
(C) Three-fourths (75%)
(D) Unanimous (100%)

44. A condominium declaration can be changed by a vote of the unit owners. Unless the declaration provides otherwise, the required vote is
(A) 50% plus one.
(B) two-thirds, plus one.
(C) 75%.
(D) 100%.

45. After a condominium was created and in operation, the unit owners association decided, by vote of the unit owners, to assign certain spaces in the parking lot for the exclusive use of certain owners. Under the Oregon Condominium Act,
(A) this is illegal.
(B) the unit owners must vote to approve a change in the declaration, setting forth the parking spaces and the units to which they will become a limited common element.
(C) each parking space must be deeded to the unit owner who owns the unit to which the space will appertain.
(D) both B and C are required.

46. Alec Sanders is a contractor who created a 100-unit single-stage condominium project. In the declaration, Alec provided that he would keep full control of the unit owners association for two years, or until 75% of the units had been sold, whichever came first. Under the Oregon Condominium Act,
(A) this is illegal.
(B) control must be relinquished when 50% or more of the units have been sold.
(C) control must be relinquished when 75% or more of the units have been sold, or within three years of the date the first unit was sold, whichever comes first.
(D) both A and B are correct.

47. Several unit owners in Clackamas Condominiums agree that the property is obsolete and should be removed from the provisions of the Oregon Condominium Act and sold. To accomplish this, they need the agreement of
(A) two-thirds of the unit owners.
(B) three-fourths of the unit owners.
(C) 90% of the unit owners.
(D) all of the unit owners.

48. A property can be removed from unit ownership if
(A) the improvements have become obsolete and 90% of the owners agree to do so.
(B) the improvements have become extensively damaged and 60% of the owners agree to do so.
(C) the consent of all lienholders is obtained.
(D) either A or B occurs, and the consent of all lienholders is obtained.

49. If a property is removed from unit ownership,
I. the unit owners become tenants in common to the entire property.
II. each unit owner has a percentage interest in the entire property equal to the interest they once held in the common elements when it was a condominium.
III. liens against individual units are not extinguished.
(A) I only
(B) I and II only
(C) I and III only
(D) I, II and III

50. Madelon DeBeck owns a unit in a condominium that is being removed from the provisions of the Oregon Condominium Act and sold as obsolete. Two percent of the common elements appertain to DeBeck's unit. Her unit has been appraised at $20,900. The total appraised value of all units is $866,000 and of the common elements is $74,100. What percent of the net proceeds of the sale will she receive?
(A) 1.59%
(B) 2.38%
(C) 2.77%
(D) 3.45%

51. Sam Weatherstone owns a unit in a condominium that is being removed from the provisions of the Oregon Condominium Act. Together with his unit, he holds a 2½% interest in the common elements. The valuation of his unit is $150,000, including the interest in the common elements which appertains to his unit. The valuation of all the units together is $5,600,000 and of the common elements $800,000. If the units were sold for cash, what percent of the total sales proceeds would Sam get?
(A) 2.30%
(B) 2.34%
(C) 2.50%
(D) 2.67%

52. Before a new condominium can be sold in Oregon, the buyer must receive a copy of
(A) the condominium information report.
(B) the declaration.
(C) the bylaws.
(D) all of the above.

53. If a condominium is sold by a developer, the buyer has the right to cancel the transaction provided the buyer gives the developer written notice at least
(A) three business days from the receipt of all required documents.
(B) four calendar days from the date the receipt for the required documents was signed.
(C) five business days from the date the receipt for the required documents was signed.
(D) seven calendar days from the receipt of the condominium disclosure statement.

54. In the sale of a residential condominium the buyer has a right to cancel the transaction. This right can be waived by
(A) the seller.
(B) the buyer.
(C) either the buyer or the seller.
(D) neither the buyer nor the seller.

55. Which of the following kinds of financing requires the use of a collection escrow when buying a condominium from a developer in Oregon?
(A) Conventional mortgage
(B) Federally insured mortgage
(C) Full price cash sale
(D) Land sale contract

56. When a developer sells a condominium unit in Oregon on a land sales contract,
I. the deed to the unit must be placed in a collection escrow in Oregon with a person or firm authorized to receive escrows.
II. a copy of the preliminary title report relating to the unit must be placed in a collection escrow in Oregon with a person or firm authorized to received escrows.
(A) I only
(B) II only
(C) Both I and II
(D) Neither I nor II

57. Which of the following terms best describes a modern form of real property ownership that involves the guaranteed right of occupancy and use of a specific property for a specific portion of each year for either a fixed number of years or forever?
(A) Life estate
(B) Periodic tenancy
(C) Recreation lease
(D) Time sharing

58. A "planned community"
I. involves the use of cluster zoning.
II. is a subdivision which is self-contained.
III. usually includes a mix of commercial and residential property.
(A) I and II only
(B) I and III only
(C) I, II and III
(D) II and III only

ANSWERS

To practice questions. If you chose the wrong letter, here's the right one! The explanations are designed to clarify your understanding.

1. **D** There are certain special rules for residential condominiums, but any interest in real property can be owned as a condominium.

2. **B** A condominium is individual ownership of a volume of space, together with an interest as a tenant in common to the common areas which surround it.

3. **C** When you own a condominium you own a volume of space individually, together with an interest as tenant in common with the other unit owners to the common elements (the areas surrounding all the units). One part of the definition of real estate is that it is a volume of space. Therefore, ownership of a condominium is ownership of real estate, which could be a life estate, but is usually held in fee title.

4. **C** A condominium is ownership of a volume of space, together with an interest as a tenant in common to the common elements. In a cooperative you own a share of stock in a corporation. The corporation, in turn, owns the building. Your ownership of the share of stock entitles you to a proprietary lease in one of the units.

5. **A** When you own a condominium you also own an interest as tenant in common to the surrounding areas. These areas are called the common elements. A cooperative is ownership of stock in a corporation which owns the entire building. Ownership of the stock entitles you to a proprietary lease in a particular unit.

6. **D** When you own a condominium, any portion of the real property that is not someone's unit is common area. The Oregon Condominium Act distinguishes between general common elements, which are available for use by all unit owners, and limited common elements, which can be reserved for the exclusive use of individual unit owners. Unless specifically stated otherwise in the declaration, all common elements are considered to be general.

7. **B** When you buy a condominium, you get a deed which conveys title to the unit, as a volume of space, plus an undivided interest as tenant in common with the other unit owners to the areas surrounding all the units (the common areas). A cooperative is an arrangement where you own a share of stock in a corporation, which in turn owns the building. Your share of stock entitles you to a proprietary lease in one of the units.

8. **A** When you buy a condominium you normally get a deed which conveys title to the unit, as a volume of space, plus an undivided interest as tenant in common with the other unit owners to the areas surrounding all the units (the common areas). A cooperative is an arrangement where you own a share of stock in a corporation which owns the building. Your share of stock entitles you to a proprietary lease in one of the units.

9. **C** When you own a condominium you own a volume of space, together with an interest as tenant in common to the surrounding common elements. Any portion of the real property that is not someone's unit, is common area.

10. **B** In a condominium the unit itself (the airspace) is owned exclusively, plus an interest as a tenant in common to the common areas is included as an inseparable appurtenance to each unit. The common areas usually include amenities such as recreational facilities, grounds and landscaping, parking areas, and so on.

11. **D** The bylaws of the association of unit owners must state what expenses and services are to be paid by the association. The association then levies an assessment (sometimes called "fees" or "dues") against each unit for that unit's share of the expenses. The assessment is a lien against the unit and can be enforced by foreclosure, if necessary. By vote of the unit owners, the bylaws can be amended to include any expense the owners desire. Typically, the assessment covers matters such as exterior maintenance, garbage collection, water and sewer bills, common insurance policy, maintenance of common areas, salaries and wages of officers and maintenance personnel, and so on.

12. **C** The bylaws of the association of unit owners give it the authority to determine what services the association will provide and how much each unit owner's dues will be. Normally, the association takes care of all matters relating to the common areas.

13. **B** The Oregon Condominium Act provides that once a property has been declared to be a condominium the interest in the common element for each unit as listed in the declaration becomes an inseparable appurtenance to the unit. Therefore a sale of the unit automatically includes the sale of the common interest that appertains to that unit. The most direct method used by the county tax assessor to determine the true cash value of the units is to base the values on the sales prices of comparable sold units. Since the price the buyers paid for such units included the value of the common elements, the resulting tax value of each unit includes the value of the common elements that appertain to the unit. Therefore, there is no separate bill for the common elements. The proportionate value of the common elements is merely included with each owner's bill.

14. **B** When you own a condominium you own a volume of space individually, together with an interest as tenant in common with the other unit owners to the common elements. Since it is an ownership of real property, it is conveyed to a buyer by a deed. One deed conveys both the unit and the interest in the common elements. Such deeds are commonly called unit deeds. The declaration is the document that creates the condominium form of ownership. The bylaws provide the rules by which the association of unit owners is to be operated, but the rules have nothing to do with conveying title to the units.

15. **B** Ownership of a condominium is normally a freehold interest in the unit (a volume of space), together with a freehold interest as tenant in common to the areas surrounding all the units (the common areas). Since it is a separate ownership, each owner receives an individual tax statement. In a cooperative you own a share of stock in a corporation. The corporation, in turn, owns the building. Your ownership of the share of stock entitles you to a proprietary lease in one of the units. There is one tax bill for the entire building, and each shareholder is required to pay his or her share of it.

16. **D** A condominium is an individual ownership of real property. It can be held in the same ways as any other real estate. Normal ownership is a fee title. Ownership for one's lifetime only is a life estate (estate for life). An estate for years is a lease, which is also possible with a condominium.

17. **C** Unlike a cooperative, where you own a share of stock in a corporation, which in turn owns the building, in a condominium you own your own individual unit, normally in fee title. Therefore, you obtain your own title insurance, the same as any other property owner. Sometimes the association of unit owners will obtain fire insurance to cover the entire building, but usually owners obtain individual policies.

18. **C** A condominium is ownership of a volume of space, together with an interest as a tenant in common to the common elements. Both interests are normally freehold interests. To hypothecate means to pledge as collateral for a loan. When a condominium unit is mortgaged, or the owner gives a lender a trust deed on it, it has been hypothecated. The mortgage and the trust deed are lien instruments which make the real estate collateral for a loan.

19. **D** Ownership of a condominium is normally a freehold interest in the unit (a volume of space), together with a freehold interest as tenant in common to the areas surrounding all the units (the common areas). Since it is a separate ownership, each owner receives an individual tax statement and each unit can be separately pledged as collateral for a loan. In a cooperative you own a share of stock in a corporation. The corporation, in turn, owns the building. Your ownership of the share of stock entitles you to a proprietary lease in one of the units. There is one tax bill for the entire building, and each shareholder is required to pay his or her share of it. If there is a mortgage, it covers the entire building.

20. **B** Owning a life estate in a fee condominium is a possibility, but no more likely than owning a life estate in any other kind of real estate. However, owning a condominium means that the owner holds a completely separate interest in real property which can be separately financed or liened in any manner the same as a property on an individual lot.

21. **A** Oregon laws provide that leasehold condominiums are assessed and taxed the same as if they were fee title, including the value of the land. The bill cannot be paid by the lessor, but must be billed to the lessee (unit owner), included with the value of the unit. The purpose of these laws is to simplify the assessment process.

22. **D** By statute, the lien of the association of unit owners for the unit assessment is prior to all other liens except property taxes, income taxes, special assessments, first mortgages and first trust deeds. Land sales contracts are not included in this exception.

23. **C** Ownership of a condominium is normally a freehold interest in the unit (a volume of space), together with a freehold interest as tenant in common

to the areas surrounding all the units (the common areas). The ownership could be a life estate, but is usually a fee title. There is an association of unit owners (called a homeowner's association in residential projects). In a cooperative you own a share of stock in a corporation. The corporation, in turn, owns the building. Your ownership of the share of stock entitles you to a proprietary lease in one of the units.

24. **D** A condominium is ownership of a volume of space, together with an interest as a tenant in common to the surrounding areas (common elements). Both interests are in fee title. In a cooperative you own a share of stock in a corporation. The corporation, in turn, owns the building. Your ownership of the share of stock entitles you to a proprietary lease in one of the units. Stock is personal property, and is not conveyed by a deed.

25. **B** A condominium is ownership of a volume of space, together with an interest as a tenant in common to the common elements. A condominium, like any other property, is normally owned in fee title, although it could be owned as a life estate. A fee title is perpetual ownership, where a life estate is ownership for one's lifetime. Since a condominium is a separate ownership, it is conveyed and mortgaged individually. In a cooperative you own a share of stock in a corporation. The corporation, in turn, owns the building. Your ownership of the share of stock entitles you to a proprietary lease in one of the units. In a cooperative, if there is a mortgage, the corporation is the borrower, and the entire building is the collateral.

26. **C** A condominium is ownership of a volume of space, together with an interest as a tenant in common to the common elements. Both interests are normally ownerships in fee title, and are therefore conveyed by deed, the same as any other interest in real estate. You may also pledge the condominium as collateral for a loan by giving a lender a note and mortgage or note and trust deed. If you mortgage your unit, the lender gains a lien on your unit only. In a cooperative you own a share of stock in a corporation. The corporation, in turn, owns the building. Your ownership of the share of stock entitles you to a proprietary lease in one of the units. In a cooperative, if there is a mortgage, the corporation is the borrower, and the entire building is the collateral.

27. **A** A condominium is ownership of a volume of space, together with an interest as a tenant in common to the common elements. Both interests are ownerships (freehold interests). In a cooperative you own a share of stock in a corporation. The corporation, in turn, owns the building. Your ownership of the share of stock entitles you to a proprietary lease in one of the units.

28. **C** Ownership of a unit in a cooperative means owning stock in a corporation, which in turn owns the building. A condominium means individual ownership or lease of a volume of space, with collective ownership of the common areas as tenants in common. A planned community is a subdivision which has an association of homeowners.

29. **B** A condominium is ownership of a volume of space, together with an interest as a tenant in common to the common elements. Both interests are normally ownerships in fee title. In a cooperative you own a share of stock in a corporation. The corporation, in turn, owns the building. Your ownership of the share of stock entitles you to a proprietary lease in one of the units. Shares of stock are personal property.

30. **D** A condominium is ownership in fee title of a volume of space, together with an interest as tenant in common to the common elements. In a cooperative you own a share of stock in a corporation. The corporation, in turn, owns the building. Your ownership of the share of stock entitles you to a proprietary lease in one of the units. If an owner of a condominium defaults on the mortgage loan, the lender forecloses on just that owner's unit. But in a cooperative there is a common mortgage on the entire building. Each owner is responsible for his or her share of the payment, but if someone defaults there may not be enough to pay the lender, potentially resulting in a foreclosure on the entire building.

31. **C** When you buy an apartment in a cooperative you receive a share of stock in a corporation. The corporation owns the building. Your share of stock entitles you to a proprietary lease to a particular unit. In a condominium you receive a deed conveying the unit, plus an interest as tenant in common to the areas surrounding the units. A real estate trust is similar to a mutual fund, but for real estate investments.

32. **A** When you buy an apartment in a cooperative you receive a share of stock in a corporation. The corporation, in turn, owns the building. Your share of stock entitles you to a proprietary lease to a particular unit. In a condominium you receive a deed conveying the unit, plus an interest as tenant in common to the areas surrounding the units. Ownership in a planned community is simply ownership of a separate lot, but in a subdivision which has an associ-

ation of unit owners which takes care of maintenance and other matters, the same as in a condominium. A townhouse can be an apartment, condominium or cooperative unit. It is not a specific legal term. Most agents use "townhouse" to describe a unit which is two stories.

33. **B** When you buy an apartment in a cooperative you receive a share of stock in a corporation. The corporation owns the entire building. Your share of stock entitles you to a proprietary lease to a particular unit. In a condominium you receive a deed conveying the unit, plus an interest as tenant in common to the areas surrounding the units.

34. **D** When you buy an apartment in a cooperative you receive a share of stock in a corporation. The corporation owns the building. Your share of stock entitles you to a proprietary lease to a particular unit. Community property is a term used when describing rights of spouses in commonly held property.

35. **B** A conversion condominium is defined in the statute as one that is residential, at least in part. Other types of property may be "converted" to condominium status, but if they are commercial or industrial in nature, then they are not "conversion condominiums." For the protection of tenants, in an conversion condominium the declarant must give the tenants at least 120 days notice before recording the declaration, unless all the tenants agree to waive the requirement.

36. **D** For the protection of tenants, in an residential property, the declarant must give the tenants at least 120 days notice before recording the declaration, unless all the tenants agree to waive the requirement. The tenants also have a first right of refusal unless there are to be substantial alterations to the premises. According to the Oregon Residential Landlord and Tenant Act, if tenants are on month-to-month tenancies the tenancies can be terminated with 30 days notice. There are no additional requirements in the case where the units are being converted to condominiums.

37. **C** For the protection of tenants, in an residential property, the declarant must give the tenants at least 120 days notice before recording the declaration, unless all the tenants agree to waive the requirement. The tenants also have a first right of refusal unless there are to be substantial alterations to the premises.

38. **D** In a residential property the declarant must give the tenants at least 120 days notice before recording the declaration, unless all the tenants agree to waive the requirement. The 120-day notice does not constitute a notice to terminate a tenancy, so if the owner wishes to evict the tenants a separate notice must be given. The tenants also have a first right of refusal for 60 days, unless there are to be substantial alterations to the premises.

39. **C** In a residential property, the declarant must give the tenants at least 120 days notice before recording the declaration, unless all the tenants agree to waive the requirement. The tenants also have a first right of refusal for 60 days, unless there are to be substantial alterations to the premises.

40. **C** Converting a property to a condominium follows essentially the same procedure as if a property were built new as a condominium. But when residential property is converted to condominiums, the tenants have certain rights. The declarant must give each tenant at least 120 days advance notice before recording the declaration, unless 100% of the tenants agree to waive the notice. And if the property will not be substantially altered, the declarant must offer to sell each unit to the tenant in the unit and leave the offer open for up to 60 days. For an additional 60 days the declarant cannot offer a unit to the public on terms more favorable than the terms on which it was offered to the tenant in the unit. However, if the tenants are all on month-to-month tenancies, the landlord and tenant laws allow the owner to give each tenant 31 days' notice to vacate, without needing a reason. Once the units are vacant, the declarant need not give the tenants notice or an offer to sell, since there are no longer any tenants.

41. **C** The Oregon Condominium Act specifies that if a declarant creates a management contract before the initial turnover meeting its term cannot exceed three years. The date the first unit was sold is irrelevant.

42. **D** The heart of the creation of a condominium is the recording of the declaration. In the declaration the declarant (owner) declares that the property is now a condominium. Floorplans must also be recorded in order to create a simplified legal description. The Oregon Condominium Act also requires that the declarant record bylaws for the association of unit owners.

43. **C** The declaration of a condominium is the document that creates the condominium form of ownership and provides that the provisions of the Oregon Condominium Act will apply to the property in the future. Since it is a basic document in the formation of a condominium, the statute requires a

vote of at least 75% of the unit owners, or more if the declaration requires a higher percentage.

44. **C** To amend the declaration, or create a supplemental declaration, ORS 100.135 requires a minimum 75% vote of the unit owners, unless the declaration requires a higher percentage.

45. **B** The unit owners can vote to approve an amendment to the declaration at any time. Common elements can be general (available to all unit owners) or limited (reserved for exclusive use of certain unit owners). Whether general or limited, the description of the common elements must be set forth in the declaration. Therefore, changing portions of the common elements from general to limited requires amending the declaration.

46. **C** For ordinary condominiums, the Oregon Condominium Act allows the declarant to retain control of the association of unit owners until the earlier of the time when 75% of the units have been sold, or three years from the date the first unit was sold. For a flexible condominium, it is the same except that the time can be as long as seven years from the date the first unit was sold. Of course, if the declarant still owns units, this statute does not prevent the declarant from exercising his or her right to vote as the owner of those units.

47. **C** A condominium is created when the developer (or person converting the property) records a declaration, thus placing it under the provisions of the Oregon Condominium Act. If the unit owners desire, it can be removed from condominium status. The statute normally requires a 100% vote in favor, but only 90% is required if the property is obsolete.

48. **D** An entire condominium project can be removed from condominium status at any time by recording an agreement to that effect. The removal must be approved by 100% of the unit owners, although only 90% approval is required if the units are obsolete, or 60% if the units have been substantially damaged. In all cases, the consent of lienholders must be obtained. After removal from condominium status, each unit owner will be a tenant in common to the entire property. Each tenant's interest as a tenant in common will be apportioned according to the market value of his or her unit in relation to the market value of the entire property. Liens against the unit simply become liens against the percentage interest as tenant in common.

49. **C** After removal from condominium status, each unit owner will be a tenant in common to the entire property. Each tenant's interest as a tenant in common will be apportioned according to the market value of his or her unit in relation to the market value of the entire development. Liens against the unit simply become liens against the percentage interest as tenant in common.

50. **B** If the unit owners desire, a condominium can be removed from condominium status. The owners then become owners of the entire building as tenants in common. In order to determine the percentage of interest for each former unit owner, the tax assessed valuations are used. In this case, the total value of the entire project is \$940,100 (the value of the units plus the value of the common elements, or \$866,000 + \$74,100). She has a 2% interest in the common elements, which is worth \$1,482 (\$74,100 × 0.02 = \$1,482). Therefore, the total value of her unit is \$22,382 (\$20,900 + \$1,482 = \$22,382). Therefore, she is entitled to 22,382⁄940,100 of the whatever the units sell for. To convert a fraction to a decimal, divide the numerator by the denominator (divide 22,382 by 940,100). This comes to 2.38% (22,382 ÷ 940,100 = 0.0238081).

51. **B** To calculate, divide the value of the unit and its share of the common elements by the value of all the units and all the common elements. The value of the unit and its share of the common elements is given as \$150,000. The value of all the units is given as \$5,600,000, and of the common elements as \$800,000, so the total value of all the units is \$6,400,000 (\$5,600,000 + \$800,000 = \$6,400,000). Dividing the value of the unit (\$150,000) by the total value (\$6,400,000) gives the percentage, which comes to 2.34% (\$150,000 ÷ \$6,400,000 = 0.0234375, or 2.34% rounded).

52. **D** The Oregon Condominium Act requires condominiums to be filed with the Oregon Real Estate Agency, which will then issue a disclosure statement called a "condominium disclosure statement." The developer must give a copy of the disclosure statement to each buyer. The buyer is also entitled to copies of the declaration and the bylaws. The buyer has five business days to cancel the transaction from the time the buyer received the last of the documents.

53. **C** When the condominium information report, declaration and bylaws have been given to the buyer, the developer must obtain a receipt from the buyer for them. The developer must retain the receipt for three years. An agreement for the sale of a condominium by a developer must contain a notice that

the buyer has a right to cancel the transaction for five business days from the date the receipt was signed. The buyer can waive this right, provided the waiver is in a document separate from the sales contract.

54. **B** Since the law was designed to protect the consumer, only the consumer has the right to waive the right to cancel the transaction. The consumer must do so in a document separate from the sales agreement.

55. **D** When you buy on a land sales contract, the seller is obligated to deliver a deed only when the full purchase price has been paid. This may be many years in the future. A condominium developer may no longer be in business at that time. Therefore, for the protection of buyers under land sales contracts, the Oregon Condominium Act requires that all sales that are financed with a land sales contract be set up in an escrow which collects the payments. The deed is to be held by the escrow for delivery when the final payment has been made. This requirement applies only to the sale from the developer to the first consumer; thereafter it does not apply.

56. **C** Normally, when you buy on a land sales contract the seller is obligated to deliver a deed only when the full purchase price has been paid. This may be many years in the future. A condominium developer may no longer be in business at that time. Therefore, for the protection of buyers under land sales contracts, the Oregon Condominium Act requires that all sales of condominiums by the developer on a land sales contract be set up in an escrow which collects the payments. The deed is to be held by the escrow for delivery when the final payment has been made. The escrow must also have a preliminary title report showing that the seller has adequate title so that the buyer's deed will convey good and sufficient title.

57. **D** Every piece of real property, even a volume of space, as in a condominium, involves a bundle of rights. These rights can be divided any way the owner desires. In modern times it is fashionable to give all the sticks in the bundle of rights to a buyer, but only for a specific week during the year, recurring each year. Such ownerships are called timeshares. A timeshare can be a leasehold or a fee title.

58. **C** Cluster zoning is a zoning ordinance that provides a total number of units for the area, but lets the developer decide whether to put all the units in one place and have other space open, or disperse the units evenly over the total area. Cluster zoning is typical of a planned community development. Planned communities are frequently created as a self-contained community, complete with shopping, banks and other services within the development.

Index

*Items in **bold** are main locations where the item is discussed in the text.*